Star Guide®
To
Predictive Astrology

Star Guide® To Predictive Astrology

Bhavas—Planets in the 12 House

Pandit K.B. Parsai
Pandit D.K. Parsai

RUPA

Published by
Rupa Publications India Pvt. Ltd 2001
161-B/4, Gulmohar House,
Yusuf Sarai Community Centre,
New Delhi 110049

Sales centres:
Bengaluru Chennai
Hyderabad Kolkata Mumbai

Copyright © Pandit K.B. Parsai & Pandit D.K. Parsai 2001

The views and opinions expressed in this book are the authors' own and the facts are as reported by them which have been verified to the extent possible, and the publishers are not in any way liable for the same.

All rights reserved.
No part of this publication may be reproduced, transmitted, or stored in a retrieval system, in any form or by any means, electronic, mechanical, photocopying, recording or otherwise, without the prior permission of the author.

P-ISBN: 978-81-716-7601-9
E-ISBN: 978-81-291-2151-6

Twenty-seventh impression 2025

30 29 28 27

Typeset by Pandit D.K. Parsai at New Delhi

The moral right of the authors has been asserted.

Printed in India

This book is sold subject to the condition that it shall not, by way of trade or otherwise, be lent, resold, hired out, or otherwise circulated, without the author's prior consent, in any form of binding or cover other than that in which it is published.

(October 11, 1922 – July 16, 2009)

Astrologer Pandit K. B. Parsai

To my father, guru, guide and friend –
As knowledge, you live forever

Author & Son D.K Parsai

(February 13, 1924 – November 5, 2000)

Dedicated to
Smt. Krishna Kumari Parsai

My life companion of 56 Years, she firmly stood by me as my real-half through the ups and downs of life, particularly the downsides. She is very much present even now amongst our four children (Vidyashankar, Gargi, Aparajita & Divyanshu) and myself, as our guide on the path of life and as our shield in adversity.

To my mother, whom I thank for all I have today. Not only did you give me unconditional love and affection but also your trust and faith enabled me to do and become anything I wanted. You live in my heart and soul and I know you guide and protect me always. Together with father, who is also my guru and guide, you suffered to give us the best this world has to offer, for which I feel fortunate and blessed.

Author Husband, K.B. Parsai

Co-Author Son, D.K. Parsai

CONTENTS

PREFACE TO THIS EDITION	XXXIII
PREFACE TO THE FIRST EDITION	XXXV
INTRODUCTION TO ASTROLOGY	1
HOW ASTROLOGY WORKS	2
Why a chart of planets when one was born?	3
Time is important, but why the place?	3
WHAT IS A BIRTH CHART?	4
How does one place the planets on those 12 spaces in the chart?	5
WHAT ARE THE CONSTELLATIONS?	5
12 *Rasi's* or the Signs of the Zodiac	5
WHAT IS "*AYAN*-ANSH", "SA-*AYAN*", AND "NIR-*AYAN*"	6
THE THREE LAWS OF ASTROLOGICAL ZODIAC	9
HOW IS A CHART CONSTRUCTED?	12
Are there any other kinds of astrological charts?	16
Time-Charts	16
Event-Charts	17
DIFFERENCE BETWEEN WESTERN SUN-SIGN SYSTEM AND INDIAN SYSTEM OF ASTROLOGY	18
TO SUMMARISE IT ALL	19
The Signs – Rasi	19
Houses	19
ADDITIONAL INFORMATION	21
BASIC CONSIDERATIONS	25
MORE ELEMENTARY CONSIDERATIONS	41

SUBJECTS TO BE CONSIDERED UNDER

THE FIRST HOUSE	43
THE SECOND HOUSE	49
THE THIRD HOUSE	55
THE FOURTH HOUSE	61
THE FIFTH HOUSE	73
THE SIXTH HOUSE	81
THE SEVENTH HOUSE	87
THE EIGHTH HOUSE	99
THE NINTH HOUSE	107
THE TENTH HOUSE	113
THE ELEVENTH HOUSE	123
THE TWELFTH HOUSE	127

PLANETS IN THE 12 HOUSES

SUN IN THE 12 HOUSES	137
SUN IN GENERAL	137
SUN IN THE 1ST HOUSE	139
Sun and Moon in the 1st House	141
Sun and Mars in the 1st House	141
Sun and Mercury in the 1st House	143
Sun and Jupiter in the 1st House	144
Sun and Venus in the 1st House	145
Sun and Saturn in the 1st House	146
Sun and Rahu in the 1st House	148
Sun and Ketu in the 1st House	149
SUN IN THE 2ND HOUSE	150
Sun and Moon in the 2nd House	152
Sun and Mars in the 2nd House	153
Sun and Mercury in the 2nd House	154
Sun and Jupiter in the 2nd House	156
Sun and Venus in the 2nd House	157
Sun and Saturn in the 2nd House	158
Sun and Rahu in the 2nd House	160
Sun and Ketu in the 2nd House	161

SUN IN THE 3RD HOUSE	162
Sun and Moon in the 3rd House	163
Sun and Mars in the 3rd House	164
Sun and Mercury in the 3rd House	165
Sun and Jupiter in the 3rd House	166
Sun and Venus in the 3rd House	167
Sun and Saturn in the 3rd House	168
Sun and Rahu in the 3rd House	169
Sun and Ketu in the 3rd House	169
SUN IN THE 4TH HOUSE	170
Sun and Moon in the 4th House	171
Sun and Mars in the 4th House	172
Sun and Mercury in the 4th House	174
Sun and Jupiter in the 4th House	175
Sun and Venus in the 4th House	176
Sun and Saturn in the 4th House	177
Sun and Rahu in the 4th House	181
Sun and Ketu in the 4th House	182
SUN IN THE 5TH HOUSE	183
Sun and Moon in the 5th House	184
Sun and Mars in the 5th House	185
Sun and Mercury in the 5th House	186
Sun and Jupiter in the 5th House	187
Sun and Venus in the 5th House	188
Sun and Saturn in the 5th House	189
Sun and Rahu in the 5th House	190
Sun and Ketu in the 5th House	191
SUN IN THE 6TH HOUSE	192
Sun and Moon in the 6th House	193
Sun and Mars in the 6th House	194
Sun and Mercury in the 6th House	196
Sun and Jupiter in the 6th House	197
Sun and Venus in the 6th House	199
Sun and Saturn in the 6th House	202
Sun and Rahu in the 6th House	204
Sun and Ketu in the 6th House	204

SUN IN THE 7TH HOUSE ... 205
    Sun and Moon in the 7th House ... 206
    Sun and Mars in the 7th House ... 208
    Sun and Mercury in the 7th House ... 210
    Sun and Jupiter in the 7th House ... 211
    Sun and Venus in the 7th House ... 212
    Sun and Saturn in the 7th House ... 214
    Sun and Rahu in the 7th House ... 216
    Sun and Ketu in the 7th House ... 217

SUN IN THE 8TH HOUSE ... 218
    Sun and Moon in the 8th House ... 220
    Sun and Mars in the 8th House ... 222
    Sun and Mercury in the 8th House ... 225
    Sun and Jupiter in the 8th House ... 225
    Sun and Venus in the 8th House ... 227
    Sun and Saturn the in 8th House ... 229
    Sun and Rahu in the 8th House ... 231
    Sun and Ketu in the 8th House ... 231

SUN IN THE 9TH HOUSE ... 232
    Sun and Moon in the 9th House ... 233
    Sun and Mars in the 9th House ... 234
    Sun and Mercury in the 9th House ... 236
    Sun and Jupiter in the 9th House ... 237
    Sun and Venus in the 9th House ... 239
    Sun and Saturn in the 9th House ... 240
    Sun and Rahu in the 9th House ... 242
    Sun and Ketu in the 9th House ... 242

SUN IN THE 10TH HOUSE ... 243
    Sun and Moon in the 10th House ... 256
    Sun and Mars in the 10th House ... 256
    Sun and Mercury in the 10th House ... 257
    Sun and Jupiter in the 10th House ... 257
    Sun and Venus in the 10th House ... 258
    Sun and Saturn in the 10th House ... 259
    Sun and Rahu or Ketu in the 10th House ... 260

SUN IN THE 11TH HOUSE	261
Sun and Moon in the 11th House	264
Sun and Mars in the 11th House	265
Sun and Mercury in the 11th House	267
Sun and Jupiter in the 11th House	269
Sun and Venus in the 11th House	270
Sun and Saturn in the 11th House	272
Sun and Rahu in the 11th House	274
Sun and Ketu in the 11th House	275
SUN IN THE 12TH HOUSE	275
Sun and Moon in the 12th House	279
Sun and Mars in the 12th House	281
Sun and Mercury in the 12th House	285
Sun and Jupiter in the 12th House	287
Sun and Venus in the 12th House	290
Sun and Saturn in the 12th House	292
Sun and Rahu in the 12th House	297
Sun and Ketu in the 12th House	298
MOON IN THE 12 HOUSES	**301**
MOON IN GENERAL	301
MOON IN THE 1ST HOUSE	302
Moon and Sun in the 1st House	305
Moon and Mars in the 1st House	305
Moon and Mercury in the 1st House	306
Moon and Jupiter in the 1st House	308
Moon and Venus in the 1st House	309
Moon and Saturn in the 1st House	311
Moon and Rahu in the 1st House	313
Moon and Ketu in the 1st House	315
MOON IN THE 2ND HOUSE	316
Moon and Sun in the 2nd House	317
Moon and Mars in the 2nd House	318
Moon and Mercury in the 2nd House	321
Moon and Jupiter in the 2nd House	323
Moon and Venus in the 2nd House	324
Moon and Saturn in the 2nd House	326

Moon and Rahu in the 2nd House	328
Moon and Ketu in the 2nd House	329

MOON IN THE 3RD HOUSE — 330

Moon and Sun in the 3rd House	332
Moon and Mars in the 3rd House	332
Moon and Mercury in the 3rd House	333
Moon and Jupiter in the 3rd House	334
Moon and Venus in the 3rd House	335
Moon and Saturn in the 3rd House	336
Moon and Rahu in the 3rd House	338
Moon and Ketu in the 3rd House	339

MOON IN THE 4TH HOUSE — 340

Moon and Sun in the 4th House	343
Moon and Mars in the 4th House	343
Moon and Mercury in the 4th House	345
Moon and Jupiter in the 4th House	346
Moon and Venus in the 4th House	347
Moon and Saturn in the 4th House	350
Moon and Rahu in the 4th House	353
Moon and Ketu in the 4th House	355

MOON IN THE 5TH HOUSE — 356

Moon and Sun in the 5th House	360
Moon and Mars in the 5th House	360
Moon and Mercury in the 5th House	363
Moon and Jupiter in the 5th House	366
Moon and Venus in the 5th House	367
Moon and Saturn in the 5th House	369
Moon and Rahu in the 5th House	371
Moon and Ketu in the 5th House	372

MOON IN THE 6TH HOUSE — 373

Moon and Sun in the 6th House	378
Moon and Mars in the 6th House	378
Moon and Mercury in the 6th House	379
Moon and Jupiter in the 6th House	380
Moon and Venus in the 6th House	381
Moon and Saturn in the 6th House	383

Moon and Rahu in the 6th House	384
Moon and Ketu in the 6th House	385
MOON IN THE 7TH HOUSE	**385**
Moon and Sun in the 7th House	388
Moon and Mars in the 7th House	390
Moon and Mercury in the 7th House	391
Moon and Jupiter in the 7th House	392
Moon and Venus in the 7th House	393
Moon and Saturn in the 7th House	394
Moon and Rahu in the 7th House	396
Moon and Ketu in the 7th House	397
MOON IN THE 8TH HOUSE	**398**
Moon and Sun in the 8th House	401
Moon and Mars in the 8th House	402
Moon and Mercury in the 8th House	404
Moon and Jupiter in the 8th House	405
Moon and Venus in the 8th House	406
Moon and Saturn in the 8th House	407
Moon and Rahu in the 8th House	408
Moon and Ketu in the 8th House	410
MOON IN THE 9TH HOUSE	**411**
Moon and Sun in the 9th House	413
Moon and Mars in the 9th House	414
Moon and Mercury in the 9th House	416
Moon and Jupiter in the 9th House	418
Moon and Venus in the 9th House	419
Moon and Saturn in the 9th House	420
Moon and Rahu in the 9th House	422
Moon and Ketu in the 9th House	423
MOON IN THE 10TH HOUSE	**424**
Moon and Sun in the 10th House	426
Moon and Mars in the 10th House	427
Moon and Mercury in the 10th House	428
Moon and Jupiter in the 10th House	429
Moon and Venus in the 10th House	430
Moon and Saturn in the 10th House	431

Moon and Rahu in the 10th House	434
Moon and Ketu in the 10th House	435

MOON IN THE 11TH HOUSE 435
    Moon and Sun in the 11th House 437
    Moon and Mars in the 11th House 437
    Moon and Mercury in the 11th House 438
    Moon and Jupiter in the 11th House 439
    Moon and Venus in the 11th House 440
    Moon and Saturn in the 11th House 441
    Moon and Rahu in the 11th House 443
    Moon and Ketu in the 11th House 443

MOON IN THE 12TH HOUSE 444
    Moon and Sun in the 12th House 446
    Moon and Mars in the 12th House 446
    Moon and Mercury in the 12th House 447
    Moon and Jupiter in the 12th House 448
    Moon and Venus in the 12th House 449
    Moon and Saturn in the 12th House 451
    Moon and Rahu in the 12th House 452
    Moon and Ketu in the 12th House 453

MARS IN THE 12 HOUSES **455**

MARS IN GENERAL 455
    Mars In the 1st House 457
    Mars and Sun or Moon in the 1st House 457
    Mars and Mercury in the 1st House 457
    Mars and Jupiter in the 1st House 458
    Mars and Venus in the 1st House 458
    Mars and Saturn in the 1st House 458
    Mars and Rahu in the 1st House 459
    Mars and Ketu in the 1st House 460

MARS IN THE 2ND HOUSE 460
    Mars and Sun in the 2nd House 461
    Mars and Moon in the 2nd House 462
    Mars and Mercury in the 2nd House 462
    Mars and Jupiter in the 2nd House 463
    Mars and Venus in the 2nd House 463

Mars and Saturn in the 2nd House	463
Mars and Rahu in the 2nd House	464
Mars and Ketu in the 2nd House	464

MARS IN THE 3RD HOUSE 465

Mars and Sun in the 3rd House	466
Mars and Moon in the 3rd House	466
Mars and Mercury in the 3rd House	467
Mars and Jupiter in the 3rd House	467
Mars and Venus in the 3rd House	467
Mars and Saturn in the 3rd House	468
Mars and Rahu in the 3rd House	469
Mars and Ketu in the 3rd House	469

MARS IN THE 4TH HOUSE 469

Mars and Sun in the 4th House	472
Mars and Moon in the 4th House	472
Mars and Mercury in the 4th House	473
Mars and Jupiter in the 4th House	473
Mars and Venue in the 4th House	474
Mars and Saturn in the 4th House	475
Mars and Rahu or Ketu in the 4th House	476

MARS IN THE 5TH HOUSE 476

Mars and Sun or Moon in the 5th House	478
Mars and Mercury in the 5th House	478
Mars and Jupiter in the 5th House	479
Mars and Venus in the 5th House	479
Mars and Saturn in the 5th House	480
Mars and Rahu in the 5th House	481
Mars and Ketu in the 5th House	481

MARS IN THE 6TH HOUSE 482

Mars and Sun or Moon in the 6th House	483
Mars and Mercury in the 6th House	483
Mars and Jupiter in the 6th House	484
Mars and Venus in the 6th House	484
Mars and Saturn in the 6th House	485
Mars and Rahu in the 6th House	486
Mars and Ketu in the 6th House	487

MARS IN THE 7TH HOUSE	488
Mars and Sun in the 7th House	491
Mars and Moon in the 7th House	492
Mars and Mercury in the 7th House	492
Mars and Jupiter in the 7th House	492
Mars and Venus in the 7th House	493
Mars and Saturn in the 7th House	494
Mars and Rahu in the 7th House	496
Mars and Ketu in the 7th House	496
MARS IN THE 8TH HOUSE	497
Mars and Sun or Moon in the 8th House	499
Mars and Mercury in the 8th House	499
Mars and Jupiter in the 8th House	500
Mars and Venus in the 8th House	501
Mars and Saturn in the 8th House	502
Mars and Rahu in the 8th House	503
Mars and Ketu in the 8th House	504
MARS IN THE 9TH HOUSE	504
Mars and Sun in the 9th House	506
Mars and Moon in the 9th House	507
Mars and Mercury in the 9th House	507
Mars and Jupiter in the 9th House	507
Mars and Venus in the 9th House	508
Mars and Saturn in the 9th House	509
Mars and Rahu in the 9th House	510
Mars and Ketu in the 9th House	510
MARS IN THE 10TH HOUSE	511
Mars and Sun or Moon in the 10th House	515
Mars and Mercury in the 10th House	515
Mars and Jupiter in the 10th House	515
Mars and Venus in the 10th House	516
Mars and Saturn in the 10th House	517
Mars and Rahu in the 10th House	519
Mars and Ketu in the 10th House	519
MARS IN THE 11TH HOUSE	520
Mars and Sun or Moon in the 11th House	521

Mars and Mercury in the 11th House	522
Mars and Jupiter in the 11th House	522
Mars and Venus in the 11th House	522
Mars and Saturn in the 11th House	524
Mars and Rahu in the 11th House	525
Mars and Ketu in the 11th House	525
MARS IN THE 12TH HOUSE	**526**
Mars and Sun in the 12th House	528
Mars and Moon in the 12th House	529
Mars and Mercury in the 12th House	530
Mars and Jupiter in the 12th House	530
Mars and Venus in the 12th House	532
Mars and Saturn in the 12th House	533
Mars and Rahu in the 12th House	535
Mars and Ketu in the 12th House	537
MERCURY IN THE 12 HOUSES	**539**
MERCURY IN GENERAL	**539**
MERCURY IN THE 1ST HOUSE	**540**
Mercury and Sun, Moon or Mars in the 1st House	541
Mercury and Jupiter in the 1st House	541
Mercury and Venus in the 1st House	542
Mercury and Saturn in the 1st House	542
Mercury and Rahu in the 1st House	543
Mercury and Ketu in the 1st House	544
MERCURY IN THE 2ND HOUSE	**545**
Mercury and Sun, Moon or Mars in the 2nd House	546
Mercury and Jupiter in the 2nd House	546
Mercury and Venus in the 2nd House	548
Mercury and Saturn in the 2nd House	549
Mercury and Rahu in the 2nd House	550
Mercury and Ketu in the 2nd House	550
MERCURY IN THE 3RD HOUSE	**551**
Mercury and Sun, Moon or Mars in the 3rd House	552
Mercury and Jupiter in the 3rd House	552
Mercury and Venus in the 3rd House	552

Mercury and Saturn in the 3rd House	553
Mercury and Rahu in the 3rd House	554
Mercury and Ketu in the 3rd House	554
MERCURY IN THE 4TH HOUSE	**554**
Mercury and Sun, Moon or Mars in the 4th House	555
Mercury and Jupiter in the 4th House	556
Mercury and Venus in the 4th House	557
Mercury and Saturn the in 4th House	558
Mercury and Rahu in the 4th House	560
Mercury and Ketu in the 4th House	560
MERCURY IN THE 5TH HOUSE	**561**
Mercury and Sun, Moon or Mars in the 5th House	562
Mercury and Jupiter in the 5th House	563
Mercury and Venus in the 5th House	563
Mercury and Saturn in the 5th House	565
Mercury and Rahu in the 5th House	567
Mercury and Ketu in the 5th House	568
MERCURY IN THE 6TH HOUSE	**568**
Mercury and Sun, Moon or Mars in the 6th House	571
Mercury and Jupiter in the 6th House	571
Mercury and Venus in the 6th House	573
Mercury and Saturn in the 6th House	575
Mercury and Rahu in the 6th House	576
Mercury and Ketu in the 6th House	577
MERCURY IN THE 7TH HOUSE	**577**
Mercury and Sun, Moon or Mars in the 7th House	579
Mercury and Jupiter in the 7th House	579
Mercury and Venus in the 7th House	580
Mercury and Saturn in the 7th House	582
Mercury and Rahu in the 7th House	583
Mercury and Ketu in the 7th House	584
MERCURY IN THE 8TH HOUSE	**585**
Mercury and Sun in the 8th House	586
Mercury and Moon in the 8th House	587
Mercury and Mars in the 8th House	588
Mercury and Jupiter in the 8th House	589

Mercury and Venus in the 8th House	591
Mercury and Saturn in the 8th House	593
Mercury and Rahu in the 8th House	595
Mercury and Ketu in the 8th House	596

MERCURY IN THE 9TH HOUSE — 596
- Mercury and Sun, Moon or Mars in the 9th House — 597
- Mercury and Jupiter in the 9th House — 597
- Mercury and Venus in the 9th House — 599
- Mercury and Saturn in the 9th House — 600
- Mercury and Rahu in the 9th House — 601
- Mercury and Ketu in the 9th House — 602

MERCURY IN THE 10TH HOUSE — 603
- Mercury and Sun, Moon or Mars in the 10th House — 604
- Mercury and Jupiter in the 10th House — 604
- Mercury and Venus in the 10th House — 605
- Mercury and Saturn in the 10th House — 606
- Mercury and Rahu in the 10th House — 608
- Mercury and Ketu in the 10th House — 609

MERCURY IN THE 11TH HOUSE — 610
- Mercury and Sun, Moon or Mars the in 11th House — 610
- Mercury and Jupiter in the 11th House — 610
- Mercury and Venus in the 11th House — 611
- Mercury and Saturn in the 11th House — 612
- Mercury and Rahu in the 11th House — 614
- Mercury and Ketu in the 11th House — 615

MERCURY IN THE 12TH HOUSE — 615
- Mercury and Sun in the 12th House — 617
- Mercury and Moon in the 12th House — 617
- Mercury and Mars in the 12th House — 618
- Mercury and Jupiter in the 12th House — 619
- Mercury and Venus in the 12th House — 621
- Mercury and Saturn in the 12th House — 623
- Mercury and Rahu in the 12th House — 624
- Mercury and Ketu in the 12th House — 625

JUPITER IN THE 12 HOUSES 627

JUPITER IN GENERAL 627

JUPITER IN THE 1ST HOUSE 628
    Jupiter and Sun, Moon, Mars or Mercury
    in the 1st House 629
    Jupiter and Venus in the 1st House 629
    Jupiter and Saturn in the 1st House 630
    Jupiter and Rahu in the 1st House 631
    Jupiter and Ketu in the 1st House 632

JUPITER IN THE 2ND HOUSE 632
    Jupiter and Sun, Moon, Mars or Mercury
    in the 2nd House 633
    Jupiter and Venus in the 2nd House 633
    Jupiter and Saturn in the 2nd House 634
    Jupiter and Rahu in the 2nd House 635
    Jupiter and Ketu in the 2nd House 636

JUPITER IN THE 3RD HOUSE 636
    Jupiter and Sun, Moon, Mar or Mercury
    in the 3rd House 638
    Jupiter and Venus in the 3rd House 638
    Jupiter and Saturn in the 3rd House 639
    Jupiter and Rahu in the 3rd House 639
    Jupiter and Ketu in the 3rd House 640

JUPITER IN THE 4TH HOUSE 641
    Jupiter and Sun, Moon, Mars or Mercury
    in the 4th House 642
    Jupiter and Venus in the 4th House 642
    Jupiter and Saturn in the 4th House 643
    Jupiter and Rahu in the 4th House 645
    Jupiter and Ketu in the 4th House 646

JUPITER IN THE 5TH HOUSE 646
    Jupiter and Sun, Moon, Mars or Mercury
    in the 5th House 648
    Jupiter and Venus in the 5th House 648
    Jupiter and Saturn in the 5th House 650
    Jupiter and Rahu in the 5th House 651

Jupiter and Ketu in the 5th House	653
JUPITER IN THE 6TH HOUSE	**653**
Jupiter and Sun, Moon, Mars or Mercury in the 6th House	654
Jupiter and Venus in the 6th House	654
Jupiter and Saturn in the 6th House	655
Jupiter and Rahu in the 6th House	657
Jupiter and Ketu in the 6th House	657
JUPITER IN THE 7TH HOUSE	**658**
Jupiter and Sun, Moon, Mars or Mercury in the 7th House	660
Jupiter and Venus in the 7th House	660
Jupiter and Saturn in the 7th House	661
Jupiter and Rahu in the 7th House	663
Jupiter and Ketu in the 7th House	664
JUPITER IN THE 8TH HOUSE	**665**
Jupiter and Sun, Moon, Mars or Mercury in the 8th House	670
Jupiter and Venus in the 8th House	670
Jupiter and Saturn in the 8th House	672
Jupiter and Rahu in the 8th House	674
Jupiter and Ketu in the 8th House	674
JUPITER IN THE 9TH HOUSE	**675**
Jupiter and Sun, Moon, Mars or Mercury in the 9th House	677
Jupiter and Venus in the 9th House	677
Jupiter and Saturn in the 9th House	678
Jupiter and Rahu in the 9th House	679
Jupiter and Ketu in the 9th House	679
JUPITER IN THE 10TH HOUSE	**680**
Jupiter and Sun, Moon, Mars or Mercury in the 10th House	681
Jupiter and Venus in the 10th House	681
Jupiter and Saturn in the 10th House	682
Jupiter and Rahu in the 10th House	683
Jupiter and Ketu in the 10th House	684

JUPITER IN THE 11TH HOUSE	685
Jupiter and Sun, Moon, Mars or Mercury in the 11th House	686
Jupiter and Venus in the 11th House	686
Jupiter and Saturn in the 11th House	687
Jupiter and Rahu in the 11th House	688
Jupiter and Ketu in the 11th House	688
JUPITER IN THE 12TH HOUSE	689
Jupiter and Sun, Moon, Mars or Mercury in the 12th House	690
Jupiter and Venus in the 12th House	690
Jupiter and Saturn in the 12th House	692
Jupiter and Rahu in the 12th House	693
Jupiter and Ketu in the 12th House	695
VENUS IN THE 12 HOUSES	**697**
VENUS IN GENERAL	697
VENUS IN THE 1ST HOUSE	700
Venus and Sun, Moon, Mars, Mercury or Jupiter in the 1st House	701
Venus and Saturn in the 1st House	701
Venus and Rahu in the 1st House	703
Venus and Ketu in the 1st House	703
VENUS IN THE 2ND HOUSE	704
Venus and Sun, Moon, Mars, Mercury or Jupiter in the 2nd House	706
Venus and Saturn in the 2nd House	706
Venus and Rahu in the 2nd House	707
Venus and Ketu in the 2nd House	707
VENUS IN THE 3RD HOUSE	708
Venus and Sun, Moon, Mars, Mercury or Jupiter in the 3rd House	709
Venus and Saturn in the 3rd House	709
Venus and Rahu in the 3rd House	711
Venus and Ketu in the 3rd House	711
VENUS IN THE 4TH HOUSE	712

Venus and Sun, Moon, Mars, Mercury or Jupiter in the 4th House	713
Venus and Saturn in the 4th House	713
Venus and Rahu in the 4th House	714
Venus and Ketu in the 4th House	716
VENUS IN THE 5TH HOUSE	716
Venus and Sun, Moon, Mars, Mercury or Jupiter in the 5th House	718
Venus and Saturn in the 5th House	718
Venus and Rahu in the 5th House	720
Venus and Ketu in the 5th House	721
VENUS IN THE 6TH HOUSE	721
Venus and Sun, Moon, Mars, Mercury or Jupiter in the 6th House	723
Venus and Saturn in the 6th House	723
Venus and Rahu in the 6th House	724
Venus and Ketu in the 6th House	725
VENUS IN THE 7TH HOUSE	726
Venus and Sun, Moon, Mars, Mercury or Jupiter in the 7th House	730
Venus and Saturn in the 7th House	730
Venus and Rahu in the 7th House	733
Venus and Ketu in the 7th House	733
VENUS IN THE 8TH HOUSE	734
Venus and Sun, Moon, Mars, Mercury or Jupiter in the 8th House	736
Venus and Saturn in the 8th House	736
Venus and Rahu in the 8th House	737
Venus and Ketu in the 8th House	738
VENUS IN THE 9TH HOUSE	739
Venus and Sun, Moon, Mars, Mercury or Jupiter in the 9th House	741
Venus and Saturn in the 9th House	741
Venus and Rahu in the 9th House	742
Venus and Ketu in the 9th House	743

VENUS IN THE 10TH HOUSE — 744
   Venus and Sun, Moon, Mars, Mercury or
   Jupiter in the 10th House — 747
   Venus and Saturn in the 10th House — 747
   Venus and Rahu in the 10th House — 749
   Venus and Ketu in the 10th House — 750

VENUS IN THE 11TH HOUSE — 751
   Venus and Sun, Moon, Mars, Mercury or
   Jupiter in the 11th House — 753
   Venus and Saturn in the 11th House — 753
   Venus and Rahu in the 11th House — 756
   Venus and Ketu in the 11th House — 757

VENUS IN THE 12TH HOUSE — 757
   Venus and Sun, Moon, Mars, Mercury or
   Jupiter in the 12th House — 759
   Venus and Saturn in the 12th House — 760
   Venus and Rahu in the 12th House — 761
   Venus and Ketu in the 12th House — 762

SATURN IN THE 12 HOUSES — **763**

SATURN IN GENERAL — 763

SATURN IN THE 1ST HOUSE — 765
   Saturn and Sun, Moon, Mars, Mercury,
   Jupiter or Venus in the 1st House — 767
   Saturn and Rahu in the 1st House — 767
   Saturn and Ketu in the 1st House — 769

SATURN IN THE 2ND HOUSE — 769
   Saturn and Sun, Moon, Mars, Mercury,
   Jupiter or Venus in the 2nd House — 772
   Saturn and Rahu in the 2nd House — 772
   Saturn and Ketu in the 2nd House — 773

SATURN IN THE 3RD HOUSE — 774
   Saturn and Sun, Moon, Mars, Mercury,
   Jupiter or Venus in the 3rd House — 776
   Saturn and Rahu in the 3rd House — 776
   Saturn and Ketu in the 3rd House — 777

SATURN IN THE 4TH HOUSE	777
Saturn and Sun, Moon, Mars, Mercury, Jupiter or Venus in the 4th House	781
Saturn and Rahu in the 4th House	781
Saturn with Ketu in the 4th House	783
SATURN IN THE 5TH HOUSE	784
Saturn and Sun, Moon, Mars, Mercury, Jupiter or Venus in the 5th House	786
Saturn and Rahu in the 5th House	786
Saturn and Ketu in the 5th House	787
SATURN IN THE 6TH HOUSE	787
Saturn and Sun, Moon, Mars, Mercury, Jupiter or Venus in the 6th House	789
Saturn and Rahu in the 6th House	789
Saturn and Ketu in the 6th House	789
SATURN IN THE 7TH HOUSE	790
Saturn and Sun, Moon, Mars, Mercury, Jupiter or Venus in the 7th House	791
Saturn and Rahu in the 7th House	791
Saturn and Ketu in the 7th House	792
SATURN IN THE 8TH HOUSE	793
Saturn and Sun, Moon, Mars, Mercury, Jupiter or Venus in the 8th House	796
Saturn and Rahu in the 8th House	796
Saturn and Ketu in the 8th House	797
SATURN IN THE 9TH HOUSE	797
Saturn and Sun, Moon, Mars, Mercury, Jupiter or Venus in the 9th House	800
Saturn and Rahu in the 9th House	800
Saturn and Ketu in the 9th House	800
SATURN IN THE 10TH HOUSE	801
Saturn and Sun, Moon, Mars, Mercury, Jupiter or Venus in the 10th House	806
Saturn and Rahu in the 10th House	806
Saturn and Ketu in the 10th House	807

SATURN IN THE 11TH HOUSE	808
Saturn and Sun, Moon, Mars, Mercury, Jupiter or Venus in the 11th House	810
Saturn and Rahu in the 11th House	811
Saturn and Ketu in the 11th House	811
SATURN IN THE 12TH HOUSE	812
Saturn and Sun, Moon, Mars, Mercury, Jupiter or Venus in the 12th House	817
Saturn and Rahu in the 12th House	817
Saturn and Ketu in the 12th House	818

RAHU IN THE 12 HOUSES — 821

RAHU IN GENERAL	821
RAHU IN THE 1ST HOUSE	821
Rahu and Sun, Moon, Mars, Mercury, Jupiter, Venus or Saturn in the 1st House	823
RAHU IN THE 2ND HOUSE	823
Rahu and Sun, Moon, Mars, Mercury, Jupiter, Venus or Saturn the in the 2nd House	826
RAHU IN THE 3RD HOUSE	826
Rahu and Sun, Moon, Mars, Mercury, Jupiter, Venus or Saturn in the 3rd House	827
RAHU IN THE 4TH HOUSE	827
Rahu and Sun, Moon, Mars, Mercury, Jupiter, Venus or Saturn in the 4th House	829
RAHU IN THE 5TH HOUSE	829
Rahu and Sun, Moon, Mars, Mercury, Jupiter, Venus or Saturn in the 5th House	831
RAHU IN THE 6TH HOUSE	831
Rahu and Sun, Moon, Mars, Mercury, Jupiter, Venus or Saturn in the 6th House	832
RAHU IN THE 7TH HOUSE	832
Rahu and Sun, Moon, Mars, Mercury, Jupiter, Venus or Saturn in the 7th House	834

RAHU IN THE 8TH HOUSE — 834
  Rahu and Sun, Moon, Mars, Mercury,
  Jupiter, Venus or Saturn in the 8th House — 836
RAHU IN THE 9TH HOUSE — 836
  Rahu and Sun, Moon, Mars, Mercury,
  Jupiter, Venus or Saturn in the 9th House — 839
RAHU IN THE 10TH HOUSE — 839
  Rahu and Sun, Moon, Mars, Mercury,
  Jupiter, Venus or Saturn in the 10th House — 841
RAHU IN THE 11TH HOUSE — 841
  Rahu and Sun, Moon, Mars, Mercury,
  Jupiter, Venus or Saturn in the 11th House — 842
RAHU IN THE 12TH HOUSE — 842
  Rahu and Sun, Moon, Mars, Mercury,
  Jupiter, Venus or Saturn in the 12th House — 843

KETU IN THE 12 HOUSES — **845**
KETU IN GENERAL — 845
KETU IN THE 1ST HOUSE — 845
  Ketu and Sun, Moon, Mars, Mercury,
  Jupiter, Venus or Saturn in the 1st House — 846
KETU IN THE 2ND HOUSE — 846
  Ketu and Sun, Moon, Mars, Mercury,
  Jupiter, Venus or Saturn in the 2nd House — 847
KETU IN THE 3RD HOUSE — 847
  Ketu and Sun, Moon, Mars, Mercury,
  Jupiter, Venus or Saturn in the 3rd House — 848
KETU IN THE 4TH HOUSE — 848
  Ketu and Sun, Moon, Mars, Mercury,
  Jupiter, Venus or Saturn in the 4th House — 850
KETU IN THE 5TH HOUSE — 850
  Ketu and Sun, Moon, Mars, Mercury,
  Jupiter, Venus or Saturn in the 5th House — 851

xxx | Contents

KETU IN THE 6TH HOUSE	851
Ketu and Sun, Moon, Mars, Mercury, Jupiter, Venus or Saturn in the 6th House	851
KETU IN THE 7TH HOUSE	852
Ketu and Sun, Moon, Mars, Mercury, Jupiter, Venus or Saturn in the 7th House	853
KETU IN THE 8TH HOUSE	853
Ketu and Sun, Moon, Mars, Mercury, Jupiter, Venus or Saturn in the 8th House	854
KETU IN THE 9TH HOUSE	854
Ketu and Sun, Moon, Mars, Mercury, Jupiter, Venus or Saturn in the 9th House	855
KETU IN THE 10TH HOUSE	856
Ketu and Sun, Moon, Mars, Mercury, Jupiter, Venus or Saturn in the 10th House	857
KETU IN THE 11TH HOUSE	857
Ketu and Sun, Moon, Mars, Mercury, Jupiter, Venus or Saturn in the 11th House	858
KETU IN THE 12TH HOUSE	858
Ketu and Sun, Moon, Mars, Mercury, Jupiter, Venus or Saturn in the 12th House	858
GLOSSARY	**861**

LIST OF FIGURES

Figure 1	Movement of Sun by *Nir-ayan* System	7
Figure 2	Movement of Sun by *Sa-ayan* System	8
Figure 3	Table of the Constellations with their Polarity, Mode of Action and Element	10
Figure 4	Table of ownership of the 12 Signs (Rasi's) of the Zodiac by the seven planets	11
Figure 5	Table of Planet behaviour	11
Figure 6	First Layer of a Chart	13
Figure 7	Second Layer of a Chart	14
Figure 8	Third Layer of a Chart	15
Figure 9	Approximate proper motion of each planet	20
Figure 10	The Exaltation and Debilitation for Planets in various Rasis	21
Figure 11	Length of Major Periods (Maha Dashas)	21
Figure 12	Nakshatras and their duration in each Rasi /Sign	22
Figure 13	Chart – North Indian Style	30
Figure 14	Chart – South Indian Style	31
Figure 15	Explanatory Chart – South Indian Style	32
Figure 16	Chart South Indian Style for 17th Aug. 1963	33
Figure 17	Chart – North Eastern Style	34
Figure 18	Chart 2 – North Eastern Style	35
Figure 19	Western symbols for the Planets and Signs (*Rasis*)	36
Figure 20	Pictorial Symbols of the Twelve Signs of Zodiac/Rasis	37

PREFACE TO THIS EDITION

Knowledge is immortal and must live forever. So does Pandit K.B. Parsai's immense and exceptional knowledge of Astrology in the books written by him, and in me, his son Pandit D.K. Parsai, in a family legacy I am proud to inherit.

With deep sadness I share that Pandit (Kanhaiyalalji Bhawanishankar) K.B Parsai, one of the greatest scholars of Astrology, Dharam Shastra and life itself, passed away during Brahma Muhurt on July 16, 2009, in New Delhi, barely a few weeks after he finished writing a book on Saturn – **Star Guide to Saturn**® – **Transit of Saturn in the 12 Rashi's (Signs).** He was determined to finish the book before he joined his partner of 56 years, my mother Krishna Kumari, in *vaikunth-dham*. This rarest of rare book will be published early next year.

Recognizing the mortality of human beings and the immortality of knowledge *(gyan)*, the great educationist and an institution in himself that he was, Pandit K.B. Parsai's greatest desire was *"to leave behind my knowledge in books for people"*. Time and again he told me that *"a lot of knowledge, especially in India, had perished because it was not documented and passed on to others"*. He did not want that to happen with the knowledge he had inherited through 25 generations and accumulated by him since the age of 13 years at the feet of his father, Pandit Bhawanishankarji Parsai, and father-in-law Pandit Nathulalji Dwivedi, in a small village in Central India.

He put into practice, in the leaves of the various books he wrote, his firm belief of sharing his knowledge in the tradition of Vasudhaiva Kutumbakam (the whole world is my family).

He was happy that ever since this books—**Star Guide**® **to Predictive Astrology** was first published in 2001, it rekindled the interest of many – laypersons and students of Astrology who all have learnt immensely from this book. For the layperson it is a book for self-analysis of their horoscope and for those interested in the study of Astrology, it is an invaluable tutor and guide, giving insightful information about the science of Astrology. You cannot turn any chapter without getting some incisive information into the various aspects of Astrology that was honed specially by Pandit K.B. Parsai through his practical experience of over 70 years, along with our ability to relate the ancient science of Astrology to current times and situations. It was most satisfying to him when others came to him reporting that many had become amateur Astrologers by studying and understanding the principles detailed in this book.

However, it is truly a sad comment on today's times that while pulp fiction are sold for thousands of rupees, rare treatise containing unprecedented knowledge such as this, are sold for a lark. Yet plagiarising and piracy of such books is rampant. So if you have received a copy of this book any other way, please get rid of it and go to your nearest book store and buy a copy for yourself. Let this be your *"guru dakshina"* to the great scholar and teacher Pandit K.B. Parsai, who shared his knowledge with you without any restraint or hesitation.

It is most befitting that I dedicate this edition to my father, Pandit K.B. Parsai, along with my mother, Shrimati Krishna Kumar Parsai.

November 5, 2011
New Delhi.

Pandit D.K. Parsai
(ptparsai@gmail.com)

PREFACE TO THE FIRST EDITION

This book—the sixth in the series of STAR GUIDE from the PARSAI FAMILY—is born from the recognition of the mortality of human beings and the immortality of knowledge (*gyan*). Normally the concepts and precepts of an ancient knowledge like astrology, (particularly the predictive side) are passed on from the father to his progeny; in other words, kept a closed family secret. But I, born in a small village of Laduna in Madhya Pradesh, who had to struggle hard to acquire knowledge and educate myself to obtaining double M.A. and *Sahitya Ratna,* believe that knowledge must be spread and passed on to generations of people in the tradition of '*Vasudhaiva Kutumbakam'* (the whole world is my family).

Let me make it clear that despite controversies, astrology—the scientific study of the influence of the visible planets in the cosmos on the life and events on earth, based on mathematical calculations of their placement at the time of an individual's birth—is under no threat of becoming extinct. The kind of people irrespective of their class, religion, background and nationality seeking astrological guidance, is incredible. Whether considered a science or an art, a craft or a skill, astrology is here to stay and my co-author son, Pandit D. K. Parsai, an IT professional based in USA, and I have explained in great detail in the forthcoming chapters, why so. At 79 years of age today, I have attempted to include in this work much of the experience, knowledge and wisdom acquired by me from 13 years of age, from *25 generations of astrologers* in my family and it looks Pandit D. K. Parsai will carry on the tradition. As in any other field, there are people who are genuinely knowledgeable and those who feign to be so. This book should enable readers to differentiate between chaff and the grain.

The book was conceived two years ago, but it assumed an urgency after the passing away of my beloved wife, Krishna, my companion of 56 years, on the most auspicious day of

*Akshay Navmi **on November 5, 2000. Indeed her's has been the guiding hand in completing this work in record time for release on her first anniversary. Krishna herself was the daughter of the widely known** Raj-jyotishi **of his times from the erstwhile princely State of Sitamau in Madhya Pradesh, Pandit Nathulalji Dwivedi. He was also my guru, along with my own father, Pandit Bhawani Shankarji Parsai, who was famous for about 90 per cent accuracy of his predictions.** Many times while writing the book, I turned around to seek Krishna, only to realise that now she lives only in spirit...*

For readers new to astrology, the science of reading the stars to predict the future, it must be explained that there are two aspects to it. One is drawing a birth-chart and its various combinations as a Horoscope, and the other is interpreting it for predicting the future. We have detailed both these aspects in this book. Most people are familiar that the zodiac is divided into twelve equal parts each representing the Sign of Aries, Taurus, Gemini and so on. It is also known that the earth rotates around the Sun but it is the Sun which appears to move around the circle of zodiac. It is this apparent position of the Sun at the time of birth of an individual that determines the rising Sign of Sun in a Horoscope, known as the Ascendent or the starting point of the 12 houses in a birth chart.

In India, the 12 Houses are known as *'Bhavas'*. Knowledge of every event, development, progress, rise and fall, virtually every aspect of life from the time of conception of a human being, till death, and sometimes even beyond, is covered under these 12 Houses. While we have tried to cover as many subjects as affecting an individual, it is not humanly possible to enlist every minute event between the earth and the sky and it must be borne in mind that an astrologer is not a god. He/she can predict the future, *not change it.* The book gives broad guidance about the rules pertaining to the subjects governed by each of the 12 Houses.

Often, more than one House is directly or indirectly involved in making accurate predictions on a particular subject. Care has been taken to mention the co-related Houses as "Referral Houses", but in this regard too, students and scholars have to devise their own rules. To give an example: conception of a child is related to the 5th and the 7th House; but a safe or difficult delivery is related to the 5th, 8th and the 12th Houses. Herein lies a reason for half-baked astrologers or computer astrology going inaccurate in forecasts. There is no escaping experience and knowledge for accuracy of predictions.

As in all other sciences, astrology cannot be fully learnt from books or by theory alone. A student or scholar attains greater expertise on the subject by practical work and continuous study based thereon, just as accuracy in any branch of science is also reached by experimenting through the years, be it in nuclear power or in genetic engineering. As part of this process, the student or scholar must check up the accuracy or otherwise, of the predictions given, at least in some cases by follow-up.

A word about whether astrology is scientific or not. It has become somewhat fashionable these days to deride astrology publicly and seek it privately. My co-author, Pandit D. K. Parsai, has dealt with the subject at length in *Introduction to Astrology*. This article should clear the confusion. The problem is that the bogey of astrology being hocus pocus is not being raised by the ignorant, but by those knowledgeable people who do so only for argument's sake. The authors have no means to satisfy such die-hard opponents of astrology. Had astrology been a superstition or hocus pocus, it would have died a natural death, instead of surviving through the centuries. What is required is sustained funding for proper and objective research on the subject in public domain.

On our part, this treatise is our humble contemporary contribution in the chain of epic studies on the subject as in *Parashar Hora Sastra, Garg Hora, Lagadh Muni's "Rhik"*, the world famous works of *Aryabhatta, Lall, Laghujatak* of *Varah Mihir*, also works of *Brahmagupt, Shreepati, Bhaskaracharya, Brihaspati* and many others in the ancient times, *Neelkanth, Ganesh Daivagya,* and several others in the medieval times, who have highly enriched the knowledge about calculations as well as predictions in astrology.

It is in the fitness of things, that I acknowledge the faith in me of thousands of people from all walks of life, strata, and nationality who have consulted me over the years and thus enriched my experience and wisdom. These include VVIPs, scientists, artists, students, professionals, bureaucrats, industrialists, politicians, filmstars, as also poor, resourceless and the ordinary people. I also thank several friends—and they know who they are—who helped in various ways in the production of this book.

November 5, 2001   **Pandit K.B. Parsai**
New Delhi.

INTRODUCTION TO ASTROLOGY
by
Astrologer Pandit D. K. Parsai

Everyone wonders, at some time or the other, what the future holds in store for him/her; even the skeptic. Astrology is one such medium, based on established criteria, that tries to shed some light into a dark tunnel of future events. The first few chapters will give the reader a basic understanding of the subject of Astrology – what it is and what it is not.

It has now been, more or less, universally accepted that astrology – (*Jyotish*) has been in existence in India for many millenniums now, along with the *Vedas*. Jyotish consists mainly of two parts: astronomy and astrology.

Astronomy, as defined by the Living Webster – Encyclopaedic Dictionary of English language, is *"the science that treats of the location, magnitudes, motions, nature and constitution of celestial bodies and structures."* Or basically, charting of the motion and the nature of the heavenly bodies.

Astrology is the science of effect and influences of the celestial bodies on life on earth, especially of the *observable planets, and constellations considered nearer in relation to Earth.* As civilisations have evolved, each generation of Astrologers have added their own research and experience to the vast knowledge, with the existing socio-economic structures of their own current eras.

Astrology is the knowledge of relationships based on a study of planetary influences, on man and his environment. It includes the entire galaxy and is true of the planetary bodies. Their radiations affect each other, including the earth and all the things on it. There is no doubt that Sun has the greatest influence on the life on earth.

Without it there would be no life, for without it there would be no warmth, no division into day and night, no cycle of time, no plantation and no seasons, and no life at all. The influence of Sun is clear and easy to see. The influence of Moon on the other hand, is more subtle, though no less definite.

There are many ways in which the influence of Moon manifests itself on earth, human, plant and animal life. It is well known fact that large movement of water on earth, that is the flow of tides, is caused by Moon. Human body, too, which consists of 70 percent water, falls within the scope of lunar influence. The menstrual cycle of many women correspond to the lunar month; the human period of pregnancy is 273 days, or equal to nine lunar months. Many a mental illness, suicides etc. have been noted to increase during periods of lunar activity. Agriculturists have established that the Moon has a distinct influence on crops, which explains why for centuries people have planted according to the movement of Moon. Migratory birds depart only at or near the time of full Moon. Just as certain fish, eels in particular, move in accordance with certain phase of the Moon.

It is been established in physical sciences that everything in the universe has an effect on everything else, and it is useful to know that this is also true about the various constellations and planets in the visible heaven. Let us see how astrology works.

HOW ASTROLOGY WORKS

Astrology is based on a pure science. This may come as a surprise to many readers. But the fact *is* that the astrological chart is based on astronomical data. The astrological chart is the exact chart of the heavens showing the various planets, *as they could be seen* in the heavens at that particular time, and from that particular place on earth. If an astronomical chart were to be constructed of that time, indeed all the planets and constellations would be visible in the sky same as shown in the astrological chart. Similar charts are given everyday in newspapers. In simple terms, the astrologer prepares the chart of the exact position of the planets as could have been seen from the place where a person was born, and at the time when the person was born.

Why a chart of planets when one was born?

Astrology is a system of analysis, based on the effect of different planets (of our solar system) on the life on Earth. The major planets of consequence are – Sun, Mercury, Mars, Venus, Jupiter, Saturn, and Moon (and also Moon's Nodes Rahu and Ketu).

Predictive astrology is an immense catalogue of cause and effects of the various positions, combinations of the planets and constellations that have been found to influence all aspects of life and civilisation through the ages. Because birth is the first major event of a person's life, therefore it is indeed the starting point in astrological studies too. Fundamentally, a person comes into existence at a specific time, at a specific place. This is the first time that person comes in direct contact with the external world and its surroundings, radiations, waves of the various planets and other celestial entities. Therefore, there is this specific chart showing the positions and combination of planets that were in effect for that person, and that chart is called the birth-chart. It's like a *unique* and *natural* **identification** for that individual.

Time is important, but why the place?

The standardisation method of Sun rising time has shown that the sunrise time varies from place to place. Just as the warmth of the sunlight, and length of the day differs at different latitudes and longitudes (like the variations prevalent from the equator to the poles), the view of the planets, and consequently, their influence too varies from place to place. With the place of birth, the positional *co-ordinates* get fixed for the exact planetary and celestial combinations for that particular place (location) on the globe.

For very refined calculations, one can fix the co-ordinates of place in the same town or city too if one is born in a geographically large city like Mumbai, London or New York.

WHAT IS A BIRTH CHART?

The birth chart may be thought of as the 'photo' of the position of planets and the constellation 'frozen' at the time of the person's birth. For the sake of simplicity, the observable sky above the earth is represented as a square or a circular space and divided into 12 parts. Each part is called a 'house'.

Daily life cycle is divided, biologically and also by convention, into a 24-hour period, with the rising of the Sun generally taken as reference indicating the beginning of a day. (By western convention, now midnight 00 hours is taken as the end of the previous day and beginning of the next day). Taking the Sun as the major observable planet (interchangeably called star for astrological purpose) around which our conventions were made, each house represents an average of 2-hour period. Thus, these 12 houses represent the 24-hour movement of the Sun in relation to the earth at any given time and place on earth. If it is night in India, it will be day in the US. This is one way to check if the birth chart is reasonably correct or not. If a person was born at around noon and the birth-chart shows the position of Sun to be at the other side of the globe, it means the chart is cast wrong.

For this reason, in astrology, the *place of birth*, the *date & time of birth* are of vital importance. This data should be as accurate as possible to cast a correct birth chart.

It is important to note here that many people may not have correct birth data, that is the *date & time of birth,* and consequently the birth-chart made for them could be from slightly inaccurate to grossly inaccurate. Like with any other science, the accuracy of the input data is very essential to get accurate output results, in this case accurate predictions. Many astrologers do not bother to check the accuracy of the birth-chart and if the birth-chart they have used for predictions is inaccurate, the predictions are bound to be wrong. This simple fact cannot be emphasised enough.

Can any one imagine any doctor performing surgery or even prescribing medications on the basis of inaccurate laboratory results?

Astrology gets a lot of bad name for inaccurate predictions but there is never any mention of inaccuracy of the input data. By the same token, there are many people who call themselves "astrologers" but do not have the basic knowledge and understanding of astrology, which too goes to giving a bad name to astrology.

So, date and time of birth is required to fix the exact moment **in time** and *place of birth* is required for the exact **co-ordinates on the globe** from which the position of the various planets and constellations is observed. This is recorded on the chart in those 12 spaces (houses or *bhavas*).

How does one place the planets on those 12 spaces in the chart?

This is the second part of the birth chart. The first part was the **planets**. The visible sky was called heavens by our ancients. The heavens, having presence of various *constellations,* is known as the *Zodiac* in the Science of Astrology.

WHAT ARE THE CONSTELLATIONS?

On a clear night, many stars are visible. A **constellation** is a group of stars. Many of these stars have always been observed together, in a group in a particular formation. Many of these star-groups resemble some sort of a shape or form that humans sensibly and *culturally* identify with. For example, some groups seen together resemble the shape of a fish or a bull. The observable constellations were grouped together and roughly 2¼ of each constellation is grouped under some recognisable and predominant characteristic associated by us humans and called a **Sign** (of the Zodiac) or a *Rasi.*

12 *Rasi's* or the Signs of the Zodiac

See below for the 12 Signs of the zodiac, with the predominant characteristic associated with each one of them, their graphical representation, and the time of the year when each constellation-group (or Sign) rises and sets by s*aayan* position of Sun. These constellation groups (Signs) are fixed in relation to each other (like position of planets Mercury, Earth, Mars, etc. in our solar system is fixed in relation to each other). Which means that Taurus follows Aries, and Gemini follows Taurus, in much the same way as the 12 months in our calendar follow each other.

WHAT IS "*AYAN*-ANSH", "SA-*AYAN*", AND "NIR-*AYAN*"

Before proceeding further we would have to understand the two terms, "Nir-ayan" and "Sa-ayan", and also the difference in calculations under each of these two systems. In this connection we have to understand a little bit about "*Ayan*-ansh".

After roughly every 25,800 years, the meeting points of sidereal and tropical zodiacs coincidence, the two points start moving separately, by the speed of roughly every 72 years for approximately one degree of arc. This distance created by separate movements of the sidereal and tropical zodiacs has been named as "*Ayan*-ansh" by the forebears of Indian Astrology.

> It may be mentioned that Ayan-ansh given basically by "*Grah-Laghav*" (author *Ganesh Daivagnya*) was earlier prevalent in India. Later on some learned astrologers, on basis of new scientific research, corrected it, and this corrected Ayan-ansh was named "*Chitra*" (name of a constellation=*Nakshatra*), and experience has proved that this Ayan-ansh is most dependable.
>
> But some learned astrologers in India in the 20th century introduced further revisional corrections in the Ayan-ansh and let it be known by their personal name, like *Lahiri's* Ayan-ansh, (B.V.) *Raman's* Ayan-ansh, and *Krishnamurti's* Ayan-ansh.
>
> The senior author claims to have known Mr. Krishnamurti on personal level. In the early sixties, Mr. Krishnamurti was on a short visit from South India to Delhi and was staying with his friend, Mr. Venkataraman, a Section Officer then in the Directorate of Visual Publicity, Govt of India, at a flat in Pandara Road. The senior author was residing

in the same colony. It was then that Mr. Krishnamurti consulted the senior author daily for about 8 days to discuss preliminaries of astrology. It didn't appear then that he could devise his own system of Ayan-ansh. But he did, and got the due publicity, and now his Ayanansh is mentioned in astrological books and yearly Panchangs as an independent system of Ayan-ansh.

However, the author takes the liberty to mention that his practical experience of working with Ayan-ansh proves "*Chitra*-based Ayan-ansh" as the most correct. Anyway, astrological scholars are free to adopt any Ayan-ansh after their own practical experience and what appears to work best for them.

Coming back to "Nir-ayan system" and "Sa-ayan system", it should be understood that virtually all astrologers in India (and specially the *Panchangs* = yearly almanacs or ephemeris giving day-wise or week-wise information about position of the planets in terms of degrees and minutes go by the *Nir-ayan* system. The western world goes by the *Sa-ayan* system.

To understand the difference, these terms are derived from Sanskrit. *Nir* means 'no' or without, so **nir-ayan** means without consideration of the *ayan* (ayanansh); similarly *Sa* means 'with' or included, so **sa-ayana** means with *ayan* consideration included. In other words, NIRAYAN means without using the element of ayanansh for calculating the positions of the planets in the degrees and minutes, and SAAYAN means inclusive of the element of ayanansh.

The two charts given below indicate the approximate dates of entry of Sun into each Sign (*Rasi*) of the zodiac, first by *Nir-ayan* system, and then by the *Sa-ayan* system:

Figure 1		Movement of Sun by *Nir-ayan* System		
		Sankranti=entry of Sun into each *Rasi*		
1.	Mesh	Aries	from	14 April
2.	Vrishabh	Taurus	from	15 May
3.	Mithun	Gemini	from	15 June
4.	Karka	Cancer	from	17 July
5.	Simha	Leo	from	17 August
6.	Kanya	Virgo	from	17 September
7.	Tula	Libra	from	18 October
8.	Vrishchik	Scorpio	from	17 November
9.	Dhanu	Sagittarius	from	16 December
10.	Makar	Capricorn	from	14 January
11.	Kumbha	Aquarius	from	13 February
12.	Meena	Pisces	from	15 March

A Sanskrit term *"Sankranti"* has been used in the table above. *"Sankramana"* means to cross, and thus *"Sankranti"* means Sun's crossing (transit) from one *Rasi* to another *Rasi*. The dates given above are approximate, and the transit might be a day earlier or a day later. The correct dates of transit are given in every reliable *Panchang*, which in India are published in every language in use over the country, viz., Hindi, Gujarati, Marathi, Bangla, Oriya, Bhojpuri, Tamil, Telugu, Malayalam, Kannada, Gurumukhi (Punjab), Sharda Script in Jammu and Kashmir.

Figure 2		Movement of Sun by *Sa-ayan* System	
1.	Mesh	Aries (the Ram)	from March 21 to April 19
2.	Vrishabh	Taurus (the Bull)	from April 20 to May 20
3.	Mithun	Gemini (the Twins)	from May 21 to June 21
4.	Karka	Cancer (the Crab)	from June 22 to July 22
5.	Simha	Leo (the Lion)	from July 23 to Aug. 23
6.	Kanya	Virgo (the Virgin)	from Aug. 24 to Sept. 23
7.	Tula	Libra (the Scales)	from Sept. 24 to Oct. 23
8.	Vrishchik	Scorpio (the Scorpion)	from Oct. 24 to Nov. 22
9.	Dhanu	Sagittarius (the Bow)	from Nov. 22 to Dec. 21
10.	Makar	Capricorn (the Goat)	from Dec. 22 to Jan 21
11.	Kumbha	Aquarius (the Water-pitcher)	from Jan 22 to Feb 19
12.	Meena	Pisces (the Fish)	from Feb. 20 to March 20

THE THREE LAWS OF ASTROLOGICAL ZODIAC

A look at the way the zodiac is divided in astrology shows that the Signs are arranged in such a way as to express first **the Law of Two**, or the law of duality or polarity; also known as male-female, positive-negative or active-passive.

Next, the Signs are divided so as to express **the Law of Three**, the principal of relationships. The presence of a man and a woman is not a sufficient cause to produce a child; there must be a feeling of love or a desire to do so.

In astrology, **the Law of Three** finds expression in what is called the 'mode of action'. A Sign may be positive or negative, in accordance to the principal of duality, but at the same time they reflect the principal of triplicity. The third law is superimposed upon the Law of Two. The *modes* are superimposed upon *polarities*. Thus in astrology, the modes of action are called:

'Cardinal' – that upon which all else depends

'Fixed' – that which is acted upon; and

'Mutable' – that which effects the exchange of forces.

(Normally they are referred to as Fixed, Cardinal and Mutable, but the reader can see from the chart below, why I have mentioned them in this order)

Three terms, however, are still insufficient to describe either a thing or event. A relationship is theoretical; it cannot be said to exist. Like date/time-place-people is not an event. The subject matter makes it an event. In most ancient traditions, this foursome is the four 'elements': fire, earth, air, and water – from which all matter is derived.

In astrology, then, the four elements are superimposed upon the modes and upon the polarities. Each Sign is different, no two are alike, and there is no repetition: all possible permutations of polarity, triplicity and quadruplicity work themselves within a twelve-Sign system.

Figure 3   Table of the Constellations with their Polarity Mode of Action and Element

	Sign (English Term)	Sign (Hindi Term)	Polarity	Mode of Action	Element
1	Aries	Mesh	Positive	Cardinal	Fire
2	Taurus	Vrishabh	Negative	Fixed	Earth
3	Gemini	Mithun	Positive	Mutable	Air
4	Cancer	Karka	Negative	Cardinal	Water
5	Leo	Simha	Positive	Fixed	Fire
6	Virgo	Kanya	Negative	Mutable	Earth
7	Libra	Tula	Positive	Cardinal	Air
8	Scorpio	Vrishchik	Negative	Fixed	Water
9	Sagittarius	Dhanu	Positive	Mutable	Fire
10	Capricorn	Makar	Negative	Cardinal	Earth
11	Aquarius	Kumbha	Positive	Fixed	Air
12	Pisces	Meena	Negative	Mutable	Water

The diagram of the zodiac, constructed as above, is the celestial language that the astrologers try to interpret. The point here is that this system called Astrology is a simultaneous fusion of polarity, triplicity and quadruplicity and harmonically determined aspects and angles as a whole. It has been scientifically developed and is internally a consistent system. In short, it can be said that our ancients never dreamed up astrology.

Further, each Sign or *Rasi* has a planet that 'rules' it.

Figure 4   Table of ownership of the 12 Signs (Rasi's) of the Zodiac by the seven planets

Constellation (*Rasi*)	Planetary Ruler	Constellation (*Rasi*)
Cancer	**Moon**	
Leo	**Sun**	
Virgo	**Mercury**	Gemini
Libra	**Venus**	Taurus
Scorpio	**Mars**	Aries
Sagittarius	**Jupiter**	Pisces
Capricorn	**Saturn**	Aquarius

The order reflects the distance from various planets to the Sun: Mercury is the closest planet, followed by Venus, Mars, Jupiter and finally Saturn. (Earth not counted because she is our frame of reference.) The order is forward from Sun and reverse from Moon. (This is another proof of Astrology as a logical system and not something that was concocted by our ancients.)

The various planets have different behaviour and generally govern that behaviour in the humans too.

Figure 5   Table of Planet behaviour

Planet	*Behaviour*
Moon	Mind
Sun	Soul
Mercury	Communicator
Venus	Desire
Mars	Action
Jupiter	Wisdom
Saturn	Renunciation

<u>Planets</u> in astrology are those planets of the solar system that are considered of major consequence on the human life on earth; there are nine major planets of consequence to an individual's life.

Herschel (Uranus), Neptune and Pluto too are included, but since their movement is so slow and they are so far away removed from Earth, that their effect is on very long term events, having no worth mention influence on individuals independently.

Signs are the 12 constellation groups that have been refined to an easily identifiable icon of human social life, which instantly remind of the primary qualities and characteristics associated with such an icon. Just as one can be born in any one particular month of the year, similarly, one is born under any one constellation-Sign of the zodiac. That Sign is called the rising Sign or the **ascendant** (the Sign that was ascending on the eastern horizon at the time of birth). In Indian astrological language it is called the *Lagna*.

HOW IS A CHART CONSTRUCTED?

The chart itself is a composition of three layers superimposed on each other, having a relationship to each other and giving meaning to each other. The chart is the simplified representation of the sky, divided into 12 parts. There are twelve constellation-Signs in the zodiac; so each Sign must get representation on the chart. This chart is like a plan of the sky made on paper. The plan of the sky is divided into 12 parts. Each part is called a 'house' (or Bhava); the top most space is called the First house.

Each house has been allotted to represent an area of activity in our life – for instance mother and mother related events to the 4th house, marriage and life partner to the 7th house and so on. Detailed list of main subjects to be considered under each house is given in further chapters of this book.

The central, top most space in the chart is the First house. Then, working anti-clockwise, is the 2nd house, the 3rd house, the fourth house and so on. The position of each house is fixed. This is a convention. And like all conventions, it is followed because it works.

This plan of the sky on paper is the first layer of your birth chart. This consists of a chart with 12 fixed positions, called the houses. Mind you, the house 'numbers' are ***not*** *actually written* *in the houses* because the notation of the houses, beginning from the *first house*, is always fixed by convention and therefore **not** written into the chart.

Figure 6 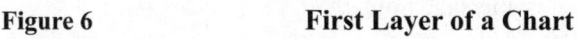 **First Layer of a Chart**

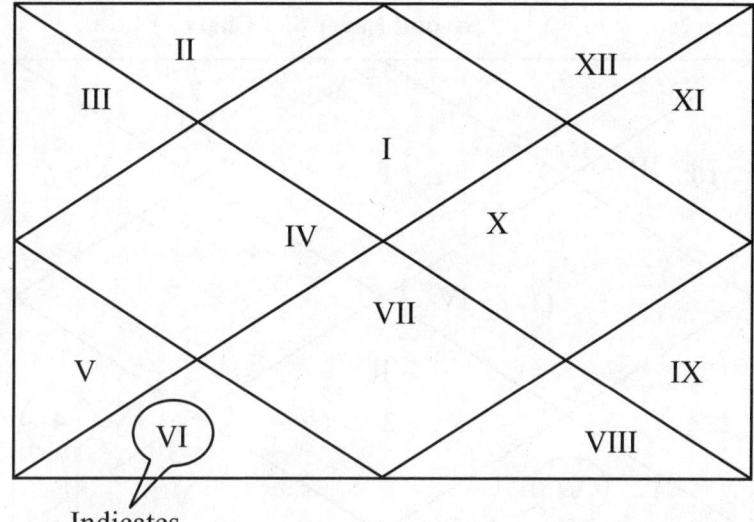

Indicates House Number

Note: These numbers indicating the House number are not given on the chart and their placement is always fixed in each drawing of the chart.

From your date, time of birth and place of birth, the *rising Sign* or the ascendant is calculated, this is the rising Sign of the zodiac that was there in the eastern horizon particularly at that date, time and particular place. Since the Signs of the zodiac are also in a fixed sequence, the rest of the zodiac belt can also be written down. This is the second layer of the birth chart.

Superimpose the second layer on the first layer. Begin with the first house of the chart and write the *Sign-number* of the rising Sign in the First house (North Indian System). Then, working anti-clockwise on the chart, complete the sequence of the rest of the Signs of the zodiac. For instance, if the rising Sign of a person is Scorpio (Sign no. 8), put down the numeral 8 in the first house of the chart. Next, working *anti-clockwise* put down the other Signs in sequence, e.g., Sagittarius (no. 9) in second house, Capricorn (no. 10) in third house and so on till Libra (i.e. Rasi No. 7) occupies the last house.

Figure 7   **Second Layer of a Chart**

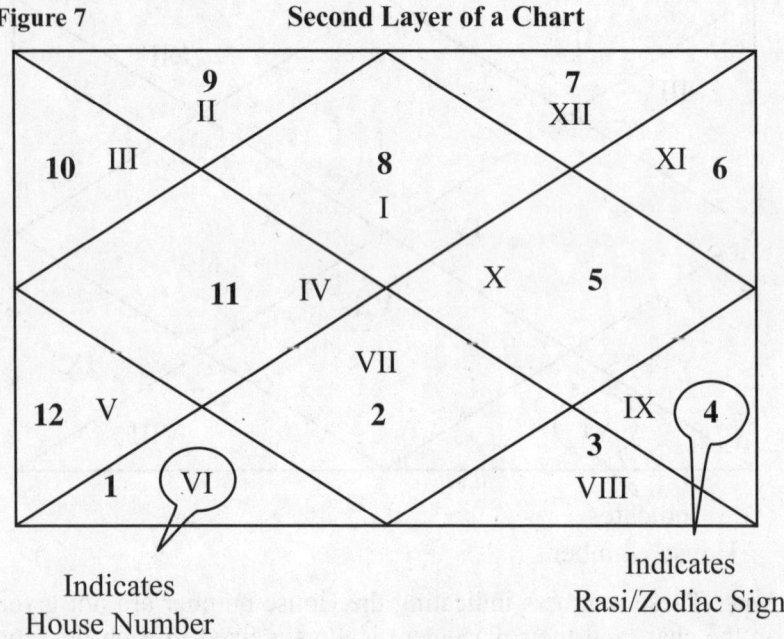

Indicates House Number

Indicates Rasi/Zodiac Sign

How do the planets come in all this?

The daily movement of the all the planets is calculated and recorded in book form called the ephemeris or almanac. Such almanacs are widely published all over the world. In India, the usual time for issuing these almanacs is prior to the Hindu New Year, which is the first day after Diwali, or 15 or 16 days after the "Holi" festival. (The Almanac is also called <u>Panchang</u>: *Panch* = five, *ang* = limb or branch; a panchang has five important limbs or parts)

    (Tithi, Day of the week, Nakshatra (Constellation occupied by Moon), Yoga and Karana.

    From the almanac, you can get the precalculated position of each and every planet for any particular day *in the relevant year.*

The position is given in terms of Signs or Rasis. For instance, Mars may be shown as traversing through Aries. It means that on that particular day, the position of Mars was coinciding with the position of the constellation-Sign Aries. *Thus Mars is said to be in Aries.* This may be verified by any astronomical laboratory or from the data issued in newspapers. The system of tracking and marking the position of heavenly bodies is the same in Astronomy and Astrology.

Once the position of each planet is known, enter each of them with the appropriate Sign in the chart (for instance, from our above example, enter Mars on the Sign of Aquarius, and so on). This is the <u>third layer</u> of the chart. With the three layers in position our chart gets completed.

Figure 8   **Third Layer of a Chart**

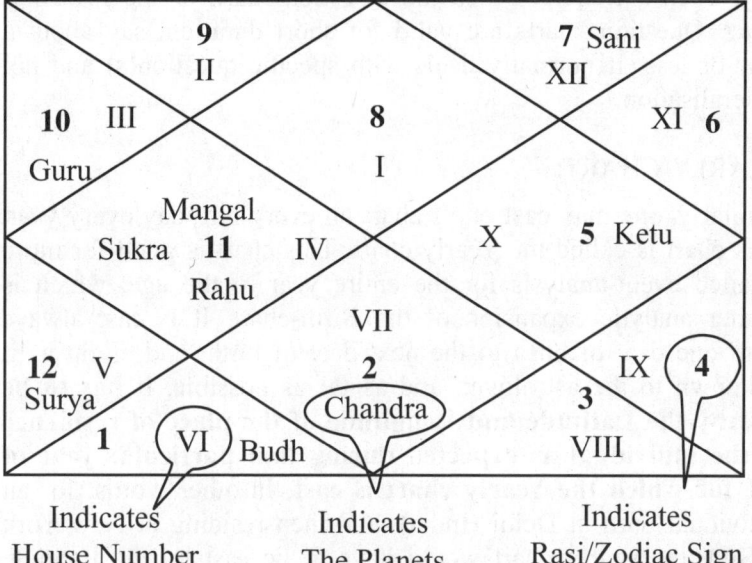

What is the difference between this chart and Birth-Chart?

None. Different charts can be made for different points of time. The process of assembling the layers is the same. A chart constructed from date of birth, time of birth and place of birth is called the **Birth-Chart**.

Are there any other kinds of astrological charts?

Charts can broadly be differentiated as Birth-chart, any particular event(s)' chart, Yearly-chart, Monthly-chart, Two and a half days' Hora-chart (a particle of the Monthly-chart), and a Question-chart.

BIRTH CHART has already been explained above in full details.

Time-Charts

QUESTION CHART:

Sometimes, one may wish to know about short-term events, or events of specific nature. In such a case the time of the question (or desire to know) formed in the mind of the Questioner is noted. The birth of the question is treated the same way as the birth of an individual, and a chart is *cast,* in the same three-layer way. Such a chart is called the Question-chart, or the *Prashna-chart*. Question charts are valid for short duration, say about a year or less. It normally deals with specific question(s) and not generalisation.

YEARLY CHART:

Similarly, one may cast one's chart on every birthday every year. This chart is called the Yearly chart. This chart is good for more detailed event-analysis for the entire year of the age, which is further analytic expansion of the Birth-chart. It is cast always from one date of birth to the next date of birth, and as far as it is known to the astrologer, and as far as possible, **it has to be cast by the Latitude and Longitude of the place of residence of the individual as expected during that particular year of age for which the Yearly chart is cast.** In other words, for an individual born at Delhi (India), and then residing at New York (USA), the yearly chart would have to be cast by the Latitude and Longitude of New York (USA).

It is really laborious process, because conversion of calculation based on Delhi timing (cast by Latitude and Longitude of Delhi) would have to be converted by detailed calculations on the basis of New York timing (cast by the Latitude and Longitude of New York)

It is to be remembered that a yearly chart is progression of birth chart, year by year, calculated to bring the birth chart in the context of the planets, as they stand on the date of birth in the given year of age.

MONTH-WISE CHART:

Yearly chart is the magnified view of one whole year starting from the relevant birthday. Monthly chart is a still more magnified view of events for any given month of the year of your age.

HORA CHART (particle of MONTHLY CHART):

One can go up to the Hora chart, which is the 2½ day chart, based on the movement position of the monthly chart vis-à-vis the position of Moon from one Sign to the next. (The Moon takes 27 to 28 days to complete one cycle of the 12 Signs or Rasis; that is, it covers each Rasi in roughly 2¼ days.)

These are all *Time*-charts, valid for different periods of time.

Event-Charts

Certain events and their achievements in the life of a person are standard, like Education, Career & Profession, Love & Marriage, Progeny (children), Parents, Money, to name a few. Priority and weightage of certain events may vary from society to society and culture to culture. But the basic nature of these events remains, by and large, the same across entire civilisation. Charts for such events follow a different treatment—the particular house pertaining to that particular event is magnified, its chart is cast and studied by the learned astrologer.

For instance, to study the married life of a man, a **Navamsha chart** is constructed and studied (*Navam* means ninth, *ansh* means part; Navamsha means the Ninth Part chart, or one-ninth of the main horoscope).

Similarly, in case of a woman, the question of marriage and married life is considered from the Trinshansha chart, One-thirtieth (1/30) part chart is constructed and studied. No doubt the

7th house in the birth-chart is the preliminary relevant consideration in this behalf.

OK. So now the Charts are prepared. So then what?

The charts are like the Laboratory reports in a medical case. The more accurate the reports, the better and detailed the analysis.

A learned astrologer, like an experienced specialist doctor, can see various permutations and combinations of planets, their Signs, their effects on each other, beneficial effect, malefic effect, neutralising effect, particular combinations leading to particular type of event, timing of that event and so on.

DIFFERENCE BETWEEN WESTERN SUN-SIGN SYSTEM AND INDIAN SYSTEM OF ASTROLOGY

The orthodox Indian school of astrology basically did not rely much on the concept of Sun-Signs, to a certain extent justifiably so, because its wider canvas leads to covering the humans under the transit of Sun in each house of the zodiac. All people born between March 21 and April 19 are considered to fall under the (Saayan) Sun Sign of Aries. In contrast, the Indian system goes by individual horoscope cast on the basis of date, time and place of birth of each individual. This system gives *much greater precision* and greater depth of analysis regarding an individual as compared merely to the Sun Signs.

The individual horoscope changes, on an average, every two hours (in India). All the twelve Signs of zodiac rise in the east horizon, turn by turn, within 24 hours every single day. A person born in Delhi on say Jan 14, 1985 between 7:20 am and 9:04 am will have Capricorn as the ascendant, while another born between 9:05 am and 10:32 am will have Aquarius as his ascendant. That is, two people born on the forenoon of Jan 14, 1985 itself would have different charts and different future growth, development and events in life.

But under the zodiac Sun Sign system both would be Aquarius. So for general and rather broad characteristics zodiac

Sun Signs may be used but for accurate and pinpointed predication, specially with regard to the actual time in life when the event is likely to occur, individual horoscope is the best to be used.

TO SUMMARISE IT ALL

The Signs – Rasi

The heavens, as the visible sky, consist of various constellations (Nakshatras) also known as the Zodiac Signs. The observable constellations are grouped together, according to similarity of characteristics. Roughly 2¼ constellations are grouped together under one Sign or Rasi and their sequence is fixed in the zodiac belt.

Houses

The entire heavens around us, the earth is divided into 12 parts. Each part is called a 'house' (or a Bhava). The eastern horizon is considered as the first house or the starting point and rest of the houses in the sequence of their order constitute the rest of the horoscope. At any given point of time some Sign (Rasi) is rising on the eastern horizon which is called as Ascendant (Lagna).

To repeat, whichever Sign (Rasi) is present in the East Horizon at the time of birth of a person (or even an animal such as calf etc.) constitutes the Ascendant (Lagna) of that person (or the animal). As a matter of fact, the senior author's father, who was a learned and accuracy oriented astrologer, always cast a birth chart of a calf born of any cow in the family, just to determine whether the calf was beneficial to the entire family.

ADDITIONAL INFORMATION

Retrogression begins when the Earth sits between planets (Mars, Mercury, Jupiter, Venus and Saturn) and the Sun. As earth orbits the Sun, we repeatedly seem to 'lap' the other planets. When this happens, our frame of reference makes it appear that these planets are moving backward. This seeming backward movement is termed *retrogression*. Jupiter and Saturn move backward once a year. Mars is not cyclical in retrogression. These movements are called 'crooked' (*Vakra* – Sanskrit for retrograde). Also note that Rahu and Ketu, the two shadow planets are always in retrograde movement.

Figure 9   Approximate proper motion of each planet

Planet	Time per Rasi (Constellation)	Time per Sun revolution
SUN	30 days	N/A
MOON	2¼ days	365 DAYS
MERCURY	30 days	88 DAYS
VENUS	30 days	224 DAYS
MARS	1½ months	687 DAYS (1½ YEARS)
JUPITER	1 year	12 ½ YEARS
SATURN	2 ½ years	29 ½ /30 YEARS
RAHU / KETU	1 ½ years	18 YEARS
URANUS	7 years	84 YEARS
NEPTUNE	13 ¾ years	165 YEARS
PLUTO	20.67 years	248 YEARS

While diurnal motion never changes its direction, the proper motion of every planet except Sun and Moon does.

Figure 10   The Exaltation and Debilitation
for Planets in various Rasis

Planet		Exaltation Highest Point			Debilitation Lowest Point		
Sun	Surya	10°	Mesh	Aries	10°	Tula	Libra
Moon	Chandra	3°	Vrishabh	Taurus	3°	Vrishchik	Scorpio
Mars	Mangal	28°	Makar	Capricorn	28°	Karka	Cancer
Mercury	Budh	15°	Kanya	Virgo	15°	Meena	Pisces
Jupiter	Guru	5°	Karka	Cancer	5°	Makar	Capricorn
Venus	Sukra	27°	Meena	Pisces	27°	Kanya	Virgo
Saturn	Sani	20°	Tula	Libra	20°	Mesh	Aries
Rahu	Rahu		Vrishabh	Taurus		Vrishchik	Scorpio
Ketu	Ketu		Vrishchik	Scorpio		Vrishabh	Taurus

Figure 11   Length of Major Periods (Maha Dashas)

Planet		Length of Major Period in years	Rounded Percentage
Sun	Surya	6	5 %
Moon	Chandra	10	8 %
Mars	Mangal	7	6 %
Rahu	Rahu	18	15 %
Jupiter	Guru	16	13 %
Saturn	Sani	19	16 %
Mercury	Budh	17	14 %
Ketu	Ketu	7	6 %
Venus	Sukra	20	17 %
Total:		120 years	100 %

Figure 12 Nakshatras and their duration in each Rasi /Sign

#	Name	From	In Rasi	Sign	To	Rasi	Sign
1	Ashvini	0°	Mesh	Aries	13°19	Mesh	Aries
2	Bharani	13°20	Mesh	Aries	26°39	Mesh	Aries
3	Kritika	26°40	Mesh	Aries	9°59	Vrishabh	Taurus
4	Rohini	10°	Vrishabh	Taurus	23°19	Vrishabh	Taurus
5	Mrigashira	23°20	Vrishabh	Taurus	6°39	Mithun	Gemini
6	Ardra	6°40	Mithun	Gemini	19°59	Mithun	Gemini
7	Punarvasu	20°00	Mithun	Gemini	3°19	Karka	Cancer
8	Pushya	3°20	Karka	Cancer	16°399	Karka	Cancer
9	Ashlesha	16°40	Karka	Cancer	29°59	Karka	Cancer
10	Magha	0°	Simha	Leo	13°19	Simha	Leo
11	Purva Phalgu	13°20	Simha	Leo	26°39	Simha	Leo
12	Uttara Phalgu	26°40	Simha	Leo	9°59	Kanya	Virgo
13	Hasta	10°	Kanya	Virgo	23°19	Kanya	Virgo
14	Chitra	23°20	Kanya	Virgo	6°39	Tula	Libra
15	Swati	6°40	Tula	Libra	19°59	Tula	Libra
16	Vishakha	20°00	Tula	Libra	3°19	Vrishchik	Scorpio
17	Anuradha	3°20	Vrishchik	Scorpio	16°39	Vrishchik	Scorpio
18	Jyeshtha	16°40	Vrishchik	Scorpio	29°59	Vrishchik	Scorpio
19	Mula	0°	Dhanus	Sagi.	13°19	Dhanus	Sagi.
20	Purva Ashad	13°20	Dhanus	Sagi.	26°39	Dhanus	Sagi.
21	Uttara Ashad	26°40	Dhanus	Sagi.	9°59	Makar	Capri.
22	Shravan	10°	Makar	Capri.	23°19	Makar	Capri.
23	Dhanistha	23°20	Makar	Capri.	6°39	Kumbha	Aquarius
24	Satabishak	6°40	Kumbha	Aquarius	19°59	Kumbha	Aquarius
25	Purva Bhadra	20°00	Kumbha	Aquarius	3°19	Meena	Pisces
26	Uttara Bhadra	3°20	Meena	Pisces	16°39	Meena	Pisces
27	Revati	16°40	Meena	Pisces	29°59	Meena	Pisces

BASIC CONSIDERATIONS

1. Whatever non-believers in astrology may say and shout from roof-tops, faith in this branch of knowledge is increasing rapidly, specially after horoscopes are now being cast by computers, and its spread is not restricted to any one country or continent. There is much scope for research and expansion on the calculation side of casting the horoscopes, because science has no limits, but whatever progress has been made so far on the calculation side can be deemed to be sufficient for making predictions correctly to a great extent. **Though most calculations have been computerised, some of the very minute and specific calculations have not yet been programmed into any software.** For example, the correct calculations in terms of sub-degree of the Indian system of aspect (*drishti*) of planets on the 12 houses (*bhavas*) and inter-planetary aspecting, as also yearly charts (*varsh-phal*) of a person settled in a country *other than that of his birth* have yet to be correctly calculated by a software program, and likewise, calculations of monthly charts related to the yearly chart made by computers have been found to be basically incorrect.

2. Similarly, the calculations of degree of Moon's position at the time of birth or at the time of start of a yearly chart of a person as calculated by computers in India, Europe, North and South Americas, Australia and Africa have been found not quite correct. The result is that consequential calculation of *Vimshottari Mahadasa* (which means the effectivity-periods of the influence of planets) has also not stood the test of accuracy.

3. It is to be appreciated that most people have come to depend solely on computer-made horoscopes and yearly charts because they are cheaper and easily available. While on the subject of computer-made horoscopes, it has to be understood

clearly that one must not depend, under any circumstance, on the predictions given by computers, because they are more stereotype than unique. They are not capable of taking into account the overall position of the planets, coordinated study of the Bhava-Chalitam + Navamsha chart + periodicity of effectivity of planets (Vimshottari Mahadasa and its sub-periods etc.) + the yearly chart and several other factors relevant to the study of a horoscope.

Experience has it that analysis of the computerised software in match-making, business partnership, litigation and political opposition/competition have been found to be rather misguiding and sometimes far removed from reality.

4. Thus, though there is no harm in getting a horoscope made by a good computer software (accurate though not necessarily the most popular), it would be in one's best interest to have the predictions read by an expert astrologer. Bear in mind that computer's software is the creation of the HUMAN BRAIN. On the other hand nothing so far can synthesize the experience and knowledge of a human mind.

For readers totally new to this branch of knowledge, it needs to be explained that any horoscope consists of 12 houses, which are known as 'Bhava' in India. Every event, development, progress, rise and fall, virtually everything from the time of conception upto death, and sometimes subsequent to death, is covered by these 12 houses.

5. Thus it is most important to know, at least in a broad manner, the subjects covered under each of the 12 houses in a horoscope. Often, even practising astrologers do not know which particular subject falls exactly under which particular house or houses, because often one subject may be related to two or more houses. For instance, conception of a child is related to 5th and the 7th house normally; however, whether delivery of the child will be safe or difficult or will it be a still-born is related to the 5th, 8th and the 12th houses!

6. Further, just like the 12 houses, the Zodiac too has twelve

Signs, each broadly occupying one of the houses by serial system (continuity of rotation). In India, these Signs of the Zodiac are known as the twelve Rasis. These twelve Signs of Zodiac (Rasis) rise in the eastern horizon by regular rotation and thus complete one full round in 24 hours.

7. It is under this compulsion that this book has to be divided into two parts in this and the same volume. The first part deals exclusively with preliminary understanding of a chart (it can be birth chart, yearly chart, monthly chart, 2 ½ days' Hora chart, Question chart) and the subjects falling under each house of the given chart. All the 12 houses have been given or assigned names depending on the principal subject or subjects related to that particular house, e.g. the first house is called Lagna, (or Ascendant in western systems), the second house is known as the 'Dhana' bhava, i.e. House of Wealth. Names of houses and subjects ruled by them are given in the first part of this book.

8. The primary element in the study of a chart is the Ascendant (*Lagna*), the first house. During the 24 hours of the day and night, all the 12 houses take rotation, which roughly allocates 2 hours per house. *But each house is not of exactly 2 hours duration*, because the duration depends on the latitude and longitude of the place for which the chart is being cast. **Because of inequality of the space occupied by the twelve houses in a chart, the *Bhava Chalitam* chart becomes very important.** Bhava Chalitam means fixation of planetary positions in the 12 houses. It is done on the basis of calculating the exact degrees and minutes of the positions of planets at the time of casting the chart, and calculating the boundary lines of the 12 Houses. In the process of fixing the positions of the planets in the 12 houses, it maybe found that a planet might have shifted from one house to another, which can be either forward or backward. In places lying north or south of 36 degrees of latitude, this shifting sometimes jumps even to the 3rd place forward or backward. This means that a planet broadly occupying the 2nd house might shift to the 3rd or even the 4th house, and backwards might shift to the 1st or 12th

house. The net result is that the particular planet would give the results of the *house* to which it has shifted.

In this context it has to be noted that despite the shifting to the adjacent house, the planet would continue to give the results of the *Sign* of the Zodiac actually occupied by it (i.e. the Rasi of its original position.)

9. This point has been explained in detail, because the Bhava Chalitam position explained above is most important in predictive astrology. **A majority of the clients want the predictions to be given merely on the basis of the broad birth chart without further details calculated, and the astrologers also do not insist on getting the calculations done for the Bhava Chalitam. The final result is that the predictions are the victim of this 'short-circuit' in consultation.** When predictions do not turn out to be correct or the point of time of the predicted event or predicted development does not stand accurate, astrology gets a bad name!

10. The rotation of the Sign of the zodiac (Rasi) is not uniform, neither from day to day, nor round the year. Its duration depends on the Latitude of the place for which the calculations are undertaken. For example, on Equator, the duration of the Sign of a Zodiac (Rasi) passing through the eastern horizon (normally known as the Ascendant or Lagna) is roughly between 1 hr. 51 minutes to 2 hrs 10 minutes. In contrast the time taken by the zodiac Signs on the eastern horizon at Latitude 60^0 varies from zero hour 29 minutes to 3 hrs 14 minutes.

11. The information in the above paragraph has been given to explain that a Sign of the zodiac rising (present) on the Eastern Horizon at the birth has to be determined by calculations. The same principle applies to determine the Sign of the zodiac rising on the Eastern Horizon at the time of casting a Question chart (that is when a person reaches an astrologer, without prior appointment, to get answers to his/her questions).

12. Thus it has to be clearly understood that accuracy of predictions would primarily depend on the accuracy of the determination

of the Sign of zodiac (Rasi) rising in the Eastern Horizon at the time of birth or putting a question. The Sign of the zodiac rising (or present) on the Eastern Horizon is known as the (Lagna) or Ascendant. Once the Ascendant (Lagna) has been determined, the chart is cast and the planetary positions are shown according to the Sign of the zodiac (Rasi) occupied by each planet at that time of birth or putting a question.

13. It may be noted carefully that after casting the chart, detailed calculations are necessary to draw the Bhava Chalitam chart, which has been explained in paragraph 8 above. It has also been explained above that the planet would give results of the Rasi (Sign of zodiac) occupied by it, and of the House occupied by it by original position or by the shifted position in the Bhava Chalitam chart. It is so because sometimes one House is spread out partly to two Signs of zodiac (Rasis), while sometimes two Houses occupy the same Sign (Rasi).

14. For attaining greater accuracy, the astrologer should then go further into calculating the inter-relationship of the planets vis-à-vis their permanent relationship, their positions in dissections of the birth chart known as Hora chart (division into ½), Dreshkana chart (division into one third i.e. 10 upon 30), Saptansha chart (division 7 upon 30), Navamsha chart (division: 9 upon 30), Dwadasansa chart (division: 12 upon 30), Trinshansha chart (division: one upon 30), and Shasatyansa chart (division: ½ upon 30).

15. The computer horoscopes contain many other dissective charts, but they are intended to increase the volume of the horoscope rather than for actual utility in the study of horoscope, because hardly one or two among one thousand astrologers have the competence to study and make genuine use of those charts relating to some specific point.

16. For reaching much greater accuracy in predictions, two more charts are essentially needed. They relate to aspect (*drishti*) of the planets on the 12 Houses (normally known as the "Bhava *drishti*), and other one is inter-planetary aspecting, commonly known as the "Grah *drishti*". The computer generally gives you just a broad idea of these two tables, but horoscopes

manually made by astrologers carry the exact calculations, which then lead to precise predictions. *"Ashtak Varga"* of the 'planets-and-the-ascendant' are also useful for reaching greater accuracy in prediction. Note that inter-relationship of planets, strength of planets, inter-planetary aspecting and aspect of planets on the 12 Houses, as also the Ashtak Varga relate to only the 7 planets from Sun to Saturn, and do not include Rahu, Ketu, Uranus, Neptune and Pluto.

17. The last essential calculation needed for correct predictions is the tables of <u>*Vimshottari Maha-dasa*</u> and <u>*Antar-dasas*</u> (also known as the main periods and sub-periods). These tables are unavoidable, because they determine when a particular planet would be more or fully effective and also give the correct idea about the point of time when a particular event or development would take place in life. The sub-periods can be further divided into pro-sub-periods, known in India as *'Pratyantar-dasa'*. When very precise point of time has to be determined, say with regard to hearing/judgement of a court case, delivery of a child, written test or interview for a job, meeting for important transaction in business or real estate, undertaking a journey for an important purpose, voting for an election, ambition for a post of power, nomination to any prestigious body, elevation as a High court or Supreme court judge, further division of the pro-sub-periods (Pratyantar Dasa) would help in reaching accurate conclusions.

18. Lastly, an important element needed for accurate predictions is the progressive charts also known as the yearly charts or *'Varsh-phal'*. The yearly chart can be further progressed into "Monthly charts" for further precision of time with regard to predictions, particular or general. There was a time in India upto mid-fifties of 20th century when rulers, nobles, *zamindars*, rich men, high officials used to get their detailed 'month-wise' yearly charts made and read by the astrologers on their birthday. When as mentioned in paragraph 17 above, predictions were needed precisely for a week-to-week basis or even on day-to-day basis, the monthly chart would be further reduced into 12 charts covering 2 ½ days each, known as Hora Charts.

Readers need to be informed that so far the monthly charts and in many cases also the yearly charts drawn by computers have been found to be inaccurate.

Calculations of month-wise charts and charts for 2 ½ days (Hora charts) are complicated jobs and need expertise on the part of the astrologer. If the calculations of the yearly chart/ monthly chart etc are basically wrong, naturally the predictions too would be wrong.

19. How to cast the detailed calculations portion of astrological work is not the subject of this book. However, the above information has been given by way of elementary acquaintance with the basics of horoscope/yearly chart/question chart, because predictive portion of astrology wholly and solely depends on calculation part of it.

As in the case of family doctors, it is often advisable to have a family astrologer. Because, however learned and experienced the astrologer, he/she would be more accurate in the predictions and about the point of time, if the astrologer has knowledge of the background and surrounding circumstances of the person requiring consultations. And continuity of this knowledge of background helps the astrologer in reaching much greater accuracy, as much as 80 to 90%. Though some inexperienced and less learned astrologers claim 100% accuracy of their predictions, bear in mind that perhaps only the SUPER POWER has retained with ITSELF the power of complete knowledge of the FUTURE. Great care needs to be taken in choosing a family astrologer.

20. Having understood what is a birth chart/yearly chart/Question chart, it is better to understand now the different methods of writing the charts. There are three main styles prevailing in India, which have travelled to other countries and continents. In India they are known as the North Indian style, East Indian style and South Indian style (which is in use to a great extent in American countries also). Briefly they are explained and illustrated below.

21. The North Indian style is in use from Maharashtra to Kashmir, including Pakistan, Rajasthan, and Punjab to Bihar. This style

is either circular or a square/rectangular chart (diagram). In this method, the chart starts with the Ascendant (Lagna) at the Top-Central point and then proceeds anti-clockwise. Given below is an illustration of the rectangular style, while the circular style is not given here because it is not presently in use for the last several decades because all horoscopes made by computers all over the world generally use a rectangular formation of the chart:

Figure 13 **Chart – North Indian Style**

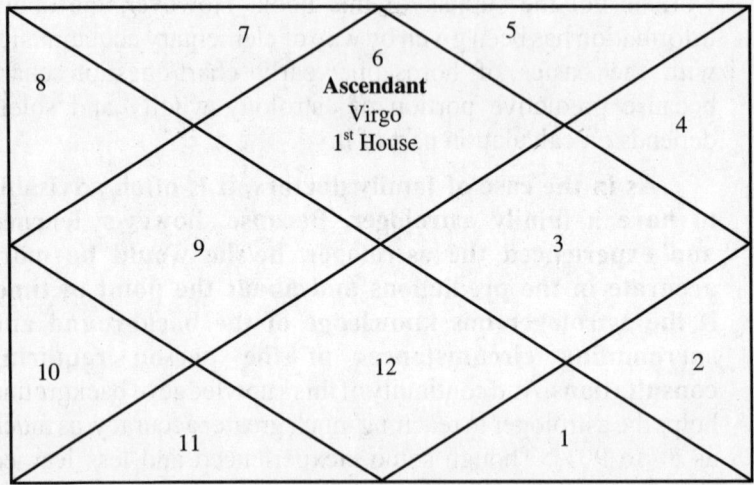

22. In the above given illustration of chart, Virgo (Kanya) has been taken as the Ascendant (Lagna), and is given at the top-central point, and the chart has then been completed anti-clockwise. In other words, Ascendant (Lagna) is the first house, Libra (Tula) is the 2nd house, Scorpio (Vrishchik) is the 3rd house, Sagittarius (Dhanu) is the 4th house, Capricorn (Makar) is the 5th house and so on. The figure given in each House (column) indicates the Rasi, starting with Aries (Mesh) as 1, Taurus (Vrishabh) as 2, Gemini (Mithun) as 3, Cancer (Karka) as 4, Leo (Simha) as 5, Virgo (Kanya) as 6, Libra (Tula) as 7, Scorpio (Vrishchik) as 8, Sagittarius (Dhanu) as 9, Capricorn (Makar) as 10, Aquarius (Kumbha) as 11 and Pisces (Meena) as 12. The names of Rasis (Signs of zodiac) are not written in

the chart; they are indicated numerically only. In this method, the position of any House can be known at a glance and no counting from the Ascendant (Lagna) is needed. It is for this reason that this method is very popular in India and now virtually all over the world.

23. The South Indian System is just the opposite of the North Indian system. Firstly, the South Indian System moves clockwise. Secondly, it is not written with the Ascendant (Lagna) at the top. In the North Indian system, the <u>Houses (Bhavas) are fixed</u>, while in the South Indian system, <u>the Signs of zodiac (Rasis) have fixed positions</u>, and the Lagna (Ascendant) is mentioned in whichever Sign (Rasi) it occurs. The diagram below explains the South Indian system:

Figure 14   **Chart – South Indian Style**

Pisces (*Meena*) 12	Aries (*Mesh*) 1	Taurus (*Vrishabh*) 2	Gemini (*Mithun*) 3
Aquarius (*Kumbha*) 11	**Birth (Rasi) Chart South Indian Style**		Cancer (*Karka*) 4
Capricorn (*Makar*) 10			Leo (*Simha*) 5
Sagittarius (*Dhanu*) 9	Scorpio (*Vrishchik*) 8	Libra (*Tula*) 7	Virgo 6 (*Kanya*)

It may be noted that the top column at the extreme left is always the Sign Pisces (Meena Rasi), and then it moves right hand side clock-wise. Thus, the next column to Pisces (Meena) is Aries (Mesh), next to which is Taurus (Vrishabh), and then top corner on extreme right is Gemini i.e. Mithun. <u>Below-it</u> is Cancer, <u>below that</u> is Leo (Simha), and below thereto on extreme right is Virgo (Kanya). From Virgo (Kanya) we move left-ward which is Libra (Tula), next left to it is Scorpio

34 | Star Guide to Predictive Astrology

(Vrishchik), while next to it on the extreme left lower corner is Sagittarius (Dhanu). Then we climb upwards thereby next is Capricorn, above which is Aquarius (Kumbha), which is in other words just below Pisces (Meena).

24. Another notable point in the South Indian system is that no numericals or names of Rasis (Signs) are given in the chart to indicate the placements of Signs (Rasis), because Signs are fixed and thus understood automatically. However, the Ascendant (Lagna) and the planets are duly mentioned in the Signs (Rasis) occupied by them in chart. Given below are two diagrams, one for facility of easy grasp, shows the placement of Signs (Rasis) in their fixed (and understood) positions, while the other chart denotes how actually the charts are written in South India. In many a western countries, South Indian style is prevailing because the software of the computers got prepared under the guidance of the South Indian astrologers, who are quick to adaptation, and in South India the common public too has some grasp and understanding of the basics of astrology.

A diagonal line is drawn in the House where the Lagna (Ascendant) occurs. For example Virgo (*Kanya*) is Lagna in these two charts given below.

Figure 15   Explanatory Chart – South Indian Style

Pisces (*Meena*) 12	Aries (*Mesh*) 1	Taurus (*Vrishabh*) 2	Gemini (*Mithun*) 3
Aquarius (*Kumbha*) 11	Explanatory Birth (Rasi) Chart South Indian Style		Cancer (*Karka*) 4
Capricorn (*Makar*) 10			Leo (*Simha*) 5
Sagittarius (*Dhanu*) 9	Scorpio (*Vrishchik*) 8	Libra (*Tula*) 7	Virgo 6 Lagna (*Kanya*) Ascendant

Elementary Knowledge | 35

Figure 16   Chart South Indian Style for 17th Aug. 1963

Jupiter (*Guru*)			Rahu
	Rasi Chart as it is written in the South Indian Style Chart as on 17th August 1963.		Moon (*Chandra*) Venus (*Sukra*)
Saturn (*Sani*)			Sun (*Surya*) Mercury (*Budh*)
Ketu			Ascendant (***Lagna***) Mars (*Mangal*)

25. For a beginner, in the above style of writing the charts, the actual location of Houses (Bhavas) has to be counted, and one does not get an idea about the inter-planetary relations and their mutual aspecting at a glance, nor the relationship and aspecting of the planets with the Houses. One has to count them and then grasp what is what. Yet another problem in this system is the shifted position of a planet in the Bhava Chalitam cannot be indicated very correctly, because suppose a planet has shifted from the 3rd house to the 4th house, and the third house supposedly falls in Scorpio, then the moment the planet is shown in the shifted position in the 4th house, it would misrepresent the planet's shifted position in Sagittarius, while apparently it is not so. The planet continues to stay in Scorpio but for purpose of effectivity, it is giving the results of the 4th house.

      This situation becomes all the more confusing in Bhava Chalitam of persons born at places north of 36° Latitude, because in those cases, sometimes a planet shifts (or jumps) two houses in the Bhava Chalitam. For example in the basic birth chart, a planet is in the 3rd house (Sign = being Scorpio), and in the Bhava Chalitam, the planet has by virtue of its degrees and by virtue also of the boundaries of the Houses shifted to the 5th house. The mention of this position in the Bhava Chalitam would show if the planet has come to occupy Capricorn (jumping from Scorpio). It has, therefore, to be understood that a Sign may get wrongly divided between two Houses, and similarly a House may be wrongly shown as occupied by two Signs (Rasis).

26. Next we come to the East Indian style, which is in vogue in Assam, Bengal, parts of Orissa and the Northeast India's border states carved out of Assam. This method is a compromise between North Indian and South Indian methods in the sense that the chart runs anti-clock-wise like the North Indian system, and Signs (Rasis) have fixed positions in the South Indian style and therefore, the Ascendant is mentioned in whichever Sign (Rasi) it falls. Given below are two diagrams, the first one is explanatory in nature, while the second one is the reproduction of the actual style of writing (practical illustration)

Elementary Knowledge | 37

Figure 17   Chart – North Eastern Style

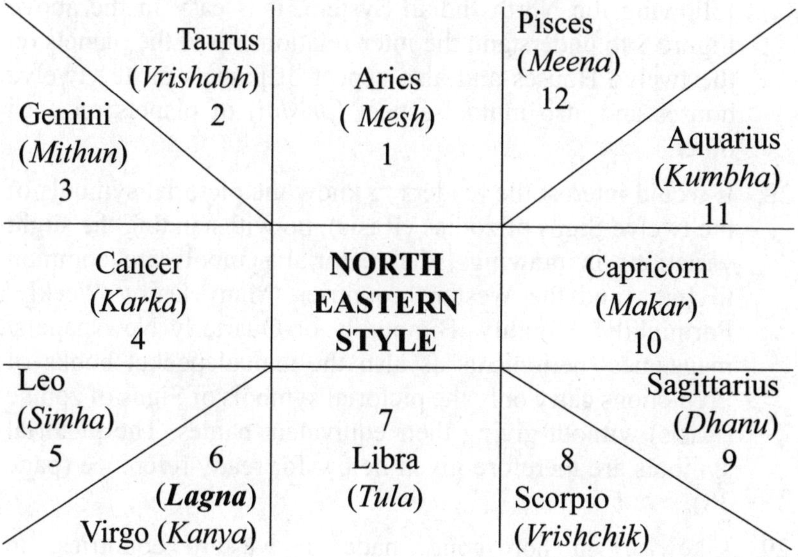

Gemini (*Mithun*) 3	Taurus (*Vrishabh*) 2	Aries (*Mesh*) 1	Pisces (*Meena*) 12	Aquarius (*Kumbha*) 11
	Cancer (*Karka*) 4	**NORTH EASTERN STYLE**	Capricorn (*Makar*) 10	
Leo (*Simha*) 5	6 (*Lagna*) Virgo (*Kanya*)	7 Libra (*Tula*)	8 Scorpio (*Vrishchik*)	Sagittarius (*Dhanu*) 9

Figure 18   Chart 2 – North Eastern Style

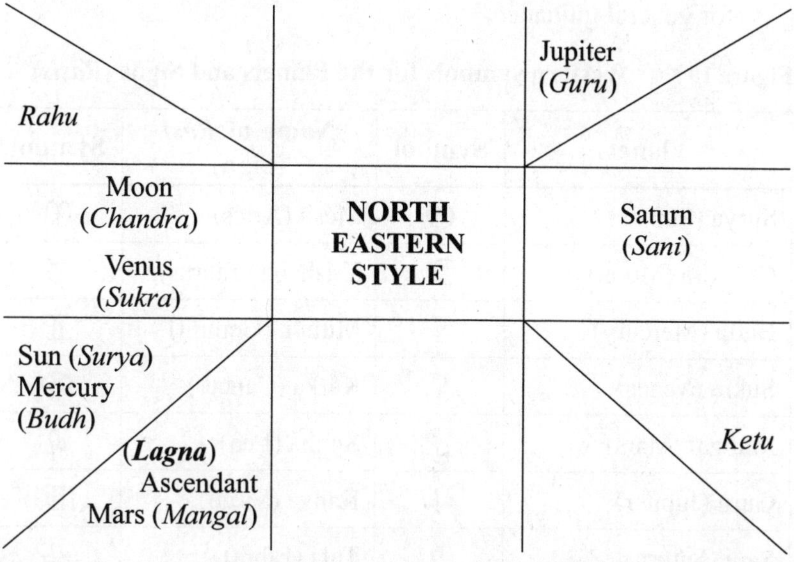

Rahu			Jupiter (*Guru*)	
	Moon (*Chandra*) Venus (*Sukra*)	**NORTH EASTERN STYLE**	Saturn (*Sani*)	
Sun (*Surya*) Mercury (*Budh*)	(*Lagna*) Ascendant Mars (*Mangal*)			Ketu

27. The planetary positions are as on August 17, 1963. By following the North Indian System, it is easy in the above Figure 8 to understand the inter-relationship of the planets on the twelve Houses and also aspect of planets on the twelve houses and also mutual aspect (*drishti*) of planets on each other.

28. It would interest the readers to know the pictorial symbols of the twelve Signs of zodiac (Rasis), notwithstanding the slight variations in drawings, the pictorial symbols are common to India and the Western countries. Many Daily/ Weekly/ Fortnightly/ Monthly/ Bimonthly or Quarterly Newspapers/ magazines/ periodicals as also the annual pocket books of Predictions carry only the pictorial symbols of Signs of zodiac (Rasis) without giving their equivalent names. The pictorial symbols are therefore given below for ready reference (page 38).

29. Likewise, in horoscope made in western countries, in astrological magazines/periodicals and books also, instead of giving the names or abbreviations of names of the planets, only their indicative symbols are given; they are given below for general guidance.

Figure 19   Western symbols for the Planets and Signs (*Rasis*)

Planet	Symbol	Name of *Rasi* (Sign)	Symbol
Surya (Sun)	☉	Mesh (Aries)	♈
Chandra (Moon)	☽	Vrishabh (Taurus)	♉
Budh (Mercury)	☿	Mithun (Gemini)	♊
Sukra (Venus)	♀	Karka (Cancer)	♋
Mangal (Mars)	♂	Simha (Leo)	♌
Guru (Jupiter)	♃	Kanya (Virgo)	♍
Sani (Saturn)	♄	Tula (Libra)	♎

Planet	Symbol	Name of *Rasi* (Sign)	Symbol
Rahu (Moon's North Node)	☊	Vrishchik (Scorpio)	♏
Ketu (Moon's South Node)	☋	Dhanu (Sagittarius)	♐
Uranus	⛢	Makar (Capricorn)	♑
Neptune	♆	Kumbha (Aquarius)	♒
Pluto	♀	Meena (Pisces)	♓

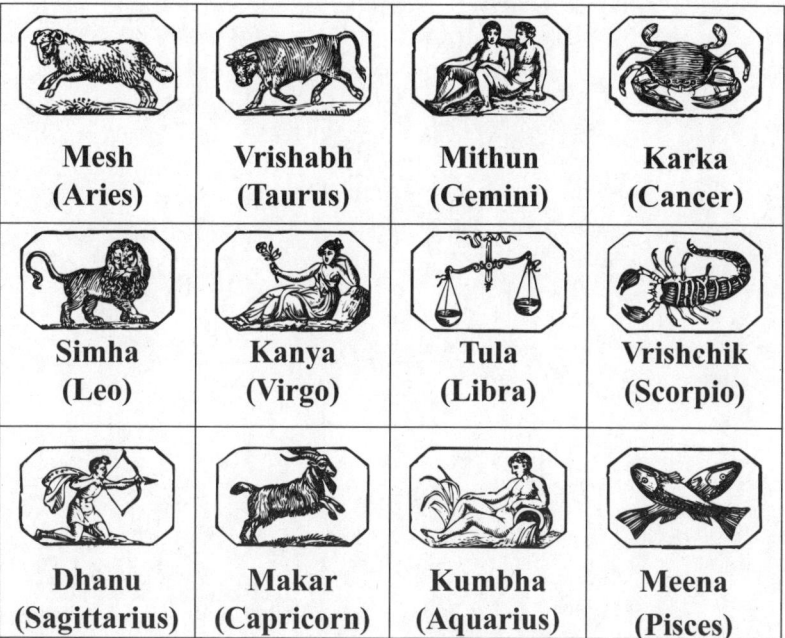

Figure 20 Pictorial Symbols of the Twelve Signs of Zodiac/Rasis

MORE ELEMENTARY CONSIDERATIONS

A. At the very outset it has to be mentioned that everything under the sky is believed to be covered by these twelve Houses in any birth chart/yearly chart or a Question chart. In other words, all activities, personality, cult, habits, nature, trends and traits of thoughts/ utterances/ action, all events, all developments and all elements of life and its associates are covered by and thus divided among these twelve houses.

B. Therefore, before proceeding with the study of horoscope i.e. the birth chart as such, it is necessary and advantageous for one and all interested in astrology to know which house rules which subject or is concerned with which element in life. The second stage would discuss the main attributes/ jurisdiction and area of control of each HOUSE as also those of combined/ conjuncted control. Then comes the study of each of the TWELVE HOUSES in a horoscope.

C. As things stand, very often a particular subject or element falls within the jurisdiction of more than one House of the horoscope, and in such cases, coordinated study of all the houses concerned with that subject/ element is very necessary. Concentration and experience normally help in this coordinated study. In the following chapters relating to each House of the horoscope, the term, "Referral" has been used to indicate the Houses warranting a coordinated study of a particular subject or element or event etc.

SUBJECTS TO BE CONSIDERED UNDER

THE FIRST HOUSE
(The Ascendant or the Lagna)

This house has several names in Sanskrit but most commonly known names are, *Lagna* (Ascendant) or *"Tanu"* (Self). Often the names of birth-chart, yearly-chart, monthly-chart, question-chart are prefixed to the word 'Lagna' for the sake of clarity, distinction and quick grasp, viz., *Janma-Lagna* (Ascendant at birth), *Varsh-Lagna* (Ascendant in the yearly chart), *Masa-Lagna* (Ascendant in the monthly chart), and *Prashna Lagna* (Ascendant in the Question chart).

In a way, the First House (Ascendant or the Lagna) is concerned with every aspect/ event/ development in life because it is the House of Self, and everything that affects or concerns the Self, is co-related to this House. However, the more important and directly related subjects to this House are as given below:

1. Personality, physical built, complexion, height, general physiology, facial appearance, first-glance-impression created on or carried by others.

2. Physiognomy, cult, culture, nature, habits, traits and tendencies, attitude towards self and others; style of walking/ sitting/ eating/ gesturing while talking; facial indications exposing the inner traits of thought and action; exposition of sexual personality (for example, while walking/ talking/ laughing/ eating/ gesturing some males appear or behave like females, while females appear/ behave/ act like a masculine person).

3. Built of body, body weight; special feature of some particular part or limb of body including of head/ neck/ eyes/ nose/ lips

shoulders/ chest/ belly/ waist/ arms and hands/ thighs and legs/ feet etc.

4. Behaviour towards parents and grandparents (of self and spouse), teachers (Guru/ priest), elders and youngsters in the immediate family and in the wider family and towards near distant relations of self/ spouse; towards seniors and juniors in school/ college/ university/ training institute, towards colleagues/ co-workers/ co-commuters, towards superiors and subordinates, towards associates/ partners, towards employers or employees/ servants/ domestic help, towards general public and other people with whom the individual comes in contact.

5. Basic instinct of honesty and dishonesty, integrity and otherwise, that of kindness and generosity or of conservativeness/ cruelty, liberal or miserly attitude towards those needing help/ compassion.

6. Maternal grandfather and paternal grandmother.

7. Natural faculty of intelligence/ IQ/ grasp, thinking/ imagination, capacity for guess-work/ intuition, to express one's self so as to become understandable to listeners.

8. Parts of body from neck/ throat/ upwards of chin including eyes, ears, mouth, lips, cheeks, teeth, tongue, head, skull, hair on head and other parts of the face, entire vocal chord and mechanism.

9. 3rd pregnancy or the 3rd child; 6th brother or sister.

10. Mistress of husband and paramour of wife (sexual relationship in it).

11. Tendency to dominate the spouse or vice versa; likewise domination over the opposite sex or vice versa.

12. Participation or tolerance of group orgies.

13. Courage and capacity of oratory/ to speak/ lecture to a gathering/ audience/ general public or lack of these qualities, quality and capacity of teaching and imparting knowledge.

14. System and order (or lack thereof) in style of living/ working, general cleanliness, quality of handwriting, drawing, sketches, colouring and painting etc.

15. Vocal power, including capacity for singing/ crying/ shouting etc.
16. Brother/ sister of daughter-in-law and son-in-law.
17. Baldness, pimples, skin ailment of any part of the head/ cheeks, any other ailment of skull, eyes, ears, lips, teeth, tongue, mouth, tonsils, nose, jaw bones, chin; inner or external injury to any of these parts; disfigurement of face or any of these parts by birth or subsequently by any accident or injury by a human being.
18. Physical invalidity/ deformity by birth, by accident, by human mistake or by human mischief.
19. Odor of the body including that of mouth, armpits, thigh joints, private parts; its good or bad impact on spouse or companion.
20. Sense of shyness/ shame/ modesty vis-à-vis expression on the face, physical gestures, apparent lack of these qualities, veil/ *purdah*/ *burqa* for females (its use and non-use) by custom/ tradition/ own choice.
21. Malicious and hideous attitude/ behaviour (by thought/ words/ action).
22. Courageous/ humane/ dignified behaviour/ attitude (by thought/ words and action).
23. Boldness mixed with patience and tolerance or absence of these qualities; the opposite of these qualities (including arrogance and bragging, insulting others).
24. Addiction to drinks/ drugs from childhood/ youth/ at advanced age.
25. Faithfulness and honesty in conduct, dealings and behaviour towards parents, teachers, Guru, elders, friends and outsiders, or lack thereof.
26. Exhibitive tendency.
27. Sexual impotence, complete or partial, physical/ psychological or both, dislike for sex in spite of competence/ capacity and stamina.

28. Frigidity in females, complete or partial, physical or psychological, dislike for actual sex without physical reasons.
29. Fickle-mindedness/ insanity/ madness – occasional or chronic; partial or complete, causing depression or violence.
30. Secretive or open-mindedness, if secretive, would it lead to any job related to spying/ intelligence/ investigations.
31. Appearance – younger/ older to one's actual age; includes mental maturity or immaturity visibly reflecting in personality.
32. Habits influencing eating/ gulping – slow or fast; heavy or light and fond of eating as if living only for eating, or eating for living and Critical/ fastidious or simple-natured about quality/ variety/ cooking of food/ water/ drinkable items (referral house 4th).
33. Fashionable/ critical/ fastidious in dress including its quality, colour, stitching, make, manufacture, texture, overall presentation or accepting whatever comes one's way.
34. Critical or non-critical about dress/ eating habits/ style of eating by spouse, members of immediate family/ wider family, outsiders.
35. Habit of gossip/ carrying stories/ anecdotes/ jokes/ humours/ rumours or lack of this type of habit.
36. Qualities of leadership or lack of it – total or partial.
37. Active and self-oriented worker with initiative or without initiative; attending entrusted work only; lazy/ lethargic/ time-killer.
38. Eyes (big or small) communicating/ expressive/ impressive, sober, average, squint or any other abnormality of the eye(s).
39. Blind by birth or by subsequent event; reduction in or loss of vision in one eye or both eyes, by natural causes or human cruelty, or by old age. This includes night blindness, or colour blindness by birth or subsequent development, causes thereof.
40. Ears – large/ long/ small/ well-formed or deformed, lobes distinct and unjoined or joined to the skin – any defect of

hearing since birth or subsequent – attributable to any injury (accidental or intentional).

41. Deaf, complete or partial, by birth or by subsequent event; natural or man-made.
42. Back hunch, by birth or subsequent development; causes thereof. It includes any defect or deformity in hand/ legs or deformity of any other part of the body by birth or subsequent development, causes thereof (remedies too).
43. After-effect of diseases like child polio/ small pox/ high fever.
44. Epilepsy, by birth or subsequent development, causes and remedies.
45. Extra thin or extra fat body by birth or by subsequent development, likeable or unlikable, its impact on self & others.
46. Adoption within the immediate or wider family; by outsiders; its impact on relations with natural parents/ brothers/ sisters. It includes outcome of adoption with regard to rights of inheritance in the original family of birth, disputes/ litigation etc. It also includes disputes/ litigation with regard to inheritance in the family of adoption.
47. Impact of adoption by such persons as have own child; problems/ disputes/ litigation with regard to inheritance.
48. Status and situation of the adopted person in the event of parents getting a child/ successor of their own by natural birth subsequent to adoption; Legal status of a child born by insemination some-times vis-à-vis adopted person.
49. Fondness for music/ dancing/ painting/ sculpture/ sports/ games/ hunting – involvement of self or mere interest.
50. Fondness for farming/ agriculture, gardening and such other hobbies as involve manual labour and attention by self and also by others.
51. Intellectual hobbies such as photography, knowledge and practice of medicine/ any future-telling science/ other branches of science.

Important Note:

Many of the subjects listed above fall within the scope of 1st House (Ascendant=Lagna) as well several other Houses in the birth chart. For example, illness/ disease fall under the 6th and 8th houses; adoption of child falls under the 4th, 9th and 10th houses; disputes about ancestral property/ inherited assets come under the 4th, 6th and 9th houses, and if violence figures in with relation to these disputes, the 8th house is directly concerned. Effort has been made to refer to the other concerned Houses wherever feasible by mentioning them as the "Referral House". However, one's own experience would gradually give an insight as to which particular Houses have to be studied in coordination with a particular House. Advice may be sought from the authors too in cases of special and genuine doubt.

THE SECOND HOUSE

The 2nd house is generally known as the *"Dhana Bhava"* (House of wealth), however it rules many other important subjects and among them, the important ones are listed below:

1. Savings and investments, returns from them.
2. Riches and loss of riches, poverty
3. Cheating and getting cheated in the matter of money, ornaments, jewellery, books, paintings, valuable assets, and investments.
4. Collection of *piece de art*, paintings, musical instruments books, magazines, journals, manuscripts, and rare postage stamps/ rare coins.
5. Decoration/ beautification of residence/ office/ other premises.
6. Death of self and risk to the life of spouse.
7. Health of or injury to spouse/ lover/ beloved person, or pet animal.
8. Discouragement by spouse/ lover/ beloved in matters relating to sex, savings, investments, wealth, collections, decision-making process.
9. Stepbrother or sister related through father.
10. Risk of life or limb at the hands of spouse/ lover/ beloved person or his mistress or her paramour or friend.
11. Deprivation of wealth, money, ornaments, jewellery, collection of valuable/ important items by spouse/ lover/ beloved.
12. Harassment/ torture/ black-mail/ litigation/ violence by spouse/ lover/ beloved or by family thereof.
13. Ailment/ deficiency to ear/ eye/ jaw/ cheek/ mouth/ tongue/ neck/ throat/ vocal machinery/ teeth or any part/ portion of

the right side of the head. Any disease of thyroid gland group has to be determined mainly by the 12th house in coordination with the 2nd house.

14. Cancer or allied disease of the throat, tongue and disease like AIDS/ venereal complaints have to be determined from the 2nd and 7th Houses, coordinating therewith the 6th and 8th house also.

15. Gains or losses to self/ spouse/ lover/ beloved by speculation, gambling, card games, kitty party/ betting at races/ betting on games and matches, or losses by chit fund companies or Financing forums (referral house 8th).

16. Treaty between nations/ armies, or between governments of states/ countries.

17. Compromise between enemies/ adversaries/ opponents/ competitors, or with lover/ beloved of the spouse (specially out of fear/ intimidation/ threat/ tactics).

18. Source of income to and actual accrual of income to mother/ stepmother.

19. Mental attitude and actual help or refusal of help towards social, religious and charitable causes.

20. Good or bad (secret) intentions of uncles/ aunts/ cousins towards self, and/ or spouse (referral houses 3rd, 7th and 9th).

21. Cordial or non-cordial/ quarrelsome/ fighting relations with neighbours, colleagues, co-workers, co-commuters, associates and partners in commerce or crime (referral houses 6th and 10th).

22. Open or clandestine collection/ storage or custody (sometimes on behalf of others) of money, encashable or moveable assets, ornaments, bullion, precious stones, valuable items, and items of antiquity etc.

23. Tolerating or taking liberty in behaviour mainly for gains of any kind (referral houses 4th and 7th).

24. Poverty and difficulty or inability to provide bare necessities of life for self/ spouse/ children (referral houses 4th and 10th).

25. Riches or poverty in childhood adversely affecting or not affecting education and up-bringing at early stages of life (referral houses 4th and 5th).
26. Receiving education in childhood upto the age of 20 years by borrowing/ begging/ scholarship/ freeship/ returnable loan from a Trust (includes books, writing material, clothes, food, residence, etc.).
27. Enjoyment/ luxury/ comfort/ other facilities/ conveniences at the cost of others in the family or outsiders/ friends (referral house 4th).
28. Gains or losses to self from brothers/ sisters/ cousins, or gains or losses to them from self (referral houses 3rd and 9th).
29. Gains from mother/ stepmother as one's right or by deprivation of rights of others (referral houses 3rd, 4th and 9th).
30. Gains from progeny including use or misuse of progeny or of its name in its childhood under necessity or greedy motive (referral house 5th).
31. Gains from enemy/ opponent/ adversary/ competitor by way of compromise, showing any favour, bestowing an honour, withdrawal from a given situation/ position/ status (referral houses 4th, 10th and 11th).
32. Gains from spouse/ lover/ beloved by genuine means or misuse or blackmail (referral houses 7th, 9th and 12th).
33. Due or extracted gains from father/ uncle (referral houses 9th and 10th).
34. Gains in terms of money/ prestige/ publicity etc. as compensation for defamation (referral houses 6th, 9th, 11th and 12th).
35. Gains or losses to self from paternal grandmother or maternal grandfather or gains or losses to them (referral houses 4th, 9th and 10th).
36. Gains or losses to father of spouse from self, directly or indirectly, or by fair or unfair means (referral houses 4th and 7th).

37. Gains or losses to self from any distant relation of the spouse, or gains/ losses to him/ her by self (referral houses 6th, 7th and 8th).
38. Extracting money by dishonest/ violent methods and tactic (referral house 3rd).
39. Loss of money owing to lust and debauch nature or tendency of self or spouse (referral house 7th).
40. Loss of money/ assets given to win over or compromise with an enemy, adversary/ opponent/ competitor (referral houses 6th and 7th).
41. Loss of money/ assets by government action (referral house 12th).
42. Loss of money/ wealth/ assets by theft, fire, floods, arson, earthquake, storm, tornado and similar other natural calamity (referral houses 4th, 10th, 11th and 12th).
43. Loss of money to escape defamation or payment of compensation (referral houses 9th and 12th).
44. Reduction in money or wealth by giving of donations/ contributions to social/ religious/ charitable/ educational causes (with or without motive) (referral houses 9th, 10th and 11th).
45. Loss of money by acts of commission and omission by parents/ brothers/ sisters/ other relations of self or of spouse, by children or grandchildren (referral houses 3rd, 4th, 9th, 5th and 10th).
46. Size of immediate family and wider family vis-à-vis system of joint living or otherwise, capacity and will to maintain/ help or otherwise with regard to the joint family or the wider family (referral houses 3rd, 4th, 5th, 8th, 9th and 12th).
47. Capacity and will to maintain/ help people outside the periphery of the family (referral houses 9th and 12th).
48. Illness/ injury/ death of paternal grandmother and maternal grandfather.

49. All matters relating to (a) Friend's son's wife or friend's daughter's husband, (b) mother-in-law of son, and (c) father-in-law of daughter.

Important note:

i. With regard to wealth and money possessions of any individual, the astrologer must bear in mind the contradictions/ conflicts/ contrast existing in the positions of planets concerned with or affecting the 2nd House directly or indirectly and then come to final conclusions. Chances of windfall/ sudden loss should not be lost sight of.

ii. Every individual relation (parents, brothers/ sisters, grandparents) is basically governed by his or her own stars and another person's stars have side-effect only.

THE THIRD HOUSE

The 3rd House is normally known as the "*Parakram Bhava*" or the "*Sahaj Bhava*" (i.e. House of Effort, brothers/sisters). Its important subjects are:

1. Brothers and sisters; also step-brothers/sisters; and cousins (more so if residing in joint family) (referral house 9th).
2. Right shoulder, right armpit, right arm, right-side upper ribs just above the nipple, upper side of the right portion of the back.
3. Capacity and ability to use the parts of body mentioned at No. 2 above; any injury/ailment/disability of these parts of the body.
4. Capacity and ability for normal and hard work or lack of it; tendency and intention to make use of this capacity and ability or lack of it.
5. Boldness, courage, bravery, daring and dashing nature, roughness and rashness in nature; or lack of these qualities/ shortcomings.
6. Short journeys for purposes of self or brothers/ sisters/ cousins.
7. Normal/ natural attitude to help brothers/ sisters/ cousins; or not helping morally/ financially/ physically.
8. Improvement or deterioration in tendency/ attitude mentioned in No. 7 above after marriage of either self or brother/ sister/ cousin.
9. Similar tendency/attitude of brother/sister/cousin towards self before and after marriage of brother/sister/cousin or of self.
10. Firmness or trembling of the hand in its use while writing, lifting weight, cooking, performing surgical and medical operations, holding and using weapons/firearms (big and small).

11. Illness and medical treatment or surgical operation to mother or step-mother; any injury/risk to her life (referral houses 8th and 11th).
12. Gifts given to or received from mother/step mother; in cash or of ornaments/jewellery/assets/property; loss of any of these gifts (referral houses 2nd and 11th).
13. Source of income/ livelihood of mother or stepmother, mother working for livelihood.
14. Any assets inheritable (shareable or not by self), which might be given or gifted away by mother or stepmother (in contravention of rights and claims of self) to entitled or non-entitled other persons (referral houses 2nd and 11th).
15. Any brother/ sister/ cousin depriving the individual of rights on inheritable/shareable assets (referral house 11th).
16. Skill, or absence of it, in use of arms, weapons, on a battlefield and in other circumstances (referral houses 6th and 8th).
17. Revenge upon self by enemies of father/ adopting father/ stepfather.
18. Interest/ skill/ expertise/ excellence in games/ sports, in use of arms and weapons as a part of education or training (or as a part of job).
19. Skill/ strength/ boldness/ bravery for hunting game, participation in competitions, running, facing and chasing enemies and criminals, at fights, battles and in war;
20. Skill and fame in the art of boxing, wrestling, karate, *"kabaddi"* etc.
21. Encouragement/cooperation/support or lack of it on part of spouse/ lover/ beloved with reference to social/ religious/ charitable activity (referral houses 7th and 9th).
22. Skill and expression of "Mudras" (gestures of face/ fingers/ feet) in dance etc., (referral houses 1st and 4th).
23. Self's relations and cooperation/ non-cooperation with brother-in-law, sister-in-law/ cousin-in-law of husband/ lover/ beloved (referral house 7th).

24. Success or failure of medical treatment/surgical operation etc.; change in medical practitioner/ surgeon/ *Vaidya/ Hakim/ Tantrik/* spiritual healer (referral houses 6th and 8th, also 12th which rules expenditure and capacity to spend).
25. Domestic help/domestic servants/agricultural labour/bonded labour; others functioning as such for self or self functioning as such for others; also honesty and dishonesty thereof (referral houses 4th, 6th and 9th).
26. Circumstances/situation leading to serving others in capacity mentioned in No. 25 above; relation with employers; period of working in such capacity (referral house 1st, 10th, 11th and 12th).
27. Attitude and relations among brothers/sisters/cousins/other relations/outsiders for fulfilment of these needs (referral houses 9th and 10th).
28. Provision/supply of food and water for self and immediate family; capacity of self to fulfil the needs; dependence on brothers/sisters/cousins/other relations/outsiders for fulfilment of these needs (referral houses 9th and 10th).
29. Lower parts of the speech-machinery of body and upper portion of the respiratory system.
30. Number of real and step or half brothers/sisters.
31. Number of pregnancies lost to mother, stillbirth to mother, loss of brother or sister by death/kidnapping/entry into renounced life/running away from home.
32. Appointment/nomination to a post (paid or honorary) under the govt., its rank; its point of time (referral houses 9th and 10th).
33. Method of appointment or nomination mentioned in No. 32 above, i.e. by way of written test, interview, recommendation, compensation, compassion, replacement or substitution or under political contingency, its point of time (referral houses 9th or 10th).
34. Purely temporary or fixed term appointment in or under

government including as personal staff of the VIPs as a matter of political favour/pay-back in kind for services rendered to keep the devil busy or under vigil (referral houses 4th, 9th and 6th).

35. Tenure or duration of appointment/ nomination with reference to No. 34 above.

36. Nomination to parliament/ legislative assembly/ cantonment board/ municipality or other similar bodies (referral houses 10th and 11th).

37. Introduction into political/ social/ religious/ charitable/ educational life by brother/ sister/ cousin of self or of spouse (referral houses 9th, 10th and 11th).

38. Introduction by self, of brother/ sister/ cousin of self or of spouse into politics/ social/ religious/ charitable/ educational activity and determination of point of time for such introduction (referral houses 9th, 10th and 11th).

39. Gains to self on death or renunciation of '*grihastha*' (family) life by brother/ sister/ cousin of self or of spouse and determination of point of time for such event, (referral houses 4th and 10th).

40. Gains to brother/ sister/ cousin of self or of spouse on death or renunciation of *grihastha* life by self, and determination of point of time for such an event (referral houses 2nd, 8th, 1st and 7th).

Important Note:
Points No. 39 and 40 above involve the time of death of an individual, which is the most difficult study in the science of astrology, and its determination should be avoided as far as possible, and if under any special circumstance, such a study has to be undertaken, it ought to be done with full devotion/honesty truthfulness of purpose, going into detailed calculations, and it is always better to have the calculations and predictions checked by another expert astrologer before handing over the predictions to the person concerned.

41. Disputes/ jealousy/ quarrels/violence with brother/ sister/ cousin, brethren, people in caste and community, sometimes involving ex-communication from caste/ community/ society as also general social boycott by an entire village/ locality/ area/ region etc.
42. Giving up one's share in money/assets for sake of brother/ sister or cousin and vice-versa.
43. Marriage with fiancée/widow/widower/divorced spouse of brother or sister or cousin; or his/her maintenance without marriage or any kind of immoral or sexual relationship.
44. Polyandry as prevailing in certain regions of Himalayan Ranges (even in 20th & 21st centuries) (Reference: Pandavas/ Draupadi in Epic of Mahabharat)
45. Expertise and skill in formation of strategy against enemy, specially with regard to battles (and entire war) as also relating to arms, ammunition, weaponry, ordnance, other equipment and manpower needed for battles, and for care of dead and injured personnel.
46. Reward/Award/Decoration/grant of title/grant of land or any other immovable or moveable asset/grant of family pension or hereditary pension for acts of gallantry, heroic bravery, outstanding leadership in a battle or on war-front or for spying and 'intelligence' activity (referral houses 10th and 11th).
47. Cowardice in any individual fight or at a battlefield, also withdrawal from a battlefield or act of defection or acceptance of defeat and surrender, double-dealing in spying or 'intelligence' activity (referral houses 6th and 8th).

THE FOURTH HOUSE

The ancient *acharyas* call the 4th House as *"Sukh Bhava"* or *"Maatri Bhava"* i.e. House of comfort or House of Mother, and the following subjects fall under its jurisdiction.

1. Mother or step mother; mutual relationship between mother and self.
2. Mother's qualities personality/nature/ habits/ character/ shortcomings including compulsions and bindings on her attitudes / actions.
3. Gains or losses owing to acts of commission and omission on part of the mother.
4. Health of mother, planetary influences leading to ill health/ injury to her; medical treatment and recovery.
5. Impact on one's education/ welfare owing to attitude and actions on part of mother.
6. Mother's influence on domestic help and other servants/ employees, and/ or their influence on mother; impact thereof on self.
7. Any dispute or litigation between mother/ step-mother and self for inheritance of property and other assets, specially those falling within the WILL left by father or grandparents to the ownership of the mother or the stepmother (referral houses 2nd, 9th and 10th).
8. Convenience/ inconvenience to mother or step mother with regard to residential accommodation/ transport/ domestic help with special reference to attitude/ action of self or vice versa (referral house 1st).
   - 8.1. Death of natural mother/ step-mother/ adopting mother; events and developments from it; subsequent impact on the individual and matters/ problems of inheritance/ succession therefrom and their settlement/ solution or quarrels and litigation/ violence etc.

9. Comforts/ discomfort/ convenience/ inconvenience to self on account of neighbours, and vice versa; chances of perpetual dispute or court cases or violence (referral house 6th and 8th).

10. Giving up rented or ownership accommodation on account of disputes with the neighbours, or neighbours giving up ownership accommodation owing to disputes with self.

11. Comforts/ discomforts/ convenience/ inconvenience to self with regard to ownership or rented or usurped premises/ accommodation of residence, shop, office, workshop, industrial unit (referral houses 6th, 9th, 10th and 12th).

12. Inheritance of property used/ usable as residence, shop, office, workshop, industrial unit, agriculture, farm, garden, orchard etc., and their use by self or giving them on rent, lease, partnership, contract, sale etc.

13. Acquisition by purchase, hiring, lease, contract etc. of property or premises for own use or, by other members of family or by partners, on responsibility or liability of self and the question of relations between Landlord and self, relating thereto.

14. Or, with regard to No.13 above, between self and the actual user, vis-à-vis relations between land lord and self.

15. Any and all kinds of matters or disputes relating to ownership of hired or rented out property such as farm lands, agricultural property, groves and orchards, gardens, woods, jungles, pastures, lands with tree-plantations.

16. Change or shifting of self-owned or hired residence, shop, office, workshop, clinic, industrial premises; point of time for such shift or change; easy or difficult shift or change.

17. Construction of property, making additions/ alterations; disputes and problems related thereto; difficulty in obtaining sanctions from municipal body or other concerned agency, electricity board/ company telecommunication authority; delays, overhead expenses/ losses resulting from acts of commission and omission by these agencies.

18. Breeding and maintenance of cattle, cows, buffaloes, horses, donkeys, ponies, camels, goats, sheep, dogs, cats, elephants,

hares, pet animals, birds like parrots, poultry farms, pigs, bulls, oxen, deer, antelopes, fish and fisheries; problems and disputes relating thereto, and using it as side or sole means of income (referral houses 2nd and 10th).

19. Losses in regard to No.18 above, owing to drop in demand, cut-throat competition, theft, fire, diseases and epidemic, distress sale owing to governmental/ municipal restrictions and change in policy or other reasons.

20. Immediate and long term Impact of No.19 above on means of livelihood (referral houses 11th and 12th).

21. Sale, purchase and maintenance of animals meant for and used in circus activity; gains and losses therefrom; if circus is run by self or it is owned or managed by others (referral houses 10th and 11th).

22. Availability or non-availability of one's own means of transport for source of livelihood, for family, for pleasure, for plying on rent.

23. Loss/ damage to means of transport by fire/ theft/ accident/ arson etc., as also damage/ injury to self or others by means of transport owned by self or owned by others and gain or loss by way of compensation/ litigation, harassment/revenge (referral houses 8th, 11th and 12th).

24. Claims on insurance; problems/ disputes in settlement of claims, relating to No.23 and losses and inconvenience/ discomfort owing to delays in settlement of claims by insurance (referral houses 4th and 12th).

25. Normal repairs; repairs in the event of accident vis-à-vis delay by surveyors, relating to item 23 above.

26. Means of transport pulled by human beings or driven by animals including bullocks, horses, camels, buffaloes, dogs, ponies, donkeys, elephants, goats, and costs and various problems relating thereto vis-à-vis restrictions imposed by municipality (local bodies) etc. (referral houses 8th and 12th).

27. Payment of compensation and litigation/ penalties/ punishment arising from accidents by auto-vehicles or animal-driven

vehicles; to be considered both ways – when self is the victim/ sufferer in the accident, or when self is held responsible for the accident (referral houses 11th and 12th).

28. Means of transport used for conveyance of goods (auto-vehicles) and animal driven vehicles including hand carts pulled by human power, and gains or losses therefrom; and in cases of accident, consequences both ways – when self stands to gain and when self is liable to pay the compensation/ damages (referral houses 8th, 11th, and 12th).

29. Air travel/ train journey/ journey by public auto-vehicle and chances of accident/ injury in such journeys, or loss of kit/ luggage in the custody of self or in the custody of the transporters (referral houses 8th and 12th).

30. Compensation for injury/ loss of limb/ loss of life/ loss of valuables and other possessions by lapse on part of self or the transporters (referral houses 11th and 12th).

31. Repairs to or recovery from accidental injury caused to animals in use for transport purposes; cost thereof; cost vis-à-vis amount of compensation.

32. Use of means of transport for smuggling/ criminal activity.

33. Seizure of means of transport mentioned under No.32 above; also the question of release on payment of penalty or absolute confiscation by the authority (referral house 12th).

34. Theft of means of transport; theft for sake of re-sale for financial gains; re-sale after disassembling it; abandonment in good or damaged condition after its misuse for smuggling or other illegal/criminal activity and its impact on the real owner including legal and financial implications (referral house 12th).

35. Claims arising out of theft, damage by accident on the insurance company as also on the thief or on the person liable to pay full or part of the compensation; mutual position of the claimant and the party liable to pay cost or compensation for damaged/ stolen vehicle; litigation arising from such claims; delays in settlement of claim and impact thereof on repairs to or replacement of vehicle (referral houses 11th and 12th).

36. Appetite; digestive system; problems of digestive system; food poisoning; any other kind of poisoning.
37. Success or failure of treatment of ailment mentioned in No.36 above.
38. Eatables and drinks including beverages/ alcohol/ wines/ "Bhang"/ "Gaanja"/ "Charas" / opium/ intoxicants; fruits and vegetables, ice cream, cold and hot drinks.
39. Good and bad effect of No.38 above on health; and in case of bad effect, treatment thereof; success or failure of treatment.
40. Cost of and facility for treatment of ailments generated by eatables and drinkables consumed.
41. Success or failure of surgical treatment; subsequent consequences (referral houses 2nd and 8th).
42. Heart; blood pressure; its functioning, problem relating to it.
43. Medical including surgical treatment; in one's own country or in another country; success or failure thereof; its subsequent impact (referral houses 2nd and 8th).
44. Cancer of the breast; medical treatment including surgery; results (referral houses 2nd and 8th).
45. Lower ribs, lower portion of spinal bones and its allied bones; bones around waistline; abdomen; uterus (to be considered in relation to the 5th house); liver, kidneys; intestines.
46. Ailments/ diseases/ injuries to any of the above parts of the body, and their treatment; success or failure thereof.
47. Menstrual cycle and procreatory system; gynaecological problems relating to the system; failure or success of treatment (referral house 5th).
48. Hernia, appendicitis; defects in any of them and medical and/ or surgical treatment; impact thereof on normal life and on sex life (referral houses 7th and 8th).
49. Adoption of a child in case of childlessness; or having a male child and adopting a female child or having a female child or children and adopting a male child (referral house 5th).

50. Birth of a natural child after adoption of a child; their mutual relationship; relationship with adopting parents vis-à-vis the adopted child's natural parents.
51. In case of No.50 above, question of succession and inheritance; problems and quarrels related thereto; litigation related to it; result of litigation and subsequent developments on the family (referral houses 9th, 11th and 12th).
52. Care of and attendance on parents by adopted child, and in the event of there being both natural child/ children and adopted child, attitude of both categories of children towards the parents; when parents are active/ working/ earning; when parents are not active nor working nor earning; and in the event of parents illness/ old age etc (referral houses 9th, 10th and 12th).
53. Death of natural mother/ step-mother/ adopting mother; events and developments following from it; subsequent impact on the individual (referral houses 11th and 12th).
54. Matters/ problems of inheritance/ succession flowing from No. 53 above; their settlement/ solution or quarrels and litigation/ violence etc (referral houses 9th, 11th and 12th).
55. Losses/ gains at horse-races/ card-games/ kitty-parties/ gambling with friends/ gambling with unknown people/ gambling at casinos (referral houses 8th, 11th and 12th).
56. Transport business; competition in it; damage to or theft of vehicles used for passenger transport/ goods transport; compensation payable by owner or the transport company or by insurance company.
57. Points 28 to 33 above referred to ownership of vehicle on an individual basis, while No. 56 above relates to Transport companies and their owners (in other words relating to fleet of public transport vehicles used for passenger or goods movement. Distinction to be achieved by experience.
58. Compensation for damage and death caused by transport vehicles of companies; litigation; public reaction to mass damage or deaths (referral house 12th).
59. Public transport vehicles falling victim to militant activity

which has become a common phenomenon to almost all countries in the World (referral house 12th).

60. Clubs/ casinos/ discotheques/ gambling houses; running these outfits; using these outfits as a means of entertainment/ recreation/ games and gambles (referral houses 11th and 12th).

61. Unlawfulness of the outfits mentioned in No.60 above, action by law and order establishment against the above outfits and persons using them or running them (referral houses 9th and 12th).

62. Misuse of outfits mentioned in No.60 above for illegal/ criminal purposes and consequences thereof; sometimes acts of violence thereof (referral houses 6th, 8th and 12th).

63. Contraband goods, smuggled goods; storage/ custody/ carriage; carrier.

64. Consequences of No.63 above vis-à-vis law and order establishment.

65. Drugs, intoxicants, alcohol, wine, bhaang, gaanja, charas; their production/ preparation; storage/ custody/ carriage/ carrier; action by law and order establishment.

66. Legal action with reference to No.63 and 65 above; consequences; subsequent impact on personal and social life of the convict (referral houses 8th and 12th).

67. Rewards and promotion for officers achieving success in apprehending the culprits connected with drugs/ contraband goods and their seizures (referral houses 10th and 11th).

68. Risks/ dangers involved for officers/ informers working on detection of drugs, contraband goods, smugglers, carriers; sometimes by the boss behind the gang (referral houses 6th and 8th).

69. Consumption of smack, intoxicants, drugs, alcohol, bhang, charas, gaanja, opium, effect on health; effect on efficiency in work (referral houses 6th, 8th and 10th).

70. Impact of No.69 above on social life/ family life/ earning capacity/ income of the individual; impact on habits/ tendency

to steal/ beg or borrow; impact on total longevity of the individual (referral houses 2nd, 5th, 8th, 11th, 10th and 12th).

71. Impact of No.69 above on progeny; sometimes leading to loss of pregnancy or birth of a defective/ invalid/ dull/ under-developed or undeveloped child; blindness/ deafness/ dumbness/ child-polio and other major physical/ intellectual defects/ deficiencies in the child as a result of drug-addiction of one or both of the parents (referral houses 5th and 10th).

72. Organising/ controlling/ running of smuggling rings, mafia gangs, criminal groups, terrorists, and hired killers.

73. Confrontation/ conflict between No.72 above and the law and order Establishment; consequences for either side.

74. Disposal of contraband goods/ drugs/ alcohol/ bhaang, gaanja, charas seized by law and order Establishment.

75. Trade in human flesh/ bones/ limbs/ kidneys/ eyes/ heart/ blood etc., (referral houses 7th, 8th, 9th and 10th).

76. Theft/ kidnapping/ exchange of children with criminal intents/ motives.

77. Impact of No. 75 and 76 above on the affected children/ persons/ parents, immediately and subsequently in life.

78. Running of brothel/ prostitution group/ prostitution home/ dance-homes; centre for group sex orgies (referral houses 7th and 12th).

79. Acquisition of individuals for the purpose of No.78 above.

80. Organising thefts from graveyards, trading in items stolen from graveyards, cremation ghats and elsewhere.

81. Finding/ hiding the finds of treasure troves; retrieving goods and treasure from sunk boats/ ships/ crashed aeroplanes/ accidented trains and vehicles; Role of law and order machinery in these matters.

82. All and every kind of activity relating to mines and minerals; also trading/ smuggling mines and minerals.

83. Injury or death by snakebite; attack by wild animals like lion, tiger, bear, wolf, panther etc., (referral houses 6th and 8th).

84. Death in sleep by heart attack (referral houses 8th and 2nd).
85. Death while sleeping by way of murder/ fire/complete or partial falling down or demolition of the shelter/ roof/ house/ hut/ cottage where the individual was sleeping (referral houses 8th and 2nd).
86. Escape from death in the event of No. 85 above; subsequent events; developments, after effects like disappearance/ revenge etc.
87. Individual and/ or collective effort/ contribution for construction of schools, hospitals, dispensaries, temples, night shelters for poor and homeless, inns, 'safari', 'dharamashala', ponds, tanks/ wells.
88. Maintenance and management of public-welfare works mentioned at No.87 above; lapses and corruption in maintenance/ management of above and consequences on the beneficiaries.
89. Organisation, maintenance/ management of orphanages, blind homes, *'Nari Niketans'*, *'Mahila Raksha Samitis'*/ shelters, etc. including building and premises for such public welfare schemes.
90. Mismanagement and corruption in running the institution mentioned at No.89 above; misuse of inmates for sexual purposes or for use as domestic help and labour; impact on the inmates; impact on the society around and society as a whole; good or condonable role of law and order establishment with the guilty persons in this behalf.
91. Domestic unhappiness/ mental disturbance/ sleeplessness on account of jealousy within the family, interference by relations from outside, interference by outsiders in family matters.
92. Development of No.91 above on account of non-approvable activity of the individual, lethargy, mistakes, non-earning of livelihood by an able and capable member of the family, supporting such a member of the family by mother and/or grandmother or an elderly lady.

93. Jealousy and disturbed family atmosphere owing to support given by mother or grandmother or an elderly lady to the earning member of the family.

94. Attitude of mother and/ or grandmother towards spouses of sons and grandsons leading to disturbed atmosphere in the family; it includes ill treatment/ violence towards the younger females in the family (referral houses 7th and 1st).

95. Ill-treatment by younger females in the household towards mother or grandmother, aunt or grand-aunt of the husband (referral house 7th).

96. Receipt of gift of assets, property, ornaments, jewellery without any kind of adoption (referral house 11th).

97. Any near or distant relation foregoing his/ her rights/ claims on any cash/ assets/ property in favour of the individual (referral houses 3rd, 9th and 10th).

98. Loss of cash/ assets/ property by individual yielding own rights and claims in favour of brother/ sister/ cousin/ near or distant relation (referral houses 3rd, 9th and 12th).

99. Deprivation of breast feeding by natural mother on one's birth, because (a) mother developed no milk/ not enough milk worth feeding, (b) mother avoided breast feeding (c) mother died on birth, or (d) mother and child separated (referral house 1st).

100. As a consequence of No.99 above, breast-feeding by a wet nurse, or a wet relation on parental side, or by an adopting mother or just a merciful wet woman knowing the plight of the child.

101. Separation from natural mother in infancy or childhood owing to causes other than her death (reference No. 53 above) like divorce, desertion by mother, kidnapping/ snatching from her or any other compelling circumstances.

102. Upbringing by someone else even while living with the mother or in the event of temporary separation from her, or permanent separation owing to her death/ divorce/ kidnapping.

103. Upbringing in affectionate circumstances by paternal/ maternal

grandparents or any other relation of father or mother; impact of it on the foster person and on psychology of the child.

104. Upbringing in difficult, loveless, trying or pains-giving manner by a cruel relation of any of the parents or by a kidnapper or by an adopting parent or a buyer or a tormentor (who sometimes leads the child to begging/ smuggling/ immoral/ criminal activity or life).

105. Upbringing in an orphanage or poor-home under well-managed atmosphere or alternatively under tormenting and criminal environments.

106. Loss of both parents by accident/ murder/ natural calamity/ suicide; its impact on the growth/ upbringing/ personality/ psychology of the child.

107. In the event of No.105 above, care/ possession/ deprivation of the child of ancestral assets/ property/ cash/ investments by the parents (referral house 12th).

108. Impact of good/ bad character or surroundings of the parent/ other person upbringing the child on child's education, mind, personality, habits and psychology.

109. Living with and upbringing by two mothers under the same roof or under two fathers, one living with mother and the other visiting the mother on regular basis (referral house 10th).

110. Facility or problem about mobility without owning a mode of transport or with ownership of a mode of transport.

111. Comfortable or uncomfortable periods in life determined by Vimshottari Mahadasa, its sub-periods, transit of planets and yearly progressive charts, because 4th house relates to comfort and discomfort.

112. Quality and composition of residential unit with special reference to flats in multi-storeyed buildings, community living, farm houses, collective living, living in joint family system with common or separate kitchen; living in own house/ palace/ bungalow; living in towns and cities or in rural areas, hamlets, tribal areas etc.

113. Living in temple/ church/ mosque/ gurudwara as a priest/ helping hand/ tenant/ refugee or as a favour of someone.
114. Ownership of several residential units and other properties; some lying vacant or unused, or going into dilapidation by non-use or misuse by tenants, care-takers, encroachers or by government occupation.
115. Release of property by tenant or encroacher or govt. acquisition, and time of release.
116. Usurpation of or encroachment on, property (inclusive of vehicles or animals).
117. Confiscation or sale by auction of property/ vehicles by govt. or court.
118. Property brokerage as source of livelihood.
119. Speculation in property; colonisation; contractor-ship, in constructive line; speculation in unconstructed property like plots etc. like buying a large piece of land and then selling it by converting into smaller units.
120. Ex-communication by caste/ community/ social/ religious group; sometimes leading to groupism/ quarrels/ violence/ litigation; consequences thereof.
121. Individual or a group instigating/ forcing a widow to become *Sati* with her dead husband's body/ sword/ *turban*/or husband's any item of personal use.

THE FIFTH HOUSE

The prominent among the names of the Fifth House are *"Putra-Bhava" "Vidya Bhava"*, *"Buddhi Bhava"*, i.e. house relating to progeny, intelligence, education etc. and the following subjects fall under its jurisdiction.

1. General intelligence; capacity for grasp of what is taught or told.
2. Capacity for learning including memory for what has been learnt.
3. Instruction and education; performance in school/ college/ university.
4. Capacity for independent writing, for imagination, for guesswork, for reproduction, for translation, for original ideas.
5. Command on language(s) (spoken and written).
6. Capacity and competence for expression, that is to put forth in writing or while teaching, preaching, public speaking, one's ideas in clearly understandable manner to make them go home to the listener/ taught/ reader.
7. Lack of clarity/ understandability in spoken and/ or written language.
8. Willingness/ keenness/ inner urge to impart knowledge to others; alternatively lack of these qualities.
9. Grasp and accumulation of knowledge of 'Mantra/ Yantra/ Tantra' (spiritual or occult usages) including practical experience.
10. Grasp/ knowledge/ experience of Yoga-Marg and Bhakti (devotion)-Marg.
11. Capacity and willingness to impart to others knowledge mentioned at No. 9 and 10 above.

12. Trust or distrust between Teacher and Disciple in the field of No. 9 and 10 above.
13. Capacity/ efficiency/ effectivity for management/ control/ supervision/ training (in individual or institutional capacity).
14. New ideas and their implementation in management/ control/ supervision/ introduction of new subjects or methods in school/ college/ university or any other institution or in administrative/ commercial/ industrial/ educational establishment.
15. Capacity and initiative in establishing a library for personal use or for limited circle's use or for general public use (referral house 2nd).
16. Insight and initiative for managing funds for establishing a school, college/ university or any other public-educational institution (referral house 9th).
17. Insight and initiative for arranging recurring funds for running the institutions mentioned at No. 16 above.
18. Defect in speech (stammering/ stuttering, repetition of words/ coughing or a kind of clearing throat before speaking); its rectification/ remedy.
19. Without defect of speech, problem of shyness and defeatism in speaking to an audience/ gathering/ crowd/ meeting/ conference/ class of students or disciples (referral 2nd house).
20. Bad handwriting; shaking of the hand while writing; difficulty in holding a pen/ pencil correctly; rectification and remedy.
21. Defect/ deficiency/ default in systematic thinking, organising ideas and their effective/ continuous expression; rectification/ remedy.
22. Defect/ deficiency/ default of the brains and their rectification/ remedies (referral 1st house, sometimes 8th and 12th if caused by injury).
23. Perverse mind, its reflection and impact on physical actions, and also on society, environments, neighbours, colleagues, co-workers and co-commuters; occasional consequences; (referral house 7th).

24. Trends of thought, and their effect on one's actions in social, political, religious, charitable, communal fields of activity.
25. Analytic process of thought and speaking in general, specially in teaching and preaching or public speaking.
26. Procreation; capacity/ competence or lack of it (referral houses 7th, 4th and 8th). Further because of abortion/ miscarriage as a result of deficiency in one or both husband and wife.

    26.1. Two or even three embryos in the womb; their continuity; or clearance medically of all the embryos or of selected one(s) which is now medically possible.

    26.2. Normal delivery or caesarean delivery with reference to 26-1 above.

    26.3. Post-delivery survival with normal health or any kind of physical, mental or intellectual deficiency in the new born(s) with reference to 26-1 and 26-2 above.

    26.4. Any kind of health problem to the new-born(s) upto one year of age, when they are governed more by the stars of the parents than by their own stars.

27. Loss of pregnancy due to physical pressure (referral house 7th and 12th).
28. Diseases of the womb (uterus), rectification, remedy or ultimate removal (referral houses 4th and 7th and also 8th if surgery is involved).
29. Complaints of the menstrual cycle, including scanty/ excess flow of blood, intermittent flow of blood, bleeding extending to several days (referral houses 7th and 12th).
30. Menstrual cycle of less than 26 days or more than 29 days and its effect, if any, on capacity for procreation.
31. Sexual activity during menses, its physical and mental consequences on male/ female partner (referral houses 7th, 8th and 12th).
32. Adoption of a child; (if from within the blood relation referral house is 4th, if from outside the family referral houses are 9th and 10th).

33. Adoption of pet animals in place of or in addition to children.
34. Incestuous relations if any with adopted child (referral houses 7th and 12th).
35. Violence towards one's progeny or towards stepchildren or towards adopted child; its physical and mental consequences on the child (referral houses 8th and 12th).
36. Illicit/ immoral relationship with one's natural or step child with the child's consent/ connivance or without it (referral houses 7th, 9th and 12th).
37. Temporary genuine or assumed insanity, failure of memory, madness, frickle-mindedness (referral house 1st).
38. Violence under influence of real or assumed insanity/ madness/ failure of senses; consequences for self and victim; legal consequences too (referral houses 5th, 8th and 12th).
39. Sexual intercourse with animals (referral houses 7th, 8th and 9th).
40. Grand children (referral houses 1st and 9th).
41. Functioning as real or bogus 'Guru' or 'Guide' for religious/ Taantrik/ spiritual/ Mantrik/ astrological disciples (referral houses 3rd, 9th, 10th and 11th).
42. Wealth/ assets of mother/ stepmother, and succession to them (referral houses 4th and 11th).
43. Functioning as a Minister/ Adviser/ Draftsman/ Policy-maker/ legislator/ Parliamentarian (referral houses 1st, 3rd and 10th).
44. Functioning as a Priest/ preacher/ Granthi/ Maulavi/ Imam/ Bishop/ Padre/ Sewadar/ Mahant/ Director/ Manager of a religious place like temple/ Mosque/ Church/ Gurudwara/ Sthanak/ Chaitya/ Ram-dwara (referral house 9th).
45. The 5th house is linked to failure or malfunctioning of liver, one or both kidneys, appendicitis, ovaries and fallopian tubes.
46. Once or repeated conception (pregnancy) in fallopian tubes and failure or success of medical treatment to stop the process; indigenous medical treatment or surgical operation (referral houses 7th and 8th).

47. Real devotion or a mere show of devotion to God Almighty, religious scriptures/ preachings/ prayers/ recitation/ Bhajans and songs (referral houses 9th, 10th and 11th).
48. Knowledge and skill (or a mere show) of performing Yagyas (religious sacrifices in the Holy fire), Murti-sthapana/ Pratishtha (installation of statues/ idols), inauguration of Church/ Mosque/ Sthanak (of Jains) Chaitya of Buddhists (referral houses 9th and 10th).
49. Knowledge and skill as a medical person (Doctor/ Vaidya/ Hakim or practitioner of any system of medical treatment (referral houses 6th and 8th).
50. Genuine or unjustified/ unearned fame for expertise in any knowledge.
51. Authorship (genuine or ghost) of books/ articles/ treatise/ essays/ notes or commentary on textbooks or on Important Books by other authors, poetry, dramas, stories, stories for films and serials of TV, columns in newspapers/ magazines/ periodicals/ Souvenirs/ leaflets/ advertisement.
52. Publication or non-publication/ popularity or non-popularity of items mentioned at No. 51 above (referral houses 9th and 12th).
53. Only income or only fame or both Income and fame from items at No. 51 above (referral houses 9th, 10th and also 11th).
54. Systematically trained/ untrained but experienced/ untrained and also inexperienced/ competent or incompetent reporter, editor, feature or column writer, translator, compiler/ index-writer etc (referral houses 9th and 10th).
55. Specialisation/ top expertise in any branch or discipline of knowledge/ learning/ research/ compilation of knowledge (referral houses 9th and 10th).
56. Determination of causes of natural miscarriage/ abortion/ still birth/ loss of child in infancy; rectification and remedy (referral houses 7th, 8th and 9th).
57. Medical/ surgical/ religious/ spiritual/ Tantrik remedies to No. 56 above.

58. Examination of curses of this or previous birth as the cause for childlessness (medical causes included) (referral houses 7th and 9th).
59. Birth of own child after several years of marriage.
60. Safe and comfortable/ uncomfortable term of pregnancy, causes and remedies (Psychological/ religious/ medical/ precautionary etc) (referral house 7th).
61. Delivery of child/ children, normal, forceps-aided, caesarean; and after effects thereof on mother or the child or both (referral house 8th).
62. Death of mother and/ or child in the process of delivery or within little time after delivery/ within one week or one to four months of the delivery); causes thereof and remedy (referral houses 2nd and 8th).

Note:
It is virtually difficult to predict whether it is a boy or a girl or twins in the womb in spite of too many calculations, and this type of prediction is better avoided.

63. Medical or mid-wifery pressure-tactic (method) or medicinal termination of pregnancy; consequences thereof (physical and psychological on the mother).
64. Termination of pregnancy owing to female embryo in the womb as ascertained by latest medical methods (referral houses 2nd and 8th).
65. Illegitimate pregnancy or birth; within/ outside the knowledge of the lawful husband (referral houses 7th, 9th and 12th).
66. Determination or non-determination of the father of the child or of the pregnancy in the event of illegitimacy or group sex orgies; (referral houses 7th and 12th).
67. Relationship between adopted child and natural child with special reference to succession to assets/ liabilities (referral house 4th).
68. Death of father (referral houses 4th, 9th, 10th and 11th).

69. Gains to spouse from sources other than direct inheritance.
70. Gains from self to paternal grandfather or maternal grandmother or gains from them to self (referral houses 9th and 11th).
71. Brother/ sister of domestic help or employee at shop or office or of the worker at the agricultural farm/ garden/ orchard; relation thereof with self.
72. Capacity/competence to stick to one's ideas/decisions/ actions etc.
73. Second brother/ sister; grandchild's relations by marriage; relations by marriage of the brother/ sister; all similar other relations by marriage in the family (the list can be very long).

THE SIXTH HOUSE

This House is known as the "*Shatru Bhava*" and also as "*Rog Bhava*" and naturally it concerns enemies, illnesses, diseases, injuries, wound, worries of the mind which include depression and introvert tendency. Its territorial jurisdiction is described below (routine referral house is 8th).

1. One's own progeny behaving/ functioning like an enemy (referral houses 5th and 11th).
2. Enemies amongst the people around you, within the family/ neighbourhood, at place of work, in society, community, organisation, public body, politics, management committee, Board of Directors, in games and sports.
3. One or both parent of self or spouse behaving/acting like enemy; (referral houses 4th and 10th).
4. Enemy caused physical/ mental/ financial/ professional trouble/ problems/in domestic or family life (referral house 4th).
5. Enemy-caused troubles/ problems in service/ business/ industry, self-employment, in joint family system or partnership business (referral houses 4th, 9th, 10th, 11th and 12th).
6. Enemy-caused grievous injury/ illness/ disease ultimately leading to death or directly causing death (referral houses 2nd, 8th and 12th).
7. Spouse or beloved or lover behaving/ acting as an enemy (referral house 7th).
8. Victory to self or to the enemy or a drawn affair.
9. Victory/treaty/compromise/cease-fire/cooperation/ cessation of hostility and its tenure, specially when the confrontation is between two countries or between two groups within the same country (referral houses 3rd and 9th).

10. Victory/ compromise/ treaty as directed by third-party intervention or through litigation or by Authorities or through politicians in power.
11. Whether victory/ defeat/ compromise/ treaty involves payment of ransom, compensation, surrender of territory/ property/ assets/ money/ human beings/ exchange of prisoners-cum-criminals/surrender or exchange of knowledge or know-how/exchange of experts, and conditions of the surrender/ compromise/ treaty etc., (referral houses 3rd 7th, 9th and 10th).
12. Death of one or many people/ animals or destruction of assets/ property/ industry/ markets/ institutions of education and Hospitals etc. owing to action by own side or by the enemy (referral houses 2nd, 4th, 5th, 7th, 9th and 12th).
13. Whether individual fighting an individual or individual fighting a group of persons or groups fighting groups; both sides well-equipped and well-armed or only one side (self or enemy) well-equipped/ armed (referral houses 3rd, 7th and 11th).
14. Final outcome/consequences of No. 12 and 13 above; after-effect on one side or both sides (referral houses 3rd, 4th, 7th, 11th and 12th).
15. Position of law and order system or of the national or international law in the context of the fight/ hostilities/ terrorism/ border skirmishes (referral houses 10th, 11th and 12th).
16. Whether the fight would turn into a regular gang-war or communal continuous fights or race war or hostilities between two states or countries or groups of countries or would lead to a World War (referral houses 10, 11th and 12th).
17. Effectivity of intervention by individual/group of people/ politicians in power/ authorities/ central-cum-federal government/ nation/nations; outcome of the Intervention (referral houses 10th, 11th and 12th).
18. Immediate effect and after-effect of No. 16 and 17 above on the neighbourhood/ surroundings/ families involved or

affected/ general population in one state/ country or all states/ countries involved or non-involved or neutral to the fight/ battles/war (referral houses 11th and 12th).

19. Role of Red Cross/ St. John's Ambulance/ United Nations and its various allied Formations/ Amnesty International and allied Organisations and their effectivity (referral houses 7th, 9th and 12th).

20. Aliens; Prisoners-of-war; exchange after cessation of hostilities/war.

21. Enemy property; confiscation (temporary/ conditional/ absolute); compensation; exchange of property after cessation of the hostilities. Damage/ non-maintenance during hostilities and afterwards and effect on the owners (referral houses 4th, $7^{th,}$ 11th and 12th).

22. Criminal cases on individual basis/groups on either side or only on the defeated side; subsequent bitterness and revival of hostile attitude in the defeated and punished people (referral houses 7th and 12th).

23. Consequences of revival of hostile attitude; after-effect on the next generation (referral houses 7th and 8th).

24. Armament and disarmament; dissolution or reduction in fighting forces of the defeated party by treaty or pressure/ compulsion method.

25. Contribution of race-based and colour-based/religion-based hatred in national and International affairs; these factors leading to War (regarding both No.24 and 25, referral houses are 3rd, 4th and 7th).

26. Common and short-term illness like fever, cough and cold, minor cut or burn injury, skin ailment, sore eyes, indigestion, constipation, nausea, temporary gynae complaints for females etc.

27. Causes, remedies, precautions for future prevention, duration and recurrence of illness of routine type or of short duration.

28. Spread of these routine illnesses by contact, joint living, sexual

association, working in close vicinity of the ill person etc.
29. Contacting infectious diseases, knowingly/ unknowingly; because of unsanitary and unhygienic conditions in and around the residence or place of work; medical treatment; preventive measures; success or failure of the preventive measures; default on part of neighbours/municipality.
30. Short term or long term or fatal illness/disease such as T.B. Cancer, AIDS, hernia, gout, arthritis, rheumatics, pleurisy, epilepsy, different kinds of leprosy, asthma, diabetes, migraine, kidney's failure or weakness in its functioning, liver trouble, schizophrenia, insanity (partial or complete), madness, troubles of blood system, ailments or malfunctioning of the heart and its allied mechanism, venereal diseases, cancerous or non-cancerous but malignant growth anywhere in the body, skin ailments, eye trouble ultimately leading to blindness, defect in hearing leading ultimately to partial or complete deafness, dumbness, stammering and stuttering, other defects of the speech mechanism, polio, effects of child-polio, problems in use of hands, feet, legs, fingers etc., expansion of bones as in the old age, other problems of bones, pain in spinal chord and waist-line bones, disease of the uterus/ovaries/fallopian tubes, vaginal complaints, appendicitis, death of white blood cells, impotency, frigidity, psychosis of any kind, any kind of phobia, psychological problems; loss of memory/ speech as a result of injury/accident; sterility, disease of the thyroid-gland, thrombosis, diseases of the throat and tonsils, small-pox, cholera, plague, encephalitis and other killing fevers, etc. etc.

Note:
It is not possible to give a very exhaustive list of diseases of mind and body, because it is a book on the science of astrology and not medical sciences.

31. Septicaemia and wounds getting septic (curable or non-curable); final termination into death; causes and remedies.
32. Death owing to any of the diseases mentioned in No. 26 and 30 above.

Important Note:
Where question of illness/ diseases or risk to life or limb are involved, it is taken for granted that the 2nd, 6th and 8th houses are directly and deeply inter-linked, and all the three houses be taken into consideration before venturing any important prediction. In the items below from No.33 to 36 therefore the term "referral houses 2nd and 8th " is not being repeated.

33. Risk to life or limb by water (drowning, sinking) or non-availability of drinking water as in deserts and sometimes on mountains.

34. Risk to life by fire, fire-arm, electricity, poisonous and other gasses, inflammables, bomb explosion; earth-quake, eruption of volcano, land-slide in mountain areas, hitting glacier, snow-storm, torpedo etc.

35. Risk to life and limb by rabies, bite by poisonous snakes other similar creatures, attack by wild or pet violent animals.

36. Risk to life or limb by robbers, dacoits, thieves, snatchers, proud and arrogant new rich, rash drivers of auto-vehicles, killers for fun, killers for racial/ communal/ religious hatred, rivals in love, anarchists, adversary in politics/ business/ smuggling, associates in crime or criminal activity, criminal bosses once the utility of the individual is over or on failure in an assigned criminal task, person hurt in a love affair or in married life, persons involved in extra-marital love affair, by a member of family or by other relation in matters relating to property/ succession or any other interest.

37. Mental worries of any and every kind, very often springing from money, property, succession, love, supremacy in tribe or community/society.

38. Mental worry/ harassment/ torture/ black-mail/fear of violence from within the family, from relations, from neighbours, from colleagues, from frustrated lovers/beloveds, from jealousy springing from third angle's emergence in married life; remedies; ultimate results.

39. Fear phobia created by train journey, sea journey, air journey,

high rise buildings, heights of mountains, hills, dams, hydrophobia, river banks etc. also that created by cockroaches, worms, poisonous insects/creatures etc.

40. Mental anxiety and worries created by money involved in speculation, gambling, lotteries, loans, card games, kitty parties, chit funds etc.

41. Lower abdomen, tieing line, waist line, loins, portion of the body immediately above anus and genitals, lower part of spinal cord and neighbouring bones; their ailments/ injuries/ remedy and recovery etc.

42. Lower lumber region, thigh joints, buttocks, hip, upper thighs etc.

43. Forgery, fraud, perjury, felony, rape and sexual crimes; results on victims; detection and action by law and order machinery; penalty and punishment including jail sentence (referral houses 7th, 8th, 10th, 11th and 12th).

44. Bullet/pellet injury, knife-injury, in any portion of the middle part of the body; surgical operation in this connection, results thereof.

45. Sufferings/harassment/ torture for false charges/ allegations, and managed court judgements or political decisions, action by authorities with powers or no powers in that particular behalf (referral houses 3rd, 8th, 10th and 12th).

46. Consequences of introvertness, reserved nature, tendency of secret spying on spouse and other members of the family (referral houses 2nd and 7th).

47. Maternal uncles and aunts; relations with them; gains or losses from them to self or gains and losses to them by self; their relations and attitude towards mother and in the event of conflict between self and mother (referral houses 4th and 12th).

THE SEVENTH HOUSE

It is known as the "*Kalatra Bhava*" (i.e. *Stree Bhava*) or the House of Love, Marriage, Married Life, Marriage Partner (spouse), sex life etc. However, many other subjects with wide ramifications are also governed by this House. Its main subjects are detailed below:

1. Love; virgin, extra-marital, platonic, genuine on both sides, real on one side and unreal on the other side; selfishness under cover of love; extreme emotionalism in love affair; one-sided love, silent one-sided love, love based on physical charm only; love based on some intellectual/ educational quality; love based on some outstanding achievement of the party opposite.
2. Love-based marriage, formal, recognised by law/ society (in a sense real).
3. Love-based marriage; snag in its formal shape; based on falsehood or fraud springing from motives; not recognised by law/ society/ family.
4. Arranged marriage, recognised by law and society.
5. Arranged marriage, wilful snag and thus not recognisable by law or society or family in general.
6. Marriage for a fixed/ limited period by contract, agreement, lease etc.
7. Formal or informal marriage by deceit such as under (false/ fraudulent) misrepresentation, temptation, or suppression of facts.
8. Marriage involving change of religion, faith, community, domicile etc.
9. Mistress/ concubine/ keep/ retainer/ paramour/ club friend involving physical relationship.
10. Physical relationship with neighbour or colleague more as a matter of closeness and convenience (rather without emotions).

11. Marriage by sale/ purchase of the individual either by self or others.
12. Extra-marital affair involving only one partner in marriage with a married/ unmarried person.
13. Extra-marital affair involving both partners in marriage either in a triangular/ four cornered arrangement or each partner not knowing about the activity of the other.
14. Group sex orgies of married couples or married people and singles, or by unmarried boys and girls, including impostors who are married but claim to be unmarried.
15. Collective physical relationship with one person by more than one person of opposite sex, in the presence of one another or keeping other(s) waiting outside, by free will or force/ fraud/ compulsion/ temptation/ greed or by fondness for this type of sex activity.
16. Physical relationship between man and woman, in the presence of other(s) but without involvement of the other(s) present in this act.
17. Physical relationship with female or male prostitute.
18. Emotional involvement with female or male prostitute without indulgence in sexual acts, sometimes leading to formal/ genuine marriage.
19. Male or female prostitute as a retainer.
20. Helping a prostitute morally/ financially or receiving help from a prostitute morally or financially.
21. Helping a prostitute with regard to its progeny or a prostitute helping the progeny of a lover/ beloved.
22. Physical satisfaction with the help/ assistance of animals/ artificial items.
23. Physical relationship between teacher and taught; between guru and disciple; between priest/ preacher/ *granthi/ imam/ maulavi/* padre / bishop/ *mahant/* monk/ *sadhu/ sanyasi/* musician attached to religious palaces on one hand, and the worshipper/ follower of faith/ visitor/ devotee on the other.

24. Physical relationship with any person falling under prohibited degree, including close relations of self or spouse within immediate family or wider family.
25. Physical relationship with teacher's spouse or teacher's any other relation, or with spouse or any other relation of the taught/ disciple.
26. Physical relationship with spouse of friend/ colleague/ superior boss or sub-ordinate, or with any other relation thereto.
27. Physical relationship with visitor/ co-traveller/ sales-person etc.
28. Physical relationship with steno/ secretary or member of the personal staff.
29. Physical relationship with employer or friends/ associates of the employer.
30. Physical relationship with domestic help/ servant/ employee or any other relation of such a person.
31. Physical relationship with politician or bureaucrat (often motives matter on either side); or with a judge or an official of the court or with an officer of the taxation authority. Astrologer to examine whether ulterior motives are involved or not involved on either side. Sometimes it could be pure and simple love without strings and motives.
32. Solitary or repeated sexual act, casual or secluded, purely for monetary gain or any other favour such as favour in Examination-result, in court judgement, in Tax assessment, approval of thesis, favour in Departmental Promotion Committee, favourable opinion in Press or on an Awards/ Reward Body.
33. Solitary or repeated sex act for getting name/ photograph/ interview/ opinion appear in print.
34. Physical relationship as a stopgap arrangement, awaiting marriage.
35. Physical relationship between flying/ ground staff of airlines (sometimes under compulsion/temptation/persuasion/ force

threat), or between flying staff and a passenger on the airline.

36. Casual physical relationship between passengers on train/long road travel/aeroplane.

37. Casual or long-term relationship between staff of sailing ship; between passengers themselves on a sailing ship; between passenger and members of staff of sailing ship.

38. Physical relationship between staff of hotel/ motel/ boarding house club/ rest house/ circuit house/ dak bungalow; or between guests themselves at such places; or between guests and staff at such places.

39. Physical relationship between members of management and inmates of *nari niketan*/ orphanage/ blind-homes/ blind school/ *ashrams*/ *dharmashalas*/ inns/ *sarai*/ destitute women's Home/ transit camps for refugees and displaced persons/ training centres/ workshops/ Scout & Girl Guide jamboree/ NCC camp/ camps organised around national day sports etc. (often compulsion/ use of force/ persuasion/ threats/ torture work in this category).

40. Physical relationship between officers of superior cadres under govt.

41. Physical relationship between self and one of the parents of the spouse (within or without knowledge/ suspicion of the spouse of either.

42. Physical relationship between practitioner in medicine/ surgery etc. and the patient or the person accompanying/ attending on the patient; (element of compulsion/ force/ temptation/ greed/ threat to be studied).

43. Physical relation between inmates of hospitals and nursing homes; mutually between patients; between doctors and patients or their attendants; between other staff and patients or their attendants; between doctors or members of staff themselves (element of compulsion/ temptation/ greed/ force/ torture/ threat to be examined).

44. Physical relationship at national or international meetings or conferences (sports/ games/ competition gatherings).

45. Physical relationship between travel guide(s) and tourist(s).
46. Failure of marriage; by divorce; contested litigation or mutual consent or by uncontested divorce degree or divorce degree obtained by fraud/ forgery/ impersonation/ any other kind of falsehood.
47. Failure of marriage by physical separation; without divorce/ without litigation, including physical separation beyond the control of the husband and the wife.
48. Failure of marriage because of separate residence at difference towns or different states/counties/countries; also owing to problems of visa, religion, hostilities between governments; cold war between two nations; or owing to restrictions by law authorities, or owing to one person being in jail or being a prisoner or a prisoner-of-war, etc.
49. Failure of marriage because of invalidity/ long illness of one partner.
50. Failure of marriage because of partial/ complete impotency/ frigidity of one partner.
51. Failure of marriage owing to interference of the family on either or both sides, specially the ladies.
52. Failure of marriage because of past (suspected/ narrated/ imagined pre-marriage friendship of either of the partners to marriage).
53. Failure of marriage by death of one of the two.
54. Failure of marriage because of insanity/ madness of one of the two.
55. Failure of marriage because of childlessness or having no male issue, and sometimes second marriage crops in such a situation.
56. Failure of marriage because of social/ communal/ financial/ political consideration and compulsions/ restraints.
57. Failure of marriage because of entry of a third person between the two.

58. Failure of marriage because of a religious vow (common feature in Jain and some other cultures), restriction by a guru/ sage/ sadhu/ *sannyasi*/ future teller.
59. Failure of marriage because of one partner renouncing the grihastha ashram (giving up the married life to live as a saint/ sadhu/ *sannyasi*).
60. Failure of marriage because of incompatibility based on difference in age/ education/ intelligence/changed faith or newly acquired faith by one in a different than the original religious sect/ cult/ faith, specially after the marriage.
61. Failure of marriage because of perversity and unnatural manners in sexual matters by one of the two, including one partner's inclination or preference for homosexuality or lesbianism or dislike for the partner on basis of personality/ appearance/ body odour/ difference in ideas on cleanliness or dress or club-life or group orgies or bringing mistress/ paramour into the married life or forcing one partner to accept the presence of a mistress or paramour or joint life with mistress/ paramour.
62. Failure of marriage because of sudden poverty or sudden riches thereby vast changes in the style of living and social/ community status.
63. Failure of marriage because of change in appearance/ physical disability befalling on one of the two owing to accident/ attack/ injury-in-fight/ battle/ war/ illness/ disease with less or no chance of returning to normalcy.
64. From this 7th house has to be considered the private parts of the human body known as genitals, testicles, anus and the internal and external areas around them, including any defect in these private parts, injury to them; treatment and results thereof.
65. Sex transmitted diseases; treatment, results and after effect; risk to married-life/ love affair/ risk to life itself/ deformity of organs/ deformity of limbs/ resultant other diseases, including that of skin.
66. Sizes/ suitability to partner of the procreational organs vividly

described by '*Vatsyayana*' in his world-wide known treatise "*Kama Sutra*"; defects in these organs; problems in sex activity and to the partner in sex; effect on satisfaction/ dissatisfaction.

67. Effect on procreational organs/ sexual capacity and competence caused by homosexuality/ lesbianism/ unnatural sex habits/ masturbation by hand, by other objects/ sex with pets and animals.

68. Medical treatment of effects mentioned in No.67 above; full or partial recovery; consequences on subsequent sex life and on married life; psychological impact on marriage-partner/ mate/beloved.

69. Sexual intercourse during menstruation cycle and its good or bad physical and mental effect on the female partner/ male partner.

70. Menopause in females; premature or at right age; its psychological and mental impact on the female and her subsequent attitude towards sex life, towards husband or male partner and towards children etc.

71. Effect of menopause on childless females and their subsequent attitude and outlook on sex life; sometimes leading to suspicion on the male partner to marriage or love.

72. Medical treatment of premature menopause and its results; failure can lead to mental depression and state of withdrawal attitude from physical relations.

73. 72 Menopause (a kind of impotency) in males (temporary/ permanent; partial or complete) and its psychological and physical impact on both partners in marriage.

74. Medical treatment of No.73 above; its success or failure; impact on both husband and wife.

75. Impact on spouse or beloved and its consequential withdrawal or aggressive and violent change in nature in the event of impotency existing since adolescence or occurring in mid-youth; impact also on other members of the family; impact on social-life/ work-life of the individual concerned.

76. Impact of partial or complete impotency in males on their other habits, sometimes leading to homosexuality.
77. Impact on physical development/ nature/ psychology/ habits of dry female (that is who doesn't get the menstruation at all, or gets just for name's sake); success or failure of medical treatment; impact on lover or husband and also on the married life and on attitude on life in general.
78. Conversion of a partial or complete impotent man into a eunuch.
79. Forcible or deceitful conversion of a sexually potent man into eunuch (prevalent in South Asian countries including India); impact on the mind and body of the man concerned; after-effect on capacity and competence to normal work which he used to do before the event.
80. Physical relationship with eunuchs; impact on the mind and health of the man doing so.
81. Impact of No.80 above on physical relationship with wife and on the married life in general.
82. Diseases begotten from sexual intercourse with prostitutes and eunuchs; their treatment; success or failure of treatment; impact on spouse and on self, psychologically and physically.
83. Husband and wife's mutual relationship while jointly running a business, industry, profession; impact on domestic life, on other members of the family and on upbringing of children including their education/ career.
84. Re-marriage of a widow/ widower/ divorcee/ separated or deserted person; (referral houses 4th, 9th and 12th).
85. With reference to No. 84 above, to examine whether the second/ third marriage is likely with the brother/ sister/ cousin or any relation of the previous spouse (referral houses 2nd, 3rd, 8th and 9th).
86. Cheating/ deceit through enactment of assumed marriage; consequences on money/ assets/ liabilities of one on the other; impact on family of one or both.

87. Consequences of No.86 above if the female becomes pregnant and the man deserts/ separates/ withdraws from the relationship, and disowns the impregnation; special reference to the female and her family (referral houses 5th, 8th and 12th).

88. Rape; consequences – mental/ physical/ social/ futuristic for the female and her family, more specially if she conceived as a result of rape (referral houses 2nd, 5th, 8th and 12th).

89. Mental and social impact on the female if the rape-case reaches a court of law; infamy for her; impact on marriage and married life, in view of the fact whether the rape is of unmarried or married woman (referral houses 9th and 12th).

90. Murder, suicide, death of a female or young boy/ man as a consequence of rape or sex action; consequence for the family of the victim; determination of cruelty and torture involved (referral houses 8th and 12th).

91. Physical and mental impact on a girl or a boy of pre-adolescence age subjected to forced/ induced temptation-oriented/ misguidance-oriented sex by opposite sex or by persons of the same sex (referral houses 1st, 4th and 5th).

92. Impact of drugs, drinks smoking or any other kind of intoxication on mental/ physical/ sexual faculties and on procreational capacity (success or failure of medical treatment) (referral houses 1st and 12th).

93. Physical desires and reaction of such desires on medical persona of all systems of medicine while examining or treating patients for sex-related/ procreation-related complaints and other diseases not related to sex and procreation, including mental and physical impact on the patient (referral houses 4th, 5th, 8th and 12th).

94. Harassment/ taunts/ abuses/ torture/ death including burning or poisoning or strangulating or pushing to death at the hands of the spouse and his/ her family; mostly it is the bride at the receiving end (referral houses 2nd, 4th, 8th and 12th).

95. Successful or unsuccessful attempt to suicide by the harassed or tortured person with relation to married life; consequences

for person attempting suicide if the bid fails (referral houses 2nd and 8th).

96. Consequences of No.95 above for the spouse and his/ her family with special reference to society/ neighbours/ police/ law court and family of the person who attempted suicide (referral houses 2nd, 4th, 8th and 12th).

97. Clandestinely motivated financial gains from death of the spouse to the surviving partner in marriage; or his family or the progeny (referral houses 5th, 9th and 11th).

98. Dispute/ litigation by the family of the victimised person with reference to No. 97 above (referral houses 2nd, 6th, 8th and 12th).

99. Husband dependent for livelihood/ maintenance on wife with assets and/ or earning/ unearned income etc; impact on mutual relations and relationship within the families of both or one (referral houses 2nd, 8th, 11th and 12th).

100. Violence as a part of nature, without vested/ greedy interests, between husband and wife, between lovers, or among persons involved in extra-marital relationship (which in some cases might be more than one relationship (referral houses 2nd 8th, 9th and 12th).

101. 101 Consequences of No. 100 above if violence ends in unintended death of any one person or matter reaches police and law agencies/ court (referral houses 2nd, 8th and 12th).

Subjects other than love/ marriage and it's failures etc.

102. Fights/ battles/ War/ cold-war/ confrontation/ conflict between two persons two groups of people, between states, between nations, or between groups of nations; it includes withdrawal of diplomatic relations.

103. Indirect support to terrorists/ insurgency/ infiltrators' groups in a hostile state/ country/ territory/ region/ area; sometimes direct support, financial help and training and providing other facilities such as arms and ammunition etc.

104. Compromise/ treaty/ arbitration/ cessation of cold war or active hostilities or border skirmishes, end of battles and fighting by

organised or stray troops/ groups/ individuals.

105. Civil and criminal litigation; costs and consequences (referral houses 9th, 10th, 11th and 12th, sometime 5th and 6th also if another generation is involved).

106. Litigation between citizen and the government/ tax authority/ local administration/ state; cost and consequences (referral house 10th and 12th).

107. Litigation between members of the family; between husband and wife; between close and instant relations of male and/ or females or of the entire family; between individual and club or between employee(s) and employer or any other similar formation or organisation; or between two communities/ societies/ groups of people or two clubs or organisations/ forums/ consumer and suppliers of goods or services.

108. Rivalry between political parties/ social workers groups/ trade unions, religious groups/ charitable and educational formations or institutions.

109. Litigation between educational/ social/ charitable/ welfare formations on one side and the state on the other.

110. Rivalry between groups of doctors/ lawyers/ other professionals.

111. Litigation between individuals or Common-cause and Housing societies or between Administrations, between Development (Housing) Authorities.

112. Relations/ disagreements between partners in business/ industrial units, those in smuggling and other criminal activities; consequences for individuals and groups of people or organised gangs; fights/ killings/ litigation.

113. Victory or defeat in any of the above litigation/ fights/ quarrels/ battles/ war etc.

114. After effect on individuals/ society-at-large/ population/ productivity in factories/ fertility of land/ vegetation/ civil life/ wild life after cessation of fighting/ battles, war and hostilities.

115. Disposal of unwanted/ damaged arms-weapons/ arsenal/

vehicles/ aeroplanes, scrap of used/ damaged weapons/ vehicles/ debris of buildings etc. etc.

116. Rehabilitation/ re-marriage/ settlement-in-source-of-income of war widows/ widowers (husbands of females working as doctors/ nurses, combatant and auxiliary forces of females in army/ navy/ air force, observer and intelligence corps); creation of reserve forces and placement of disability-discharged or otherwise discharged male and female personnel.

117. Return and rehabilitation of prisoners-of-war on cessation of hostilities and/ or after signing of treaties of peace/ surrender.

118. Medical treatment arrangement including allocation of hospital beds to wounded and diseased personnel back from battle-fields/ war, its impact on civilian medical facilities and hospital beds.

119. Post-war reconstruction with an eye on prices, destroyed/ damaged industries/ roads, railway lines, airports/ seaports, army air-bases, other facilities of human and animal life, availability of fodder for cattle and raw material for construction/ revival of industries manufacturing units and other reconstruction activity.

120. Financial burden in the shape of (i) cost of reconstruction (ii) rehabilitation of war-returned personnel (iii) taxes on the public, (iv) servicing and repayment of national loans obtained for post-war reconstruction; and (v) in the case of defeated party or nation, cost of damages claimed by the victorious party or nation (referral houses 2nd, 4th, 9th, 10th, 11th and 12th).

121. Reconciliatory steps taken to assuage the bitter feelings of the defeated people/ nation; impact on preparation for retaliation in future by the defeated people/ nation (vide the case of Germany after the wars of 1914 and 1939).

122. Impact on the mind/ development/ withdrawalness on the young or the next generation of the defeated people/ nation.

123. Over-all impact and reaction on the victorious people/ nation.

THE EIGHTH HOUSE

The 8th House is known as the "*Aayu Bhava*" (House of Longevity). It rules the following (8th House is very much inter-linked with 7th and 2nd Houses)

1. Internal structure of the private parts of the body (genitals), anus, liver, kidneys, urethra, fallopian tubes, ovaries, vaginal passage upto uterus, intestine, testicles, appendicitis, spleen, thighs and joints.
2. Any injury, wound, disease to body parts mentioned in No. 1 above (referral house 7th).
3. Injuries, wounds, diseases leading to invalidity or to <u>death</u>.
4. Diseases/illness related to blood system (excluding the heart and its ancillaries), all kinds of fever, left eye of self or right eye of spouse, typhoid, TB, small-pox, dysentery, diarrhoea, piles, fistula in the region mentioned at No.1 above, venereal diseases, AIDS, diseases other than venereal diseases and AIDS (referral houses 6th and 7th).
5. Contagious diseases, including those of the epidemic category.
6. Chronic illnesses.
7. Injury/fracture to bone in any part of the body, including skull/face/legs.
8. Invalidity resulting from injury mentioned in No. 7 above.
9. Cancer of any part of the body, but specially of genital organs and the uterus.
10. Leprosy of any kind, plague, diseases generated by influenza and bronchitis.
11. Injury by fire, any kind of gases, acid, fire, firearms of any size and category, cannon, bomb of all types/varieties, electricity, chemicals and inflammable items.

12. Risk, injury or death from water including sinking or drowning or injury inside water, water-oriented diseases, hydrophobia, injury by diving etc.
13. Poisoning of any kind, including by food, snake bite, rabies gangrene, sepsis, septicaemia, morphine, *gaanja*, *bhaang*, *dhatura*, in a sense any and every kind of poison entering into the body or the blood system.
14. Injury/wounds sustained/suffered by a fall from height; sometimes death caused thereby.
15. Injury by rains, hail-storm, cyclone, snow-fall, avalanche, strong dusty winds, and wind-storm, hit by glacier, current of dashing waves in sea or ocean.
16. Injury by any means of transport, whether animal driven (like bullock-cart, camel-driven cart, dog-driven sleigh, horse-driven tonga/ bugghee) or carried by human beings (such as rickshaw and palanquin) or auto-vehicle (such as motor car, lorry, bus, truck, scooter, pick-up van, container, crane, tractor, trolley, motor-cycle), passenger or goods train, or rail bogies being shunted with or without an engine, single engine or trolley running on rails, tram, single animal used as transport such as horse, camel, pony, donkey, ass, elephant, yak, ox, buffalo.
17. Injury by stone, rock, land-slide, bamboo-stick, knife, sword, piece of glass, sharp edged or blunt iron/steel element, block of ice, sharp edged piece of snow, hail-storm, tree or branch of tree, fruits of tree, hitting by a flying bird (specially large sized as vulture etc.).
18. Injury caused by animals with horns/claws/nails/teeth/thorns, fish, crocodile, tortoise, animals under the water including poisonous animals.
19. Injury or risk to life in mines, exploring; digging operation, oil drilling, ammunition used in mines and explosives, explosion, outbreak of fire; spread of germs/worms/insects as a battle-tactic; spreading of poisonous chemicals to kill population; earth-quake, eruption of volcano.

20. Injury or death by natural calamity like cloud-burst, lightning, and man-made calamities and by killing devices generally leading to mass-death and injuries to a large number of people.

Important Note:
While considering the possibility or post-event query about injuries and deaths owing to causes listed above special attention need be given to the 2nd house (which rules actual death), 6th house which rules enemy-action, diseases and illnesses (caused naturally or by enemy) 7th house which rules war, battles, fights, conflict with or without violence involved in it, and the 12th house which rules injuries mostly to the upper parts of body sometimes leading to death or death as a punishment by court/ state/ military-rule/ dictatorship/ terrorist groups/ anarchists group/ smugglers gang/ mafia gang and others in due coordination with the study of the 8th house.

Further, with the help of the Vimshottari Mahadasa, its Antardasas and Pratyantar Dasas (main period/ sub-period and pro-sub-periods) and with the help of the yearly chart = Varsh-Kundali (progressive chart) as also transit of planets causing injury or death, the astrologer should determine the year or the month or the day or the period when the injury, disease or death is likely to happen to the individual, its duration and intensity and chances of full or partial recovery and its due time, or no recovery at-all.

21. Insults and miseries, quarrels and enmity generated by insult or any kind of defamation or boycott (referral houses 6, 9th and 12th).

22. Recovery or non-recovery and loss of old dues (referral houses 2nd and 11th).

23. Recovery or non-recovery and loss of money arising from side-business or secret/clandestine/contraband sources of income; if pressure/wild tactics adopted for recovery, consequences thereof including gang-war.

24. Gains and losses from card games, gambling of any kind, betting on horse races/bull fights/ buffalo fights, matches of

cricket or football or baseball, or tennis; betting at wrestling or boxing-fights; financial consequences on self and sometimes on the family (referral houses 11th and 12th).

25. Gains or losses from criminal acts, illegal transactions, trading in contraband goods/ controlled goods/ prohibited goods/ smuggled goods; black market and profiteering; financial and legal consequences thereof, (referral houses 4th, 10th, 11th and 12th).

26. Acts of kidnapping for ransom/for revenge/for political bargaining/for securing release of culprit or accused and arrested person or prisoner or political detainee; consequences for the individuals/ kidnappers/ politicians/ bargainers etc., (referral houses 9th, 10th, 11th and 12th).

27. Acts of kidnapping to influence legal process/ proceedings/ judgement; or to influence politics and diplomatic relations; or to influence any elections/ nomination for appointment or election/ assignment/ marriage/ contract/ agreement/ deputation/ representation etc., (referral houses 4th, 7th, 9th, 10th, 11th and 12th).

28. Any and every kind of consequences of No. 26 and 27 above for the kidnappers, for the kidnapped person, for the family/ group/ party of the person kidnapped (referral houses 6th, 7th, 10th and 12th).

29. Torture and/or death of the kidnapped person while in the custody of the kidnappers or due to events subsequent to release from the clutches of the kidnappers; also sometimes death of one or more of the kidnappers too (referral houses 2nd, 7th, 9th and 12th).

30. Consequences of No. 29 above for all concerned including the family of those killed or deceased persons; also legal and social or political consequences arising therefrom, (referral houses 7th and 12th).

31. Sheltering of guilty persons, criminals, smugglers, kidnappers, contraband traders, religious or communal refugees (referral houses 3rd, 4th and 9th).

32. Consequences (legal/political/social) of No. 31 above for the person given shelter and for the persons/ parties/ groups/ nations giving the shelter (referral houses 4th, 9th, 10th and 12th).

33. Concealment and storage of contraband goods, normal merchandise goods of high value on behalf of others without involvement in sale or purchase of the goods; consequences with regard to responsibility or legal implications for the custodian (referral houses 4th and 12th).

34. Organising rallies, demonstrations, *'dharanas'*, picketing, *'gherao'* etc. consequences for the organiser/ followers/ hired hoodlums if everything goes on peacefully, or if there is violence, arson, loot, injuries and deaths of public or of law and order personnel (referral houses 4th, 10th and 12th – sometimes also 2nd house).

35. Religious or social or spiritual rallies, demonstrations, processions or meetings; peaceful functioning disturbed by rival groups; anti-social gangs, by hoodlums with ulterior motive of looting, molesting or terrorising or giving communal colour to the disturbances/ riots (referral houses 4th, 9th and 12th).

36. Slogan-shouting including "in-house" agitational meeting by way of demonstration by employees or ethnic groups of people against employers or residents in a high-rise or other building etc., consequences and sufferings for other unconcerned people/ residents; consequences for the people against whom slogan-shouting or the demonstration is aimed; consequences for the slogan-shouters and demonstrators without disturbing peace or creating problems of law and order, or consequences if law and order machinery or hoodlums make an appearance in the process or on the scene (referral houses 4th, 7th, 9th and 12th).

37. Criminal acts like theft, dacoity, robbery, murderous attack, murder (intentional or non-intentional) consequences for self and for the victims and/or their families and neighbourhood/ society in general; (referral houses 2nd, 4th, 11th and 12th – sometimes also 7th house).

38. Injuries caused to others or self in the course of commitment of acts mentioned in No. 37 above; consequences for self and sufferer.

39. Rape and forced or consented sodomy; intentional and unintentional injuries or suffering in the process of the act to self or the victim (referral houses 7th and 12th).

40. Unnatural acts with pets and animals; consequences on health and mind of self; legal implications if detected where law of the Land prohibits it (referral houses 4th, 6th and 7th).

41. Piracy of goods, literature, source material; consequences for the pirates and for the sufferers of the acts of piracy; (referral houses 4th, 5th, 9th, 11th and 12th).

42. Writing under pseudonym or any action under pseudonym; using (rather piracy of) names of ancient writers, poets, authors experts in music/ medicines/ painting/ architecture/ sculpture by way of adoption of their names or adoption of their works.

43. Consequences of No. 42 above on contemporaries and the coming generations as a result of this piracy of names and/or works of the ancients (referral houses 9th, 10th and 11th).

44. Different kinds of Phobia, including that of water, river, sea, darkness, height as that of mountains/hills/high-rise buildings, valleys, road journeys by auto-vehicle, train journey (specially that across the water or on mountainous regions), riding a horse, camel/ elephant, phobia of rabies and dog-bite or jackal-bite; phobia of weapons including fire-arms; phobia of poisonous snakes, reptiles and scorpions, lizards etc.; phobia of school-teachers; phobia of police personnel or any person attired in police-type uniforms (referral houses 6th and 12th).

45. Nausea or any other allied illness owing to phobia mentioned in No. 44 above (referral houses 6th and 12th).

46. Phobia of hangman or operator of electrical chair or the shooting squad.

47. Formation or organising of groups and gangs for criminal acts, arson, any kind of illegal/ anti-social/ rebellion or anarchist activity.

48. Usurpation of wealth/ assets/ jewellery/ money/ literary production/ work or film or film-story of art/ any other creation earning fame for self or by the spouse or result of the effort of the spouse (referral houses 4th, 6th and 7th also 10th and 11th).

49. Loss of pregnancy, by natural causes or by lapse on part of the husband or the wife herself or by medical method (referral house 5th).

50. Still birth (referral house 5th).

51. Death of child in the process of child-birth including caesarean section in the normal course or by lapse on part of the surgeon/ doctor/ nurse/ midwife/ untrained *Dai* (as in rural/tribal areas) (referral houses 5th and 12th).

52. Loss/Death of spouse (referral houses 2nd and 7th).

53. Poor performance in written test/ examination owing to slow or bad handwriting (referral houses 5th, 10th and 12th).

54. Rejection by medical board for appointment or promotion to a high or higher post/assignment (referral houses 1st and 6th).

55. Weak eyesight; use of spectacles or other aid; consequences in job, work selection for appointment (referral houses 2nd, 10th and 12th).

56. Disease/illness of the eyes or injury to the eyes, leading to weakness in eyesight or ultimate or immediate blindness (referral houses 2nd, 6th and 12th).

57. Loss of money, bullion, jewellery, ornaments, loaned money or any valuable item given on loan (referral houses 2nd, 4th and 12th).

58. Unexpected and higher gains from investments, speculation, casino games, gambling, card games, kitty parties, betting on horses and any other kind of betting; windfall of money or inheritance/gift; higher perquisites; (referral houses 2nd, 4th and 11th).

59. Payments of out of recorded accounts, a part of the pay or perks by the employer, any lump sum gift or unaccounted string-less loan by the employers (referral houses 2nd, 4th, 10th and 11th).

Sometimes under strain in employer-employee relationship or on quitting the job, question of recovery of any gift, lump sum payment, interest free loan, etc. arises (referral houses 2nd, 4th, 9th, 10th, 11th and 12th).

60. Expenditure on religious/social/ educational/ charitable/ spiritual causes and works for it; these include poor homes, Nari Niketan, Night shelters for homeless males and females, hospitals, dispensaries training centres, Yoga-school, any other work of public utility or public welfare (referral houses 9th and 12th).

THE NINTH HOUSE

This House is known as the *"Bhagya' Bhava"*, *"Dharma Bhava"* (House of luck, faith, religion). In South India it is considered as the house of father, but it is not very correct. It is actually the House of Inheritance from the father. Anyway, the following subjects are under the jurisdiction of the 9th House.

1. Good and bad luck; time of rise of good luck (Bhagyodaya) (referral house 10th).
2. Relations with paternal and maternal uncles/ aunts/ cousins (referral houses 3rd, 6th and 12th).
3. Relations with spouses of brothers/ sisters/ cousins (referral house 3rd).
4. Ancestral inheritance including that individually from father/ mother (referral houses 4th and 10th).
5. Interference from within the family/ outside the family with regard to ancestral inheritance through parents in tact or with damage, sharing by a wrong person, reduction in it, or its total loss (referral houses 3rd, 4th, 10th, 11th and 12th).
6. Quarrels, fights, disputes, litigation, violence relating to inheritance from ancestors/ parents; consequences thereof for self/ family (referral houses 6th, 7th, 8th and 12th – sometimes also 10th and 11th houses).
7. Influence of inheritance from ancestors and parents on education, career, habits, nature, sociability and life-in-general (referral houses 1st, 3rd, 4th, 5th, 6th, 7th, 9th, 10th, 11th and 12th).
8. Effect of inheritance on development of personality and effort in life (referral houses 1st and 3rd).
9. Influence and contribution of brothers/ sisters/ cousins and their spouses on success or failure of the individual in education, effectivity of effort, in matters relating to career/

marriage and married life (referral houses 3rd, 5th, 7th and 10th).

10. Harassment/ torture/ physical injury to spouse of self by brothers/ sisters/ cousins and their spouses; sometimes even leading to death, consequences for the victim, for individual, for torturers, for other members of the family not involved or concerned in the matter (referral houses 2nd, 4th, 7th, 8th and 12th).

11. Relationship of mutual or one-sided affection, hatred, aloofness, give and take attitude, reciprocity with brothers/ sisters/ half-brothers/ step-brothers/ sisters of self and spouse (referral houses 3rd, 4th, 10th and 12th).

12. Faith and devotion in religion/ spiritualism/ cult/ sect/ God Almighty/lower deities/ Congregation/ Unitarianism/ Cosmopolitanism; some times faith but no attendance at religious place and no activity at home or at any religious place or gathering or at place of worship or prayers etc.

13. Malicious use, misuse, exploitative use of religious faith/ doctrine/ cult/ sect/ *'panth'*/ group/ organisation/ congregation/ *'math'*/ school for religious thought for selfish or organisation purposes (referral houses 5th and 11th).

14. Joining merely as a layman-follower or as a preacher or as an active worker or as an organiser of any religious sect/ cult/ *'panth'*/ group/ formation/ organisation, while staying in family life or having given up the family life (i.e. giving up the *"grihastha jeewan"*) (referral houses 5th, 11th and 12th).

15. Ideals, principles, known or hidden activities of any religious or spiritual formation, organisation, *'panth'*, *'marg'*/ *'math'*, sect/ cult or religious group.

16. Having once joined an organisation/ *'panth'*/ *'marg'*/ cult/ sect, formation or organisation, after duly knowing or without knowing its ideals, principles, open or hidden activities, the individual's agreement or disagreement, participation or non-participation in the prescribed/ given/ adopted activities/ teachings/ preachings; consequences thereof for the individual and also for the organisation/ formation etc.

17. Creation/ Establishment of a religious/ spiritual order/ *'panth'*/ marg/ organisation/ formation/ group etc; its ideals and principles; other legal or illegal, social or unsocial activities under the cover of that organisation or formation etc.; its impact on society and on the individuals and their families; on the general neighbourhood.
18. Creation of an educational/ social welfare/ medical welfare formation/ organisation/ group/ order/ association for the given ideals and principles; or for some other hidden activities under the cover of that formation or organisation.
19. Working as an active participant/ active worker, paid or unpaid for No. 17 and 18 above.
20. Giving or refusing financial or any other kind of concrete help or moral support to formation/ organisation mentioned at No. 17 and 18 above; consequences thereof (referral houses 11th and 12th or 1st).
21. Working as a paid or honorary Head of formation/ organisation/ group mentioned at No. 17 and 18 above or as a Head of any public welfare or Public utility or Sectional Welfare/ Utility Institution such as school/ college/ hospital/ orphanage/ poor-home/ Nari Niketan run by No. 17 and 18 mentioned above (referral houses 5th, 10th, 11th and 12th).
22. Favourable or adverse effect/ impact on social/ political/ personal image of the individual connected/ associated with No. 17, 18, 19 and 21 above.
23. Generous or miserly attitude towards public welfare/ educational/ medical/ welfare/ social welfare/ orphan and abandoned persons welfare/ charitable institutions/ bodies/ formations/ organisations in general.
24. Generous or miserly attitude toward kith and kin, near or distant ones, whether of self or of the spouse (referral houses 1st, 3rd, 4th, 5th and 12th).
25. Renouncement of worldly life ("Grihastha life") and staying at one place/ Ashram/ own premises/ secluded permanent cottage; or leading a constant nomadic life except four months

of the rainy season, or nomadic life even during the rainy season (referral houses 1st, 4th, 5th and 7th – sometimes 12th house also).

26. Individual's last wishes/ will/ sermons and guidance for others for the post-renouncement period or the post-death period, including brief etc., including donation of eyes or kidney, last religious rites/ gifts/ charities/ contributions/ *'daans'* etc.

27. Respect or disrespect, obedience or disobedience towards one's Gurus, Teachers, priests, preachers, other elders in general.

28. Partnership in business/ professional/ self-employment/ industrial venture or any other income-generating activity (referral houses 4th, 10th and 11th).

29. Criminal activity connected with kidnapping of children, girls, female and male youths, sometimes old and infirm persons too for begging, for prostitution, for forced labour, for disfiguring/ maiming or creating invalidity of body for purposes of begging/ smuggling/ any criminal activity/ immoral activity with changed identity (referral houses 1st, 8th, 10th, 11th or 12th).

30. Partnership in business/ industrial venture/ profession/ self-employment with one's spouse/ brother/ sister cousin of self or of spouse, with other kith and kin of self and of spouse whether near or distant ones; success or failure; impact on financial position; impact on mutual relationship (referral houses 4th, 7th and sometimes also 10th, 11th, and 12th houses).

31. Partnership with colleagues/ co-workers, friends (such partnerships normally for side or part-time business/ activity); financial implications and results; success or failure with impact on relationship.

32. Incest-type physical relationship or forced relationship of sex with brother/ sister/ cousin/ uncle/ aunt/ step-brother/ step-sister/ half-brother/ of self or of spouse, or with stepmother or step-father, (involving prohibited degree) referral house 7th).

33. Extra marital relationship with the approval of or within the knowledge of the spouse (referral houses for above No. 32 and 33 above are 3rd, 5th, 7th and 11th).

34. Partition of inherited assets/ property/ moveable possessions; gain or loss in it; reactions and consequences thereof (referral houses 2nd, 4th and 12th).

35. Abandonment/ total relinquishment, by self or family, of (rightful/ bogus) rights/ claims to properties/ assets/ titles/ privileges/ decorations/ entitlements/ inheritance of any other kind or in favour of none or in favour of the next person in the line of succession or in favour of another claimant.

36. Confiscation/ cancellation/ withdrawal by the authorities/ state/ 'giver' of moveable/ immovable property or assets; impact on social/ financial/ communal/ political status of self or on the family; ultimate consequences for self and all other concerned; (referral houses 4th, 10th, 11th and sometimes also 1st and 2nd house).

37. Gains and losses in political/ social/ communal/ collective activity (referral houses 4th, 10th, 11th, 12th and sometimes also 7th house).

38. Organising and running of chit funds, kitty parties, savings circles/ and other similar activity; success and failure; consequences thereof (referral houses 10th, 11th and 12th).

39. Capacity/ competence or lack thereof in selecting candidates for employment for one's own Establishment or for representation of self, or selection or representation on behalf of others including employers of self (governmental or private sector) or for friends or for any organisation/ formation/ body.

Note:
Regarding No. 39 above, if it is a Profession of self or of the firm/ company of self or of the employers of self, then the 10th house would be applicable, instead of the 9th House.

40. Fulfilment or non-fulfilment of obligations related to No. 37 above, consequences; disputes, litigation, violence, sometimes murder or killing (referral houses 6th, 8th, 11th and 12th).

41. Cheating/ fraud/ forgery/ falsehood/ lies as part of personality (referral houses 1st and 5th).

42. Strain/ run-down in relations with mother, step-mother, divorced or separated mother; disputes over property and assets; quarrels, litigation, violence; impact and consequences; (referral houses 4th, 7th, 11th and 12th).
43. Second progeny, its education and upbringing (referral house 5th).
44. Tendency and intentions to help and serve others without any motive, selfishness, without reservation/ restriction of any kind, neither of caste/ colour/ community/ religion/ status (referral houses 1st and 5th).
45. Stipendiary or honorary appointment/ nomination/ election to Governing Body of school/ college/ university/ Institution running any Hospital or charitable formation or training institution, poor-home, *Nari-Niketan*, Legislative body, municipal bodies and similar other organisation/ formations; (refer to item No. 21 above) (referral houses 1st and 10th).
46. Touring/ repeated travels, inland/ foreign for education/ official/ social welfare/ religious/ spiritual/ charitable/ pilgrimage or any other purposes of self or related to source of income or duties and responsibilities (referral houses 4th, 5th, 10th, 11th and 12th).
47. Help and assistance or refusal to give it by progeny of self in any kind of good or bad activity of self (referral houses 5th and 7th).
48. Marriage/ physical relationship with brother/ sister or cousin of the dead spouse (referral houses 3rd, 7th and also 5th in case of any child or children from the first marriage).

THE TENTH HOUSE

The Tenth house is known as the "*Rajya Bhava*", "*Pitri Bhava*", "*Karma Sthaan*" and "*Vyapar Bhava*", and as these names indicate, this house rules father (both real and one who adopts), source-of-income such as profession, vocation, business, industrial venture, self employment, political activity, etc., and in addition, this house rules the following subjects:

1. Father, if the individual is adopted by someone else, the adopting gentleman.
2. Foster father.
3. Source of income/ livelihood (at different stages of life) (referral houses 9th and 11th).
4. Lack of source of livelihood (to determine at what stage in life, and what would or what could become the alternative).
5. Career (it normally means service of others, that is working in a job, which can be a government job, public or private sector job, non-corporate or corporate job, totally private job, domestic servant's job, agricultural work or self employment; daily wage earner, etc.,
   - 5.1. Including service in central or state government, be it through open or restricted or reserved competition (referral houses 3rd and 5th), or
   - 5.2. Service in central or state govt. (whether or not through competition, open or restricted/ secluded) (referral houses 3rd and 5th), or
   - 5.3. Service under local administrative/ municipal bodies etc., and under public-sector undertaking including banks and insurance companies; through open or restricted competition or otherwise (referral houses 3rd, 5th and 9th), or

5.4. Service in private sector – corporate or non-corporate or totally in an individual's employ or in the employ of a group of people or an association of people (referral houses 3rd and 9th and also 5th if through open or restricted competition).

6. Entry in a regular cadre at a superior level; public or private.
7. Entry in a regular cadre at middle-level, public or private sector.
8. Entry in a regular cadre at low/lower level; public or private sector.
9. Elevation to senior cadre/ superior posts, posts in 'selection-grade'.

Note:
Four items given from No.6 to 9 are given separately because different planets (stars) work in case of each item from No.6 to 9.

10. Enquiry and/or investigation against a person in service.
11. Consequence of the enquiry/ investigation – emotion/ reduction in rank or stoppage of increments with or without cumulative effect or dismissal from service or minor punishment or total exoneration with all benefits that became due during the period of enquiry/ investigation.
12. Reference No.11 above – prosecution as a consequence – resultant punishment, or total or conditional acquittal, reinstatement if suspended.
13. Political work as a whole-time or main-time career/occupation; gains expected and received; gains expected and not acquired/ received.
14. Politics of decency and dignity; service to the public as the aim.
15. Politics of dishonesty, crime, violence, unethical practices (referral houses 8th and 11th).
16. Politics for resemblance of public service; underneath serving self-interest (referral houses 4th and 9th).

17. Politics openly for enrichment/ influence/ domination of self and the family/ friends and followers (referral houses 4th, 3rd and 11th).
18. Politicians in reality functioning as stooges of capitalists, trade unionism, criminals of every kind (referral houses 8th and 9th).
19. Politics purely for on behalf of trade-unions (referral houses 4th and 8th).
20. Politics through educational institutions/ students' organisations/ teachers' associations and groupism (referral houses 5th and 9th).
21. Politics for or on behalf of agricultural lobby, *zamindars*, gentlemen farmers (referral house 4th).
22. Politics with readiness for sufferings, sacrifice, beatings by police or para-military services, including temporary or long imprisonment, (referral houses 8th and 12th).
23. Political game from behind the scene (referral houses 1st and 4th).
24. Political game of king-making without risk of 'negative-side' of politics (referral houses 1st, 8th and 9th).
25. Politics of ex-ruling elite or the ruling class including the former ruling princes, *'zamindars'*, *'nawabs'* and members of their families or their descendant persons who were in power once and therefore power is considered as birth right by them (referral houses 5th and 9th).
26. Defeat or falling from grace in politics; temporarily or for all times (referral houses 6th and 12th).
27. Financial and social consequences (good or bad) of No.26 above.
28. Business and trading as source of livelihood.
29. Business and trading – wholesale or as selling agents of the manufacturers and producers; also as indenting agent; commission agent.
30. Business and trading – retail, petty, small-scale.

31. Business as middlemen/ hoarders/ storage agents/ mortgagors.
32. Business as brokers and commission agents, exclusively for Industrial houses/ multinationals, or general for one and all in the particular commodity or general commodities.
33. Business as hawkers, vendors on heads and hand-carts/ trolleys/vans.
34. Business on footpaths in market places, by roadside, at street corners, and door-to-door selling by self or through salesmen/ girls.
35. Business as sales-promoters (large-scale and door-to-door style.)
36. Business of tricksters, cheats, con-men and women, forgers, counterfeiters; sellers of sub-standard/artificial/ inferior quality goods; sellers of rags and paper-waste instead of real goods in packing.
37. Business of manufacturing and marketing of inferior quality or duplicate goods/ spurious medicines and chemicals or other consumer items.
38. Manufacturing, production, industrial activity as source of income.
39. Agency business/ sole or regional/ jurisdictional selling agents.
40. Manufacturers and producers themselves functioning as selling agents, distributors or suppliers to retailers through self-managed formations.
41. Manufacturers' and producers' own retail outlets and exclusive shops; also exclusive shops run by shopkeepers.
42. Small-scale industries, home industries, cottage industries.
43. Agriculture product-oriented large industries or small-scale industry.
44. Garden and orchards.
45. Poultry farms and fishery and breeding/ marketing of other

animals such as pigs, goats, lambs by way of meat-food or seafood.

46. Growing and marketing vegetables, flowers and other fruits etc.
47. Selling irrigation facilities.
48. Medium-scale industries.
49. Big industries; also closely held industrial companies of large/ big industrial houses.
50. Large-scale industries manufacturing capital goods/ heavy machinery.
51. Large scale industries manufacturing ships, rail wagons and bogies, aeroplanes, other rolling stock for railways, automobiles, large-size equipment, tractors, agricultural equipment, textile mills, jute mills, railway engines, cranes, oil exploring machines, machines used in mining operations, all other kind of large-size equipment and machines; machines ancillary to big industries.
52. Small and medium scale industries functioning mainly as ancillary to big industries.
53. Manufacture of spares.
54. Disposal of industrial scrap, industrial waste material, defective and damaged goods, out-moded unusable goods, irreparable goods etc.
55. Supply agents, contracted suppliers, wholesale suppliers, suppliers of small and stray items, suppliers of service material (this includes whole-time employer of industrial companies).
56. Brokers and sub-brokers in share market.
57. Brokers arranging finance for businessmen and industrial companies.
58. Financial companies on large scale, medium scale and small scale.
59. Private persons and business firms functioning as bankers, both as legally licensed and unlicensed.

60. Sleeping partner / financier-partner in business and industries.
61. Clearing agents at seaports including for customs clearance.
62. Clearing agents / cargo handling agents at airports.
63. Clearing agents at railway goods yards.
64. Clearing agents handling local transport / movement of goods cleared from ship-yards, airports, railway-goods-yards; it would include such firms and parties or transport groups who handle transhipment of goods from ship-yards and airports to rail-heads, road transport centres and centralised 'wholesale' market places for produce, etc. called *mandis* in India.
65. Transporters running goods-trucks for local transport, short-distance transport, long distance transport of goods of all kinds.
66. Transporters running containers of medium and large size as are used in westernised countries.
67. Transporters running pick-up vehicles, medium and small sized vans or vehicles for transport of goods locally.
68. Means of livelihood as handcart puller, cycle-rickshaw operator, rickshaw puller on foot as at hill stations in India and at Calcutta and other towns.
69. Coolies at railway stations, railway good sheds, loaders at airport, loaders at shipyards and transhipment yards of railways, at bus-stands, at goods truck centres, in markets generally carrying load in baskets on heads.
70. Domestic help, full-time, part-time working for several households.
71. Washer-women who wash clothes in several households like domestic help; also sweepers and those earning livelihood by petty jobs or running hand-cart-type stationary stalls that are easily removed under pressure of police and municipal staff.
72. Boot-polish (shoe-shine) boys, barbers, road-side shoe-repairers, road-side fruit and eatable vendors, tricksters and sellers of duplicate or sub-standards or spurious goods by

roadside, trolley-boys selling drinking water or cold drinks or other drinks as *'lassi'* etc.

73. Manpower employed as local courier service, auto-rider messengers, and delivery boys.

74. Technicians, technocrats, artists, polishers, washers, cleaners, packers, shop boys, canvassers by road-sides, petty brokers, who earn their livelihood by working in various markets as job-workers or daily wage earners, including farm-labour on daily wages, masons, carpenters, house painters, electricians, plumbers, furniture repairers and painters, other daily wage earners on odd jobs in residential localities, markets and *'mandis'*, as well as people earning livelihood by other odd jobs/self employments such as tailors, road-side auto-repairers, bicycle repairers, rickshaw repairers, cart and hand-cart repairers, people fixing horse-shoes.

75. People mobile from street to street and village to village, town to town for livelihood such as the monkey-man, snake-charmers, people doing acrobats, magicians, juggler, mobile priests, match-makers in marriage market, boys and girls ironing clothes by the road-side and at street corners.

76. Regular-career-type membership of election-based or nomination-based legislatures, municipal bodies, *'panchayats'*, community councils, regional and country or district advisory boards, governing bodies of Institutions, social welfare boards, board of directors of banks and insurance companies, board of directors of public sector undertakings.

77. Membership of the council of ministers, cabinet, governing body, management committee, ruling junta, dictatorial group, council of military rulers, advisory council to the king/queen/ruler/emperor.

78. Holding elected and nominated high offices in the governance of a country or state, viz., president, vice-president, prime minister, governor, chairman/member of the election commission, house of lords, chief justice and judges of the supreme court / high court / governor of the reserve bank or

the state bank of the country / state, administrator, chairman of autonomous bodies, chiefs of staff of defence services.

79. Appointment as envoy, ambassador, charge d'affairs, special envoy, or on diplomatic corps, *non-diplomatic* employees in embassies, high commissions, consulates and allied establishment, including part-time employees, job workers, daily wage workers etc.

80. Speakership or chairmanship of the federal / union legislature and the state legislatures.

81. Service under the Commonwealth Secretariat or European Common Market, other similar administrative or cooperation organisation / formation.

82. Service under the United Nations organisation and its allied Organisations such as UNESCO, International Agricultural Organisation, Human Rights Organisation etc.

83. Service under World Bank, International Monetary Fund, Interpol, International Narcotics Control Board, and other allied formations, also Asian Development Fund, and other regional cooperative bodies of nations/countries.

84. Partnership in profession/firms of accountancy, law/medicine, or banking etc.

85. Relationship with father, adopting father, foster father, deemed father, father by re-marriage of mother.

86. Inheritance or partial or complete deprivation of inheritance by oral decision or a written formal Will executed by the father/step-father/adopting father etc.

87. Acquiring knowledge of ancestral professional knowledge/ arts or craftsmanship etc.

88. Migration to another village/town/city/state/country for livelihood.

89. Upbringing by father before reaching the age of adulthood or lack of it even if father be alive; reasons thereof such as disharmony in family or poverty or separation by any circumstances.

90. Adoption of another country's nationality for sake of livelihood.
91. Investment in another country to acquire its nationality.
92. Permission to migrate into and conferment of nationality status on a person in recognition of the person's achievement in any field of specialisation such as education, arts, science, law, accounts, craftsmanship, music, dance, acting on stage or in films, serials and episodes etc.
93. Livelihood by means of writing, free-lance journalism, poet or poet-laureate, court musician, court dancer, royal priest, royal astrologer, royal/court-adviser on religious or legal/social matters.
94. Recognition of services by the government/university, other social or educational body/trust/foundation/statutory body and conferring any award, title, *honoris causa degree*, with or without pecuniary benefits attached thereto (Noble prize and other prizes too included in this category).
95. Inability of a person to earn livelihood for self and/or the family; consequences thereof and alternative arrangements; consequences/ impact.
96. Effect on father by acts of commission and omission of self and friends of self; favourable/ unfavourable reactions of father and the family in the matter, instantly and subsequently.
97. Succession to titles, awards, *'jagir'* lands and hereditary grants, decorations etc., continuity or discontinuance by the grantor and his/her heirs and successors; acceptance / refusal of continuance by the descendant beneficiary; social consequences of relinquishment.
98. Effect on self by acts of commission and omission on part of the father during father's lifetime or subsequent to father's death.
99. Custody of self in the event of separation or divorce between the parents; consequences thereof on upbringing/education and also inheritance, marriage, relations with other members of the family on father's side and on mother's side.

THE ELEVENTH HOUSE

Chiefly it is known as the House of Income, but it also covers other subjects viz.

1. Health of mother and the father-in-law, relationship between mother and self as also between self and father-in-law (referral houses 4th, 7th and 8th).
2. Health of the heart, its ailments, and success or failure of treatment including surgical treatment.
3. Relationship with friends; good friends, bad friends; helpful friends; parasite friends (referral house 4th).
4. Income or loss resulting from side business (referral house 12th).
5. Receipt of gratifications and bribes in cash or kind.
6. Receipt of gifts, donations and contributions for justified cause.
7. Left arm and left shoulder and left upper ribs, upper portion of left chest/ breast.
8. Getting children, comfortable or difficult delivery (referral houses 5th and 12th).
9. Spouses of children; their selection; side effect of marriages of children (referral house 5th).
10. Gains and losses involved in marriage of child(ren) (referral houses 5th and 12th).
11. Adoption of a child, in the event of childlessness.
12. Adoption of a child besides one's own child (the question relates also to adoption of a child of the opposite sex than that of one's own child) (referral houses 4th and 5th).
13. Adoption of pet animals, such as cat, dog, hare, squirrel, birds;

14. The 5th brother or sister; also elder brother or sister (referral house 3rd).
15. The 3rd pregnancy or the 3rd child.
16. Love affair of a child including reaction of the parents.
17. Love based marriage of the child, (with or without approval of the parents and subsequent relationship between the married couple and parents of both the persons) (referral houses 4th, 5th and 10th).
18. Post-marriage achievements of the spouse in the field of education, literature, writing, music, reciting poems including performance for public (referral house 1st, 9th and 10th).
19. Birth of or begetting illegitimate children (referral house 5th).
20. Relationship with son-in-law and daughter-in-law vis-à-vis their spouses (referral house 5th).
21. Animosity of or with maternal uncle and/or aunt (referral house 6th).
22. Concealed wealth/ assets/ money of natural or adopting father (referral houses 4th, 5th, 9th and 10th).
23. Helpful or unhelpful attitude of family-in-general in the event of one's ill health, injury and financial disaster (referral houses 6th, 8th and 12th).
24. Serviceful or non-serviceful attitude of domestic and other servants in the event of one's ill health, injury, long illness or a financial disaster (referral house 4th).
25. Employment/ Investment of old savings/ ancestral wealth for earning current income (referral houses 2nd and 10th).
26. Maintenance of second spouse, mistress/paramour on a regular or casual basis (referral houses 7th, 9th and 12th).
27. Sudden risk to longevity of natural or adopting father including his death.
28. Relationship with family members of the son-in-law or daughter-in-law including their brothers and sisters; this question crops up prominently when there are disputes and

litigation within the family and near as well as distant relations or members of the family appear directly or indirectly on the scene to help solve the situation or to intervene making things difficult and worse (referral houses 2nd and 12th).

29. Buying of ornaments and jewellery (referral house 12th).
30. Gifting away of ornaments and jewellery (referral houses 2nd and 12th).
31. Use of unfair means and threats or influence in respect of Tests, Examinations and Interviews (career-connected and academic).
32. Good or bad consequences of No. 31 above, including punishments (referral houses 5th, 12th and sometimes also 10th house).
33. Benefits with regard to business, profession, career, self employment etc. under threats and influence; consequence thereof.
34. Bad habits and connections begotten solely on account of high earnings in black money or mere possession of black money or being in bad company (referral house 4th).
35. Trade in contrabands, smuggling, and also ransom money through kidnapping, trade in flesh (referral houses 7th, 8th, 10th and 12th).
36. Money or property-oriented disputes between father and members of the family at his level, that is his brothers/ sisters/ cousins etc (referral house 9th).
37. Claims of children against the parents for share in property, assets, inheritance etc., disputes and litigation related to it (referral houses 5th, 9th and 10th).
38. Step-sons, step-daughters; children from previous marriage or illegitimate children before marriage with the spouse; relationship with them as well as their maintenance and acceptance in the family (referral houses 4th and 5th).
39. Claims and disputes relating to money and assets, with parents and other step brothers and step sisters, half brothers and half

sisters; consequences of it (referral houses 5th, 7th and 12th).

40. Cousins on the maternal side and relationship with them (referral house 9th which relates to cousins on the paternal side).

Note

Note that 9th house (relating to good or bad Luck), 10th house (relating source of income or livelihood) and the 11th house (ruling actual income and gains) are very much interlinked and influence one another.

THE TWELFTH HOUSE

The 12th House is commonly known as the *"Vyaya Bhava"* (House of Expenditure, outgo of money), subjects ruled by this House are given here under:

1. Outgo of money including expenditure on self and family.
2. Expenditure on children's education, children's health, children's entry into career, private tuition for them (referral houses 5th and 9th).
3. Illness, injury, fine, penalty, punishment to the children by parents/ teachers/ tutors/ govt. agencies/ employers or society (referral house 5th).
4. Loss of educational year of the child owing to ill health or change of school/ college/ Institution or expulsion, or agitational action of the child itself (referral houses 5th and 9th).
5. Behaviour of the child at the school and playground, picnics, excursions, games, specially upto the age of 12 years (referral house 5th).
6. Success or failure of business, industry, profession managed or run by brother/ sister/ uncle/ cousin or spouse of self, specially in partnership with other members of the family (referral houses 2nd, 3rd, 7th and 9th).
7. Second wife, mistress, paramour, openly or secretly.
8. Expenses on maintenance of No.7 above.
9. Reaction of the first wife (if alive and living with husband), on her individual level or with the help and support of other members of the family with regard to No. 8 above (referral houses 2nd, 7th and 9th).
10. Effort and expenses related to profession, business, career,

job, self-employment or any other source of income of self (referral houses 9th, 10th and 11th).

11. Casual physical relation with anyone other than legal/ social spouse (referral house 9th).
12. Complications of health/ diseases resulting from No.7 and 11 above (referral house 7th and 8th).
13. Expenditure on drinks, intoxicants, drugs, artificial sex, etc.
14. Impact of No.13 above on health of self vis-à-vis wife and other members of the family.
15. Swapping spouses or partners in physical relationship, other than group situations (referral house 4th and 7th).
16. Psychological/ health-wise and financial impact of No.15 above on self and partner.
17. Spending money on bribes, gifts, gratifications for gaining favours or without any immediate selfish motive/ by way of security for future (referral houses 10th and 11th).
18. Expenditure of self *and* friends, *or* of self or friends, for the purpose of engaging call-girls, gigolos, any kind of sex-worker, dancing girls, musicians, entertainers, jesters, massage persons.
19. Natural miscarriage/abortion or medical termination of pregnancy (referral house 5th).
20. Subsequent physical and psychological effects of No.19 above, on wife (and husband).
21. Still births/ instant death of infant after delivery/ death of children within one year of birth and its effect on the parents and others (referral houses 5th and 8th).
22. Being bonded into labour contract/ service agreement/ retention contract (referral house 8th).
23. Salvation or discharge from No. 22 above.
24. Losses in trade, business, industrial venture, self-employment, profession or vocation.

25. Losses in speculation, gambling, card games, kitty parties; chit fund ventures, mutual investment programs of banks; loan and deposit schemes of companies in private or public sector (referral house 8th).
26. Losses in circulation of money or circulation of sale and purchase of goods.
27. Losses through fines, penalties, punishments by government agency and any law court/ tribunal.
28. Loss of job, service, part-time employment, contract work etc.
29. Loss owing to normal or pre-mature retirement/ retrenchment from temporary job or regular/ permanent service (referral house 10th).
30. Enquiry and investigation against conduct in government service or political activity or misuse of political power and also political corruption (referral houses 9th and 10th).
31. Enquiry and investigation against private individual/ companies/ firms/ organisations/ association of persons/ groups.
32. Prosecution/ court case/ departmental proceedings for punishment resulting from No.30 and 31 above.
33. Anonymous and pseudonymous complaint against conduct in office (public or private) and consequential result thereof (referral house 10th).
34. Investigations by taxation agencies such as income-tax, customs, excise, foreign-exchange regulation agency, sales-tax, profession-tax of the central/ federal government or the state governments.
35. Results and impact of No. 30 to 34 above on prestige/ privileges/ powers/ social status/ financial standing reputation, and other such results as prosecution, fines, penalties, imprisonment etc.
36. Downfall from elected office, by vote of no-confidence or any other development or casualty.
37. Minor and major punishment by government as an employer,

by courts of law or tribunals, or by military-junta and dictators, military-rule, martial-law, emergency-rule of an elected government, etc.
38. Minor and major punishments for criminal acts/ anti-social acts, anti-governmental acts, anti-national acts, violent activity etc.
39. Punishment of simple and rigorous imprisonment.
40. Punishment as externment from state/county/country limits etc.
41. Death penalty (referral house 2nd).
42. Getting injured or killed in riots, police or army action, general arson and violence in the area/ region/ state/ country or in the massacre etc (referral houses 2nd and 8th).
43. Getting injured by creditor/ debtor or by rival in politics, by rival in love matter, by members of one or the other family disapproving the love affair or love-based marriage or any other action, or in caste-war, in communal hatred (referral houses 2nd and 8th).
44. Injury or death caused in disputes relating to inheritance or property and assets (referral houses 2nd and 8th).
45. Injury or death owing to competition/ opposition/ adverse attitude related to source of income (referral houses 2nd and 8th).
46. Feuds and rifts in the parental family or family of the spouse, its reactions and repercussions in general and on self and/or the children.
47. Partition in the parental family/ joint family/Hindu-Undivided-Family (HUF).
48. Walking-out of self from the joint family (alone or with one's spouse and children) without demanding/ taking share in assets/ liabilities of the joint family.
49. Disappearance of a person of own-free-will or by kidnapping.
50. Disappearance of a person to escape governmental/ police action, or action by creditors or under fear of enemies/ rivals/

opponents/ adversaries.
51. Kidnapping for ransom.
52. Kidnapping for political/ communal/ social/ marital/ enmity reasons.
53. Loans and debts.
54. Bribes/ gratifications/ initial cuts in connection with getting loans, security, surety/ guarantee etc. or that paid in court case or in securing a loan from a banking/ financial institution.
55. Problems arising from loans.
56. Litigation related to loans including civil imprisonment.
57. Disputes resulting to property/ assets/ valuable and litigation relating thereto.
58. Disputes related to tenancy including litigation and fights or violence (referral house 4th and sometimes also 6th and 8th house).
59. Infringement of copyright.
60. Arbitration in disputes.
61. Functioning as a middleman/ arbitrator/ broker/ taut/ agent/ attorney.
62. Spouse of the maternal uncle or aunt.
63. Illicit relations with spouse of maternal uncle or aunt (referral house 7th).
64. Father's immediate elder brother or sister
65. Spending money on charity, social work of public good, on any institution of public utility or educational or medical facility for common public and/or for running such institutions (referral house 9th).
66. Deriving undue benefits in cash/ kind/ flesh/ domestic help/ help in office/ help for political activity by running the institutions mentioned in 65 above.
67. Renunciation of worldly life by mother or any member of her family.

68. Renunciation of worldly life by self and indirectly by spouse.
69. Taking to *"pad yatra"* i.e., walking for some public cause; or for gaining political mileage.
70. Relinquishment of one's right in property/ assets/ valuables for benefit of another whether belonging to the family or outside the family or for a charitable/ social/ political/ public utility cause.
71. Left eye/ left ear/ left jaw/ left side of the skull/left side of the chin and upper throat/ left cheek/ left forehead etc.
72. Teeth on the left side/left nostril/ left side of the two lips.
73. Litigation connected with separation or divorce or maintenance matters between husband and wife (referral houses 6th and 7th).
74. Litigation regarding custody of children either between husband and wife or between one of them and other relations in the family (referral houses 5th and 7th).
75. Interference and instigation by the members of one or both families in the affairs of husband and wife or their progeny (referral houses 5th and 7th).
76. Open or secret expenditure on general family and objection of the spouse thereto (referral houses 2nd and 7th).
77. Driving while drunk and consequences on self and others (referral houses 4th and 8th).
78. Accidents involving losses and damages to property/ vehicle/ machinery/ labourers/ other individuals.
79. Compensation for No. 78 above.
80. Losses by fire, floods, arson, general looting, political disturbances, communal riots, robbery, theft, cheating etc.
81. Loss by picking of pocket, lifting of baggage/ luggage/ brief cases, snatching of jewellery, purse and brief cases.
82. Loss by looting, pilferage by police or investigating taxation agencies while carrying on a search of person/ premises; or in arson, riots, disturbances owing to an accident.

83. Excuses of loss without actual loss (mischief and falsehood) very often by "trust members" and members of the immediate or wider family.
84. Excuses of theft, robbery, dacoity etc without actual loss just to deprive others of their genuine share or dues.
85. Smuggling activities.
86. Under-valuing and over-valuing Invoices.
87. Loss by way of payment of bribes, gifts and gratification where promised job is not done or got done by the person accepting the bribe/gift etc.
88. Loss by fraud and forgery committed by self to cheat others.
89. Loss by fraud or forgery committed on self by others.
90. Hush money paid for suppression of facts, removal of evidence, non-appearance of witness; planted witness, planted guarantor or surety or security.

PLANETS IN THE 12 HOUSES

IN THIS PART

SUN

MOON

MARS

MERCURY

JUPITER

VENUS

SATURN

RAHU, and

KETU

in the 12 Houses

SUN IN THE 12 HOUSES

SUN IN GENERAL

Sun is deemed to be the king, chief or head among all planets. The reason is not far to seek. Sun is the brightest of all planets. It gives us life through its light, and rest at the night through its absence. It causes rains without which human, animal and plant life would be no more. It reflects its light to the Moon.

If the term 'epicentre' be used, Sun is the epicentre of our visible universe. All planets including the Earth revolve around it. As far as humans are concerned, it is the epistemology of our knowledge, wisdom and experience.

During a Lunar eclipse, one does not find the animal life disturbed, perturbed, or restless; but during Solar eclipse, the entire animal life becomes terribly restless, as if it is the end of life, end of Earth is on the verge.

One must have noticed that life can exist, and it does exist, under extreme heat, but it is difficult to survive in extreme cold (absence of sunlight). As an example, compare the population in areas near Equator (extreme heat) and areas near South Pole and North Pole (extreme cold). Light and heat granted by Sun are the main cause of this vast difference.

It is not without reason that our entire system is called the SOLAR SYSTEM, instead of Mercury System, or Venus System, which are so close to Earth, or even perhaps Lunar System.

To check for Signs of life in humans (and in animals), the body warmth (temperature) is checked, and the warmth is caused and given by Sun.

No other planet is so regular in its rising and setting as Sun is, and that is why our entire *time* system is based on Sun. In every country on earth, a day is linked with the time of one Sun-rise to another Sun-rise. Methods of counting the months may have been different during different civilisations and different lands on the globe but again, the counting of the year is linked to one particular position of Sun in the zodiac and back again to that very particular position in the zodiac. The solar year of the Indian System and the counting of the year by the Pope Gregory III system is one and the same. The only difference is that India adopted this system thousands of years ago, while the western system adopted it in the 16th century after Christ.

The Lunar System of counting the year has also to follow and come in conjunction with the Solar System by adding an extra month to the Lunar System every 3rd or the 4th year. Simply put, the Lunar system has ultimately to follow the Solar System of counting time and counting Years.

It is also a fact that Sun is *self-luminous*, while all other planets, including earth, receive light and heat from the SUN, and Sun alone. The Sun contains stored heat and emits light. The humans discovered fire and its subsequent offshoots into electricity and power from Sun's heat only. Fire in itself, whatever its form and shape, took and even now takes its origin from Sun's rays and Sun's heat.

It is not without reason that ancients in most lands on earth worshipped Sun from the very start of the human life. In India, '*Surya Namaskaar*' (bowing to the Sun) is prescribed with offering of water to Sun, known as '*Surya Arghya*', after every day's prayer program.

Many parents and elders advise their youngsters to arise before Sun-rise, saying : the Sun has risen, the day has begun, the Sun is already on its job, its duty, and therefore the Sun enjoins the young people to wake and proceed with daily routine.

The earliest ancients in India have fully justifiably named the Sun as "*Prana*" (life-cum-soul). Heat caused by Sun gives vitality and activity to all humans and animals, and that is why our most work-activity is during the daytime. If we work at night under artificial illumination (electricity), it is an outcome of heat granted by Sun. We light our candle or lamp by a match, which too found its origin from heat of Sun.

In so far as astrology is concerned, Sun is neither wicked nor cruel. As a loving parent gives punishment to an erring child, similarly, even when in an unfavourable position, Sun doesn't cause extreme damage, harm or hurt. It does so only when in conjunction with other hard planets like Mars or Saturn (or even Rahu/ Ketu causing an *eclipse* combination). Why it is so? An Emperor, a King, a President, a Chieftain, a Prime Minster or even a Dictator doesn't get up from his or her throne or seat of Power to punish a culprit. He or she *orders* the subordinates to mete out the punishment.

Likewise, when Sun is alone, it is rarely extremely harsh, harmful, wicked or cruel. Sun needs at least *drishti* (direct aspect) of another hard planet to be extra harmful. Because Sun has the qualities of a Monarch or King, it gives an individual, when favourably placed in the horoscope, qualities of efficient administrator.

For example, check the horoscope of any recruit in the Administrative Service of a country. If the recruit has entered the Service on own merit, the person, without doubt, must have a favourable placement of Sun in the horoscope.

SUN IN THE 1ST HOUSE

This position of Sun gives a bad temper, non-flexible nature, unadjustable with persons lacking in integrity, sometimes resulting in earning annoyance/ anger/ revenge from government officials and politicians. If these individuals have any dues from government offices or from government owned Organisations or local bodies, municipalities etc., payments get delayed and sometimes great spokes are put in by greedy or jealous officials. There are chances of goods produced or supplied by these individuals being partially or fully disapproved for non-official (or personal) reasons and selfish motives. These individuals fall easy victim, if in government or semi-government service or in government owned formations, to transfers to inconvenient posts and places. They might have to face enquiries and investigations about their conduct in office, extending even to their personal and private life, whether warranted or not.

In fact, Sun in the 1st house is a double-edged sword. It can provide strength for the individual, and also a source of harassment and torture. However, these individuals are rarely labelled as inefficient or sluggish.

If these individuals find an entry into active politics, they have good chances of rising to power and prestige, irrespective of whatever little work they actually do or whatever duties are assigned to them initially.

Sometimes these individuals do not jump into political arena, but they remain in close contact with high placed dignitaries in politics and governance. If this Sun in 1st house is in its own Rasi (Leo) or in Virgo or Pisces or in Aries, these individuals earn a bad name for insubordination, whether they actually are so or not.

These individuals are vulnerable to poor eyesight, trouble with eye(s) in childhood, mild skin ailment now and then, and headache. Otherwise Sun doesn't have much adverse effect on health.

This does not mean that these individuals do not go in for self-employment, business or any private venture or private service. Those fields are also open to them, but for any remarkable success, these individuals have to depend on the support of other stars to Sun in the 1st house. No doubt, in profession or self-employment, they make a mark for their devotion to work and honesty of purpose. But competitors and jealous persons often try to cut throat of these individuals, so much so that even their subordinates, employees, students and disciples try to harm them financially or hurt their feelings.

Often these individuals appear outwardly very ambitious, but inwardly, they are reserved and somewhat timid too, avoiding big risks. If Sun is alone in the 1st house, they stay honest, straightforward and rather outspoken, but not to the extent of hurting the feelings of others.

One special influence of Sun in the 1st house is that these individuals have a limited number of progeny from their legal spouse, but do not hesitate to have progeny outside the wedlock (more applicable to men!).

Sun and Moon in the 1st House

This individual is reserved by nature, somewhat secretive too, observing more and talking less, hesitant to express own ideas and thoughts very openly, nourishing unfulfilled desires and ambitions, and might sometimes suffer from insomnia. These results are valid if Sun is ahead of Moon in terms of degrees.

If however Moon is ahead of Sun in terms of degrees, the individual would work hard for fulfilment of desires and ambitions of self or spouse, would not disclose own mind and often would try to read the mind of others, is over-desirous of foreign travel. If the 1st house consists of a watery Sign (Cancer, Capricorn, Aquarius or Pisces), the individual would want to settle in a foreign country, and if that be not possible then in a distant state/ county/ town in own country.

Some of these individuals, specially with a Rasi owned by Mars or Saturn in the 1st house, are used by their own governments or by government of a hostile country to work as a spy in a country different to that of their birth.

If Moon is ahead of Sun in terms of degrees, these individuals have a firm mind, unwavering in decisions, reflecting a positive stand in talks and discussions; and they rarely change their statements and versions, even where monetary or other gains are involved. They do not mind remaining in middle or even lower strata of financial status.

Sun and Mars in the 1st House

These individuals are given to irritation and anger, cause or no cause, sometimes between self and spouse, without leading to failure of marriage (just keep pulling on sweetly and sourly)!

They very often try to prove unapproachability of self, specially when in position of power or prestige, though tactful people penetrate into the fortress of their unapproachability. These individuals do not hesitate in speaking evil of A in the presence of B or C and speaking evil of B or C in the presence of A. Another bad habit generally found in these individuals is that they criticise or speak evil of A or B or C, in the name of such other person who is not present there, going to the extent of quoting (imaginary) words of that other person. If ever confrontation takes place, these individuals do not express regret, but make an excuse that they quoted a wrong person, while they actually intended to quote someone else!

Because they are given to irritation and anger rather quickly and easily, they are fickle minded, not hesitant to indulge in wrong deeds. They rarely become overweight bodily, but more often they're void of pleasantness in life. However, one commendable point about them is that they are equally at ease in the company of high placed dignitaries and lower-placed workers, labourers and those in menial jobs. So much so that to show a kind of outer affinity with those lower placed people, these individuals join them in eating, drinking (not alcohol, but other beverages, cold drinks), in games and sports.

Thus these individuals prove very useful in gathering crowds for rallies, processions, meetings, electioneering, and what not! They do desire their price for these acts and activities, but that price is not exorbitant, just within reason.

Health-wise, Mars and Sun in the 1st are capable of giving headache, weak eyesight, eye trouble now and then, ailment or disorder of the middle parts of the body. They also give fluctuating blood pressure, complaints of menstrual system, and uneven teeth or trouble with teeth even at a young age or in childhood itself. If the complaints of fluctuating blood pressure become more frequent, chances of heart trouble are also there for the individual.

These individuals are devoted and faithful servants, subordinates and employees, and if they are masters, in spite of their anger, irritation and abusive language, they prove to be considerate masters or employers or superiors.

Another speciality of Mars being in conjunction with Sun in the 1st house is that it removes that touch of internal (hidden) timidity from the individual, and gives a sense of boldness and bravery.

Sun and Mercury in the 1st House

Remember that Mercury is *always* within a 25-degree distance from Sun, whether ahead or behind it. Therefore Mercury, unlike other planets, never suffers from combustion on account of being with Sun. Thus, whether with Sun, or ahead of Sun in the next Rasi, or behind Sun in the previous Rasi, Mercury is always effective. In this context also remembered that Mercury is a very soft planet; it never acts harshly or harmfully. Mercury is lord of intelligence and therefore also of formal education. Even when in a harmful placement, the maximum harm Mercury does to an individual is that it obstructs proper (formal) education, and gives higher education after breaks and gaps.

Being a soft planet, Mercury adds softness to the temperament of Sun, reduces to a great extent the element of irritation and anger in the individual, improves quality and quantity of formal education, increases wisdom and experience, and bestows capacity for very quick grasp of any subject taught or learnt.

Mercury with Sun in the 1st improves the complexion of the individual, gives good appearance to personality, gives high quality to written and spoken word of the individual, and depending on other helpful stars, gives the individual talent and capability for producing literature, poetry, or expertise in journalism. Generally these individuals are very good teachers, preachers, priests, orators, public speakers. But unless Mercury has the support of Jupiter, these individuals do not grow into top-level lawyers, advocates, judges, or arbitrators.

Being in the company of Sun in the 1st house, Mercury induces these individuals (or a good number of them) to join public services directly in government departments or in government-owned formation/ organisations. And these individual prove their efficiency in table-work (as opposed to executive work), or in any other line mentioned above. With the direct support of Mars from 3rd, 4th, 9th, 10th or 11th house, these individuals get into senior Civil services of their country or into active politics, rising quite high in the field of power and position. Otherwise too, these individuals become well known for their knowledge and learning and use thereof. They are normally known as supporters of truth and straightforwardness.

Now that globe-trotting has become common and within reach, it can be taken for granted that if a water-Rasi is in the 1st house, or Sun with Mercury gets the support from Moon or Venus occupying a water-Rasi, these individuals would get easy and repeated chances for foreign travel.

The adverse effect of Mercury is when it is retrograde. Then Mercury disturbs the educational progress, encourages use of falsehood and unfair means in life, and sometimes while speaking, forgets at the spur of the moment, the important point or argument the individual intended to make, and recalls it subsequently.

Sun and Jupiter in the 1st House

This combination generally makes good lawyers, advocates, judges, jurists, legislators, lawmaker, qualified accountants, appraisers, arbitrators, jewellers, goldsmiths, artisans for making ornaments and decorative items of gold and silver, village *Pradhans* or *Panchayat Pradhans* or *Pradhans* of castes and communities. These individuals are normally good looking with impressive personality, vehement argumentators, stubborn while accepting defeat in any debate or argument or confrontation with opponent on public stage.

Whether men or women, these individuals are fond of wearing jewellery and presenting themselves in decorative dress. Otherwise too, these individuals are fond of collecting gold and gold items, gold utensils, costly jewellery, and if Mars is in 2nd or 12th house, they wouldn't hesitate to borrow money and invest it in gold items and jewellery. They are fond of being in constant touch with and being publicly seen with important political or social personalities.

They are not religiously committed to tell only the truth and nothing but truth. They are more interested in self-interest or in the interest of people towards whom they stand committed. If Saturn or Rahu is in the 10th or 11th house, these individuals would not hesitate to create false evidence, present false witnesses and go to the extent of forgery.

If this combination in the 1st house is in Cancer, Aries or Sagittarius, there are strong chances of these individuals joining the judicial services, and with the support of other stars, they have chances of rising to the High court or even to the Supreme court. If Pisces be in the Ascendant, Sun and Jupiter together in the 1st house can take the individual to an International organisation or Commonwealth Secretariat or any similar or allied formation.

This combination can take the individual to a legislative body, like Parliament, Senate, Provincial Assembly, university court, Election Commission, and Consumer Grievances Redressal Court by nomination method. In some cases if the 10th or 11th house has the support of Mars, rise of the individual can be through election process.

If Sun with Jupiter be in the 1st house and Saturn or Mars be in the 12th house, the individual might be subjected to an enquiry or investigations for deeds and decisions of commission and omission, and is likely to suffer disgrace. However if Rahu alone is in the 12th house, an enquiry or investigation is likely to be conducted against the individual, but subsequently, either as a result of the enquiry/ investigations or for some other political and legal complications in the matter, the individual might be exonerated.

Sun and Venus in the 1st House

This is an interesting combination. The individual would have charming and impressive personality, fairer than average complexion of that geographic region. The individual will neither be fat nor thin but good built of body, dark hair even into declining age, voice with a touch of sweetness mixed with influence, knowledge (or even practice) of any fine art like music, dancing, acting, painting, writing poetry or songs. Because of Sun's status as King of planets, these individuals, with combination of Venus with Sun in the 1st house, do not prefer to become playback singers or substitute stunt actors, actresses; (poverty or destitute or adverse circumstances may be a totally different matter, where human beings become helpless!).

Another important avenue open to these individuals is that they learn any branch of medical sciences/ systems, and later on join government or semi-government services, including hospital administration. These individuals are fond of going abroad for education or migration, specially if Cancer, Capricorn, Aquarius, or Pisces, is in the 1st house.

One major shortcoming of this combination is that these individuals are quite romantic in their attitude and utterances, sometimes indulging into activity of that type, and in due course they earn a bad name on this account.

It equally applies to women too. The question is the same i.e. if Mars, Saturn or Rahu be in the 12th house (which automatically means 12th position to this combination of Sun and Venus in the 1st house). This combination leads to chances of an enquiry or investigations being started against the individual for misconduct, misbehaviour, lapse or mistake in work, acts of commission and omission, including that relating to moral character.

Since both Sun and Venus normally move from one Rasi to another within a month on an average, if any enquiry or investigation has to take place, it would more likely take place during Venus-Mahadasa and Sun-Antardasas or Sun-Mahadasa and Venus-Antardasas. Chances are also likely during transit of Saturn or Rahu in the 12th house, or by transit movement Mars going retrograde in the 12th house and staying there for about 6 months as against its normal one and a half month's stay in one Rasi.

Sun and Saturn in the 1st House

This is a difficult combination to predict about. Though the mythological belief is that Saturn is son of Sun, astrologically they are considered die-hard enemies of each other. Saturn's evil effect is not marred to any mentionable extent even on its combustion in Sun's vicinity. Also special attention has to be paid to the Rasi in the 1st house. If it is Virgo, Libra, Capricorn or Aquarius, then Saturn would have the upper hand in the 1st house. If it is Leo,

Cancer, Aries or Pisces in the 1st house, Sun would have the strength and stamina to oppose any kind of influence of Saturn there. Other Rasis like Taurus, Gemini, Scorpio, Sagittarius are inclined equally to both Sun and Saturn.

Another factor to be considered about this combination is whether, in terms of degrees, Sun is ahead of Saturn, or Saturn is ahead of Sun. If Saturn is ahead of Sun, Saturn's effectivity is limited, but if Saturn is behind Sun, even by Saturn's retrogression, Saturn has the greater say in the 1st house. Then regarding this particular combination, the Navamsha position of both these stars should be taken into account, and if it is the birth chart of a woman, consider the Trinshansha chart too with Navamsha chart. Only then the predictions would come to some point of accuracy.

The above mentioned principle relating to Sun and Saturn's combination in the 1st house may be borne in mind even when considering their joint effect *in any house in the birth-chart*, or yearly-chart or month-wise chart of yearly chart or Question chart.

Somehow, a misconcept got attached to Saturn that it is always an evil or harmful planet. This is actually not so. The first advantage of Saturn in the 1st house, whether alone or with some other planet is that it gives a firmness and positive determination to the individual, which proves 75% helpful (and 25% detrimental) in life. Saturn gives capacity for hard work, also capability to handle more than one hard job at one and the same time, without causing damage to any other work.

When in combination with Sun, Saturn positively reduces the touch of (internal) timidity caused by Sun. This combination often gives close contacts with the top brass in the government, but rarely allows or helps the individual to rise to the top position, whatever the field of activity, job, profession or self employment. These individuals do not brag or boast, but for no reason or rhyme, they cause annoyance to their fellow-workers, immediate superiors, subordinates and employees, despite the fact that they are helpful and serviceful to any or all of them, whenever the occasion. These individuals have no discrimination or distinction in their attitude and behaviour because of class, category, status, rank, or caste & colour of people. They are equally free with Kings, Rulers, Presidents and Prime Ministers, as also with clerks, peons, labourers, bullock-cartmen and everyone, with old as well as young, with men as well as women. They are often truthful, fair-minded, straightforward, outspoken, frank and honest. But because Sun and Saturn are adversaries of each other, these individuals fall victim to blackmail and unfair criticism or complaints by concerned and unconcerned people. Thus, it is all the more so if these individuals happen to be in active politics, social work, public services, or any job having dealings with public.

In the same breath it can be said about these individuals that they do not give up their path of fairness and honesty under fear of blackmail and criticism. They suffer and do not mind the sufferings, take the sufferings too as God-given fate and fortune

Note that when Saturn transits over the 1st house, that period of roughly two and half years, proves to be beneficial and of rise for the individuals, and compensates them for the loss and sufferings given by Saturn's transit over the 12th house. If Sun with Saturn combine in the 1st house has Mars or Rahu in the 12th house, these individuals should stay preventive about legal action and penal proceedings, with or without cause and justification.

Sun and Rahu in the 1st House

Though Rahu is considered a shadow (virtual) planet, its presence in combination in any house with Sun puts Sun in an 'eclipse' combination, thereby undermining the results of Sun and uplifting the results of Rahu. *It is a known principle that when Rahu is alone in any house, it is not fully effective*, but when it is with any real planet in a house, Rahu becomes 100% effective.

Whenever Rahu is in the 1st house, whether alone or with any other planet, it gives a typical sense of 'ego' to the individual. It has already been stated above that Sun in the 1st house gives a touch of irritation and anger, therefore it can be concluded that these two together would give anger and ego to the individual; exceptions being rare.

Further, these two in conjunction often bar and mar

chances of progress of the individual in the field of politics or public service. And because Sun applies its influence, there are strong chances that sometime or the other, the individual would join a public service, may be for a short while or take interest in active politics for a limited period. It is immaterial whether the political arena is of national character or state level or only limited to one's own town or village. Slogan shouters and adding to the crowds at rallies and processions or political meetings is also a kind of association with politics.

Another favour that Rahu grants, when in the company of Sun in the 1st house, is to courage, boldness and bravery in any field, be it in argument, public speaking. It includes indulgence in a quarrel or fight at one-to-one-level or by groups, or even in a battle or any kind of confrontation with enemy. In other words, Rahu wipes out from the mind and action of the individual any touch of internal hidden fear or timidity created by Sun in the 1st house.

These individuals are quick to pick up an argument or verbal quarrel, they talk a lot and with self-confidence creating impression on others. Rahu's conjunction with Sun protects the eyesight of the individual in spite of Sun's adverse effect on eyes, which might at the most give sore eyes or some other minor tolerable ailment. No doubt, Rahu would give a little bulge around mid-body, be it a man or a woman.

Individuals with this combination are likely to earn a bad name without substantial fault about morality of their character, but it is difficult to help this situation, because the individual might try to change own nature but Rahu wouldn't give up its natural influence on the individual.

Sun and Ketu in the 1st House

It has to be noted while going through this book from any chapter and from any angle that in its effect Rahu (normally and in general terms) *follows the pattern of Saturn*. While Ketu *follows the pattern of Mercury*, and there is not any substantial change in this pattern whether Rahu or its counterpart Ketu be alone in a House or with any other (real) planet. Wherever there is a deviation in this rule of similarity of Rahu with Saturn or in Ketu with Mercury, it has been specifically mentioned in that particular context.

Thus this combination would give sharp intelligence, quick grasp of what is taught and learnt, appreciation for poetry and other literature, capacity to write on civics, politics/ social services etc., or at least good understanding of these subjects. This individual normally helps or supports brothers and sisters and even distant brethren, but without good response from them; instead they prove a source of drain, botheration and sometimes loss of face publicly for the individual. Another adverse impact of this combination is that Ketu adds to the internal hidden timidity in the individual, and sometimes this tendency too might lead to loss of face publicly, at least sometimes.

In the field of public service or politics, they are virtually unable to fight for their seniority, their rights, their claims and their due place in the line of promotion. Even if they put in a fight, they often lose the battle, or have to depend on kindness and mercy of someone else.

In spite of these adverse results of this combination, these individuals are respected and honoured by a majority of people for their knowledge, learning, wisdom and experience. They prove very efficient teachers (whatever the level of students in the school or college or university), preachers, priests and public speakers, or reciting poetry (but not singing). As far as possible, these individuals neither cheat any one financially nor pirate the literary or journalistic work of others. They are in reality contented, though their immediate family is not.

SUN IN THE 2ND HOUSE

This is normally a beneficial position for all individuals, though somewhat unfavourable to the spouse, being in the 8th position from the 7th house which rules marriage and married life.

Sun in the 2nd house invariably gives wealth, at least better monetary position than what was in the childhood or at the start of the career. It gives a fondness for gold ornaments and jewellery according to the individual's status and finances. Very few people know that Abdur-Rahim-Khankhanaa, a Cabinet Minister of the Mughal Emperor Akbar was a very learned and experienced astrologer, and out of many books he wrote on Astrology, some two or three are still available in published form. He has highly praised Sun's position in the 2nd house with relation to money and power, including great success in source of income and savings.

Being in the 5th position from the 10th house (which rules career, joining public services and politics) Sun in the 2nd house gives outstanding success in career, job in public services and in politics, and being in Kendra position from the 11th house, Sun ensures high grade regular income too. However this position of Sun being in 6th place from the 9th house (which rules luck, fate, fortune), success would not drop into the lap of the individual without effort and hard work.

Similarly, this position of Sun being in the 8th place from 7th house (which as stated above rules marriage, married life, love affair etc), the spouse might sometimes undergo a setback in matters of health (headache, weak eyesight or skin ailment). And in some rare cases, it gives differences between wife and husband about overall management of money.

2nd house is considered one of the KILLER (*Maarak*) houses in every school of astrology. But Sun being the King of the planets, rarely indulges in ending the life of an individual in the same manner in which a King himself doesn't descend from his throne to lash a guilty person himself. Instead the King entrusts the task to one of the subordinates or employees. Similarly, Sun doesn't directly involve itself in ending life of an individual. Sun leaves this task to other planets. This is more a result of study and practical experience of Sun's position in the 2nd house for several years and generations.

It has also to be clarified here that even if Saturn's Rasi is in the 2nd House, Sun alone would rarely end the life of an individual. It is also noteworthy that Sun has got the shortest duration of its Mahadasa, just a total of 6 years as compared to 20 years of Venus and 19 years of Saturn.

Being in the 12th position from the 3rd house which rules brother(s) and sister(s) or cousin(s), Sun in 2nd house makes the individual spend money and energy in helping and supporting this category of relations. But at the same time, the individual gets financial and moral help from mother or motherly persons.

Sun in the 2nd house is in Kendra relationship with 5th house, which besides other subjects rules progeny too. The individual becomes extra involved in the education and upbringing of the children to the extent of interfering in their affairs when the children are adults and sometimes even after the children are married. Some schools of thought in astrology take this position of Sun as detrimental to the progeny, but experience does not indicate this theory to be correct.

Sun and Moon in the 2nd House

Though Moon normally becomes combust when with Sun, it is quite effective in the 2nd house. Moon adds silver ornaments and utensils, silver images of deities (idols of Gods) to other costly possessions owned by the individual by grace of Sun. Moon also adds to the wardrobe, so much so that it adds such silken and artistically prepared apparel with gold embroidery (which may rarely be used or not used at all). Moon makes an individual fond of collecting silver coins (old and new). These two stars together give a very pleasant and presentable personality to the individual worthy of wearing the costly clothes mentioned here. Moon cools down the irritated or angry voice of the individual, makes the individual more tolerant, charitable, and generous in outlook.

Sun and Moon together bring the individual in contact with foreign dignitaries or foreign traders and gives opportunities for business or professional links with them. There is no use predicting foreign travel, because in modern times it has become quite popular for a large portion of the population.

In the normal course, these two stars bestow on the individual good capacity to grasp and analyse matters related to foreign trade, foreign relations between nations, rules and regulations relating to foreign travel and customs etc. These individuals know when to talk and when to keep silence, thereby becoming more suitable for Foreign Service of any country. They are sometimes able to read the mind of others but often are unable to read the mind of own spouse or lover or beloved.

A Note About Moon

Thus this point relating to own spouse or lover or beloved presents the other side of this combination in the 2nd house with regard to the spouse. Moon is unilateral lord of Mind in all human beings, including the spouse. Moon makes the spouse suffer mental harassment by the attitude or maltreatment by the individual or family thereof. The spouse is in a dilemma: if expresses own ideas and thoughts, there are repercussions including criticism, confrontation and conflict; if keeps silent, the harassment increases, sometimes by leaps and bounds. Normally these two stars do not give physical violence, but short of that every kind of harassment or torture is likely, if not at the hands of the individual, at the hands of the individual's family. If the 7th house is in Cancer or Leo (owned by Moon and Sun), matters go worse for the spouse.

Spouse or lover or beloved of an individual with Sun and Moon in the 2nd house combination needs to be protected against accident by or in water. Also against food poisoning, and mental disorder under duress from the family of the individual, or sometimes even the individual himself or herself.

Sun and Mars in the 2nd House

This combination needs to be watched and studied in proper perspective, because Sun grants riches/ wealth, while Mars brings wealth and riches down. Very few know, understand and realise this hidden influence of Mars in the 2nd house on money, wealth, riches of the individual. The conflict between Sun and Mars in the 2nd house is thus strong and practically effective.

Then these two together sometimes introduce physical violence between the wife and husband or between male and female lovers, and if Saturn gets placed in the 7th house or gets associated by *drishti* or by ownership of the 2nd house or involved in 6 : 8 relationship with this combination from the 9th house, the physical violence can be injurious, and if the stars of spouse also run against the spouse in a serious and strong manner, the physical violence can be fatal too. Many cases of bride burning in India indicated Sun and Mars in the 2nd house of the individual and stars of the bride were also at the given time dangerous for herself.

An individual with Sun and Mars in 2nd house should avoid dabbling in shares and stocks, specially of speculation type, otherwise financial ruin might not take many years. The individual should avoid giving cash loans and accumulation of bullion, and gold ornaments/ jewellery/ items/ deities' images or statues. If the individual owns firearms, care be taken that the firearms do not lie loaded at any place or on any person. Precautions must be taken against fire and electric short circuit. Acid and inflammables be kept under locked security, specially not to be reached by spouse, women and children.

Normally these individuals are bold and brave, dare-devil type, physically strong and capable too, but these qualities have to be suitably guided and utilised only on demanding occasions. If left unguided they can do greater harm than good to the family/ friends and the individual's own self.

Another important point about this combination in the 2nd house is that these individuals know how to earn money, assets, property, respect and prestige too, but they are not good masters in preserving them. Someone else (spouse or any other relation or sometimes even a true and dependable friend, faithful employee or co-worker or associate in business/ profession) has to be their guide, controller or protector of their money, assets and property. Even efficient astrologers can prove a correct guide in this behalf.

Sun and Mercury in the 2nd House

Others normally feel jealous of the individuals who have combination of Sun and Mercury (or Sun and Jupiter or Sun and Venus or Sun and Rahu) in the 2nd house. Reason?

These individuals save money and prestige, self-earned and that coming from father to son or from grandparent to grandson.

They always maintain a vast and useful accumulation of books, magazines, newspaper clippings, informative pamphlets, and if their money permits, even manuscripts of old or ancient or rare books by famous authors and poets, the choice of subjects depending upon the education, tradition and liking of the individual.

A businessman in Calcutta had a rare collection of books and volumes on Saint Poet Kabirdas of the medieval times, the difficulty being that he kept his library in a room adjoining his Puja-room and bed-room on the top floor of the house and everyone didn't have access to it. And this businessman had Sun and Mercury in the 2nd house!

These individuals are normally rich enough to afford a good library of their own, and they are experts at money-earning, money-generating and money management. However it has also been noticed that they normally do not take interest in a large number of progeny of self. It can naturally be assumed or concluded that these individuals are very well read, at least in subject(s) of their own choice. If Gemini, Virgo or Pisces is in the 2nd house, these individuals are rare birds with their spouse in the bed, and the spouse grudges it through major part of the youth. These individuals leave it to their spouse to adopt their own line of reading and educating themselves, making facilities available to the spouse for this purpose, but rarely they make practical effort to educate the spouse themselves!

Being well read means intelligent, knowledgeable and experienced, though sometimes unpractical in maintaining friendly relationship. These individuals are respectful and keen to render every kind of service to their elders, though they expect the same attitude from their youngsters, which is often not easy-coming. Normally, they have great attachment and devotion to their religion or faith or cult, but they refrain from being die-hard or violent towards others for sake of religion, faith or cult.

These individuals prefer to be believers and followers of Truth in their dealings and behaviour, other than that applied to their source of earning. In source of earning, income is the main aim and ambition, truth or no-truth!

They do not mind migrating to other town, city, province or country for earning money and for getting rich. The hidden desire of getting rich is there in 90% of these individuals, if there is no obstacle from any other planet in their this aim and ambition. And riches would naturally lead them to a comfortable (if not luxurious) life.

However it is also noteworthy that these individuals are not much inclined towards pleasures of physical relationship in bed, but often platonic relationship with more than one person of the opposite sex drops into their lap automatically on account of their knowledge etc., and they too do not mind it.

Sun and Jupiter in the 2nd House

The main difference in results of Mercury with Sun in 2nd, and Jupiter with Sun in 2nd is that these Sun+Jupiter individuals collect such books and knowledge as would help and support them to earn more and more money. And often their collection would have books and other material on:

(a) accounting and audit, (b) the art of invoicing, including over-invoicing and under-invoicing, (c) preliminary knowledge of general law but specially commercial law, (d) economics and foreign trade, (e) marketing in own country and other countries, (f) exchange of money including foreign exchange, (g) law relating to industries, labour matters, and (h) public relations.

However collection of books and knowledge runs parallel to their desire for collection of bullion, gold and silver jewellery, gold and silver utensils (if affordable by them), wooden/ timber items of use, utility and decoration, and gold or silver embroidered clothes, shoes, turbans etc.

Normally these individuals get married to a good-looking spouse belonging to well-possessed family or background, if need be, these individuals do not mind deriving direct or indirect help and support from the family of the spouse or the spouse's own self to become rich and well possessed. In the same breath it can be said that they often stay happy and try to keep the spouse also happy, comfortable and in good disposition. There might be arguments between wife and husband or between lovers, but never in violent manner nor in disturbing the mental peace of each other.

In some cases, specially if Mars or Saturn cast their direct *drishti* on the 2nd house, these individuals have poor health upto the age of 19 years, but subsequently they are healthy and strong. However these individuals should stay preventive against asthma and diabetes, which might lead, after the age of 56 years, to a long-term ailment.

Some astrologers categorise these individuals with problem of ego, pride and vanity. Naturally when an individual has wealth of knowledge or money or beauty, the touch of ego or pride or vanity would hover over the individual.

Sun and Venus in the 2nd House

These individuals are creative in their ideas, thoughts, and actions, generally prefer to work alone without colleagues but with helpers. They are fond of collecting good pictures, paintings, decorative items, rich and fashionable garments, musical instruments, decorative and ornamental items of silver. They also collect drawings and architectural books and plans, material on fittings and furnishings, books and material on textiles, their texture and system of manufacture, knowledge about garment-making or textile designing, growing of variety of cotton/ real silk/ artificial silk/ and allied textiles. They collect books and pictorial material on sex sometimes bordering on pornography.

They talk fluently and impressively, and keeping the listeners in view, add a touch of romanticism to the talks. They are fond of making friends of the opposite sex, with or without indulgence in actual sex. These individuals do keep an eye on the wealth and possessions of opposite sex, and would try to obtain a portion of it for own use and utility. They are not generally mindful of returning items borrowed, even for a short while, from others.

They normally give no loans without proper security, but do not hesitate in obtaining loans without security, on just word of the mouth and then delay repayment and do not pay in one go. Sometimes, if Mars, Saturn or Rahu be in the 11th house or Jupiter be in the 5th house, they even pretend to forget the loan or dispute the actual amount of loan taken and also about the interest payable on the loan. They have less hesitation in borrowing even clothes/ garments and items of daily use, and in that case too, often forget to return the borrowed items. And often they put in better appearance in public than the person from whom they borrowed money, garments or other items.

They are very fond of sex, producing good number of progeny, and thereto they try to benefit gradually in relation to the progeny or later in life from the progeny as each member grows. If money liability is involved in the marriage of a child, these individuals do not mind delaying the marriage to the maximum extent possible. And these are the individuals who expect a big dowry in a child's marriage, all the moreso if Mars, Saturn or Rahu is in the 11th house or Jupiter in 5th house and consider it no loss of face in demanding it indirectly or directly.

In business line or industrial venture matters, they deal in or manufacture silver items, cloth, silk and imitation silk, sugar, ghee, cotton, cotton-seed, medicines and herbs, basic essence and constrict of medicines and perfumery, scents, cut flowers and garlands, tailoring, ready-made garments, long cloth. And also criminal type trade in humans (specially children and women). Suppliers to brothels also come under this combination of Sun and Venus in the 2nd house.

One big disadvantage of this combination is that these individuals, specially when Mars, Saturn or Rahu be in the 7th house or the 1st house indulge in deriving material benefits by sharing their spouse with others, and benefits or no benefits. Swapping of spouses is also an outcome of this combination, specially if Pisces or Libra is in the 2nd house.

Sun and Saturn in the 2nd House

It has to be remembered, as it is stated in reference to this combination in the 1st house, that though astrologically Saturn is deemed as a son of Sun, both are die-hard enemies to each other in so far as predictive astrology is concerned.

However they both generate money in the hands of the individual, but keeping him or her restricted and miserly in using the money, and keeping an eye on usurping money and possessions of others, provided loss of face and dignity is not involved. For accumulating money, no means are unfair so far as risk of an enquiry or punishment is not involved. These individuals sometimes exhibit their tendency of getting money initially by minor thefts in own house or by snatching from youngsters or helpless members of the family. In later life, they turn into smugglers, profiteers, hoarders, black-marketeers, and agents of this class of people. These individuals generally deal in iron, steel, placement services, petrol, diesel, lubricating oils, edible oils, machinery and machinery parts, skins and hides and utility items made thereof, rubber, leather, shoes and other footwear made of rubber/ leather, capital machinery, grabbing of industrial sheds and cattle-sheds, stealing or usurping goats, sheep and buffaloes (both male and female), supply of agricultural labour and exploiting the labour as well as the employer in this context, and no doubt working as liaison person between others and government officials, against normal fees or other gains.

These individuals are open minded to forget and forgive the faults/ offences (not severe crimes) of others, and expect the same treatment to their own faults and offences (even crimes). But they neither forget nor forgive even minor mistakes and faults of own spouse and do not feel ashamed to settle the core with the spouse by violent methods. They are however more accommodative towards own progeny but not towards progeny of others.

In so far as self interest or selfish motives are not involved, these individuals try to speak the truth, sometimes lies with decorative borders of truth and where selfish motives are involved, they succeed in turning half-truth and pure lies into acceptable truth. Because of this nature, they sometimes become patent witnesses in courts of law, specially on the criminal side. Unless Mercury or Jupiter is with this combine of Sun and Saturn in the 2nd house, or Mercury or Jupiter be in the 5th or 11th house, these individuals avoid forgery and forged documents. Though they claim and present themselves as handwriting experts, they are none of the kind. Because of their tact and talent, they however succeed in establishing themselves as an expert of handwriting in a court of law. That is possible only in cases where the presiding officer of the court has been won over by the concerned litigant.

These individuals prove to be efficient and tolerably honest as Treasurers and collectors of money/ funds for a political or social party or person.

Sun and Rahu in the 2nd House

It may be noted that when in combination with Sun, Rahu doesn't exactly follow the pattern of Saturn's combination with Sun, because Rahu exerts in its own manner, since it creates an 'eclipse' combination when with Sun.

The first and foremost thing is that these two stars would give birth to the individual in a well-to-do family. And then would constantly lead his family on the path of financial progress till the individual becomes adult, and then these two stars collectively help the individual to generate money and become rich in own right.

Some school of astrological-thought opine that Rahu (with Sun) in 2nd house gives the individual unfair and rather illegal means and methods of generating money, while the other schools of thought do not agree with this opinion. On some rare occasion, the individual might use unfair (not illegal) means of making money, but not always. The individual is rather encouraged to work hard, with full application of mind and body towards earning money, and saving a good portion thereof effectively. It also encourages the individual to invest the savings very profitably and in safe/ secure avenues. Rahu normally discourages an individual to tread on the path of speculation, including in avenues of shares and stocks.

This combination is normally inclined to give sophistication to wife and husband relationship or that between lovers in a even if the couple do not have a label of formal education. The 'ego' problem surfaces between them, anger also shows its face now and then, but not to the extent of violence jumping in between the two. If somehow Venus gets associated with this combination from the 8th or the 12th house, or in the 2nd house itself, a third angle might make an unwanted appearance casually or regularly, and then strained relations figures in between the couple in a routine manner.

This individual develops intimacy with persons of all categories, class, community and colour, behaving in a manner suiting to the person opposite, whether it is a male or a female.

The individual also contributes towards political parties and activities and at the same time derives full returns or benefits for the contributions given.

These individuals do not spend much money on paintings, musical instruments, library, items purely and exclusively for decoration without any iota of utility. In other words they are more practical and utility-oriented where the question of spending money is concerned. No doubt, they welcome gifts of these items, whether or not they are termed as (unfair or illegal) gratification.

Sun and Ketu in the 2nd House

Ketu doesn't interfere much with the results of Sun's position in the 2nd house. Ketu rather helps the individual on the pattern of Sun to earn better and save and invest savings profitably. Ketu makes the individual rather more miserly than any other planet in the 2nd house with Sun. Except element of irritation and anger which Sun brings into the life of the married couple, Ketu doesn't much interfere this way or that way in married life too and gives Sun a free field to operate.

The individual, under influence of Ketu, doesn't much look eye to eye with the family of the spouse, doesn't hesitate to utter bitter words with any of the relations of the spouse, or towards the family of the spouse as such.

Further Ketu's combination with Sun gives, after the age of 56 years, or during Mahadasa of Sun or Ketu trouble in the teeth line or any complaint of the throat (but not of ear and nose). It can give any complaint of the blood system or piles ailment or any complaint on the lines of venereal disease to the individual's spouse, the last one being a result of Venus in the 6th, 8th or 12th house (but not in 2nd house).

Ketu with Sun doesn't allow the individual to see eye to eye with government machinery, and lower level politicians, and doesn't mind exchange of harm with them in a mutual manner!

SUN IN THE 3RD HOUSE

This is one of the best positions of Sun for the individual. It grants success in whatever the individual undertakes on his or her own, or is assigned to undertake. It grants success in political aims and ambitions, or those relating to entry into public services at high, medium or low level. Whether in active politics or not, Sun gives political clout and influence to the individual, and also wisdom and courage to make best use thereof for self and others in whom the individual is interested.

The individual helps and supports brother(s), sister(s) and cousin(s), but doesn't normally get reciprocity from them. Instead from the elder brother(s) or sister(s) or cousin(s) the individual might get exploitation, blackmailing and backbiting. The elder ones might go the extent of putting blame on the individual for losses or other troubles suffered by them on their own! Another allegation that is sometimes levelled against the individual by own brother or sister or cousin is that the individual is more helpful and supportive to friends rather than to blood relations, whether it be correct or not. Sometimes mother also puts blame on the individual that he or she is not rendering financial or physical service to the mother or other motherly woman, even if the individual is duly dutiful towards mother to the best of capacity and capability.

Some of these individuals join defence services, and they prove very efficient, duty-oriented and hard working, but in some cases their integrity faces question-mark. They are good commanders but not very clever in implementation, if the implementation is their responsibility. They do not stand disobedience though they themselves indulge in disobedience to their superiors and political bosses. They do not prove very brave and forceful leading commanders or soldiers on a battlefield. However they prove useful from behind the battle scenes.

They are on the other hand successful in handling administrative matters, negotiations, committee and conference discussions, preparation of returns and reports, minutes and descriptions.

These individuals are helpful and serviceful to members of the wider family of self and spouse so long as their name and prestige is not adversely involved, otherwise they have no hitch in turning the face towards the wall.

They are kind and accommodating towards domestic servants, other employees, subordinates and menials, but always within limits, and sometimes during any long absence of the spouse, these individuals do not mind being a little extra romantic towards the domestic help or employee or subordinate (in office, shop or factory).

These individuals are particular about their physical built-up and appearance in public or outdoors.

Sun and Moon in the 3rd House

Though Sun and Moon are intimate friends and Moon is dependent on Sun for its light, Moon is not supportive of Sun in the 3rd house in so far as hard work, valour, fearlessness, and helpful attitude are concerned. Moon reduces the degree and force of all these qualities which are normally bestowed upon an individual by Sun in the 3rd house. Moon has a typical touch of lethargy in the 3rd house. Then where a question of actual combat fighting crops up, Moon generates a withdrawn tendency in the individual. Moon also reduces Sun's willingness of the individual to help and support own brother(s), sister(s) and cousin(s), and creates a desire in the mind of the individual for instant reciprocity, because Moon is the fastest moving among the stars (it takes on an average 54 hours to transit from one Rasi to another and in all only 27 days to complete its round of the entire zodiac).

Though Moon alone or with Sun makes an individual

lethargic, it gives a strong desire for riches/ wealth, all kinds of comfort and items of luxurious living.

If aspected by Jupiter or accompanied by Mercury in the 3rd house itself, the individual is fond of literature and poetry. If however Mercury is in the 2nd house, the individual would have a good collection of books and other reading material but would rarely read them, and if Mercury is in the 4th house, the individual would exhibit love for literature for sake of show and name in the society.

One typical quality of these individuals is that they can maintain their outer pleasant disposition even in adverse circumstances because of Moon in support of Sun in the 3rd house.

If a Rasi owned by Mars or Saturn be in the 3rd house and Moon be ahead of Sun in terms of degrees, loss of a younger brother is indicated in childhood. However if Sun is ahead of Moon in terms of degrees, the loss would be of an elder brother of the individual in childhood. Then upto the age of 15 years, the individual remains reserved in talks, though not in the classroom or in any debating society.

Sun and Mars in the 3rd House

One of the best combinations in the 3rd house; both are intimate friends, both become extra beneficial in the 3rd house independently and collectively. They enhance the power, position and prestige of the individual gradually and steadily, irrespective of the fact whether the individual is in business, industry, profession, politics, job, self employment or in social work. The individual gets the support of own kith and kin and also of servants, employees and subordinates, as also of colleagues and co-workers, so much so that even superiors and bosses (if any) try to help the individual.

There is commendable reciprocity between the individual and brother(s), sister(s) and cousin(s) of self and also those of spouse, without reservation. This mutual tendency of help and support brings success to the individual as well as to these relations. If this combination of Sun and Mars be in a Rasi owned by Venus or Saturn, or if Rahu too becomes a member of this combination or Saturn be in the 9th or the 12th house, loss of a brother or sister in childhood is clearly indicated.

These individuals are hardly in tight financial position and therefore there rarely arises an opportunity for them to borrow money, leave aside the present trends of borrowing money from banks, financial institutions and share-holders for running public limited companies and multinational formations.

These individuals are bold, brave, fearless fighters, chivalrous by nature, but at the same time they know the importance of forgiveness. Because of martial planet Mars (deemed commander-in-chief among the stars) with its king Sun in their best position in the 3rd house, under favour by these two stars, the individual becomes an efficient strategist in matters concerning strained relations between two states or governments or nations, or in the event of battles or war between two nations. These individuals are best suited for popularising feeling of patriotism among the masses.

In local troubled areas, these individuals are well suited for managing the situation or suppressing the revolt or social disturbance. Normally individuals having Sun with Mars in the 3rd do not agree to buy peace by money or by paying ransom or by any other costly method of establishing peace. These individuals quickly learn use of small and big firearms, guns and canons and other modern missiles. However, unless other stars induce them, these individuals do not misuse their strength and expertise for any illegal or immoral purposes. They are however not very clever, cunning and alert to prevent other mischievous elements to misuse their name here and there.

These individuals either inherit agricultural lands or other landed property, or acquire it by own effort or get it as a reward or grant for some chivalrous act, and sometimes they gracefully share it with their brother or sister.

Sun and Mercury in the 3rd House

Mercury doesn't disturb the functioning and results of Sun in the 3rd house, except that it makes the individual more thoughtful, slow in decision-making and consequential action/ activity, adds to the internal hidden timidity or withdrawnness if these shortcomings already exist in the individual on account of any other planet's influence. But in this regard too Mercury's conjunction with Sun makes the individual outwardly bold and daring, if nothing else, at least in words, utterances and shouting threats. In written word too, the individual is bold and daring.

The individual has intentions of helping and supporting kith and kin of own and of the spouse, and without any desire for reciprocity.

In the field of writing or composing poetry or songs, *Ghazals* or any musical items or producing literature, these individuals are often lethargic, their works remain lying incomplete, and often they miss the target date too. They are much sought after poets and singers, but there too, their response is slow, sluggish and rather discouraging the hosts. But they spellbind the audience once they are on the stage and at the mike! They do not run after members of the opposite sex, but if anyone chases them with romantic intentions, they often respond to it.

Sun and Jupiter in the 3rd House

These individuals trust that everything ought to drop into their lap without much effort on their own part, whether it is the field of law or accounts or economics or management or legislature or arbitration or *Panchayat* or functioning as a special envoy or emissary. However if Mars or Saturn or even Rahu be in the 3rd, 10th or 11th house, often they get things without much effort on their own part, just by sheer good luck, specially where membership of a Legislature or *Panchayat* or arbitration or job of a special envoy or emissary is concerned. The reason is that before the age of 38 years, these individuals work very hard and achieve recognition in their field of study or profession, which counts for achievements subsequent to 38 years of age.

These individuals have chances of being elected or nominated to Parliament, Senate, Legislature, *Panchayats*, Higher Courts, Public Service Commission or Election Commission,

Tribunals, International bodies like ILO, UNESCO, SECURITY COUNCIL, INTERNATIONAL COURT at The Hague or similar and allied organisations of the United Nations or the Commonwealth.

These individuals often make efforts to keep their kith and kin happy and prosperous, even at own cost. They are miserly in spending money on unjustified or unfair or illegal venues, but quite generous for spending on deserving cause or for such public utility purpose, charitable and social formation, as is sincerely active in the field. If Mercury is in the 4th house and Mars or Saturn or Rahu is in the 9th or 11th house, these individuals, like ancient Emperor Harshvardhan, do not mind nor feel hesitant to donate or sacrifice a major portion of their assets for educational or social purposes or for public utility services or for medical purposes. For example, Sir Harisingh Gaur established the Sagar University in the then Central Provinces or Pandit Madan Mohan Malviya (a highly learned scholar with no money of his own) established the Banares Hindu University. Because of their this type of charitable and philanthropic nature, these individuals sometimes face financial tightness in their old age, but they rarely regret or repent their past actions of charity and nobility.

Sun and Venus in the 3rd House

These individuals are generous and helpful to nephews and nieces of self and of the spouse, sometimes towards brothers and sisters too of self and spouse, but with reservation. Romantic more in words, less in practice and also unmindful of who the listeners are when talking in romantic mood, and thus earn criticism.

These individuals start learning any one of the fine arts, like music, dance, painting, photography, sculpture, producing or directing films and serials or publicity episodes for vision media, stage acting or acting in films and serials or episodes. Some others function as models for publicity-stuff (print media and vision media), production and sale of garments (cotton, silken or of artificial fabric), manufacture and sale of yarn. Those with combust Venus leave the learning in between. If Venus is stronger than Sun in the 3rd house, the individual not only completes learning, but is effortful to attain expertise in the line chosen and undertaken by him or her.

The question is that Sun in 3rd makes an individual hard working and devoted to work, while Venus in 3rd makes an individual lethargic and intent upon taking benefit or advantage of work of others. In that case, these individual make a greater show of work than actual work.

These individuals are fond of wearing beautiful upper garments, not bothering about the clean or unclean under garments.

Sun and Saturn in the 3rd House

As mentioned previously, in spite of being father and son and in spite of being die-hard enemies to each other, they together give very great success to every stroke of effort when both are in the 3rd house. These individuals generally work hard, are efficient workers, attach importance to use and utility of their work, always want due returns or rewards for their work. They are capable administrators and also remarkable craftsmen.

They make outstanding commanders of forces, able fighters, far-sighted strategists, successful investigating and intelligence-collecting officials, expert spies, respected envoys and special representatives. They are very clever observers in any location and situation. Their reporting is always minute and perfect, though sometimes delayed to the extent that the report loses its value for the recipient.

The only drawback of this combination in the 3rd is that they lose a brother or sister in childhood, and they are often very strict with their younger brother(s) and sister(s), and do not hesitate in beating them severely.

There are rare chances of these individuals being superseded in service, they get their due promotions and rise without litigation.

They involve themselves in controversy and conflict specially during Saturn Mahadasa and Sun Antardasas or Sun Mahadasa and Saturn Antardasa, or when Saturn transits over the 9th house from Ascendant.

Sun and Rahu in the 3rd House

This combination gives more or less the same results as those by Sun and Saturn in the 3rd house, but to a less degree, because Rahu is after all a shadow planet.

These individuals are hard working, expect full results and rewards for their work, but do not run after rewards.

They are rather fast workers than those individuals who have Saturn and Sun in the 3rd. They take care that their work and reporting do not lose their value and importance, and therefore whether perfect or not, the reports are on the due desk at the right moment.

They sometimes go jealous of the achievements of their brother(s) or sister(s), or feel bored and bothered if these individuals are required to help and support close relations often. Sometimes their spouse also poisons the mind and put hurdles in help or support going out to brother or sister.

They are not so bold and brave in actual fighting as they are in forming strategy, plans and projects that would make the actual fighting a sure or near-sure success.

Sun and Ketu in the 3rd House

Though an 'eclipse' combination, Sun has full freedom to function in its own way, Ketu either contributes help to Sun in its functioning or keeps aloof. These individuals are very efficient in table work, preparing notes, minutes and proceedings of meetings and conferences, managing meetings and conferences, writing reports, co-ordinating the work of those working on intelligence, investigations and spying, or any kind of field work or performing executive jobs. As far as possible, these individuals neither interfere in the working of others, nor do they tolerate interference by others in their work.

These individuals attain remarkable command on foreign languages and some of them become experts too, in reading, understanding and writing therein. Sometimes they undertake translation work from one language to another.

Sun in the 4th House

Normally astrological experts are full of praise for Sun in the 4th house, because it has direct *drishti* on the 10th house, while practical experience of others fails to confirm this viewpoint fully or unconditionally. There is no doubt that Sun in 4th house helps those individuals who are in government, semi-government or local government or municipal or public sector service or in active politics.

However, Sun in 4th house, specially if in Aries, Leo, Libra or Aquarius creates hurdles in getting full care and affection of the natural mother in childhood, i.e. upto the age of 12 years. Even in later life, hidden differences or a typical type of dislike or distrust develops between mother and son, whether natural mother, stepmother or adopting-mother.

The individual is often arrogant whenever he/ she commits any traffic offence or violation of routine system of law and order. These individuals take pride in dropping names, whether they actually know those important persons or not, or have contacts or not with the name-dropped.

Some of these individuals, depending on the position of Mars in 6th, 9th, or 10th house or that of Jupiter in 2nd, 5th, 7th or 10th house, get respect and recognition from Rulers, Presidents, Prime Ministers, government or Very Important Political and Social Formations or individual leaders.

If these individuals hold any administrative or management charge in any big establishment, organisation, office or industry, they boast of their impartiality, which they hardly exercise. If Virgo or Capricorn is in the 4th house, sometimes their integrity also faces a question mark and undergoes an enquiry or even a regular investigation.

These individuals often help in works of public utility, such as widow homes, night shelters for poor, tanks and ponds, irrigation projects, small dams for collecting rain-waters, small schools, dispensaries, and old-age-homes, etc. But their actual monetary contribution is not so large as they brag about their all kind of service to the cause undertaken.

Because these individuals are given to flattery, they indulge in it towards their employers, superiors and Godfathers, and unfortunately expect the same from their subordinates and juniors. When they do not get it to their estimation, they put hurdles in the progress of those non-flattering employees, subordinates and juniors.

These individuals often tell their grown up children as to how much trouble and sacrifice were involved in the children's upbringing, more with a view to high expectations from the children than to acquaint the children with the past years of their childhood.

These individuals have bright chances of inheriting residence from the parents or from maternal side, and if Cancer or Leo is in the 4th house, they either get adopted by someone on the mother's side or get a gift of money and immoveable asset from that source.

These individuals are quite sincere and helpful to their friends. They rarely suffer want of domestic help. If these individuals ever go out of their way to help the domestic servant or any other employee, they do not miss the chances of putting a burden of obligation on that domestic servant or other employee.

Sun and Moon in the 4th House

Naturally Moon would be in combust position, but even then it would have its full functioning, because of its capacity of giving results in the 4th house. These individuals get their full due of affection and care from the natural mother, breast-feeding too for the normal phase of infancy. But in later life the reciprocity on part of these individuals towards their mother is not of equal proportion to the affection and care they got from the mother in infancy and childhood. Whatever the Rasi in the 4th house, these individuals are more inclined towards their father in physical service and financial support.

This combination gives to the individual facility of residence and conveyance, of own or at the cost of others. There are good chances of inheritance too from parents or others with regard to residence and conveyance.

These individuals are helpful to their friends and colleagues, without consideration of caste, creed, colour or sex. They do not expect reciprocity, but do expect sometimes sense of obligation in the friend thus helped.

Similarly they help, in an hour of need, their domestic servant and other employees, and in that case too, they expect sense of obligation from the employee helped. However in a sense these individuals are generous and graceful.

They help also in works and constructions of public utility, such as temporary or permanent bridges, prayer halls, marriage ceremony halls, schools, dispensaries, night shelters for pilgrims, shelters for widows and destitute women.

These individuals prove reliable spies and national representatives to another country or international or commonwealth organisations etc. They do not talk out of turn, and generally talk to the point and impressively too, and in so doing, they do not carry sense of 'ego' in their utterances. On the other hand they are polite and whatever sense of inner pride or vanity Sun might have created in these individuals, that too cools down when in responsible positions.

Sun and Mars in the 4th House

These two stars are intimate friends, and when together though they are opposed to each other in chart of spontaneous relationship among stars, they function as friends in any situation or circumstances, even when facing enemies or adversaries or opponents or competitors.

They make the individual very influential or a follower of influential people normally called Very Important Persons (VIPs). They often use that influence for their own good and also for the good of their friends and relations or subordinates and employees. They are not much inclined to help totally unknown persons, it being a different thing that they might help a charming person of the opposite sex. In doing so, if nothing else, they enjoy and cherish talking to a young person of the opposite sex, under influence of Mars in the 4th house, and to create an impression because of Sun in the 4th house.

These individuals have no middle path of relations with mother and motherly persons, either they are affectionate and obedient to mother or they do not see eye to eye with mother owing to influence of spouse or family of the spouse.

They deem mother as an obstacle in their happy married life, even if mother is non-interfering type, polite and aloof or co-operative and of service to the spouse. However this tendency does not stop them from expecting inheritance of jewellery, cash and property from mother or even from maternal uncles and maternal grandparents.

But if this combination is in Aries, Leo, Capricorn, Libra or Aquarius, the mother is hard taskmaster, affectionate and caring but strict and restrictive in the same breath. Such mother is helpful to the spouse but not submissive, mother might even be harassing and going to the extent of torture to the spouse. It needs deep study to determine whether mother is a bridge of happiness in the married life of her progeny, or mother adversely influences the married life.

These individuals often wear a cloak of pride and vanity, and throw it around to influence people, concerned and unconcerned. No doubt, having full direct *drishti* on the 10th house, these individuals have close contacts with top category authorities on political and civil administration side, or they themselves wield influence on their own by their post and position in government or semi-government.

They are charitable and generous towards a selective class or portion of the society, and donate money and physical service where necessary. But they try to derive some personal benefit too for such services rendered. They donate generously when there is national calamity caused by nature's fury (such as earthquake, floods, famine, landslide, devastating fire, or an accident to a passenger train, aeroplane, passenger bus, volcano, battles and widespread war). However often they are mute observers in cases of atrocities on masses by robbers and dacoits as well as kidnappers, and if they are on any administrative post or political position of power, they adopt policy of appeasement towards the robbers, dacoits, and even towards mass-murderers.

These individuals are normally trustworthy friends, always ready to help in hour of need of a friend, even after reaching a higher post and position in government or in public or private sector.

These two stars together guarantee these individuals residential premises on ownership basis, and facility of conveyance too, whether of own or at the cost of others. And Mars helps them to acquire property for speculation or earning rental income.

Sun and Mercury in the 4th House

Highly educated professors and teachers, writers on political and civic subjects, impressive public orators and speakers, convincing preachers, efficient priests, competent revenue officials specially on the menstruation side, investigating journalists, hard-hitting editors have this combination in the 4th house.

These are the people who get recognition and rewards from government sources as also from social and semi-political organisations, sometimes genuine ones and sometimes inspired ones.

Some of these individuals turn into ghostwriters for their political, social, wealthy masters and patrons. They might indulge in acts of piracy while in journalism, but not in the field of literature. No doubt sometimes these individuals adopt names and surnames, pen names, pseudo-names corresponding to very famous writers, poets and literary stalwarts of the ancient and medieval times.

Another shortcoming of these individuals is that quite often they do not acknowledge the source of their information, including texts and references from literary works of others. They forget to acknowledge the help, guidance and assistance received by them from colleagues, guide and others for writing and publication of their works. They do not admit that they are ungrateful. For example, a colleague of a pseudo-writer wrote three-fourth portion of a book published by the latter. The understanding between the two was that the book would be published under joint names. But the pseudo writer published the book under his single name, mentioning the colleague as helping in proof reading of the book. That pseudo writer had Sun and Mercury in his 4th house, while the colleague had Mercury and Sun in the 1st house. The deceptive pseudo writer's book didn't sell because it was for a limited number of non-Hindi speaking students learning Hindi. On the other hand, the colleague wrote and published 6 books subsequent to that event which received high class warm reception among the readers, and in the market!

Sun and Jupiter in the 4th House

These individuals become known figures in judiciary, sometimes in higher judiciary, or in any field of law and legislation. Otherwise they become experts in accountancy, in economics, in management of business, in taxation laws, in commercial statistics, in drafting and preparation of law and legal documents, in writing constitutions for a nation or any public body or private formation, in arbitration, in settling disputes between countries, states and nations.

Some of these individuals write very useful books on law, economics, political science, history, accountancy, business management, statistics, tax laws, and edit law reporters, economic surveys, laymen books of taxation.

They often get big name and fame for their knowledge, expertise and hard work, and also recognition from political bosses and general public. They are rarely in want of money, because generally they become well possessed. They are given to comfortable and luxurious style of life. They are genuinely charitable and generous, without any kind of distinction. They are fond of woollen garments, because they feel cold, and sometimes suffer a bad throat.

They are open hearted to help any cause of public utility, and are willing even to go out of their way to help that cause. The problem with them is that in spite of being educated and experienced, they trust a person easily, and thus sometimes they provide protection and shelter to violators of law and criminals. They get cautioned about these mischievous elements quite late in the day, sometimes after the individuals themselves have suffered at the hands of these wrong type of elements.

    Rarely these individuals have lean and thin built of body. They have got strong built physique, sometimes bordering on fatness or actually fat. But it has come to observation, whether on the Bench or at the bar, these individuals reach old age, and continue to be working quite actively too.

Sun and Venus in the 4th House

This combination gives the individual a beautiful mother with noble qualities and capacity for bringing up her progeny under love, affection, care and due control. The individual, whether male or female, inherits charming personality and some of the noble qualities of the mother. The mother would be gifted with neat and clean habits, keeping the house and household in neat and clean condition. The mother would have an open-minded attitude towards all relations in the wider family as also friends of the family, and would be free from the vice of jealousy.

    Whatever the attitude of the individual (after reaching adulthood age), towards the mother, there would be no drop in mother's love and affection towards the individual.

    The individual normally develops, (specially if Taurus, Pisces, Libra or Gemini is in the 4th house) understanding and knowledge about one or more of the fine arts, by effort of self or by a touch of inheritance from mother (or father or a grandmother). If the individual would not acquire knowledge in any fine art, at least she/ he would have the capacity for appreciation of fine arts, which could be dance, music, painting, photography, sculpture, acting, directing or producing films and allied items, designing (including of garments), landscape ideas, knitting, embroidery, etc. Further, whether they know or not, these individuals decorate their residence with some musical instruments, and sometimes try to possess a collection of rarely available musical instruments, paintings, and medieval time royal or rich garments of gents and ladies' wear.

The individual is likely to acquire expert knowledge of medicines and herbals, whether the individual is in the medical profession or not.

These individuals are fond of living in a fashionable house or entire-floor-flat in a posh locality or open area, and sometimes are able to build their own house of their liking and design, with luxurious fittings and furnishings.

Being noble hearted, these individuals do not refuse, if within their capacity, to help or support any needy person, specially on being approached. Further they have a passion for getting built water-supply resources for drinking water (useful for human beings and animals as well) and also for irrigation purposes, and donate swimming pool to their club, or society or town. Some others establish institutions for educating young generation in music, painting, acting etc. And others more capable and resourceful take great pains and establish medical school and college (though of late, greedy persons too are starting medical colleges for generating big money without providing even basic facilities and clinicals and laboratories at least in India, moreso on the south of the Vindhyachal Ranges).

These individuals are normally helpful to wider family and circle of friends, but in this case they are sometimes restricted in their generosity.

They have got very romantic ideas, and sometimes they develop romantic relationship with a member of their maternal family. Because Sun is also in the 4th house with Venus, often afraid of their reputation, these individuals do not go beyond a certain limit, because normally these individuals are competent administrators (for others) and thus have the quality of self-restraint too.

Sun and Saturn in the 4th House
It is useful to remember that the 4th house concerns mother, property, digestive system, domestic and non-domestic employees, conveyance, safety or non-safety in journeys specially by road (includes journeys by train, auto-vehicles, bicycles, bullock-carts

and on foot and also crossing of rivers etc.). It also covers domestic happiness or otherwise, general comfort, heart, ribs, chest (breast in case of women) and ailments relating to these parts of body.

It has been mentioned more than once that in spite of Sun being father and Saturn being his son, these two are die-hard enemies to each other. Thus these two adversary stars in the 4th house generally affect all these subjects concerning the 4th house adversely at one time or the other. It is all the more so when Saturn is in transit over the 4th house (thank God, Saturn's cycle repeats to the 4th house after 28 to 30 years), or Saturn has its Mahadasa or Antardasas in any planet's Mahadasa including that of Sun itself.

Though the general belief is that Saturn is helpful or favourable for the house it occupies and unfavourable for the house on which Saturn has direct *drishti*, experience shows that it is not so in the case of the 4th house. Saturn normally gives adverse results in the 4th house and all the more so when in the company of Sun. However one point needs special observation. If Saturn is behind Sun in terms of degrees (say Cancer is in the 4th house and Sun is on 18th degree of Cancer and Saturn is at 14th degree), Saturn is all the more rash and rude in the 4th house, influencing Sun too, to give adverse results. However if Saturn is ahead of Sun in terms of degrees, Sun and Saturn both would give results independent of each other, whether the results are good or bad depending on their respective Navamsha positions (or Trinshansha in case of women). Their strength, company or aspect of other stars on each of the two (in such cases precise *drishti* needs to be calculated in terms of degrees).

Another confused impression is that Saturn (and Sun) in the 4th house do not affect the mother so much as they affect (adversely no doubt) the 10th house which includes element of father. Experience shows that it is not exactly so. Both or either of them would adversely affect any of the subjects mentioned in para 1 above (under Sun and Saturn in 4th house).

Thus during the periods mentioned in para 2 above, the individual should be very cautious in driving a vehicle (whether auto one or driven by bullocks, buffalo, horse, ponies, dogs or pulled by men as in Calcutta and some hill stations in India). Caution is needed in walking on or crossing a road, walking in bathroom and on any slippery ground. Extra care is required to prevent theft of any vehicle. If the individual gets injured, besides normal medical aid, examination be conducted whether there has been any injury whatsoever to skull or any other part of body, specially to a bone.

Second point is that during the periods mentioned in para 2 above, extra care has to be taken of the health of mother (natural, step mother or adoptive mother), and also of father (though step father is not so much affected). Care has also to be taken of individual's relations with mother to keep them as sweet, soft and serviceful as possible.

Very often influence of spouse works in the opposite direction in this matter. That is ultimately harmful to everyone concerned, and injurious to the interests of the individual and the spouse.

Third point is that these individuals should not take to regular or heavy drinking or smoking, and should adopt all such precaution as would avert any trouble to the normal functioning of the heart. In case of women, care and caution needed to keep away any cancerous ailment of the breast and vaginal region.

Fourth point is that the parents should take better care of digestive system of such children, upto the age of at least 16 years, when the child has Sun and Saturn together in the 4th house.

Fifth point is that these individuals should be very selective and careful with regard to friends, partners in business (whether from within the family or outside the family), associates, colleagues, subordinates and servants and employees, including domestic help, lest any one indulges in theft or cheating!

Sixth, during construction of any premises, house, shop or industrial shed, or any other property, these individuals should take preventive steps against theft and pilferage of cement, bricks and iron or steel stuff.

Seventh, if in government or semi-government service, or in active politics or holding any political office of profit, these individuals should keep themselves above nepotism, favouritism, gratification and groupism. If they come to adverse notice, it would be a big task to clear the allegations, and if any iota of substance is found in the allegations, punishment of some kind or the other awaits at their door.

Eighth, if these individuals have to undergo any surgical treatment, they should obtain second expert opinion and, then have it done by the best surgeon available. There are chances (to an extent depending upon the position of Mars in the birth chart, the yearly chart and transit of Mars at the time of surgery), that some defect might be left in the surgery calling for further surgery or other medical treatment lasting longer period.

Ninth, unless these individuals are willing to tolerate usurpation, they should avoid giving entire house/ building/ premises to a single tenant, whatever the temptations offered by the tenant. Vacation and getting back possession of the property would be very difficult, and sometimes the vacation has to be obtained by paying a huge amount as "Pugree"(i.e. monetary gratification for vacating the property) or the property might be usurped by the tenant. This position is equally applicable to agricultural land and orchard etc. Unless Jupiter is very favourably placed in the birth chart and the transit of the Jupiter is also favourable, litigation might not prove very helpful in the matter.

Tenth point, which is rather favourable is that these individuals have bright chances of being adopted by any man or woman or couple, who would be much richer than the natural parental family of the individual.

Yet another favourable point of this combination is that some of these individuals stand to gain substantially from maternal family, from adversaries, opponents, enemies and competitors. If the gain is not always in terms of money and assets, it is at least in terms of knowledge, success in exams, settlement of claims, or compromise in terms of enemy's surrender and material gains thereby in the shape of compensation for losses in war. These individuals always fare extremely well in settlement of claims with defeated enemies!

Sun and Rahu in the 4th House

Rahu with Sun in 4th house would give in reduced degree the same results as that of Saturn with Sun in the 4th house, except the following points:

i. Rahu would not normally give fracture of the bone;

ii. Rahu would not lead to adoption by any male or female or a couple within or outside the family; chances of adoption are really remote;

iii. The individual would be generous and social-service-minded but would not normally contribute money from personal resources;

iv. Rahu doesn't create chances of any major accident by vehicle or mode of transport or while walking on foot. In towns with heavy rush of vehicles, also in rural area without much of vehicles, chances of minor accident or accidental injury are not ruled out.

v. Friends and employees might cheat or embezzle funds but not heavily;

vi. Very little chances of tenants usurping the entire premises, though trouble from or with tenants not ruled out;

vii. Routine enquiries or explanations likely in government or semi-government jobs, but not such developments as might invite major punishment for the individual;

viii. Less chances of any major or severe surgery, and if at all it becomes unavoidable, very little chances of its failure or it proving fatal.

ix. This combination would no doubt give fatness to the individual, whether a male or a female, specially around the middle parts of the body, but normally wouldn't give an unpresentable appearance.

x. Relations with natural mother, stepmother or adopting mother will fluctuate between sweet and sour, but not to the extent of complete break off.

xi. No strong chances of substantial gain from maternal family or enemies and opponents, just the normal routine gains, if at all any!

Sun and Ketu in the 4th House

Being an innocent planet, Ketu in the 4th house doesn't much interfere with the functioning of Sun, in spite of creation of 'eclipse' combination for Sun. This combine of Sun and Ketu would not give, even in a reduced degree, the results which Sun and Rahu combine can give in the 4th house.

No doubt, Sun and Ketu combine can give any of these results:

1. Minor differences and hot arguments between individual and mother (natural, stepmother or adopting mother), absence of the individual during mother's illness or hour of her need for help and support.

2. Minor accident to vehicle or by vehicle to the individual.

3. Non-repayment or delayed payment of loans given.

4. Allegations of mismanagement or misappropriation of funds belonging to any social or charitable or educational organisation.

5. Low level of educational progress of any of the first two children is one of the results of this combination in the 4th house.

Normally the above results will occur during Ketu Mahadasa and Sun's sub-period or Sun's main period and Ketu sub-period, or during Ketu's transit over the 4th house, which on an average repeats every 18 years, and is of 18 month duration.

Sun in the 5th House

a) Unless the stars of the spouse are more powerful, or Sun is accompanied by Mars or any soft planet, the progeny remains limited to 3 or at the most 4 pregnancies, and if stars of spouse are helpful, the first one will be a male child.

b) Outstanding capacity for management and administration, sometimes bordering on harshness or ruthlessness.

c) Educational progress would often be above the average, but rarely at the top of the class or very high level results.

d) Good grasp, but outside help needed for developing equally good memory. In some cases, given to copying homework and difficult exercises from fellow students and depending on private tuition. If Saturn or Rahu or Ketu is also in the 5th house, the individual would be given to copying in the Exam hall too.

e) Given to dropping of names and exercising influence over the teachers in school as well as in college life, though normally respectful towards teachers and elders.

f) Given to more than average annoyance, irritation and anger, more so from the age of 24 years onwards.

g) Less chances of indulging in bad character or any kind of criminal activity as such, though if associated with Saturn or Rahu by conjunction within 10 degrees or aspected by Mars or Saturn fully from the 11th house, the individual might provide protection, shelter to hard-core political leaders, and to such social reformers as believe in hard-line approach.

h) Normally charitable by nature, specially in giving monetary help or manpower support to any political party, politician, political or social cause.

i) Bold and courageous relating to matters mentioned in (g) and (h) above.

j) Desirous of political rise of self or spouse and if unsuccessful in gaining grounds directly in political arena, the individual become helpful to or follower or patron of high-level politicians and bureaucrats, resulting in importance to self.

Sun and Moon in the 5th House

Both of them are friends in permanent relationship, but because of togetherness in one house, they become opposed to each other at the time of birth. However it should be taken that they do not lose their importance in giving results. Moon is unable to give full results because it goes combust when in the same House with Sun. Being Sun's permanent friend, it does give at least 50 to 60% results of its presence in the 5th house. In this connection it has to be noted that the 5th house is a Trikona and therefore considered very important in study of any birth chart, yearly chart or Question chart.

This combination gives sensitive nature, emotional attitude and easily irritable trend of mind, but not with much expression of inner feelings. The individual suffers or enjoys own feelings often inwardly only. If Mars is also in the 5th house with these two, the inner anger damages the process of thinking of the individual, and the anger element becomes unbearable for the individual as well as for those people towards whom the anger is directed. It is better not to cause provocation for anger, if it could be avoided.

These individuals are often keen for early progeny after marriage, and unless Venus too is in the 5th house with these two, the individual avoids indulgence in physical involvement before actual marriage. The individual gets both male and female progeny, though the matter depends equally on the stars of the spouse too. If there is natural loss of conception or pregnancy upto the 4th month, these individuals blame each other for it, without going into causes thereof.

Since both these stars directly aspect the 11th house, these individuals often have an eye on the financial outcome of every effort, contact or event or development around them.

Moon being lord of Mind, these individuals are always much concerned for doing everything possible for the progeny, irrespective of the fact whether the progeny is responsive or not. Sometimes these individuals are classed as over-protective bordering on 'possessiveness', which in turn is often resented by the progeny.

These individuals are very sensible but at the same time sensitive too in matters of management and administration, particularly if they hold any office of responsibility relating to manpower. Females are all the more harsh and sometimes ruthless without much justification.

Sun and Mars in the 5th House

The 5th house rules the Mind, thoughts, planning, capacity and competence for management, progeny, education and wisdom-cum-experience. Thus this combination often proves quite difficult for others to tolerate the attitude in the individual, who gets into fits of iron-hot anger and determination too with it. In school life, these individuals do extremely well in languages, specially a language foreign for the individual, for example English, French, Spanish or German for an Indian student, and Tamil or Malayalam or Telugu for an individual from North India or other countries. Further these individuals do very well in science subjects such as Chemistry and Biology, but unless Mercury too is in the 5th house, they are not so efficient in Mathematics, accounting, higher level of literature. They prove successful monitors in class and very capable in sports and games requiring physical capability.

If this combination is in a Sign owned by Sun or Mars or in Gemini or Capricorn, these individuals get success in and get selected for superior services on the administrative or defence side of the country.

Depending on planning by both husband and wife, these individuals get more male progeny (provided the stars of the spouse are also supportive for it), and at the right age too, though special care is needed to avoid natural loss of pregnancy during the 3rd and 5th months. Generally the progeny is sturdy and physically active depending on the birth chart of the child itself.

These individuals are efficient in administration and in the art of deriving full capacity work from subordinates and employees and sometimes also from colleagues. Otherwise too, these individuals are very able administrators, managers, rulers, bureaucrats, public servants, guards, defence Personnel, organisers, ordnance experts, security-heads for top personalities in any country. They are remarkable marksmen. They do not generally prove very successful spies and envoys because they tend to lose temper rather quickly and openly, thereby sometimes they invite trouble for themselves and also for the employer-country or organisation.

These individuals are dependable friends, specially where political or physical help and support is needed.

They respect and obey their parents, teachers and elders or seniors, but they are often harsh or hard towards juniors, subordinates and employees and do not hesitate to indulge in violence for protection of those whom they respect. They normally have faith in Almighty God, and do not tend to change their religion, faith or cult, but at the same time they are rough in spreading their religion, faith or cult.

Sun and Mercury in the 5th House

Because generally Mercury is often in combination with Sun, and 5th house is favourite of Mercury, these individuals often attain high standard in educational achievement, specially in languages and literature, in writing essays or material for publication anywhere and everywhere. They make efficient (sometimes rude or ruthless) teachers, professors and tutors, guides for research work, journalists, writers, poets, orators, preachers and *"Katha Vachaks"*. Also they make efficient Mathematicians, advisers to rulers or administrators of any country, province, state, organisation, proof readers, editors of books and literature, critics, letter writers (though the art is gradually disappearing with advent of Radio, TV. Internet and what not), story-writers, dialogue writers, and all such activities which require high level of intelligence.

These individuals are more or less always good in written tests, and also at in interviews or viva voce, or as examiners and interviewers. They avoid harshness in their criticism of literature, specially if the writer or poet is senior to them. They generally get rewards, awards and recognition for their achievements in education, or as a writer or poet or editor or journalist or for any intellectual work of quality.

They are generally lenient in matters of management, administration and punishment, maybe initially harsh and angry, but merciful and lenient in decisions and orders. Most of them are vigorous readers and have a personal library.

They do not, normally, adversely affect a pregnancy.

Their progeny is often intelligent and good at studies but not equally good in sports and games, specially which require physical stamina.

Sun and Jupiter in the 5th House

It is generally believed that Jupiter is the teacher (Guru), adviser, priest and guide to Sun, and Sun is the King. Being Teacher, Jupiter is commonly known as "Guru" in Sanskrit, Hindi and other Indian languages. Thus Sun and Jupiter combination is a happy one, moreso because Jupiter is helper-planet of the 5th house, which is a *Trikona*.

In school life these individuals have sharp memory, though often they avoid written work and homework. They make outstanding economists, jurists, judges, advocates, solicitors, petition-writers, draftsmen, drafters of law and legal literature, written constitution for any country or public formation, accountants, bankers, treasurers, cashiers, historians, researchers in law, economics, history or political science. They give a good account of themselves as political advisers, private tutors for girls in their teens, brokers in stocks and shares, middlemen for fixing marriages, counsels in divorce matters, revenue officers responsible for land management and soil conservation. They are successful in managing and running hotels, restaurants, eating houses, preparing and selling sweets and all kinds of eatable and drinkable delicacies, managing Inns, motels and night shelters, destitute-women-homes, orphanages, *Gurukuls* (i.e. residential boarding houses for students and scholars).

However these individuals are easily open to political or social influence and legal or illegal gratification, whatever their field of work, including judiciary. They are capable of embezzlement of funds of their clients and customers, cheating, piracy, taking credit for work of others. In spite of these minus points, these individuals are widely respected and trusted, because they know the art of concealment of their weak points.

As advocates, negotiators, arbitrators or even as judges, they are capable of double dealings, including cheating and backing out of a promise, assurance, word of honour, commitment, undertaking, understanding, or gratification or no gratification.

If these individuals are ever caught for any misdeed, often political influence is available to them and they manage to get out of trouble. Otherwise they get harsher punishment than what average persons get.

Sun and Venus in the 5th House

Though basically with attitude of animosity towards each other, Sun and Venus go very well for the individuals in the 5th house. They get patronage and recognition from Emperors, Kings, Rulers, Presidents and Prime Ministers, Governors, political and social bodies for their ability and efficiency. It can be in music, dance, painting, architecture, sculpture, embroidery, needle work, flower growing and flower arrangement, preparation of scents and perfumes (*Itra* in India). It can also be organising parties, concerts, dance programmes, music and other conferences, religious gatherings, acting, direction or production of films and episodes or serials. Besides that it can be in hotel management, guides to tourists and travellers, dress designers, rural arts, tree plantations specially in an artistic manner, swimming pools, arrangements for mountaineering, etc. They make efficient and middle-path-followers in management of hospitals and nursing homes, and prove capable of managing troublesome leaders of trade unions.

These individuals are believed to be open to giving and seeking patronage, help, support in exchange of physical favours either for self or spouse or for progeny or for others too under monetary considerations. They have less sense of self respect where seeking any favour is concerned. They often overlook and want to be overlooked for lapses in character of self, spouse or progeny too. They get into the habit of drinks and even if they themselves do not drink, they offer drinks to others.

These individuals make good courtiers, flatterers, suppliers of human flesh to those who want and can afford this luxury.

They are favoured with, depending on the stars of the spouse, both male and female progeny.

Their progeny is beautiful, charming and good at one or two branches of the fine arts.

These individuals are specially kind to the spouses of their progeny and do not mind going out of their way to extend help and support to them.

Sun and Saturn in the 5th House

Indian mythology (and astrology) believe that Saturn is son of Sun, and in spite of that relationship they are die-hard enemies.

The first target of this combination in the 5th house is the embryo in the womb. It gets adversely affected by any lapses on part of the mother, and sometimes it becomes difficult to avoid natural clearance of the pregnancy. Mother gets lengthy and intermittent labour pains, delivery is difficult sometimes leading to caesarean or forceps delivery of the child. After birth the child needs greater care than normal during the first year of its age, whatever its own stars in birth chart.

When at the school, the child is slow in grasp, quick in irritation, alert in becoming violent even towards seniors and teachers, tends to become ring leader, group-commander-type in school. The child doesn't hesitate to use unfair means at examinations and manages somehow to get promoted to the higher class, if necessary by threatening the examiners. The child is clever in collecting information about examiners. In competitive examinations, sometimes this individual gets caught while using unfair means, or at the stage of evaluation of the answer books, but manages to escape adverse outcome thereof.

This combination gives somewhat unattractive appearance to the legs, feet, thighs and even the waist region including front and back portions of the body below the tying line. It can also give intermittently skin ailment on the legs, in some cases hernia trouble, problems to liver, kidney or intestines, problems of the urinary system, stone in the gall bladder or elsewhere, peptic ulcers (particularly if Mars gets associated with this combination by presence in the 5th, 8th, 11th or 12th house).

Sun with Saturn combine gives, if a moving Sign (Aries, Cancer, Libra, Capricorn) be in the 5th house, considerable tours and travels, including journeys abroad, tendency to undertake difficult tasks, to indulge in acrobatics, stunt actions in films and serials, daring acts in fighting individually or on a battle field. The individual proves an efficient member of the Observer Corps, actions of risk on sea or in flying.

This combination makes an individual expert on arms, ammunitions, weapons, ordnance, warfare strategy and guiding any acts of offence and defence on a battlefield. The individual might shoulder big responsibilities in organisations responsible for peacetime and wartime use and usage of Atomic and Nuclear energy.

These individuals generally work as employees, may be low or even high, including in politics, with specialisation in labour, agriculture, defence, mining, minerals, industry, hydes and skins.

Sun and Rahu in the 5th House

In this combination, influence of Sun becomes less important and that of Rahu becomes prominent. Among more important influences of these two planets together in the 5th house are given below:

a) Risk to the safe running of the pregnancy upto the completion of the 5th month, but moreso till completion of the 3rd month. However Rahu doesn't interfere at the time of delivery at full para stage. Sun sometimes gives excess bleeding at the time of delivery.

b) Adverse effect on the grasping power of a child at its studies, moreso upto the age of 17 years. Parents and teachers have to take extra precaution to make the studies go home with the child by one or two repetitions. Such children needn't be burdened with advanced *Maths* (the tragedy in India is that Maths is compulsory in all courses of study, without exception upto the stage of the 12th class, i.e. completion of the Higher Secondary education). However if Mercury too is in the 5th house the child would not have much problem with grasping capacity nor with Maths, and it is a good thing that Mercury is often with Sun as it always is within 25 degrees of Sun.

c) These individuals have a divided mind, often a confused thinking on matters relating to administration (particularly in government and semi-government formations), and management (moreso in non-government firms and formations), and often seek from others confirmation of their ideas, decisions and actions.

d) These individuals have more artificial and less real respect and obedience towards teachers and elders, and a hidden sense of 'ego' works in their mind.

e) Dirty ideas take origin and get developed in their minds more easily and quickly than noble ones, but if Mercury too is in the 5th house, the dirty ideas would not get converted into practical shape.

f) They put on a greater show of their intelligence, wisdom and performance than what they actually are; and many a time they exhibit ideas and performance of others as their own; which can be classed as piracy.

g) Rahu reduces Sun's gift of the individual in the field of politics, reduces the understanding and effectivity of actions in that field.

h) Because of 8th position of the 5th house from the 10th house, which rules father, it should be examined carefully whether Rahu's conjunction with Sun in 5th house would give differences and ultimate confrontation between the individual and the father.

Sun and Ketu in the 5th House

Ketu is not as hard as Rahu and Ketu carries attributes more of Mercury than Saturn, which Rahu carries.

Thus firstly, it doesn't interfere much with functioning of Sun in the 5th house, in spite of forming an 'eclipse' combination.

Secondly because Sun too adversely affects, though to a smaller extent, the grasping capacity of a child, Ketu reduces Sun's adverse influence on the grasping capacity of the child, though not to the extent Mercury helps.

Further Ketu would help Sun in clear thinking, firmness in decisions and no looking towards others for confirmation of ideas and actions. It also enhances the individual's ability and capacity for administration and management, whether he is working for government, semi-government or for private sector.

Ketu would not give showy tendency to the individual, would give rather modesty, without, no doubt, damaging the administrative capacity granted by Sun to the individual.

Ketu also does not interfere with pregnancy of any woman, unless Sun is intent upon doing so, because of Capricorn or Aquarius in the 5th house.

SUN IN THE 6TH HOUSE

This is one of the most helpful positions. It gives very cordial relations with mother's brothers and sisters, and they too on their part try to be helpful to the individual.

It helps the individual fight illness and diseases, specially those relating to blood system and skin.

Sun helps in a positive and constructive manner in the field of politics and political activity, as also in the field of administration and management, specially in government and public sector.

If Jupiter too is 5th, 9th or 10th house, or even in the 4th house, Sun and Jupiter together help the individual in reaching a legislature at state or national level. But if Mercury is with Sun in the 6th house, the individual is rather unable to or at least ineffective in speaking from public stage as also in the Legislature and the chances of a second term becomes difficult for him or her.

Sun helps in suppression of or gaining favourable relationship with opponents, adversaries and to an extent die-hard enemies too.

The Western theory believes that Sun in 6th house gives differences with father, but Indian system does not attribute to this belief, because in reality 10th house rules father, and 6th house has 9: 5 relations with 10th house; therefore the question doesn't arise. 9th house rules inheritance of assets and liabilities from father (and grandfathers), but 6th house doesn't have relationship of confrontation in this case too because of Kendra relationship between the two houses.

One important point is that Sun has no connection with business and industry as such, and being a service-oriented planet, Sun doesn't help much in self-employment too, unless it is in the field of politics or administration or diplomacy of any kind. And conducive to these fields of activity, Sun gives an impressive personality with good health.

Sun and Moon in the 6th House

In terms of degrees, whenever Moon is within 11 to 12 degrees behind or ahead of Sun, Moon remains combust. Thus it is always better to know the positions of these planets in terms of degrees. Normally Moon, unless in its own Rasi (Cancer), is less effective when in combust position; however when it gets ahead of Sun, Moon resumes effectivity as it proceeds ahead, and when it gets 12 degrees ahead of Sun it is fully effective in its own right. Suppose Moon is on 18th degree and Sun is on 4th degree in the same house, Moon has regained its effectivity, in fact it started regaining gradually as soon as Moon reached even one degree ahead of Sun in the same Rasi.

This principle is applicable to all combinations of Sun and Moon in any house. This point should be kept in mind while determining Moon's effectivity in any house with Sun.

Moon invariably gives depression of the mind, tendency to think more about the past and less about the future, which can be called as retrograde thinking and brooding. If both Sun and Moon are in Capricorn or Aquarius, or even in Gemini, some kind of temporary mental disturbance (or even disorder) is likely during the Mahadasa or Antardasas of Sun and Moon mutually under each other.

Sun is a strict administrator, but Moon gives a sense of regrets over strict commands and orders, and such regrets are sometimes expressed to the persons giving the commands or orders, and often it carries reactions on part of the person giving commands or orders.

Moon diverts the mind from studies every now and then, and to save the Exam results likely to be caused by this diversion from studies, Sun encourages use of influence over the Examiners or school and college authorities to save loss of a year to the child.

Some astrologers feel that Moon in 6th house with Sun gives bad health in childhood, but it is not always so, because to a great extent it depends on the lord of the 6th house and its position in the birth chart. Further if Mars, Saturn, Rahu or Herschel be in the 3rd, 6th or 11th house, the child would enjoy perfect health in childhood too. On the other hand, parents or guardians in residential schools try to keep the child overdosed with nutritional medicines, which the child resists, and secretly avoids, giving the impression of having consumed them.

Moon, now and then, adversely affects the cordial relations with maternal uncles and aunts, though not on a permanent basis, because Moon is a fast moving planet.

Moon also gives a tendency of jealousy to the individual. However when the individual perceives jealousy of others towards self, the individual grudges it, forgetting that it was initially the individual who gave origin to jealousy. Moon encourages quarrels and fist fights or even more violent fights, and the conjunct planet Sun has to descend to the individual's rescue. If the fight is at the level of a group or political entity, Moon is not an efficient strategist and Sun again comes to the individual's rescue.

Sun and Mars in the 6th House

To correctly describe this combination, there is a very suitable saying in Hindi, "*sone mai suhaga* (sweet fragrance in gold)".

Sun and Mars, whatever the Rasi in the 6th house, protect the individual in every manner possible, all the time and virtually everywhere, except the bedroom or in a quarrel between husband and wife.

They give a sturdy physique, perfect health, capacity for hard work and ability to endure hardships.

These individuals overflow with valour, energy, boldness, courage and feel brave inside and outside, in individual fights, in-group fights and also on battlefields. They achieve success in competitive tests and interviews for administrative services, defence services, police service, in electrical and electronic trades. They prove able administrators and also capable engineers, specially in electrical and electronic lines. They can endure hard work and long hours of work.

They are always keen to have a self-owned residence, and actually they come to own more real estate than their actual needs. They believe more in sale and purchase of property every now and then, and always no doubt on profit. They prove more honest and straightforward brokers in real estate as compared to others in the field.

They rarely suffer from any disorder of the blood system or skin ailment, and if they get any blood injury, it gets cured easily and quickly. Women rarely get trouble with their menstrual system, nor do they get their menopause earlier than normal age.

They are not jealous of others and do not tolerate unwarranted jealousy. They are normally friends or neutrals to all and rarely enemy of anyone, though this theory doesn't apply when they are functioning on behalf of their state or country or province or nation or any administrative set-up, or when functioning or behalf of their community, religion or cult.

They keep very cordial relations with maternal uncles and aunts, and many a time it happens that for some special reasons or circumstances, they are brought up in childhood by their maternal family. If the 4th or 9th house is owned by Sun or Mars, there are strong chances of their going into adoption to a member of the maternal family, or be favoured with substantial moveable or immoveable gifts.

Unless these two planets are under influence of Jupiter, these individuals do not take any initiative in litigation. If need be they manage the matter by mere threat or at the most by physical valour-cum-violence.

Sun and Mercury in the 6th House

It has to be remembered that Sun and Mercury are often together, and Mercury is equally effective even in a state of combustion in the 6th house. If the 6th house belongs to Mercury or Venus, Mercury becomes more effective than Sun.

The first hit of Mercury is in the childhood of the individual, by getting a dull and slow grasp of studies, resulting in rebukes, scoldings and sometimes corporal punishment (though prohibited, teachers still take recourse to it!)

At the time of delivery, the mother suffers labour pains for longer than anticipated and if a hard planet is in the 8th or 12th house and a Rasi owned by Mars or Saturn be in the 6th house, recourse is taken to caesarean delivery.

The individual has poor command on language as also on grammar and composition. If, because of influence of Sun in the 6th house, the individual finds a table job, or a teaching job, or a journalistic job under government or government controlled formation, at least in India, they are able to pull on, no need to explain the reasons (most readers know them). However, if in a journalistic job in Media or in an organisation producing pamphlets, booklets and books, these individuals either seek active help from colleagues and subordinates or change their job every now and then.

They are often originators of jealousy, backbiting, undeserved criticism of others, and at the same time taking the safeguard against litigation for witch-hunting and defamation.

In school and college and at playground they create situation of getting beaten up by other boys and girls, notwithstanding whether the individual getting the beating is a boy or a girl. It is good luck that protectors from beatings also come forward at the same time, because of Sun too in the 6th house.

They are neither good warriors at battlefield, nor efficient strategist, but one quality of these individual is that they can produce impressive and convincing publicity material for propaganda of any and every kind.

Being in the company of Sun, they always develop quality of 'Yes-Sir' 'Yes-Madam' in them and they rarely betray in the field of flattery, including true or false praise. This quality has often been noticed in the birth-charts of *Bhaats, Chaarans,* even bards of cheap type. They can talk and sing very loudly and effectively from public stage, in demonstrations, in leading protesting groups, rallies and at any occasion of slogan shouting. They are better in this type of work than in written work, right from the stage of attending to homework in school, to the stage of job-work in later life. But they are less talkative in bedroom, and patiently listen to love-mixed or love-lacking talks and rebukes of the partner in the bedroom.

These individuals are often keen to leave a legacy of good collection of books to their progeny, though they do not directly bother much about the education of the progeny. In this behalf they depend more on the self-effort and on good or bad luck of the child.

Sun and Jupiter in the 6th House

This can be classed as both happy and unhappy combination in the 6th house, more unhappy than happy.

This combination gives unhappy results in the matter of memory related to studies in school and college (which is generally made up by written notes). It also gives unhappy results in the matter of litigation (specially one initiated by the individual), in economy planning on behalf of self or family, non-cordial relations with maternal family, unwanted and unwarranted misunderstandings, quarrels, fights and break off of trustworthy friendships.

The worst unhappy results are in the field of material possessions.

Loss by cheating, by speculation, by theft, by highway robbery, by theft from a safety vault, dissolution of partnership in business, by payment of compensation for loss to others deemed to have been caused by the individual.

Loss by payment of ransom for kidnapped person or for kidnapping of self, embezzlement or pilferage by own staff and employees. It can be by dropping of jewellery or costly items by spouse, payment of dowry, money paid for buying divorce from the spouse (there have been cases where wife paid heavy money to buy her divorce, because she had another man waiting for marriage with her or even otherwise).

Loss of lands-in-grant, on change in government or change in law or change in policy of government, or by malefic intentions of the descendants of the grantor, confiscation of property or assets under a decree of a court of law or under order of the Head of a government or under law of the Land.

Then Jupiter tries its best to give health problems relating to respiratory system, kidney, liver and pain in abdomen above the naval point. No doubt, Sun helps in preventing these complaints of health, but much depends on the strength of the two planets as also association of other planets. If nothing else, Sun helps in quick recovery, though Sun is unable to cut the heavy cost of medical treatment imposed by Jupiter.

Jupiter doesn't give fear of verbal fights and unimplemented threats. No doubt Jupiter adversely affects the masculinity of the male partner, sometimes leading to unhappiness with wife or leading even to separation or ultimate divorce.

The happy results of this combination in the 6th house are that the individual gets compromise easily and quickly in quarrels and even in civil cases in courts or before any other forum of law. Sun gets help and support to the individual from unexpected quarters like government officials, economists, teachers of student life, advocates and jurists, also from Legislators, and this support helps in getting out of trouble so long as the trouble doesn't relate to any serious criminal charge. In student life, grace marks or grace addition to percentage often helps in saving the year of studies.

In hour of need the individual gets loans from banking institutions and private sources easily, quickly and on easy terms and conditions, which money is often needed by the individual to meet losses in business and speculation.

The opinion of these individuals counts in matters of diplomacy, and they themselves prove as successful envoys and ambassadors or consuls general or as representatives at United Nations and its various organisations.

Sun and Venus in the 6th House

This is a difficult combination, because even in combust position, Venus is fully effective. It has always to be kept in mind that because Venus (and Mercury) being nearer to both, Earth and Sun in Solar system, Venus never moves more than two houses away from Sun, and as a result Venus too goes combust often, though less often than Mercury. That is the main reason why Venus (and Mercury) does not become ineffective.

Factually, none of Mars, Mercury, Jupiter, Venus and Saturn becomes remarkably less effective with Sun (in a combust position). It is only Moon, which becomes less effective when with Sun, provided Moon is behind Sun in terms of degrees.

Another equally important point is that Venus is, correctly speaking, exclusively ruling planet, astrologically, of love, marriage, marriage-partner and married life. No doubt Mars too has an important role in matters related to marriage and married life. Others planets play a role, in a limited sense, important to matters relating to the marriage partner or the partner in love. And it has not to be forgotten that Venus is the exclusive overriding planet of the 7th house (which concerns love and marriage etc.) and when in 6th house it is in a damaging position to the 7th house being in 12th position from the 7th house. In plain language, with Sun or not, Venus in 6th house is often giving unpleasant results to love and marriage, even if 6th house has Taurus or Libra owned by Venus itself, or Pisces (house of exaltation for Venus).

Venus is capable of giving damaging or hurting, initially or in later life, the capacity to satisfy the partner in the bed, reason can be any. This lack of capacity adversely affects the love life or the married life. Separation is easy and less hurting to the feelings of either of the two in love life or married life. In orthodox families, sometimes the spouse is intent upon tolerating the situation. In all other cases, the ultimate result is separation and ultimately divorce.

Yet another position in this regard is that because Venus is intent upon disturbing or damaging the sex life of anyone of the two partners or of both, it can be by circumstances also. For example, such as being stationed at different places, as in the defence services, one being posted at a non-family station, or one partner residing or working in different country and the Visa problem standing between the two. It can also be the restrictions imposed on the two by their elders. (There have been several cases where the father of the boy died of lack of vitality resulting in failure of heart, the mother of the boy allowed her son to have sex on very restricted scale. The mother sometimes forced the boy to sleep in the mother's bedroom to keep the boy away from wife, and kept both of them under observation even during daytime). It can be lack of proper or suitable accommodation, moreso in cities where several families share two rooms or even one room in all. Therefore the couples fix weekly or bi-weekly turns for use of the room at night, moreso where climatic conditions allow sleeping in the open or in the veranda.

Because of 'dowry' problem or demands of one family on the other family subsequent to marriage, the bride goes back to her parental family, and for sake of social upkeep of status, legal separation and divorce proceedings are not gone into. At least this is very common in India and some of the middle-east countries too. Another reason can be childlessness of the couple, and without verifying the reasons thereof specially those relating to the capacity of the boy, the bride is sent back to her parents.

In some cases, after the marriage, one of the couple comes under some serious disease or suffers such injury as prevents conjugal life for a long time or might be even for the rest of the life, leading to absence of sexual relations between husband and wife.

Yet in other cases, one partner, more often the husband, is

involved even before marriage with another girl, or gets involved with another girl after marriage, and therefore avoids cohabitation with own wife. Cases are there of wife too avoiding the husband for this purpose but they are very rare cases. It is often so, because in every country the husband has an upper hand over the wife, whatever be the dominating nature of wife and her independent income, or capacity to earn an income enough for her living.

Sun and Venus together are capable of giving illness of the chest (breast), cough, cold and rough throat leading to breathing trouble too. It can be general weakness not affecting the bedroom life, tuberculosis, sometimes cancer of the breast specially if Mars is in the 8th or 12th or in 4th house. It can also give lack of feeding milk after child birth to the woman, thin built of body resulting from less flesh, pain in palms and soles of the feet, with or without reason swelling of any fleshy limb or part of the body, rather frequently.

Another very important trouble caused by this combination is quarrels, fights, litigation, criminal charges owing to any woman or wife. Also quarrel and fighting at casinos, chess games, at gambits, dance-houses, at brothels, competition between two lovers or suitors for one and the same girl, at places of group orgies, and similar other reasons or at similar places.

Many of these individuals receive support and relief from politicians, legislators, administrators, police officials to get out of trouble of any kind described above, no doubt for a price, sometimes in terms of supply of a girl.

Otherwise too, some of these individuals are expert in trading in women, running brothels, kidnapping of girls for ransom or other criminal activity. Whether men or women, these individuals indulge in smuggling as also in sea piracy, because they are assured of protection from law and order system by their contacts and also by those in their pay. Otherwise too, these criminal-activity-oriented individuals prove very helpful to the politicians and legislators at election-time, because all those who run a crime ring have to maintain a gang of vagabonds and mischief-mongers, team of lower and inferior-status workers. Even when these individuals run pubs, public houses, bars and taverns, they definitely need the service of vagabonds and mischief-mongers without whom it is virtually impossible in modern times to run these formations.

Sun and Saturn in the 6th House

Sun and Saturn are deemed as father and son in mythology as well as in astrology, and even then they are die-hard enemies to each other. In spite of this fact, they are both very helpful to the 6th house in their own individual way.

They both protect the individual against illness and any disease of long-duration, against opponent, competitor, adversary or enemy, against any blackmail, generally also against kidnapping.

Normally Sun and Saturn do not give an attitude to the individual to create enemies. These two planets provide protection against any serious injury in an accident (though it depends on transit-position of Saturn and Saturn's placement in the yearly chart).

If the individual stands for election to any office of profit, including for Legislature (Senate or Parliament included), they secure help in a clandestine manner from government staff. They also seek open help of slogan shouters, mob collectors for meetings, arranging street-corner meetings, mobbing of crowds, reaching the voters by several other methods. Thus in their own way, they put in best effort for securing success to the contesting individual.

The individual normally doesn't feel immobilised because by not owning a means of transport of own, though in the normal course, the individual does come to possess some means of transport.

Unless when the individual is on path of progress to active politics and office of profit or to appointment to at least a middle-level post in bureaucracy, the individual prefers buying or owning old vehicle, appearing like a new one.

If the individual is a candidate for any middle or senior

level post in government service or in public sector, these two planets in their own independent way see to it that the individual gets selected, or is at least on the "wait-list". However in this case, the individual suffers from embittered relationship between Sun and Saturn in the sense that the individual gets harassment at the hands of superior bosses, or at the hands of organised subordinates. It might also result in either very heavy work unmanageable during office hours or no work at all leaving the individual ideally sitting at desk. Another harassment can be in the shape of frequent transfers, often to posts or places inconvenient or discomfortable to the individual. Refusal of any kind of leave is another method of harassment in offices.

However in spite of these harassment, the individual stands firm in the saddle.

This combination gives very fluctuating relations of affection and jealousy with maternal uncles and aunts and their children. It can be embarrassment and comfort both, if the individual has to stay in maternal home for any long duration. And all hell descends on the individual if question of or actual adoption takes place by a maternal grandparent or even by a maternal, uncle or aunt.

In person to person quarrel and fighting these individuals excel others. Even in exchange of blows and serious violent attack, they don't get defeated, and if defeated by any trick or chance, they do not take it easily; revenge figures soon.

If the fight is between two communities, two religionists, two countries, they do not formulate the strategy, but once the strategy is handed over to them, they ardently implement it even at the cost of own limb and life!

They often render very personal and useful service at the time of any mass calamity such as famine, floods, earthquake, epidemic and they mobilise support from others, including financial and medical aid.

The last and more important point, a kind of minus point of this combination of Saturn and Sun or a weakness of the individual is more often he (than she) is unkind, and has unhelpful attitude towards ailments, complaints of health and paucity of funds where own spouse is concerned. It can be to the extent that the individual considers complaints of the spouse as exaggerated and untrustworthy, or underrates the complaints for remedy, or delays the remedy.

At the same time the individual is quite demanding of the spouse in physical relationship, making no secrecy of the demand.

Sun and Rahu in the 6th House

Nothing much to say about this combination except that in spite of it being a kind of 'eclipse' combination, Rahu allows Sun to function in its own way, and Rahu does not impose too much of interference upon Sun.

In matters of health and defence of self or community or own religionists or own country, this combine gives the same results as Saturn but not with the same solidity and vehemence, because Rahu is after all a shadow planet

In the matter of physical relationship with spouse the individual is very adjusting and co-operative by nature. The individual is more attentive and active in attending to complaints of health or paucity of funds from the spouse. However the spouse of the individual does interfere in individual's relations with his or her parental family, and if the couple happens to be living separately or distantly from parental family of either, the spouse does not approve of individual's frequent visits to the parental home. The attitude of the spouse is more cordial towards a brother or a sister of the individual. Further, the spouse of the individual doesn't easily and quickly forget any inconvenience, discomfort, embarrassment or insult by the parental family of the individual, be it the husband or the wife.

Sun and Ketu in the 6th House

Unlike Rahu, Ketu does interfere in day-to-day life of the individual and spouse thereof. Instead of any act and action, Ketu with Sun functions against the spouse only by words and critical behaviour on part the individual, and the spouse retorts it by unwelcome-type behaviours towards guests and visitors, whether they are guests of the husband or of the wife.

The criticism is all the more bitter where the individual meets with failure in any venture about which the spouse had given an adverse or unapproving opinion at the initial stage itself.

In virtually all other matters, Ketu is a mute spectator of Sun's functioning.

SUN IN THE 7TH HOUSE

In marriage matters, the individual gets a spouse full of ego and mild-type anger with no regret over its exposition. The spouse might belong to a family of bureaucrats or politicians or a person in senior management in private sector. The spouse has no doubt good and presentable personality infusing self-confidence.

The mutual relations between husband and wife can be described as a mixture of sweetness and sourness. The couple get better results if both are in active politics, but if only one is in active politics or is back-bencher, the life is unhappy now and then at home.

These gentlemen are sometimes considered a little below the expectation of the spouse, in virtually majority of matters, including physical relationship. If however Venus too is in the 7th house, or Saturn is in close vicinity of Sun (in the 7th house), the husband would prove worthy of wife's expectations in bed.

If the individual stands for any office based on election, a severe fight is ahead and sometimes even trusted lieutenants and followers go absent at the right moment. And if Saturn or Rahu or Herschel is with Sun in the 7th house, victory is difficult to achieve. The individual should take clues from initial sources of support or opposition.

If it is a question of selection for a coveted post or cadre in government or semi-government formation, selection is not within easy reach. If however Mercury is in vicinity of 10 degrees to Sun, or Jupiter or Venus be in the 5th house, or Moon be in the 10th house (or at least in the 9th house) selection would be easy. Saturn and Rahu too can help if situated in 3rd, 6th or 11th house, but more at the interview than at the written test. If Moon, Mercury, Jupiter or Venus is in the 6th or the 8th house, it is better to get out of the competition. Non-selection would dishearten in attempts for other posts for which selection is without written test, based only on an interview or on approach of the right type to the right person on the Selection Board.

Litigation should be avoided as far as possible, specially if the individual has no approach to any important person in politics or bureaucracy. Even then sometimes the judge on the Bench doesn't bother about any approach and goes by own opinion and impression, who often moves on one track only that gets registered in the judge's thinking.

Sun alone normally does not lead a marriage towards long-term separation or legal separation or ultimate divorce. Sun can however cause ailment of the skin, any disease generated by physical contact, all the more so if Venus is in the 6th or 8th house, or Mars is in 4th, 7th, 8th or 12th house. Timely treatment is effective. Sun in 7th house can cause ulcers, specially peptic ulcers, but doesn't lead on its own to any cancerous complaint of health.

The individual is not very clever in any sale and purchase deal, specially of property or any valuable item like jewellery, gold ornament or pure gold. It is always better to examine the position of Mars with respect to property and position of Jupiter with respect to other items or assets of high value.

Sun and Moon in the 7th House

Some people think that because Moon goes combust with Sun rather in totality, Moon becomes inoperative and practically ineffective when with Sun. No it is not so in all cases.

This combination gives ups and downs in married life, no break off and no compromise. Life just drags its feet on concrete road full of pitfalls and rocks lying here and there. The more the husband and wife try to understand each other, the more they misunderstand the partner opposite. Each one thinks not having got a spouse of own liking. Whether factually a better choice was ever available or not, the partner claims better 'left-out' choices available, even if they be imaginary.

Same as above is the case with mental and physical health of the two. Complaints are constantly there, solid grounds or slippery grounds. Exaggeration is not lacking. It takes longer time for both to understand the psychology of each other and strike adjustment.

The husband and wife have to be more careful and preventive against mental torture, as it might lead to serious mental trouble to the sufferer.

Where question of quarrel or fight with others is concerned, the husband and wife normally join hands, forgetting mutual differences, but if it is a question of physical fight, the couple proves defeated as coward and weakly.

This combination is neither helpful nor harmful in matters of litigation before any forum of law; not these two planets ensure victory or defeat. It is better for the couple to avoid litigation, unless it is between themselves. Then matters depend to a great extent not on Sun and Moon combination, but on what Rasi is in the 7th house, where is the lord of that Rasi. Also where Jupiter and Venus are, what are mutual relations between Jupiter and Venus and what relations Jupiter and Venus have with the lord of the 7th house.

In matters of sale and purchase of any costly item, the husband and wife rarely have agreement. The opinion of the dominating of the two prevails depending on the Rasi in the 7th house and position of its lord. If that lord is friendly with Sun, husband's opinion would prevail, if it is friendly to Moon, wife's opinion would prevail. Further if Moon is behind Sun in degrees, wife would have to surrender to the wishes of the husband. If Moon is ahead of Sun in terms of degrees, wife would bring the husband round to her opinion.

Sun and Mars in the 7th House

In this house, undoubtedly, Mars prevails over Sun, whatever subject relating to the 7th house is under consideration.

In the matter of marriage and married life, the spouse has temperament full of pride and anger. The life of the individual becomes that of a constant sufferer. Often the ultimate result is failure of the marriage, by divorce or death. It starts with separate living of the married couple. In some cases deprivation of physical relationship between husband and wife for anything from one to seven years is likely. The break-up periods, in continuity or intermittently can be owing to other unavoidable circumstances, such as one of the two residing in different towns or in different states or county or in different countries. Or one of the two is suffering from some such ailment or disease as warrants avoidance of physical relationship. Or there prevails pressure of the parents or guardians to avoid frequency of physical relationship owing to fear of existing or anticipated ailment or health complaint. Angry outburst of one of the two leads to avoidance of physical relationship the same day or for several days and or a few weeks but not for long period. Compromise on this account would depend on the relations prior to the quarrel.

Whenever it is found that the individual has these two (Sun and Mars) in the 7th house, it is always better to have the horoscopes of the boy and the girl matched before marriage. It is possible only if the parents get a birth-chart drawn (if not a detailed horoscope which is always more useful in this behalf) as soon after the birth of the child as possible.

No doubt, the argument always goes that in love-based marriages, it is not possible for the boy or the girl to get the birth-charts examined and then proceed with love affair. Love takes origin and develops without birth-charts. In such cases, if correct time, date and place of birth of both become available (if not the original horoscope), the birth-chart be got prepared as soon as differences and quarrels begin to take origin between husband and wife. Some times remedial suggestions based on matching of the planets in the two horoscopes work wonders to bring harmony between the husband and wife.

In matters relating to quarrels and fights with others, be they relatives or blatant outsiders, the husband and wife are always together in putting up an effective fight and as far as possible, the husband and wife strive to be victorious. And they often are victorious!

In matters of sale and purchase, the individual does not possess the acumen of a businessman, and it is always better for him or her to consult some expert before finalising any important deal. While negotiating the transaction, the individual shouldn't lose temper whatever the provocation from the party buying or selling. If the individual loses temper, he or she would be at a disadvantage if the deal is finalised with the same party. Sometimes the buying or selling parties (or at least their brokers or go-betweens) have mutual contacts with one another. In that case the stories of angry behaviour of the individual travel to other prospective buyer or seller with added tails and tales.

In matters of fights, the individual proves a good fighter or warrior or commander of a situation, or commander of a battalion. But the strategy for the fight should be formulated by experts other than the individual. The individual may associate with formation of the strategy if invited. Otherwise the individual should stay contented with implementation.

While sending troops for liberation of Bangladesh from Pakistan, Mrs. Indira Gandhi the then Prime Minister of India, adopted a strategy based on astrological consultation – of selecting retired Brigadier S.S.Uban, conferring on him the rank of an acting Major General for commanding the operation of this important project. The date of start of the operation was fixed according to the favourability of stars of both Mrs. Gandhi and Major General S.S.Uban.

This astrological consultation is not hearsay but a first person account, because the senior author was the astrologer who gave the astrological consultations on both questions – of selection of Major General S.S.Uban, and fixation of the date for commencement of the operations.

Sun and Mercury in the 7th House

Mercury is during most part of the year, in conjunction with Sun. Whether combust or not, Mercury is fully effective in the 7th house.

The individual often finds an educated person as spouse. And education of the spouse helps in mildly controlling the hot temperament of the individual whether towards the spouse or towards others. Unless Mars interferes in the matter directly, Mars being in 8th, 12th or 1st or even 2nd house, Mercury not only protects the marriage, but also leads it to peaceful and sweet running, irrespective of the Rasi in the 7th house. Mercury gives capacity to the (educated or at least intelligent) spouse to create an atmosphere of understanding between husband and wife.

In matters of sale and purchase of any important item, the wisdom of the spouse often proves helpful and profitable for the couple. Mercury doesn't let the spouse feel opposed to consultation with experts in any transaction related to real estate.

In matters of litigation, Mercury tries to stop Sun from going into litigation. But if litigation starts, Mercury always gives very useful suggestion with regard to the wording of the complaint or its reply as the case may be. If the individual is required to give an oral statement before any Legal forum, because of Mercury, the individual stands the ground well with regard to cross-examination. It becomes very difficult for the party opposite to bring out any contradictions in the statement of the individual. However Mercury neither helps nor harms the outcome of the litigation.

Mercury with Sun in the 7th house helps the individual against minor ailments and short-lived diseases, but not much in matters of serious illness and long-term disease. On the other hand, Mercury makes the individual feel greater suffering and pain than what actually is. In any case of this type, it helps a lot if family members and friends (or even visitors) lead the sick individual into repeated conversation, no doubt with gaps; it would reduce the individual's impression about the intensity of suffering and pain.

Sun and Jupiter in the 7th House

It be remembered that Sun is the King, and Jupiter is Sun's Guru (Teacher, priest, Adviser, all combined). Thus Guru enjoys a bit dominating influence over Sun. Going combust too doesn't mar the capacity of Jupiter to function and show results.

Jupiter in 7th house is always very helpful in finding a suitable match for marriage and for running the married life sweetly and peacefully, without much impact of the occasional annoyance expressed by one partner towards the other. If there be any problem in begetting children, Jupiter's presence in 7th house helps solving that too. The King and Priest together do not allow economic problems of high magnitude to crop up in married life. If under the influence of other planets, say Mars in 2nd or 12th house or any other planet in 12th house, any difficult position crops up in financial position of the couple, Jupiter tries to solve it. It has to be remembered that Mercury and Venus can never be in the 12th house when Sun is in the 7th house, because both these stars move within the vicinity of Sun. Jupiter in 7th house with Sun helps in quick repayment of loans obtained or debts incurred by the couple.

Jupiter's conjunction with Sun helps the individual securing a post in Economic services of the country or the state, failing which secures the individual a career in accounts and audit system. These two planets together help in getting an appointment as a public prosecutor or government lawyer. Selection from Bar to the Bench is another avenue of reaching judgeship. Whether the individual (man or woman) would stay honest and straightforward or would go corrupt as a judge would depend on the Rasi in the 7th house and the position of its lord in birth-chart and Navamsha chart.

If the individual goes into own business or into service of any business concern, he or she proves successful and gains confidence of the customers as well as the employers.

The individual secures victory in any litigation, so long as the litigation is not against any government organ or public sector undertaking. The individual proves an expert in drafting plaints and replies to plaints for submission to any forum of law. But the individual doesn't gain big reputation and impressive success while working as a member or partner of any lawyers' firm, because on account of Sun being with Jupiter in the 7th house. The individual's mind is more government-side oriented.

The individual proves a good adviser in any matter of sale or purchase of big magnitude. If the transaction relates only to husband and wife, or family of either of the two, then too good gains are assured. No doubt when the sale or purchase is on behalf of the family of either husband or wife, the individual would keep an eye on what is 'in it for him or her'.

The individual is an efficient adviser on the financial side of any defence services project, but nothing beyond that. The individual can neither formulate a strategy, nor implement it successfully.

In cases of kidnapping, the individual believes more in paying ransom, with or without the help of a politician or a bureaucrat, but certainly not with the help of law and order system.

Sun and Venus in the 7th House

Though Venus too goes combust in the company or vicinity of Sun, Venus is fully effective in the 7th house, because Venus is the "*Kaaraka*" (main result-giving or ruling factor) in matters related to marriage, marriage-partner i.e. spouse and married life)".

With Sun, Venus is more inclined to lead the individual into love-based marriage. Failing this, into love-based marriage converted into arranged marriage. In other words, a matrimonial match eyed by the family and planted for the individual to develop a love affair. The family of the individual or families on both sides keep an eye on developments between the boy and the girl!

Whether the marriage is a love-based or an arranged one, greater emphasis is on beauty, complexion, height, and presentability of the personality of the two. But the bow is often held by the family taking the initial step. Rejections often happen, not only in India but in other developed and advanced countries too. Once the alliance has been fixed and finalised, the question of "give and take"(in other words dowry) arises in at least 60 percent of proposals. It is better to do so. Sometimes the fully ripe proposal approaching fixation of date of marriage also gets dropped under this phenomenon.

Otherwise too, it is good, specially for the girl, because often the girl (now bride) gets tortured for dowry in cash or kind or securing favours for the son-in-law. No doubt, bride burning and physical torture cases are rare in countries with white population, because the course to divorce is easy and quick in those countries. Also because the status and prestige of the families on the two sides are not involved. In India, joint family system is fast breaking, but even where the husband and wife reside independently, that is separately from the joint family or parental family, the ghost of this or that demand for cash or kind from the husband or his family looms over the head of the bride in many a case.

It is always advisable to finalise the question of demand for cash and kind (named *dowry*) once for all before the marriage itself. It is not very difficult to detect whether the parents of the boy or the boy himself are very greedy for easy money and prosperity, no doubt at the cost of the bride or her family. It is the experience of the author that girls are deemed burdens by 50% of the parents of the girls, who are not bothered as to what happens to the girl after marriage. In such cases the girls suffer all taunts and torture without the path to parental home open to them.

The main question is whether the individual is a boy or a girl. In spite of Sun's presence in the 7th house with Venus, it is common to impose allegations of bad character on the girl.

What can happen is like this. The husband narrates own affair with one or more girl(s) he has had or falsely claims to have had before marriage. Sometimes these stories are true, but often they are imaginary. Then the boy (husband) persuades or compels the bride to open out about her own love affair before marriage. It is all initially treated as a joke by the husband. Sometimes the foolish girl also narrates her own affair (true or half-truth or even a crush, or infatuation), which is then used by the husband to blackmail the girl or her family for demands of money or, assets, or other favours.

There could be some more dark sides of this matter, but it is better left to the readers to guess!

In matters of sale and purchase, the individual generally goes by outer appearance of the item, whether it is real estate or any costly item, and overlooks the inner weak points. But there the wisdom of the spouse normally helps, provided the spouse is in the picture or taken into confidence before finalisation of the transaction. In many cases, the individual is sufferer or at a loss, because the spouse was not taken into confidence! It cannot be helped, because the impact of Sun with Venus is like that.

These individuals are good neither in drafting plaints (petitions) or their replies nor in advising on any matter involving point of law (and litigation). These individuals are good neither in economic nor in accounts and audit nor in management of big finances, except running own household or own business venture. In business venture too, it is better for these individual to take help of experts in economics, accounting and financial management, if the size and investments in the business have scope for doing so.

It is always better for these people to keep off defence Matters, even if in the government employ.

These individuals make good actors and actresses, whether on stage or in films etc attracting the masses. They make very impressive singers or instrumental musicians, or players on musical programs including dancing. These artists are more eager to be attached to any government formation or having approach to various *Darbars* (courts) of rulers, Kings, Emperors, Governors, and Viceroys.

One weakness in these individuals often is that of loose character physically or mentally, often with their co-workers, their students, their followers and casual visitors. They rarely get caught on the wrong side.

Sun and Saturn in the 7th House

Recall that Sun and Saturn, despite being father and son, are enemies to each other and when together, they become bitter enemies. However, Saturn being stronger and often has an upper hand on Sun, unless both are under *drishti* from or in combination with Mars. Soft planets do not bring any remarkable variation in the effect of Saturn in the 7th house, which rules love affair, marriage, married life, mutual relationship between wife and husband. Saturn (with Sun) rules sale and purchase, struggle in formation of plans and their implementation when they relate to self, vis-à-vis source of income or profession.

Let us take the most important subject of the 7th house first of all – it is marriage and married life. The spouse often has ego, irritation and intention to pick up a quarrel or at least heated exchange or one-sided utterance of harsh words, between husband and wife. It might be meant for the spouse or family of the spouse but the target of the oral outburst is the spouse. Actual exchange of blows and violence is not ruled out and neither of the two remains a silent sufferer whatever the Rasi in the 7th house.

Exchange of violence and beatings would depend to certain extent on position of the lord of the 7th house, presence of any other planet in the 7th house or direct *drishti* of any planet from the Ascendant. Respective positions of Sun and Saturn in the Navamsha chart of the husband, and Trinshansha chart of the wife also matters in this behalf. In this type of event, there can be severe injury to either of the two, needing hospitalisation too. If Jupiter is in 6th, 8th or 12th house or even in 2nd house, law and order system is likely to figure in, ultimately proceedings in a forum of law or arbitration.

In spite of oral and sometimes physical exchanges, the marriage keeps working, and it doesn't fail in giving progeny. Progeny too helps to a great extent continuance of the marriage. It avoids a step leading to divorce or permanent separation, legal or otherwise. The main reason is that Saturn (with Sun) helps the spouse or a companion in the bed, and this keeps the marriage dragging its feet and running!

It is always better to examine the position of Mars in the horoscope of the individual, or of both. If Mars is not damaging it, the marriage may work well and good. If Mars on its own (wherever it is in the birth chart), and Sun with Saturn in 7th house are bent upon disturbing, damaging or destroying the marriage as such, it is always better to examine the planets of the boy and the girl before actual engagement and marriage. Unless Venus is directly and favourably associated with Sun and Saturn in 7th house, chances of love-based marriage of the individual are rare and remote. Positively the position of Venus and Mars (and indirectly of Sun and Saturn too) be carefully examined also in the Navamsha chart of the boy and Trinshansha chart of the girl. All this exercise is not possible in love-based marriages moreso in countries with white population or in undeveloped country with majority aborigine population, where divorce and remarriage are always easy, not as difficult as in India!

These individuals are good neither in sale and purchase nor in negotiations for sale and purchase or any other matter. These individuals are often rigid in approach and exhibit irritation in face-to-face talks. Similarly, litigation is not the subject of these individuals. They must always engage efficient and loyal lawyers. Cases are not rare where lawyers got purchased by the opposite party for one consideration or the other.

It is very important that these individuals keep off extra marital affair, casual indulgence in physical relationship with persons other than the spouse. Chances of venereal disease or even AIDS are not rare and remote. This type of activity doesn't remain hidden from the spouse and rarely fails to give differences and quarrel, or the spouse develops unwelcome attitude towards physical relationship.

Sun and Rahu in the 7th House

Undoubtedly it is a kind of 'eclipse' combination and Sun functions in a subdued condition with Rahu close-by. Another important point is that whatever house Rahu occupies, it gives a sharp sense of 'ego' to the person or relation governed by that house.

Thus it is clear that Rahu gives a sense of sharp ego to the spouse and once the spouse feels hurt ego, the sense of annoyance is created by Sun there.

Rahu gives extra flesh to the middle parts of the body, but

it doesn't go flabbiest, because occasional generation of annoyance and anger keep the flesh sturdy (if not tight).

Rahu with Sun creates disturbed moments in married life, but because of Ketu in the Ascendant, things would stay within manageable wisdom. This combination generates threat of violence, but not actual violence unless there is interference of Mars, Saturn or Herschel from the 1st, 8th or 12th house in the birth chart of husband or wife quarrels. If Venus joins this combination in the 7th house, or occupies 9th or 12th house the third person makes an appearance in the marriage. This appearance of the third person can be casual or on a regular basis or it can be just meeting with call girls or male gigolo. Then Rahu and Sun combination becomes more actively operative towards disturbance in married life. However if it is Venus in the 6th house, there is a general suspicion in the mind of the one of the two without any substance about a third person. This suspicion gets cleared at the maximum within 18 months.

Since 7th house concerns sale and purchase of costly items, Rahu doesn't fail in bringing to the forefront the question of payment of a part of the price in unaccounted money. Often both parties agree to this arrangement, finally mutually settling the percentage of unaccounted portion of the price.

The question of strategy relating to any cold war or exchange of firing or actual battle in defence matters at national level, crops up with relation to Rahu and Sun combine. But Rahu being a shadow planet, the individual just gives, if asked to do so, non-committal opinion, and would try to get out of the situation of active action.

This combination is quickly sustainable to outward injury to the genital parts of human body, and routine precaution is necessary in the course of physical relationship.

Sun and Ketu in the 7th House

Ketu is concerned neither with ego problem between husband and wife nor with appearance of third person in the married life. On the other hand, it (even with Sun) creates and maintains sensible understanding between husband and wife. The fact remains that Rahu (occupying the 1st house) does try, though unsuccessfully, creation of egoist differences between the two.

Ketu has nothing much to do directly or indirectly with battles and/ or defence strategy. This combination normally keeps the individual aloof from these matters, more under fear of leakage of secret information or theft of secret documents pertaining to these subjects. This combination generates a peculiar fear of legal action of any kind in the mind of the individual.

In matters of sale and purchase, these two planets together do not feel much concerned with element of unaccounted money in the payment of price. At the same time, the individual would not mind if it takes place on its own, as is the general practice in business world these days.

SUN IN THE 8TH HOUSE

The main subject of the 8th house is health, with or without impact on longevity. Sun would not normally cause any such injury or ill health as would adversely affect the longevity. Sun is directly concerned with fever (of any kind and any duration and on any account), skin ailment, burning sensation, heat stroke, and indirectly with functioning of the blood system, with any ailment relating to anus and the area around it, because anus region is ruled by the 8th house. It is a different matter that Sun would cooperate with other planets in causing any other kind of health trouble or long-term health problem, irrespective of the fact whether that planet is a friend or foe of Sun.

Sun gives trouble related to health either during its own Mahadasa, which is of 6 year-duration (shortest among duration of Mahadasa of all other planets), or during its Antardasa under any other planet. Otherwise Sun gives trouble when placed unfavourably in the yearly chart. Sun's periodicity of stay in any Rasi by transit is of one month (one or two days minus or plus), and therefore Sun doesn't create any long-term adverse effect on health except an injury or sudden fever or temporary skin ailment or burning sensation to any part of the body. Thus Sun does not do any substantial harm to the health during its transit in 4th, 8th or 12th house, even in the 1st house.

Because 8th house is concerned about stunt acting, Sun doesn't give any mentionable injury in this connection. Sun is not much concerned with accidents or injuries of serious kind. It gives minor injuries, curable easily and quickly. However Sun gives serious and severe beatings sometimes at the hands of government investigating agencies like police, customs and excise, anti-narcotics, anti-smuggling. Smuggling activities are directly concerned with the 8th house, and Sun concerns directly with government and administration.

Sun might however give injuries at an election meeting, at any procession, demonstration, picketing, political and religious rally, religious disturbance, because all these items reflect on efficiency of the administration.

Sun is not much or directly concerned with injury by animals, such as fall from horse, camel, donkey, elephant, or an attack or biting by cow, buffalo, dog, jackal, bear, tiger, panther, lion etc.

Sun is, in fact, very much concerned with bribes, whether one is in government or semi-government service or not. From this point floats the question of investigations about an individual's corrupt conduct, ultimately leading to punishment, if any, including fine, penalty, simple or rigorous imprisonment. But never a sentence of death, if any hard planet is not directly involved with Sun and the 8th house. Simple ownership of the 8th house by a hard planet also does not matter in this regard.

On the favourable side, Sun helps success in a competition or interview for entry into government or semi-government service, entry into active politics, liaison work in government departments, rendering help and support to politicians and bureaucrats in powerful positions (low or high).

However it is wrong on part of some less experienced astrologers that Sun in 8th house is harmful for father, his health or longevity. No it is not so. On the other hand, Sun in 8th house is helpful to father with regard to his health, longevity and source of income. Sun helps in very cordial and helpful relationship between individual and the father.

Sun and Moon in the 8th House

Again the same thing, Moon is effective even being in combust condition. These two stars together give a lot of inner annoyance and anger, unexpressed discontentment, mental depression, any other kind of trouble or disease related to mind.

The Rasi in the 8th house, its lord and the placement of its lord in the birth-chart, Moon's and Sun's positions in the Navamsha chart assume great importance with relation to any kind of trouble with the mind. The least is depression and dissatisfaction over minor events and developments in life, and highest is insanity, partial or complete. The distance in terms of degrees between Sun and Moon would have to be examined, and also whether Moon is behind Sun or ahead of Sun. If Moon is behind Sun but in close vicinity of 10 degrees, the mental trouble would perhaps not reach the state of any kind of insanity. If Moon is ahead of Sun at a distance of more than 5 degrees, the question of insanity must be thoroughly examined and necessary remedies suggested and taken. Without examination of Navamsha position of Moon, no prediction should be given related to question of insanity. Then there is the question of Mahadasa of Moon. If it does not occur upto the age of 28 years, the fear of mental disturbance to any great extent might not crop up at all.

In this context it must be noted that sex has very direct connection with state of mind vis-à-vis mental disturbance. There have been several cases where a boy or girl between the age of 14 and 28 went partially or completely insane, because there was no sex relief available to the individual. On consultation, sex relief, even by the outer method of body-touch with a member of the opposite sex was taken resort to, and the insanity disappeared. In modern times, late marriages also play a vital part in this behalf.

All this analysis should not mean that everyone with Moon in 8th house suffers at one time or the other from mental trouble. Mental trouble is quite different from depression and disturbance, which are caused by events and developments in life. Mental disturbances or depression are temporary phases, they come and go. There are 12 houses in all in a birth chart, and so on an average every 12th person in the world would have Moon in the 8th house. Mental trouble depends on position of other stars, their connection with Moon (and Sun) in the 8th house, and on Navamsha chart too. One shouldn't give predictions on this subject without having Bhava Chalitam and Navamsha of the birth chart.

Moon and Sun in the 8th house is a funny combine in the 8th house. Sun normally give a touch of masculinity, while Moon with it in the 8th house gives males a touch of feminine habits, gestures and qualities. In the birth charts of females, this combination positively gives a good percentage of masculine habits, gestures and qualities.

These individuals are often keen for journey(s) across the seas, and if Cancer, Capricorn, Aquarius or Pisces is in the 8th house, they desire a settlement either by seashore or in a different land across the seas.

These two planets are responsible for repetition of fever, cough, cold, bad throat, or even diphtheria in the infancy or childhood, combined with high fever. It is always advisable that any physical trouble caused by Moon alone or by Moon and Sun in the 8th house must receive medical treatment without delay.

Another important point is that individuals with Sun and Moon in the 8th house must not take risk with waters (stationary or flowing) in childhood and adult life too. It is always better for these individuals to learn swimming under strict and constant help and supervision. Even then they should not take to swimming as a regular hobby. Several accidents prove the correctness of this theory.

A daughter of an erstwhile Maharaja had this type of planetary influence in her birth chart (Moon and Saturn in the 12), and the senior author predicted that she would lose her husband by taking risk with water within twelve months of marriage. After marriage the couple on honeymoon trip went to the swimming pool of the hotel. The husband took a dive in water, and owing to wrong judgement about the depth of the water, his head hit the floor at the shallow end of the swimming pool. He died instantly, and it was on the eighth day of that marriage. The boy had Sun and Moon in the 8th house, besides damaging stars of the girl. Because of Sun in 8th house, both belonged to lineage families of Maharajas (feudal lords in India).

The 8th house concerns a fall from a height and injury thereby.

These individuals are often intent on smuggling activity or any kind of link or association with it. Risk of severe action by government agency often looms over these individuals. Risk to limb or life at a group fighting or at a battle or border skirmish is also there for these individuals. Outwardly, they show boldness and courage and inwardly they are cowards. It is always safe for these people to keep away from active fighting, individually or in a group.

And these individuals must avoid any kind of unnatural physical relations, even if one partner insists for it.

Sun and Mars in the 8th House

A difficult combination indeed, something warranting extra care about health, accidental injury or multiple injuries (specially by fire, electricity, fall from a height and attack by thief or robber), illness and diseases including ulcers (and cancerous trouble not ruled out). Loss of pregnancy (one or more) to females.

But this combination is very favourable indeed for income, earnings, savings, returns from investments, property, and gains by upward trend of gold, precious stones, jewellery and other valuables in the possession of the individual.

Fever, even high temperature (casual and repetitive), more in childhood upto the age of 12 or sometimes upto the age of 20 years is the first trouble these two planets give. For these individuals, whether male or female, blood pressure and purity of blood should be checked at regular intervals always and more so after the age of 45 years, and positively after the age of 60 years. These individuals must stay extra careful while handling fire, electricity, acids, inflammables of any kind. Their medical treatment must be at the hands of or under consultation from experts of the particular complaint of health. In case of heart trouble or approaching complaint of cancer, it is always better to obtain guidance and consultation from two different sources, independent of each other.

These individuals often suffer from cut injuries and an injury from any source giving little or more bleeding. Delay or carelessness in medical aid might make the injury septic or risky to the life itself.

A student of medical college at Indore (Central India) suffered a cut injury while shaving, and because he had to rush for some urgent work, he didn't bother about taking any antiseptic step. It might surprise most readers that the boy (a medical student of the 3rd year) died on the 4th day, in spite of all medical care subsequent to injury on cheek going septic!

If surgical treatment by operation is advised, take a second opinion or even without it, take resort to the surgery. The patient mustn't apply own opinion or impression or excuse to avoid surgery. In certain cases of ailment or disease like cancer, repeated surgery might be essential, no need to make excuses to avoid it. Though in very rare cases, specially where Saturn is also involved in the 4th, 8th or 12th house, amputation of a limb or part of the body might become unavoidable. Take it without grudge. However one special care has to be observed in cases of major surgery. Extra care be taken that the surgeon or the assistants or nurses do not leave any small surgical instrument or even cotton piece in the wound. At least in India, several cases of this type of lapse on part of those in the operation-theatre have come to notice, through Print Media. Though rarely, there have been cases of amputation of a wrong limb or part of the body by mistake of the surgeons.

Mars is directly concerned or in a sense, the 'ruler' of radiography and pathology. Sun and Mars in the 8th house might get a patient wrong reports of their X-ray tests or pathological tests. Or report of one person is given to another person. This ultimately results in wrong treatment or wrong surgery. The patient and the persons looking after the patient must be more vigilant in this matter. Mars in 8th house (with support from Sun there), in a Rasi owned by Mercury, Venus or Saturn can cause it.

The above discussion should be taken as guidance for prevention, not as to create any kind of fear whatsoever.

These individuals are good fighters, warriors, experts in defence strategy, and do not hesitate to go to active fighting on battlefield, nor are they afraid of injury or even loss of life. In this matter, Mahadasa and Antardasa should be studied, with transit of Saturn and position of Saturn, Mars, Rahu and Sun in the yearly chart.

These individuals are efficient detectives to locate smuggling and take action. However, if they themselves get involved in smuggling, it is rather difficult to detect or apprehend them. It is the same case with other crimes. They are good at detection, but if they involve themselves in theft, robbery, criminal attack or murder with unlawful intents or purposes, it is very difficult to detect them or to apprehend them, also because their colleagues and superiors would directly or indirectly help and support them!

They are efficient stunt actors or actresses, and if they happen to be in the role of hero or heroine or the villain, sometimes they offer to perform the stunt action themselves instead of getting the action done by a duplicate expert. In the main role, they prove very successful as strong-headed or strong-action-oriented, but sometimes do not fit-in or appear very successful or impressive as a 'soft-conduct'-oriented (romantic) hero or heroine.

These individuals become the first victims in accidents of fire, earthquake, looting in times of acute famine, and in fire-fighting operations. Because of brave nature, they are not afraid of taking risk or meeting with death.

Sun and Mars combine in the 8th house often see to it that the individual comes to possess real estate of own, whether for use of self or for earning rental. Sometimes the individual owns property more than own needs or needs of the wider family. Even if a property is sold, another property is acquired. The individual would not hesitate to gift property to any near and dear person.

Sun and Mercury in the 8th House

As mentioned before, Mercury is often with Sun. The first adverse effect that is caused by Mercury (with Sun) in the 8th house is the capacity of grasp of a child at school (and college) level. This adversely affects the progress in studies. Generally private tutors have to be engaged.

The second adverse effect is that these individuals do not make very efficient and successful writer, journalist, poet, and stenographers. If they become a judge in legal system, their written judgements and orders are of poor quality in language, sometimes in grammar too. These individuals are no doubt good administrators, headmasters of schools, principals of colleges, chancellor or vice-chancellor of universities, registrars in universities and courts of law. They have loud voice and they are good at delivery of prepared text given to them, but if they themselves have to write the text, they fail to impress much.

They are not good sufferers in physical or even mental torture. In smuggling and other unlawful activities too, they cannot tolerate too much of torture and cross-questioning and quickly give out the secrets of the trade. They are not good in fighting or functioning on a battlefield, and if by chance they are taken as prisoners of war, to save their skin, they give out whatever (secret) information is known to them.

Whether the individuals themselves are very intelligent or not, they are often critical of intelligence of others, moreso of their spouse.

Sun and Jupiter in the 8th House

This combination is apt to cause serious trouble related to asthma, diabetes, kidney, liver and to stomach, generally an ailment of limited nature. It is always better to have a child, with this combination in the 8th house, tested for asthma and diabetes, and even if a remote indication is apparent, medical remedy must be taken resort to without delay. Spiritually, wearing a real quality yellow sapphire in gold helps, but only when the child is of an age capable to protect self and the ring from theft and snatching.

Asthma and diabetes often carry hereditary effect. In cases where a parent or a grandparent on either parental or maternal side (even an uncle or aunt or cousin) has or had the trouble, it is always better for the child with these two planets in the 8th house to be subjected to medical test by the eighth year of age. It should be noted that these two diseases are curable, but warrant long-term medical treatment.

The next question pertaining to this combination is loss of money and moveable but costly assets including jewellery, currency and ornaments. The loss can be by own carelessness or by theft, by snatching of the item or the purse, by robbery, by speculation in shares and/or loss of any other kind. It can be loss in business or in industrial venture, loss owing to cheating, by non-recovery of loans given, by litigation, by any kind of punishment involving penalty in terms of money by any court of law or other statutory authority or civic body. The loss can also be by confiscation of goods or assets by any government agency or by seizure of irregularly imported or exported goods by the Customs authorities, and their complete confiscation or sale by auction at the cost of the party involved. Some individuals or their spouse or progeny or authorised representative carelessly operate a safety deposit vault, drop some costly item and loss is incurred. Embezzlement and pilferage are two other sources of loss. Division of assets between partners in business or between members of the family can also often lead to loss to the individual with Sun and Jupiter in the 8th house.

As far as possible these individuals should not enter into or initiate litigation, and if they are named as respondent, they should try for a settlement outside the court, if possible. These individuals often suffer owing to lapse or deceit on part of their legal representative or by false evidence given by partisan witnesses.

These individuals can suffer loss on account of under-invoicing and over-invoicing in goods imported or exported, by keeping duplicate accounts, because it becomes difficult for them, in case of detection or seizure of duplicate books, to prove which account books are true and correct.

These individuals are fit for issuing orders and commands, but not for their implementation in peacetime or wartime. They make good judges of any low or high courts, but often come to suffer bad reputation. They are efficient teachers and professors with such forgetful nature as is criticised by students and disciples. These individuals suffer from weak memory right from childhood and from school days.

They shouldn't undertake such jobs and acting roles on stage or in films which involves risk to limb or to life itself. They might fall from a height. It is immaterial whether the fall is from a low level or from very high height, they are due to get a serious injury. They should always be careful against scorpions, snakes, poisoning of any kind and on any account, also against biting by any dog or wild animals including cats and rats, also against attack by animals with hurting horns.

Their injuries, with even a little bleeding can get septic without notice and cause more trouble subsequently.

Sun and Venus in the 8th House

It is an interesting combination indeed. Sun rules masculinity while Venus gives desire for all good things including dance, music and sex, and also capacity to enjoy. Thus these two together can give all pleasure to human beings. Sun and Venus together in the 8th house reduce the stamina for frequency and intensity of sex action, specially in males. Therefore while matching horoscopes for marriage purposes, several astrologers attach due or undue importance to this factor, and in the process many a workable marriage proposals get turned down. The reality of this combination is that it doesn't bestow unlimited capacity for frequency and intensity, but there is no lack of competence for normal sex life throughout the normal youthful years of age. . In horoscopes of females, because Sun rules heat too, the desire for sex and its frequency and intensity is rather very strong. Not that the ancients didn't know it. They knew it very well, and therefore they have described that the desire for sex in a woman is 8 times stronger than that in a man.

Then there is the question of illness and diseases brought to bear on the individual because Venus and Sun both in their individual capacity give complaints of health now and then. Further Venus goes combust in vicinity of Sun and then both are enemies to each other, and being in the same house, they become diehard enemies. Thus cornered, Venus struggles hard to gain effectivity and as a consequence it gives complaints of health every now and then. The individual is vulnerable to diseases related to sex including venereal diseases and in modern times to AIDS too. Another reason for this dogma is that the individual, male as well as female, entertains an inner desire for variety in partner. In some societies, it is easier for the male partner to have access to variety, but the female partner has difficulty, specially in joint families, to have access to variety. They then take resort to any other male member available within the joint family or within the wider family including distant relatives, or failing all resources, within neighbourhood, or on the occasions of festivals and at marriage gatherings. Now because a large number of females are working outdoors, away from residence, such an access has become easier for females too. And the ultimate result, sometimes at least, is contacting diseases related to sex.

Unfortunately these individuals are fond of unnatural sex too, without bothering about the results thereof to self or to the other partner.

These individuals get tempted towards acting, and if somehow they find a place in the film world, they want to acquire roles of a King or Queen or a role of person of importance or authority – all this because Sun's presence in 8th house with Venus. And if Mars too is in the 8th house or has direct *drishti* on 8th house or is lord of the 8th house, these individuals further desire to take to stunt acting and actions. This applies to both males and females, whether they are in film line or theatre or in Circus. They very much overestimate their capacity in this regard.

They are fond of presentable wardrobe, and its use, even when they are not in a financial position to afford it. Where medical treatment is concerned, whether money allows or not, they would prefer consultation only of top experts. They are fond of dropping names of top personalities in any field about which they enter into conversation, whether they have even a passing acquaintance with that personality or not.

They are not very vulnerable to injuries by falling from an animal like horse, camel, elephant etc., or fall from a height, or bite by poisonous insects. But they are undoubtedly vulnerable to injury or death by consumption of any poisonous item by mistake or with the intention of a show of attempt at suicide. They are vulnerable to injury or death in water (flowing or stationary) or in floods or by sinking of a boat, sailing ship or steam-ship or any other vessel moving on water, a train or aeroplane accident by falling in the water. Though both Sun and Venus transit from one Rasi to another more or less in one month (except when Venus is retrograde), both these planets are capable of giving long-term disease, sometimes making medical relief practically impossible, resulting in death.

Sun and Saturn the in 8th House

Again two diehard enemies (son and father) together in a house meant to give injuries, illnesses, diseases, and sometimes death too. Death could be caused by long illness or any unnatural cause, including an accident. All other results become secondary in this house in so far as this combination is concerned. However one point be noted that general tendency of Saturn in the 8th house is to give injuries, and some times invalidity too, moreso in the waistline and the region lower thereto, but at the same time Saturn gives long life to the individual. Common belief is that Saturn's very nature is to give sufferings by one hand and some kind of relief or compensation by the other hand. Some people might take long life with invalidity as a curse, while some others take it as a boon that they are at least alive, having a full-term life!

These individuals are very much concerned with their name and fame, for good acts and actions or for unsocial and unapprovable causes. These individuals have no hitch or hesitation in taking up jobs or duties and responsibilities involving injury and risk to life. It may come from either source, to *defend* or to *offend* an attack, injury or hurting a person with intention to kill and murder. Even *Mario Puzo* has described this attitude in his famous novel *Godfather*, wherein the Don says that some people are bent upon getting killed.

That is why many individuals, with Saturn in 8th house in company of other planets or alone, are often readily agreeable to join police force, anti-smuggling squad, narcotics prevention force, combatant wing of the army, while many others willingly join any and all kinds of criminal gangs. Another result can be punishment by imprisonment for any crime or even for activity opposed to the ruler(s) of the country or state or province at the given time. In such cases, the administration highbrows attempt through hired or paid or employed goons and followers to cause injury or hurt with an intention to kill the individual opposed to the Ruler(s) at the given time. Because Saturn rarely causes death, these goons or followers often do not succeed in actually killing the individual. Poisoning is another method applied in such cases.

A fall from a height or from ground level, or from any animal of transport, is common for these individuals from childhood itself. If nothing else, in infancy they fall from *"jhoola"*(baby bed), from their tiny bicycle. Accidents on road, by train or from airplane are also results of Saturn (with Sun) in the 8th house. Had Saturn been alone in 8th house, it would normally not cause death by any of these unnatural causes.

Injury by animals with horns or large teeth or paws with nails is also a result of these two planets together in the 8th house. Minor or serious injuries in stunt acting in films or in acrobatics in circus is a common result of this combination. And individuals under Sun and Saturn in 8th house must always avoid extra marital relationship and unnatural sexual acts, as it would lead to serious complaints of health, curable by serious effort and lengthy process.

One of the important plus points of these two planets in the 8th house is that they ensure regular, slow and steady increase in the income by the main or side sources of income. If the individuals happen to be in government or public sector employ or actively whole-time workers in any trade union or labour movement or in agricultural field, the work of these individuals brings rich results in progress of one kind or the other.

Sun and Rahu in the 8th House

Though Rahu generally follows the pattern of Saturn, here in the 8th house Rahu would not give results, even shadow results parallel to those of Saturn. Rahu would give fatness to the body, especially to abdomen and parts of body lower to it, despite all efforts of Sun in 8th house to keep body weight under control.

Secondly, in case of an injury, chances of recovery therefrom are slow and chances of it going septic loom over the injured part or limb.

Thirdly this combination would give differences between husband and wife, especially under suspicion of backbiting and leaking family matters to unconcerned outsiders.

Fourthly Rahu and Sun would encourage the individual to interfere and dabble into affairs of others, though the individual generally minds outsider's interference in affairs of self and family.

Fifthly, these two together would easily give complaints of health related to sex life (at home or outside). Venereal disease also stands in the corner to contact either of the two or both husband and wife or the friend in love. Extreme preventive caution is needed.

But the same combination helps in easy and quick recovery of dues and loans, especially those related to place of work or from colleagues and companions. Not much need to take recourse of a Lawsuit. Sometimes government officials extend a helping hand in recovery, no doubt privately.

Sun and Ketu in the 8th House

In this case Ketu gives more or less, results similar to those of Rahu, and not Mercury. The individual has sometimes to suffer theft or loss of low-cost items of daily use at home or at place of work. Colleagues and co-workers are jealous instead of being co-operative. Injuries certainly take longer time to cure, and chances of going septic are very much there. Loans and dues get recovered easily.

SUN IN THE 9TH HOUSE

It is important to keep in mind the subject concerned with the 9th house according to Indian system of astrology, especially that of North India. The variation is that in South India system and some of the Western Systems, everything relating to father is attributed to the 9th house, which is not correct. No doubt the 9th house rules father's money and losses, any kind of cheating to father or punishment to father, but not father's longevity and other general matters relating to him. Admitted that inheritance of assets or liabilities from father (or for that matter even from paternal grandparents) is the subject of the 9th house. Similarly good luck or bad luck, good name or bad name, happy or unhappy relations with grandparents and with wider family including uncles and aunts etc are covered by the 9th house.

Except for those in government service or in active politics or in management of social and religious institutions, Sun stays, more or less, neutral to the 9th house. Sun leaves a majority of subjects related to the 9th house to the Rasi in 9th and position of its lord in birth-chart and its Navamsha, as also on other planets in the 9th house. Therefore combination of other planets with Sun in 9th house is all the more important.

Sun in 9th house generates a touch of distrust between or among partners in business, industrial venture, profession, or even in criminal activity of any kind. If there are more than two actively working partners, generally grouping takes place as soon as the source of income takes steady roots, and proceeds on path of fast profits. This groupism ultimately leads to dissolution or driving out one or two partners not belonging to the more powerful or effective group. More often this process continues driving partners out till only two of them are left in the field. It happens that those who walk out or get driven out of the partnership are often the losers, because rarely they are paid or allowed to take out shares equivalent to real value of their portion of the partnership.

Sun when alone in the 9th house grants better fortune to active politicians, deemed social workers and government employees. Others have to depend on their own work, results in terms of income depending on the quality and quantum as also demand and supply position in the field.

In wider family, uncles, aunts, cousins, brothers and sisters of spouse, brothers-in-law and sisters-in-law often suspect the intentions of the juniors in age or status, with or without reason. It happens that a sister-in-law or brother-in-law or cousin, on their own make romantic advances towards the individual, if the latter person responds favourably and quickly, direct or indirect complaints are made to the elders against the individual. At the same time if no response is made, the individual is considered coward, discourteous and heartless. A tricky and rather risky game indeed!

When directly concerned with management of any social, religious, charitable institution or formation, firstly these individuals do much less work themselves and make a greater show of their work, secondly they do not miss any opportunity to interfere with the work and working of others. In matters of donations and contributions in cash or kind, they are nearer to miserliness than being liberal.

In regard to inheritance from father or from one generation above father's level, others in the family or any kind of relationship make efforts to give these individuals less than their due share. But with unofficial help and support from government employees, these individuals manage to get their due share in full, and sometimes, by adopting various ways and means, cut an extra slice from the share of others.

Sun and Moon in the 9th House

Moon being a soft planet and being a good friend of Sun (though in the friendship table at the time of birth they are opposed to each other), Moon reduces in volume and quantity the adverse effect of Sun in the 9th house. Then both planets together help the individual in granting good fortune. These two planets help the individual in becoming more active and real worker for social, religious and charitable causes, in a concrete manner, and sometimes involve their immediate family too to extend cooperation towards social, charitable or religious activity. These individuals encourage their family to offer prayers regularly. If Moon is not in waning position, the individual would not suffer any kind of suspicion in any matter from or regarding uncles/ aunts/ cousins/ sisters-in-law and brothers-in-law. Moon would make the individual more liberal and charitable, subsiding the miserliness given by Sun in 9th house.

No doubt in the matter of inheritance from any source, whether of assets or liabilities, Moon would not make any contribution worth mention to the effect of Sun there. Moon would encourage the individual to consolidate assets and properties (if scattered here and there), and also to dispose of or part with assets not needed by self or immediate family. The assets in the form of property which may be surplus than personal needs, then both Sun and Moon would need the help of Mars by conjunction in 9th house or by direct *drishti* from 3rd house for its management or disposal.

In matters related to partnership in business, profession or industry etc., Moon would make the individual more alert towards correct share distribution on dissolution or parting company.

Sun and Mars in the 9th House

Though normally Mars helps Sun when in combination with it, since they are friends in permanent relationship and both are 'birds of the same feather', but Mars has totally different type of effect in the 9th house for the individual.

The first effect is that it doesn't help protecting the interest of the individual in getting due share in inheritance. Where assets are concerned, the individual gets less than due share in actual assets, or less in value and compensation. Fighting and litigation do not help much, unless stars of spouse or of a progeny above the age of 18 years come to the help of the individual.

The same is the effect in dissolution of or in parting company from any partnership in business, industry or profession, and in this case, the stars of the spouse or of progeny do not count much. Anger and fight descend unfavourably on the individual.

Others blame him or her, even without understanding the totality or inner situation of the matter. The correct suggestion is that individuals with Sun and Mars (or Mars alone) should avoid, as far as possible, entering into any partnership. Generally in partnership within the family, between brothers, or between brothers and sisters or between brothers-in-law or sisters-in-law, the more clever or cunning partner (also often the more active partner) maintains the partnership so long as own progeny doesn't grow old enough to join and actively participate with the parent. As soon as that partner's own progeny is grown up and is competent to join hands with the parent, the partner(s) in inferior position (even if the percentage and investment is equal) is (are) asked to walk out with nominal compensation or placed on a side-board, virtually inaction and helpless. Things go so much difficult for the inferior partner(s) that the progeny is secretly encouraged to question and bitterly criticise, also find faults with, even minor actions of the inferior partner(s) relating to the business, industry or profession. Such insulting position descends on the partner(s) reduced to inferior status that only choice left to him or her or them is to walk out of the partnership with whatever little is offered by the overall in charge of the partnership, by way of terminal compensation.

These individuals are not much afraid of suspicion and bad name for their conduct and behaviour towards uncles, aunts, cousins, brothers-in-law and sisters-in-law, and go ahead rather shamelessly with their plans and activity of making advances towards the opposite sex in the joint family or wider family.

These individuals have no hitch or hesitation in usurping part of real estate or other assets or funds of the social, religious or charitable formation or organisation for which they pretend to work. They are afraid of neither criticism nor bad name and are often extra-ready to fight litigation too, if their action, right or claim is questioned or challenged.

In a sense, rather unknowingly and involuntarily they compensate themselves by usurping assets and funds outside the family to make the loss suffered in the inheritance.

Most of these individuals are religious and offer prayers, no doubt, for fulfilment of their ulterior motives, whatever they be, and for whatever purpose they are.

When confronted with a physical fight or violence, they face it very willingly, because they are generally over-confident of own victory, the only exception being that males do not enter into a combat with females. However these individuals have very correct sense of judgement of the force and strength opposite and where they feel inferior in the situation, they have no hesitation or shame in pronouncing surrender.

These individuals take interest in politics, some of them passively to the extent discussing it in private meetings, while some go more active in the field. If they stand for any election to a Legislature or local or civic body, they fight for their victory vehemently and sometimes violently too, through their goons and followers, and manage a victory.

Sun and Mercury in the 9th House

Mercury is effective in conjunction with Sun, though to a reduced extent. Mercury insists on documentation of every agreement, contract, mutual understanding etc., if not signed by both parties, at least recorded by self for use when needed.

Mercury makes an efficient teacher, professor, journalist, ghost-writer, printer, publisher either in a government institute, school or college, or on behalf of the government or public sector. The individual is properly paid or compensated directly (or under the table) for the labour, responsibility and quantum of work involved. The individual doesn't mind working within the framework or norms fixed which are often there.

Mercury doesn't help or support Sun in putting up strong resistance in any fight, quarrel or dispute, if violence is involved. Mercury helps considerably where the situation remains limited to words and shouting.

Mercury provides the intelligence, wisdom and willingness for working actively for any social, charitable or religious formation or organisation, but if the individual's motive and intentions start moving to wrong path, Mercury remains passive with Sun engaged in all activities of this type.

In the field of politics, they prepare very effective speeches and publicity material, and also deliver speeches from public platform, which reach home with the listeners. In matter of election whether of self or their boss or colleague or follower, they are more passive than active.

Sun and Jupiter in the 9th House

This is a combination which produces efficient and effective judge, members of law commissions and judicial tribunals, public prosecutors, government lawyers on the civil side, members of consumer-redressal forum, members of appellate authorities in taxation departments or similar formations of the government or public sector. Sun and Jupiter together can produce economists, qualified or unqualified accountants, finance experts for the government, as also government budget-makers, and draftsmen of government Legislature of every kind.

These individuals rarely prefer to function as independents working on their own or in the private sector, because Sun in conjunction with Jupiter is directly concerned with government side. They do not cherish private practice of own or joining a professional body, and always keep an eye on an opening on the government side.

These individuals do not bother much about minor or major loss of their share in inheritance, more because they are confident that they would make up the loss by own earnings in life.

Because of the above self-confidence, they are often helpful, not so much physically, as morally and financially to brothers/ sisters/ brothers-in-law and sisters-in-law or even to first-degree uncles, aunts and first cousins, whether of self or of spouse. And they keep self-restraint on their conduct and behaviour and thus stay above suspicion. Except in the field of their profession or work, they do not respond to romantic glances and gestures. In the outside field they are active in response, provided the person making this type of move is really attractive and charming, and no loss of name or fame is involved in going ahead with romance. And they do not much hesitate to casually mentioning it to spouse, not in its totality, but just such a slight indication as would not make the spouse feel that there is any significant interference in their marital relationship.

These individuals are religious, social, whether they are able to offer regular prayers or not, or are able to render any social service or not. They are charitable but rather conservative in giving donations, "*daans*" and contributions. Except for becoming figureheads for sake of status, they are not given to any active work for religious and charitable organisations. These individuals are not of much service at the time of any natural calamity or national trouble, unless their own interests or own family is involved with adverse effect, be it floods, famine, earthquake, big fire, major accident by bus or lorry or train or aeroplane, drought, landslide, cloud-burst or any similar event.

These individuals have helplessly to enter into partnership business or industry, while working in government or holding any office of profit under the government. But then they take necessary precautions that they are not put to loss at the time of dissolution of or withdrawal from the partnership.

They neither avoid long or short journey nor are they extra fond of tours and travels. They are moderate in this matter. It also depends on what Rasi is in the 9th house, which planet is its lord and where is that planet sitting. However they are quite liberal in allowing journeys to spouse and children. When they themselves travel their luggage or baggage is overloaded with this thing or that thing. Over-possession is their weakness otherwise too in their day-to-day life so long as they are able to provide for it.

In physical person-to-person fighting, they are neither competent nor do they welcome it. If they see any chance of physical fight, either they try to escape from the spot, or surrender to the opposite party in a calm and dignified manner. Because they are very protective of their spouse, even if the individual opposite is a woman, they would not indulge in getting into a physical fight. They would try to buy peace at any cost, and would not like the women-folk of their family to indulge in physical fighting.

This combination in the 9th house is capable of bringing civilian award or decoration for the individual, if holding a senior position in the Judiciary, Economic or Accounting Establishments, and financial benefits too, if any, connected therewith, though financial benefits are rarely there.

Sun and Venus in the 9th House

Astrologers should stay careful and restricted in giving predictions about conduct and character of these individuals, because often they are very romantic by nature, if not to the extent of physical involvement, at least in talks, gestures and physical touches here and there. It is all the more so if the person opposite is attractive and charming, generally in the joint family itself or in the wider family or from amongst distant relatives. Often they suffer insults or even a teach-him-a-lesson kind beating depending on the status, standing, actual relationship bond and the extent of the misdemeanour.

These individuals may take keen interest in sexually oriented group situations, and make the spouse agree against her or his initial objection or hesitation.

When faced with a situation of loss in inheritance, if the individual is a male, he would put forth his wife for quarrel and dispute in the matter. If she fails to acquire full benefit due, the individual would surrender and accept whatever comes in hand and would not indulge in physical fight or litigation. However the situation would be sometimes different if the individual has grown-up son(s) residing with the parents. Then the grown-up son on his own, or on encouragement from parents would come forward to dispute the claim to full share in the inheritance.

These individuals often take active part in social religious, public service activity, less under urge of service, more under thrust of lust, if nothing else at least to come in close and intimate contact with opposite sex. And if they succeed in fixing something of their personal interest, they do not hesitate in making liberal donations and contributions. Additional interest is to attract the attention of the person in whom the individual has started taking interest with romantic idea in mind. The third purpose this generosity serves is to gain name and fame. If they do not render physical service or make any donation and contribution in terms of money, others notice their romance-oriented activity, and try to discard them and ultimately oust them from that association or organisation. However if some of the top management people also belong to the same feather as these individuals are, they manage to continue even without fishing out any substantial money or without rendering any physical service to that organisation or association.

These individuals generally enter into any partnership in business or industry in the name of the wife and keep a strict eye on developments and profits. As soon as they find the going is not good to their interests, they withdraw from the partnership without loss of original investments and profits thereon. Sometimes in the course of partnership, the wife gets attracted and physically involved with another partner or a worker therein. Even on its knowledge, the husband may make a show as if he does not know the developments, for the simple reason of gains from the partnership. There have also been cases of wife disobeying the husband and refuses to withdraw from the physical relationship or the business partnership.

Sun and Saturn in the 9th House

The results are much similar to those described under "Sun and Mars in the 9th house" supra. A major difference between Mars and Saturn in 9th house (with Sun) is that Saturn has scope for extra-marital sex or freelance physical relationship on a rather large canvas, while Mars is strict in moral character matters.

Saturn generally provides the labour class or agriculturists and agricultural labour as followers for the individual, and whenever a question of physical fight or violence crops up, Saturn helps the individual to remain in the background and operate through those employees or followers.

When the question arises about forming strategy for battle or war on behalf of the nation or for actual fighting on the front, Saturn encourages the individual to go ahead without fear or hesitation.

Saturn and Mars (with Sun) both are capable of winning a gallantry award or decoration or grant in the shape of higher pension or family pension or grant of land. Saturn, however, brings lower awards, while Mars brings higher awards and decorations. Neither of them (with Sun) brings a civilian award or decoration.

Saturn often connects the individual with trade unions, labour movement, movement on behalf of the agriculturist and farmers. Saturn (and Sun) would otherwise give leadership of human-power suppliers vis-à-vis placement service people, leadership of destitute women and prostitutes, orphans, low-paid employees in government or Public sector or private field, leadership of hotel or motel employees. The individual carries out responsibility quite successfully, though simultaneously the individual also keeps climbing the political ladder ultimately for membership of state legislature or national parliament/ senate etc.

If the individual goes into partnership business, industry or communication services or transport line (all are fields for Saturn's operation), the individual would not allow the other partners to drive him or her out when the partnership concern starts making big profits and grows into expansion and diversification. The individual would give, through other sources, threats of violence or damage to the business or industry, and the cleverer partners would go mute on the matter of dissolution of the partnership or driving the individual out.

Where the question of association with social, religious, charitable or any public service formation or organisation is concerned, the individual will first of all find out what is "in it" for the individual, and then walk into it for rendering any real or superfluous service. However it is also a reverse fact that the individual would work hard and make others too work hard for the progress and advancement of the organisation, no doubt retaining a slice for personal benefit!

Saturn has little faith in religion or prayers etc., but gives the individual a talent to make pretensions of any and every kind of religious activity to make others believe the individual's religious trend, trait and tradition. The individual's eyes are only on the personal benefits therefrom.

Sun and Rahu in the 9th House

Sun actually becomes ineffective in Rahu's conjunction in 9th house. Rahu is a shadow planet given to pretensions also pretentiousness. Since Rahu follows the pattern of Saturn, it has an eye on what the individual can get from any political, social, religious, charitable or public service body.

In matters related to moral character, Rahu's influence would stop the individual from proceeding further than talks, gesture and mild physical touch, without giving rise to misunderstanding or suspicion of any kind. Rahu generally promotes this kind of behaviour *outside* the periphery of family limits, not in immediate family or wider family.

As far as possible Rahu doesn't concern itself with defence matters, strategy or actual fighting. If by chance, the individual joins any branch of the defence services, he or she tries to quit at the slightest indication of hostilities, and never hesitates to employ all kind of approach and pressure to get relieved from active-type defence service.

Rahu doesn't make the individual willing for physical fight and violence, keeps the matter to verbal exchanges, more in subdued tone, critical remarks and leakage of weaknesses of the party opposite. Rahu doesn't encourage the individual for litigation too.

Because of the above attitude, the individual has to tolerate loss in division of inheritance or dissolution of partnership or forced exit from the partnership.

Sun and Ketu in the 9th House

This combination literally follows the same pattern of results as that of Rahu and Sun combination, though it is a rare case, because normally Ketu follows the pattern of Mercury. The only exception is that Rahu has no hitch in handling any dispute roughly, while Ketu with Sun goes with the matter intelligently and gentlemanly.

Ketu and Sun would not encourage the individual to any romantic talks, gestures or physical touch whatsoever. These two planets together have greater sense of self-respect and dignity of relationship in the family or society. The individual would not normally respond to similar gestures and advancement by the opposite sex, and would mildly and politely indicate indirect 'no' ultimately.

SUN IN THE 10TH HOUSE

This is one of the most favourable positions of Sun in the birth-chart. Sun is Raja (King) among planets, 10th house is the *Rajya-Bhava* (profession, career, calling etc.) ruled by Sun (and also by Mars to an extent).

The 10th house concerns father and if Sun is there, it is beneficial to the father of the individual. Father is strict in discipline and affectionate in the same breath for such individuals. Sometimes the father is in government service or in active politics. In either case, the father finds less time to spend on upbringing of the individual, and makes it up by employing domestic servants and private tutors. The individual too serves the father very well in the latter's old age or in any other kind of disability of the father. Even to grown up age, the individual has a kind of inner fear from father owing to father's strict discipline in the individual's childhood.

Father doesn't normally interfere with married life of the individual. However father rarely approves of any love affair of the progeny upto the age of 18 years, and in case of any such development, tries his level best to put an end to it by all means and methods, direct or indirect.

In this context, remember that every individual is ruled by own planets, and the planets of the progeny or vice-versa have very little influence in the life of the other person, whatever the relationship between the two. The child can have at the most 15% influence on the planets of the father, while father has hardly 5 to 10% influence on the fate and fortune of the child, whether the father has only one child or more than one child.

The 10th house chiefly rules the question of main source of earnings and income. Therefore the matter needs to be studied in its full perspective, with special reference to the Rasi in the 10th house, position of its lord in the birth chart and an overall study of the Navamsha chart, in case of both male and female individuals. Ancient *acharyas* of astrology have attached importance to the lord of the 10th house from the 10th house in the birth chart (which means the lord of the 7th house) and its position in the Navamsha chart of both males and females. The *Sapta-Varga* strength of these two lords respectively of the 10th and 7th houses in the birth chart, and their relationship with the 10th house of the birth-chart has to be studied.

It is all the more important in this context to study the influence of the 5th house, as element of education is ruled by the 5th house and its lord. Thus the planets in the 5th house as also relationship of the 5th house lord with the 5th house and also with the 10th house assumes importance while studying the career and source of livelihood of any individual.

It has been observed in several cases that the individual has totally departed or separated from the education received, and has gone into totally different profession, calling, employment, business or self employment, sometimes including active politics and social work. Thus while dealing with an individual's source of livelihood, besides a study of the 10th house (also 7th house), in the birth chart and in the Navamsha chart, the study should include the 5th house and its lord too. The 10th house has another importance as it rules father. In several cases, the individual follows the line of livelihood of the father, for example, a lawyer's son or daughter becomes a lawyer, medical man's son or daughter is deemed fit for medical line, and quite often best efforts are made to bring the child into father's line of livelihood. A father having main source of livelihood from rental income from properties or from agriculture often wishes that the son or the daughter too continues in the same line of livelihood, no doubt besides other line of livelihood too.

It is in the above context that Sun in the 10th house assumes special importance (no doubt other planets too in the 10th house have similar importance). Sun is more concerned with employment under government, semi-government or public sector or civic bodies like municipal services, or otherwise with active politics, or social and religious work (under the banner of the government or having a touch of governmental system).

As stated above, Navamsha position of Sun read with birth-chart-cum-Navamsha position of the lord of the 10th house and the Navamsha position of other planets in the 10th house will also matter with relation to the main source of earning or income of the individual (both male and female). These stars would concern themselves with the field of employment under government or semi-government department or civic body or public sector undertaking (including banks and insurance companies owned by government or working under the banner of government as in India). With regard to social work too, these associated stars would directly affect the field of activity of the individual. Even with regard to religious activity, the associated planets always have their 'say' in the matter. It is so because there are many different fields of activity and duties related to religious work. For example, such as management, finances, construction and maintenance, security of the jewellery on the deities/ statues, security of the visitors, preparation of offerings to the main deity, preparation of *'prasaadam'* to be given to the visitors, recitation of scriptures and arrangement of discourses, etc

> Normally, some main fields of livelihood of all the seven real planets (i.e. barring the 'shadow' planets Rahu and Ketu) may be as given below:
>
> (a) **Sun:** Functioning in the fields of indigenous medicines, gold, gold ornaments, and precious stones (Jupiter too is concerned with these), production and trading in wool and woollens, goods used in sports and games to a certain extent (which are main concern of Saturn). Trading in molasses, dry fruits, perfumery (it concerns Venus also), hay and fodder, wood used as fuel and timber, wholesale trading in wheat and coarse grains, pulses and cereals, indigenous system of medicines. Functioning as agents and advisers in legal matters (specially non-judicial process and procedures), representing general public or any individual before government machinery, drafting and writing

or preparation of applications and petitions to be submitted to government machinery. It can be service or employment as Envoy or Ambassador or Counsel General or on any other post in an Embassy or High Commission or Trade Representation (in the last one Jupiter too is concerned). These sources of livelihood are in addition to what sources have been described above in general terms on Sun's position in the 10th house.

(b) **Moon:** Science and scientific instruments, navigation and navy, medicine, fluids and liquids, water and all items that flow, pharmacy and pharmaceuticals. Trading in sugar, ghee, cotton including its different uses in cloth etc., cotton-seed (its oil is concerned with Saturn), paper (specially white paper), and paper products, pearls and ashes thereof for medical use. Trading or providing free or using for own purpose only the irrigation facilities. Production of earthen pots (including of china clay), producing comic literature, bringing out and trading in sea products, production and trading in vegetables and garden produce, fruits etc. Because Moon's cycle of waning and waxing is directly related with Sun, Moon's pattern of sources of income get influenced by those described in the above paragraph under Sun. Moon rules the Mind in every human being, and therefore sometimes it happens that the individual wants or prefers to adopt a particular source of livelihood, but owing to circumstances or lack of education in this behalf or lack of means and resources, the individual is obliged to adopt some other line of livelihood. If this point is not kept in mind, predictions might miss accuracy.

(c) **Mars:** Police, army, weapons and ordnance, electricals, electronics including computer/ TV/ Radio. Then iron-smithy, acids, inflammables, fire, firearms, arm, ammunition, artillery in every line of defence (army, navy and air force). Atomic energy and all its branches and productions, Nuclear in any shape and form. Production of and trading in facial cosmetics (Venus too is concerned with them). Gold (including smuggling), manufacturing of and trading in gold ornaments and other items of gold. Theft, robbery, dacoity, kidnapping (for ransom or revenge) and other related crimes. Working as a cook or nanny or baby-sitter or domestic servant. Search of treasure troves and treasures retrieved from damaged trains, sunk ships, fallen aeroplanes. Mining and trading in minerals. Functioning as a surgeon (specially of heart, brains, blood system and cancerous trouble), Radiologists, Pathologist, Cardiologist, Cartographer, expert in treating skin and diabetes trouble. Nursing, assistant in operation theatre. Speculation in real estate, brokerage in real estate, construction and sale of multi-storied buildings, apartments, any kind of construction (real construction work is more related to Saturn and to some extent to Mercury too). Renting, buying and selling of plots and properties concern Mars. Wrestling and arranging wrestling fights. Races and fights of animals and birds etc. Managing threats and violence on payment on behalf of others. Running training institutes for use of weapons and firearms. Manufacturing or trading in acids and inflammables, running metal-melting industries (electric furnaces etc.). Repairs to any kind of electric and electronic systems (from motor vehicles to domestic appliances), Radio, TV and Computer. Manufacture and trading in Atomic Energy's and Nuclear System's operational machinery and all material and elements (scientific and others) needed for the purpose. Construction and running of power houses and other similar systems for generating electricity, either owning these companies or working in them on scientific and technical side.

(d) **Mercury:** Fields related to education, journalism, writing, printing, publishing books, booklets, pamphlets, any kind of publicity or other material. Spiritual or religious recitations and public speaking on these subjects. Ghost writing. Functioning as priest or worshipper in temples, maulavi in Mosques and padre in Churches, converting people from one faith or religion to another, also running religious cults. Preparing designs and drawings for machinery and instruments, houses, buildings, industrial sheds, defence and aviation buildings and hangars. Manufacturing and trading in artificial flowers and decoration items of paper, plastic, timber. Manufacture and trading in other coloured papers and products thereof. Astrology, palmistry, numerology or any other method of forecasting the future. Living on charity or annual grants and stipends (normally given to religious preachers and 'pandaas' (record-keepers of generations of customers when they visit holy places and places of pilgrimage). Functioning in any capacity in science or medical laboratory, writing and scrutinising reports of medical and science laboratories. Trading in emeralds, manufacture of semi-precious stones, chemically produced artificial precious stones and application of wisdom to sell these items. Owning and running advertisement, publicity and propaganda agencies. Managing educational or training institutes for any line of learning, running semi-educational institutes of coaching for competitive tests for recruitment to any cadre of employees in government, semi-government, public sector, private sector, for commercial and private services jobs. Running a daily, biweekly, weekly, fortnightly, monthly, bi-monthly, half yearly and yearly newspaper or magazine or periodical or any other kind of publication for public circulation. Production of and trading in any kind of paper for printing including newsprint, or that used for packing purposes. Production and sale of plastic covers and containers for retailing productions of consumer goods (Jupiter too is concerned with plastic and plastic items manufacture and sale).

(e) **Jupiter:** Fields of law, economics, accounts, finances, budgeting. Advisership in any of these fields. Business, management or employment therein. Money lending, helping moneylenders in recovery of money by ordinary and crude methods. Functioning as priest or worshipper in temples or as Maulavi and Mulla in Islam religion or as Bishop, Nun or Padre in Christianity. Trading in horses, camels, elephants, donkeys, ass, ponies. Trading in minerals (mining is concerned with Mars and Saturn). Giving discourses on religion, faith and spiritualism. Receiving charity at holy places and places of pilgrimages, including outside temples, mosques, churches. Membership of Panchayats, county councils, district advisory boards, municipalities, legislature, Houses of Parliament, Senate. Marriage making and intermediaries in marriage disputes, marriage brokers. Import and export of manpower (Saturn is also concerned with it). Priesthood at marriages and at death-connected ceremonies. Functioning as representative or member of any judicial or semi-judicial tribunal or any other similar forum. Agents and brokers in the field of law, judiciary, religion. Arranging (merely as an agent) loans and their recovery for other people, including commercial houses. Also malpractice in business, accounting including under-invoicing and over-invoicing in export and import trade. Embezzlement of funds and pilferage of stocks and stores by malefic practices in keeping of accounts and stock registers.

(f) **Venus:** Trading in precious stones (Sun, Mars & Jupiter are also concerned with it), specially in pearls and diamonds and making of jewellery therefrom and also in trading in them. Silver and all kinds of silver items, silver-coated or artificial silvery items. Trading in milch animals like cow, she-buffalo, goat, sheep (camel too in deserts and adjoining regions). Decoration items including those made of paper or plastic or any other material. Producing and trading in wine/ liquor/ alcohol/ cold drinks/ ice/ ice-cream and all other consumable items including Indian bhang, opium and other allied narcotics or semi-narcotics items. Trading in milk, curd, ghee, butter, other preparations of milk and sugar (including all kinds of sweets and drinks). Poison and preparations of poison for normal consumption and sometimes with evil intention of intoxicating, sending a person into unconsciousness or causing illness, with or without intention of causing death. Costume jewellery and real jewellery. Manufacture and trading in paper and paper products, cloth and all products from long-cloth including garments, and medicines. Medical practice (including as a physician). Adulteration in medicines and drinkables of every kind including intoxicating items, like opium and its products. Working as actors, actresses, performing supporting roles, all other whole-time or part-time or occasional work in films and stage performances. Writing of scripts and dialogues for films and drama etc. Dancers, singers, supporters working on musical instruments for dances and vocal music. Dressmaking for actors, actresses and other supporting roles. Production, trading and supply of hospital equipment including all kinds of instruments for operation theatre, supply of nurses and ward-boys, supply of medicines to hospitals and nursing homes, running and management of nursing homes.

(g) **Saturn:** Production and trading in big and small machines, capital goods for industrial units, railway system, naval system and aeroplanes. Manufacture and trading in rail engines of all kinds and system (locomotives etc). Manufacture of rolling stocks, and laying of tracks for railway system for both passenger traffic and goods traffic. Manufacture and trading in cars, lorries, trucks, heavy vehicles for road transport and all other kinds of transport vehicles of auto-type and non-auto type like bullock carts/ carts for snow regions, horse-carts. Trading in all and every kind of pet animals and transport-animals including horses, donkeys, ponies, ass, camels, elephants, monkeys, cows, buffaloes, sheep, goats, dogs, cats, snakes and other reptiles. Preparation of poison and poisonous elements for medicinal purposes and criminal purposes too. Theft, robbery, dacoity, plundering, pick-pocketing, forcibly snatching purses, handbags, and any other kind of criminal activities or association with criminal groups and gangs. Working or actively helping as information agents for police, custom, anti-narcotics, other taxation offences. Working as informers for defence intelligence. Working as any kind of cover for criminals or other unlawful activists. Working for or actively helping politicians in gathering crowds, arranging meetings, and managing propaganda and publicity outfits. Managing other legal and unlawful activities connected with politics and elections. Supply of every kind of manpower for domestic work, offices, shops, and commercial establishments. Finding (as an open or secret agent) recruits for police and defence services. Managing export and import of manpower including females and children for domestic work and use as victims for acrobatics in foreign countries. Establishing and working of communication-system. Working as peon, postman, driver, cabman, and working on manpower operated transport system. Working as stunt actors and actresses. Supply of workers for industry and transport systems of any and every kind. Supplying labour for farming, agriculture, gardening and allied works. Working as labourer in industries, transport system and field of agriculture, farming, and gardening. Manufacture and supply of all kinds of instruments and equipment for agriculture, farming and gardening. Running poultry and trading of its products. Running and managing veterinary hospitals and clinics. Establishing and managing big market places for trading in all kinds of cattle, and holding annual fairs for trading in cattle. Construction-line including construction of railway line, roads, residential houses and apartments, multi-storeyed buildings for residential or office or factory use, industrial sheds, cottages and farm houses, construction of barracks and other housing units for police and defence services. Demolition of constructed buildings etc., reconstruction after war/ battle/ floods/ earthquakes/ large-scale fires or after any man-made or natural calamity. Construction of bridges, over-bridges, parks, play-grounds and parking places.

AGAIN GENERAL: The important point to be noted in this context is that above given are brief indications of means of livelihood, of earnings, of income for individuals. The above list is neither exhaustive nor complete. There are thousands of trades and activities that cannot be enumerated within the scope of this book. Many a subject and sources can be allied to what have been detailed above. The astrologers and amateurs in astrology have to make own rules depending on their knowledge and experience.

Reverting to Sun's effect in 10th house, it is enough to go through the subjects listed above under Sun. Add thereto recruitment to civil services including senior cadres, working on administration side of government or semi-government establishment, on any post in bureaucracy. Working as head of government, head of County, head of state (normally with designation of Governor), as Prime Minister, as member of the Council of Administration (i.e. on Cabinet), as President, as Dictator, as Chief Executive, or with any other designation while functioning as head of administration of a country. Heads of police department and defence service chiefs come under Mars and Saturn. Jupiter rules appointments as judges and chief judges of superior court. However in all these cases SUN is *also directly concerned*, because it is the head of the country or state who selects or finally approves these appointments and issues necessary orders/ warrants of appointment

Downfall from elected posts of Governors, Presidents, Prime Ministers, Chiefs is also covered by Sun in the 10th house. This point includes resignation, dismissal, termination, non-election for a second or third time, sudden change in system of Governance owing to revolt as was the case in Russia in 1917, or owing to grant of Freedom as in the case of India and Pakistan in 1947. All these changes in the head of government are ruled positively by Sun, though in association or conjunction with other planets, responsible for that particular post or portfolio. Change of government or change of system of Governance by results of war or treaty is also the concern of Sun in the 10th house.

However it is not possible to discuss these causes in detail as the matter depends much on the horoscope of the individual. **Some of the planetary influences which lead an individual to the rank of Governor, Prime Minister, Chief Minister, President etc are given below, because it is one of the very important points connected with the 10th house:**

A. Exchange of houses between lords of the 9th and the 10th house.

B. Three or more planets occupying self-owned Rasi or Rasi of exaltation (short of peak point of exaltation), provided soft planets are not in 6th, 8th or 12th house and hard planets are not in 4th, 5th or 9th house. It won't matter if a hard planet is in the 12th house, because that position being 3rd from the 10th house is helpful for reaching a top-post or top-rank of power.

C. Also any of the following planet-positions:

    a) Lord of 4th house in 10th house and lord of 10th house in 4th house and both under direct *drishti* of lord of 5th or 9th house.

    b) Lords of both 5th, 9th and possibly with lord of the 1st house also, occupying the 7th house (achievement would mean to an extent with the support of the spouse or stars of the spouse).

c) Lords of 1st, 9th and 10th houses together in the 10th house.

d) Lord of 4th house in the 9th house, Jupiter with Venus in 4th house, lord of 9th in 1st, 4th, 5th, 7th, 9th or 10th house.

e) If lord of 2nd house is exalted (short of the peak point) and is in 1st, 4th, 7th or 10th house.

f) Moon and Jupiter in 5th house with good strength (Moon shouldn't be in waning state of motion).

g) Waxing Moon in 1st house, Jupiter in 4th house and Venus in 10th house with strong Saturn in own Sign or in exaltation.

h) Waxing Moon in 4th, 7th or 10th house directly aspected by Jupiter or Venus.

i) A planet in debilitation occupying its Exaltation Rasi in Navamsha.

j) If Jupiter is in 1st house and Mercury in non-combust position in 1st or 4th or 7th or 10th house aspected directly by lord of the 9th house.

k) Jupiter in debilitation-Rasi in 1st and lord of 9th occupying 5th, 7th or 9th house with exchange of at least 50% *drishti* on each other.

l) Jupiter in 12th house, Sun in 3rd house and Saturn in 11th house (what Rasi these planets occupy is immaterial).

m) In the Moon chart (also known as Rasi chart), Sun with Saturn in 3rd house, Mercury or Venus in 4th house and Jupiter in 11th house.

n) Jupiter in 1st house, Sun is in 4th or 7th house and retrograde Venus is in 4th, 5th or 7th house.

o) Mercury in Virgo in the 1st house, Jupiter in Pisces in 7th house (just opposite) and Mars in Scorpio in 3rd house and Sun in Leo in 12th house (which means Sun in 3rd position from the 10th house).

p) Taurus or Scorpio in 1st house, Saturn in Capricorn in 9th

house or 3rd house, and Mercury or Venus or Jupiter in the 5th house.

q) If all 7 planets from Sun to Saturn are in Aries or Cancer or Libra or Capricorn.

r) Leo in the 1st house, Exalted Saturn in 3rd house, Venus in Taurus in 10th house and Sun in Aries (i.e. exalted) in 9th house It is additional support if Mars is in 6th house which would mean in its Exaltation-Rasi.

s) Lords of 9th and 10th house are in 1st or 4th or 7th or 10th house and Lord of 5th house is extra strong.

t) If any 3 planets are in exchange of ownership Rasis or 3 planets are in their debilitation Rasis. (Smt. Indira Gandhi, Prime Minister of India for a total of 16 years had three pairs of planets exchanging ownership Rasis with one another. That was the planetary influence in making her Prime Minister).

u) If Aries or Cancer or Libra or Capricorn is in Ascendant and Sun, Mars and Saturn are in 3rd, 6th or 11th house, together or separately.

v) Libra as Ascendant and Moon is in 10th house, Saturn is in 1st house and Mars is in 4th house.

w) Capricorn as Ascendant and Moon in 7th house Mars in 1st house and Saturn in 10th house.

x) Cancer as Ascendant and Moon (not near its combust point) with Jupiter there.

y) In Moon (Rasi) chart, if Moon is in its own Rasi (Cancer) and at least any two planets are in their own Rasis or in their Exaltation house, short of peak point.

z) Aries or Cancer in Ascendant and Mars in its ownership Rasi and Jupiter in Exaltation Rasi (short of peak point).

These are some of the combinations that make an individual reach high and highest position of power in administration or judiciary or any of the defence services or even in the police set-up. It is repeated that the above-given are only a few of the combinations, there are many others, which all cannot be covered in the limited scope of this book.

As stated above, there are combinations that bring the downfall of an individual in high position of power. In this context of elevation and downfall, it has to be noted that Mahadasa and its sub-periods as also transit of long-term planets as Saturn or Jupiter or Rahu (and to some extent Ketu too) carry great importance. Transit of Sun and Mars too at the given point of time, say, elections or appointment or usurping a high post of power certainly play a very important role.

Another important point is the yearly chart (known as *Varsh-phal* in India) plays indeed a very important part, and this has also to be noted that yearly charts cast by computer system are rarely accurate. *One should depend only on manually made yearly chart by a learned astrologer, not a quack!*

Then we come to Sun's combination with other planets. In a general way, it has been the experience of many learned astrologers over centuries that excepting Saturn, no other planet proves harmful in the company of Sun in the 10th house. Saturn too helps in rise or elevation if it is in its ownership house or in its exaltation Rasi. In either case, Sun becomes weak, because Saturn is diehard enemy of Sun, and Sun in Capricorn or Aquarius loses its strength and result-giving capacity. If Libra is in 10th house, which is Exaltation for Saturn, it is debilitation for Sun.

It has often been observed that Sun and Saturn together bring the downfall too for the individual from the high position of power and that too in a shameful or disgusting manner, with loss of reputation.

Now in so far as the question of conjunction (combination) of Sun with other planets is concerned, the ancient *acharyas* of astrology have gone into detailed discussion not only of one planet's conjunction with Sun but of more than one planet's combination with Sun in the 10th house. The authors of this book however have kept themselves restricted to discussion of Sun's combination with each planet independently and separately. When there are more than one planet in the 10th house with Sun, readers are advised to read discussion of each of those planets by means of combined study of these combinations, and reach a co-ordinated conclusion.

Sun and Moon in the 10th House

Positively Moon helps Sun very much, because whether combust or in debilitation or whatever Rasi be in the 10th house, Moon in the 10th house always brings success and wide-spread reputation to the individual. Moon also gives good complexion (depending on climate of that region), dignified behaviour, never harmful to any one unless some wrong has been done to the individual. No doubt these two planets in the 10th house make an individual rather ruthless in revenge.

Sun and Mars in the 10th House

Mars is another planet whose effectivity is very much attached to the 10th house as compared to all other houses. In this context it is important to note that Abdur-Rahim-Khankhanaa, a Minister in the cabinet of Moghul Emperor Akbar in the 16th century AD, (who was a very learned astrologer and was author of several books on astrology), has opined that if an individual has Mars in the 10th house, all population around him or her would bow at the feet of that individual.

Normally Mars and Sun are friends in permanent relationship, though they would be slightly opposed to each other being together at the time of birth. But it does not make either of them inoperative.

Both, Sun and Mars help the individual very much in reaching a high or medium or low position of power and authority, not by help and support of others to a weakling individual, but more by individual's own effort, capacity and suitability.

The individual comes to own substantial immovable property and wealth in one shape or form or the other.

Sun and Mercury in the 10th House

Normally Mercury is always with Sun because it is never more than 25 degrees away from Sun. Mercury attributes the element of intelligence, wisdom and experience to the individual to make serious efforts to reach a position of power, low or high is immaterial. Further Mercury gives a very good collection of books, and other reading (readable too) material to the individual. The individual indeed reads in full or merely a portion of the books, and gains knowledge and experience thereby. The individual gets a lot of books by way of gift or for retention after review. In many a case, the individual receives not only high education, but also obtains high educational degrees by self-effort, including those bestowed honoris-causa. He or she gets honours, titles and decorations in the field of education and literature. If ever in the field of teaching or in journalism, or writing as the whole-time source of livelihood, the individual earns a very big name and widespread reputation. The individual comes to hold a senior appointment as headmaster, principal, registrar, vice-chancellor etc in the field of education and teaching, but generally misses the rank of chancellor. In the field of journalism, the individual often remains restricted to a post under or connected with government or administration, with less chances of working in the private field, because of Sun, being in the 10th house, exerts more influence than Mercury in the 10th house.

Sun and Jupiter in the 10th House

This combination generally makes the individual reach a high position at the Bar or on the bench in the field of law and judiciary. Otherwise a high position in the field of economics, accounting, business management, ambassadorial post, Chancellor or Vice-Chancellor or Registrar of a university, may be even of a deemed university. The individual has chances of attaining the post of President, Prime Minister or a Minister in the Council of Administration or a self-appointed Dictator or Chief Administrator. Otherwise he or she becomes a Governor or a Chief Minister or Minister at Provincial level, Head of a county or District or if nothing else, Head of a *Panchayat* – in any case a *Head* person!

Or the individual becomes famous in the field of taxation, specially Income Tax and Sales Tax, whether the individual is on the governmental side or in advocacy and pleadership or chartered accountancy or costs and works accountancy. A majority of judges, court officers, commissioners and junior officers in Income Tax or Sales Tax have this combination in their 9th or 10th house.

The individual doesn't have any restraint or restriction in giving or accepting bribes and any kind of illegal gratification or obligation, or functioning as middle-man (females included) in bribery etc.

As a dark side of this combination, the individual sometimes indulges in gambling, card games, betting at horse races, buying lottery tickets in bulk, speculation on large scale. The damage and destruction in money, finances and material-shape often takes time to descend on the individual and the process is a slow one leaving margin for the individual to get rid of the destructive habits or at least reduce them to a great extent.

NOTE

So far discussed combination do not give downfall from a position reached, though continuing to occupy the same position after the expiry of the fixed term is a different thing altogether. It is not so exactly in the case of combination of Sun with Venus or with Saturn or with Rahu or Ketu. These combinations can bring a regrettable downfall too, even before the expiry of the fixed term.

Sun and Venus in the 10th House

The individual becomes famous in the field of fine arts, painting, drawing, architecture, sculptor, vocal and or instrumental music, dancing, acting and medical line including the indigenous ones. The individual also becomes expert in marriage-making, broker in marriage market, smuggling of goods as well as of manpower, cheating in Customs and Excise taxation, indulging in under-invoicing and over-invoicing for cheating the Tax system. Other fields for the individual's activity are show business like running theatre, cinema house, film production Centre, Studios, Distribution offices, agents for procuring part-time extras needed for forming groups in films etc. The individual sometimes becomes known for getting things done in offices and rather everywhere under temptations (to the concerned person) in the shape of supply of wine, woman, costly clothes, perfumes, domestic decoration items, smuggled goods etc. Other lines of activity open to these individuals are supplying domestic servants for serving known and secret purposes, conveyance/ transport facility for occasional use or permanent use.

The dark side of this combination is that quite often the individuals become notorious in public for these nefarious activities, and this notoriety might lead to enquiries and investigations. Sometimes the individual escapes the actual downfall, while other times suffers the actual downfall with added loss of reputation, and sometimes loss of source of livelihood or other assets. The matter warrants minute examination and detailed study.

Sun and Saturn in the 10th House

This is another risky and double-edged combination with hidden and sudden results, favourable and unfavourable. As stated earlier in this book, Saturn is the only planet that gives a slap and in the same instant sweets by the other hand, sometimes openly and sometimes secretly.

Saturn gives a tendency for indulging in unusual actions, without bothering about the opinion of others or about good name and bad name. And when Saturn is in conjunction with Sun, though both enemies in permanent as well as birth-time relationship, Saturn has a hidden feeling in mind that after all Sun being father would come to rescue at the time of any physical, financial or legal trouble.

To achieve any end in view, specially in the field of politics, job or work related to main source of livelihood, Saturn itself doesn't bother, (and influences Sun too not to bother) about appreciation or criticism, approval or disapproval of means, sources and actions used for reaching the desired aim or result. Saturn has its eye only on the final result, ultimate outcome. It applies to upright and noble acts, actions and activities, viewpoints, approach, and also to unhealthy, anti-social, semi-criminal or fully criminal deeds, actions, approach and activity.

Saturn has no hesitation in leading the individual to theft, robbery, dacoity, beating, even injuring fatally for achievement of the object or objective. Smuggling of goods, narcotics, intoxicating items are all in the routine course of life in the context of Saturn and Sun in the 10th house. Saturn is competent to organise groups and gangs, and also making them available to self and near relations, to any parent, to friends, and people paying for the individual's force at command. Truth and false-hood too do not have much value for Saturn (with Sun no doubt), because Saturn holds the view, "everything is fair in love and war".

If Saturn (and Sun) lead to a love affair for the individual, it is a whole-hearted affair, no falsehood. However even the slightest iota of doubt or suspicion about the beloved or the lover results in Saturn not only finishing the affair, but also making the opposite party not to easily think of repetition in these terms throughout life. It applies to Saturn (and Sun's) approach of mind and action in politics and job-competition also.

This combination leads the individual to position of power slowly and gradually, from a lower rank to a higher and then highest too, but the path is neither an easy one nor a clean road. Generally help and support comes from labour class, agriculturists, low ranks of service class, hidden help from capitalists and money-people. It is also a fact that Saturn forces its enemy-father (Sun) never to become ungrateful to these people who extended help and support in time of need, whether Saturn is able to do any favourable thing to those helpers and supporters in return or not.

Sun and Rahu or Ketu in the 10th House

In this combination Rahu and Ketu have been taken together, because there is not much difference in their results with Sun in the 10th house. The fact should not be overlooked that both are Shadow planets and both Rahu and Ketu are always in a 7: 7 parallel position to each other.

Unless Sun in 10th house has help and support from other planets either from lord of the 10th house or from some friendly planet casting full or direct *drishti* on Sun and 10th house both, Rahu or Ketu create hurdles for the individual in reaching the highest or even very high position of power. These shadow planets create problems for Sun to function freely in the 10th house, specially if either of them is within 12 degree vicinity of Sun in terms of conjunction.

These two are in no way less mischievous than Saturn (with Sun) in 10th house. Saturn tries its best to keep unhealthy and nefarious acts and actions secret as far as possible or at least till the desired result is achieved. On the other hand Rahu or Ketu (with Sun in the 10th house) openly leak out the unhealthy deeds, actions and the individual's association with undesirable elements. It is so when the individual is working for a recognised position of power or authority. Thus the result achieved becomes more or less bitter in the mouth of the individual.

No doubt, Rahu or Ketu does not lead the individual to very serious type of criminal or illegal acts and actions or association, but at the same time they are not noble, gentle and approvable too.

SUN IN THE 11TH HOUSE

The 11th house is mainly concerned with Income, earnings, actual arrival of money in hand, and also mental disposal of self towards progeny, and in later life with fiancée or lover or spouse of son and daughter respectively. Other subjects for 11th house are loss or gains from a brother or sister, illegitimate children, left arm, left lower ribs, left breast or left portion of chest.

Sun, at least in the case of government servants, politicians in power, officers and staff in semi-government or public sector, gives a mixture of honest and dishonest income in cash or kind. Even if a government servant is honest, corrupt persons seeking favours make him or her dishonest. An example would make the point clear.

An officer in the rank of Commissioner of Income Tax was known for his (real, not assumed) honesty. One very rich assessee wanted a favour from this Commissioner in an unjustified appeal in his tax assessment. When the Commissioner was out of town for a whole week on official duty, this businessman went to his residence, did not disclose own identity, and returned after enquiring from the Commissioner's wife as to when her husband was expected back in town. The businessman found that even holding the rank of Commissioner, the officer had no fridge(refrigerator) at his residence. This businessman had a fridge sent to the Commissioner's residence without disclosing the identity of even the dealer who supplied it. The unloader and an electrician installed it in the house of the officer. His wife enquired from the electrician but could not know who had sent it. The simple reply was, "the boss had ordered it".

On return from tour, the officer couldn't trace who had sent it. What could the officer do! He could not put it outside his house, as it was not known as to whom to return it. After an expiry of about six months, when the businessman's appeal was to come for hearing, he just casually enquired of the Commissioner if the fridge was working all right. Then the Commissioner came to know the source of supply. After six months use, it was not proper to return a used fridge. He sent a crossed cheque to the businessman, which naturally the businessman never encashed. The appeal had to be granted, and the innocent Commissioner sought and got his transfer to another province!

Not that it happens to be so in the case of every government servant. No, some of them, at least in India (a widely known fact that), are known to drop indirect and direct hints for gratification, like demanding precious-stone rings, jewellery for daughter's or son's marriage, free air passage to go abroad, etc. The senior author remembers examples from personal experience, and believes that now many officers in public dealing departments, like Income-tax, Customs, Central-Excise, Sales-tax, Police, Telecommunications, Public Works, Law Courts, Irrigation directly demand bribes in cash and openly haggle on the amount of the bribe. Some do so directly, while some have agents or family members as agents and conduits.

And many such corrupt officers and members of staff have their own agents and sources to secretly invest this ill-gotten money.

One such officer of the Public Works Department would often obtain loans from his own Provident Fund in office to establish that he was honest and needed money for day-to-day expenses, while the fact was that he was running a business in joint names of his wife and wife's brother and was investing the loans from the Provident Fund into that business.

Sun is normally not a planet injurious to general health or any limb or part of the body, unless it is associated with some injurious planet. Sun causes at the most fever (sometimes high fever if it is harmfully placed in the yearly chart), minor and easily curable skin ailment, or tolerable type of fluctuation in blood system. Sun generally does not associate itself with disorders of the menstrual cycle in females, unless linked with Mars, Venus or Saturn or Rahu.

One point is more or less certain about Sun. It doesn't tolerate any love affair or even casual intimate (platonic type) friendship of the child with any member of the opposite sex, be it in the school or college or in neighbourhood or with an equal-aged child of a relative of the family. After the child reaches the normal age for marriage, the individual (father or mother) with Sun in 11th house would be willing to consider, in an unbiased manner, any marriage-oriented love affair of the child, simply on merits and demerits. One major problem in this connection is that the individual would attach due or undue importance to own family and its status as compared to that of the fiancée or the lover. However being a dignified planet, Sun is an easy surrender to convincing pleas of the child itself or of the individual's spouse or any senior member of the immediate family, or outsider intimate friend of the individual. Therefore in a case of controversy, it is always better for the child concerned to apply these sources of approach.

An individual with Sun in the 11th house is much concerned with sharp sense of self-respect. If after marriage, the individual finds that the daughter-in-law or the son-in-law is in a mood of challenge or confrontation, the individual (if a man) would withdraw from the scene or the situation. If the individual were a woman, she would first put in a fight on basis of her viewpoint, and on defeat would try to make the person opposite her to withdraw from the situation or from the joint family itself.

These individuals with Sun in 11th house would lose temper rather quickly too, but often suppress the anger and hot words, and would take resort to silence. When angry, they do shout, and later on regret it and often attempt a compromise and fresh understanding.

It is general belief that Sun gives only male children or at least a male child first of all, but it has not been found a very correct belief. Sun can give progeny of both sexes, of any sex in the first instance, and secondly, getting children or their sex depends on the planets of the spouse too, because no single individual can produce a child, whatever the progress in the science of the modern world.

Sun and Moon in the 11th House

This combination doesn't deter a person from dishonest ways and means to make money, nor it interferes with the working of the individual, whatever may be the manner of one's working or functioning. Moon with Sun in 11th house, though combust normally, controls the individual's bad temper towards the children or even towards outsiders, if Sun happens to put the individual in public dealing work or post.

Further, this combination gives the individual a strong desire for immigration to another town, another state or county or another country for higher earnings and is generally successful in doing so. No doubt Moon with Sun in 11th house suppresses the initial failure of the individual, in doing so, Moon brings undue pressure on the faculties of the mind of the individual, and rather gives mental worries, mental depression and forgetfulness too.

Moon and Sun in conjunction in the 11th house do not prove a hurdle in getting both male or female children, and the couple do not bother whether the first child is a son or a daughter.

One important point is that these individuals should always stay careful about their diet, what they eat, when do they eat, and what is the climate of the place where they are residing or staying temporarily or permanently. Any lapse in carefulness would adversely affect the health, even before the lapse is recognised and corrected.

Sun and Mars in the 11th House

Sun and Mars combination is a profitable and co-operative event in every respect. Mars with Sun increases the frequency and intensity of anger, on own progeny, on any child, on others at home or in the school and college or at play-ground during student days. This tendency of quick anger at others continues when grown up, moreso if the individual happens to occupy a post or position of public dealing. The reason is that both these planets are rage-generating ones and more so when they are in conjunction, and all the more so because they cast direct *drishti* on the 5th house, which rules thinking, emotions, feelings and mental disposition.

Then Sun and Mars together make an individual very bold and courageous in giving or accepting unlawful gratification in cash, in kind, and in extreme cases, even a plot of land, building material (or even a ready-to-occupy flat, apartment or a small house). There are real life cases within the knowledge of the senior author where dishonest officers have accepted bribe of a motor car or a flat, if not directly, in the name of the spouse or a son or daughter or even in the name of the son-in-law. However generally only those individuals indulge in this high type of malpractice who have a protective Jupiter in their birth or Navamsha chart.

These individuals are very rough with their progeny in the matter of education, irrespective of the individuals' own level of education. They often want to have their children, at least one daughter or one son selected for the senior civil service or in police or in defence services as a full-fledged commissioned officer. In so doing these individuals do not bother about the choice of the progeny itself nor about the progeny's own stars whether the stars are helpful or unhelpful for that particular line of career desired by the parent(s).

Some of these individuals with Mars and Sun in 11th house are employed directly in police or in defence services or on such an administrative or accounting or finance controlling post as is directly concerned with police or defence services or with Customs and Excise or anti-narcotics services.

Health-wise, this combination, because of pressure from Mars, gives pain or ailment to the females in the left breast (swelling, or less milk on childbirth) or left side of chest to males. Otherwise it can be pain in upper ribs, or in rare cases the pain goes upto the range of (generally dry) pleurisy, injury with bleeding to the upper left arm, below armpit, the left portion of body between left breast/ chest and spine bone. This combination however does not give directly any ailment connected to blood pressure or leading to heart trouble.

A normal belief is that Mars (and Sun) in the 11th house protects the individual against any illness and keeps the health alright. In actual life, even a very affectionate parent or guardian sometimes gives a harsh beating to own progeny. Similarly even a protective planet can give some jilt or jerk to the health of the individual when Mars (or even Sun) has its unfavourable Antardasa under the Mahadasa of a planet which is in opposition to Mars or Sun or is an enemy to either of them.

Because of holding an obliging or harming post or position, these individuals, in spite of their short temper and malpractices, enjoy good or cordial relations in the public. They prefer to be associated to some well-known Club, social-work body or religious formation or similar public-service and public contact organisation, more to stay respectful in society, with less interest in the work concerning to that body, and with an eye to their own prestige.

Unless Venus is in the 10th or the 12th house, these individuals generally maintain good character, also because of the impression that a bad character would bring bad effect of the same type on their own progeny.

Another important result of this combination in the 11th house is that even slightest provocation would cause loss of pregnancy to a woman, more likely in the 2nd, 3rd or the 5th

month. If the medical advise has prohibited physical relationship between husband and wife during any stage of the pregnancy, the couple must follow the advice strictly. Even kissing and touch of the woman's body might lead to loss of pregnancy, because her desire gets awakened, and pushes the embryo out of the uterus.

Yet another important point is that this combination in 11th house is apt to give full-para delivery of the child by caesarean section. Sometimes it is so because the pregnant woman does not want to suffer the labour pain for long duration, sometimes because the doctor attending on the pregnant woman is in a hurry to 'do with' the delivery of the child. It is not rare that the gynaecologist makes caesarean section delivery to earn a higher fee. In any case, whether it is a miscarriage or abortion or full-para delivery of the child, there are chances of excess bleeding, sometime making it necessary to give blood transfusion to the woman concerned. The family of the woman should stay prepared for such a contingency, at least at the time of full-para delivery of the child. Sometimes it becomes difficult to get the blood of the needed type for transfusion, moreso in smaller towns.

Sun and Mercury in the 11th House

Mercury tries to bring an element of honesty in the demeanour of the individual, but is generally unsuccessful in doing so because Sun is always more powerful than Mercury, and secondly because Mercury stands in a combust position. Then Mercury generates better wisdom into the individual to conceal the ways, means and effects of dishonesty, and also to secretly use or invest the unlawful gains from dishonesty. One peculiar drawback of Mercury in the 11th house is that it casts full *drishti* on the 5th house of intelligence and wisdom. Mercury is prompt in keeping accounts in written form somewhere or the other, in tiny note-books, on loose slips hidden under the postal receipts and acknowledgements, within bunch of bills for water, electricity, property tax and receipts of payments, or similar other places. Some individuals keep coded jotting at the binding side of a notebook or casual account-books. This is normally done by business community earning black money in very large amounts and also by judges and government officers and junior staff, advocates and chartered accountants who function as middle-men in conveyance of bribes, who are all given to extreme type of dishonest practices.

Now what actually happens is that the investigating officers belonging to anti-corruption outfits have also gone so expert in the line of searches that they somehow reach these hidden spots and locate the written proof of dishonesty and black money. Unfortunately the state of affairs in this regard in India is that a good many of these investigating and search-conducting officers too have gone dishonest.

For example, in Mumbai (old name Bombay) a search party traced about 2 kilograms (a little over 4 pounds English weight) of gold. But in the 'seizure memo' (called "panch-nama", i.e. a written statement signed by at least two independent eyewitnesses), they showed only 8 ounces (about 250 grams) of gold seized. The three Customs officers conducting the searches usurped the remaining large quantity of gold, and a little share was given to the two independent witnesses too. Normally these corrupt officers in any department take along with them their patent (so-called independent) eye witnesses, who would share a small part of the booty.

Mercury with Sun in 11th house gives softness to the nature of the individual and the individual applies faculties of mind before using harsh language towards anyone outside home. But the same Mercury rather encourages the individual to be harsh to own progeny for progress in education.

In a love affair or friendship with a member of the opposite sex, Mercury makes the individual quite talkative, and indulging in exchange of written letters or love-oriented poetry, *ghazals*, poems, songs, or Sanskrit verses etc., which ultimately serve as a source of leakage of the love affair. Sun is a matured planet, while Mercury is deemed to be young. Their conjunction sometimes leads to love affair, friendship or even marriage between an aged person and a young one, under force of some consideration, temptation or pressure, for some need of self or of the family, or under certain uncontrollable circumstances.

Mercury has no direct concern with good or bad health or with good or bad diet habits or other habits of the individual having good or bad effect on health and it doesn't interfere with protection provided to health by Sun.

Mercury is willing to help or support a sister-in-law or brother-in-law without direct involvement in their difficulty or problem, and the individual rarely needs their help or support, in return.

Sun and Jupiter in the 11th House

A typical combination in the sense that Jupiter tries to keep the individual above board in matters of integrity and honesty, but often it fails in doing so, because of Sun's presence in the 11th house. Then helplessly (like its predecessor Mercury), Jupiter and Sun together help the individual in accumulating a big hoard of unlawful income in his or her hands. Jupiter encourages the individual to maintain some record somewhere of the illegal money coming in hand, but when seized, unlike Mercury, Jupiter is often able to produce proof of that money's accountability and lawful character.

Jupiter (even with Sun) in the 11th house encourages the individual to help and support the real or adopted or foster parent(s) in every manner feasible. Jupiter has a tendency to extend an occasional helping hand towards other near and distant relatives of self or spouse, and simultaneously desiring a return in some manner or the other, if nothing else at least expression of grateful feelings repeatedly. This combination rarely makes the individual in need of financial support from mother or other relatives, except in legal matters. However the individual is always keen on full share or even more than full share in inheritance from real parents or adopting parents.

The individual has to be careful in matters of diet and drinks, because Jupiter (with Sun) might cause problems with digestive system, diabetes and pain on verge of getting (wet) pleurisy. However unless Mars is in the 4th or 8th or 12th house, this combination would not cause peptic ulcers.

Motherly women (but not real mother) should generally stay alert, because of Jupiter (with Sun) in 11th house creating a suspicion in the minds of the women that their rights are being encroached upon or are being interfered with by the individual. On his or her part, the individual would not hesitate to issue a legal notice to the motherly woman, and in case of not getting the desired relief from the particular woman, the individual would not hesitate to take recourse to legal action in the matter.

Jupiter in conjunction with Sun in 11th house normally doesn't encourage the individual towards extra marital affair, nor towards any untoward affair towards relatives of prohibited degree. When bachelor, the individual would not jump from person-to-person quickly or deliberately for any kind of romantic relationship. On the other hand, in case of formality-based behaviour of the other party, the individual would wait for the normal formality of marriage according to the traditions or customs in the family or community or tribe. Otherwise too, the individual would not have more than one spouse, and in the event of death or divorce of the first spouse, would hesitate to go in for second marriage, unless the age and circumstances and family pressure lead to a second marriage.

However Jupiter (even with Sun) in the 11th house tolerates and normally approves of any love affair of own progeny, and if consent for marriage is sought for, it is given without much a-do.

Sun and Venus in the 11th House

The first effect of this combination in 11th house is that the individual has romantic ideas towards opposite sex. A platonic or physical love affair does find place in the life of the individual at one stage or the other, irrespective of the age.

A woman had this combination in the 11th house, with Mercury on border of 11th and 12th house in Bhava Chalitam chart, and Venus alone was in the 7th house in her Trinshansha chart in own Rasi (Taurus). She was 43 years old in 1953 and she had four grown up sons, three of them working in responsible positions and the youngest one in the 4th year in the University. By chance she casually consulted the senior author astrologically who predicted to her that even at that age and even after being mother of four grown-up sons, she did not know the real pleasure of sexual satisfaction. The astrologer predicted further that within four months she would meet a young man of about 25 to 27 years in age, fall in love with him and derive the best-ever-felt satisfaction of sex. By chance, she developed fever after 3 months of this prediction. Her husband ran a charitable dispensary, and she was his second wife, the age difference between them being 14 years. He directed his compounder (a medical assistant) to give an intra-muscular anti-fever injection to the wife. The manner in which this assistant rubbed her upper thigh portion after the injection aroused the woman's sexual sensation on the first occasion itself. On the third meeting, the assistant and the wife of this very senior officer arranged to sleep together, and she derived the best pleasure of her life. She then summoned the senior author and confirmed to him that his prediction came correct. The astrologer retorted by saying that it was because of Saturn's transit over the 7th house in her birth chart, and the love affair would not last more than two and a half years. The affair ended with the departure of that compounder (after expiry of exact two and a half years of love affair with that woman) to his home-town as he had lost his father and he had to give up his job to look after the big agricultural farm of the family. The astrologer and the woman last met after 40 years of that event, and she was full of praise for the knowledge of the astrologer!

An important point for study from astrological point is that because Sun and Venus were in the 11th house, they cast full *drishti* on the 5th house which concerns getting progeny at an early age (the woman had her first child before completion of her 15th year of age). Saturn comes back to the same Rasi (Sign of zodiac) by transit after a gap of 28 (to 30) years. When Saturn was in transit in the 7th house the first time, the woman got married. When it was in the 7th house by transit after exactly 28 years, she got into the extra marital affair, when the elder son was about 27 years old. This establishes the faith in astrology, if the calculations are correct and the astrologer has his knowledge to a good degree of perfection.

These are the individuals who sometimes entertain romantic feelings and emotions towards even motherly woman or fatherly figures in the case of females. What happens in the conclusion depends on the planets of both, and prediction about it depends on the knowledge and experience of the astrologer!

Generally these individuals honour their commitments in love affair, whatever the kind, depth, duration and quality of the affair.

At the same time, these individuals are normally given to extend unconditional help and support near relatives, if not always, at least in hour of their need, whether financially or otherwise

Venus normally doesn't give problems of health, unless Mars is in the 8th or 12th house or Saturn is in the 4th house with 6: 8 relationship conflict with combination of Venus and Sun in the 11th house. Then the health trouble would depend on the planet causing it. Saturn would give muscular pain or any injury to any bone or to the skull. Mars would give some dreadful disease related to sex with person suffering from that type of disease or disorder of the blood system, complaints of menstrual cycle or skin ailment repeatedly.

Sun and Saturn in the 11th House

The first and foremost result of this combination is that it gives an in-built tendency for dishonestly begotten money, whatever the individual's source of income. Even highly placed persons in politics, defence, judiciary, public bodies and organisations of the country go corrupt. Why look at the highly placed persons. Even a vegetable vendor, fruit seller would try to earn dishonest profits. A daily wage labourer, if nothing else, would try to indulge in petty thefts, picking up items in a clandestine manner wherever he works, or even while walking on roads or narrow streets. There is not much difference in theft, pick pocketing, picking up goods, purses and packets from parked vehicles or even from vehicles waiting for the green light on roads, robbery or dacoity, single-handed or as a member of a well organised gang.

It is extremely rare that the top dignitaries get apprehended or booked, though the lowly, unconnected person does get caught and perhaps convicted too. Such has become the system today. The public in its heart of heart believes that many highly placed persons –be it ministers, other senior authorities of the government accept illegal gifts in cash and kind, directly or through their kith and kin. But the public, the common man would not openly talk about or disclose, in spite of reliable knowledge, for fear of reprisals of all kinds.

Where health of an individual is concerned, normally this combination helps keeping the individual fit. All that one might suffer is from pain in the regions described at the beginning of the chapter on Sun in the 11th house.

These individuals are more confident of their physical strength. At the drop of the hat, they would indulge in a physical bout. In such an event as this, they too might receive a severe blow on the chest or near about that area, which might give pain in the long run. If these individuals ever fall down with a force, a few muscles get ruptured. Another trouble generally caused by Saturn with Sun in 11th house is hernia, or kidney problem or liver ailment, as these parts of the body are on the borderline of 10th and 11th houses.

These individuals are often very helpful to near and distant relatives as also to outsider who approach them for help of any kind, including financial help. They expect nothing in return, except loyal feelings from the recipient on getting a call from the giver of help.

These individuals are quite often dry-natured and not given to emotional love, except physical relief according to their needs or whims. They are slow to fall in love and slow to declare the love dead. They are cruel and revengeful if the other party in the affair betrays their confidence. It is sometimes true even in developed countries like USA, Canada and France or other European countries where starting and breaking love affair is quite common and a routine matter. These individuals go in for customary marriage as per standards of the family. And they stay loyal to the spouse, notwithstanding their platonic love for others outside the marriage.

Unless Moon or Mercury has any direct association with this combination, these individuals do not entertain too much or too many emotional approaches to their life plans and programs. And thus they have less scope for worries and depression of the mind. They believe in action, and they themselves plan implementation thereof.

In case of pregnant women, Saturn (with Sun) in 11th house gives prolonged labour pain at the time of delivery of the child, sometimes the labour pain is intermittent and also fluctuating. But this combination rarely gives caesarean section delivery.

Sun and Rahu in the 11th House

In this particular house Rahu (with Sun) gives more or less the same results as Saturn gives, no doubt to a reduced degree. Sun is more or less ineffective in this eclipse-type combination. Being a planet connected to fatness, Rahu normally gives big breasts to a woman, and expanded chest to a man. Nearing the old age, even a man's chest gives an appearance of medium size breast of a woman, sagging. If no where else, one can observe it in pictures appearing on the visual media.

Rahu makes a bigger noise and bigger show of giving help to near and distant relations, but sometimes is more liberal towards outsiders seeking help. Financial help is less in virtually every case, but moral support, verbal or written recommendation, threat and even actual physical action are given without reservation indeed.

Rahu (even with Sun in 11th) is not very bold and courageous in commitment of theft, robbery, dacoity, and generally uses others for the purpose, the individual remaining in the background, but in case of trouble helps that agent or operator whole-heartedly.

Another result worth note is that Rahu is capable of causing loss of pregnancy to a woman, and because of conjunction with Sun, it is capable of giving excess bleeding in the process of miscarriage, abortion or full-para delivery of the child. Rahu, however, does not cause so much loss of blood as to necessitate blood transfusion.

Sun and Ketu in the 11th House

With regard to Sun and Ketu combination, just read the matter given under "Sun and Mercury in the 11th house", and it would be enough for Sun and Ketu combination too. The only difference is that Ketu, being a shadow planet, functions to a reduced degree of actual action. In every sense it thus operates as a junior to Mercury.

However Mercury doesn't create trouble to a woman at the time of delivery of a child, but Ketu does cause longer labour pain or other kind of trouble to the woman at the time of delivery of a child.

SUN IN THE 12TH HOUSE

Sun is a mixture of hard and soft planet. It is the 'ruler' among planets. Like any parent, it exercises discipline on the individual as well as has deep affection. But in the 12th house, Sun often functions as a hard planet.

Whether the individual is in government employ or in private employ or in own business or industry or self-employment or profession or in active politics, Sun would bring an enquiry or investigation against the individual. The enquiry or investigation might relate to the employer or an employee of the individual, but it would arrive at the door of the individual. If nothing else, the individual might be detained for interrogation or arrested for a minor civic offence or just a casual or negligible violation of traffic rules. God forbid it might not be some over-enthusiastic police officer who could unhesitatingly shoot an individual for something as trivial as a traffic offence (happened in August 2001)! However it would happen only if Mars or Saturn too would be in close vicinity of Sun in the 12th.

The individual might be dragged to a court of law under various Sections, only to give a big dimension to the minor offence or to the hollow imagination of the law and order outfit.

Sometimes framed charges also descend on the individual and it becomes difficult for the individual to get out of it. The system of law is so defective in virtually all countries that the judge hearing the case would often show inclination to believe the police version, and overlook the version of the individual howsoever truthful and correct the individual's version is!

For example, I am told that in Middle-East countries, their local resident is treated as always true and correct, and a national from another country is considered more at fault. Once in Iran, two cars of local residents (Irani nationals), driven from different directions, banged into each other, because one of the drivers was on the wrong side the road, and heavily drunk. As a result, one of the cars in the crash bounced in the air and fell on a third car, parked in the curb, but belonging to an Indian, working in Iran on deputation to the Iran Government. The impact of the crashing car falling on the parked car was so much that the Indian's 13-year old daughter sitting in the parked car, was crushed to death. In the final enquiry, the Iran Police booked the Indian for parking his car in a wrong manner! Though fact was that the car was parked correctly at the proper parking space. No action whatsoever was taken against the two Iranian nationals whose cars crashed. The Indian national was repatriated to India. Neither the police nor the court of law took any cognisance of the death of the 13 year old girl crushed in the parked car. The Indian gentleman had Sun and Saturn in the 12th house and had been cautioned about governmental action, a good time before he left for Iran.

In India and in virtually all other countries, if police or any other agency of the government like customs, excise, or anti-narcotics) want to harass an individual, the officials themselves would plant a small quantity of opium or narcotics or illicit liquor, or a small piece of smuggled contraband within the premises of the individual. Then a search would be conducted of those premises and the individual would be booked for a severe type of offence or crime.

I know the case an individual who was asked to remove clothes for a more effective search of his person, and while one official was frisking his body, another official placed a packet of contraband in the 'removed' clothes in a clandestine manner. Thus the person was found in possession of contraband, and booked for non-bailable offence.

Political vendetta and vandalism, suppression, unlawful arrest and imprisonment, physical attacks, even murders are quite common in more or less all countries, and there is virtually no rescue or relief for the sufferers. There is no need for the government machinery to make any special effort to frame an individual in a crime. Unfortunately, the judges in a court of law, for one reason or the other, tend to believe and trust the version of the police, often, if not always.

Therefore, one should always stay alert and preventive against any framed or exaggerated charge(s), when Sun is in the 12th house.

The question of causing a loss is also connected to Sun in the 12th house. The loss can be on any account, viz., speculation, gambling, betting on person-to-person level about outcome of an uncertain event, betting at horse races, card games, buying lottery tickets in bulk, and getting no compensating gain in the result thereof. Any fine or penalty in terms of money imposed by a court of law or any department of the government has to be deemed as a loss for the individual concerned. Any fine or penalty imposed correctly or wrongly by community or restricted cult or club or village *Panchayat*, or any other similar organisation or body would naturally amount as a loss for the individual. However an important point in this context is that the kind of losses enumerated in this paragraph would not normally be caused by Sun alone in the 12th house, unless Sun is in conjunction with any other planet(s).

In this connection an example would explain the better An individual has Sun, Mercury and Venus in the 12th house, and he has suffered big losses by way of fighting police challans (tickets) for no fault whatsoever on his part, except that he feels because he is from an ethnic minority community in the USA. He also suffered losses in connection with matrimony, as also by way of paying big bribes in his home country to various officers of even *non-concerned departments. Because the combination of Sun with Mercury and Venus is in a moving (cardinal) Rasi (Cancer) in the 12th house, the individual suffered loss of considerable money on useless journeys with no productive and useful purpose, and also on paying sky-high fees of the advocates in the USA!*

Another result of these three planets in the 12th house for that individual was that he was dragged to a court of law in his first marriage for not much fault on his part. The under-current was his refusal to join his father-in-law in his civil construction business. This individual has Jupiter in the 5th house, which means in the 8th position from the 10th house which rules father (and sometimes father-in-law too).

These examples have been stated to for easy understanding of the results of Sun in the 12th house. Interference by a government agency in the matter of immovable property of the individual is also an outcome of Sun in the 12th house, with the result that the individual is unable to use the property for the purpose it was constructed, bought or obtained on lease or rent.

Sun in the 12th house means in the 8th position from the 5th house, which rules mainly education of self and the progeny. As a result the person sometimes gets education, at least at the higher stages in a piece-meal manner, after much hard struggle and effort on part of self. She or he gets any progeny also often late in life after the marriage.

Yet another result of Sun in 12th house is that a lot of money, even beyond the financial capacity of the individual, gets spent on paying bribe and other illegal gratification, some of which never bring the desired results. It is also true that the individual indulges in giving gifts to members of the family, to children of self and others, without bothering himself or herself whether the costly gifts etc. are easily affordable or not.

But, it may be added here – if regular prayers for Sun are offered, and head is bowed before the rising Sun (at least within 3 hours of rising whether Sun is actually visible or not), the extreme results of Sun in 12th house can become somewhat less or toned down. The Sun is regular and punctual in its rising and setting.

It is unavoidable that the individual should undertake the remedy of Sun in a regular and undisturbed or unbroken manner, because piecemeal or sporadic efforts would not bring much relief.

Sun and Moon in the 12th House

The combination of Sun and Moon in the 12th house gives losses or unbearable heavy expenditure through consumption of or trading in liquids, liquors, alcohol, drugs, narcotics, poisonous items, that is any kind of intoxicating items. Losses might be suffered in trading or hoarding of cotton, cottonseeds, long cloth, medicinal goods, running a pharmacy and trading in pharmacy products. Losses can be on account of medical expenses on self or a member of the family (specially suffering from any health-problem connected with brains, mind and sanity).

Yet another source of outgo of money is emotional spending of money, often in an unjustified manner. This combination tempts an individual or spouse to spend on wanted or unwanted journeys, as also on gifts to friends of the other sex, for sake of creating an impression or winning over the friend for romantic purpose. One thing is very often possible that Moon (with Sun) attracts the mind of the individual (whether married or single) towards members of the opposite sex, and naturally it leads (sometimes) to wasteful spending.

Another source of wasteful outgo of money or other costly items is demands by members of immediate family or even wider family. It is not unheard of thing that a relative expresses liking (really or artificially) for a costly item in the household, and expresses regret that the relative is not in a position to afford it. Then the individual feels obliged to offer that item (or equivalent money to buy it) as gift, whether the individual was in position to afford it or not. These events can be termed as tricks of the trade on part of the relative!

Moon very often gives wasteful expenditure on securing admission to a medical college or a specified course of study in science, with no gainful result to the individual or a child of the individual.

Similarly, import and export trade also give losses, or under-invoicing and over-invoicing gets detected and the individual is punished in terms of fine and penalty and excess taxes on the differences in the amount shown in papers and the exact amount of duty due. In many cases it happens that an importer in a foreign country claims that the goods supplied were not of the quality ordered, or were not received in time and purpose for which goods were ordered was lost owing to delay. Then the importer in foreign country wants to return the goods at the cost of the exporter or wants a big cut, sometimes 50% or more in payment of the price of the goods. In a sense of cunningness, the importer does not get the goods cleared and does not take delivery from the Customs. Since the exporter cannot afford to get back the goods owing to heavy cost of transport by air or sea, the goods cross the time limit of being kept in the warehouse of the Customs. The goods are then sold by the Customs at a public auction, resulting in a big loss to the exporter. Many a time it transpires later on that the same importer had purchased the auctioned goods at a throwaway price. Sometimes the importer too suffers a loss because wrong goods were sent or the goods were short in quantity claimed or goods were of inferior quality or sometimes the goods were spurious in nature. These are also tricks of the trade, and even a very alert or smart importer or exporter might suffer heavily, with no actual relief or remedy. Neither the exporter nor the importer wants to suffer loss of the trade link between them, because it is difficult to find and establish a new link. And then, what is the guarantee that the successor importer or exporter would not play the same or even bigger tricks. And all this happens on account of the suffering trader having Sun and Moon combination in the 12th house.

Similarly, when smuggled goods get within the investigation trap, and they are seized and confiscated, the smuggler does suffer a heavy loss. The loss can be in terms of bribe, in terms of getting the confiscated goods released on payment of heavy fine and penalty or complete loss of the goods in Customs hands.

Another source of loss can be in transmission of the goods (from one town to another, from one state to another or from one country to another) by theft, looting, natural calamity, accident etc. No need to go into details on this point, which are normally known to the readers and the astrologers.

The losses caused by Sun and Moon conjunction are much subject to remedy by prayers and charity etc. Prayers for Sun and Lord Shiva (for Moon) can bring some relief, at least where the loss or heavy expenditure is connected to health problems, relating to brains, mind and sanity. Eating from silver vessels, wearing silver anklets (in case of women sufferers), using white linen including bed sheets also appeases Moon to some limited extent. At least no harm whatsoever is there in trying these remedies.

Sun and Mars in the 12th House

In this case, the loss can be through failure of electricity (power) resulting in stoppage of manufacturing process or production, fire, short-circuit, pilferage, embezzlement, theft or looting,

Then there can be losses by fire, theft, pilferage or embezzlement of money or profits. It can be by natural calamity too. It can be by confiscation of goods produced, workers' strike in the factory or market of carriers' network, etc., or differences or dispute between sellers and buyers. Damage and loss can be due to an accident to the factory-shed or shop or residential building or to any other property or assets in riots, religious disturbances, by hooliganism of hoodlums on occasions of festivals or communal disturbances, by damage and destruction by pleasure-seeking youngsters. Loss can be by stoppage of production or manufacture for non-supply of raw material or base material. Loss can also be by the owner of the industry or business suffering loss at some other source (say in share market or unthoughtful spending or failure of a banking institute). Owing to that loss at other source, the industrial production gets stopped, leading to allied losses. If production or manufacture gets stopped for one reason or the other, other losses flowing therefrom would be:

    (i)   by cost of unused raw material,

    (ii) rent or lease-amount of the industrial shed,

    (iii) interest on bank loans and market credits,

(iv) wages of the idle labour force, and

(v) loss of prestige in the market.

Similar loss can be on account of closure of shop or any other business.

Several times, governmental action is also responsible for heavy expenditure that can be deemed as a loss, because it reduces the money-content in the hands of the individual or spouse or the family. This type of expenditure might include money spent on getting bail, money spent on fighting any criminal charge or civil litigation.

This combination gives a touch of mischief to the young kids in the house, or even those staying in hostels for education. This combination adversely affects the educational progress and standard of those children who too have unfavourable Mars or Sun or both for their education. Naturally, such children as those with unfavourable Mars and Sun would avoid full attention to studies or to prescribed homework. Loss can also be caused by any kind of damage to moveable assets or immoveable property by the youngsters within or outside the household.

Yet another point that deserves attention in the context of Sun and Mars combination in the 12th house is that it can cause physical injury by any instrument, by short circuit, by live electric wire, by fire, by a firecracker or by a severe attack by anyone (may be a thief, robber, or an enemy or opponent or competitor) to the individual himself or herself or to a member of the family. In any case, medical treatment would cost money, and it has to be deemed as a loss. The level of expenditure can be higher if surgical treatment or treatment at outstation is involved. The astrologer must examine the stars like Saturn and Rahu, if either of them happen to be in the 12th house by transit. Or whether Mahadasa or sub-period of Mars or Saturn or Rahu is current simultaneous to the illness, injury or accident. Under these Mahadasa or sub-periods too, the individual or the spouse or any other member of the family might suffer an illness, injury, or accident, requiring costly medical expenses. If the current year's yearly chart too has harmful stars in the 6th, 8th or 12th house, it is better to caution the individual about risks to his or her person during that year of the age. Unless the astrologer is three times sure, he or she should not frighten the individual by prediction of risk to life itself.

Sun and Mars in 12th house very often develop strain in relations with neighbours and distant relatives. Both categories often expect some help or support in one form or the other from the individual or from the family of the individual. If due to some circumstances the help or support is not given, at least at the right moment, it would cause annoyance to the seeker of the favour.

Another source of loss can be damage or any other kind of loss through property due to man-made mischief, unfair division of property, usurpation of or encroachment on such property as has been lying unoccupied or unused.

Complete or partial loss of property can be under any court order or government order or acquisition by government for one purpose or the other, which is ultimately not released by government. It is a common knowledge that any government normally offers very little value of the property thus acquired. Loss can be by a tenant not paying rent, or turns hostile and tries to become owner of the property by force or by other unlawful methods, or by top-class cunning methods.

There has been such a case in New Delhi in a posh colony. A nice big bungalow was vacant. One businessman from Bombay approached the landlord for renting it. The landlord quoted ₹1,00,000/- per month as rent for it. The prospective tenant remarked that he would be honest to the landlord, adding that the correct market rent should be ₹1,50,000/- per month. The prospective tenant further offered 12 months rent as deposit. The landlord was naturally very happy over this rental agreement. The tenant paid ₹18,00,000/- in all as deposit, and also paid another ₹6,00,000/- as advance rent for 4 months. After four months, the tenant did not pay any money as rent. For further two months, the landlord did not demand rent, depending on the security deposit in the shape of 12 months' rent. After six months, the landlord residing in the same locality demanded the rent. The tenant scolded the landlord claiming that the latter had sold the bungalow to the former for the amount already paid. The actual money paid was ₹24 lakhs, while the house was probably worth 20 times more. The landlord filed a civil-suit in a court of law, which is dragging on for the last 6 years or more now.

Untimely death of a member of the family can be another cause. An example would explain the position.

An old man had hidden a large quantity of gold underground in the house of residence. On the old man's death, his two sons dug open the entire floor of the house but could not trace the treasure trove. Some dacoits, robbers too sometimes hide their looted gold and jewellery away from the village or town. Either they forget about it or do not get an opportunity to take it out subsequently, or they die before taking it out, and others reach it after his or her death. This type of loss can happen also in the case of householders, due to Sun and Mars in the 12th house.

There are some gains too from this combination. It gets support from unexpected quarters and sources in matters related to job, career, profession, and political activity leading to position or post of power. The reason is simple. These matters concern the 10th house and planets like Sun and Mars in the 3rd position from any house are beneficial to that house. Thus, Sun and Mars in 12th house are beneficial to the 10th house.

However, it is not so in the case of the 7th house, which rules marriage, married life, relations with spouse or beloved or lover. It is so in spite of the fact that Sun and Mars together in the 12th house are in 6th position from the 7th house. (The 6th position for Sun and Mars from any house is deemed favourable). Similarly, the Sun and Mars in the 12th house are not favourable to the 2nd house (which rules wealth), though Sun and Mars are considered favourable in the 11th position from any house. On the other hand, Sun and Mars in the 12th house might give a competitor to the spouse, or at least suspicion in the mind of the spouse about a competitor. If actually a competitor exists, the individual would take extra care to keep it completely secret from others, and positively from the spouse. Even being in the 11th position from the 2nd house of wealth, these two stars together lead to severe losses ultimately resulting in reduction to the net wealth, instead of adding to it.

The quantum of wealth, savings and investments, might reduce also by drop in prices, by theft or loss caused in any other manner.

Another very important damage this combination can cause to the human life is that of medical termination of pregnancy, or natural miscarriage or abortion. Not only the patients with illegitimate pregnancy but even married couples go to quacks for termination of pregnancy or post-abortion treatment, and suffer (as is natural) injurious results of such quack-oriented medical treatment, which often leads to permanent ineffectivity to the child-bearing system or even death of the patient.

This combination is directly responsible for excess bleeding in the process of abortion or full-para delivery of the child normally or by caesarean section. It is always advisable, after due examination of the blood system of the patient, to make arrangement for blood transfusion (by keeping blood ready or for prompt supply of blood of the type needed), because quite often, moreso in smaller towns, blood of the type needed doesn't become readily available.

This combination can lead to sentence of simple or rigorous imprisonment or even to capital punishment.

Sun and Mercury in the 12th House

First of all, these two in the 12th house adversely affect the education of such a child, as already has his or her own stars weak for education. The causes may be many. Some of them are diversion of attention from textbooks to comics and other books, too much attention to newspapers and magazines. Company of similar children in the school who have diverted attention from studies. Then another cause is going to places of worship and spending much time there under the impression that the God or Goddess worshipped would grant high results. It is actually not so, because nothing else than real hard studies would secure a bright result. The children neglect their written work at home and also neglect taking written notes of what is taught in the class. Generally, percentage of attendance in school or college also falls short and they lose a session or semester or a year in this process.

Then, in adult life, loss or notional loss can be by keeping duplicate or false accounts, and collecting or recording documents in support of those accounts. It is such a common feature these days that it needs no analysis or details. And when these accounts face challenge in an enquiry or investigation by taxation authorities or any other agency of the government, or even by a litigant in a court of law, the individual has to spend considerable money in an attempt to prove them correct and acceptable as legal.

Another source of wasteful expenditure can be by buying books and magazines, subscribing to periodicals, which neither the individual nor the spouse nor the family uses or reads. Books become a showpiece on the shelves in the drawing room, or the stuff is considered useless and is thrown into the dustbin or sold as 'waste paper' where the system exists.

Then another source of loss of prestige or loss of money or loss by heavy expenditure is to get caught on the wrong foot on account of having given wrong testimony in some formal case or submitting forged or false document or papers, in investigations or before a legal forum. It costs money either to prove the legitimacy of the documents or saving the skin from such misleading testimony or documents etc.

The individual might suffer a loss of large amount of currency in theft, snatching of purse or brief case, fire, landslide, floods, earthquake or any other event.

Yet another source of loss can be at races, in betting or gambling or speculation or at casino etc., or buying lottery tickets in bulk and getting nothing out of them.

Another source can be hiding love letters, photos of romance, and similar other items from the spouse, from the family or from the investigating searches and seizure.

In one instance, a family had six daughters-in-law. In an official search to detect smuggling and evasion of Income Tax and Customs Duty, the youngest daughter-in-law had to beg for mercy to take back her love-letters and photos of herself with her pre-marriage lover from the officer in charge of the search party. The senior author was a member of that search party, and he prevailed upon that officer concerned to release and return the mementos to the daughter-in-law of the house. Then the author had them burnt in a brass-bucket in the lady's room and in her presence.

One source of loss is wasteful expenditure on getting features or stories or photos of self, spouse or of progeny printed in print media or on being shown on visual media, without estimated gains therefrom. Extra money gets spent on obtaining (officially or clandestinely) copies of petitions, reports, orders, etc. in cases of enquiry, investigations or commercial assessment, or of secret documents submitted by the prosecution before a court of law. Similar expenditure also is incurred in obtaining copies of secret or confidential documents from any government office or secret agency.

However, one gain from this combination is that the individual gets support in election campaign from print media and visual media, through reporters and editorials etc., for which the individual has, no doubt, to spend money on the concerned journalists.

Sun and Jupiter in the 12th House

The combination of Sun and Jupiter in the 12th house gives more or less the same results as the Sun and Mercury combination give in that house. No doubt, a little variation has to be there because Mercury and Jupiter, though both are soft planets, have their own independent attributes and effect. Jupiter is more concerned with law, economics, accounts, taxation, and certain health problems too. Jupiter is deemed as Guru (*acharya* and adviser) of the deities and planets including Sun, and because of such stature Sun on its own gives preference to Jupiter in effectivity.

This combination concerns itself less with the education of children, and certainly more with expenditure on their education, private tuition etc. It's another concern is spending huge amounts on admission of the child first in any worth-the-name school or residential school, and later on selection for desired course of study for the child on reaching the standard IX or equivalent in the school. Later on, heavy amounts get spent on seeking and securing admission for the growing child in a desired course of study, like medical, engineering, accounting, law, science discipline, aviation, courses connected with police and defence services, and in last two decades of the 20th century on computers and their software. Only those parents and guardians who have suffered the running about, spending heavily on obtaining recommendations from influential persons and paying gratification to the authorities of the school or college or specialised institute for admission at any level or stage know the problem in its intensity and depth.

The next problem is from various government agencies, moreso from taxation authorities. In several countries it is now an order of the day that assessment and appellate authorities desire, both directly and indirectly, illegal gratification in cash or kind even from civil servants and semi-government servants! It was an unheard of thing till the end of World War II in 1945. Searches of premises, of persons, and seizure of this item or that item is a routine thing and then comes up the question of settlement of tax liability, above the table and under the table.

If by chance, the individual or spouse or a member of the family gets involved, by own action or as a respondent, into any litigation, comfort and cash money find easy sources of parting company from the individual and family. Running after lawyers, solicitors and advocates, attending courts to face mere adjournments for one reason or the other, efforts for out-of-court settlement with involved failures and cost thereof, are some of the evils resulting in heavy cuts on the purse of the individual.

Often one needs the services of accountants for one reason or the other. Cost of their fees has jumped sky-high, and when they negotiate bribe-amounts with taxation authorities, the accountants add their own share in the bribe in the name of and under cover of the Tax-man. Ultimately, whether for the individual or the spouse, it is loss of money.

Payments of fines and penalties imposed by courts of law, taxation authorities and other similar agencies of the government as also by civic bodies and semi-government undertakings is another source of outgo of money of the individual and the spouse, whosoever is in the catch of these gentlemen looters!

Jupiter (with Sun) in the 12th house leads to loss of gold, jewellery, costly items, hard cash in theft and looting. Blackmail by gangsters or individual criminals is yet another source of loss of money. Money demanded by and paid to kidnappers is also concerned with this combination in the 12th house. Sometimes near or distant relatives make demands of money, or in cases of divorce and judicial separation, the spouse (husband or wife) makes demands for heavy maintenance and one-time settlement of claims for maintenance, which also falls under the jurisdiction of Jupiter with Sun in the 12th house.

In so far as health problems are concerned, this combination is concerned with troubles related to kidney, liver, respiratory system, lung region, front as well as the back area falling between navel point and the heart area. Unnecessarily, Sun and Jupiter give an impression to the medical world that the patient is well-to-do in money matters, and the medical people find ways and means to extort more money than usual from the patient. And the patient thinks that the world has become like that and there is no escape from it. The medical people know that the patient has to have the treatment or surgery and the patient is helpless in the matter. One medical man may suggest this test and that test, and if he has no laboratory of his own, the patient is recommended to another medical man, pathologist or radiologist or some or the other 'logist'. The patient is the sufferer who has to pay for this lengthy exercise, which costs him or her a lot of money. In the process, the first medical man who had suggested tests and recommended to another medical man gets his cut from the fees charged by the other doctor for tests etc.

The only relief which can sometimes be granted by this combination of Sun and Jupiter in the 12th house is a favourable attitude from the judges in litigation related to elections and allied subjects, that too at a cost in cash or kind. Even at a cost, it is very seldom. It is the nature of a majority of judges that as a result of one-track mind, they catch one point in the case and pay exclusive attention to the arguments on that point and overlook many other important submissions in arguments of both parties.

Sun and Venus in the 12th House

It is in the very nature of Venus that even in a combust position on account of vicinity of Sun, and also under enemy-type relations with Sun, Venus is fully effective in the 12th house. Often Venus either overpowers Sun or secures the support of Sun in its romantic attitude towards opposite sex, and sometimes other anti-social deeds and actions.

First of all, Venus (with Sun) gives a romantic touch to the actions of the individual, at least sometimes, if not always. If Venus is stronger in strength or is in Pisces, Taurus, Gemini, Virgo, or Libra in the 12th house, it gives physical relationship with a person of the opposite sex (though sometimes more than one at one and the same time). It can happen in both, in pre-marriage and post-marriage days. The individual doesn't mind extra expenditure involved in the matter. Not only that men spend on women. No, it is not so. Women also spend on men, and quite lavishly too. Another source of extra expenditure in this connection comes from keeping the relationship secret, because 12th house directly concerns with secrecy. And secrecy becomes more essential for married individual as also for such individual who has serious and constant vigilance from parents and the family, including brothers and sisters or their spouses, or even servants. In the case of political and social workers and leaders, common public also keeps an eye on this type of relationship and the public derives pleasure and talking about it freely, within hearing level of the Press and other Media.

Extra-marital or unethical physical relationship with opposite sex, can be in the open or in a clandestine manner or there be no relationship of this type at all; but still some of these individuals spend considerably on advised or advertised drinks, drugs, one or the other element of intoxication, merely to enhance sex capacity.

These individuals do not bother to find out whether the drug or remedial element is actually effective or not.

These days young and ageing or old folk too spend a lot, and lavishly too, on clothes, ward-robe, on apparel, on linen, on other similar accessories, on cutlery, on any and all kinds of household goods, needed or unneeded. The reason for thus spending money lies in the tempting advertisements, which forcibly attract the individual to invest in this type of goods. Visual media as well as male and female models have added extra spices to the attraction for the advertised goods.

Gifts are another source of not so necessary (sometimes rather wasteful) outgo of money, moreso on the occasion of marriages, anniversaries, birthday, etc. And it is rarely that the individual gets similar gifts on similar occasions in life of self or spouse or children etc. Venus (with Sun) gets very much concerned with outward show of one's affection or care or links attached on their tops for exhibition of money, whether in reality one can easily afford doing so or not.

Outside-court-settlement of disputes with spouse relating to judicial separation, divorce, maintenance or similar type of compromise with a friend of the opposite sex also involve extra expenditure, whatever the capacity of the individual in this behalf. No doubt, Venus (with Sun) in 12th house is also concerned with this kind of settlement, irrespective of the position of both these stars in Navamsha chart of the man or Trinshansha chart of the woman.

This combination often proves a hurdle in securing admission in a medical college, and sometimes resort has to be taken to "capitation fee" or big cash donation to the political party in power or bribe to the authority deciding the admission.

On the favourable side, this combination gives chances of travel abroad, migration to foreign country, shifting of work place or residence from a smaller town to a bigger town, or from one state to another in the same country. This combination also helps in securing H-1 or H-1(b) visas or Green Cards or later on natural citizenship of countries like USA and Canada, UK or Australia, or some European countries.

Medical treatment (not related to major surgery or amputation of any limb of the body) generally proves very costly under this combination, but effective too, specially if Venus happens to be stronger than Sun in the 12th house.

Venus and Sun in the 12th house makes an individual a competent and efficient officer or staff for naval force as also for the merchant navy. And it is said in a lighter vein that a navy-man has a wife in every port. It is but natural too, because especially in the merchant navy, the individual has to be away from spouse and the family for anything from 6 to 8 months at a stretch.

Sun and Saturn in the 12th House

Again die-hard enemies (in spite of being father and son) sitting in combination in a house concerned with loss of money, fines or penalties or punishments (including imprisonment and death sentence). The interesting part is that both planets are equally effective and harmful in their own way, independently and jointly too, in the 12th house. It is all the more so if both these stars are occupying harmful positions in the Navamsha chart too.

The first effect is physical injury, illness, and disease concerning bone-structure of the entire body, including the skull. Therefore, brain injury or any ailment or disease related to the brain is direct concern of Saturn, whether Sun is concerned with it or not. Otherwise too, 12th house itself concerns the brain area, including the neck and upper-most part of the two shoulders, moreso the left shoulder. Saturn gives hard injury and generally no bleeding unless Mars is also actively involved in the injury from one angle or the other in the birth and Navamsha charts. Navamsha chart would in addition indicate if an injury or a disease in any part of the body not visible outwardly, is in existence or not inside the body-structure.

Another impact of Saturn (with Sun) is that medical treatment takes very long and patient as well as the family mustn't become impatient with due or undue lengthy period of the treatment. Saturn is not very much in favour of change of treatment-giving medical person, but Sun's presence in the 12th house favours treatment in government-owned or government-aided hospitals. It is in the best interests of the patient. But lately in India, those working in government-owned or government-aided hospitals pay less attention in the hospital itself, and recommend going to their private clinic. If private practice is prohibited, they ask the patient or patient's relatives to take treatment from a relative or intimate friend or associate of the government hospital doctor treating the patient. Sometimes the spouse of the doctor is in private practice and the patient is given direct or indirect hint to go to the spouse.

One problem with this combination in the 12th house is that it leads to medical termination of pregnancy, or natural miscarriage or abortion. In cases where the termination of the pregnancy is desired for illegitimacy of the pregnancy, the concerned people generally take the patient to quakes. The result is great damage to the childbearing system or to the entire middle-part of the body of the patient, and cases are not rare, in which the patient even died at the hands of the quacks. This is the outcome of secrecy element. Often even married couples go to these quacks and the result is the same.

Saturn is directly concerned with surgery too, whether of skull or for joining or rectification of any injured or damaged or fractured or broken parts of a bone of the body. It is natural that any surgical operation would cause bleeding, though bone fitting and correcting might not give bleeding at all. When such a case as this comes to an astrologer for consultation, the consulted astrologer must check up Mahadasa, Antardasa, and the position of stars in the yearly chart with special attention to position of Mars. Then should be studied the inter-relationship of Saturn and Mars in birth-chart, in Navamsha and in the yearly chart. If any problem relating to need of blood transfusion or any problem with blood system appear in the astrological study even casually, the astro-consultant must give correct guidance to the patient's family or relatives who have approached for consultation.

Then comes the question of loss of money or other valuable assets and possessions including jewellery, cash and bullion etc. While Mars and Jupiter are concerned only with gold and gold jewellery or bullion, Saturn is concerned with Gold, Silver and all other costly metals. Loss can be caused by theft, looting, dacoity, and highway robbery. The loss can be of valuable assets, even those placed underground for safety and security. Several other causes of loss of this type have been given in detail under paragraphs supra relating to "Sun with Mars" and to some extent in "Sun with Jupiter". Instead of repeating them, the readers may please re-read those paragraphs above.

One important point is in case of Saturn and Sun together in the 12th house. It is not there with regard to combination of Sun in the $12t^h$ with other planets. Saturn (with Sun) sometimes prompts the individual to indulge in theft, looting, dacoity, robbery, plunder, and similar other acts. Only theft can be performed in individual capacity. In all kind of illegal activity, the individual has either to constitute own gang or join a gang of criminals. And because of presence of Sun in the 12th house, the individual gets apprehended at some stage sooner or later and is brought to book in the normal course of law.

Individuals with this combination in the 12th house prove very efficient investigators, intelligence personnel, efficient police or army or air-force officers.

Saturn has no concern with the navy and its officers. It has an indirect concern with a plane moving in the air, firstly because after flying, the plane has to come down to earth. Secondly, if a plane meets with an accident in the air, it has to fall on the ground. Earth is under the sole control of Saturn. Thus flying objects are also concerned with Saturn. Further, in perhaps every country, the flying planes have to obtain a license from the government of that country. Thus, Sun too becomes concerned with this subject. In other words, the Sun and Saturn combination concerns with air flying objects. If a flying object falls in the ocean or sea or water, Moon, Mars and Venus would be concerned with that fall of the air vehicle. However it is rather difficult to expect all these investigating officers from police, para-military force, army or the air force, whatever their rank and authority to be honest or impartial or unbiased. After all they too have an eye on getting appreciation for good work, and their promotion too depends to a great extent on showing success in the investigations and ultimate results thereof. Therefore very often they cannot be expected to be honest in the investigation work. They should not be blamed, their stars and circumstances drive them to dishonesty.

Trading (including smuggling) in all kind of contraband goods, including drugs, liquors, wines, alcohol preparations, intoxicating elements is not very rare for such individuals as have Saturn (and Sun) in the 12th house.

If they themselves do not indulge in activities of this type, at least they consume any of these items, and because of Saturn, they store the items of their consumption. The storage sometimes drops these individuals into the network of law and resultant prosecution. Now the whole field involves bribery and gratification and so there are strong chances of the accused individuals coming out scot-free from the legal network.

Another important aspect of this matter is that if they themselves are not directly involved in trade or smuggling of these items they clandestinely help and support persons who trade and smuggle these items.

A good many among these individuals are given to some kind of gambling, whatever its shape and form or formality. It can be speculation in shares, in property, in food grains, in other goods. It can be card games, it can be betting at racecourses. In some towns in Central India, people indulge in betting on rains and clouds. Just a habit, and a habit is a habit. Readers might have noticed some people indulging in gambling or speculation or large-scale betting on horse races leading to their downfall in money and finances. Many individuals exist and survive on loans and rarely they are able to repay their debts. Insolvency and bankruptcy are common events in the life and career of people of this type. Another fact is that once an individual adopts this line of existence and survival on a whole-time basis, he (now some women too) are unable to do anything else for livelihood!

In some rare cases, and definitely not in case of all individuals, these persons could get sentenced to imprisonment, simple or rigorous, for short or long terms, or even for life (which is generally limited to 12 or 14 years in many countries). Death sentences are also not unheard of in some countries, excepting where death sentence has been totally abolished by law. In all cases of this type, the astrologer must work very hard. He or she should study the Bhava-Chalitam (that is fixation of planetary positions) of the birth chart, its Navamsha chart, strength of all planets, *drishti* element of all planets on the 12th house and the *effect giving capacity* of Saturn and Sun stationed in the 12th house. The astrologer must study the Mahadasa with Antardasa, and if by transit any long-term planets like Jupiter, Mars and Saturn are in 12th house, or any of these stars is in retrograde position while in transit in the 12th house. In addition, examination is unavoidable of the transit positions of Rahu, Herschel (Uranus) and Neptune and impact of these transits on the 12th house and Saturn and Sun in the 12th house. Then finally the yearly chart for the current and the next year should be studied properly. Only after this detailed study, the astrologer should predict on the question of imprisonment and death sentence. If possible the stars of the spouse may also be examined, because the stars of the spouse would indicate whether there is separation between husband and wife owing to imprisonment or permanent separation of one of the two on account of the sentence as such.

It is also desirable that in above type of consultations, the astrologer bears in mind the relationship of severe enmity between Sun and Saturn, all the more so because they are together in the same house. Whether this relationship provides any scope for "differences of opinion" among the judges of the apex court of the country, or any scope for grant of clemency or reduction in sentence of imprisonment, or that of death.

Another point to be examined relates to death in the family. Saturn is very much concerned with causing death and the 12th house, besides the subjects discussed above, is directly concerned with the parental family (2nd house rules the family acquired by marriage or adoption). In this context, study may be based on Saturn's *saadhe-saati* (explained in the glossary), and also Saturn's transit over the 12th or the 7th house (which is 8th position from 12th house), and on the yearly chart. These three elements form the best basis for finding out chances of death in the family. It may be noted that Saturn normally affects, in matters of death, either persons older than 60 years of age, or very rarely, babies within the first two years of their birth.

Saturn (and Sun) does present chances of premature retirement (volunteered by self or imposed by the employer), specially in the case of public and semi-public servants. It might be even termination of job or outright dismissal, with or without pension benefits or without other gains attached to the job. In any case end of job is end of job, whatever name be given to it!

Sun and Rahu in the 12th House

Rahu gives more or less the same results as those described under "Sun with Saturn in 12th house", but never with the type of severity as that of Saturn and Sun in that house.

For example, Rahu (with Sun) rarely makes a person totally insolvent or bankrupt. This combination generally does not lead to deaths in the family. It does not give extreme type of legal punishment like rigorous imprisonment or the death sentence. Similarly, this combination does not completely ruin the health or education of the progeny, though it does affect the progeny adversely upto the age of 18 years, in matters of health and education, both.

Rahu (with Sun in 12th) gives affiliation to gambling, speculation and other similar sources of unearned gains and losses, sometimes in larger quantum even more than what Saturn and Sun combination gives in 12th house.

Rahu and Sun combination gives arrogance and wasteful spending habits to the progeny, depending on the progeny's own stars. One or two children in the family or the household might take to drinking or consuming other intoxicating drug, moreso at an immature age.

Rahu (with Sun) is more effectively capable of bringing loss of job to a permanent or semi-permanent employee, moreso if the job is under the government or in government-linked service. In case of Saturn or Jupiter in 12th house (with Sun) might give loss of job, but generally not with loss of pension and other benefits. Rahu is, (because of eclipse-type influence over Sun) capable of loss of pensionary or other benefits too with loss of job, which situation is brought about on the employee by obtaining the employee's resignation instead of termination of job. This situation can be reached also by outright dismissal of the individual from service.

Rahu very often gives secret extra-marital type relationship within the wider family or the broader circle of friends and acquaintances, and if ever detected, it is claimed to be a platonic one. God and the two persons concerned alone would know the inner secret of the relationship. In India, often this type of relationship is given the cover of brother-and-sister relationship, more often under the bond of '*rakhi*'.

This combination sometimes, and that too in very rare cases leads an individual to lead a life of renouncement, even while living with the family, and without dressing like a '*sannyasi*'. It happens after some difficult type of tragedy or calamity takes place with the individual or within the family or after great loss of money or property or assets, chiefly between the age of 42 and 66.

Sun and Ketu in the 12th House

Positively Ketu behaves like Mercury in this house, not on the pattern of Saturn or Rahu, in spite of having eclipse influence over Sun.

This combination is more concerned with education of the progeny. The individual or the spouse gives corporal punishment (beating etc.) to the progeny for inferior progress in education or for failure in an exam. It leads to further deterioration in the progress of the child in the next one or two classes. Therefore corporal punishment, at least for educational progress, should be given after getting the stars of the child examined in this behalf.

Ketu (with Sun) causes mild-type trouble to the eyes, hearing power, slight stammering, any kind of mild nasal ailment, and very rarely it concerns itself with indigestion, or liver or kidney trouble, no doubt with support of other hard planets.

Ketu might lead the individual to take part, (often not alone but with other dishonest employees), in embezzlement, pilferage or directly minor thefts from factory or household, but it doesn't bring any severe punishment for these offences. It brings, at the most, dismissal from the job. Once indulged in this type of malpractices, Ketu makes it a habit with the individual.

Ketu (with Sun) is generally good at preparing false documents or accounts or invoices, whatever the individual needs for submission to any government agency or semi-government formation or organisation, or even to a court of law.

This combination leads to loss and theft of books from the charge or custody of the individual, and they get hardly traced, because the individual's connivance is involved.

Ketu and Sun in combination generally lead an individual to give self-oriented resignation as soon as the individual finds that the "going" is not in favour, or events have developed for termination or dismissal from the job. Often in the resignation process, the individual tries level best to protect the pension benefits and other allied gains.

MOON IN THE 12 HOUSES

MOON IN GENERAL

At the initial stage itself, one must remember that Moon is the exclusive ruler of the MIND in case of all humans. Sharpness in thought, tendency to maintain secrecy are all basic attributes of Moon, irrespective of the house occupied. Further it is deemed to be concerned with travels across the waters (sea and ocean), sometimes with settlement in a country other than that of one's birth. Moon is also concerned with higher education in science or medical line (branch or system is immaterial) in own country or in a foreign country. No doubt, with regard to subjects other than the MIND, Moon gives results depending on support from or conflict with other soft or hard planets, as also Moon's relationship with the lord of the house occupied by it.

     One very important point to be borne in mind is that Moon takes on an average 54 hours (in all) to move from one Rasi to another, and generally, within 27 or 28 days, Moon completes its one round of the entire zodiac (i.e. all the 12 houses). We all know that Moon is directly concerned with Tide, and also has control over storms and other troubles in the waters (of seas and oceans).

     Moon's fast movement (fastest among all planets) has its own advantages and disadvantages. It is fast in giving good and bad results, but the impact of the results sometimes last for long. Virtually every month (one day short or one day in excess) it goes combust in the company of Sun, and then as soon as it moves out of Sun's vicinity, it starts growing in size as it is visible from Earth. Similarly, it is visible in its full size on Full Moon Day, and simultaneously its size starts reducing in visibility from Earth, so much so that when it reaches the vicinity of Sun, it becomes invisible from Earth. In astronomy, the size of the Moon is the same throughout the month, and it is only a question of Earth coming between Moon and Sun and thereby increasing or reducing its visibility.

However it is a different story in astrology. The waxing Moon, from the 5th day of the Bright Half (*Shukla Paksha* in Indian languages) till the 5th day after the Full Moon Day (*Poornima*), is considered not so harmful and trouble-giver, in whatever house the Moon is in the birth-chart or the yearly chart or in transit.

On the other hand, it is considered more harmful and trouble-giver from the 5th day of the Dark Half (*Krishna Paksha* in Indian languages) till the 5th day of the Bright Half, i.e., when Moon is in a waning position.

Above given are a few points that should be kept in mind while giving predictions about Moon in a birth chart or in a yearly chart.

Moon in the 1st House

The individual is often self-centred and feels lonely even when sitting in any company of one or more persons or even in an audience, or hearing a case, or speaking from public platform. When speaking from public platform or arguing before any court or tribunal or officer, the individual dwells upon the same subject for long. While talking about one point, the individual starts talking about another point just in between, and in the process, either returns to the previous point abruptly or forgets the previous point altogether. The same thing happens when the individual is participating in any talk or conversation with one or more persons.

Judges in courts of law, in tribunals, in appellate authority, often pick up a single point in the arguments or submissions, and deal that point in great detail. In doing so, they often neglect or overlook other points even if the other points were more important to the subject matter before them than the single point grasped by them. This tendency quite often leads to injustice or wrong justice, making the litigants or applicants or appellants suffer the consequences without any fault on their part.

These individuals are sometimes considered as given more

to the objective side of a matter, and get governed more by their emotions than by factual position.

If Moon is in waning process at birth, sometimes (not always, and not in every case) it gives partial or complete deafness, squint in the eyes, tendency to utter critical and taunting remarks in conversation as also in written language. Moon is quickly affected in giving results by the other planet(s) in conjunction with it, and Moon's results get increased or diminished accordingly.

It is believed that if Moon is in waxing position, it gives a fair complexion and a charming face thereby influencing the personality of the individual. Now fair or dark complexion is a relative matter depending on several factors, including family traditions, the country's nearness to or distance from Equator and climate of that region. The same theory applies in with regard to charming face. The outlook on this point differs from person to person.

If it is in waning process, it adversely affects the facial appearance (not necessarily and not always). Moon adversely affects the financial status of the individual as compared to others in the family or in the same source of income or in the same social status.

Moon has got direct concern with the education of the individual, specially when with soft planets. It helps in receiving complete education at a stretch without break. If Moon is with hard planet(s), including Rahu or Ketu, it gives gaps in education, often reaching the final aim in education by self-effort.

Moon is very much concerned with chances of survival of the infant within the first one or two years of birth, which would depend to a great extent on the Rasi in the first house, placement of its lord, and Moon's relations with that lord of the 1st house. However after the age of two years, Moon doesn't keep direct concern with the longevity of the individual.

And lastly the question of mind is there. Many an individual with Moon in the 1st house are given to whimsical thinking, often reflecting in their actions and conversations or decisions and judgement, a hint to which has already been given above. The whims and fast-changing mood lead to correct or wrong deeds, actions and decisions or judgements. Special care of mental health of the individual is needed if Scorpio or Capricorn or Aquarius is in the 1st house, and the lord of that Rasi (Mars or Saturn) is in 2nd, 12th or 6th or 8th house. Then the individual develops mental disturbance or even disorders now and then, warranting medical examination and treatment. If Mars is lord of the 1st house, it would give uncalled for bad temper and anger to the individual. If Saturn is lord of the 1st house, it would give obstinacy and stubbornness bordering on unstable mind and mentality. These conditions of the mind are the preliminary indications of partial or slow and steady insanity. All the more so if Moon is in Aries, and things go worse if Mars too is in the 1st house with Moon. The chances are that complaints of mental trouble start to give indication latest by the age of 28 years. If Saturn is lord of the Rasi in the 1st house, and Saturn is in conjunction with Moon or casting more than 45 out of 60 *drishti* on Moon, the complaints of mental trouble start giving indications before the age of 46 years, rather after the age of 30 years.

But an astrologer shouldn't jump to conclusions at the first glance of the ownership of the 1st house, and that lord's placement in the 2nd/ 6th/ 8th or 12th house. One must examine in detail the Mahadasa and its sub-periods as also transit of Saturn in the 2nd, 8th or 12th house, or transit of retrograde Mars in the 2nd, 7th, 8th or 12th house. And the astrologer mustn't overlook the positions of Moon, Mars and Saturn in the Navamsha chart, be it a man or woman. Further full attention has to be paid to the yearly chart(s) covering the specific periods of transit of Mars and/ or Saturn. Only then an astrologer should arrive at a conclusion and even then he or she should be careful in choosing the actual words for communication of that conclusion to the person concerned or her or his relatives and others. Cases of this category must always be treated as top secret, not for quoting even as an example!

One point is repeated concerning Moon in the 1st house. It gives considerable self-confidence, as also the capacity to maintain secrecy (where needed), and varied capacity to think and plan with undivided attention. The same rule applies to the working of the individual, who generally dislikes interference in the course of working, no doubt having an open mind towards constructive and really useful suggestions (rather than commands)!

Moon and Sun in the 1st House

This has already been discussed in the chapter on Sun.

Moon and Mars in the 1st House

Though these two are friends in permanent relationship, they go unfriendly when together in a house. In this case, Mars dominates the effectivity of Moon, whether Moon is waxing or waning.

The individual develops hot temper and to an extent unmanageable temperament too, specially if Aries, Leo, Scorpio or Capricorn is in the 1st house. The individual is very mischievous and quarrelsome both at home and in the school and at the playground in the very childhood, besides being bold and daring. In later life the individual develops brave nature, but use of that nature depends on his or her mood at the given time, place and atmosphere around.

The individual likes swimming, use of weapons of any kind, which he or she tries to learn in adolescence and early youth, specially because girls too join the National Cadet Corps or target shooting in the school or join similar organisations as extra-curricular activities. These boys and girls like travelling, single or with family or with school-and-college groups. They do not hesitate to pick up a row with fellow passengers and others, wherever they go in the course of travelling and in Camps and later on in university Campus too.

Generally these individuals do not disclose to others the quarrels and fights at home or to those not present at the spot of the group travelling together, and indulging in a fight.

They are good in sports, welcome any competition and friendly matches, in races and in use of weapons etc. They entertain ambitions and often work towards achieving them, if not all, at least a few of them.

However this combination adversely affects the marriage and married life, unless the matrimonial match too has similar or equivalent position of Mars or Saturn. Rahu/ Herschel and Neptune do not cut much ice in this context. The problem with these individuals is that Moon has at least three-fourth *drishti* on the 7th house (of marriage and married life) from the 1st house, and Mars has full *drishti* on 7th house from the 1st house. The net outcome is that the individual suddenly brings separation with the spouse suddenly as bolt from the blue, without giving any pre-indication of it to the spouse.

Some astrologers hold the view that this combination makes the individual prone to accidents. No, it is not totally true. An accident rather very rarely can occur from water, fire, electricity, acid or any inflammable items, as also from excess consumption of alcohol or intoxicating drug or any other intoxicating item. It is only rarely, with Moon and Mars in the 1st house that an individual would be given to these intoxication items, while she or he is alone, generally alcohol and drugs are consumed when in company. In this context, periods of retrogression of Mars or Mars's transit over the 1st, 2nd, 8th or 12th house and presence of Mars in any of these houses in the yearly chart should be studied properly.

Moon and Mercury in the 1st House

The individual is very intelligent and also conscious of it. She or he is very talkative in the company of known people, but less talkative otherwise, doesn't hesitate to make acquaintance with totally unknown people. He or she has keen interest in literature of own language as also of other languages, often tries to become a writer or poet, orator or journalist or a teacher or priest, preacher, publicist, propagandist. The individual very rarely entertains any request or suggestion for change of religion, faith, cult, and often gives valid arguments for not doing so, because he or she knows own religion better and has a nature given to prayers and penance according to capacity and availability of time and facility.

The individual is rarely in need of borrowing money from others, at least not outside the family or outside the circle of intimate friends, because the individual knows "to cut one's coat according to cloth available". If he or she ever borrows, there often is the inner urge to repay it as early as possible.

The individual often collects books from all sources possible, buy, borrow or even steal, and not for storing them, but often reading them and putting the knowledge to use.

The individual is talented in speaking effectively and keeping the listeners or the audience attentive to what he or she is talking. Whether he or she has charming personality or not, people are impressed and influenced by his or her qualities, talent, eloquence, learning and capacity to use the knowledge to the benefit of others.

In some rare cases, the individual gets attracted towards opposite sex, not beyond the decency of talks or romantic writing in normal correspondence. No physical indulgence except with own spouse enters into the behaviour. It is also the case with these individuals, moreso regarding males, that women get attracted towards them because of their knowledge, experience and capacity to put this quality to use. Women are often keen to make friends with them, without any bar or fear of any kind.

These individuals are often very impressive in preparing drafts of petitions, applications, appeals, and letters for others. Their writing suffers neither from ambiguity nor from lack of communication. Often their handwriting is nice and easily readable by one and all. They always take extra care of their books, exercise books, correspondence, documents and record of papers. They are keen on prompt filing of papers, and if they are unable to do it themselves, they entrust the work to another person or employee or subordinate.

Whenever these individuals go for a meeting or conference, they generally take a written note or slips containing scribbled points meant to be discussed there. As far as possible, they are keen to talk to the point and not waste words and time of self and others to talk irrelevant.

A weakness in these individuals is that sometimes they

behave like an highbrow and others present feel belittled or even insulted, with or with out expression of opposition or annoyance.

Moon and Jupiter in the 1st House

Several learned ancient '*acharyas*' and astrologers of the modern day take Jupiter in the 1st house as very favourable and beneficial. Experience indicates that it is not so always. Jupiter whether with Moon or alone in the 1st house is capable of giving headaches and worries about finances of self vis-à-vis pressing needs of self, spouse and the immediate family. It can give trouble with or from law and order machinery, misunderstanding with the family of the spouse, and also unexpected, sudden and rather unmanageable expenditure, leading to borrowing even on hard terms.

Undoubtedly, these individuals are well educated, specially in law or economics or accounts or business management or law making, and are often keen to put their education and knowledge in full use. They are very particular about being paid properly for their work, whatever the field of work. They are also prompt in recovery of their money and other dues. In joint family matters too, they do not give up their demand for dues, though do not insist on prompt recovery of dues. Women and men are careful about security of money, jewellery, ornaments, items made of gold and silver whether of daily use or meant for preservation.

Jupiter exercises a control on Moon in its conjunction with Moon in the 1st house and generally does not allow Moon to disturb the newborn's life as such during the first two years, which otherwise Moon does. However, if the parents or the grandparents on either side have a history of diabetes or asthma or any trouble of the respiratory system, the baby or child or the young-man should be protected against cough and cold through mother's habits related to eating and drinking. And the individual, upto the age of first 19 years of life, shouldn't be exposed to climate causing any of these troubles.

The individual generally has presentable personality, better complexion than an average person of that region or climate. There are less chances of the individual going bald at an immature age.

These plus points of personality often help the individual in getting married to a beautiful or charming spouse, and sometimes the gentleman's matrimony brings a fortune at the time of marriage or within 3 years of marriage. Subsequently too, the wife proves very lucky for the husband.

Generally the individual gets good fame in the field of work or occupation, and he or she tries to keep up that reputation. Therefore the individual keeps instinct of greed suppressed, and keeps moral character too above direct or indirect criticism and infamy.

The individual gets helped during unfavourable transit of Saturn or retrograde transit of Mars. Normally Mars takes one and a half month on an average to move from one Rasi to another, but when it goes retrograde it stays in a Rasi, continuously or in two phases for 6 to 8 months. Therefore emphasis in predictions is more on retrogression-period of Mars. However Jupiter does not very much interfere with any unfavourable planet's Mahadasa or sub-period therein, and generally remains a silent spectator!

In spite of judicious outlook on any matter for decision or judgement before the individual, Moon does interfere with Jupiter's presence in the 1st house, and allows the individual to take sides.

Moon and Venus in the 1st House

Initially itself it is a mischievous combination, Moon ruler of Mind and Venus ruler of romanticism, both fond of good living, nice atmosphere, and attractive company. Romanticism starts appearing in their looks and glances, talks and attitude towards opposite sex even from the start of adolescence. If nothing else, they like to talk to the members of the opposite sex, any age and any level. Sometimes they are caught on the wrong foot, and get rebukes, scolding and even a brief beating, and if nothing else, at least hurting critical remarks from the person concerned or from the person accompanying that girl or boy. Till about the end of the 19th century, this type of activity was found more in upper class and middle class population. The tendency started spreading first from the end of the First World War and expanded fully after the Second World War, affecting one and all without distinction of colour, class, region or religion everywhere.

These individuals are generally fond of reading romantic literature, listening and learning songs of the same type, using romanticism in talks and hints. They are often fond of sweets, cold drinks, beer and wine or alcohol, very spiced and tasty food, top class attractive clothes or garments or apparel, fresh flowers and perfumes (scent of which they intend to reach others, even passers by). They neither mind cost thereof, nor hesitate in borrowing these items whenever going on any special occasion, where there is likelihood of meeting opposite sex. If nothing else they borrow money heavily and beyond capacity to buy these items.

On the favourable side, generally these individuals get easy admission into medical college or courses, and succeed in becoming a doctor, '*vaidya, hakim*' or a spiritual healer. Some of them go for higher studies in medicine and allied subjects. Most of them, specially those void of greedy nature, are very successful in their treatment of patients suffering even from long-term illness or serious disease. They earn high reputation in the field or region of their functioning and for their system or style of work and attitude towards patients.

If they do not go into medical line or become highly qualified physicians, these individuals make very efficient actor/actress, singer, expert in instrumental music, all kind of dancing or any other branch of fine arts, including painting and sculpture.

Whatever line of career they choose, they like travelling within the state or country of their normal residence and also to foreign lands. Some of them achieve success in migrating to another country and earning good name and fame there too.

Some of these individuals are fond of mountaineering, on mountains with heavy snowfalls or covered with snow the year-round.

In sex matters, these individuals are satisfactory in bed, pay full attention to the partner in bed and also to the actual act of lovemaking. But rarely they stay restricted to one partner, if not at the same period of time, at least one after the other, when separated from the first one.

It has to be remembered that Moon and Venus are enemy in permanent relationship and become bitter enemy when together in the same house, but they are birds of the same feather and therefore co-operate with trend and tendency of each other, instead of interference.

Moon and Saturn in the 1st House

This is yet another combination of two diehard enemies, and it has been noticed that generally, Saturn overpowers Moon in giving effect to its presence with Moon in the 1st house.

The first effect is on the appearance of the individual, which is not very presentable from the very childhood. The complexion is just on the average of the particular region or climate, though Moon does try to give a glare to the complexion, if not the fairness.

Saturn, over-riding Moon, gives an unusual formation to the nose and the lower lip, which is often fatter than normal. Sometimes it gives an unnoticeable very mild limp in walking, which gets cured as the individual grows in age, but in rare cases it persists all along life. Much depends in this behalf on the Rasi in the 1st house, and its lord and placement of that lord in the birth chart. If Capricorn or Aquarius or Aries is in the 1st house, the mild limp in walking would persist, the theory does not hold water that any planet's presence in a house of its ownership doesn't cause harm to that house. Saturn (with Moon or any other planet) sometimes gives swollen-type cheeks, or uneven shape to one cheek from the other.

Some astrologers believe that Saturn (with Moon) in the 1st house gives lack of self-confidence or lack of sense of responsibility or gives merely limited talents, but experience of several generations doesn't prove this theory correct. On the other hand, Saturn (with Moon) gives rather unshakeable self-confidence, sense of responsibility and unlimited talents.

No doubt in childhood, the individual gives more attention to sports and extra-curricular activities, and some inexperienced people conclude it to be lack of self-confidence. No, it is not so. On the other hand, just before Exams or valuation of the year's or session's or semester's work, the individual makes up the negligence in studies by hard work, and the result is not inferior to more exhibitive co-students!

Because the individual is very particular in recovery of salary, other dues, payment for work done, sometimes makes people think that he or she is mean-minded or very miserly or lacking in good manners! But none of these attributes are befitting. The individual is not prepared to suffer due payment for labour or hard work. It is normally the case with virtually all those individuals, who work with undivided attention on the job on hand or undertaken. Then why shouldn't they expect full compensation for their work? They often have no evil eye on the money of others. They are neither snobbish nor clumsy in their attitude to work vis-à-vis money therefor.

These individuals are generally obstinate/ stubborn and do not disclose their mind easily to others. If they ever enter into field of criminal activity or supporting that type of activity, it is very difficult to get truthful disclosure thereof. They know how to make the investigator wander in wildness and un-knowledgabilty. They are hard nut to crack.

These individuals are ruthless, cruel and revengeful towards informers and also towards such member of the group or gang as revolt against them or who discloses information about the gang or its activities, its whereabouts, its system and style of functioning, its movements. The term 'gang" naturally includes the individual too. These individuals give good care in all matters including liberal financial help to the family of the gang's such members as are in police custody, or in imprisonment or got seriously wounded or got killed or got murdered or got hanged by law machinery.

On the favourable side of Saturn with Moon is that it

makes the individual very efficient sailor, boatman (women included), engineer and technician related to jobs in naval force and merchant navy. They are efficient in providing directions to the sailing ship at the time of storm or tornado, and also in collecting other useful information and intelligence relating to navigation, including sea rovers and sea dacoits.

In other fields too, these individuals are good engineers, technicians, technocrats, good at gathering intelligence, keeping an eye on trouble from keepers of law, also on competitors and trouble-makers within or without their field of working. They have no distinction between truth and a lie where their or party's or group's or gang's interests are involved.

They do not spend wastefully, but are not miserly where the need of the hour demands to be liberal or charitable or helpful. It is often a privilege to work with or under this type of individuals. Though they are obedient to their seniors, employers, and masters, they do not stand wrong orders, questionable directions and insults of any kind, whether in private or openly before others. Thus they are more suitable for public service or self-employment rather than in private sector where employment and dismissal are quick, depending on the decision or whims of the employer or senior boss enjoying that authority.

Moon and Rahu in the 1st House

Poor Moon gets eclipsed in this company, and is rendered less effective, whatever the distance in degrees with Rahu.

If the 1st house has Cancer or Leo, Rahu grants high standard of living, depending more on the money or facilities provided by others, a lot of arrogance and vanity, outwardly carefree, but inwardly bothering about every event and development in life of self, spouse or the family. In spite of these inferior qualities, these individuals are very much given to taking good care of education, well being, health and fulfilment of needs of every member of the family including the spouse. However they do not stand disobedience from their progeny and sometimes from the spouse too. If a wife has the same combination of Moon and Rahu in her first house, she too gets angry and rises to hit the husband.

Rahu (with Moon) does exhibit too much religionism in the individual, and whatever prayers the individual offers every day, or now and then, are personal affair of one's own self.

At the same time Rahu doesn't believe in exhibitionism in charitable acts or charity in terms of money and in kind. Rahu doesn't take advantage of others' work, and gets very hurt when his or her work's advantage is derived by others or goes to others by mischief. Like Saturn, Rahu too in the 1st house gives ample self-confidence, capacity for hard work (if it is according to one's liking in accordance to education received). Otherwise Rahu doesn't hesitate to do job superficially or superfluously.

Rahu (with Moon) gives sharp ego to the individual, and has little or no tolerance to any insult to his/ her ego, by anyone, howsoever senior or older or deserving respect. Ego is Ego, nothing more and nothing less!

With Rahu, Moon too becomes very touchy in the 1st house, at least towards spouse and married life. The individual often cautions the partner that tolerance has a limit, and going beyond, carries dreadful results. It is for the other partner whether she or he takes the hint, or continues in behaviour as prior to caution. This combination doesn't give hesitation to the individual to break a marriage by separate living, judicial separation or even divorce. And in such instances, a successor to married life is often available at hand to both the partners, sooner or a little later. A weak point in this context is that though the individual expecting tolerance from the other partner, often gets exposed for own intolerance. That one-sided attitude hurts the marriage more than any other shortcoming on either side.

Some astrologers allege greediness and eyes on another's money, assets and wealth, but actual experience does not support this viewpoint. As already mentioned above, they do not want to benefit unfairly from possessions of others and at the same time do not want others to snatch their own possessions.

Some people maintain the impression that Rahu grants immense wealth and growth in worldly possession and all the more so after the age of 42 years. No, it is not so. Rahu on the other hand develops source of income for the individual from the age of 18 years onwards, and the sources go on expanding, depending on the capacity for hard work on part of the individual.

One unfavourable aspect of Rahu (with Moon) in the 1st house is often a potbelly, and change from better to inferior complexion after the age of 36 years. Remedies do not help much.

Rahu is more effective during its Mahadasa or sub-period under any other planet. Rahu is less effective when alone in a house, but more effective when with any planet, and actually full effective when with Moon (or Sun) be in the same house in which Rahu is.

Rahu gives a desire for travel, but not so much of actual travelling, and very rarely for just pleasure's sake. No doubt, Rahu (with Moon) would mix pleasure with work for purpose of travelling. At the same time, this combination is not too keen on travel abroad or settling in a foreign land. One weakness with these individuals is that they always strive to return home as soon as the work, for which travel was undertaken, gets completed or postponed by circumstances other than those under control of the individual.

All said, Rahu is given to discipline both at home and at place of work, discipline binding on self as also equally binding on others.

Moon and Ketu in the 1st House

In spite of this being an 'eclipse' combination, on the whole it is not very unfavourable to the individual. In this house, Ketu carries the attributes of Mercury, and thus gives remarkable concentration resulting in good progress in studies, and the studies get retained in the mind of the learner for long time, because of Moon too in the 1st house.

These individuals talk very relevantly whenever they talk, and create an instant impression on the listeners, whether one or two or many. If these individuals take to writing, they are successful in it, and often get published in print media or in a book form.

No doubt, they are very particular about prior fixation of royalty and prompt payment thereof.

Some modern astrologers predict short life for these people, but the authors and their ancestors have had hundreds of cases, where individuals with this combination in the 1st house have enjoyed long and active life. No doubt, it is very likely that they (physically) fall down very easily and often too, but normally do not suffer from any long-term disease, and recover from illness quickly. Their main complaint is about cough, cold, bad throat (rather) caused by disorders of the digestive system. They do not fall ill quickly if they consume a lot of pure drinking water and take minimum of cold drinks, wine, beer and alcoholic items.

Some other astrologers' fear that this combination of Ketu and Moon in the 1st house might cause marital unhappiness, but experience of other astrology-experts does not confirm this fear. Both Moon and Ketu function as soft stars and do not disturb the married life, more than it is common to every married life in present-day top materialism.

MOON IN THE 2ND HOUSE

Even a waning Moon gives favourable results in this house. The individual normally doesn't suffer from paucity of funds, no doubt, money supply being strictly by the family's standards and the sources of the individual's earning, sometimes added with the earnings of the spouse or from rental income or from returns on investments. Whatever the Rasi in the 2nd house, the individual remains within own resources and budget rather strictly.

Moon prompts extra spending on clothes and wardrobe of self and spouse and children too, and on medical treatment, moreso of spouse and general family. These individuals are not fond of consuming drugs and drinks heavily, but they do sometimes store a good quantity of wines, beer, and other alcoholic drinks and cold beverages for consumption in company of friends and guests.

These individuals are fond of putting up a rather artificial show of status by using silverware, high quality tapestry and linen, furniture and items of decoration in the house. But if any of Mars,

Mercury, Saturn is with Moon in the 2nd house, the artificialism gets exposed easily and quickly too.

These individuals take a lot of trouble in training the spouse according to their own liking for a particular life style (and also artificialism in that style), but spouse doesn't normally fall in line, and the effort falls flat.

The 2nd house being related to wealth, collection of costly assets and valuable items of daily use, the individuals are often fond of collecting all these in life, no doubt keeping in mind the position of their resources to possess, without access to loans and debts.

Moon and Sun in the 2nd House

Moon being lord of mind and entire thinking process of an individual, Moon enjoys rather a dominating influence over the 2nd house as compared to Sun there. Therefore the discussion has been brought here instead of giving it under "Sun with Moon in the 2nd house" supra.

Sun is lord of rule, administration, powerful authority, and Moon being lord of Mind, the individual often tries to reach closeness to the Ruler, King, President, Prime Minister, Governor, if the individual enjoys some worth-the-name status. Otherwise, the individual makes efforts to come in close contact with any person in position of power and authority in the state or country or district or sub-division of a district. If nothing else the individual tries to get into close contact with the local Heads of departments and offices, at least all such departments and offices as come in direct contact or have dealings with the public. Some of them are local police, revenue, municipal or civic body, electricity and water supply system, controller (if any) of market and consumer goods, doctors and senior staff in hospitals and nursing homes.

The individual gets fond of amassing as much bullion and items made of gold and silver or gold and silver-plated items, similar to those in the household of dignitaries.

It all means outer show. However, Sun in the 2nd house is well known as giving very good savings and income from investments, and Moon has a tendency to accumulate wealth and costly items of household. Therefore to an extent it becomes possible for the individual to make a show of wealth befitting dignitaries.

Individuals who have had very wealthy and dignitary ancestors, even upto the level of grandfather or father (if dead), also try to make their household and style of living a showpiece of the past dignity. If they are unable to afford financially, they try to retain domestic servants or other retinue of the late father's time, even by incurring debts. Moon gives them support in this type of thinking and actual acting.

Moon and Mars in the 2nd House

Moon and Mars is a very funny combination indeed. Moon wants savings and heavy investments for sake of returns therefrom. Mars is invariably bent upon giving losses and downward trend in money content in the hands of the individual (spouse included)!

Whatever the Rasi in the 2nd house, Mars has dominating influence over Moon in the 2nd house. Mars rarely fails to bring down the financial status of the individual at least twice in life. Its periodicity depends on Mahadasa or sub-period of Mars under any other planet, transit of Saturn or Rahu or Herschel in the 12th house, or very unfavourable placement of planets in the yearly chart.

While writing this chapter on Moon and Mars combination in the 2nd house, an instance comes to mind.

An individual came to one of the authors for consultations. The moment, the author noticed Mars, Sun and Ketu in the 2nd house, the author predicted for the individual that he would suffer, or might already have suffered heavy losses of money either by speculation or gambling or by unrecovered loans or by cheating in investments. Till then the individual hadn't spoken even a word about self, and it was his first visit to the senior author. Hearing this prediction, tears came to the eyes of the individual and he remarked that he had been ruined in 1999-2000 by sudden fall in prices of shares. And he added that none of the other 4 or 5 astrologers whom he had been consulting for over about a decade had ever predicted or cautioned him that he would be ruined in this manner. The author told him that though Sun had helped him in accumulating wealth by its position in the 2nd house (specially in his case Sun was in its own house Leo in the 2nd house), and Mars was combust because of vicinity to Sun. But nothing could stop Mars from giving its results in the 2nd house, neither Sun, nor Ketu.

Even if Mars being combust, Sun couldn't stop Mars running down financially the above-mentioned individual. Readers should not expect Moon to be able to stop Mars from giving heavy losses to any individual. No doubt, Sun in 2nd house had given unearned income to the above-mentioned individual to invest heavily on shares, Mars brought about heavy losses.

In this context it has to be noted that Sun is capable of reviving the money content of the individual, though not to the full extent as in the good old days. However Moon doesn't carry even that much of strength as that of Sun so as to revive the wealth of the individual, who suffered heavy losses owing to Mars in the 2nd house. A strong planet like Saturn cannot stop losses to be caused by Mars, and so no other planet in the 2nd house can help in the matter. No doubt, other planets can revive the financial status of the individual to an extent possible for that planet but it is impossible to stop Mars from functioning adversely in money-content matters when in the 2nd house. Mars in the 2nd house in the yearly chart would also function likewise, though sometimes not as harshly as in the 2nd house in the birth chart. In this context it must be noted that Mars is effective if the Bhava Chalitam chart clearly indicates that Mars is positively in the 2nd house.

Apart from loss of wealth or money-content in the hands of the individual or spouse, Mars gives complaints of skin and blood system to the spouse of the individual, and sometimes leads to heart trouble too, provided the stars of spouse are under harmful influence of Mars. If the spouse has stars protecting from these complaints of health, either nothing would go wrong, or just a mild touch of the complaint would descend on the spouse and get cured easily and quickly. Therefore it is always better in cases like this, that stars of both husband and wife should be examined simultaneously.

It is also important in this context that the spouse of this individual should always protect self while handling fire, electricity, acids and any inflammable items, or while swimming or taking any kind of risk with flowing or stationary water, or while consuming any drinkable item including medicines. Extra caution has also to be observed about the spouse in a matter of any surgical operation.

If either of the couple doesn't have correct data of birth (date of birth and time of birth), a Question chart be drawn by the date and time of arrival of the couple or the individual for consultation at the astrologer's place (residence or office whatever it is). The Question chart would not work with equal effect and accuracy if the astrologer is called to the place of the consulting person or the place where the individual is staying at the moment, or in case of consultation by telephone or e-mail service. If the e-mail message is exchanged by the both sides at the same moment, it can be effective and accurate to at least about 60%, but not that accurate as the surprise visit of the individual to the place of the astrologer.

The above guidance holds equally good with regard to consultation about all matters relating to any subject in the horoscope.

Mars and Moon in the 2nd house help any cause of charity, social service, religious activity started or planned by father, because 2nd house is the 5th position from the 10th house which rules affairs of father. Similarly these two (Moon and Mars) do help in any matter relating to mother's health, money etc. or in matters concerning means of transport or relating to any residential premises or other property, if it is self-owned. It is so because Moon and Mars in 2nd are in the 11th position to the 4th house, which rules these subjects.

However this combination disturbs the implementation of any plan or scheme of the individual, because 2nd house is in 12th

position to the 3rd house of effort and planning and implementation of schemes.

It also adversely affects relationship with brothers and sisters (at least one or two of them, if they are more in number) because of the same rule of 2nd house being in 12th position to the 3rd house.

These individuals are sometimes unable to protect their book-collection. Books lent by them do not come back; sometimes the personal library suffers from rains, white ants, and fire or for any other reason. Because these persons are not bookworms, these individuals do not bother to re-build their damaged library or replace the lost or damaged books.

Moon and Mercury in the 2nd House

Moon is lord of thoughts, and Mercury rules brains, intelligence, wisdom, imagination, experience. Both in the 2nd house do not fail to make the individual richer in knowledge and experience than original background, and family status. The individual doesn't indulge in risks to money-content and general wealth, flowing from speculation of all kind (including buying and selling shares), gambling, betting at horse races, or by cheating in investments or loans given. The individual often keeps the past developments in mind, studies plus and minus points of each category of investing money, and goes ahead with caution (without risking the capital). Thus the individual rarely suffers severe losses. Ordinary loss and gains is a common thing in everyone's life.

Secondly Mercury leads the individual to observe, and to remember in memory, all developments in the line of investment, which might be of interest to self, leaving out other lines in which interest of self is not involved. Normally what happens with other people that they keep concern with all lines of investments, even those in which they have no interest and this trend of thinking lands them in jumble of many things with exclusive mastery in none, which might be of real interest to them. The final result is that they tumble down in unanticipated and sometimes unmanageable losses in hard cash or of assets.

Moon and Mercury in 2nd house give a strong tendency to the individuals to establish a library of own, by buying or by borrowing and not returning books, but not by stealing. They not only store books for a show in the drawing or general sitting room, but they very often read every book completely or at least the relevant portion of interest to them. Though they borrow from others, but generally do not lend books to others, wiser in this behalf by actions or experience of self.

Mercury (with Moon) in 2nd house always gives the individual the gift of quick grasp of whatever is taught or learnt by effort of self. This gift helps not only at the education-stage, but also in later life in understanding and assessing the truth of every situation, whether it concerns money or any other subject. And because of this quality supported by good memory, the individual proves to be a very worthy teacher, professor or holding any office efficiently in the field of education.

They are equally careful about safe custody of their useful documents, papers and files of correspondence. They actually keep their papers, documents and correspondence systematically, and promptly destroy what is not relevant for further use or utility.

Some of these individuals turn out to be very successful writers, authors of serious readings, poets, dialogue-writers for films and dramas, moreso when they have Gemini, Virgo or Libra or Pisces in the 2nd house.

One problem with Moon and Mercury in the 2nd house is that sometimes the individuals are unable to stop piracy of material from their books, essays, articles, poetry-collection, though they are particular in getting paid in terms of royalty for their works.

Another problem is that if the spouse lacks in good education, they often try to make her educated, either by effort of self or by engaging tutors, in rare cases encouraging the spouse to join school or college. Depending on the stars of the spouse, the response can be very good or very discouraging. But one thing is sure; the individual doesn't easily stand a stupid or foolish spouse, if married by mistake of self or parents or by an attempt of some greedy middleman. It is not unknown at least in India that very often wrong information is tendered to the individual about the educational standard of the spouse (matrimonial match). In an arranged marriage, it is difficult to verify the fact of real education standard. It is also common in Indian society that even in a love-based marriage, the lover gets influenced by other charms of the beloved, sometimes the monetary gain angle too. A proposal for a match with an inferior education, or little education is accepted by the individual because of other reasons such as money offered or for better chances in career or business or the high social status of the parents of the match under consideration.

Moon and Jupiter in the 2nd House

Moon and Jupiter combination is a favourable one in the 2nd house. These two definitely make the individual richer than financial position in pre-career stage. Another favour is in the shape of gold, silver, jewellery, ornaments, costly furniture, much better style of living, rich wardrobe, presentable appearance outdoors, social connections.

Even if the individual makes investments in risky avenues, Moon and Jupiter in 2nd rarely give losses, and if by chance any loss descends upon the individual, these two stars make their best effort to revival from the loss, and reaching the same standard of money-content and wealth as before. Speculation in shares and investments as sleeping partner in business or industrial venture, or permanent investments in shares in business and industrial ventures normally do not lead to losses, provided investments are not made under any kind of pressure or obligation. But gambling and betting on horse races can lead to losses, moreso if Mars or Saturn or Rahu or Herschel be in the 12th house in the birth chart or yearly chart. Even transit of Saturn, Rahu or retrograde Mars over the 12th house can lead to losses in gambling and races etc., in that particular period of time.

Normally these individuals have very strong memory studies and in money matters, also good understanding of avenues of investments and the market trends. They are very careful to keep their savings and money in banking institutions or similar organisations, that is they rarely keep their money in a place of risk.

Another cause for their money growing and not leading to major losses is that generally their investment-oriented money generates from genuine and honest sources of earning. It is not in the shape of unearned money.

These individuals are impressive orators and their talk or speech is often enriched by useful and befitting quotations, reciting of relevant pieces of poems/ poetry etc.

They are liberal in giving charity to deserving people or purposes, and if they do not have own funds, they try to get funds from others capable of helping in such cases.

Because of all these good virtues and qualities, the individual enjoys very good status and respect in society. If the individuals are judges in any court or tribunal or forum or are members of legal body like Law Commission etc., they enjoy high level of respect and reputation in the public because of their honesty of purpose.

These individuals are fond of good food and have very good appetite for it. For this purpose, generally they do not miss going to a party, where good and tasty food is likely to be served. This also raises their social popularity, instead of harming it in any way.

Moon and Venus in the 2nd House

Moon and Venus together in the 2nd house give all good things in life, namely, good knowledge of navigation, of music, dance, fine arts, acting, directing actors and actresses, production of films and their distribution. They give good clothes, good decoration to house and sometimes to work place too (provided it belongs to the individual). They can give, depending on the Rasi in the 2nd house and relations of Moon and Venus with the lord of the 2nd house, a beautiful spouse (many a time an envy and attraction-point for others). Ancient authorities have said:

"roopvati triya shatru"

meaning a beautiful wife proves an enemy because many people have an eye on her!

This combination generally easily gets an admission in a medical college or school, and ultimately the individual turns out to be an efficient and well-known physician, or a Radiologist and pathologist or at least working in the field of medicine, radiology or pathology.

For the individual's knowledge, education, profession or any other reason, the individual is a centre-point of attraction of the opposite sex, and sometimes of the same sex, though ancients have said that a woman doesn't get attracted towards another woman. Wide spread lesbian and homosexual relations in virtually all civilised countries have proved our ancients false, and the funny part is that it has been accepted as legal by the concerned societies.

Moon and Venus combination generally gives a sense of self-confidence as well as sense of vanity and ego; some individuals wear their ego rather sharply, as reflected in their talk and behaviour that sometimes pinches others.

In rare cases, this combination gives a second or third marriage, during the lifetime of the first one or during the first-one still living together with the spouse. Where law of the Land prohibits it, the individual doesn't hesitate from keeping mistress or enjoying casual or one-night friendship with opposite sex, no doubt, in a very secret manner.

These individuals (men and women alike) are fond of costly jewellery or costly costume, including headwear and footwear.

These individuals are usually without knowledge of music or dance or any other fine art, like painting, drawing, architecture, or art and technique of landscape. But they at least enjoy exhibiting drawings/ pictures, piece-de-art, or paintings of these items of fine arts or good fruits and good musical instruments, cassettes of high class music (including classical music of India) in their drawing rooms.

Some of these individuals get interested in collecting ancient costumes, jewellery, decorative ornaments and paintings. Some others are interested in attending dances, musical concerts, meeting film and stage personalities, and obtaining their autographs.

Whether personal resources and financial status allow or not, some of these individuals like to live and behave like aristocrats, whatever the cost and ultimate effect on their finances.

These individuals are often fond of mountaineering or going to places known for snowfall and cold climate etc. Instead of taking the spouse along, they take a friend of the opposite sex with them. But if the spouse has a strong nature by influence of own stars, the individual is obliged to take the spouse along.

These types of individuals have hardly any hesitation in borrowing money and other items from others, and they conveniently forget repayments or return of the items thus borrowed. Because they are experts in sweet words, more or less flattery, very rarely they are discarded or totally refused a loan. They manage to obtain a loan, if not in full, at least a part of it, and to cover it up, they always demand higher loan than their actual need at that moment. Sometimes to create an impression of their honesty of purpose and genuineness of the demand for loan, they take their spouse along.

Moon and Saturn in the 2nd House

Moon and Saturn combination means actually two die-hard enemies together! Moon becomes more or less ineffective in the company of Saturn, which rules the individual or to use a proverb, rules the roster.

The most important effect is that the individual becomes very wise in saving money slowly and steadily by hook or by crook, and rarely fails to invest it wisely and profitably. The individual is also clever in recovery of own dues, and easily manages to forget what the individual owes to others.

These individuals do not hesitate to borrow items of daily use or household items on promise of return, which is rarely kept. Truth and lie are equal for their policy. Honestly borrowing or cheating or even stealing enjoys no distinction in their conduct and behaviour.

They have no hitch in using unfair means in examinations or annual valuation of their work and performance. If unfair means do not meet with desired success or fall short of the prescribed standard, they use influence from here and there, try to drop names of influential people, and if this source also fails, they indulge in giving direct or indirect threats. In school, these tricks work, but not at the university level education. Then they have to drop midway.

Another recourse is that easily they attain high standard in games and sports, and it helps them in school or university or college, because they are very successful in earning a good name for their school or university or college.

In the matter of married life, they are rarely satisfied in it, even if the marriage and selection of the marriage-partner had been of their choice. Whether man or woman, these individuals do not have any restraint or reservation in beating the spouse, without bothering about immediate effect thereof on the physical condition of the spouse, and about the after-effect on the mind of the spouse. They generally have little fear of the family of the spouse. They think they are all-powerful and resourceful, and remain prepared for separation or divorce. If a wife has this combination in the 2nd house, she too does not hesitate in beating the husband.

Taking a second source of marital happiness, openly or very secretly is a common fact and feature with them.

Whether they have ample money or not, they prefer to live in ordinary or poor style and as far as possible, conceal their money and financial worth. Only people having first-hand knowledge of their investments have an idea about their wealth.

They often keep their investments and hidden wealth a secret from their spouse and immediate family also. It happens then on their death that their hidden wealth and secret investments are lost to their heirs and successors. So far as investments in shares or stocks are concerned, sometimes the family finds the certificates and other papers from their concealed files. If the family doesn't find these documents, others with first-hand knowledge of their investments manage by forgery and false means to derive advantage of those investments.

So far as money deposited with private parties is concerned, it is complete loss to the family, because the people having the deposits are not fools to reveal the existence of that money. Old times are gone when people were more honest and loyal to their friends and customers.

Similarly, if some people had advanced loans, they may make true (or false) claims of money lent of this individual. The heirs and successors either get cheated in the matter of repayment, or they try to totally deny the existence of the any loans obtained by the deceased individual. Litigation is the only final outcome in the matter, and it is all a time-consuming and difficult exercise.

Moon and Rahu in the 2nd House

There is nothing much to say about the combination of Moon and Rahu in the 2nd house. The question of taking loans normally doesn't arise, because Rahu generates wealth, and makes the individual miserly in style of living, so the wealth is preserved. If however the individual makes a false show of obtaining a loan, the matter is always covered by some method or the other in the matter of repayment. So neither of the two parties suffers in any way. Generally this process is adopted to cheat the taxation system or as a cover in litigation or government recovery on some account or the other.

The second result of this combination is ill treatment of the spouse, but generally it doesn't reach the extent of beating and violence. Another problem in married life is miserliness of the individual adversely affecting comfortable living and also the education of the progeny. The third problem in married life is that of suspicion on the moral character of the spouse, which sometimes gets cleared in due course, and even if stays between them, it does not ruin the marriage in any way. The marriage just drags on its feet, at least for consideration about the progeny.

Rahu generally gives a fat body to the spouse, but much in this behalf would depend on the stars of the spouse herself or himself. Even fatness descending on the spouse doesn't make much difference in mutual relationship between the couple.

Rahu also gives extra-marital relationship, but more of the platonic type than involving physical relationship, because Rahu generates fear of reputation as also fear of any disease, risky to the life, also because Rahu has no liking for using preventive items in this behalf.

In other matters, Rahu gives shadow results on the pattern of Saturn discussed in the paragraphs above.

One typical effect of Rahu with Moon in the 2nd is that, unlike Saturn, this combination gives a liking to the individual for travels, walking all alone, going to remote and reclusive places or sites.

Moon and Ketu in the 2nd House

Like Rahu and Moon in combination, there is not much to say about Moon and Ketu together in the 2nd house.

Ketu gives problem of constant or intermittent complaint of mouth, nose or ear, and medical treatment costs a lot. But these individuals are not miserly like other hard planets with Moon in the 2nd house. Ketu spends liberally on self and spouse and also on own progeny, but generally not on the wider family. This combination makes the individuals fond of storing large stocks of food-grains of any and every kind for domestic consumption or for profiteering in trading. Ultimate result is that food-grains go a rot and have to be thrown away or sold or given free to those owning cattle. Sometimes the stock are so badly rotten that they are unfit even as cattle-feed and have to be thrown away. It happened like that once in USA for their wheat stocks and the stuff had to be thrown into the ocean.

These individuals are neither very social nor helpful to the common public in its troubles and natural or man-made calamities. They always keep the profit point in view while extending any help, whether the profit is in cash or in gaining cheap popularity in the masses.

Like Rahu in 2nd house, these individuals too have no distinction or dividing line between truth and falsehood.

They too entertain suspicion about spouse with regard to character and needs of money. But these elements do not disturb the mutual relationship between husband and wife. They are not much inclined to platonic or physical relationship outside the arena of marriage.

These individuals too maintain secret finances, and therefore others feel that they are poor, but in reality it is not so at all. They are miserly, but at the same time they dislike taking loans from any source.

They prefer to use their own money. Further, if they know about their likely death in the near future, they acquaint their spouse and progeny (if grown up enough to understand) their investments and deposits of money with private parties. Thus nothing much gets lost to the heirs and successors.

MOON IN THE 3RD HOUSE

Moon is lord of mental faculties, while the 3rd house concerns chiefly work, efforts, brothers and sisters. Some astrologers carry the theory that 3rd house concerns only the elder brother/ sister, and every 3rd house from the 3rd house concerns others brothers and sisters one by one. For example the second brother or sister is governed by the 5th house, the third brother or sister from the 7th house, and the fourth brother or sister from the 9th house and so on. Practical experience does not support this theory.

The 3rd house rules also jewellery, domestic help and other employees (in fact both the 3rd house and the 4th house rule full time or part time servants and domestic help). Undoubtedly the 3rd house rules side sources of income.

The main result of Moon in the 3rd house is that the individual is given to working by mood. If the mind directs to work hard, the individual does so, if the mind directs 'go slow' vis-à-vis lethargy and laziness, the individual bows to that inner command too. Generally it is the experience that Moon leads more towards lethargy than towards hard work, as other soft planets too have the same influence on work attitude of the individual.

No doubt, the individual has fondness for wearing ornaments and jewellery, very attractive clothes (apparel or costume).

The individual has great inner affection towards brothers and sisters. If their number is large, at least towards one brother and one sister, but the individual doesn't much express that love and affection under the impression that no undue advantage may be taken thereof.

These individuals encourage others towards boldness and bravery, but they themselves often remain in the background, unless there is some obligatory or compelling circumstance to move to the front or forward position. Normally they are neither daring nor dashing. This withdrawn tendency sometimes affects others too adversely, but not often.

The individual is often alert towards health and public image or public relationship of the father. He or she extends moral and financial help to the father, but not so much physical support in any fight against father by father's enemy or adversary. In father's illness, the individual gives all physical service too, because it doesn't involve any physical risk to the individual. It can be called in an overall manner, a 'fear complex'.

This very fear or hesitation to taking risk is responsible for these individuals to make serious effort to migrate to another country, specially across the waters (sea or ocean), and look towards others for help and support, and not getting it, continue quietly wherever and whatever they are!

These individuals do not normally work very hard, but they are keen to become wealthy and well possessed, without minding the support and help of brothers, sisters, friends, or by secret money from mother.

These individuals consult a doctor even on a slight complaint of health and start taking medicine. But when they start feeling better, they become irregular in taking medicine and stop it suddenly and abruptly, Unless under pressure from other planets, these individuals do not suffer from any such trouble as might warrant major surgery. Since the 3rd house rules hearing faculty, they are very alert about their hearing capacity. They do not generally suffer from heart ailment, or any complaint of health leading to it. They stay preventive in this regard. During pregnancy days, these women have greater confidence about continuance of the pregnancy as also about own health, and they try to avoid delivery by caesarean section or forceps delivery.

Because these individuals do not prefer themselves to attend to domestic chores, they are generally tolerant and liberal towards domestic help.

Moon and Sun in the 3rd House

Please refer to chapter on Sun, relevant paragraph on "Sun with Moon in the 3rd house.

Moon and Mars in the 3rd House

Though Moon and Mars are permanent friend, these two become opposed to each other being together in the same house, and thereby Mars gains a dominating influence over Moon.

The first effect is that Mars rather compels the individual to work hard and to drop the tendency to delaying work under any excuse. Mars without bothering about Moon's presence in the 3rd house, makes the individual bold and brave indeed, also dashing and daring, never afraid of proceeding forward or to the front line, taking initiative in any job entrusted or undertaken, preferring own independent decisions and judgements.

Mars does give loss of one or two pregnancies of the mother, or infancy death to a brother or sister after birth, within maximum 18 months of birth. Otherwise too, the individual often exercises domination and pressure over the mother, whether the mother is real or adoptive.

The individual is often very good at games and sports, and is often keen to learn use of weapons, including light and heavy firearms. The individual acquires efficiency also in different uses and utilities of electricity and electronics. Generally top quality cooks and chefs are also born under this combination. Mars (and Moon with it) make an individual a good policeman or an efficient army-man. Professional butchers and criminals are also born with this combination in the 3rd house.

The big contribution of Mars with Moon in 3rd house is that it gives concentration of mind to the work or job in hand, without any noticeable touch of lethargy.

These individuals do not hesitate to handle domestic cores too themselves, and therefore, though liberal and accommodating towards domestic help, towards other servants, employees and subordinates, they do not tolerate any act or attitude of insubordination or lack of discipline.

They are often keen to ownership of real estate, if nothing else, at least of own residential unit, and when needed, do not hesitate to work hard for it.

Moon and Mercury in the 3rd House

Moon and Mercury are soft planets, and though Mercury (being deemed son of Moon) is friendly towards Moon, the latter one has inimical attitude towards Mercury (own son). Therefore their being together in 3rd or any other house is always a matter of mixture of happiness and unhappiness.

However in matters of lethargy and laziness, postponement of job in hand, diversion of attention, both Moon and Mercury co-operate with each other. In student life too, the individual is not keen on very bright result, just passing from one class to another is deemed enough. Instead of paying attention to studies, home work and written work related to studies, the individual generally works a bit harder on days nearer to the Exams, and sometimes, because of gift of intelligence granted by Mercury, manages to get through to the higher standard. The individual generally gets extra valuation because of good handwriting, and is normally good in Mathematics, whereby the percentage gets much improved.

When in career, the individual relies more on personal talks and discussions rather than on written communication etc. However the individual has helplessly to use fax machines and E-mail system, where the dependence is on written matter.

The individual is expert at convincing others merely by talks, discussing and oral arguments over a point. If the individual functions as an advocate, lawyer, solicitor or even as a judge in a court of law, preparation of petitions, appeals and writing judgements remain pending, generally much to the inconvenience and impatience of the litigants concerned.

The same is the case in teaching line too. The individual proves to be an efficient teacher in the class room, making the students fully understand the subject, but is lethargic in checking written work of the students or answers-books for the Exams conducted.

In the profession of future-telling science, the individual attains high proficiency in his learning, but prefers to give oral predictions, instead of written ones. If the listener insists, the listener is asked to take down written notes, while the individual is discussing the future in terms of predictions.

Because of this trend of laziness or lethargy, this type of individual hardly indulges in keeping duplicate accounts for cheating taxation system. On the other hand, the individual is not careful about the custody of documents and papers, nor prompt in filing system, unless colleague or subordinate or employee helps and takes over the responsibility of this type of work.

Moon and Jupiter in the 3rd House

Most of the characteristics and habits created by Moon and Jupiter combination in the 3rd house are similar to those created by Moon and Mercury in the 3rd house. The main difference is that the lethargy and laziness do not totally overpower the individual, who becomes a calculated worker, for obtaining expected or anticipated particular result or return, and for that this much quantum of work would prove sufficient.

Brevity and writing to the point, be it an agreement, treaty, contract, undertaking, petition, appeal, judgement or written arguments is the speciality of these individuals. They may be verbose in oral talk, discussion or argument, but not in writing, because in lecturing on religion, cult, faith, performance of assigned or undertaken duties, one has to be elaborate for the matter going home with the listeners.

In business deals and as goldsmiths, these individuals stay within tolerable limits, and therefore, their customers impose greater faith in them and their goods-in-trade.

These individuals do not prefer physical violence, fighting, proceeding to the front-line, because they give very useful and valuable suggestions for achievement of the aim, without moving to the Front.

Moon and Venus in the 3rd House

Moon and Venus together in the 3rd house make an individual partly lethargic (not lazy) and partly hard working, given to the situation, circumstances, importance of the job in hand and whether the work is interesting or causing boredom. If the job relates to a brother or a sister or close or distant relation of the opposite sex, or a female member of the uncle's or cousin's family, these individuals often take keen interest and have no hitch in putting in hard work. And if it is a matter involving romance on either side or a developing love affair, these individuals are all out to achieve the desired result.

These individuals are specially interested in all kind of ornaments and jewellery, for use of self or the spouse or the beloved one or the family. They sometimes enter into active trading in diamonds, all kinds of precious stones, gold and silver ornaments, bullion, gold and silver utensils, gold-plated or silver-plated items, even in costume jewellery and artificial jewellery. They are always fond of best quality and nicely made clothes, garments, apparel, cosmetics, beautifying elements, to the extent that they undertake business in any of these lines, tailoring and beautician-clinic included. They are fond of milk, butter and other products and sweets of milk, curd, butter etc. They have no reservation in taking to trade in this line too. Automatically they get interested in keeping and maintaining milch cattle, for use of self and family or for extensive trading in this line. Some of these individuals take to trading in liquor, wine, alcohol and allied items on a regular basis under the usual license.

The individual often helps and does not put hurdle in any love affair or love-based marriage of brother, sister or cousin or even nephew and niece, and expects this category of relations to prove helpful to the individual when the need arises. The individual has the correct sense of secrecy, whether the affair is of own or of any one else in whom the individual is interested on account of blood relationship or mere friendship.

One dark spot in this regard is that barring the real brother or sister, the individual doesn't much hesitate in developing love relationship with a half-brother or half-sister, stepbrother or stepsister, cousin, nephew or niece. But he or she is always careful to go ahead only if the response from the other person is there. Otherwise the individual has the decency to drop the idea at the initial adverse response.

The same is the case with regard to love-based marriage of the individual. If both or even one parent on either side has firm opposition to the individual's love-based proposal, instead of adopting the path of revolt, the individual drops the matter. There have been cases within the experience of the authors, their father and grandfather (who have been eminent astrologers with wide reputation) that the two individuals involved in the love affair waited for the death of the opposing parent and then went into formal marriage.

Another angle to this matter is that if one of the two in the love affair is waiting for entry into worth-the-name career or betterment in job and status, the other party waits till the desired aim or ambition is achieved, and then goes for formal marriage.

Because of Moon, the individuals concerned are secretive, at least till they become sure of response of acceptance from the other person in the love affair.

Moon and Saturn in the 3rd House

It has to be remembered that Moon gets dominated when in combination with any hard planet. Saturn is not only hard but rather the hardest planet among those who are nearer to the Sun (and the Earth) and is very effective in giving results. Going by this principle, Saturn is fully effective and operative actively in the 3rd house (with Moon), because Saturn has full influence on the positive side in the 3rd house.

Saturn makes the individual very hardworking, given to the aim or ambition in view or the responsibility or duty assigned or undertaken. Saturn's slowness gets reduced to noticeable extent owing to swift (rather swiftest among all planets) speed of Moon.

Saturn is dutiful towards brothers, sisters, cousins, uncles, aunts and their spouses, but very rarely Saturn creates any remarkable sense of attachment to these blood or near relations. Saturn is 3rd house (even with Moon) has the same trend and attitude towards friends of either sex, so long as the friendship doesn't take the colour and attitude of love relationship. In love affair and married life too, the individual doesn't tolerate infidelity, and returns it with sudden break off in the matter of love affair, and with violent treatment of the spouse, be it husband or wife. If the infidelity continues in spite of this attitude, the individual, under forceful effect of Saturn (with Moon in the background) takes resort to physical or judicial separation or ultimately to divorce proceedings. Further, because of Saturn, the individual has no hesitation is washing dirty linen in the court or arbitration hearings.

One very favourable point of Saturn (forcefully obtaining support of Moon) for the individual is that it gives him or her capacity, and also competence to reach achievement of the result desired or expected. Because of this success-oriented impact on life, the individual is hardly ever in need of obtaining loans or entering into heavy debts. It's a different matter altogether that the individual has to take resort to debts (often in the shape of investments) when starting and running large-scale business or industrial venture, in the fashion of private limited or public limited company.

Career-wise most of these individuals are in service line, public or private, senior job or a lower job, depending on educational qualifications, competence and experience. Mostly a majority of them have the quality of being bold and brave in any and all circumstances. Many among them have to suffer and tolerate under-employment too. Saturn's aim is more on completion of job, duty and responsibility rather than on status and rank of the employment.

No doubt, some rare individuals are able to start their own venture in the field of trading, business, industry, or self-employment. It becomes possible when either Saturn is in Taurus, Libra, Capricorn or Aquarius or is receiving very strong and active support from such planet(s) as be concerned with that source of livelihood as has been adopted by the individual.

This position of Saturn (with Moon) often causes loss of one or two pregnancies to the mother, unless her own stars are helping otherwise, or death of a brother or a sister in its childhood, before the age of 10 or at the most 20 years. Much in this regard would depend on the stars of that individual too. Therefore it is safer not to give predictions in this behalf on the basis of examining the stars of the individual alone.

Moon and Rahu in the 3rd House

It becomes an 'eclipse' combination, to a great extent nullifying the effect of Moon in the 3rd. The individual is given either to hard work or at least to a show of hard work. Rahu is able to achieve the desired or expected or aimed results, if not on its own, at least with the support of other stars, including its counterpart Ketu in the 9th house, which house rules fortune, faith and devotion and prayers to God.

The individual with Rahu (and Moon) in the 3rd is not bothered whether the source of income is considered good or bad, nor the individual is much bothered about reputation of the field of work or reputation of self in that line. Rahu and the individual both are concerned with final results and income from that source of livelihood. Borrowing money, resources or items of daily use is not uncommon with Rahu in 3rd house, but the return or repayment is often prompt and within the period mutually agreed.

With regard to relations with brothers, sisters, cousins, uncles, aunts, nephews and nieces, the actual attitude and performance are on the basis of 'give and take', nothing more and nothing less.

In the same sense, Rahu (with Moon) doesn't shoulder the responsibility for loss of pregnancy to mother or death of brother or sister in childhood. Except leading to medical termination of pregnancy, Rahu keeps aloof and leaves matters to the stars of the mother and the individuals born to her.

Moon and Ketu in the 3rd House

In spite it being an 'eclipse' combination in a sense, Ketu doesn't give results similar or parallel to Rahu, except hard working tendency.

Ketu doesn't concern itself with pregnancies of mother nor to those born to her. All these matters are governed by the stars of mother or of those born to her. No doubt Ketu too maintains 'give and take' approach towards all blood relations and friends in the inner circle.

Ketu no doubt makes the individual liberal, charitable and helpful to real needy people, and often goes by own judgement, neither by recommendations nor by approaches, requests and entreaties.

In love matters or married life, Ketu is neither violent nor revengeful in case of infidelity, and gives an opportunity to the other partner to improve and become befitting to the intimacy in the mutual relationship. Failing utterly to bring about a visible or noticeable improvement in the other party, Ketu believes in quiet end to the relationship, whatever the mode thereof is acceptable to both, husband and wife.

As compared to Rahu in 3rd (even with Moon), which doesn't take much interest in starting and running any trading, business, industrial venture, alone by one's own self, Ketu doesn't entertain reservation in this behalf. Ketu whole-heartedly and with full attention takes to a career of self-employment or trading or business or running an industrial unit, big or small, whatever the circumstances and financial capacity of the individual permit.

Moon in the 4th House

This house chiefly rules mother (including breast feeding by real mother or otherwise), inheritance of knowledge, experience and quality of character or absence thereof from the mother. In addition, this house rules conveyance, friends, property, food and diet, digestive system, thinness or fatness of body, moreso of the middle part of it, comfort or lack of comfort in bedroom, and sound or disturbed sleep. This house rules also keeping and maintaining cattle for milk (cow, buffalo, goat, sheep, sometimes camel too) and also as means of transport (male-buffalo, horse, pony, donkey, elephant, camel), dogs in much higher latitude (lands of extreme snow like Iceland).

Moon being a soft planet but given to waxing and waning condition in so far as residents on Earth are concerned, it tries its best to give good results with regard to the above stated subjects. But being a fast moving planet and also having the weakness of being dominated and overruled by other soft and hard planets, its capacity for giving good results becomes limited. Then it very much depends on the Rasi in the 4th house, its lord, placement of the lord in the birth chart and intra-relationship with Moon. Navamsha chart too plays a very strong effect with regard to Moon in the 4th house. Moon gives diminished results when Aries, Scorpio, Capricorn or Aquarius is in the 4th house and all the more reduced results if Mars and Saturn have 6:8 inimical relations with Moon.

In all these considerations, recall that Moon is lord of the Mind in every human being. The individual's pleasant or unpleasant attitude towards events and developments concerning or surrounding him or her would to a great extent depend on the attitude of the individual's mind. Lord Krishna has said in Shrimad Bhagwat Gita:

"Mind alone is the cause of an individual's bindings (and bounds) and salvation".

The first point relates to breast-feeding. If **Aries** or **Scorpio** is in the 4th house in birth-chart or its Navamsha or its *Kaarakaansh* chart, mother lacks in sufficient supply of milk in the breast, and has to take resort to bottle-feeding. If **Capricorn** or **Aquarius** be in the 4th house in birth chart or Navamsha or *Kaarakaansh* chart, the mother, for sake of her beauty and personality doesn't prefer breast feeding, even if she is capable of it. In either case bottle-feeding or employing a surrogate (feeding-nurse) becomes unavoidable. If the parents are financially poor, the baby has to suffer poor development of body and ill health too till the age of at least 4 years.

As regards mode of transport, conveyance facility, even when alone in the 4th house, Moon makes it available, whether owned or borrowed one or getting lift every now and then. If Moon is in Taurus, Cancer, Virgo or Pisces, the individual enjoys more than one mode of transport, owned by self or parents or spouse or provided by the employers. The mode of transport doesn't meet with repeated accidents or breakdowns, unless a Rasi owned by Mars or Saturn is in the 4th house and Moon is under unfavourable impact of Saturn, Mars or Rahu.

In so far as food and diet are concerned, the individual likes sweets and drinkable items, and often gains extra weight than medically prescribed for the individual's height and age. But food habits otherwise do not adversely affect the health. Normally the individual doesn't believe in fasting for religious purposes (even if a staunch religionalist), but agrees to fasting on medical grounds or for presentability of the personality.

With regard to comfort in the bedroom and also of sound sleep, Moon gives both in the normal course, provided it is not in combination with Sun, Mars, Saturn, Rahu or Herschel, or is not in Aries, Scorpio, Capricorn or Aquarius. Much would depend on the *Kaarak* chart at the time of birth (expert astrologers do give this chart in the detailed horoscope). If the *Kaarak*-planets (doer=giver of comfort from) for mother and/or spouse is a soft planet, these comforts are assured. If the hard-planets Mars, Saturn or even Sun rule over these aspects of mother and/or spouse, the comfort in childhood would be less than needed or desired, and comfort in married life would be adversely affected, undoubtedly.

Further the position discussed in the preceding paragraph would also determine whether the baby or the child would stay in the company or under the care of the natural mother or in the custody or care of other blood relation, or under a nurse or nanny. Bringing up by someone else than the natural mother adversely affects, at least to a certain extent, the mentality of the baby or child when it grows into adolescence and adulthood.

One boy spent his childhood from the age of 6 months to 6 years in a separate town with the maternal grandmother. The result was that when he was sent from India to the US, for higher studies in a special career-oriented subject, he returned to India just after four months, though the study-course was of three-year duration. The parents approached the senior author, and he suggested to the mother to shower greater affection and nearness to the boy mentally and physically. The natural mother acted as advised by the author. The result was that within just 4 months, the boy returned to USA and completed his studies with good honours.

The individual, on volition of self, is sincere and helpful to the friends within the inner circle, sometimes even when the response from the friends is not encouraging. But on achieving adulthood and entry in career, this attitude of one-sidedness changes, and response from the other side becomes unavoidable. After marriage, vast change comes into the basis of friendship, often remaining limited to one or two persons. Friendship on face or surface is a different matter, because it falls within sociability of the individual.

With regard to real estate (i.e. property), the individual is a contented person, generally remaining restricted to ownership of premises needed for restricted use of self and the family. Chances of getting property by inheritance or by adoption or by gift or by way of award for gallantry or outstanding services to the nation (prevailing till 19th century and first half of the 20th century) are strong under Moon in the 4th house. The individual doesn't feel inclined to borrow large sums of money to own premises for residence or for work. But under pressure of the family or friends or circumstances, the individual might indulge in borrowing money to gain ownership of premises.

The individual generally doesn't believe in speculation in property or oft-repeated purchase and sale of property, unless driven by heavy loss in other avenues of finances!

The individual is very much interested in social work, providing facilities for drinking water to human beings and cattle, construction of shelter for the destitute and poor, building school or other sources of education, religious premises, hospital or dispensary and similar other facilities for public use. If the individual doesn't have own resources, he or she doesn't mind in securing support for any of these purposes from others, who are capable to help financially or by work force.

The individual is always very prompt and particular in medical remedy, when needed, to mother, self and spouse, as also to other members of immediate and wider family and to friends too, and observes regularity in treatment. Often the individual is afraid of medical treatment involving major surgery, and needs mental encouragement and support for getting ready for it, whether for self or others. If the need suddenly arises for caesarean delivery of child to a woman, she tries her best to avoid it or postpone it even to own risk or to the baby in the womb or to both. She has to be persuaded to go in for this or any other kind of major surgery.

Moon and Sun in the 4th House

Please refer to Sun with Moon in 4th house in chapter supra.

Moon and Mars in the 4th House

When Moon and Mars are in combination in the 4th house, a major portion of Moon's effect in the 4th is overridden by presence of Mars there.

Mars not only gives rich inheritance in terms of real estate, but also encourages the individual to own more property for the purpose of rental income. The individual naturally gets interested in speculation in property, and also frequent buying and selling for profits, and very rarely the exercise turns out to be a case of real loss (not considering notional or imagined).

Chances rarely appear for the baby to grow under the custody and care of others, instead of the real mother. That type of chances increase, sometimes owing to ill health of mother or owing to change in marital status of the mother It is all the more so, if the natural mother expires within four years of the birth of the individual. To a great extent this eventuality depends on the stars of the mother and the real father. If the conception of the baby was illegitimate, full term birth of the baby in the womb, its growth under natural mother or others is difficult to determine on the basis of the stars of the child alone. This development quite often adversely affects the mutual love, affection and relations between the mother and the child; moreso after the child has reached the age of adolescence and adulthood. In such a case as this, in spite of the mother giving great love, care and affection, the individual becomes indifferent towards the mother. Sometimes it happens to be so under pressure of her husband (who is not the natural father of the child) or under non-cordial relations between mother and her husband.

The individual makes a serious attempt to gain specialised knowledge (and experience too) in the line of electrical and electronics, real estate business, matrimonial brokerage, government or semi-government service or public sector job. The individual also tries to start and establish own industry or business connected with industrial ventures of others. Some individual makes a very serious and concentrated effort to migrate to another country and establish there, and meets with success sooner or later.

Mars too gives trouble and inconvenience related to or on account of mode of transport or conveyance facility (though not as much as Saturn in 4th house gives). And it is not oft-repeated either.

One important impact of Mars (with Moon) in 4th house is that the individual entertains intentions of violence from the school days itself, and takes resort to it, even on very minor cause or provocation. It often continues towards the beloved or the spouse too.

With regard to food and diet, the individual keeps a strict eye on health and does not allow growth of unwanted flesh on the middle part of the body. The individual is very fond of tasty and spicy food items, and doesn't mind making complaints at home or in hotels and restaurants. The individual is sometimes unable to suppress critical words even at parties and receptions, if the food is much below the liking of the individual.

This individual has often to face strained relations between spouse and mother, and things go worse if the individual takes sides with either of them. At the same time, the individual is unable to avoid taking sides, because the individual is positively given to short temper and anger.

In matters of medical treatment, the individual often avoids medical consultation and undertakes self-medication unless things reach beyond control or others interested in the well being of the individual bring pressure. However the individual doesn't entertain fear complex with regard to major surgery for self or any near and dear one, including friends, whom the individual provides encouragement, if necessary.

Moon and Mercury in the 4th House

Combination of Moon and Mercury normally makes an individual very honest to the purpose, straightforward in money matters, generally intelligent and wise for constructive ends (as opposed to destructive ends). If the individual has been able to get higher medical education, she or he would prefer to be a professor or teacher in a medical institution, otherwise too, the individual would prefer teaching line than other better paying avenues. Failing this, the individual would like to go in journalism, publishing, book selling, as a librarian, or any table job requiring more of noting and drafting or any kind of written work.

The individual generally does not entertain greedy intentions, and wants to stay off any kind of corrupt practices. The individual is not much bothered about the standard or size or location of the residential unit, nor bothers about buying a better or bigger one, so long as any residence has space for personal collection of books (and magazines etc.)

The individual wants to be of service to both parents, with no considerations of gains or loss, and as far as possible guides the spouse too to remain service-minded, financially and physically towards parents. The individual maintains cordial relations with own brothers and sisters, but often doesn't get very intimate with their spouse, nor with own uncles, aunts and cousins, though goes to their help whenever needed by them. If the individual, by circumstances resides away from parents, in the same town or in another town or even in another state or country, the individual keeps constant contact with parents of self and spouse.

Some of these individuals take interest in music, dance and any other branch of fine arts, but they acquire neither expertise in, nor remain attached to any of these arts for long periods. They however contribute reviews on performances of artists in those fine arts in which these individuals are interested. They therefore acquire deeper knowledge for the limited purpose of writing reviews on performance.

These individuals exercise command on spoken and written words, and become popular among the public. Unless Sun is in the 4th house or Mars is in 3rd, 4th or 10th house, these individuals keep no concern with active politics beyond expressing their ideas in their writings for print media or otherwise, but not for the visual media.

Moon and Jupiter in the 4th House

The combination of Moon and Jupiter has given some of the well-known personalities in the field of law, whether at the Bar or on the Bench (low and high in rank) or in legislature or legislation or drafting laws and Acts or writing material for constitution-making.

These individuals are often very much interested for proper payment for their work or services, wherever and whomsoever they work for. They maintain the desire for a bursting-out bank balance, comfortable and nicely built residence in a posh locality.

They are always keen for social recognition for their knowledge and work. If not in the field of law, they prefer to be in Legislature or Parliament or Senate or District Council or Village *Panchayat*, depending on level of their education and background for this purpose, as also their approach.

They want an impressive mode of transport, nice food at home or elsewhere as a customer or as a guest. But they are rarely a paying customer at any hotel or restaurant, unless they want to go out for food with the whole family or with the spouse. Otherwise they prefer to be guest only.

They enjoy good sleep and want a short siesta during work hours too, and do not want to be disturbed when sleeping or taking rest.

They are serviceful to parents, more financially than physically. They want others in the family or in their employ to *render* physical service to the parents, and they are willing to pay for it. In the same breath, these individuals have a vigilant eye on inheritance from parents, and if they cannot get a lion's share in it, at least they do not want to surrender even a part of their share in favour of another needy co-sharer!

Unless this combination is in Cancer or Pisces, these individuals are not keen on migration to another state or another country across the waters. They are fond of travelling, more from income point of view than that of unadulterated pleasure and enjoyment (with or without family). However they do not mind providing money and facilities for the family or for the progeny to go on pleasure trips.

Moon and Venus in the 4th House

Both, Moon and Venus are soft planets, but enemies of each other and both are independently and jointly effective in the 4th house.

Going by its nature, Venus gives, even to pious individuals, romantic ideas, which Moon keeps unexpressed. Mercury and Venus are generally in combination or occupying adjacent Rasis. Thus if Mercury is in the 3rd house, these individual would not utter out their romantic ideas and romantic opinion to concerned persons in their presence. However if Mercury is in the 4th or in the 5th house, the romantic ideas get expressed, at least, by way of praise and appreciation for the beauty of the person before them, or passing by, or in talk to a third person referring to that person with charming personality.

Since Venus has greater influence over women, the women folk too discuss with friends or neighbours the attractive personality of a young or youthful man. In this matter, Venus does not spare women of motherly age or status, though it might be by way of praise and appreciation only. Even Chhatrapati Shivaji Maharaja, who established the Maratha Kingdom initially, used to talk about his mother, Smt Jijabai's personality.

Normally, being soft planets, Moon and Venus in 4th house do not induce these individuals to make any advances towards persons other than own spouse. But if the initiative comes from the opposite side, these individuals do respond, may be with hesitation and restraint. Then the ultimate result depends on stars of the opposite party who initiated the advances.

Because 4th house rules mother also, these individuals are always very respectful and serviceful to the real or foster or adopting mother. In return they get high quality response from the mother. On birth, they get enough of breast-feeding and that too for anything from 8 to 18 months, or even more. Financial adjustment too between mother and the individual is perfectly all right. This understanding works in favour of the individual in matters relating to inheritance. There are several cases where father wasn't impartial in the matter of inheritance, if the division took place in father's life time, but the mother intervened in favour of the individual (with Moon and Venus combination in the 4th house), and helped her or him in getting due share.

However it has to be noted that if Saturn or Mars be in the 4th or 10th house or Rahu be in the 4th house, mother is unable to help in the matter of correct share in inheritance. If any one of these three planets in the 4th house has greater strength than Moon and Venus, even the mother would harm the interests of the individual. Ketu in 4th house (with Moon and Venus) in 4th

house would not cause or help any injustice of this kind to the individual.

These individuals do not generally suffer in the matter of conveyance. Some facility, either of self or of others, or convenient public transport is at hand, when needed.

The 4th house rules residence, and Moon and Venus both are interested in cleanliness, system, order, decoration to the residence. So the residence gets decoration, no doubt, as per means of the individual. However in present times, so many financial institutions and even dealers or shop-keepers are allowing debit facilities that often the individuals indulge in buying semi-utility or rare-utility items of furniture, furnishings and decoration beyond their means. The consequence is that they suffer when the hour and demand for recovery of due payments reaches their door. It is generally so, if Saturn or Rahu is in transit over the 4th or 12th house, or Rahu, Saturn or Mars or even Sun or Jupiter (with unfavourable attitude towards matters relating to money and wealth) is running its Mahadasa or sub-period at the repayment junction of time.

Generally these individuals keep good health, and so any problem related to heart or trouble leading to heart ailment doesn't arise. No doubt, capacity for physical relationship of the husband might suffer downward trend if it is Venus Mahadasa and Moon sub-period or Moon Mahadasa and Venus sub-period at the time this process of deterioration in masculinity commences. Then the deterioration continues even beyond those 20 months of either sub-period. Timely medical remedy can help to a great extent. One shouldn't take resort to remedies advertised in newspapers and magazines or listed in pamphlets distributed from door to door. Even in the matter of consultation with a doctor or Hakim or Vaidya, one must check up on the ability of the medical practitioner in this matter.

In matters of charitable works and social service, these individuals generally take keen interest. If they do not have their own resources, they manage by asking for donations and other kind of help from others.

These individuals are specially interested in constructing

and providing drinking water facilities for human beings and cattle, homes for widows and destitute women, and relief of some kind or the other to prostitutes including providing arrangements for education to the children of prostitutes and destitute women.

Some astrologers lay great emphasis on bad character of these individuals, but the authors have their own reservation on this view, because of coming across several individuals with this combination in their 4th house who maintained high level of moral character.

These individuals are no doubt very much interested in and make efforts for settlement in another state or country or shifting to a town or city on the seacoast. Often they are successful in doing so.

This combination generally produces very efficient and qualified medical personnel, and if Cancer or Libra or Capricorn or Pisces is in the 4th house, they positively migrate to another country, temporarily or permanently.

These individuals are sincere in their friendship with both sexes, because they have religious trend of thought and action. They are often honest in their money dealings.

However if a female Rasi (Taurus, Cancer, Virgo etc.,) is in the 4th house, these individuals get larger number of daughters, and sometimes the first issue is also a daughter, though this matter equally depends on stars of both husband and wife. No positive prediction be given in this matter without thorough study of horoscopes of both, wife and husband simultaneously.

Moon and Saturn in the 4th House

Moon and Saturn combination in the 4th house is an inconvenient one. Its first adverse effect on the new born is that the baby doesn't get, for one reason or the other, breasts feeding for enough time, sometimes doesn't get breast feeding at all. In later life relations with mother go under strain for one reason or the other. It adversely affects the matters related to inheritance too.

Generally the individual is uncomfortable at home, in

spite of all material facilities for comfort. Dissatisfaction and discontentment descend on the individual with own source of income, because Moon is lord of Mind and Saturn in 4th house generates a strong feeling of envy and jealousy. If these two happen to be in a cardinal *(char)* Rasi, the individual changes the source of livelihood rather often, at least at every gap of 10 years at the most. The individual works till old age for one reason or the other, and is generally not satisfied with achievement in life.

The individual often gets disturbed in the natural course or is disturbed by others in peaceful sleep. Sometimes perfect facilities for comfortable sleep are not available or hard to have. The same is the story with facility of conveyance and mode of transport. Even self-owned transport gives trouble, or meets with an accident or stops moving at the moment of urgency. The reason is simple. The 4th house is directly responsible for means of movement, and Saturn is lord of means of movement. Saturn on the one hand provides own mode of transport and on the other, gives trouble through it.

For example, in astrological system of division of regions among the seven solid planets, Saturn is deemed as Chief Ruler of *Saurashtra* (*Kathiawar*), part of Gujarat State in India. In February 2001, Saturn and Mars were in direct conflict, and Mars had conjunction with Pluto in Scorpio. Saturn being in Taurus, which Rasi is directly concerned with Earth, and Mars with Pluto being in Scorpio that is a watery Sign, caused the very destructive earthquake specifically in Saurashtra (which means parts of Gujarat too). Pluto being far away from Earth is not effective in case of individual human being but is very effective with regard to the **five elements** (earth, space, fire, water and air). Thus the conflict also between earth Rasi (Taurus) and watery Rasi (Scorpio) caused this destruction on a huge scale. Further, Mars is a fiery planet, and scientists believe that in inner layers of earth, when water flows into the underneath fire therein, a series of vibrations are induced in the earth's crust, which disturbs the inner structure. This is how an earthquake is caused.

Saturn in Taurus gives a touch of corruption to individuals; much of the relief sent to victims and sufferers of this earthquake went into wrong hands, not letting it reach ultimately to the sufferers! Another part of this calamity was that the transit position of Saturn is in the 4th house from Gujarat state, and in this chapter the subject being discussed is about the 4th house.

This conflict between Saturn and Mars (which are otherwise too die-hard enemies, at least in astrological thought) lingered on till 27th August 2001. Mars (fiery planet) being in Scorpio (a watery Sign of zodiac) involved in conflict with Saturn has caused eruption of Volcano too in Philippines between exactly the period of conflict between Mars and Saturn (from February 2001 to August-end 2001)!

Moon and Saturn combination in the 4th house generally brings the charge of insubordination against those in public service or even in private service, and whether at fault or not, the consequences thereof descend on the individual.

Even in the individual's actions for charity and social service, very often the public view the individual with suspicion and attribute selfish motives to the individual or criticise for even minor lapses and defaults, if at all any.

The 4th house rules digestive system also. The individual is fond of all kind of food, eating whether hungry or not, because of food appearing tasty and spicy. It ends in disturbed digestion and consequential ill health, as also extra fat on the middle part of the body. It can be avoided, to a certain extent, if the individual takes enough quantity of water, comparative to the food eaten.

The 4th house falls in 12th position to the 5th house, which is responsible for childbearing in the case of women. As a result of this combination, the women become imaginative and think about all things and events in the world, and become very keen on taking rest, and avoid work. Also they walk very little. The ultimate result is that they have trouble at the time of delivery of the child (confinement). This laziness in bed during early months of pregnancy sometimes leads to caesarean delivery.

Similarly, the individual is a back-bencher in school, and inferior in results as compared to others, but at the same time good in sports and games, on which side the individual concentrates a lot. Saturn doesn't help in securing admission to medical school or college. If the individual so wants, Saturn with Moon in 4th house helps in becoming a qualified Hakim or Vaidya of the indigenous system. Otherwise, the individual may become a good sportsman as a career, or an engineer or a technocrat, a technician, an industry-owner.

In the matter of friendship, sincere friends are less, and those with selfish motives or with lip-sympathy in the hour of need are more. Friends of the opposite sex are also not lasting long, more for the period of serving the purpose on either side.

Saturn makes the individual keen on ownership of residence, and grants success in it sooner or later. As regards premises for business or industry or self-employment, Saturn leaves the matter to Moon, which will help if it is in waxing position and very strong by occupying its own Rasi or a Rasi of an intimate friend like Sun, Mercury or Jupiter.

Moon and Rahu in the 4th House

Moon with Rahu in the 4th house, would give results similar to the combination of Moon and Saturn in the 4th house, but in a very reduced degree, sometimes just negligible or tolerable.

Rahu would give trouble with facility for movement, but would provide solution and relief too, rather quickly without causing any damage to the purpose for which movement was meant. Rahu gives trouble to the mode of transport, but not repeated or severe accidents. If Moon provides facility of own transport, Rahu would not interfere with it. Moon would provide it if it is not in waning position and is in Taurus, Cancer, Leo, Virgo, Libra, or Pisces.

Rahu with Moon in 4th house would not much disturb the comforts available or with sleep. Occasional mild disturbance is tolerable.

Rahu doesn't give very strained relations with mother, though the breast feeding after birth is not enough after the 4th month, or feeding doesn't last long, not more than 6 months in any case.

Rahu gives health problems to mother for any period upto 4 years after birth of the baby with Moon and Rahu in the 4th house. This might create troubles in upbringing of the individual, and the child may have to grow under care of other members of the family or of nanny etc.

Rahu no doubt gives strong likes and dislikes for food from the very childhood, and creation of trouble by the individual if the food is not to her or his liking.

At school, quite often the individual is absent from the class or prefers to sit on a backside bench in the class. It adversely affects the final results of the year or session. However the individual is not much given to games and sports, and spends time in the company of other fellow-students, inferior in studies. Like Saturn, Rahu with Moon in 4th house does not help in securing admission in any medical course. The individual can learn indigenous system of medicine and become a Hakim or Vaidya.

In so far as pregnancy period of a woman is concerned, Rahu doesn't give much trouble as Saturn gives, because the woman moves considerably at least upto the end of the 7th month and it helps in delivery without resort to surgery of any kind.

Rahu doesn't cause too many changes in the source of livelihood, because its counter-part Ketu in the 10th house normally helps continuance of the source without many changes, whatever be the source of income, namely job, profession, self employment, trading, business or industrial venture.

Rahu doesn't make a person very keen to migrate to another country, and even if the individual tries, success is not so easy. Moon in the 4th house creates the desire for migration to another city or district or state or country, but Moon is not very effective on account of eclipse combination with Rahu.

Rahu (with Moon) gives such friends as have a feeling of "give and take", and less number of sincere friends, who would help in the hour of need.

Rahu is not very keen on ownership of property by the individual, but if Moon is strong enough to favour the individual with ownership of property, Rahu doesn't interfere.

Moon and Ketu in the 4th House

Ketu is an innocent planet, and its combination with Moon in the 4th house does not interfere much with decisions and actions of Moon in the 4th house. If Ketu cannot help and support, it does not give hurdles or obstacles too in any important matter coming under the 4th house.

Ketu doesn't interfere with pregnancy of women. It doesn't interfere with breast-feeding of the newly born individual. Ketu keeps the same relationship between mother and the individual which she has with other children, or in other words, neither very deep affection nor any kind of dislike or hatred. Ketu remains neutral in matters related to inheritance.

No doubt, Ketu does adversely affect, though in a mild manner, the comforts of sleep and food of the individual, moreso with timings thereof. Ketu doesn't cause constant trouble with digestive system, and whatever trouble it causes is mild and tolerable in nature. Ketu doesn't affect this way or that way the structure of the body or its weight etc.

As compared to Saturn and Rahu with Moon in the 4th house, Ketu does give some sincere friends, willing and ready to help at the hour of need. Ketu simultaneously gives some selfish or greedy friends too. Ketu provides the capacity to the individual to distinguish between the two kinds of friends. Ketu is neither interested in nor discards friendship with the opposite sex.

One major defect of Ketu with Moon in 4th house is that it gives a nature of unnecessarily criticising or talking in defaming terms about other people. And if Jupiter is in the 6th, 8th or 12th house, matters go even to a court of law or arbitration or *Panchayat* relating to defamation.

In matters of education, this combination gives absence from class in school or from lectures in college or university, and less inclination to do written work. But by help of friends and fellow-students, the individual manages to reach the ultimate destination in education. However like Saturn and Rahu, Ketu too with Moon in 4th house doesn't help in receiving education in modern system of medical line, and the individual doesn't become much attracted by indigenous system of medicine.

Moon in the 5th House

This is a very important position of Moon, because this house rules education, thought, capacity for management, and progeny (which means continuance of family tree). Moon is lord of MIND in every human being and thus rules thoughts, desires, aims, ambitions, dejections, disappointments and dissatisfactions in mind, as also joy, pleasure, happiness, satisfaction and contentment or sense of fulfilment.

No doubt Moon in 5th house gives concentration on education, doesn't allow mind to divert from regular studies, and gives a touch of honesty in Exams, tests, interviews etc. Moon protects against failure at school level, provided there is no change of school. In this particular case, the child takes time and wastes a lot of energy to adjust to the changed atmosphere and get acquainted with fellow-students as also teaching system and style in the new school. Because 5th house is in 8th position from 10th house, which rules father, generally a change of school becomes unavoidable owing to change of town of work of the father.

However the post-school education progresses very well, not involving change of place or town, even if father has to change, because the individual is grown up to stay in a hostel or otherwise independently. The individual is able to reach the desired destination in studies.

If Venus is in 5th, or 1st, 4th, 9th, 10th or 11th house, chances for receiving medical education become quite strong, though the higher education in medicine, surgery, pathology, radiology (there are innumerable branches presently) would depend on other stars. If only Venus and Moon are strong in the horoscope, the individual would go in for medicine, and later on in life becomes a famous physician. There are no doubt certain individuals who, even after good medical education enter into administrative service or active politics because of stronger and better placement of Sun in the horoscope, including Navamsha chart.

After education, the individual is naturally at the threshold of marriage and getting children. Marriage would depend to a good extent on the 7th house, lord of the 7th house and its placement in birth chart and Navamsha chart (for boys) and Trinshansha chart (for girls). Unless there is considerable force from the side of Venus, these individuals do not go in for love-based marriage, though they do not hesitate getting into any love affair. Because they are very much given to inner voice of self, they judge the intentions and sincerity or showmanship of the opposite party by deep thinking and take their own time to fall into any love affair. Generally they go by the choice of the mother for matrimonial match, and normally they intend to disagree with father's choice in general terms.

With regard to getting children, depending on the stars of the spouse, the couple is keen on having children soon and rather in quick succession, because of considerations regarding upbringing and education of the children. The male individual pays full attention from the pregnancy days to the birth of the child in looking after wife and the baby in the womb. If the individual is a female, she herself looks after these matters.

If Moon is in a female Rasi (Taurus, Cancer, Virgo etc), the likely sex of the baby would be female, and if it is in male Rasi (like Aries, Gemini, Leo) the baby might be a son, as the first issue. However this matter depends on the stars of both, husband and wife, and many detailed and minute calculations are involved in predicting about the sex of the child in the womb. Since the God Almighty hasn't given 100% "insight" into the future, to any astrologer, no one should claim 100% accuracy about the sex of the baby to be born. In the last few decades of the 20th century, medical system carried out some test on the pregnant woman during the 3rd month of pregnancy and predicted about the sex of the embryo in the womb. Practical experience has shown that, the medical opinion too hasn't proved accurate in several cases!

Further it would help to a certain extent in predicting the sex of the baby in the womb by determining the lord of the 5th house and the Rasi in the 5th house. If the lord of the 5th house is Sun, Mars or Jupiter and that lord too is occupying a male Rasi, the chances are that the baby in the womb is a son. If it is female stars (Mercury, Venus, Saturn and waning Moon) in the 5th house, or any of them own the Rasi in the 5th house and a female Rasi is in the 5th house, the chances are that it is a female embryo in the womb. However, it is advisable to note once for all that it is virtually difficult to predict the sex of the baby in the womb.

Moon protects the pregnancy from miscarriage and abortion, unless the couple indulges in physical relationship after the 5th or at the most the 7th month. No use in going into detailed discussion of this delicate topic. Intelligent readers can easily grasp the caution indicated indirectly here.

No use in discussing the number of the progeny, because laws of many countries have put restrictions on the number of progeny, if not directly, at least indirectly. Further number and sex of children depends on the stars of both, wife and husband, and it needs very deep study into the horoscopes of both.

For one reason or the other, irrespective of the education, culture, religion or faith of the individual, he or she becomes interested in spiritualism, in occult science and its usage, and sometimes indulges in using this knowledge in favour of or against other people. But since the individual has constant touch of mercy, chances of severely hurting others would not arise. It is very likely that the individual might adopt the spiritualism or occult science and its practice to become very rich, beyond the normal source of earnings and income. If the individual has any planet in the 12th house in birth chart, there are strong chances of adverse results too from this kind of practice and usage to the individual or his or her spouse or children or any other member of the immediate family. Normally the individual has some strict ideology, but the greed for more and more money makes him or her blind (at least for sometime) to ideology.

Barring the above weakness, the individual would be a great devotee of God Almighty, would read religious scripts of own faith or religion, and follow the path of virtuous living, with modest behaviour to one and all.

In the normal course of life, the individual has chances of being very well possessed, resourceful for possessing all comforts and luxuries of life for self and the family. But once the greed for big money enters into the mind of an individual, no restraint and restriction stand in the way of this kind of activity.

Because Moon in 5th house would have direct *drishti* on the 11th house (which rules income), the individual would have satisfactory standard of income and earnings, and stands to receive rich gifts from the opposite sex too, without adversely affecting the moral character. The individual gains knowledge about hidden money or jewellery or ornaments or other costly possessions of mother, and in the long run stands to benefit therefrom to the exclusion of other claimants to it.

Another appreciable quality that Moon bestows on the individual is of full concentration on work on hand, including on matters related to management of any business, office, industrial venture, organisation outside the individual's work orbit.

These individuals maintain friendship in all sincerity, and do not mind extending help or support to the friend in hour of need, but they do judge whether the need is real, and what is the arena of the need.

If the individual doesn't migrate to another state or country, he or she is often desirous of sending the progeny, or at least one of them, to another country for education or better chances of career and income, and sometimes marriage too. Migration of self to a foreign country would depend on other stars of self, on the Rasi in the 5th house and lord of the 5th house and placement of that lord and inter-relationship between that lord of 5th house and Moon in the 5th house.

Sometimes, stars of the spouse might also help or lead both, the spouse and the individual to a foreign country for regular or permanent settlement there.

And as regards the question of sending one child or all children, one-by-one, abroad for education or better career or sometimes marriage too for purposes of Visa etc. it would depend on the child's own stars The parents' stars would render only side support.

Moon and Sun in the 5th House

Please refer to the earlier Chapter and relevant paragraph therein on results of "Sun and Moon in the 5th house".

Moon and Mars in the 5th House

The combination Moon and Mars in the 5th house makes an individual rough in thought and action, and if Scorpio or Capricorn or Aries is in the 5th house, the individual doesn't hesitate to adopt cruel attitude, even towards near and dear ones, including own progeny. He or she doesn't waste time or energy in thinking and taking decisions. Quick decision and quick action if often the motto of these individuals.

The individual is often unnecessarily critical of own religion or faith as also that of others, and has no reservation in adopting spiritual or occult science methods secretly to harm other persons or hurt their interest, or cause serious physical trouble to others.

In normal nature and day-to-day life too, the individual behaves in a rustic manner, towards one and all, moreso when she or he is in bad mood or angry posture.

The individual is bold, courageous, daring, dashing and brave, and even on minor provocation, takes undue advantage of these qualities in quarrelling, fighting or beating others. The individual has no hesitation in being rough and misbehaved even towards own parents, at least towards father of self or mother of the spouse, if and when the question of inheritance or possession and use of spare premises arises between the two.

Further the individual often has a greedy eye on the personal possession of the mother (whatever it be, cash, jewellery, ornaments, or other costly things). She or he has no hesitation in cheating own brothers and/or sisters by sweet talks and diversion of their attention from the question of inheritance and costly belongings of parents, specially that of the mother. She or he has no hesitation in encouraging the spouse to adopt similar tricks to usurp costly belongings of both or either parent of either of the two (i.e. husband and wife).

The individual is always keen on begetting male children only or a son from the first pregnancy. If by modern day scientific tests it is detected that the embryo is that of a female, without much thought and hitch, the couple would take action for its clearance, sometimes by surgical help if the pregnancy is at an advanced stage beyond clearance by medicine or injection alone. There are several instances where women went in for the test, and finding a female embryo in the womb, got it cleared, without prior knowledge of the husband or that of others in the family. Several countries, which are opposed to medical termination of pregnancy, have prohibited the above kind of medical tests and clearance of pregnancy by medical methods by formal law. But many a medical practitioner still continue this type of medical tests and then clearance of the pregnancy on finding that it is a female embryo in the womb.

Sometimes Mars and Moon in the 5th house cause miscarriage or abortion for natural reasons, without interference by outside causes. But it often depends on the stars of both, wife and husband. Sometimes, if Mars is more powerful in the 5th house, loss of pregnancy for natural reasons occurs repeatedly. In this type of cases, stars of both wife and husband should be examined, and then suitable correctional medical or remedy by prayers is suggested.

These individuals are often rough or even cruel to own progeny for better or very outstanding results in studies and sometimes for studies and games or sports both. It becomes a real torture for the child, at least for a child below 15 years of age.

For higher studies too, the individual prevails upon the son or daughter by own choice and selection of subject or discipline or line of higher studies, and the child has helplessly to surrender to the choice by the parent(s). It is generally one parent who takes the decision in these matters.

One example would suffice. In Central India, at INDORE, a father was a doctor, and he forced for full 3 years his only child, a son, to secure admission in medical institute at Indore. Colonel M. A. Nicholson (an englishman), an expert and well known surgeon was then the chief of that institute, he was also the Chief Medical Officer for Central India, because it was the British rule at that time in whole of India. Recommendations or illegal gratifications did not work those days for securing admission in medical courses of study. On the son's 3rd failure to get admission, the father ruthlessly turned the son out of the house, and the son's maternal grandfather took him to his house. It was vacation time, and the grandfather consulted the senior author astrologically, who advised the old grandfather to put the boy in commerce course. The grandfather did accordingly, and the boy stood 2nd in the whole University in B.Com (final) Exam. The grandfather helped the boy in starting his own business, and the boy, within three years of business, started earning more than the doctor-father. The father then took the boy home, got him married, and things went alright thereafter.

These individuals very often do not allow the progeny any freedom of opinion in the matter of marriage, because the individual (whether father or mother) has a keen eye on the riches of the matrimonial match and advantages therefrom to the individual's family as such!

These individuals should keep their blood pressure and blood system under regular check, at least every two years till attaining the age of 42 years, when medical check-up of blood should be done every year thereafter.

These individuals generally maintain very good moral character, and unless the charm in terms of material gains is very big, they do not go down their path of virtue.

However, they have always a greed for immovable property and want to possess as much as possible, sometimes even by getting into a big network of unmanageable debts. And then sometimes they are forced to sell it even at a loss to clear the debts and interest thereon. They often buy property in joint names of self and spouse, because Mars (with Moon) in the 5th house is in 11th position from the 7th house, which rules spouse. When the question of judicial separation or ultimate divorce comes before the couple, at least in countries like USA, Canada, etc., the property poses rather the biggest problem for division of assets.

The individual is often keen on earning big name for learning or chivalry or personal achievements in either of these two fields. They are also keen on honorary degrees for their knowledge and titles or decorations for any act of chivalry at some time or the other, whether war or no war, whether battle or no battle, may be even day-to-day type of service rendered.

There are very strong chances of a serious bleeding injury to these individuals in an accident or fight or in performance of the particular act of chivalry mentioned above. Chances of surgical operation are also not ruled out, at least in the case of women. It generally happens when Saturn is in transit over the 5th or 4th or 12th house.

These individuals are generally very helpful and accommodating towards brothers and sisters, with ulterior motives in inner mind, but not much helpful towards uncles, aunts, cousins etc. with or without ulterior motive. They have sometimes to face rift in the wider family whenever Saturn transits over the 12th house, or in the family of the spouse when Saturn transits over the 6th house.

These individuals are generally hard working, efficient in management anywhere and everywhere, and also maintain discipline over employees and subordinates, and sometimes do not hesitate to be critical of superiors or employers too on noticing failure in promptness in decision or action on their part. And these individuals are not much bothered about consequences including loss of job.

They work for spreading the faith or religion or cult they adopt to follow (which might be even the changed one from the religion or faith of their birth), and would use all tact and tactics or even compulsions and temptations to spread it.

Moon and Mercury in the 5th House

Though not very friendly towards each other, even being father and son, Moon and Mercury, both being soft planets in combination in the 5th house are favourable to the individual in most of the matters concerned with the 5th house.

These individuals are very good at studies from the very childhood, so much so that they are younger to the average age of the class in the school. They do not hesitate to have their doubts cleared by the teacher in the classroom itself. While in college or university, they are argumentative with the lecturer or professor or visiting speakers.

An example could make it clear. One Asharam Bhati, son of a poor widow in a small town Jaora in Central India, was very hard working and often stood first in his class. When he was in M.Sc. (first year), he wanted to do some research during the vacation holidays. Principal Padmanabhan of the Holkar College, Indore, refused him permission to do so. He left that College at Indore and shifted to Agra College, where his former professor Dr. Deshpande was then Principal. Asharam prepared a extraordinary Research Paper on some Atomic Energy subject and it was decided that the Research Paper would get published in joint names in the USA., but Dr. Deshpande cheated Asharam and got the Research Paper published in Dr. Deshpande's own single name. Asharam left Agra College too without appearing for the M.Sc. final Exam, and migrated to the U.S.A. Those days migration was not difficult at all. Asharam did his doctorate from a very leading university in the USA and reached a very high ranking post in the atomic research outfit of the USA Government. Asharam Bhati had Moon and Mercury in his 5th house.

These individuals can become very efficient researchers, scholars in any subject they study, very outstanding teachers at any level and are not given to any kind of ego or vanity. One Dr. Hermalenda, one time Professor and Head of the Department of Physics at Hamburg University in Germany, on becoming a nun and a teacher at the St Raphael's School in Central India was teaching Physics to the 9th and 10th classes with all humility and efficiency.

These individuals get a big name as authors, poets, journalists, publicity experts and propaganda masters. They are not 'jack of all trades but master of none', but master of every field of knowledge they study and work for. They are not much bothered about family matters, day-to-day functioning of the household, and even about getting progeny.

I personally knew Dr. Nagendra Singh, ICS, a great scholar and highly learned writer with eight doctorate degrees to his credit (and none honoris causa). He held the rank of and was working as the President of the International Court of Justice at the Hague, when he passed away in eighties of his age. He had no child of his own and it never bothered him from his early days of youth. He did not also adopt anyone as a son, heir or successor. He was younger brother of the 'Maharawal' of Dungarpur state in Rajputana (now Rajasthan in India), and was married to the Princess of the Panna state in Bundelkhand (Central India).

It is also likely that these individuals get, depending on the stars of the spouse too, first a daughter or more daughters than sons, but they do not bother about either matter. They similarly do not bother about miscarriage or abortion, natural or medical termination and do not interfere with the decision of the spouse. If the individual is the wife, she has to surrender to the wishes of the husband in this respect. Neutral attitude prevails over these individuals.

Because these individuals are kind-hearted, and generally casual about management matters, others (their juniors) have to look after the duties and responsibilities of these individuals.

They do not use unfair means or dishonesty for any purpose, unless Mars or Saturn or Rahu (some times even Sun) is in the 11th house. They take no bribes in cash or kind, and are not good at offering and giving bribes. Sometimes others, including some member of their family, take undue advantage of their indifferent attitude in this behalf.

These individuals do not mind platonic love or attachment to any person of the opposite sex, if the opposite party is keen for it, but if the matter reaches the point of physical relationship, in most cases, these individuals step backwards and ultimately withdraw from the platonic relationship too.

One funny thing about these individuals is that they do not bother about life or death, and appear quite indifferent on death of even a near and dear one. In this respect they are believers in fate of every person.

Moon and Jupiter in the 5th House

A majority of results of Moon and Jupiter combination in the 5th house are similar to those given in the preceding paragraphs relating to "Moon and Mercury in the 5th house". Some typical differences are given below:

(1) These individuals pay greater attention to education in law, economics, accounts, business management, government or semi-government job-oriented education, and ultimately go into the same career as is in accordance to education received. Very rarely there is diversion from the field of education received.

(2) They are not averse to receiving or giving unlawful gratifications, because they often have an eye on getting rich, and outdoing others in riches and living in a manner that pleases the eye of the observers. They are not averse to wide publicity about self, and their achievements, worth publicity or not.

(3) These individuals are very particular about marriage and gains therefrom, be it a boy or a girl. They have an eye also on future expectations of gains from the marriage. Other points take the second place in decision-making.

(4) They are often keen to get a son first and also more sons than daughters, without appreciating the fact that it depends on the stars of both wife and husband.

(5) Because they have often an eye on gains from any event or development affecting their work or life, they do not mind minor or major insults during the course of their education or work, whatever be the field thereof. In work too, they have eyes fixed on prospects and gains, not on competition.

(6) They often try to prove themselves successful in management, wherein they use courtesy mixed with tricks and underground information about subordinates,

employees, colleagues, and sometimes about seniors, employers, and competitors too. They have no hitch in using that information for something like blackmail in a mild manner, if they stand to derive some benefit or other from it.

(7) They prove efficient law – persons, on bar and on bench, both, but they should not be taken as 'above board'. They do not mind a word in favour or against any case being heard by them, no doubt only from political bosses or top-moneyed people for some consideration.

(8) They are very particular about education to their progeny, and want one or two to follow their footsteps and enter into the same line of career as they themselves are.

Moon and Venus in the 5th House

An interesting combination, one lord of normal thought, and another lord of romantic thought and action. It is the special feature of soft planets that even if they are inimical to each other, they are often co-operating with each other in the matter of results.

The most important point about this combination is that the individual takes science courses for study, makes best efforts to get entry into medical institute. Normally they succeed in becoming a medical professional or a scientist with good rank.

On entry into the medical profession, they prove efficient and devoted to their profession, but the maxim goes,

"*Prakratim yanti bhutani nigrahh kim karisyati*",

meaning an individual is governed by his or her nature, and restraints do not work. In other words, they remain romantic in their talks and general approach to fellow doctors as well as nurses and other staff of the opposite sex working with or under them. Their attitude is more or less the same towards patients of the opposite sex, no doubt of appropriate age and appearance. Some patients mind it and change their doctor; some patients show tolerance taking it to be natural instinct-cum-weakness, while some rare one responds favourably. In spite of this weakness in some individuals in the medical line with Moon and Venus in the

5th house, they prove able administrators of Hospitals and large nursing homes and similar other establishments.

If not in the medical line, some of these individuals are very successful importers and exporters, dealership in medicines, pharmaceuticals, cloth of every kind, garments, liquors and liquids (including intoxicating alcohols) or in trading with foreigners. Thus in managing the business establishments too, these individuals prove their worth. Because both Moon and Venus have direct drishti on the 11th house (that rules income), it is very rarely that they suffer an ultimate loss in their business. If in a job in any of the lines mentioned here they prove efficient and honest. However at the same time, they keep learning the tricks of the trade, and no sooner they collect some savings of own, and have no sources of getting a loan, they start own business in import and export line, or any other trade mentioned in this paragraph. The same is the case with regard to trading in cotton, cottonseeds, milk and its products, rice and other white food-grains, etc.

They are efficient at running a film studio, or managing a distribution firm in the film line or any other kind of own business. They prove their worth in any job linked to the show-business line, may be even a theatre, fun house, dance and drama school, institute of textile designing, music school, trading in musical instruments. It is rather difficult to give a list of all lines of trade governed by Moon and Venus individually and jointly.

Depending on the stars of the spouse too, these individuals are normally gifted with a daughter as a first child and more daughters than sons in all.

They are also very keen and make efforts for good education to the progeny, moreso in science and medical subjects. Otherwise too, they plan and manage good education for all children, who normally have fair complexion and charming features.

Whether these individuals are in the medical line or not, romanticism is a part of their nature and approach towards the opposite sex. Some others are romantic in talks only for joyfulness for self and for the listeners, males or females or both. They do not proceed further than talking point.

They are very sensitive about their own appearance in public and at place of work, and so dress up attractively, and use make-up methods too. Even men sometimes use cosmetics, which are common only among female-folk.

Moon and Saturn in the 5th House

Moon is soft and Saturn is a hard planet together in the 5th house, which rules education, thinking, management capacity and progeny. The 5th house concerns one's popularity or unpopularity, here, there and everywhere. With Saturn, Moon doesn't have much say in this house.

Saturn adversely affects the power of grasp as well as memory in a child, and the child struggles to pick up properly the subject taught in the class. Often the child needs help at home by elders in the family or by tutors. In spite of these drawbacks, the child manages with the help of Moon in the 5th house to go upto the aimed destination in education. No doubt, after Secondary education, sometimes there are gaps, and the individual picks up the disconnected thread of education now and then. Saturn is slow but gives steady help to the child in reaching the destination.

Till about 1950, at least in India, it was not only difficult, but impossible for any youngman to appear for BA., BSc., MA., MSc. Degree exams as a private candidate, without being a regular student of a college or university or without being a teacher in a recognised institute. Even on being a teacher in a recognised institute, the youngman was not allowed to appear privately for science and technical subjects like engineering, mining etc., on the plea that he or she had no facility of a laboratory and practical work. This restriction left very little and limited scope for their careers. The Colleges for post-degree courses were at very distant places.

Now the facility of evening and night schools and colleges has started, opening the avenues of higher education even for working adults.

In so far as pregnancy, child bearing and delivery of a child are concerned, Saturn is rather slow. Sometimes couples get their first child in late 20's of age or in 30's, because of late marriages, or owing to inner desire of women to retain their youthful appearance, and also owing to advancement in medical science leading to safe or caesarean delivery at late age. Pre-delivery labour pains also take much longer than normal time, and the medical attendants take it as an open excuse for caesarean section. But normally the child is healthy, though complexion might appear a little less fair than the family standard. Saturn doesn't hesitate in causing natural loss of pregnancy or by medical system. One risk which Saturn creates for illegitimate pregnancy or for poor and low-middle-class women is that for medical clearance of pregnancy, they take resort to quacks in the medical field, and thereby risk not only the procreation system in the pregnant woman, but also her life as such.

Saturn turns the individual into a slow, steady, quiet but rigid-type administrator and manager or supervisor on technical side. These individuals would help in domestic or other difficulty, and problems of personal life, but would not allow discrepancy in work or in speed-schedule.

With extension of facilities for technical and engineering education, so many boys and girls go in for these branches of studies. Saturn, with Moon in 5th house and support from Venus in 1st, 2nd, 7th, 9th, 10th or 11th houses, opens the doors for medical education for the individual. Later on, the individual might choose higher education in bone surgery, orthopaedics, surgery related to ear, nose and throat, surgery concerning diseases of the stomach-area (including lower spine-bone, kidneys and liver ailments). Atomic energy and Nuclear sciences are also governed by Saturn with direct help and support from Mars in 1st or 9th house (Moon support is already included, it being in combination with Saturn in 5th house which constitutes a Trikona). Because of combination with Moon, Saturn doesn't hesitate in dealing with cases of paediatrics too, though Saturn doesn't make it the main line of profession for the individual.

Because of rigidity and firmness in own ideas and principle help granted by Saturn (with Moon), with inner strength too, these individuals do not bother much about popularity and unpopularity.

They are more concerned with completion or conclusion of a job in hand or a task entrusted.

Their devotion in God Almighty, prayers as also respect for elders and teachers is not a subject of public demonstration. Both are their secret personal affairs. Even with regard to respect for elders and teachers, their sincerity becomes known only when those people are in real need of support, help or physical service. And same is the case with friendship as also love and affection towards children, including their own. They do not shout their love and affection from housetops.

Moon and Rahu in the 5th House

Though this combination constitutes clearly an 'eclipse' combination, in 5th house Rahu doesn't much interfere with functioning of Moon with regard to education and resultant career for the individual, because Rahu has no line of education attributed to it, nor any field of career given under Rahu's sole charge. In these matters Rahu becomes a support-planet to all other solid (normally regularly visible) planets. Some modern astrologers have started attributing some lines of education and also some fields of career to Rahu, but that research hasn't yet proved correct in practical application.

However if Saturn or Jupiter or even Mercury be in the 12th house, or Saturn be in the 11th house, disturbing the educational achievements and rapid progress of the child, Rahu would render indirect help to the mischief-making planet.

No doubt Rahu is alert and prompt in exercising its influence in matters of child bearing and pregnancy. It doesn't stop early pregnancy at the proper age (these days even unmarried girls bear children or take resort to medical termination of pregnancy because of late marriages). Rahu doesn't hesitate in thrusting a natural miscarriage or abortion on any pregnant woman (even unmarried girls, who very often conceive because of physical contact with boys, specially owing to late marriages now for one reason or the other). But Rahu normally doesn't concerns itself with any prolonged labour pains or with any problem at the time of the delivery of the child, nor does it, being in 5th house (which relates directly to childbearing), give any health problems to the child after birth. If other stars are out to give trouble to the newly born, Rahu would no doubt give them background support or indirect help.

Rahu doesn't grant extra efficiency or deprive the individual of it in management matters. Rahu leaves it to Moon in the 5th house and to other planets concerned with 5th house, including the lord of the 5th house, the Rasi in the 5th house and connection of the 5th house lord with the house itself.

In so far as relations with friends are concerned, Rahu believes more in 'give and take' principle. With regard to respect for the elders and teachers, Rahu is sure to make the individual respectful to this category of people, even if the individual entertains any kind of grudge in the mind towards any of them. Actually Rahu assists Moon in this respect.

Rahu doesn't give dirty or indecent thoughts and ideas to the individual, but if any other planet(s) intend to cause, Rahu stays neutral in the matter. Basically without concrete cause, Rahu doesn't have intentions of harming or hurting anyone on its own, and gets support in this regard from Moon too.

Moon and Ketu in the 5th House

Ketu behaves more or less like Rahu in a majority of matters concerning the 5th house, but doesn't interfere with intentions and actions of Moon in the 5th house.

Normally, it is helpful in matters of education, even higher education without helping or harming the powers of grasp or memory of the child, and leave Moon alone to function in this behalf.

Ketu doesn't normally interfere with pregnancy or delivery of a child, except in very rare cases when it is under influence of other damaging stars. On the other hand Ketu is helpful in health and growth of the child from the very birth. Unlike Rahu (which gives a fattish built of body in the childhood), Ketu keeps normal structure of body of the child given to family tradition, health of mother and climate of the area where the child grows into adolescence and then youthhood.

Ketu develops a feeling of respect in the individual for elders, for teachers, and normal courtesy for all others with whom the individual comes in contact, even with servants and subordinates.

Ketu gives capacity for proper management and administration to the individual, neither very rigid, nor very polite or fearful.

The only drawback of Ketu in the 5th house is that it gives a tendency to the individual to change jobs, when in service and to change the field of business or self-employment. If the individual goes into own industry, there too he or she changes the items of production or manufacture. The individual sometimes does so without proper know-how of the product or item listed for manufacture in the factory. At the same time, she or he doesn't bother much for the loss suffered in the process. Ketu and Moon both in the 5th house make this tendency rather a 'whim'!

MOON IN THE 6TH HOUSE

Initially itself it is an unfavourable position of Moon. Even in the company of other planets, Moon is effective in the 6th house. The only difference is that with soft planets, Moon causes greater trouble to the individual, while with Sun, Mars, Saturn and Rahu (and to some extent Herschel too), its strength, capacity and intention to create or give trouble get considerably reduced, though not totally washed out.

It has specially to be kept in mind that Moon is lord of the Mind, and the 6th house concerns mainly illness, log-term disease and enemies. Also it affects the longevity in childhood, sometimes adversely, moreso if in the company of another soft planet like Mercury, Jupiter or Venus.

Moon being lord of the Mind adversely affects the Mind or process of thinking. The individual becomes to some extent an introvert, broods over past events, and is sometimes absent-minded, with diverted attention from the work in hand.

Thus if Moon is powerful and alone in the 6th house, it adversely affects the studies in school and sometimes even in post-secondary education. Even very favourable placement of Mercury (lord of intelligence) is less helpful in the matter. Steps to remedy the bad effect of Moon on studies of the individual are unavoidable.

After the age and stage of education, the individual becomes introvert and often broods over events of the recent past as well as distant past. The individual rotates in the mind the bad or unsavoury behaviour of others, including members of the family, of the spouse, as also of the family of the spouse, because 6th house is in the 12th place from the 7th house, which rules spouse and family thereof.

If the individual has powers and authority to decide the fate and future of others, in her or his capacity as a judge in a court of law, or as an Administrator in public sector or private sector, or as Head of the family or Head of any organisation or establishment, this retrovert or retrograde or retrogressive state of mind often drives the individual away from the path of just and fair decision or judgement in the matter before her or him.

However that is not the end of the problem of Moon on the mind of the individuals. Moon causes delay in taking decisions, changing the finality of the decision once taken. Further Moon adversely affects such matters concerning self or family or others, and this two-minded attitude many a time snatches some very good opportunities from their hands relating to their progress, relations with members of the family and friends, marriage matters of self or of progeny in their later life. Even in minor matters whether to go out for a picnic or not, or to a theatre or not, rotate in the divided mind upto the last moment.

The further worse affect of Moon in 6th (if alone) is on the mental health. Sometimes Moon drags the individual on the verge of fickle-mindedness or insane type of thinking and decision-making. If medical attention in this type of run down of mental health is delayed, the condition worsens quite fast. In this behalf, astrologically, the Mahadasa and sub-period be examined besides the yearly chart and Moon's position in it. If in Navamsha of the birth chart too, Moon is in the 6th, 8th or the 12th position, the individual would positively need expert medical examination and treatment. It is always a case of medicinal prescription and never a case for any kind of surgical treatment. Surgery becomes necessary only when there is tumour or blood clot or some other problem in the brain region. This point of medical examination must be studied very carefully and in full detail. Quick conclusions without detailed study prove harmful and misguiding to the individual, damaging the prestige of the astrologer too!

These individuals make enemies quite soon, sometimes by spoken or written words, and in some rare instance by mere gestures in the process of conversation. These individuals are fond of back-biting (criticising a person in his or her absence), and where criticism was not at all due on part of the individual. Sometimes, no doubt, enemies crop up even without any fault or mischief or default on part of the individual, for matters beyond the direct control of the individual.

Enmity created by Moon in the 6th house, irrespective of the fact whether the individual is at fault or not, can be short-termed, medium termed or long-termed, depending on the roots of the enmity, circumstances when it developed, and the nature of the people who became enemies. In this behalf Rasi in the 6th house has a major "say", no doubt. If Aries, Cancer or Libra be in the 6th house, the enmity would be short-lived and is based on instant feeling of annoyance, anger or discomfort or temporary damage caused to the person who becomes enemy.

If Gemini, Virgo or Pisces is in the 6th house, the enmity would be of medium term, provided Moon's own Mahadasa is not intervening during that phase. If the Moon's Mahadasa is intervening it might last for the full 10-year-period or balance period of the Moon Mahadasa.

Because, if any of Capricorn (a cardinal Sign but owned by a hard planet, Saturn), Sagittarius (a mutable Sign, but considered a hard-natured Rasi) or a fixed Sign (Taurus, Leo, Scorpio or Aquarius) is in the 6th house, it tends to give long-termed enmity.

The meaning of the word "term" would also vary from individual to individual. If the individual is very sensitive by nature, even a period of few months or few years would appear long-termed to her or him. To individuals with hardened outlook, even an enmity continuing from grandfather to grandson would be considered as softly long-termed.

When Moon is alone in the 6th house, the enmity would not extend beyond mental worry and mental torture. However if any other soft planet is in the 6th house, or any soft or hard planet has direct and more than three-fourth drishti on Moon in the 6th house, the enmity might cause to the individual financial loss, loss of job, or loss of educational progress. Or it can be physical injury or damage to the individual or any person near and dear to the individual.

When Moon is in 6th house and any other planet(s) be 12th house, it might lead to temporary or partial insanity. And if Sagittarius or Capricorn or any fixed Sign be in the 6th house, the touch of insanity can go to the extent or border of complete insanity and will take long period to recover, slowly and gradually. But this matter deserves proper examination in astrology as well as medically.

Then comes the question of other illness or disease that can be caused by Moon in the 6th house. It can be repeated attacks of severe cough and cold, bad throat, development of diphtheria in childhood, pleurisy (dry or wet), or tonsillitis.

If Jupiter is in the 6th or 8th or in 12th house, the question may be examined whether serious complaint of the respiratory system, growth or development of boils between upper ribs and neck, trouble of the thyroid gland, discolouration of the skin of face and/or upper part of chest (breast) and back, leukaemia or leukoderma is likely to be suffered by the individual.

If Mars is in the 1st, 4th, 8th or 12th house, it has to be noted in this context that religious remedy in the matter of illness or disease would help to a very limited extent, and immediate medical treatment is rather unavoidable.

These individuals indulge in criticising the spouse for

overspending habits, and for his or her indifferent attitude towards the family of the individual. Ultimately this creates differences between husband and wife too. Remedy of Moon would be needed if such development takes place.

Moon adversely affects the digestive system, particularly after the age of 48 years for men and after the age of 42 to 45 years for women. It is advisable in this type of complaint to develop the habit of going for a 'walk' for sake of walking, both times (mornings and evenings) or at least one time everyday. Nothing else would work better than walking!

Some astrologers allege that Moon in 6th house makes a man lazy or lethargic, while others (more experienced astrologers) argue that it is not so, unless one or more soft planet be in the 3rd house.

Because of whimsical nature, it cannot be said in positive terms that these individuals are cruel or wicked by nature. A whimsical person can be merciful at one moment, and cruel or merciless at another. It is better not to touch this side of the nature of an individual in predictions.

Several of these individuals develop amateurish knowledge of medicine (of one system or the other), apply that knowledge in case of others, and indulge in self-treatment too, sometimes causing harm or damage, whether it is the case of others or of self. Mistake knows on distinction.

Moon in the 6th house sometimes gives one-sided trend of thinking process, and as a result these individuals go into wanted and unwanted details of a matter, thereby delaying the consideration or the decision. However individuals are unable to help it as the position mentioned in the preceding paragraph is because of force of their nature as such.

The individual generally develops strained relations with brothers and sisters of the mother and also with their families. Improvement sometimes takes place by good and compromising nature of the spouse of the individual.

Moon and Sun in the 6th House

Please refer to relevant paragraph in the chapter Supra on Sun in the 6th house, which covers also the predictions on "Sun and Moon in the 6th house".

Moon and Mars in the 6th House

Though Moon and Mars are friends in permanent relationship, Mars generally opposes every trend and attitude of the individual caused by Moon in the 6th house. Little or rare chances of any serious type of mental trouble to the individual or any other kind of illness or disease mentioned under Moon alone in the 6th house (in the above paragraphs).

This combination gives cordial relations with brothers and sisters of mother and also with their families.

The individual is very much interested in owning property, and if possible to acquire more property than needed for personal needs. The individual wants rental income too. In some cases, there are chances, though remote ones, to inherit property from maternal grandparent or from maternal uncle or aunt or spouse thereof.

In matters of education too, Mars proves helpful to the individual, even if there is lack of resources for the individual at the age of education. The principle of "beg or borrow" comes to the rescue in this behalf. Unless Mercury and/or Jupiter be placed in any damaging house like 8th or 12th house (sometimes 3rd house too), the individual would not suffer from poor grasp or poor memory in the matter of preliminary education or the higher education.

Further Mars (with Moon) in 6th house gets support, guidance, and encouragement from both parents, or at least from the real mother in the matter of education at school level. If real mother is not alive or is not staying with the child-individual, a mother-like person, including the parental or maternal grandmother would help the child in the matter of education.

Neither Mars would allow Moon in the 6th house to cause

laziness or lethargy in the individual nor make him or her cruel or merciless. It would be just the opposite. Mars would not give any digestive disorder to the individual at an immature age.

Since Mars would be protecting the mental faculties of the individual against Moon's adverse effect, the individual would neither be in divided mind, nor changing the decisions once reached, nor would be whimsical in approach to men and matters.

Moon and Mercury in the 6th House

Combination of Moon and Mercury in the 6th house is rather a very difficult phenomenon for the individual in matters of education, use of intelligence, wisdom and discretion in decision making, and also in relations with the family of the spouse affecting adversely the cordiality between husband and wife.

Mercury would, in general terms, help to add to the mental problems as also any illness or disease described under Moon alone in the 6th house.

If the family has financial or other difficulties in arranging proper education for the individual, if not at school level, at least at post-secondary level, these two soft stars together wouldn't find easy and quick solutions to the problems. Because of poor grasp of the matter taught, the individual would have shallow root of understanding and weak-rooted mastery of the subject learnt.

Mercury would, in post-education life, give the individual a tendency to reduce every thing to writing, a reaction of avoiding written work at the school stage, as also going into detailed written discussion of the subject for use of self and for use of others. It becomes a time-consuming job for others to read that stuff and comment thereon. It generates gradually a kind of dislike for the individual at the place of work, if she or he is in public or private service.

One favourable effect of Mercury (with Moon) in 6th house is that as far as possible, the individual would not indulge in self-medication and if he or she does it, would do so after consulting relevant book or material on the subject or after consulting an expert in the line.

Another favourable effect would be that the individual would not be very cruel or merciless. In matters of clemency, charity or help requested for on solid or valid grounds. Mercury would induce the individual to listen and grant the request to the extent possible in the circumstances, or to the extent within the powers and authority of the individual.

However Mercury would not be able to help much in the matter of disorders of the digestive system, and leave it to Moon's exclusive charge.

Laziness and lethargy would be in reduced degree with Mercury sitting with Moon in the 6th house.

Moon and Jupiter in the 6th House

The results of Moon and Jupiter combination in the 6th house would be more or less on the lines of Mercury's conjunction with Moon in the 6th house, except that Jupiter would make the individual very much calculative in financial matters. Further because Jupiter doesn't allow too much funds in the hands of the individual, she or he would be forced to miserliness in dealings, charity and spending money on wider family.

Further Jupiter (with Moon) in 6th house would make the individual very argumentative, and legal-minded, with or without any study or substantial knowledge of law. It is just a tendency caused by Jupiter in the 6th house (with Moon).

If these individuals function as judge at any level, they often start the hearing of the matter before them with confused or inattentive mind, or would allow influence of any kind to bear effect on their pronouncements. Sometimes, they suffer from the lapse of speaking out their mind (that is a hint of the judgement) even before the hearing is complete or before completion of the arguments by litigants on both sides.

Generally the conclusions and decisions of these individual in economic matters and in financial planning or estimates of costs of any venture or midstream estimate for any big work misfire in the end. If the persons availing of services of these individuals obtain a second opinion, that would prove beneficial for all concerned in the long run.

Moon and Venus in the 6th House

This combination of Moon and Venus in the 6th house is complicated with risky results in store for the individual. No doubt about enmity between Moon and Venus, but in the 6th house their adverse results have to be watched with caution.

These two planets together make an individual very romantic-minded, and he or she does not feel much hesitant or ashamed to throw lustful glances towards any member of the opposite sex, and sometimes, though rarely, even in the presence of but diverted attention of the spouse. These individuals are quick in responding to any romantic gesture or hint or message, without much caring for the consequences.

This type of individuals become victims of corrupt, dishonest and favour-seeking people, who influence them by arranging sex facility for them or for their colleagues and friends. Some commercial establishments employ charming girls (boys too) for throwing temptations to those individuals who sooner or later take interest in this type of evil-intended activity of favour-seekers. Wine is an ordinary addendum to these parties or assemblage.

Another side of this activity is that quite often call girls, society-women, corrupt and greedy women too trap this type of men into their charm, and either vacate their pocket when they are busy with wine and that woman, or take favours granted to them. There have been instances where this type of females got written documents from this type of trapped personalities for large sums of money or gift of some assets or immovable property too.

In all above mentioned type cases, Moon (lord of Mind) gets fully overpowered by Venus in the 6th house (which rules enemies and inimical operations) and the individuals with this combination easily fall into any of the traps mentioned above.

With selfish purpose in view, many a time, interested parties obtain either a copy of the birth chart of these individuals, who are ear-marked for above mentioned type traps or their birth data some how or other from somewhere or other, sometimes even from dishonest astrologers. Then the favour-seekers ascertain by consulting any dishonest and obliging astrologer as to whether the plan to trap a particular individual would succeed or not, and if the plan is likely to be successful, then when and how.

Individuals with this combination suffer ill health of several kinds, including cough, cold, bad throat, pain in lower abdomen below naval point, sometimes complaints of health related to venereal diseases or ultimately AIDS too. Spouses and other members of the family of individuals having Venus (and Moon) in 6th house should keep these individuals under as much strict watch as possible. On finding any direct or indirect indication of lapses, they must be cautioned about the consequences springing from the indications noticed. They should be advised, in the best interests of their health, wealth and fame to stop free-lance love making here and there.

Whether the spouse has any source of information or not, a clever spouse gets automatic hint to outdoor objectionable activity of the marriage partner from his (or her) behaviour, scent of body and change in style of love making with the spouse. Then it becomes the duty of the spouse to caution the partner about the adverse consequences of his or her objectionable character.

Unless Mars or Saturn or Rahu or Sun be in 3rd, 6th or 11th house, these individuals do not achieve victory over their enemies, opponents, adversaries or even competitors. If the matter relates solely and only to the source of income (career etc.), with Mars or Sun in the 10th house, these individuals are often able to walk over their competitors or win the favour of their superiors or employers. But defeat in this type of struggle adversely affects their prospects in job or morality. Therefore it is always advisable for these individuals to enter into the arena of fighting or hard-type competition (whether by written test or interview or both) only after thoroughly checking strength and capacity of self, without taking into account outside help or assistance or commendation etc.

These individuals are quick in consultations with medical

people about health matters, with or without any concrete complaint, buy the medicine but are often not regular in taking the medicine for the prescribed period or prescribed times during a set of 24 hours. Then again illness or same complaint of health repeats and the same process gets repeated.

These individuals do not worry much if they have hurt the feelings or emotions of the spouse. When they reject the wishes or expectations of the spouse, the feelings, expectations or emotions of the spouse get hurt badly. It is also a fact that occasions of this type do arrive often in relations between husband and wife. But because of the combination of Moon and Venus in the 6th house (which is the 12th position from the 7th house, which rules the married life), the feelings, emotions and expectations of spouse get crushed under the obstinacy of the marriage partner. It is also a hard fact that immoral character of the partner in marriage would incurably hurt the feelings and emotions of any straightforward spouse.

Moon and Saturn in the 6th House

Combination of Moon and Saturn in the 6th house is very favourable and protective for the individual. Saturn is powerful in the 6th house, whatever the Rasi be there, and Saturn is fully capable of suppressing the influence of Moon there, because being very powerful, Saturn would naturally gives its own results.

Thus the individual rarely suffers any illness or disease under influence of Moon in the 6th house. If any illness or disease descends upon the individual, Saturn sees to quick recovery from it.

Saturn gives cordial relations with maternal family, and even Moon makes best efforts, and if any temporary differences crop up between the individual and the maternal family, the relations become normal soon by intervention of the mother (with unspoken approval of father).

Saturn is also able to suppress the enemies, opponents, adversaries and competitors, whatever the field of activity. In competitive written tests or interviews or in both, Saturn tries its best to grant success to the individual. However in these matters Saturn needs the help of Mercury or Jupiter either from a Kendra or a Trikona. If the matter relates to fine arts, music, dance, medical line, painting, architecture, sculpture or designing, Saturn in 6th house (with Moon) would need the support of Venus from Kendra or Trikona. If the competition relates to any arena of active political activity or relates to bureaucracy, Saturn would need the support of Sun (or Mars or both) from the 3rd, 4th, 8th, 10th or 11th house.

In matters relating to moral character, Saturn tries to keep the individual on the path of chastity, but sometimes Moon gets over Saturn's influence and is able to exercise its power to lead the individual to wrong path, specially under pressure of friends, colleagues or neighbours.

Saturn in 6th house (with Moon) does encourage the individual to start or initiate a quarrel or fight, making her or him over-confident of strength, capacity and resources. The net result in conclusion is either "a narrow win" or a drawn affair, undoubtedly by interference of others for a compromise.

Moon and Rahu in the 6th House

The combination of Moon and Rahu in the 6th house gives favourable results to the individual with regard to enemies, adversaries, competitors, but not so much relief in matters related to competitive written tests and/or interviews.

Rahu helps in keeping illness and diseases away from the individual, but lapses occur often, because Moon too has some powers to exercise its own influence, when in the company of Rahu, specially because Ketu then in 12th house too tries to help Moon, instead of Rahu.

Rahu doesn't encourage the individual to initiate quarrel or fighting with others without cause or even with cause. It is so because Rahu knows the effect of its counterpart, Ketu, in the 12th house extending at least some support to intentions of Moon in the 6th house, leading towards defeat or disrespectful compromise.

Rahu tries its best to keep harmony between the individual and the maternal family, but even then if strain starts to seeping in, Rahu soon tries to bring normalcy and without much effort. However, Rahu doesn't help bringing all such gains from the maternal family as the individual expects to receive!

Moon and Ketu in the 6th House

The combination of Moon and Ketu in the 6th house is a risky one for the individual, as also for the spouse, because Ketu would function more as a soft planet rather than a hard planet in the 6th house.

Quarrels, fighting, resultant defeat or surrender is one result of this combination. Family and friends would suggest, "not to initiate any quarrel or fight or confrontation or conflict". If once started, accept the compromise move if any. However the individual often wants to stick to own stand and opinion, and puts up with ultimate defeat or surrender.

In so far as relationship with maternal family is concerned, Ketu doesn't affect it favourably or adversely on its own, but if Moon succeeds in deteriorating it, Ketu does render indirect help to Moon to let the relationship slide further downwards.

With regard to health too, Ketu would not give any start to an illness or disease, but if Moon brings a complaint of health at the door of the individual, Ketu remains neutral, neither helps quick recovery, nor causes further deterioration. After all Ketu is a shadow planet, and is not very effective in this "un-patented eclipse relationship". Ketu helps keeping spouse happy and non-grudging even if any concrete ground exists against the individual.

MOON IN THE 7TH HOUSE

This is one of the most favourable positions of Moon, be in waxing or waning position. Moon is very important in the 7th house, because this house relates to lover/ beloved or the spouse as such. Other soft stars in 7th house can give qualities like education, maturity of mind, beauty or charming personality to the spouse, but Moon alone can get the individual a spouse with cordiality of mind and thought, with very good mutual understanding. Disagreements are not ruled out, but no serious quarrel or fight. Disagreement ultimately ends, on elucidation of the disputed matter, into fresh mutual understanding or appreciation for the viewpoint of each other is restored in full.

If Venus is also in a Kendra or Trikona or even in the 11th house, Moon is able to give ample mental and physical satisfaction to each other in the bedroom, besides giving beauty, charm and pleasantness or presentability to the personality of the spouse. No doubt Moon gives an understanding of and feeling or need for companionship of the opposite sex at an early age, sometimes even at an immature physical growth or unripe age for the purpose.

Where complexion is concerned, firstly its concept carries a relative sense in it; secondly it depends on the parentage as well as on climate of the region of birth and growth in childhood. Thirdly it depends also (a) on the Rasi in the 7th house, (b) its lord, (c) placement of that lord in the birth-chart and (d) its relationship with the 7th house, and with Moon situated there. Fourthly it depends to an extent on other planets occupying the 7th house in close vicinity of or at a distant degree from Moon. And the last point relates to the planet ruling the *'kaaraka'* for spouse at the time of birth of the individual.

For example, with Aries, Scorpio or Leo in the 7th house, the spouse would have bright reddish-oriented complexion. With Gemini, Cancer, Virgo, Libra or Pisces, in the 7th house, the complexion of spouse would be fair. With Sagittarius or Taurus or Capricorn in the 7th house, the complexion would be a mixture of the complexion of mother and father of the spouse. And with Aquarius in the 7th house, the complexion of the spouse would be dark. However it shouldn't be taken as a hard and fast rule. It is just a casual guidance, because generally when any person approaches the astrologer for consultation about marriage, he or she naturally puts a question about the complexion of the future spouse.

It would be better to give an example. Both, mother <u>and</u> father of Maharani Sanyogitabai Holkar, (wife of Maharaja

Yeshwant Rao Holkar of the then Indore State, the largest in Malwa Region) had bright dark complexion. But the stars of Maharani Sanyogitabai Holkar were very favourable for extra-ordinarily fair complexion, and she really had it. Maharani Sanyogitabai Holkar expired sometime in the 1940's. People of Indore recall even now, several decades later, that she had such extraordinarily translucent and fair complexion that when she chewed a betel-leaf, its movement down the throat could be observed by the people sitting with her. Betel leaf is a unique item in India, which is packed with several condiments, and which on chewing gives out a fragrant smell to the mouth and red colour to the lips, perhaps better than modern lipsticks!

This point has been discussed in great length because whether a boy or girl (even parents thereof) always or often judge the suitability of the matrimonial match on basis of the complexion, and then other qualities, qualifications and virtues are taken into consideration. No doubt greedy parents first judge the monetary value of the matrimonial match and her or his family.

Saturn or Rahu in the 7th house would give noticeable difference between the age of the husband and wife. Sun or Mars in the 7th house would give a touch of short temper in the nature to a husband or wife, and also noticeable difference in the height of the two. Sometimes, though rarely only, if the individual has Saturn or Ketu in the 1st house and Moon with Mercury in the 7th house, the spouse might have quick grasp and higher educational qualifications as compared to the other partner in marriage. Jupiter with Moon in the 7th house would give sharp memory, maturity of mind and quick appreciation to the spouse. Venus (with Moon), or in the 1st house, or in any Kendra or Trikona, would grant medical qualification to the spouse, she or he may even be practising in the medical profession. Otherwise the spouse would be an expert in any branch of the fine arts, including music, painting, dancing, acting, or any concrete connection with film line. It is also likely that if Venus is in the 7th house with Moon, the spouse (wife or husband) might be an expert in gynaecology.

Concern of the 7th house is not with marriage and married life alone. Other important matters are also concerned with the 7th

house. Thus it has to be remembered that the 7th house very much concerns with quarrels, fighting, buying and selling, litigation, to some extent prosecution or a criminal charge against the individual. Moon alone is unable to grant victory to the individual in case of a fight or litigation etc. It often needs the help of other planets. Mercury's help would generate useful application of mind, brains, experience and education. Jupiter's help to Moon would give use of own knowledge, besides experience and pleadings of the lawyer on own side. Sun's help to Moon brings in use of influence or interference of persons in power or authority to the advantage of the individual. Help of Mars and Saturn would bring rescue to the individual by use of threats and use of recourses, friends and physical strength or manpower. Though Rahu is normally unhelpful to Moon, but in the present context, Rahu's help to Moon in the 7th house would bring in use of tricks and cunningness, while Venus would bring relief to the individual by recourse to wine, physical charm, through supply of casual friendship with a member of the opposite sex, specially in case of men, or use of music, dance, and providing a chance of appearance on vision screen.

In brief the point is that for ensuring victory or upper hand in any quarrel, fight or litigation Moon will need support of some other planet as such.

In so far as differences between husband and wife or physical separation or judicial separation or divorce by mutual consent or legal contest is concerned, it would be discussed in the following paragraphs with relation to Moon's combination with other stars. Similarly complaints of health related to procreational parts of the body would also be discussed in the course of discussing Moon's combination with each of the other planets. Moon alone in 7th house normally does not lead to any of these minus points in life.

Moon and Sun in the 7th House

Combination of Moon and Sun in the 7th house can lead to good or bad results in connection with active political career. In case the individual is a back-bencher in political activity, Sun is likely to drag the individual into some enquiry or investigation, including the assets of the individual and the spouse. Similar is the situation if the individual or the spouse is a big or petty employee in government service or any semi-govt service or in public sector service. The ultimate result of the enquiry or investigation would depend on (a) transit position of stars, (b) on the yearly charts, and (c) on the Mahadasa and Antardasa elements in the horoscopes of both husband and wife. A detailed comparative study would be unavoidable.

Apart from the above three elements, the Rasis in the 7th and 12th houses in birth charts of both, lords of those two Rasis, their placements in the birth charts, their mutual inter-relationship as also relationship with 7th house and combination of Moon and Sun there would also matter much. In case a Rasi owned by Saturn or Venus is in the 7th house, and there is bitter relationship between that lord and the combination of Moon and Sun in the 7th house, the results are very likely to be unfavourable. If on the other hand, the lordship of the 7th house is of Moon or Sun itself or of Mars, Mercury or Jupiter, the results are bound to be favourable.

However the combination of Sun and Moon in the 7th house is capable of giving serious differences between husband and wife, temporary separation too, interference of other members of the family for good or for bad. But these two stars, normally very friendly to each other and inter-connected in the field of Light and energy (i.e. life and energy) would not lead to permanent separation or divorce. Threats of this type remain immaterial.

This line of conclusion may be applied to all the points discussed above with relation to Moon alone in the 7th house.

As regards physical ailment, whether these two together are basically favourable or unfavourable, they are liable to cause skin ailment of any kind, of any severity and of any duration to either of the husband and wife. These two stars together might cause minor problems to a woman individual with regard to her menstrual system with impact on child bearing capacity, but not to a very severe extent. The problem would be easily curable.

Moon and Mars in the 7th House

A majority of the results are similar to those of Moon with Sun in the 7th house, but results of this combination are often more severe and last for longer period.

The more important among results of Mars with Moon is that it can very easily lead to physical separation, judicial separation, and ultimately divorce too, unless the other suffering partner in the marriage has parallel severity of Mars (alone or with any other planet in the 7th or 8th house). This topic has been discussed in greater detail in our book, "Star Guide to Love and Marriage" published by Parsai Publishers from New Delhi (ptparsai@gmail.com) and also available with Rupa Publications India Pvt. Ltd.

Mars brings in unwanted and unhealthy intervention of one or more members of the family of the spouse, and then members of the individual too start interfering in the dispute between husband and wife.

Because Moon is already in the 7th house, the mental impact of above developments in married life on the spouse of the individual often becomes unbearable, and in some rare cases the spouse (whether man or woman) loses balance of mind. This combination in the 7th house involves not only mental torture but also physical beatings and cruelty or other kinds of torture on the spouse by the individual or by (often his, and rarely her) family.

Learned, experienced and uninfluenceable astrologers therefore always advise similar position of Mars (with or without any planet) in the horoscopes of both. Cases of bride-burning or male or female spouse receiving burn injuries in the course of physical torture are somewhat common occurrence, at least in India, and all countries with predominant Muslim population. Now, at least in India, instances have come to knowledge where a wife caused burn injuries to the husband; she had Mars in the 7th house (alone or with any other planet).

As regards quarrels, fighting, threats of physical violence to the opposite party involved in the quarrel or fight or ultimate litigation are not uncommon to individuals with Mars (with Moon) in the 7th house. Such individuals have neither hitch nor hesitation nor fear of consequences about starting or initiating or forthwith responding to any quarrel, fight, physical violence or litigation. Annoyance and anger quickly overtake these individuals and they overlook the impact on the party opposite and consequences thereof.

Mars (with Moon) is capable of giving any kind of gyne ailment or allied serious disease to the female partner in the marriage. Often resort to surgery has to be taken, because in fact Mars is the main ruler of surgery of any kind and to any part of the body. Because of influence and impact of Mars, not only inexperienced surgeons but even highly qualified and experienced surgeons too commit serious or grave blunders in the surgical operation. Details not needed because virtually all readers now get this kind of information from print media, and though very rarely, from visual media too.

Other physical troubles generally caused by Mars is skin ailment, eczema, inflammation of any part of the body, migraine, epilepsy, pleurisy, venereal disease, AIDS, big fluctuation of or impurity in blood system or even cancer. It is not possible to list all troubles that can be caused by Mars in the 7th house (or 8th house) (alone or with any other planet). Individuals with Mars in the 7th house (or the 8th house) must always be cautious about food and drink habits. Heavy drinking is just an invitation to call such ailments into the body as are related to Mars through drink habits. On account of Mars and Moon in the 7th house, it is advisable to use own towels, instead of using those provided in the guest houses and hotels etc. Mars is capable of taking an individual by sheer surprise!

Moon and Mercury in the 7th House

On the whole Moon and Mercury combination is a very favourable one for the individual and her or his spouse.

The individual gets an educated, intelligent spouse, who becomes more matured and experienced after marriage, though gradually only, because normally, experience and maturity of mind are not a game of one day! Steadily both husband and wife develop good understanding of each other, maintain cordial relationship and grow accommodating and caring for each other.

The couple enjoys good health, also bedroom relationship of adjustment. They do not suffer generally in the matter of begetting progeny, because they plan it wisely and go ahead accordingly, by Grace of God, successfully.

The individual is not much given to picking up quarrels, or fights, or useless arguments with everyone, everywhere and every time, because the individual is given to intelligent thinking and wise decisions lined with maturity of mind and action. Because this combination is in 3rd place from the 5th house (which rules progeny), the individual helps the children in their educational progress and also in proper mannerism and growth of mind and experience, slowly and gradually, without imposition of any kind.

Mercury gives the quality of cutting critical remarks without causing derision, ridicule of or hurt the feelings of the listener or of other party. The individual is very good at reviewing books, introducing speakers on public stage or at conference etc., in journalism, teaching, public speaking, writing for print or vision media, writing poetry, using music and poetry to entertain the spouse or the audience, anecdotes in speaking to any audience.

The individuals do not mind mocking or jesting at self or sometimes at spouse too for amusement of the audience, and either the spouse understands the situation or the individual explains it on return to privacy.

Moon and Jupiter in the 7th House

Moon and Jupiter together in the 7th house is another favourable and pleasure-giving combination for the individual and the spouse.

The individual develops, by formal education, by normal reading and by learning on own, a kind of expertise in economics or accounts or business matters, common law, rules and regulations of civic bodies. She or he doesn't hesitate to use this knowledge at the proper opportunity, but rarely out-of-turn.

The individual also maintains cordial relations with spouse

and family on both sides. If anything seems wanting in the conduct or behaviour of the couple towards any member of the family on either side, the individual (undoubtedly with co-operation of the spouse) quickly and smartly makes amends, again normalises the relations.

Both being soft planets, the individual doesn't start or take initiative in picking up a quarrel or fight, but if needed, the individual doesn't hesitate to start litigation, rather quickly and easily, if the cause demands.

The wife and husband always try to maintain good credit in the market, as far as possible avoid borrowing cash, and if an occasion arises, the couple try to repay the loan as soon as possible. In modern times, generally, both husband and wife try to generate income by becoming actively engaged in any kind of activity for the purpose, including job, practice in law, running some educational institute (if necessary at home itself).

Health-wise, the individual makes best effort to keep good health, and not to increase the body weight much beyond prescribed limits vis-à-vis height and age, but sometimes the body weight doesn't respond to the individual's effort and goes much beyond the prescribed limits.

Moon and Venus in the 7th House

The combination of Moon and Venus in the 7th house has been taken as a mischievous one even by ancient *acharyas*, because it gives more than normal lust, if not actual, at least mental desire for more companionship with opposite sex. This excess desire, at least the mental one becomes a little uncomfortable to orthodox and conservative families, because of love-oriented marriage of the individual.

There are equally good points also of this combination. The spouse is handsome and charming, has well-proportioned built of body, whether highly educated or not but talented in a branch of the fine arts (including music, dance, stage acting, working in films, painting, architecture, sculpture), adjusting attitude in any circumstance and among any people or in any surroundings.

There are strong chances of spouse being a qualified doctor, nurse or connected to medical line working in any capacity, or having knowledge of an indigenous system of medicine.

In spite of the individual being attracted to persons other than the spouse, the spouse maintains dignity of self and doesn't pay heed to attraction of others for her or him. If the husband is the individual and the spouse is the wife, the spouse being extra beautiful, several males would naturally get attracted towards her, and wish to come in contact with her on one pretext or the other. She would, however, know how to maintain respectable distance and also her dignity in every circumstance.

Like Moon with Mercury and Moon with Jupiter in 7th house, this individual also doesn't prefer to take initiative in starting a quarrel or fight or even litigation, unless the provocation is really intolerable.

Normally these individuals keep good and working health, but if they allow Venus to operate in the matter of extra marital relationship(s), chances are strong for illness related to that-type of relationship, including venereal disease or even AIDS. It is so because at least in India, none bothers to have periodical medical check-ups of these free-lance people, hidden or open or in the brothels and other places, these days hidden even in family localities.

Moon and Saturn in the 7th House

Moon and Saturn conjunction in the 7th house is a difficult one indeed. Its first adverse result is on mutual relationship between husband and wife, sometimes owing to conduct and mutual behaviour, sometimes under interference and criticising attitude of the family of either or both. Sometimes the differences crop up owing to growth in fatness of one of the two partners in the marriage, which adversely affects (only in some cases) the pleasure in bed.

Because Saturn is a very slow moving planet, these differences between husband and wife, after taking origin for one reason or the other, keep growing slowly but positively steadily. Intervention by families of both or by the family of either of the husband and wife sometimes (not always) try to bring compromise between the two, it is well and good. However sometimes (that too not always) one or the other family adds poison to the situation, and then the families respond to each other bitterly, the ultimate result is always one and the same in every case, namely separation and divorce.

Sometimes the families of the husband and wife stop at the verge of separation point, and stop the couple too from reaching it, for either family prestige or under hope of normalisation of relations between the two in future. A deep study of horoscopes of both would give an idea about the final outcome in the disputes.

The second result is, sometimes as a result of the strain in mutual relations at home, origin of quarrels, fights and litigation with outsiders might, in some cases, include the family of the husband or the wife, as has now become common virtually everywhere. In fact what happens that once an individual gets involved as a litigant, either as a plaintiff or a respondent, the individual's intentions for litigation become more fearless and sometimes common on basis of the experience gained in it.

At least in 50% cases of married couples with misunderstanding or dispute between husband and wife, attention of one or the other gets attracted towards other source of companionship. It is often so because man (woman included) is a social animal, and the desire as well as need for a companion of the opposite sex is a natural instinct. Ancients have also counted the four most essential instincts as common in all animals (humans included) and they are food, sleep (or rest), sense of fear, and the desire and need for coupling. The original Sanskrit saying is

"*aahaar, nidra, bhaya, maithunam cha, saamanyam eitad pasubhih-naranaam*".

Higher-level knowledge is the only speciality of humans, and a human without (that) knowledge is just like an animal.

From the above point flows the question of ill health and other 'clumsy-considered' diseases also. At least in India and other under-developed or undeveloped countries, one cannot go asking a friend or companion of the opposite sex whether she or he suffers from any sex-oriented disease, before starting coupling. In developed countries the story is different, where medical tests and certificates are more or less unavoidable. Saturn helps the house occupied by it, and damages the house on which it has direct *drishti*. Thus the 7th house is for companionship with the opposite sex, and Saturn helps in getting it, and helps in its continuance also. But because Saturn in 7th generally has direct *drishti* on the 1st house, which governs the personality of self, Saturn proves harmful to the self, i.e. the individual herself or himself.

In the matter of buying or selling, Saturn takes time to finalise a deal, but sticks to it once the deal is finalised, and doesn't tolerate the other party's withdrawal from the final deal. In a case of withdrawal after finalisation, Saturn (with Moon) in the 7th house leads to quarrel, fighting, or arbitration of the market committee or ultimately to litigation.

Moon and Rahu in the 7th House

Moon and Rahu combination in the 7th house leads to growth in the sharpness of 'ego' of one of the two, and final result is serious misunderstanding between the two. The follow-up result is quarrels between the two and sometimes suspicion on character of each other.

Unless Rahu has the support of Mars or Saturn (in some cases Herschel too), Rahu doesn't normally lead to separate living and ultimate divorce. Where Saturn is in the 6th house from the Ascendant, in the normal course it is favourable in every manner. But Saturn in 6th house casts direct *drishti* on the 7th house and adds fuel to the fire of disagreements and disputes between husband and wife. Otherwise presence of Mars in 12th, 1st, 4th, or 8th house also hits the married life directly. The question of divorce would depend to a great extent on Mars or Saturn.

It is rarely that Sun hits the married life, unless it is in the 6th or 12th house. This point needs very extensive examination of Sun, Moon and Rahu read with their respective positions in the Navamsha chart of the husband and Trinshansha chart of the wife, besides transit positions of Saturn and Jupiter or retrograde Mars. Caution is needed before giving any prediction merely on presence of Moon with Rahu in the 7th house and Sun's interference in the mutual relationship of the couple.

Rahu (with Moon) in 7th house instigates an individual to cast romantic glance (with ulterior motive of developing friendship) on members of the opposite sex, but the progress is rather slow and full of fears of all kinds. Solid results are difficult to drop into the lap of the individual easily and quickly, because Rahu is after all a shadow planet and Moon is reduced to mere 50% effect because of its eclipse combination with Rahu.

Then the question of illnesses or diseases likely to be caused by extra marital relationship also appear into the backyard of life, again depending on other planets like Saturn and Mars.

Similarly, in the matter of quarrels, fight, and litigation too, this combination has to depend on position of Jupiter (for litigation), on position of Mars and Saturn in the 12th or the 1st house or at the most in the 4th house. Otherwise the quarrels would end after some heated exchanges once or twice, and actual physical fighting is difficult to find a place in the quarrels without direct support of other hard planets.

In the matter of buying and selling, the individual develops the habit of finalising a deal and then withdrawing from it under one excuse or the other, while in some other cases, the opposite party imposes it upon the individual. The final result is the same.

Moon and Ketu in the 7th House

This combination is on the whole a non-interfering one in the 7th house, because Ketu leaves matters to the wisdom and initiative of Moon with regard to married life. No doubt, quarrels limited to heated exchanges between wife and husband are common, but the quarrels generally neither travel outside the private apartment of the couple, nor outside to the family of either of them.

Ketu is not much interested in adversely affecting the finances of the husband and wife, nor with the world outside their home, nor with physical health of either of the two.

Ketu generally is in favour of honouring a deal or decision, once it has been finalised and communicated to the other concerned party.

Ketu (with Moon) in 7th house does draws attention and sometimes develops attraction towards outside members of the opposite sex. But it doesn't develop courage in the individual to proceed beyond glances and sometimes a casual talk, because Ketu is not intent on disturbing the peace in and continuance of the married life.

MOON IN THE 8TH HOUSE

It is a difficult position for the individual in some cases, because Moon in 8th house gives a man a touch of feminine qualities, habits, tendencies, while it gives masculine qualities, habits and tendencies to a woman. This situation of nature of a partner in the married life often creates problems for the individual with regard to adjustment, as also adjustment with wider families of the two and also in the social circle of the two.

Many a wife does not like timid or submissive tendency or nature of the husband, which many a time reflects on mutual bedroom life too. This type of husband generally lacks initiative, courage and welcome-type of force towards wife and bedroom affairs between the two. On the other hand, a wife given to masculine nature and tendency makes her bold, brave, very talkative, dominating. She doesn't miss an opportunity to take initiative, courage and desired force or compulsion in the bedroom, which is liked by some husbands, while disliked by some others.

In such a case, much would depend on position, help or opposition from other planets in the 8th house (with Moon) or from other houses in the birth-chart. Undoubtedly Navamsha chart of husband and Trinshansha chart of wife would carry a lot of weight in this behalf.

In so far as other effect of Moon in 8th house is concerned, it is deemed to be of generous nature, charitable in deserving cases, benevolent, fond of jokes and casual remarks (but not hurting anyone). It gives concentration of mind on the job on hand or subject under study or any matter under consideration. Some ancient astrologers have attributed to Moon in the 8th house a tendency for stealing (theft of any kind) and initiating quarrel leading to inimical relations. But by experience spread over several generations, these attributes can be called very rare and remote, instead of being common and traceable often.

It is undoubtedly true that Moon in 8th house gives easy misunderstanding in love affair, because a girl wouldn't very much like timidity, fearfulness or withdrawal tendency in a boy friend. Similarly, a boy friend would normally disapprove of a very bold, daring or daring tendency in a girl friend, vis-à-vis other qualities. Sometimes, in spite of this situation between the two, the marriage might take place. The married life then drags its feet. Interference by other stars in the married life might bring adverse results too.

However one more important function of Moon in the 8th house is the physical troubles and illnesses of any kind which Moon can cause. First thing is that being lord of Mind and every kind of mental faculty in human beings, it gives a kind of worrying nature about even minor events and ailments, and also over-cautiousness about them.

Secondly, Moon can cause tuberculosis, pleurisy, over-weight of body, partial mental or physical impotence to men. In women it gives partial or complete frigidity, sometimes absence of menstrual cycle or very scanty flow of menstrual bleeding leading to childlessness, besides frigidity. Underdeveloped breasts to women is also a result of Moon in the 8th house, resulting in very little milk or sometimes no milk at all for breast feeding to the newly born. Masculine features to women and feminine touch of features to men is also an outcome of this position of Moon.

Apart from these complaints, Moon gives a funny touch of uncertainty to the nature of any individual. Further fragility of mind, fickle-mindedness, change of mind and resultant change in decision are also results of the Moon in 8th house.

More serious consequence in the shape of a mere touch of insanity type nature, or partial insanity or even complete insanity and madness are also caused by Moon in the 8th house. In this connection it has to be specially noted that many a time, any degree of partial or near-complete insanity is caused to both boys and girls between the age of puberty to about 28 years of age. The cause is not far to search. Absence of relief from sexual desire and company of the opposite sex play the main role in it or at least the major role undoubtedly. Several cases of partial insanity have been cured, under the advice of competent astrologer, by arranging close physical contact with the opposite sex (nearly of the same age or a little older or younger in age), even without actual cohabitation. The difficulty is that the parents, guardians or other members of the family and even astrologers do not understand this point. And cases have come to notice where even medical experts could not come to the conclusion that absence of relief from desire of sex has caused the partial or near-complete insanity. It has to be noted in this context that if the insanity goes to the extent of completeness, it is difficult to cure it, one major problem being no girl or woman (even from a brothel) agrees to cohabit with a boy at that stage of insanity.

Suffering from injury in water, near sinking or near-drowning or even death by drowning are also outcomes of Moon in the 8th house. Another angle of Moon's presence in the 8th house is food poisoning, or falling ill by taking wrong liquid-medicine or out-of-date medicine or out-dated and rotten medicine. A wound going septic is also a result of Moon in the 8th house.

It is interesting to note that Moon is dependent on its light and bright side totally on Sun, and Moon is basically concerned with Mind. But even then Moon can cause all kinds of physical troubles stated above, and that is not a complete list – it is difficult to give a complete list. Allied and linked troubles can be guessed by what has been stated above.

Moon in 8th house (12th position from the 9th house) easily earns the individual a bad name in connection with management and funds of any social, religious or charitable organisation, whether the individual is at fault or not. Generally the employees of that institute or organisation start rumours and accusations. Others believe those unfounded allegations and stick to them. It is always better for these individuals to keep away from funds and management of these organisations.

Further, whether guilty or not, uncles, aunts, cousins, brothers-in-law and sisters-in-law of these individuals blame them for usurping their due share in parental or family inheritance, or encroaching upon property or other assets of these persons, guilt or no guilt becomes immaterial in this regard.

One very favourable influence of Moon in 8th house is that the individual is often desirous of repeated travel abroad, ultimately leading to settlement in a foreign land for some years or permanently. And often the individual achieves success in it.

Whenever Moon is found in the 8th house in the horoscope of any child, it is always better to have the Bhava Chalitam position of that Moon, placement of Cancer (Moon owned Rasi), and Navamsha chart should be got thoroughly examined by an expert and honest astrologer.

Moon and Sun in the 8th House

Though Moon goes combust in the vicinity of Sun, Moon doesn't become ineffective. The only result is that Moon's effect becomes reduced in degree and mild in its force, with regard to everything that has been stated in regard to Moon alone in the 8th house in the preceding paragraphs just above. This theory applies to even illnesses attributable to Moon in the 8th house. Sun (with Moon) in 8th house doesn't allow any kind of insanity or touch of even mild or partial insanity. Fragility and fickle-mindedness might be there to an extent, sometimes unnoticeable to others.

An important result of these two together is that the individual is generally keen for entry into government or semi-government or public sector job, and is often successful in it. If the individual migrates to a foreign land, there too, keenness for this category of job persists in the mind.

Then this combination gives fluctuating repeated bad temper at least towards the spouse, and rarely or mildly towards others. Some ancient *acharyas* have opined that this combination gives timidity and cowardice in battles, war, fights at local level or personal level and also in disputes and quarrels. No, experience shows that it is not exactly so. It is true that a feeling of timidity touches the mind sometimes, but under force and stronger influence of Sun it doesn't stand for long nor persists continuously.

Because the Sun & Moon's combination in 8th is 11th from 10th house (ruling source of income) and in 10th position from the 11th house (of income), Sun (even with Moon) becomes extra helpful for source of income and actual income as such. In spite of this extra help from Sun to actual income, the individual remains a kind of unsatisfied person in regard to income. He or she always tries for "still better", "all the more better", and because every time Sun doesn't fulfil the individual's wishful pursuit, he/ she remains disappointed in mind and it affects the nature of the individual, giving a greater touch of annoyance and anger or quarrelsomeness.

This combination gives use of spectacles to the individual in young age itself. It also adversely affects built of the body, being often lean and thin, generally unfit for heavy-duty use of the body.

Moon and Mars in the 8th House

The Moon and Mars combination in the 8th house is a terrible one indeed!

Mars (with Moon) in 8th house gives a faultfinding tendency to the individual from the very childhood, even in food at home. She or he doesn't miss finding a fault in the teacher at the school and at the University. This tendency develops to a full extent by the marriageable age, and operates upon friend-in-love or on the spouse. In the same breath, there is absence of liberal nature in providing funds to the spouse, be it a wife or husband. There are cases of house-wives capturing the entire income of the husband every month or every week or periodically, and then giving funds for personal expenses so miserly that the husband feels a kind of starvation for funds!

Anger and physical violence also find a place in married life, even in love affair. It is easy (and quick too) to end a love affair. But in countries like India and neighbourhood, it is difficult to reach a stage of salvation from these sufferings in the married life, ultimately leading to separation or even divorce, depending on family traditions and other surroundings and influences in the life of both, husband and wife.

That is why it is recommended that similar placement of Mars is essentially desirable in the horoscopes of both, girl and boy, before finalising the proposal for marriage. Otherwise failure of marriage is more or less certain, even if it is made to drag its feet in one manner or the other! (Those wanting detailed discussion of this aspect of Mars may consult page 58 (specially from page 75) to page 92 of our book, "Star Guide to Love and Marriage", published by Parsai Publishers from New Delhi (ptparsai@gmail.com) and also available with Rupa Publications India Pvt. Ltd.

Other important results of this combination in the 8th house are that

(1) Moon is not allowed by Mars to function freely and fully with regard to physical complaints, specially those related to brains and mental faculties;

(2) Mars gives extra touch of provoked and unprovoked annoyance and anger to the individual. This leads sometimes even to self-torture or punishment to self for real and imaginary fault(s) of self.

(3) Mars leads to illness like fluctuation in blood system, disorders in menstrual cycle, quantum of bleeding, complaints leading to inner organs of procreation in the body of women, heart ailment to anyone (men and women), unrecoverable type of cancer, even ordinary wound going septic sometimes needing surgical operation and in extreme cases, even amputation of a limb.

(4) Repeated fever, different kinds of fever, including T.B., (dry) pleurisy though Moon generally causes wet pleurisy.

(5) Headache, migraine, baldness, weak eyesight, injury to an eye, ear, nose or any trouble to throat including diphtheria in childhood, and thyroid trouble in declining years of life.

Mars gives a typical type of thirst for real estate to the individual and very often is successful, by hook or crook, to possess real estate more than actual need of the individual for use of self and the family, and generally earns rental income therefrom,

Mars is deemed, in astrology, a bachelor and male planet. Therefore some learned astrologers are of the opinion that Mars is extra unkind to women. The authors of this book neither hold nor support this opinion. They have come across several females to whom Mars has been kind and liberal in every aspect of life, even from the 8th house, except protecting their marriage or married life, unless the husband too had similar placement of Mars in his horoscope.

Moon and Mercury in the 8th House

Moon and Mercury combination constitutes two soft planets in the 8th house, granting both, favourable and unfavourable results. The favourable results are that Mercury controls the faculty of intelligence and experience flowing from brains, associated with education too, and therefore protects the individual from onslaught by Moon on mental faculties like fragility, fickle-mindedness and touch of insanity.

Mercury generates a reading habit that grants considerable relief in loneliness and dull hours. It gives an above average capacity for talking, public speaking, for explaining a speech of another speaker to the audience. It also gives a sense of self-confidence, not withstanding education level being high or low. It also provides flexibility to thought and action, moreso where they affect others, within the family or outside the family, even for the sake of unknown people, but not for unconcerned people. Mercury (with Moon) gives appreciable capacity for recitation of poems, prayers, and any verses likeable to the listeners or the audience.

If Venus is in the 7th or 9th house, this combination gives capacity for writing romantic songs and poems, and they often get published and become popular. The individual is always mindful of the needs of the spouse and does not allow matters to starvation for funds for personal and family's needs.

On the unfavourable side, because of this combination, a child's attention gets diverted from studies or gets divided by thoughts away from studies. The child generally avoids written work including notes on what has been taught or learnt. The individual is governed more by emotions than brains. These two stars together give a mentality to usurp the benefits of another person's literary work or any other work meant for income. The individual has no hesitation even in piracy of physical labour, depriving the real worker from its results and gains.

Moon and Jupiter in the 8th House

Moon and Jupiter combination is another pair of soft stars in the 8th house.

The result is more or less the same as caused by Moon with Mercury, no doubt with several differences, as given below:

(a) The individual has a tendency of giving threats of legal action and litigation, for justified or unjustified provocation. Sometimes starts litigation too, and generally the outcome at the final stage goes against the individual who initiated the litigation.

(b) The individual indulges in speculation in all kinds of shares and stocks, and often suffers an ultimate loss. Same is the outcome in betting at horse races, card games, of every activity of gambling type.

(c) The individual gets cheated easily, and then becomes wise after the event. The same is the story about theft from the possession/ purse or kit of the individual. Sometimes while operating the safety deposit vault too, the individual drops some costly items from the vault, or forgets properly locking the vault after use.

(d) The individual is often willing to give financial help or loan even to undeserving persons, again regretting own action after giving and non-recovery of the loan. On the other hand, when in need, the individual obtains loan from private sources on heavy rate of interest or on mortgage of jewellery or property, and then might suffer loss of either, because of failure to repay in time or as a result of court decree.

(e) In every case, Moon in 8th house gives excess of emotional hurt to the individual, strong feeling that the world is greedy and dishonest, but without betterment in attitude in future.

Moon and Venus in the 8th House

This is the third combine of two soft planets in the 8th house.

Exchange of blames for reason or without reason is a usual element of the nature of these individuals. No doubt these individuals have a touch of blame-worthiness in their conduct and character. If they do or can do nothing else, they at least try to be very romantic in public or in any large company of friends and followers, or even in the company of elders and superiors. They take pride in it. And generally the opposite sex, moreso the men-folk consider these individuals worth avoiding and condemning. These individuals feel happy, at home and well-received (in opinion of self) when in the company of ladies or audience of larger number of women than men, provided they have some prominent place or part to play thereat.

No doubt they (both women and men) have good physique and personality. They are always very keen for marriage with a top-class beauty or handsome person. If planets like Mars, Saturn and Rahu do not put a hurdle in this pursuit, they do get a beautiful girl or handsome boy in marriage.

Though rarely, some of these individuals become doctors, hardly sticking to the profession and to practice as a doctor. Generally they shift to some other attractive job like administrative services or in political arena or in business field. If they continue in medical line, soon they earn a bad name for their conduct and character towards the opposite sex.

They earn well and spend extremely well, generally remaining in tight financial position, and sometimes forced to borrow from private sources rather than public ones.

Some astrologers have the opinion that these individuals

go into adoption or get out-of-the-way benefit from sources of inheritance from parents of self or spouse. It is not correct in more than 40% cases, and they are often a failure in protecting what they got in inheritance. Chances of adoption are very remote, generally not noticed in practical application of this theory.

In this combination, there are ample chances of risk to the individual from water, from food poisoning and also from brain trouble, though only of mild type, and often temporary in duration.

Moon and Saturn in the 8th House

No doubt, Moon becomes subdued under Saturn in the 8th house too, as everywhere else. The individual has generally long life, though not very capable of active work after the age of 68 years, sometimes invalidity caused by an accident, illness or blunder in surgical operation.

These individuals have single track of mind and action influenced thereby, which many a time, becomes unbearable for others, specially when the individuals enjoy a position of power and authority over others. And whether they are or not in a position of power and authority, they are often given to corrupt trend of mind and actual practice. And association of Moon in the 8th house makes their demands for illegal gratification according to own whim, instead of the matter involved and the capacity of the bribe-giver. This leads to a bad name, which spreads widely.

These individuals are no doubt bold and brave, in person-to-person fight as well as on a battlefield. But they do not carry the capacity to encourage others by their words to boldness and bravery, because of Moon's presence in the 8th house.

Saturn in 8th house doesn't allow Moon to cause physical and mental troubles detailed under the heading "Moon in the 8th house". On the other hand, Saturn causes physical troubles attributable to Saturn itself, and leaves the brain and mental faculties undisturbed even by Moon.

Saturn forces the individuals to maintain good moral character, and doesn't allow them to go beyond verbal romance and at the most, minor or mild physical touch here and there, just occasionally.

However it is unavoidable that one should get proper study of Saturn's transit over the 4th and 8th houses from the Janma Lagna, because there are strong chances of an accidental injury to the individual during those transits. The injury could be casual or mild or of serious and severe nature depending on what Rasi is in the 4th or 8th house. When Libra, Capricorn or Aquarius is either in the 4th or the 8th house, the injury would be quickly curable without leaving any post-accident impact on the individual. However if it is Aries, Cancer, Leo or Scorpio in 4th or 8th house, the injury would be severe and post-accident impact would be left for long time. In case of Taurus, Gemini, Virgo or Pisces in the 4th or the 8th house, the injury would be serious but would get cured within less than nine months. In case of Taurus, Scorpio, Leo and Pisces, the injury, whether of one or both legs, would leave a limp in walking as an after effect.

In spite of the above impact of an injury, the result of Saturn in 8th house of granting a long life to the individual however continues. Injury, invalidity and long life are all there, the last one not being inter-linked to the first two.

Saturn gives good inheritance and also good current income, but even then sometimes it creates very inconvenient situation of paucity of ready cash, leading to borrowing. If manageable even with difficulty, borrowing should be avoided, because repayment and complete clearance of loan takes a long time, conditions of borrowing becoming difficult now and then.

Moon and Rahu in the 8th House

The first impact of the combination of Rahu and Moon in the 8th house is fatness of the body, at least between chest (breast) area and the tying line on the waist.

Second result is a touch of laziness and hard work, overtaking each other every now and then right from school days. Parents have to pay special attention to this tendency in a child, because it would otherwise adversely affect the educational progress of the individual.

The third influence is that the individual becomes much richer than the financial status of the parents at birth of the individual. Richness favours the individual more after marriage, though not during prolonged love affair, or during changing the partners in love affairs one after another. It is advisable to marry quickly within 9 months or at the most 18 months of the start of the love affair or the first acquaintance. If it is an arranged marriage, the engagement mustn't prolong beyond 9 months in any case for formal marriage.

Rahu (with Moon) in 8th house gives control of the major portion of the finances and investments into the hands of the spouse, and that is rather favourable in the interest of both. The individual shouldn't resent it.

These individuals suffer at least once in lifetime from hernia or allied trouble, besides piles or diabetes and other physical troubles allied thereto. Fear complex is another result of this combination, the fear could be from any source or imagination, including fear of illness or disease or accident or enemies or physical attack by a thief or robbers. It can be quarrel and fight within family of self or the spouse, no doubt involving individual too. The imagination of fear from one or the other source is nothing but a disease of the thinking process.

Some astrologers are of the opinion that Rahu (with Moon) in 8th house gives criminal tendencies, but the authors, on basis of their long experience of self and of their father and grandfather do not attribute to this opinion. In this particular matter, we have to distinguish between criminal thought and criminal acts or association therewith. No. Thoughts of mind do not go beyond thought and into action, and a majority of people have such thoughts in their mind. At least an idea of taking resort to crime finds a place in the mind of virtually everyone of us all. The reason is not far to seek. Moon is lord of Mind and Rahu is a shadow planet, and criminal tendency doesn't travel beyond mind and reach any actual act in any case. If any such tendency has been observed in an individual, the reason might be far away from Rahu and Moon combination in the 8th house.

One very important result of these two in the 8th house is that they give homosexual or lesbian tendency, though in many times not possible in actual action for want of companion, facility and availability of time or occasion. These two stars positively develop in the individual a strong desire or inquisitiveness for it in mind between the age of 18 and 36 years.

Moon and Ketu in the 8th House

This combination also gives a hidden desire for homosexuality or lesbian tendency, but lack of facilities and courage (or boldness of mind) sometimes saves the situation in real or concrete action. Not getting a suitable companion can also be another reason for not taking resort to it. But the tendency is spreading fast almost in all developed and semi-developed countries, because of publicity of approval to this tendency by print media, resulting in formation of groups and societies, which take pride in pronouncing this tendency in loud language.

This combination gives fatness of body from the age of 8 years, and it is difficult to reduce it from the level it has reached at the age of 18 years. It is therefore advisable to bring it under control prior to full puberty of the individual.

These individuals often have an evil eye on the riches or assets of others as also on the spouse of others for romantic intentions and purposes. However Ketu is a timid planet by its very nature, and so the desire rarely reaches practical fulfilment, at least with regard to desire for romance with spouse of another person. It is altogether a different matter with or between unmarried boys and girls or with divorcees or between widows and widowers!

Like Rahu with Moon, Ketu with Moon too keeps an individual well provided with necessities of life for self and family, including education and settlement in life of the progeny, and therefore the need for borrowing money rarely arises. No doubt, these individuals have the tendency to borrow items of daily use, like clothes and garments for festivals or other special occasions, food items, furniture and furnishings, typewriter or computer or any other easily transportable machine merely carried by hands. The borrowed items sometimes go back very delayed or in a rather damaged condition, and sometimes do not return to the owner at all.

The authors do not agree with the opinion of some astrologers that Ketu (with Moon) in 8th house gives rather an unhappy married life. Not at all, unless Moon owned Rasi Cancer is in the 7th house or in the 1st house, though 1st house lordship of Moon is not so vehemently applicable in this context.

This combination normally gives or can give all those physical complaints as have been listed under Rahu with Moon in the 8th house. In addition to those complaints of health, Ketu (with Moon) is liable to give oft-repeated disorders of digestive system, dyspepsia, dyslexia (because of Moon in 8th house with Ketu), diarrhoea and dysentery, or allied troubles linked with digestive system. Unless Mars is connected with this combination from the 1st, 2nd or 4th house, these two (Ketu & Moon) do not adversely affect the menstrual cycle in women. And unless Saturn is linked from the 2nd or 4th or 12th house, with Moon and Ketu combine, there are no chances of any major surgery, or amputation of a limb of the body.

MOON IN THE 9TH HOUSE

Though the 9th house relates to good or bad luck, inheritance (gains and problems in it), fame or defame, faith or absence of faith in God or in religion, and good moral or immoral character (within the knowledge of the spouse). It relates also to many a close relations. Moon very rarely becomes very effective and influential in the 9th house, because of its waxing and waning nature. This being the exactly correct position, Moon has to depend on other planets in the 9th house, and if it is alone, it depends on the lord of the Rasi in the 9th house, placement of that lord in the birth-chart and its relation with Moon in 9th house. Very few astrologers would agree with this fundamental position about Moon in the 9th house, but it is a hard fact.

Moon gives a person strong faith in God and religion or cult, it stops the individual from becoming an atheist, though several times adversity forces lack of the faith in God Almighty. Whether in a cardinal Rasi or not, Moon encourages journeys for pilgrimage with the family, or at least with the spouse. Basically the individual is generous and charitable by nature and tries to help people, in real need. The individual also gets associated with any organisation or group connected or concerned with religious activity, and sometimes the individual has to accept an office in management of the religious body or a temple or mosque or church etc. Moon being alone in 9th house would not generally bring any defame to the individual for lapse in management or suspicion about funds (collection, accounting and spending).

The 9th house being directly related to brothers-in-law, sisters-in-law, cousins, uncles and aunts on paternal and maternal side, nephews and nieces, Moon generally tries its best to maintain cordial relations with one and all of these relations, without much bothering about response from these people.

Moon does not bother to develop any kind of romantic or illicit relationship with any of the above relatives or relations. However if the endeavour comes from the opposite side, the individual, after a mild rejection at the initial stage, starts responding to the advancement from the other side. This is where the question of earning a bad name crops up, because after all, even after best care and caution to hide the fact, the illicit relationship does come to light. Because Moon (when alone in the 9th house) makes an individual shameless person, the relationship ends after exposure.

But with regard to immoral character of the spouse, for one reason or the other, the individual turns a blind eye to this development, and if the individual at all expresses disapproval, it is in mild and easily tolerable tone.

These individuals are obedient and serviceful to parents, teachers and almost all elders, unless they find some concrete drawback in the conduct or character of an elderly person. They are not miserly towards parents of self or of spouse, and are not much guided by the feelings and opinion of others in this behalf.

They are often keen for advanced education, and if necessary, at cost of self, no doubt after entry into any career for earning livelihood of self and or family. Though they are normally deemed easy going in relation to their work or career, they are hard working towards acquisition of education.

Apart from pilgrimage (including mountaineering to holy and religious places), the individuals are fond of normal tours and travels too, in connection with career or work as also for sake of pleasure and knowing new places by a visit there.

There can be gains from uncles, aunts, cousins or even from brothers-in-law or sisters-in-law, but not exclusive gain (debarring other claimants) from the mother or from father, because notwithstanding other considerations, desiring or getting exclusive gains from mother stands opposed to these individuals' principle of honesty of purpose and straightforwardness. They refuse (respectfully) even if the mother offers any gains exclusively.

Unless Venus has some direct link with the 9th house or casts full *drishti* on the 9th house, these individuals do not join any sex orgies, and if invited to join, they politely refuse.

They try their best to protect the inheritance. If they shift away from the place of birth or place of normal residence of the parents or a surviving parent, these individuals take care of both, the inheritance at the place of birth or wherever else it is located and also of the parents or the surviving parent.

Moon and Sun in the 9th House

Combination of Moon and Sun in the 9th house gives a typical type of envy, sometimes jealousy towards parents, teachers and elders, and though the individual doesn't turn disrespectful towards them, he or she is not desirous to render help, support or physical service to them. Sometimes this trend of thought and action is owing to competition or jealousy towards brother or sister residing with the parents, or parents residing with a brother or sister.

In all other respects, the individual behaves more or less in the manner described above under effect of Moon alone in the 9th house.

There are chances of the individual losing a part of the inheritance in favour of other claimants, namely brother(s) and or sister(s). But the individual is not satisfied with own share, and tries to bring influence from governmental sources (not legal sources) to acquire full share of self or even more just as a revenge for being given less share originally.

The individual or sometimes her or his spouse is in government or semi-government or public sector service or in politics, actively or as a backbencher.

These individuals make a bigger show of their faith in religion and social service though in fact it is not even 40% of what is pretended. They are not charitable in so far as cash money is concerned. They would plead to others for donation and then give it as if it were their own donation to charitable cause.

For sake of publicity or popularity, these individuals show respect for all religions and join festivals and festivities of other religions too for the purpose of a show or being photographed or getting their face seen on vision media. The main point is that their self-interest is first and last consideration for them everywhere, every time.

Moon and Mars in the 9th House

With Moon and Mars together in the 9th House, the individual does suffer a loss of inheritance, whatever her or his attitude and effort to avoid the loss. If it is not loss of the complete inheritance, at least the loss is of a good portion thereof.

If the individual is the only claimant, others will crop up to claim and fight for their share, not hesitating to indulge in litigation with the correct heir and claimant. This situation arises more where there is property or any other immovable asset involved in inheritance. The right person has to forego own right and sometimes the possession over the property, and the false or the wrong persons get the possession. One funny part of the matter is that though the individual is capable of physical violence, where inheritance is involved, and where he or she is losing the rightful share, the element of violence is somehow avoided.

One reason for the above tendency can be the keenness of the individual to earn a good name among relatives, friends, neighbours and become popular in the public for the non-violent attitude in the matter of inheritance. Somehow the false or the wrong claimants realise this weak point in the individual and do not miss to take advantage of it.

If any litigation case is in a court of law or before any legal forum or tribunal concerning the inheritance, the individual prefers to argue the case herself or himself, only by general study of law-points related to the matter under dispute.

In matters of investments, or in speculation in shares and stocks, in card games or other similar betting (barring betting at horse races), these individuals stand to suffer a net loss in the final outcome, sometimes by cheating or cunningness of others involved in the game or investment. They lose money even in deposit with private parties for sake of higher interest or as a source of secret investment of unaccounted money. One example would explain the point.

A rich man had fear of search of his premises by the Income Tax Investigation people. He and his family were going out on a month-long pilgrimage. He locked a very large amount of high denomination currency notes in a big black steel box, locked and sealed the box securely, and left it one of his best friends in the world. They both were intimate friends for over 30 years. Even on return from the pilgrimage, the gentleman didn't go to his friend to get back the box for full six months. When he brought the box home after about six months, he had found the lock and seal in tact. On opening the box, he found sheets of new blank white paper sheets in place of the currency notes. The money left in custody of the friend was not accounted money; the rich man kept silence. When he approached the author to find out the fate of the money, the author found that the man had Moon, Mars and Rahu in the 9th house in the birth chart, and Mars alone in the 9th house in the yearly chart. The senior author advised the gentleman to forget the whole loss of money.

These individuals are often keen for recognition of their work and services rendered while working in bureaucracy or in active politics. If the country has the tradition of conferring honours and titles, they are desirous of getting one, and also exhibiting it very openly and widely, virtually everywhere, even on writing pads.

Normally these individuals have good appetite and are fond of good food and drinks too, if they are given to drinking. In infancy, they generally get breast-feeding for 9 months or so, and thus have a good-built physique from the very beginning. When grown up they take special care of real mother, whether they bother about other relatives or not.

These individuals often come to own self-earned property and that is also one reason why they do not bother much about usurpation by others of ancestral property situated at a distant place from their place of work.

They are fond of travel but not without purpose, and not for pleasure only, because they often think of self-interest in any act or action of theirs.

They are not much attached to uncles, aunts and other relatives at their own level, normally have "give and take" relationship, but at the same time, no jealousy or hard feelings for anyone. They neither harm relatives, near or distant ones, nor cheat them or exploit them, and want a similar response from them.

Moon and Mercury in the 9th House

The individuals with Moon and Mercury in the 9th house are experts in spoken and written word, and therefore rarely an occasion arises for them to lose a part of their due inheritance. They know how to talk down the false or the wrong claimants. They generally settle disputes related to inheritance or any self-earned property out of a law court, and rarely initiate litigation themselves in such matters.

They have great faith in God Almighty as also in activities related to religion and faith of self, and that of others, not for sake of any selfish motive or intention. They are charitable to the extent their purse allows them. They normally do not concern themselves with donations of others, rather suggest those people to give it directly wherever they want to give. They generally have a good collection of books on religion and philosophy, *Vedas, Upanishads, Puranas,* whether they have the time and energy to read all of them or not. Their speciality is that they know what subject or point of discussion would be found in which scripture and at what point in any volume.

They often refuse to hold any office of power and authority in a religious trust or in management of charitable organisation or related to social work. They are normally of the opinion that it would be difficult for them, being simple and honest workers themselves, to stop others from dishonesty of any kind in the management of a temple, mosque or church, or religious and charitable formation.

They are often kind and generous to their servants, employees, subordinates, and do not harm them or dismiss their service unless those people themselves want to leave their job or distinctly prove dishonest or negligent in their duties and responsibilities.

These individuals like children, try to play with them, help them, and give proper guidance to the youngsters with vast knowledge of self. Sometimes they teach the children their difficult subjects. Because some of these individuals are writers and poets of repute, they sometimes write for children too. Normally too, these individuals are good teachers, well known journalists, preachers, priests, publicity men for Kings, Rulers and top politicians.

They are often kind and helpful to all relatives without expectation of any return or reward, and if they are not in a position to help financially or physically, at least they are not jealous or harmful to any relative.

They are less interested in bedroom activities with the spouse, and this leads the spouse to seek pleasure and satisfaction elsewhere. If these individuals come to know about it, they turn a blind eye and deaf ear to it. They are always away from all games, meetings, and any loose talks of this type. They have generally their own progeny, and if they have none, they are rarely keen to adopt anyone under the fear that the adopted child might prove unworthy of their standard of honesty and moral character. But if the spouse desires and actually adopts a child, they do not interfere in the matter. They accept the situation as it is.

They do not have a greedy eye on money, wealth, any possessions of other people, whether relatives or not. They have normally a saintly outlook on all these matters, though as far as possible, they do not renounce the family life just for a show. If they renounce the family life, home and assets once, they would not come back to it till death. That is the peculiarity of Mercury and Moon in the 9th house of religious activity!

Moon and Jupiter in the 9th House

This combination of Moon and Jupiter in the 9th house gives more or less the same results as those mentioned above under "Moon with Mercury", except that –

(a) The collection of books in the case of these individuals contains books also on law, economics, accounts, business management, arbitration and deciding public grievances if the individuals happen to be in a position of power or authority or in active politics.

(b) They are liberal and helpful to their staff, servants, dependants and subordinates to a justified extent only, and not in a blind manner. These individuals are given to forgiveness on faults or negligence of duty or dishonesty of small nature, and the result is either physical punishment, or it being a legal offence imposition of fine, and on second or third repetition straight dismissal from the job.

(c) They have a legal bend of mind mostly in all matters.

(d) If a dispute crops up about inheritance or their dues against anyone pending repayment beyond the mutually agreed date, these individuals do not hesitate to initiate a legal action after due warning in writing to the person concerned.

(e) They are not totally void of sense of romance or extra marital affair, but they judge the person opposite, time and place and capacity of both for secrecy of the relationship. But these individuals also do not go near group sex situations, whatever the pull from friends.

(f) They are fond of law, rules and regulations. If these individuals renounce the family life, they make their "will" and as far as possible give possession of assigned assets (losses are out of question) to the persons named in the "will".

(g) They do indulge in speculation in shares and stocks, though not in betting, gambling etc. They go in for card games but not on stake of money.

Moon and Venus in the 9th House

This combination of Moon and Venus in the 9th house is quite different in results than the two other soft planets with Moon in the 9th house.

These individuals have liking for all good things in life, including drinks, drugs, any other source of intoxication, very charming dress, giving attractive appearance to personality of self (whether a man or a woman), fond of romantic talks freely, and if opportunity permits, physical contact with opposite sex.

These individuals are keenly fond of music, dances, dramas, concerts, any conferences or meetings concerning any of these branches of fine arts, meeting actors and actresses, obtaining their autographs and pictures (photos) if possible. Whether they have learnt any fine art systematically or not, they want to actively participate in a performance of that branch of the fine art from the public stage, bothering little about praise or criticism.

They go in for another marriage, but only on divorce or death of the spouse. However, some of them do not mind having a mistress or paramour, and have no hesitation in changing the person.

They are fond of very tasty food and sweets, soft drinks, cold beverages, attending parties, functions, festivals, gatherings of social elites (sometimes even if not invited formally).

They would not tolerate any loss of their due inheritance, and they would first try to avoid any loss of it by sweet and soft negotiations with the wrong or the false claimant, and in failing to get the desired result, they would take resort to threats and underhand methods. They dislike going to a court of law for this purpose, and if the other party goes, they bravely and boldly face the drama, making best effort to win the case by any means.

They do not think of renouncing the family life or giving up their control on property and assets, and they expect the progeny to wait for their natural end. They are very much afraid of food poisoning and observe all precautions in the matter.

They are very kind and helpful to sisters, sisters-in-law, aunts, female cousins, nieces and other female relatives, though not with any ulterior motive or evil eye on any of them. They observe full decency and respectability in this matter.

If they have to give any donation in cash or kind for a charitable, religious or social cause, they check it in advance what is there in it for them, if nothing else, at least name and fame in the public or in the press.

Moon and Saturn in the 9th House

With Moon and Saturn in the 9th house, there is a strong chance of losing a portion of the due inheritance by mischief and cunningness of others greedy of the individual's inheritance. Even use of violence doesn't retrieve the lost portion. Some times, own relatives do not help the individual in such a mischief or cunning activity for personal gain, or even without it, only out of jealousy or an outcome of wicked nature.

(For sake of comparison, when Moon with Mars is in the 9th house, it leads the individual to suffer a loss by lapse on part of self or spouse or by mistake of either of the two.) But it is not exactly so in the case of Saturn and Moon together in the 9th house, because firstly Saturn is slow (though steady) in acquiring property or real estate for personal use or for rental income. And secondly Saturn is more interested in moveable assets, including arms and ammunition, weapons of any kind, investment in industrial venture, in gaining personal strength by organising follower and dependants, and maintaining them in every manner.

Saturn doesn't mind rented premises for residence or for industrial unit or for shop or office. Saturn (combined with Moon) thinks that buying property is blocking big funds, which could be used for investment purposes with higher returns than the rentals paid for hired premises.

Saturn (whether with Moon or alone in the 9th house) needs manpower for another reason, not common with other planets, except in the case of Rahu (with Moon) in the 9th house. Saturn (with Moon) in 9th house takes interest in blackmailing influential or rich persons for ulterior motives or substantial gains for upkeep of the manpower under the command of the individual.

Saturn has rarely any interest whatsoever in illicit relationship or in extra marital affair. On the other hand, if the individual finds some loophole in the spouse, the individual doesn't break the marriage, but gives up physical relations in the bedroom with the spouse. No doubt, on divorce or death of the spouse, Saturn goes in for another lawful marriage, but doesn't keep a mistress or paramour.

In some rare cases, this combination gives, specially when Saturn is in 2nd, 4th or 8th house by transit or Saturn is having own Mahadasa or sub-period, an accidental injury, resulting ultimately in some kind of difficulty in using the injured limb, for example limpness or difficulty in using a hand. If Mars aspects Saturn and Moon together from 3rd house or even from 12th or 2nd house (provided the *drishti* is at least 45 out of a total of 60), need for amputation of a limb of the body can arise in some cases, though remote. This point applies more to person injured in a War (on a battlefield) or in an earthquake or in landslide, or by fire on a large scale or in any other calamity of this type.

Saturn doesn't leave any scope for Moon in the 9th house to exhibit much emotional and binding love or affection for relatives, though these two stars together do try their best to render best help and support when any relative in trouble needs it. At the same time, the individual doesn't expect much help or support from the relatives except own spouse and progeny (if grown up or nearing adulthood in age).

Saturn with Moon in 9th house doesn't help or harm educational progress of the individual or any member of the immediate family. If a brother or sister is not upto mark in educational progress, the individual cautions the brother/sister once or twice and leaves the matter to fate of the person concerned.

These individuals are not much concerned with 'show business' type behaviour related to religious or social or charitable formations, and they try to contribute financial or other kind of help or support rather secretly. They do not exhibit too much of their feelings (of respect) for the parents, teachers and elders in a matter of making a show of it. Yet they are fully dutiful in any hour of need.

Moon and Rahu in the 9th House

The results of combination Moon and Rahu in the 9th house are somewhat parallel to those of Moon with Saturn in 9th house, but in much reduced degree, and not much on the surface.

The criminal type thinking is there, though neither actual activity, nor very violent attitude is there. Any major injury to body or its part is not indicated unless Mars or Saturn is in the 2nd, 4th or 8th house as such. Therefore the question of invalidity or amputation of a limb rarely arises.

The individual is not much or directly concerned with religious, social or charitable activity, at least in the public or for a show. Like Saturn with Moon in 9th house, whatever these individuals have to do, they do it lonely, and secretly, not even for press or publicity.

In case of loss of a portion of inheritance, these individuals try their level best to retrieve it from the wrong hands, and do not give up the effort for a long period, which actually bores or tires the encroacher or the person who has done the wrong. The ultimate result is that the individual gets back possession of that portion of the property or assets that had been encroached upon.

These individuals do not indulge in speculation of any kind, gambling or card games or betting at horse races, and so there are remote chances of loss through this loophole. They are not given to extra greed than normal in every person, and so, they have no big regrets related to losses. They do not mind spending liberally on an event, ritual, festival, function of their choice and liking, and are fully satisfied that they have spent their money by own hands and at own free will.

They are not normally fond of romance beyond own spouse, but often want the spouse to be responsive to their romantic approach and move. Otherwise too, neither women nor men under this combination are very sex-oriented by nature itself. So outside affairs rarely or seldom arise in their life. In the company of romantic type friends, companions or colleagues, they do not excuse their presence, but at the same time do not participate in physical deeds. At the most they keep observing others or absent themselves on some excuse or the other from the site.

Moon and Ketu in the 9th House

Ketu in 9th house (with Moon) behaves more or less like Mercury's combination in 9th house with Moon.

The individual is a good orator, teacher, writer, philosopher, preacher or even priest. He or she is given to quick annoyance or anger, and also getting rid of such anger similarly quickly. In criticism, such individuals do not spare their own father or male teacher or male elders, but are not critical towards mother, female relatives and female teachers or female elders anywhere. They considers the females as deserving respect only.

Generally after birth, these babies have to depend on bottle feeding or feeding by a wet nurse, because of paucity of natural milk in the breast of the mother. The result is that these individuals do not grow fat, and avoid physical fighting, hard labour or going to battlefield as a combat force.

Ketu (and Moon) in 9th house gives a religious or charitable or social bent of mind, resulting in concrete action too, depending on the power and capacity of their purse or resources. As far as possible, like Mercury and Moon in 9th house, they avoid holding any management responsibility in religious or social or charitable organisation or related to a temple, mosque, church etc.

These individuals do take active interest in orphanage, poor home, shelter for destitute women and also for people going on pilgrimage to mountain-based holy places or centres of pilgrimage. They render best help in every manner possible for the sufferers at the time of any natural calamity like earthquake, large-scale fire, landslide, famine, floods, cyclone, etc.

Moon in the 10th House

This is one of the most important positions of Moon in a birth chart or even in a yearly chart.

Moon is capable of giving great fame and widespread publicity to an individual for own work, for achievement in any field of activity, for any single great action of bravery or social service.

In so far as career by way of regular service or job or even piece-meal service is concerned, Moon gives struggle and delay in progress or promotion or a raise in salary or perquisites.

Even individuals born in a village, or ordinary family or remote areas, in less populated towns get widespread fame for their achievement in any field. Moon is concerned normally with fame only, not with notoriety, unless Saturn or Rahu is hitting Moon's effect from inside the 10th house or from an angle befitting for hitting.

It is not a path of comforts and flowers for these individuals in achieving fame and success in their effort. At every step struggle and hard work, constantly and continuously, constitute their normal fate throughout life.

Moon gives the individual a typical kind of under ground unspoken understanding with the father, rarely so much with the mother, though on birth the individual gets the longest breast feeding by the mother.

Moon often gives the individual close contact with top people in power and authority, but he or she rarely secures any gain in cash or kind or for progress in sources of income from such people in position and power. The people in position of power are not responsible for it. It is the individual who deems it fit to achieve every thing, (even success, fame and honour, progress or promotion) by effort of self and self alone, and not as an obligation from others.

The individual with Moon in 10th house very often suffers from envy and jealousy everywhere and from everyone. But at the same time, generally ladies high and low always help and support the individual.

It is a tragedy with these individuals that they are often dry natured about the fine arts (including music and dance), in romance and advancement of gestures of love, so much so that they are not responsive to such gestures made by the other side. It seems as if they have no concern with anything except their studies in school and college and their work in youth and old age. They generally have more than one source of income, but they are not given to avoidance or evasion of taxes.

Though these individuals are devoted to wife but not much sex-oriented because of their deep interest in their work, which often consists of two separate sources of income.

When in a job or regular service, they are sincere to their work, attend to such work too as is considered difficult by others, and do not mind working day and night continuously. But they cannot stand any rebuke, any scolding, any adverse comment on their face from their superiors and employers. This tendency quite often proves a hurdle in their progress, because many superiors and employers are more interested in blind obedience and total blind tolerance rather than hard and devoted work, at least in government or semi-government or public sector offices.

Very often they have to start their career with incomplete education or at an immature age, and then they have a third angle to their activity, that is two sources of income, and the third one educating themselves by own effort, standard or as required for progress and promotion etc.

It is very surprising that even ancient astrologers haven't attached much importance to Moon, when alone, in the 10th house. And then their blind followers as well as half-baked teachers and students in astrology do not go into details of Moon's extra beneficial position for the individual in the 10th house, moreso when it alone is there.

Moon gives chances of large-scale gains from foreigners, foreign countries and also by foreign travels and tours. In fact the individual gets better recognition and respect from foreigners than from own countrymen, moreso if Gemini, Cancer, Virgo, or Pisces is in the 10th house.

Moon and Sun in the 10th House

The 10th house rules two most important elements in the life of an individual: father and source of earnings. Though Moon goes combust in the vicinity of Sun, both being basically intimate friends, they become very beneficial to the individual from father's side in the matter of career, business, profession, self employment, active politics, public service, anything anywhere in the world. This combination brings closeness and respect from the top people, who are in positions of power and authority, in their capacity as bureaucrats or as politicians or as dictators or rulers and kings or queens.

Though progress and promotion in career might be slow, but rarely they have to climb down on the ladder of progress.

Whether they enter or do not enter into the profession, business, self-employment, any line of career of the father, these individuals always get the support and blessings of the father. The individuals are always ready for physical and financial service to the father (and naturally to the mother too). They do not mind exchange of help or support with brother(s), sister(s) and other brethren, or giving one-sided help or support to this category of relations. Not much love and affection is lost between the individuals and these relatives of self or the spouse. On the other hand, they are rarely able to establish rapport with brother(s) and sister(s) of the spouse.

One minus point of this combination in the 10th house is that even on minor fault, default or lapse in acts of commission and omission, these individuals suffer the consequences quite soon, whatever it be, penalty, punishment, rebuke, scolding, anything. It is unavoidable for these individuals to be on their alert and to stay active as also honest at every step in their career, business, industry, whatever is the source of livelihood.

If these individuals enter active politics, and have to face general elections at any level, they get help, support and publicity even from most unknown and unexpected corners.

Many modern astrologers attribute extra cruelty to these individuals, but long experience does not confirm this opinion. Because these individuals are often in bureaucracy or in active politics, a touch of cruelty or exhibition of cruelty is not much possible, because eye of the common public and media is on their acts of commission and omission.

Moon and Mars in the 10th House

Moon and Mars are mutually intimate friends, and therefore these two planets together grant the best benefits from father and also from the main source of livelihood. The reason is that in their individual capacity too, Moon as well as Mars is most beneficial when in the 10th house.

If these individuals join active politics, success automatically comes to their door. If they want entry into high-level bureaucracy, there too they gain success, if not in the first attempt, surely in the second or third attempt. But they do not remain left out of selection ultimately.

These individuals often own their residence, sometimes in addition to every kind of property inherited from father or grandfather or from adoption in another family. They prefer to own real estate in joint-names of self and spouse.

The spouse generally dominates the individual only within the four walls of the house, and he or she does not mind it, moreso because outside home, spouse is of utmost help and support, praise and favourable publicity for them.

These individuals help and support own brother(s) and sister(s), but there is not love lost between them and the individuals, whatever the reasons.

The individuals attain importance, fame and influence on own without looking for support from the immediate family or the wider family.

Sometimes these individuals are alleged to be very cruel. It is correct to some extent, because when in position of power and authority, they have to maintain order and discipline everywhere.

If these individuals go into industry, specially on electrical or electronic side (including computers and telecommunications), they are extra successful in their venture throughout, provided they do not take outside partners blindly, or do not have a brother or sister as a real and active partner. A brother or sister as a sleeping partner is all right.

Relationship with father is always sweet and soft, but with mother, sometimes it comes under strain on account of spouse of the individual and then mother too becomes intolerant, not only towards the spouse but towards both husband and wife.

These individuals are very respectful, obedient (even when outside the school or college or university) and helpful towards their teachers, whatever the age and status of the individual in later life.

In matters of health of self or father or even of mother, exchange of care and service is perfectly all right, no grudge on any side.

Moon and Mercury in the 10th House

These two soft planets (Moon and Mercury, who are inimical towards each other) in the 10th house make the individuals work very hard as compared to others in likewise post/ position in the same line of career. And the result of the extra hard work very rare reaches them, and never in full quantum.

No doubt, the individual receives (often) high education as compared to the level of the family background and surroundings of the individual. But again the success achieved in career or profession or in self-employment or whatever is the source of livelihood is not fully paying for the education and hard work.

And the individual can do nothing except blame own stars or own bad luck.

If the individual becomes a teacher or a writer or a journalist or a publicist, he or she might find colleagues and even juniors going ahead on the path of progress and promotion or raise in emoluments and the individual remaining lower to those colleagues and juniors.

Even if the individual reaches the rank of a Minister in the Cabinet, his or her powers are encroached upon by a junior Minister or by the departmental Secretary or one lower to the Secretary in rank. If nothing else, the personal staff of the individual exercises some powers and authority of the individual without his or her knowledge and sanction or approval.

The individual often helps brother(s), sister(s) and even their progeny in their education, because the individual is already highly educated, but the individual gets no gratification in return. The individual's bare duty is to give and forget it, then and there.

Moon and Jupiter in the 10th House

Moon and Jupiter together belonging to the same group of planetary friendship often help the individual in education and also in post-education source of livelihood. The net results are that the individual becomes rich, prefers to possess bullion and precious stones, jewellery of high cost and of royal-type choice

The individual attains expertise, either by education or by work-experience, in law, drafting of legislative acts and or in drafting the constitution of the country, state or any high level organisation. The individual attains expertise in economics, accounts, business management, advisory position to a high dignitary like president of a country or prime minister or to a large department, or to any large organisation, commercial concern, industrial empire, etc.

If the individual goes into practice of law or that of an economic or accounts adviser, the individual is quite demanding in professional fee etc. If in service, the individual is quite demanding in salary and other perquisites too.

The individual is very much aware of qualifications and practical experience of self and demands the gains accordingly.

The individual goes and comes back to foreign countries, but unless Cancer, Capricorn, Aquarius or Pisces is in the 10th house, the individual is not desirous of settling in a foreign land. He or she is more particular about respect and honour in own land.

The individuals have no hesitation in advising avoidance or evasion of taxes, use of unhealthy or dishonest means in business or industrial products, and in the process sometimes get themselves into trouble. They have no reservation in owning substantial shares of a business or industrial venture. Going a step further, they do not hesitate to attain hidden, unrecorded partnership in such industries or business empires where these individuals advise irregularity. Unhealthy or dishonest practices in the resultant process find them in trouble with the governmental establishment and investigations, but only very rarely, because government investigators are also corrupt.

Moon and Venus in the 10th House

Moon and Venus combination in the 10th house is both, favourable and unfavourable in the same breath.

Favourable in the sense that it grants very comfortable, luxurious, fashionable living, a good numbers of friends from both sexes and in all fields of life. Oft-repeated foreign journeys for work and pleasure drop into the lap of the individual. The individual sometimes desires and often succeeds in settling in a foreign land, or at least in a city by the seacoast.

The individual gets enough of breast milk feeding from the mother. The individual also gets fair complexion going by the average complexion of that region or that family. Robust built of body and good health fit for hard work till reaching an old age.

The individual commands a large family of own or a big team of followers and retinue.

Chances are strong for the individual to go into medical line as a profession or to become a well-known musician, dancer, actor, actress, sculptor, architect, painter of renown, landscape and other designer. And success is guaranteed to her or him in any of these lines.

If the individual enters into a business of perfumery, fresh fruits, vegetables, sugar, milk and milk products, long cloth, clothes and garments, royal-type costumes, in these lines too, success awaits the individual from the very start.

The unfavourable effect of this combination in the 10th house is extra romantic nature, instant desire to contact and talk to the opposite sex, known, semi-known or unknown. A strong desire and determined effort is there to become intimate with the particular member of the opposite sex, with chances of a casual or regular friendship. This attitude or tendency doesn't take time to bring adverse results in its fold. The results can be disapproval, total rejection, taking precautionary steps against the individual, making a complaint to family and or guardians, drawing confrontation to the level of open insult or beating or making a complaint to the law and order system. It becomes very difficult for the individual, at least for the males, (because females do not go to the extent of that much liberty) to get out of the situation. It ultimately hurts and damages the reputation and popularity of the individual, adversely affecting the income too, sometimes forcing the individual to change place of work or place of residence or both from that locality or town.

The above kind of possibility is greater in the case of medical personnel, actors, actresses, suppliers of "extras" in the film line, those in stage performance line, those in practice of law, those in the profession of future-telling including astrologers and palmists as also spiritual healers, and the so-called *tantriks*, and those in professions alike to those mentioned here. Real *tantriks* normally do not indulge in this type of mal-practices of romantic approach to opposite sex.

Moon and Saturn in the 10th House

Moon and Saturn in the 10th house works hard on the source of income, quite opposite of Moon with Mars in the 10th house.

No doubt this combination helps getting into service with police, defence services (specially the army or the air force), Intelligence services of the police and defence forces, Nursing Service in the army, and leads the individual to a high rank. But there are pitfalls too in the course of service, not in terms of risk to life as such, but to face enquiry and investigations for acts of commission and omission. Often, at least for those in the defence services, these enquiries and investigations result in stoppage of promotion, reduction in rank or pay, dismissal from service or imposition of severe punishment.

Services rendered do not get recognition so well and at the right moment, as even minor mistakes or lapses in any kind of job get exposed and dealt with rather seriously (if not severely).

Change of job, or transfers on the wish and will of the seniors or employers become a routine matter, causing inconvenience to parents and also worry to the spouse.

More important part of Saturn (with Moon) in 10th house is that the individual is often obliged to accept a job, high or low to the education and experience of the individual. Even if the individual is able to start business or an industrial venture, many a time, circumstances and developments beyond the control of the individual oblige her or him to revert to service-career.

This combination often gives a sense of fear in the mind of the individual from father, and in spite of very good understanding between the two, a distance stays between the two. The individual feels hesitant to put forth, to father, own ideas, plans and matters relating to career, job or industrial venture. Normally if the individual is a son, for one reason or the other, he is unable to join hands with father for livelihood, or follow the line of career of the father in this behalf. There have been several cases where the father led the son (or daughter) to such education as would lead him to the career-line of the father. But after completion of the educational program (in some cases before completion too) the son takes to another line of career, totally different from that of the father.

An example would make the point clear. A father was in

the top-rank in Civil services of India (a full-fledged secretary to the Government of India), and wanted his only son to join the Administrative Service. The father (in company of the son) consulted the senior author about the son's success in the first attempt at the IAS examination and interview. It was predicted that the son would get finally selected for the Service, securing a very high rank in the list, but at the time of actual joining, he would walk away on a different path. The son secured the 23rd rank in the list of successful candidates for the IAS, but on the day of reporting at the Training School, he left for London to join business as a partner with an old classmate from his public school days.

The individual is always keen to suppress or totally remove from path, all adversaries, opponents and competitors. Initially she/ he meets with success, but subsequently in the process of revenge by the sufferer, the individual gets a defeat.

For good deeds, or for rigid policy and strict administration or management, the individual becomes somewhat unpopular among colleagues, subordinates and the public who come in contact with the individual for the work in her or his charge or control.

If the individual didn't have distance in relationship with father, she or he would feel it acutely from own progeny who would come to observe distance with the individual.

It is also likely that a distance comes to exist between the individual and the parents because the individual goes overseas for studies or career. Then the individual's attitude towards parents and the homeland undergoes a major change, to the financial benefit of the individual and the spouse or the immediate family in that foreign land, and to the disappointment of the parents.

When Moon is in waning process and very weak in *Sapta-Varga* strength, and the 10th house is owned by Venus or Saturn, there are chances of the individual being given away in adoption to a distant place. Or the individual is sent away to a boarding school in a different town at a very young age. It also happens that the individual suffers separation from the father, by father's another marriage, and father starts living totally away.

Or the individual loses father by death before individual is even 9 or 13 years old.

Virtually all ancient *acharyas* have laid down that Saturn and Moon together give leadership qualities to the individual and also capacity to influence general public. However those *acharyas* missed to clarify the point that the individual earns bitter feelings of the followers in the leadership matter, and earns notoriety for rigidity and exhibition of ego or pride larger than necessary.

Moon and Rahu in the 10th House

Being a shadow planet, Rahu is not very effective itself, but when in combination with Moon in the 10th house, Rahu reduces the effectivity of Moon by making it an 'eclipse' combination.

Generally, the individual, on his own, changes job quite often in life, or is obliged by pressure from bosses to quit or actual dismissal from service. In the matter of business, the individual tries to become rich overnight, comparing self with others growing rich quickly. The he or she gets stumbled in losses because of hard competition in rates and quality of work, and has to change the line of business or change the place itself, if the individual is keen to continue in the same line of business.

With regard to relations with father, they are neither very sweet nor sour, just average. No doubt, the individual tries to be serviceful or financially helpful to parents in their old age, and is not inclined to listen to the spouse against this attitude. To make the point more clear, even a daughter tries to help the parents financially and would not listen to the husband if he were opposed to it.

By chance, if Sun or Mars be in the 5th or 9th house, the individual has always to be cautious not to come in adverse notice of the superiors or employers in case the individual is in a job. If the individual is in business or in industry or in any kind of self-employment, he or she shouldn't to come to adverse notice of the law and order system. If Jupiter were in 6th, 8th or 12th house, the taxation problems would loom over the head of the individual. In all such matters, Moon is unable to plan path of relief or rescue, as it is under 'eclipse' combination with Rahu, and has therefore to depend on advice of others. For this purpose, Ketu in 4th house proves helpful in formation of reliable friends' circle for the individual or spouse. Their advice proves very helpful.

Moon and Ketu in the 10th House

The results of Moon and Ketu combination in the 10th house are much better as compared to Rahu and Moon in 10th house. Firstly, the individual is always careful and alert about the good or harmful outcome of own acts of commission and omission.

Secondly, so long father is alive, he always helps the individual to the extent possible financially, by good advice, by speaking to someone in authority to help the individual in a difficult situation. The individual too maintains very cordial and affectionate relations with father (though to a less extent with mother, because of Rahu in the 4th house).

Thirdly, the individual doesn't change a job or business line very often, and doesn't give up one source of livelihood unless picks up another with certainty. The individual knows that friends cannot help always and in all situations. Therefore the individual learns to live on "self help" more than anything else.

This combination doesn't make the individual very keen to migrate to another country, though going for higher studies is altogether a different matter. The individual goes and comes back after the educational program is finished.

MOON IN THE 11TH HOUSE

Being a soft planet, Moon is helpful to the individual earning livelihood comfortably and honourably. The individual generally stays honest in money dealings, is not inclined to demand or expect or accept illegal gratifications. Sometimes the bribe-givers try to give a bribe to the progeny or try to oblige the progeny in some other manner as would make the individual too obliged, and help the bribe-giver's cause.

The question of loss from an elder brother or sister normally doesn't arise, as the individual is always careful and alert in own dealings of money.

The individual is very careful and cautious in proper growth and education of the progeny, though the question of education depends on the stars of each child. The individual is always open minded about any love affair of any child, provided it is at the proper age, and the individual tries level best if the child and that friend could get married to each other. If the chances are less or altogether remote, the individual cautions the child, but doesn't force the child to break up the relationship.

The individual is kind, considerate and helpful to the spouses of the children, provided none of them misbehaves with the elders, because Moon in the 11th house is always mindful of disrespect from the youngsters towards any elder whether in the family or outside.

The individual, whether a man or a woman, doesn't believe in causing miscarriage or abortion of any pregnancy outside a marriage bond, say during unmarried state or when one is widow or widower or a divorcee. On birth, the illegitimate child receives the same attention and love as a legitimate child would get.

Being in the 2nd position from the 10th house, which rules father, the individual is assured of due inheritance from the father. However, if the father predeceases the mother, sometimes mother causes, intentionally or unintentionally, some damage to the inheritance rights of the individual. The reason is very clear. The 4th house rules Mother, and Moon in the 11th house is in 8th position from the 4th house. Thus the mother develops a feeling, wrongly or rightly, that the individual (be it a son or daughter) is not totally serviceful and obedient to the mother. Such feelings are always very much inside the person concerned, and these inner feelings are not known to others, and cannot be remedied. These feelings get exposed only when the partition of family properties and assets is finalised by the mother.

Moon and Sun in the 11th House

Please see the chapter on Sun, the portion under heading "Sun with Moon in the 11th house". No addition or alternation needed.

Moon and Mars in the 11th House

The Moon and Mars combination in the 11th house often makes the individual very much interested in owning immovable property, owning the residence, owning any other premises needed by the individual for personal use. On account of this desire (or a kind of greed) for property, the individual doesn't mind taking recourse to even utter dishonesty in earning money by hook or crook.

The individual is, in the normal course of life, quite miserly, whether the question is of giving financial help or other support to old parents, or of upbringing and education of own progeny. It might be the question of giving any kind of financial help to elder brother or sister in his or her hour of need. If the individual gives any help in terms of money, he or she always expects its repayment in cash or return in kind in one shape or the other. Even from the parents, the individual wishes a bigger share in inheritance in return for the financial support given to them.

The individual has always to be on alert with regard to blood pressure and any minor or mild heart ailment, for two reasons. Firstly, the 11th house is in the 8th position from the 4th house, which rules the heart. Secondly, the 11th house is directly concerned with left side of chest, left ribs, left shoulder, the portion of body below the left shoulder. Normally it is believed that Mars in 11th house grants very perfect health, but generally beginners in astrology overlook the 8:6 relationship between 4th and the 11th house.

Mars induces and encourages the individual to keep a strict vigilant eye on the assets owned by the parents, specially under control of the father, because Mars in 11th house is in 2nd position from 10th house which rules father. The individual is willing to make father poorer, but would not tolerate self being made poorer for sake of father, in any manner.

Moon and Mercury in the 11th House

Mercury with Moon in the 11th house supports every point described above in discussion about Moon alone in the 11th house.

Mercury tries to give a very good collection of useful books and other reading material to the individual. This combination also gives the individual very excellent command on language, which gets expressed in praiseworthy manner. Therefore this command on language proves very useful in writing and drafting, whether for self-interest or for the employer or for customers and clients, whatever is the source of livelihood of the individual. These individuals are high level experts in spoken word too.

Therefore generally it is found that men and women with this combination in the 11th house go into teaching line or journalism or writing books and articles for print media, or for stage performances and film line. Alternative source of livelihood for these individuals is running a school or college or any training institute or functioning as a preacher or priest or on the management side of an educational institute.

Further Moon and Mercury together make an individual willing to extend physical service and monetary help to father, elder brother or sister or other elders including the mother, not taking into account any strain in relationship with mother on account of self or spouse. The problem in this case is that the spouse is not very trustful of the mother-in-law with regard to the progeny of the self and the spouse. That is the main reason for distrust in mother, and mother too realises this attitude, and remains withdrawn from the grandchildren though unhappy over this attitude.

As far as possible, the individual stays honest in money dealings, and also in a job which has public dealings in some manner or the other.

The individual pays special attention to the education of the progeny, including development of general knowledge by suggesting and providing material for reading during school and college days. The individual guides the children about the line of career and education leading to it, but does not force the progeny to follow that advice blindly or strictly. The progeny get the freedom of thinking and deciding in this behalf.

Moon and Jupiter in the 11th House

An individual with Moon and Jupiter combination in the 11th house generally goes into a profession or career related to law, economics, accounting, business management, and is always careful to receive education to that end.

The individual doesn't mind receiving costly gifts and presents from people with whom the individual has official dealings, whether one may call it bribes or not. The gifts can be in hidden cash too. The individual might drop hints about it, but is generally not observed demanding gratification directly. The best method adopted by the individual is to drop hints about needs of the family (spouse and children included) for costly items, ornaments, items of rich jewellery etc. The excuse can even be of educational high fee of the children or a marriage ceremony within the family.

The individual generally renders financial help to father and other elders in the family, but keeps a record of it, and mentions it at some crucial moment.

When the individual is in legal profession, she or he would not mind, sometimes under pressure from judge in return for a favour in some other client's case, or under any greed or other personal consideration, to indulge in double-dealing. That is working as a lawyer of one client, to give secret points of the own client, to the opposite party.

These individual are vulnerable to complaints of the respiratory system, chronic complaints of cough, cold, pain in the chest region, and in case of women having extra milk in the breast on child birth than the newly born can consume.

An important point about these individuals is that they always want to pay anyone and everyone for their purchases or for services rendered. They are honest paymasters in that respect.

Moon and Venus in the 11th House

Ancients have said:

> *"prakratim yaanti bhootani, nigrah kim karrishyati"*

meaning an individual is given to one's own nature, and (any kind) of control cannot help against it.

So, Venus means romance, loving tendency, and Moon means Mind. The two together will give the individual a nature full of romantic tendencies, even if they are not implemented in action for one reason or the other. Whether a man or woman, the individual naturally gets attracted towards a beautiful or charming personality of the opposite sex. Whatever the modern culture may advocate about homosexuality and lesbian bent of mind and action, the hard truth is that a woman does not get romantically attracted towards another woman, and the same is true of man too. If woman or man gets attracted towards a person of the same sex, the main underlying reason would be that particular woman has some evident masculine qualities or the particular man has some feminine qualities evident to others that the attraction towards the same sex works. No doubt, there can be some reasons too for indulgence in same-sex physical relationship.

In some matters, results of this combination are similar to Mercury and Moon in the 11th house and in some other matters similar to Jupiter and Moon in the 11th house (reference preceding paragraphs above).

For example, these individuals, specially men, would not always refuse offer of a charming woman to influence their judgement, order, decision, action, which was originally meant to go against the person, who supplied that charming woman. The question of supply arises in very rare cases for securing the favour of women judges, or officers in power and authority (in public or private establishments or organisations), in virtually all developing, or under-developed and undeveloped countries. Cases have been in recent past of supply of young youths to women in power and authority, in developed and very advanced countries. One reason is that in many countries, marriages at proper age have become next to impossible, number of bachelors and maidens in increasing fast, but the biological needs overrule every situation of restraint in anyone's life.

These individuals are fond of learning music, dances, any branch of fine arts, acting in dramas and stage performances, as a hobby or as a means to come in contact with people including those of the opposite sex.

These individuals are often rich enough to afford these costly hobbies. If nothing else, they like to attend at least music concerts, ballroom dances, dramas and stage performances. They do not hesitate even to finance these arts and performances.

These individuals normally want their marriage to work and continue, and if necessary, they do not mind extending the same freedom of romanticism to spouses as are enjoyed by self.

They are also fond of good dresses, ornaments and jewellery (not costume jewellery because these days people recognise real jewellery and artificial one) to appear attractive in public, sometimes inviting risk of theft, robbery etc.

These individuals have to stay preventive against repeated attacks of cough, cold, bad throat etc, because it is very likely to become chronic and lead to other complaints of health.

These individuals are on the border between being helpful and unhelpful towards father, mother and other elder relatives, depending more on own circumstances than the circumstances of these relatives, also on the needs and attitude of their progeny, if grown up enough to express an opinion.

These individuals make very good physicians of any system of medicine, and they find it easy to secure admission into a medical school or college even in modern times of cutthroat competition for admission.

Moon and Saturn in the 11th House

The individuals with Moon and Saturn in the 11th house are often fond of blue sapphires, dark colour clothes, woollens (even in summer), keeping hair on the head in disorder for adding glamour to personality, it is so even in cases of girls and grown up women.

They have no distinction between honesty and dishonesty; their main aim is to have money, more and even more money. In addition, they are granted good riches by this combination.

They normally keep very good health, are stout by physique, ladies have charming breasts. They are given to going for a walk regularly, whatever the weather round the year. They are often gifted by every kind of means of transport according to their desires, much less dependent on their actual needs. It is so, right from the school days.

Sometimes these individuals either join a gang of robbers and thieves, or work for them in a clandestine manner, going to the extent of giving them shelter and disposing of their contraband goods, providing them dresses and other means for disguise.

These individuals are harsh in maintaining discipline in the younger generation, whether it is their own progeny or children of others. However, at the same time they are fully considerate regarding needs of the younger generation under their care or responsibility.

These individuals go into industrial ventures, in building and construction line. Some of them also function as high-level contractors, if they are qualified engineers and technicians, otherwise function as small contractors. They rarely suffer loss in own venture, and they take care that their employer (when in service) also does not suffer loss as far as work of these individuals is concerned. They normally do not tolerate interference of others in their work, nor do they interfere in working of others, unless those people are subordinates, helpers or co-workers to these individuals.

These individuals do not have the least hesitation in having abortions of unwanted or untimely pregnancy. In these matters, they do not bother much about approval of the spouse.

They are inclined to giving physical or financial help to parents, brothers, sisters, any relatives, but they are less involved in emotions of love and affection. They do not expect expression of similar emotions for self. They do not bother as to what others think in this matter.

These individuals are very good in sports and games, get rewards and prizes, get recognition, and work hard for these achievements. Sometimes they neglect the studies or the academic Exams too for partaking in some special event of games or sports.

Moon and Rahu in the 11th House

Results of Moon and Rahu combination are simple and straightforward.

These individuals always want high income by any method or means. Not very keen to invest in property, and prefer to have a partnership for running an industry or business or contractor line. They never hesitate to invest money freely in a partnership venture, but keep a strict eye to avoid malpractices of anyone including the partners. They are very strict in recovery of their dues, whether it is for goods supplied of services rendered or loans given.

They allow full freedom to wife for working outdoors and generally do not suspect her conduct or character unless they have solid and confirmed grounds to do so and even then try to amend matters then straightaway go for a divorce.

In spite of 'eclipse' combination, Rahu doesn't suppress much of the free functioning of Moon in the 11th house. If the individual is keen for migration to a foreign land, she or he finds full support and help from all concerned, and somehow migration gets managed visa too to uneasy countries like USA, France and UK gets ultimately managed.

They work on average basis for studies, but see to it that they get their promotion from class to class in school, and get their degree for studies in college or university. They are good in sports and games, but do not go mad after this side of the life, nor do they avoid studies for sake of games and sports.

Moon and Ketu in the 11th House

Individuals with Moon and Ketu in the 11th house are interested in games and sports but unlike other student, they are not mad after them. It is so because they are very serious about their studies and always work for a higher rank or high percentage or an excellent report in studies. They maintain the same standard in college or university too.

If they do not take to writing, journalism, functioning as a priest or preacher, at least they remain in touch with these lines of profession. Sometimes they adopt one of these lines as a side source of income or for publicity in print media.

They have work-oriented health until late 60's of age, because they are always effortful for keeping good working health. They do not get good health automatically like individuals having Saturn or Rahu in the 11th house.

They are open to gifts, presents and gratification in any shape or form, but stay within reasonable limits, and never press for it while granting any favour to a person seeking it. Normally they do not alter their judgement, decision, and action for sake of gratification. In other words, they maintain honesty of purpose.

They do not have to go for medical termination of pregnancy, because they are often careful in avoiding pregnancy when not desired, and secondly sometimes the miscarriage or abortion takes place automatically.

They are well possessed and well-to-do financially, more because of hard work of self and/or spouse, and not so much on account of malpractice and dishonesty.

Moon in the 12th House

To get a correct appreciation of Moon in the 12th house, one must first bear in mind the subjects ruled by or concerned with the 12th house.

Briefly, they have problems in married life, owing to less capacity or desire or interest in husband-wife physical relationship. Problems in getting progeny soon after marriage, problems relating to health and education of the progeny (this being 8th from the 5th house) also face them.

They are often subject to temporary loss of or reduction in earnings from the main source of livelihood, resulting in mental disturbance. Epilepsy (full or partial, of short or long duration), a simple touch of partial insanity (of short duration or life long), and other mental worries loom over the head of the individual. It also causes heavy expenditure, loss of money, loss of prestige, arrest, penalty, punishment, imprisonment, loss by theft, cheating, robbery, dacoity or by any natural calamity.

The 12th house concerns with father's brother(s) and sister(s), also extra-marital relationship of self or spouse and attitude of one or both towards it.

Because of these important subjects relating to the 12th house and Moon ruling the Mind, one must take into account what Rasi is in the 12th house. Who is the lord of that Rasi, and where is that lord of the Rasi in the 12th house is placed in the birth chart and the Navamsha chart.

For example, if Moon-owned Rasi Cancer is in the 2nd, 5th, 6th or 8th house, and Moon in 12th house. Then Moon would give disturbed state of mind, worrying mind, fickle-mind or jealous mind towards others, even towards the spouse for achievement and progress of spouse in own work.

If Moon is in Sagittarius or in a Rasi owned by Sun, Mars or Saturn, there are strong chances of the individual getting into a trap with the law and order system, whether the individual is actually at fault or not. It might or might not come as a result of a regular enquiry or investigation against the individual.

Moon in 12th house sometimes gives drinking as a regular habit, and its adverse effect on married life, ultimately leading to extra-marital relationship. Some times, in the case of some rare individuals, the opponents or competitors try to involve the individual into an extra marital relationship to damage the reputation or good conduct record of the individual. If the competitors or opponents fail in involving the individual into an extra marital relationship, they try to develop a tendency in the individual to spend extravagantly or unnecessarily on the spur of the moment or on provocation. This would ultimately lead the individual to adopt an open mind for acceptance of gifts and other gratifications, and thereby earn a bad name. Such a situation as this might lead to an enquiry or investigation and nothing else, at least mental torture to the individual.

Moon in the 12th house thus rarely gives any comfortable results, and when joined by other planet in the 12th house, the position becomes more unfavourable and sometimes uncontrollable.

Moon and Sun in the 12th House

Please refer to the "Sun and Moon in the 12th house" paragraphs in the Chapter on Sun in the 12th Houses, which is complete in itself.

Moon and Mars in the 12th House

Generally, the results are the same as those of Sun with Moon in the 12th house. The additional point is that this combination might involve the individual in charges of criminal violence, fatal attack on someone with the aid of a weapon or without weapon, chances of imprisonment or sometimes death sentence too depending on the law of the Land. The individual might indulge, though rarely, in unapprovable acts of commission and omission to help father in his hour of extreme difficulty on any account.

Moon and Mars in the 12th house are capable of leading to serious disturbance in married life and the individual is charged with extreme anger and resultant violence towards the spouse. The final outcome is imaginable.

The individual is often very strict and sometimes violent too towards own progeny for educational progress and keeping discipline in them. The progeny do mind this strictness till the age of 14 years, but subsequently understands the value and worth of this kind of treatment from a parent, and forgets or even forgives the past.

This combination is capable of giving very serious losses owing to theft, robbery, and loss or damage or injury by fire and also by heavy cost of repairs or reconstruction or on medical treatment etc.

However, the individual pays greater attention to the main source of income and does not let lethargy to interfere in the hard work. Another favourable result is that the individual renders every kind of physical service and bears financial expenditure required for best medical treatment of spouse in any kind of complaint of health. This results into forgiveness on part of the spouse for the individual in the event of harsh behaviour or violence-mixed attitude.

Moon and Mercury in the 12th House

The first result of Moon and Mercury together in the 12th house is visible in the very childhood of the individual, who exhibits rather poor grasp with regard to studies. It leads to weak foundation and it is difficult to make amends as the individual grows in years. However, this is not an incurable problem. It can be cured by instant care from the mother's side. But this care has to be taken between the age of 3 and 5 years age of the child. It would be virtually impossible to improve this aspect after the child crosses the 12 years of age.

The individual is slow and lethargic in keeping accounts with the result that several times, losses have to be suffered. Many a time, people demand payment for supplies, a second time, or if the individual is in business, the buyers claim they made purchases only five times, though actually it is six or even seven times. If it is the supplier, he claims that he supplied six or seven consignments of goods, though he might have supplied it only 5 times.

A businessman was neither regular nor prompt in keeping accounts. He sent ₹43 lakhs in cash to another businessman in a locked and sealed briefcase, but did not keep a written record then about the day and time of sending the money. After 14 days, the receiving businessman demanded another ₹20 lakhs, claiming that the original businessman had sent only 23 lakhs rupees. Without proper records, the first businessman had to pay another ₹20 lakhs helplessly. The senior author had in general cautioned the first businessman in advance (and in writing) that without being prompt and regular in written accounts, he would suffer a big loss. And in the written predictions for that particular year-chart of the businessman, the author had again cautioned him about a big loss of money owing to his lack of keeping adequate record of accounts. After this event, the businessman paid an additional handsome fee to the author for such correct guidance.

Another example of Mercury and Moon in the 12th house is given. A lady, returning from a foreign country, was detained by the Customs officers. They had searched her baggage and had asked her to give a written statement. She already knew the law that she could refuse to give a statement without the presence of her lawyer. But she thought that there was no harm in giving a truthful statement outright. She did so, and consequently her husband (and family) had to fight a case in a court of law for next four months for grant of bail. The further story is not known to the author, because he had stopped giving consultations, since they were not taking the guidance given to them. Sometimes individuals talk loosely or out of turn, and suffer the consequences.

Those in any career connected with Mercury like teaching, journalism, reading news on radio and visual media, etc., have to change their job quite often, because they are found lacking in promptness, in punctuality, keeping attendance to the correct minute, though they are deemed very fit for the job.

Moon and Jupiter in the 12th House

The combination of Moon and Jupiter in the 12th house leads to problems with law, with banks, with insurance companies, with litigation whether started by self or involved as a respondent. Many a time, some of these individuals get involved in charges of perjury, standing patent surety, security or guarantee for every tom, dick and harry, and the result is serious trouble for them with legal action hanging over the head.

These individuals many a time estimate their capacity for repayment of a loan within a particular period totally on guesswork and on expectations, which do not stand the test of truthfulness. Then they get into the clutches of Shylock-type moneylenders, who suck virtually every drop of their blood, besides every penny available with them. Extra precaution is unavoidable for these individuals while getting into debts.

Though very rarely, these individuals get charged for participation or at least active association with any theft, robbery, fake currency, dealing in contraband goods, and supporting the families of criminals and smugglers in trouble. Some others are suspected of monetary corruption or bribery, and are subjected to thorough investigation, by Special agencies, under the impression and information that the individual is a member of a regular unlawful assembly or crime-oriented gang or group of persons.

If these individuals are before an Investigation-cum-semi-judicial authority for tax evasion or any social crime, they suffer heavy penalty and fine in cash, without thorough examination of their activity.

These individuals sometimes want but fail to get formal education in law, economics and accounts. Even then, they prove very able and successful guardians to their wards.

Another unfavourable result of Moon and Jupiter together in the 12th house is that these individuals suffer substantial loss by theft, robbery, cheating, etc., or snatching from women folk of the family, or from the spouse or from any other member of the family. Loss can be on account of dropping cash or item of jewellery by carelessness, or by giving non-justified monetary help to any member of the wider family, under one excuse or the other.

Moon and Venus in the 12th House

The individual with Moon and Venus in the 12th house would have liberal and helpful attitude towards females in the wider family, and this would be often misunderstood as undue attention to or interest in that particular person. These individuals spend, as a habit, excessively on clothes, dresses, apparel, costly costumes for self and members of the immediate family. Sometimes they are given to spending more than they can afford, and take resort to incurring debts at very high rate of interest. Because Moon too is in the 12th house, these individuals regret this unessential borrowing later on.

Some of these individuals are fond of regular drinks or any kind of drugs, if Venus happens to be lord of the 7th or the 12th house itself, or Cancer is in the 8th house, (which means Scorpio is in the 12th, which is the house of debilitation for Moon). These individuals try to drag their spouse (which generally means wife) to join them in the drinking or drug habit. Because the 12th house is in the 8th position from the 5th house, which rules progeny as also mood of the individual towards progeny, this habit becomes a disaster for the children in matters of their education, if not health too.

Extra marital relationship or having casual physical relation, like "one-night-stand" is commonly found in a good number of these individuals (though not all, because there is exception to every rule). It is not uncommon to women folk too, except that they are good at keeping it a guarded secret, (at least in India) in upper and middle class families. And it is natural with some of these individuals (not all) to get into the habit of gambling and speculation as the main source of livelihood. Often, ultimately they suffer heavy losses and then seek relief into drinking, debauchery, cheating others and to tell lies. They become less communicative with members of the family other than the spouse. An additional result of acts of commission and omission of these individuals becomes a source of worry, torture and sometimes disaster to the education of the progeny, and the children have to "endure what cannot be cured". The mental and/ or physical torture becomes double for the child where both parents are given to drinks and drugs, and allied habits.

However, unless Sun is in the 5th or 8th house, or Mars in the 2nd or 8th house or Jupiter in the 6th or 8th house, these individuals and/ or their spouses do not have to face tirades of and troubles from of the law and order machinery.

Many among these individuals form groups and gangs for debauchery, or running or helping in running brothels, centres for homosexuality and lesbian activity or unlawful sale of liquor and alcoholic stuff, kidnapping of young girls for immoral activity. Some of them go to the extent of managing sexual orgies or any sort of immoral activity, unapproved by the normal social laws.

Moon and Saturn in the 12th House

Moon and Saturn together in the 12th house is indeed a very difficult combination. Moon is a soft, easy and vulnerable planet, while Saturn hard and cruel with criminal tendency at its extreme, when it is in the 12th house. Saturn in 12th actually stands for bad habits, bad deeds and punishment, besides loss of money or assets and honour of self or of the spouse or of the entire family.

No use counting the mischievous, unlawful, or criminal activity to which Saturn might lead the individual, who cannot even claim that the serious nature and consequences of the unlawful or criminal act hadn't gone home with the individual. Saturn is capable of dragging the mind and action of the individual to any unsocial and/ or unlawful act. This might include cheating, pilferage, bribery, theft, robbery, gambling, kidnapping for ransom or for immoral acts, beating, serious violence, helping or otherwise associating with killing, murder, embezzlement, giving threats to officials or private sector bosses for blackmailing or getting favours for their patrons and money-suppliers.

One very special quality of these individuals is that they understand the consequences of their actions and seldom entertain fear for the consequences, even if it is a sentence of rigorous imprisonment or sentence of capital punishment. Some of the individuals of this category are very merciful and sympathetic to sufferers, and are often keen to help them or provide them protection from further sufferings. For sake of this deed of mercy or charity, they do not hesitate to risk their money, or any valuable possession including life or limb.

These individuals are often harsh and rough to own progeny for their educational progress or upkeep of health and good habits. They seldom find time and a few of them lack in capacity and qualifications to render practical help to the children in their studies. However all the time they try to find fault with the children for one reason or the other and are rough to them, sometimes beating them black and blue. Later on, they express regret to the children and try to appease the children by sweets and costly gifts, picnics, taking on a travel, etc.

Often these individuals are a problem for the wider family and they feel the wider family is an unwanted botheration or burden for them. In the same breath, members of the wider family seek help in terms of hard money and other favours from these individuals, and actually get them. Even then, the result is criticism and discarding these individuals by the same relatives who received all kind of help from them. God may help both sides!

Moon and Rahu in the 12th House

Rahu and Moon combination generally gives results somewhat similar to the Moon and Saturn combination in the 12th house, but the seriousness, severity attributable to Saturn is lacking in this case.

The individuals are neither helpful nor cruel and separated from the wider family. They are no doubt harsh to the children but as far as possible, do not take resort to beating the kids, whatever the fault, default or pitfall on part of the children as a group or as an individual.

Additional point about these individuals is that they have no hitch or hesitation to embezzle funds of any charitable, religious or social service formation, establishment or organisation. They presume, rightly or wrongly that those funds are being wasted on those activities related to religion or charity or social work, and also rightly or wrongly their presumption is that they (the individuals) have naturally better use and utility for those funds.

Unless Mars or Saturn, or even Sun is in the 5th or the 8th house, Rahu and Moon in 12th house rarely lead an individual to rigorous imprisonment and never to capital punishment. It is so in spite of the individual getting involved in one or other of such immoral type of criminal activities as Saturn normally leads the individual to.

Another unfavourable result of this combination is generally towards pregnant women, with whom their husbands indulge in full-fledged sex even after the 6th month. By then the baby in the womb has developed full human shape, and often the baby's head is engaged towards the mouth of the vagina. This act on part of the husband, at least when wife is in lying condition, because at that advanced stage, she can hardly physically afford to sitting or standing posture, hurts the baby straight on the head. The result is some kind of invalidity in the child when born as a full para.

Moon and Ketu in the 12th House

In Moon's combination with Ketu in the 12th house, it normally functions like a soft planet, actually very much like Mercury with same good and bad points in the result.

Sometimes this combination makes the individual interested in homosexuality and lesbian acts, but is always keen to keep it a secret. In reality, the secrecy never stands in about 90% cases.

One special impact of this combination is on the baby in the womb of the mother. Very often it is found that a newly born infant has some defect of mind or formation of limbs.

Instead of repeating what has been stated in the last para above under "Moon and Rahu in the 12th House", readers may please study the contents of those paragraphs carefully, because this phenomenon is applicable in case of "Moon and Ketu too in the 12th House". This result of hurting the baby in the womb acts more harshly in the case of Moon and Ketu together in the 12th house than what it is in case of "Moon and Rahu in the 12th House"

Ketu and Moon combination can lead to financial loss, penalty, and heavy fine in terms of cash or simple imprisonment for a short period. But this combination never leads to such severe punishments or losses as are applicable to the individual by "Moon and Jupiter" or "Moon and Saturn" or "Moon and Rahu" in the 12th house.

No doubt losses can be caused in likewise manner and by such causes as are caused by "Moon and Mercury in the 12th House".

It may also be noted that Ketu induces or encourages the individual for acts of charity and help to real sufferers without consideration of caste, creed, colour or religious inclination.

MARS IN THE 12 HOUSES

MARS IN GENERAL

Mars is lord of human skin, blood flowing through veins, and the menstrual system in females (humans & animals). Astrologically, semen is considered as the most valuable substance of blood, its protein condensate. Thus, though Venus is associated commonly (and correctly too) to be the lord of semen, it is also recognised that (ejaculation or propulsion of semen will not take place unless the male reproductive organ is engorged with blood): semen is the outcome from blood system. By implication, the entire system of procreation depends first on Mars, and then on Venus. We know that a woman is considered capable of conceiving only so long as her menstrual cycle is actively functioning in her body. This is normally from the age of 12 years to about 45 to 60 years. No doubt there are exceptions where a woman went into menopause much before the age of 45, or just after the birth of her first child. Mars is the lord of the uterus, and allied limbs in the physical structure of women. Then Mars also rules the warmth in the human body (physically – body temperature; mentally – irritation, and anger; emotionally – courage and bravery, feelings of brotherhood and fellowship, strength (vigour, power) in the human body (that of both males and females). It is this strength (vigour and power) which leads to accomplishment of hard tasks including that pertaining to defence and protection of self, family, society and the country. However problems related to neurological ailments or diseases concern both Mars and Moon, but more specifically to Mars.

Then comes another important domain of Mars, the functioning of the heart. In a sense it can be said so because heart is the prime organ in the body related to blood. If the heart stops, the body stops. The individual is dead for all practical purposes. Mars and Venus are collectively responsible for organs of procreation in males, as also orgasm in females. Thus it is the primary influence of Mars and subsidiary influence of Venus that human beings (also animals) become capable of creating another body, another life similar to that of self. Whether we go by the procreation theory or not, it has to be admitted that for pleasure of mutual physical relationship between man and woman, it is firstly Mars (and then Venus) that play the most important role.

It is in this context that Mars has been given the most important consideration in the matter of matching of horoscopes of a man and a woman for successful matrimony. This, then leads us to the theory of defective position of Mars in a Birth-chart from the angle of married life, details of which can be consulted in '**Star Guide To Love and Marriage**' from pages 75 to 92, (published by Parsai Publishers (ptparsai@gmail.com) and also available with Rupa Publications India Pvt. Ltd).

Thus though each and every planet has its importance through the Birth-chart and allied calculations, Mars has special importance on basic human life.

It should be keep in mind that normally Mars, Saturn, Jupiter (and sometimes Moon) are apt to cause fatal illness, accident, or death too. It is the speciality of Mars that it causes death by fire, electricity, acids, inflammables (fire include gun-fire or big fires like the one caused in September 2001 by the crash of aircraft into the World Trade Centre, New York and in Washington). Moon causes death by poisoning, serious illness, or drowning in water or meeting with an accident in water. Saturn would cause death by non-bleeding illness or injury (routine minor bleeding included). Given below are examples of all three kinds of deaths:

> *(a) Pandit Nehru, the first Prime Minister of India met with his death in the last week of May 1964, due to illness because of conflict of Mars+Jupiter with Moon.*
>
> *(b) Death of Indira Gandhi, also the Prime Minister of India, was caused by gun-fire on the last day of October, 1984 because Rahu had a 6:8 conflict with Mars on the one hand, and Saturn on the other. Saturn rules employees too, and she shot dead by her own security-personnel.*

(c) Anwar Sadat, President of Egypt was also killed by gunfire when Mars was involved in a conflict with Saturn and Rahu.

However, **extreme caution is required** when making predictions of such nature about political leaders, because fanatics or misguided elements, and/or state investigating agencies may hold the astrologer guilty of complicity or encouraging, or instigating any attempt caused towards a popular personality. On the flip side, if an astrologer refrains from predicting such events, questions are raised as to why not!

Mars In the 1st House

This position of Mars normally gives annoyance, irritation, anger, easily vulnerable to fever, problem in the thoracic region, skin ailment, short eye-sight (needing correction), bragging (sometimes in reality) about one's physical strength, vigour and deeds of valour, and threats related thereto.

Because Mars in the 1st House has direct aspect (*drishti*) on the 7th house, it sometimes leads to psychological maladjustment between husband and wife (or man and woman living together).

Mars and Sun or Moon in the 1st House

The results of these two combinations have been discussed under Sun and Moon's respective positions in the 1st House.

Mars and Mercury in the 1st House

Mars with Mercury in the 1st house gives the individual capacity for intellectual control on irritation and anger, and saves the situation from threats or actual violence. Persons with this combination sometimes turn out to be good writers, poets, and producers of episodes, serials, and films. These individuals work as actors or actresses or director or producer of such films, which all have elements of violence in utterances, dialogues, speeches, stimulation, provocation etc.; they prove to be efficient orators of provocative speeches capable of influencing the audience.

Mars and Jupiter in the 1st House

Mars and Jupiter in the 1st House makes a person very impressive judge, advocate, qualified accountant, negotiator in business or in diplomatic matters, envoys with limited or specialised task, cashiers and treasurers. Jupiter exercises a typical kind of restraint on irritation and anger of the individual, moreso towards one's spouse, enhancing the quality of mutual adjustment.

Mars and Venus in the 1st House

Mars and Venus combine in the 1st House makes a man or woman extra desirous and capable of marital pleasures, given to considerable liking for luxurious living, material and gadget-oriented comforts of life. If either of these two stars is lord of the 12th house, the person gets given to alcohol, fashionable dresses and fond of diamond items on body of self or spouse. These people sometimes become fond of imported items of daily use.

They have little hesitation in having extra-marital relations or having more than one spouse or companion in life, at one and the same time or one after another. In this type of cases, Navamsha-chart in horoscopes of men and Trinshansha-chart in horoscopes of women must be examined for a co-ordinated study. When Mars is lord of the 9th house in the Birth-chart, the life partner would tolerate the entry of the third element in their married (or companionship) life. But when Mars or Venus is lord of the 12th house, the life partner (or companion) would dispute the very entry of the third element in mutual life. These individuals often keep companionship in high strata of society, and are given to drinks and other titbits of club life.

Mars and Saturn in the 1st House

Mars and Saturn together in the 1st House increase the unfavourable pressure on married life, adding obstinacy to irritation and anger, and sometimes lead to violence in married life. These individuals are rough and rude not only towards children and younger generation in the house but also towards elder and outsiders, quickly aroused to quarrel, threats, and even violence. But these individuals make very good warriors, commanders in combatant forces, spies and intelligence officers, smugglers, traders in humans, kidnappers, and extortionists. They make efficient police officers, informers and tutored witnesses in courts, though they don't hesitate to double-dealing (since Mars and Saturn are bitter enemies of each other). In civilian jobs, these people get slow promotions in spite of their ability and good work, and are often victims of jealousy of concerned colleagues and unconcerned outsiders.

If Mars and Saturn are in a Rasi owned by Mars, the results are more damaging, but if Capricorn is in the 1st House, the unfavourable impact of Mars with Saturn combine would get reduced, though it would continue to be so if Aquarius is in the 1st House. Other Rasis in Ascendant would not make much difference in the impact of these two stars. One point worth note is that this combine can give complaints of health to women with regard to their menstrual cycle, pain in waist region, trouble with lower portion of spine, arthritis, etc. When Jupiter too is associated with this combination, the person might suffer from cystic fibrosis, or allied complaints.

Mars and Rahu in the 1st House

Mars and Rahu combine in the 1st House gives a sharp sense of Ego to the individual, and even a hint hurting this ego gives considerable irritation, anger and outburst to the person opposite. This sense of ego is more directly operative towards one's spouse or friend of the opposite sex. Several love affairs meet their untimely end at initial stage itself owing to this combination in the 1st House.

Rahu generally gives inflated formation of feelings, and in this case it becomes inflated formation of ego, irritation and anger, also bragging about one's worldly possessions and achievements. Another important point is that Rahu is a shadow planet and it is in full operation with regard to its results when it is in the company of Mars in the 1st house.

Mars and Ketu in the 1st House

When Ketu is in the 1st House giving company to Mars, having the attributes of a soft planet, Ketu helps in softening the irritation, anger and hard attitudes of Mars. These people should avoid consumption of large quantity of red chillies, as they are often vulnerable to piles (haemorrhoid) trouble. Ketu with Mars in the 1st House gives results similar to Rahu and Mars combine detailed above.

However, one point must always be remembered: – Uranus, Neptune and Pluto being at a considerable distance from Earth, they rarely affect an individual as such; they affect rather a group of people, population or an area of land, water or sky.

MARS IN THE 2ND HOUSE

Second House concerns wealth, monetary possessions, ownership of immovable property, gains and savings. Mars, when alone, has positive <u>adverse</u> effect on this aspect of life. Normally it strikes twice in life, more often after the person has assumed working for livelihood or holding assets even without working but leading towards livelihood.

If Mars happens to be lord of the 4th or the 10th house, Mars brings loss of money or assets to one or both parents during the childhood of the individual. Otherwise Mars operates during its mahadasa or its antardasa under any other planet, irrespective of helpful or unhelpful position of that planet. Mars hurts and harms the money position and assets even if its own Rasi is in the 2nd House. Mars spares the person if either the spouse has countermanding effect in his or her Birth-chart or Mars has assumed position helpful to wealth and money in the Navamsha and Trinshansha-charts (former in case of men and latter in case of women).

The second influence of Mars is that it adversely affects the health of the spouse, because it is in the 8th position from the 7th house. In the case of women the trouble is often related to menstrual system, pregnancy, trouble at the time of birth of a child, caesarean birth, skin or blood system problem to the newly born infant, sometimes surgery to the wife on account of some other inner trouble.

In the case of men, Mars in 2nd House gives complaints of the blood system, skin ailment, trouble to one of the eyes, trouble in hearing (at advanced age), gradual loss of teeth immaturely, and bleeding. It can give injury of any part of the body, but at least to the skull during Mars antardasa under any planet or repetitive placement of Mars in the 2nd or 8th house in the Yearly-chart.

This position of Mars normally tempts an individual to part company with old property, (moreso any inherited property) and attempts to acquire or build new property, or acquire other immoveable or moveable assets by the cost of the price sold. In the process the individual generally suffers some loss of money.

Going by the South Indian school of thought, this position of Mars sometimes hurts the married life, and in rare cases, bring separation or divorce, because that school of thought attaches much importance to Mars in the 2nd House being in 8th position from the 7th house. On a parallel level, the North Indian school of thought attaches importance to Mar's position in the 12th from the Ascendant, because it is in the 6th position (that of an enemy) from the 7th house ruling married life. In the opinion of the authors, Mars in 2nd or 12th house is harmful to married life, and sometimes to monetary possessions too.

Though Mars doesn't totally forego its 2nd House effect on wealth, money and property when in the company of other planets, it does relax and relent in its effect of causing disturbance to the married life or affecting health of spouse adversely.

Mars and Sun in the 2nd House

Mars and Sun combination in the 2nd House gives immense wealth thereby creating non-regrettable scope for loss of a part of that wealth under 2nd House effect of Mars. But it doesn't help much in giving perfect health to the spouse, though its restraints Mars to a 50% extent so that it may not disturb the married life or love life of the couple. Sun in the 2nd house provides enough money and wealth to the individual leaving no scope for help from others, but sometimes Mars in the 2nd House creates that need, at least on two occasions in adult life of the individual, though often, temporarily only.

Mars and Moon in the 2nd House

Mars and Moon combination in the 2nd house opens scope for mental disturbance to the spouse, sometimes neurological trouble too, and depending on the stars of the spouse, this combination would not hesitate to give a temporary dose of fickle-mindedness or just a touch of partial lunatic-type spell. Otherwise, this combination proves helpful in protecting the wealth and assets of the individual, if Moon is not in a waning position or, though behind Sun, but is *not* in the vicinity of Sun.

If the combination is in Scorpio, Moon gets its '*neech-bhang yo*ga' (severance of debilitation yoga) because lord of Scorpio is Mars and is in Moon's company in the 2nd house itself.

These individuals get ample chances of travel in foreign lands, and stand to derive benefits too from those travels and tours.

They are fond of collecting semi-precious stones, decorative gold-plated utensils or other items of decoration, silverware, garments of various designs, electrical gadgets etc.

Mars and Mercury in the 2nd House

Mars and Mercury combine in the 2nd house makes the individual fond of collecting books, magazines, manuscripts, pens, pencils, stationery items, notwithstanding the quantum of the person's needs for reading or using them. The individual tries to improve the general knowledge, learning and experience of the spouse. The individual gets into the habit of correct and prompt account-keeping, which sometimes saves the individual or the family from any loss by cheating or false claims etc. At the same time, the individual gets annoyed by anyone, without actual or understood permission, touching or using the items mentioned above belonging to or possessed by the individual. The individual is very much concerned about not letting others have access to her or his Manuscripts and books in the process of printing. The spouse of the person is often proud of intellectual faculties and achievements of that individual.

Mars and Jupiter in the 2nd House

Jupiter and Mars combination in the 2nd house can make a person an outstanding and successful lawyer on the criminal side, a *rigid* economist in theory and practice, a strict but qualified or experienced accountant or cashier. These two stars together can make a successful jeweller or goldsmith, an expert on quality and value of precious stones. If the individual suffers any loss of wealth, money or assets under impact of Mars in 2nd, Jupiter makes the loss good quite quickly. If the 2nd house has Capricorn, Jupiter enjoys '*neech-bhang yoga*' owing to exaltation of Mars in that Rasi.

Mars and Venus in the 2nd House

Mars and Venus combination in the 2nd house gives attraction and temptation towards persons of the opposite sex other than own spouse, and depending on other factors, it might lead to immoral indulgence, which ultimately harms the interests of the spouse, leading to quarrel, and sometimes, avoidable violence too.

The individual is very fond of every thing good, comfortable and fashionable in life, whether it is within affordable means or not. These persons don't hesitate to enter into debt for fulfilment of lust or luxury. Their fondness for diamonds, silverware, silk fabrics and fancy fabrics becomes well known. They have no restraint on shouting at the spouse, fault or no fault. But at the same time, these persons prove to be very goods lovers, both inside and outside the bedroom.

Mars and Saturn in the 2nd House

Mars joining hands with Saturn in the 2nd house is often a problem for the spouse, because it leads to maladjustment in married life, at least with the family of the spouse; for demands for this thing or that. Torture to the spouse also figures in married life on account of unfulfilled demands or for any other reason. Violence is not unknown or far to seek in these cases, though sometimes it is a two-way phenomenon – that is, the husband and wife go violent towards each other. When the individual suffers any loss of money or immoveable assets, Saturn makes it good by slow and steady process of savings as also from gains through future investments.

These persons should always be very careful during driving when the husband-wife, or the two *committed* lovers of opposite sex, are together inside a vehicle or any other means of transport. Extra precaution needs be taken against loss of vehicle by theft, or vehicle being forcibly driven away, even if it be an animal transport like horse, donkey, camel, etc.

Saturn and Mars in the 2nd house are inclined to give bone injury to the spouse during the main period or sub-period of either of these two stars, or when Saturn is harmful in transit or either of them or both are harmful in the Yearly-chart.

Mars and Rahu in the 2nd House

Mars and Rahu combination in the 2nd House is like North Pole and South Pole meeting in one and the same house. Mars is intent upon causing financial and material loss to the individual, while Rahu is intent upon making the person rich and well possessed. Thus Mars causes loss and Rahu quickly makes it up.

Sometimes it might not be loss of money or assets, but it can be in the shape of problems with blood system, menstrual cycle or the heart, leading to prolonged medical treatment or surgery etc. Further this combination is liable to give extra body weight to women after birth of a child. Even males are not spared by this combination in gaining extra pounds in body weight.

Mars and Ketu in the 2nd House

Mars and Ketu combine in 2nd House doesn't leave wide scope for Ketu to function. No doubt it tries in its modest manner to make up the loss caused by Mars. The persons concerned must avoid at all cost any kind of unnatural physical contact with opposite sex or with a person of the same sex, because this combination is most likely to give one disease or the other as a consequence of it.

These people are experts in telling lies, cooking up stories, making excuses and giving false or tutored evidence in legal forum.

MARS IN THE 3RD HOUSE

The 3rd House mainly relates to brothers and sisters of self, spouses of brothers, and sisters of the spouse, effort, capacity for effort, strength, power, vigour, vitality, muscle power, and determination to put these qualities and talents to profitable use.

In this context, Moon plays a very important role, because Moon rules the MIND in every human being, and MIND generates determination. In spite of Mars being on a strong wicket in the 3rd House, Moon has the capacity and competence to make or mar the DETERMINATION.

Moon's position in the 8th house is worst in this behalf, firstly, because Moon in 8th gives a timid and withdrawn mentality to the individual. Then Moon's 8th position amounts to 6:8 relationship between Moon and Mars. This element positively diminishes the determination of the individual in use of vigour, vitality, strength and capacity. Similarly, when Moon is in the 12th house, brothers and sisters, real and distant ones make demands on the individual for monetary and other kind of material help. If Moon is in the 6th house, though it has a *kendra* relationship with Mars, the enemies, opponents, competitors manage to hurt the determination of the individual. But there is an exception too involved in this context. It is in the sense that when Moon is in the 10th House, in spite of it being a 6:8 relationship between Moon and Mars, Moon helps the aims and ambitions generated by Mars in the 3rd house.

Otherwise in the normal course, Mars generates courage and bravery in any individual. It is also interesting to note that excepting Moon, all other planets if conjunct with Mars in the 3rd House, enhance the capacity and capability of Mars and help in giving still better results, notwithstanding the friendly or enmity relations between the planets. No doubt it is a fact that a person having Mars in the 3rd house gets moral and physical support from brothers and sisters, but at the same time, they expect financial and material help from the individual in return as mentioned in the preceding paragraph.

Mars and Sun in the 3rd House

Sun and Mars combine in the 3rd house is helpful for candidates desirous of entry into higher (or even lower) post or a junior job directly in or under the government in own country or another country. They manage to succeed in getting entry into politics, and climb a to post of power. These persons give a very bright account of themselves in defence (combatant) forces, moreso on the battlefield, where they prove efficient leaders, fighters, commanders and guides to other personnel of the force. They develop commendable knowledge and expertise in ordnance matters. This combination gives scope for lack of integrity, where money, gains and favours are concerned, because they deem it a befitting exchange for their efficiency. They are given to bragging their integrity, whether they are honest or not.

Mars and Moon in the 3rd House

This combination of Mars and Moon in the 3rd house normally causes interference by Moon in results to be given by Mars in the 3rd House.

Moon's presence in the 3rd house reduces the determination and strong will-power in the individual generated by Mars there, and sometimes Moon creates a kind of cowardice in the mind of the individual, specially in a fight, while facing any situation of danger or on a battlefield.

Moon also generates double-mindedness in the individual on important matters, more so where matters relate to property or immovable assets. In matters of extending monetary or material help to any brother or sister or relation of that kind, Moon gives a feeling of withdrawal or regret after giving it. This combination gives the individual good capacity for secrecy (against Moon's influence to open out) in matters relating to defence and diplomacy of the country, expertise in naval warfare and strategy, success in putting an end to (sea) piracy in the area under the individual's command, control or routine supervision.

Mars and Mercury in the 3rd House

Though Mars and Mercury combination in the 3rd House doesn't create the same type of confused thinking and withdrawn attitude in the individual, as Moon and Mars together do. This combination makes a person very thoughtful, philosophical, sunk in over-intelligent planning and decisions. However when this combination in 3rd house is in Aries, Gemini, Leo or Pisces, the individual proves (a) a very remarkable and success-oriented strategist in matters relating to defence, (b) in collection of secret information of the other side (intelligence activity), and (c) in preparation of deceiving documents misleading the opponents or the enemy and adversaries, like the British strategy towards Germans during the Second World War (1939-1945).

Mars and Jupiter in the 3rd House

Jupiter and Mars combine in the 3rd house makes the individual an expert on economics related to defence matters, whether for an individual or a family or a society or a country as such.

It makes competent experts on forensic matters and criminal law, whether on the Bench or at the Bar. The person is an expert in science related to economics, including matters of war equipment and ordnance weaponry.

These individuals adopt violent methods for recovery of their loans and dues on any account. They would give a loan to a person in a town in one state or county and get papers signed by the person for a town in another state or county, and then by false methods they obtain a degree of recovery for the correct amount due or for a falsely inflated amount. However these individuals prove efficient as judges or advocates or prosecutors in court-martials.

Mars and Venus in the 3rd House

When Venus joins hands with Mars in the 3rd House, they together make an individual colourful in love affairs. They have no hesitation in making romantic advances, and sometimes do not spare even near relations in this behalf.

Otherwise they are experts in the film-line, acting out fight sequences, semi-nude (or lewd) dance sequences, singing songs of love, or eve-teasing with a natural ease. Some of them do become or make others romeos-of-the-road; some others prove as experts in gynaecology, cardiology, import and export, smuggling of arms and ammunition, raw-material for medicines and films, pornographic photos, and all allied matters related thereto. These individuals exploit their partner in love (regular or casual or even in one-night affairs). But they are outstanding in bedroom. They willingly face and fight any risk in love. In any kind of emergency, they come forward to marry brother or sister of the late spouse or divorced spouse. Cases of romantic involvement between brother-in-law and sister-in-law can easily be traced to this combination.

Mars and Saturn in the 3rd House

The combination of Mars and Saturn in the 3rd house is very important.

Individuals who prove high quality warriors, fighters, dacoits, highway robbers and plunderers, daredevil smugglers, performers of fights and of stunts in films have this combination in the 3rd house. Similarly, leaders of armed forces, commanders, dashing combatant pilots in the air force, all kinds of brave persons, experts in weaponry and ordnance equipment, manufacturers of modern-day mass-killings, experts in arms and ammunition also generally have this combination in the 3rd house.

On the other hand, kidnappers, extortionists, blackmailers, traders in flesh, and owners of brothels too quite often have this combination in their 3rd House. At the same time protectors of society from anti-social elements are also very often born with this combine in their 3rd house. The main point is Mars with Saturn combine gives strength, bravery, vigour, dashing nature. It depends on the individual *whether this gift by two very strong stars is put to constructive use or destructive use.*

This combination can work both ways where brothers or sisters or cousins (of self or spouse) or their spouses are concerned. The real sense is that mutual relations can be cordial, affectionate and helpful or they can be bitter, envious, and jealous to the extent of harming each other or harming one, by forming a group of others.

Mars and Rahu in the 3rd House

Rahu and Mars in 3rd house give more or less all those results attributable to Mars with Saturn combine in the 3rd house detailed in the paragraphs above.

The only difference is that Saturn is very strong and full of vigour, while Rahu can give only half the results in all qualities, whether good or bad.

Mars and Ketu in the 3rd House

In so far as Ketu and Mars combination in the 3rd house is concerned, it would give results parallel to those given by Mars with Mercury, positively to about 40% extent or even less than that.

Ketu would often bring demands for help from brothers and sisters and cousins or allied relations, and it becomes difficult for the individual to totally refuse to give help or support, if he or she is in a position to do so.

MARS IN THE 4TH HOUSE

This is an important position of Mars, as this House concerns mother, heart, conveyance, getting moveable and immoveable assets in direct inheritance from natural parents or from adopting parents or even without adoption, just as a gift.

Results of Mars in this House depend on the Rasi in this House. If a Rasi is owned by Mars itself or by Sun or Jupiter, the individual would have cordial relations with mother, would get her full affection and protection in childhood. Mother would oppose the child being sent to a residential school. The individual would inherit property from parents. No doubt, it would be at late stage in youth for the person to own a conveyance of comfort, but conveyances of comfort owned by others would always be at his or her disposal.

The individual would acquire, build or buy own property too in addition to what has been or has not been received in inheritance or by adoption.

If these individuals keep away from smoking and drinking on a regular basis, their heart would function perfectly well even beyond the 60's of age. These people get respect and acceptance from people in position and power. When a strong Mars is in its own Rasi or in a Rasi owned by Sun or Jupiter in the 4th House, the person would wield a position of power. In this context, do not miss the point that it is Mars alone which always has full *drishti* (aspect) on a house which is in the 7th position from the House or Rasi occupied by Mars, irrespective of the distance in terms of degrees. THUS, MARS IN 4TH HOUSE HAS FULL *DRISHTI* (ASPECT) ON THE 10TH HOUSE, AND THE 10TH HOUSE RULES CAREER, PROFESSION, BUSINESS, MAIN SOURCE OF INCOME, AND POLITICS. And therefore Mars in the 4th house would prove very helpful in these matters for the individual.

Mars in 4th house makes a person bold, daring, dashing and competent to face difficult situations, and also die-hard enemies and adversaries, in life. And on top of all qualities, generally these persons are generous in material matters and liberal in helping or accommodating others, including destitute and helpless people.

But at the same time, these individuals don't tolerate insubordination, indiscipline, disobedience and lack of loyalty. They have force in what they say, and they have force in their voice too. These individuals make very efficient and successful commanders of combatant forces and armed constabulary. They are generous to a fault, if it is admitted by the wrong-doer.

Only pressure of circumstances can compel these individuals to dispose of property in full or in part, and they generally stick to the price quoted by them. At the same time, they are straightforward in any transaction, and do not have any intention to cheat or exploit anyone for own advantage.

But Mars in a Sign owned by Saturn, Venus, Mercury, or Moon is a different story. Then, they are diehard in their approach to men and matters. They often do not surrender their ground. They refuse to yield, even at a heavy cost to themselves. They sell the ancestral property at the drop of the hat. They have intentions of usurping the share of other claimants in the property. If Capricorn is in the 4th House, these people rise to position of power, high or low and assert themselves more forcefully than their actual position.

As a matter of general caution, these individuals should always stay careful against injury by accident (including fall from a high level or on slippery ground), heart ailment, disturbance in blood system, maladjustment between mother and spouse, because in the process these individuals suffer double pressure helplessly. Their vehicles meet with accidental damage more often than normal. <u>Injury to the human body may broadly be categorised of two kinds: one which gives bleeding, and, the other a blunt one, without bleeding.</u> Mars is associated with injuries causing bleeding. Thus, Mars in the 4th rarely fails to give bleeding injuries in the childhood and adolescence, including sometimes any injury of the head (skull).

When Mars is in the 4th House and Sun or Moon in the 9th or the 10th House, there are strong chances of the person enjoying inheritance by adoption or by way of gift. If Mars is in Aries, Leo or Capricorn, the person leaves the parental family in infancy itself on being adopted by someone related to the family but living separately. If Mars is in Taurus, Scorpio, or Pisces, someone living jointly with the natural parents adopts the child.

As mentioned above, Mars in the 4th creates differences between mother and spouse, which means it disturbs the married life of the person. The question whether the disturbance would conclude in continuance of the marriage or in divorce or physical separation or in death or suicide is a question for detailed examination. This point may be examined in detail by consulting 'Star Guide to Love and Marriage' by the author (pages 72 to 92 – published by Parsai Publishers (ptparsai@gmail.com) and also available with Rupa Publications India Pvt. Ltd.)

Mars and Sun in the 4th House

Mars and Sun combine in the 4th house gives opportunities to the individual, right from an early age, to come in contact with people in power and position. When these two stars happen to occupy in the 4th house, a Rasi owned by either of them or by Jupiter, ultimately the individual attains a position of power and authority or gets married to a person in that position, or gets adopted by a person with power or authority.

There are chances sometimes, while living with natural parents, the individual grows under the care of uncle, aunt, grandparent, brother, sister or an employee, formal adoption or no adoption.

Under this combination the individual often gets scoldings or beatings, or both, at least from mother or a mother-like person in childhood upto the age of 4 years or even upto the age of 16 years. There are also chances of the individual to suffer from skin ailment, headache, and disorder of digestive system intermittently upto 16 years of age.

Mars and Moon in the 4th House

The individuals with Mars and Moon combine in the 4th house get less care from natural mother and grow under the care of a relation of mother. Pretty often, they get no breast-feeding beyond four months or at the most 6 to 8 months after birth, yet they grow as adults with determination and extracting work from others, free or on short payment.

These individuals might have an interest in spying, transmission of country's weaponry and defence secrets to enemy-agents, interest in (sea) piracy, in running a trade in electrical and electronic items. Their second line of choice for livelihood can be manufacture or dealership in long cloth, garments, base for medicines, hospital supplies, ghee, cotton, sugar, juices, alcohol or interest in brokerage or speculation in real estate.

They often hide information from mother or motherly women. Present day cut-short distances encourage them to travel to different lands and to make effort to settle in a foreign country.

These persons should stay careful against food poisoning, physical trouble owing to wrong medication or treatment by a quack, which would add to their ailment or illness instead of recovery from it.

Mars and Mercury in the 4th House

These individuals with Mars and Mercury combine in the 4th house are the people who build libraries of own or for public use, run schools and other institutions for higher education.

They are capable of literary and or poetic work, journalism, and teaching and prove successful in their work. They lead to construction of premises for public utility. If nothing else, they work as architects or engineers for construction of public utility. They are apt to disagree with colleagues, superiors and seniors, though not with juniors and subordinates.

They often upgrade and refresh their knowledge by extensive reading whatever their profession, vocation or calling. They learn good ideas and develop good qualities from their mother. Unless Saturn or Rahu is in the 8th or the 11th house, these people always try to stay honest, both work-wise and money-wise. And by their honesty, they sometimes suffer harm or humiliation by dishonest people.

Mars and Jupiter in the 4th House

This combination of Mars and Jupiter in the 4th house makes the individuals good judges, lawyers, drafting acts or statues of law, or expert legislators, qualified accountants, economists, specially on the defence side or in police establishments.

Even otherwise, they have a kind of common-sense knowledge of law and rules regulating functioning of civic bodies. If Jupiter is lord of the 9th, 10th or 5th house, they become famous as judges on the civil and criminal side, or lawyers and advocates or qualified or experienced accountants. They have a judicious approach to life even in personal and domestic matters, and are often ruthless to a fault. They are very strict and prompt in recovery of their dues, and also in paying off their debts.

They take personal interest in construction, administration and successful working of hospitals, schools, colleges, widow-homes, orphanages, night shelters for homeless and destitute, collective abodes for uncared old persons, legal help institutions for poor litigants. They neither usurp another person's share in inherited property, nor give up their due share.

Mars and Venue in the 4th House

This is a difficult combination of Mars and Venus in the 4th house.

It is rather difficult to give consultations to others on delicate subjects ruled by this combination in the 4th house. These persons have a sex-oriented mind. They consider even motherly women as mere women instead of treating them with the outlook befitting a motherly lady. Sometimes, if linked with Saturn, Rahu or Uranus, they do not hesitate in indulging in incestuous relationship. They tend to resort to services of call-girls, male or female prostitution, group situations, interest in unnatural sex generally considered wild, vulgar or unconventional. Some may exhibit lesbian / homosexual tendencies too.

If this combination is vitiated by any kind of link with Saturn, Rahu or Uranus, these people do not hesitate to indulge in crime related to sex matters. If Moon is linked with Mars and Venus combination in the 4th house, the person is very secretive about sex relations of self, though not of others. She or he takes active interest in disclosing and discussing sexual acts of commission and omission of others, including of near and dear ones.

Another attribute of these people is to indulge in clandestine trade in contraband arms, ammunition, any kind of weaponry, and even large-size ordnance items. They indulge in smuggling of cloth, garments, chemicals, and ingredients for medicinal purposes, liquors and alcohols, intoxicants and drugs. Some of the Mafia leaders of international notoriety have this combination with links of Saturn either by conjunction or by direct *drishti*.

However it may be noted that these individuals make

very efficient medical experts, in medicine or surgery, pathology and radiology, and gain widespread fame for their knowledge and expertise.

Unless Mercury or Jupiter is associated with this combination, they make poor teachers or unimpressive authors on their subject of specialisation, because they lack quality and clarity in their language.

Mars and Saturn in the 4th House

Combination of Mars and Saturn in the 4th house is somewhat parallel to this combination in the 3rd house too.

This combination produces warriors, commanders, knights, and brave men (and women too). They make expert war strategists. They command their force actively by personal presence at the battlefield.

These individuals attain success even in crime, if they take to it. They make bold smugglers of arms, ammunition, weaponry and ordnance items of large size. They make expert spies, envoys and special representatives in political and national administration arena.

When angry, these persons become wild and violent. They are to be taken as obstinate and rigid, whether right or wrong in their approach.

They do not hesitate in usurping assets or property of others. They make expert encroachers on public land, and institutions of public utility. They suffer rough attitude from their mother or guardian in childhood, and they themselves become very rough when they grow up, with their spouse and sometimes with the kids too.

It is also likely that they lose a natural parent in infancy or childhood. Then if they have to grow under compulsions or rigid treatment or pressure of a step-parent or a real parent or a grand parent or a relation of a parent, or in an orphanage or destitute home, they develop the same rough attitude towards others when they reach a position of power and authority.

They suffer from upset digestive system, tend to grow fat, and later may suffer from complaints or irregularities of the blood system. This ultimately may lead to problems of heart system for them. Otherwise too, there are chances that these individuals may suffer from repeated physical ailments, whether they are given to any kind of intoxicants or not.

If either Mars or Saturn owns the 8th House, they or their vehicle(s) meet with accidental hurt or damage, and if Saturn or Mars owns the 12th House, their vehicle gets stolen and is detected later on with parts missing. These people make successful robbers, dacoits, kidnappers, or hijackers. If this combination has 6:8 relationship with Jupiter (specially in 11th house), they get into legal trouble, and if they have Sun or Rahu or Uranus in the 8th or 12th house, they get punished by law, or by group revenge parleys.

Mars and Rahu or Ketu in the 4th House

The first and foremost thing is that this combine gives extra body weight, ailments allied to it, including gastric complaints. Their belly sometimes bulges to an unseemingly large extent.

They have less respect for women elder to them, whether related by blood or not. They have a tendency to usurp assets of others in a clandestine manner. They do not hesitate to indulge in smuggling, trading in contraband items, functioning as carriers of contrabands, directing thefts and robbery for a consideration.

But these people are helpful when masses suffer from floods, draught, famine, landslide, avalanche, earthquake, widespread fire, epidemics, war or any other kind of public calamity or disaster. In the same breath they expect acknowledgement for their public service.

Ketu gives more or less the same results as Rahu, but not connected with theft, robbery, dacoity, violence, smuggling etc.

MARS IN THE 5TH HOUSE

The 5th House mainly rules progeny, intelligence, education, capacity and capability for management, administration, faith, devotion, respect towards God Almighty, and attitude towards teachers, Gurus and elders in age or wisdom.

Though the ancient *acharyas* have laid down that Mars in 5th house gives 3 sons, but experience shows that it is not so very correct. It does give a male child. Present-day limitations and restrictions on the number of progeny cuts down the total number of progeny, and thus effect of Mars gets reduced. Further Mars itself helps and causes termination of pregnancy or loss of pregnancy by natural and/ or medical causes.

Mars makes a youngster a 'hot-shot' in the classroom but actual performance in formal exams is much below the impressions given by the individual in the classroom.

These individuals are normally hard taskmasters, given to discipline and devotion to work on their own part as well as on the part of others, whether subordinate or associated with them. They respect the teachers, *gurus* and elders so long as they continue to deserve respect. Their faith in God Almighty also fluctuates with their success and failures in life.

Since Mars rules the 5th house pertaining to progeny, it naturally rules the menstrual cycle, uterus and allied organs connected with procreation in a female body. In this connection the points coming up for active consideration relate to untimely menopause, infertility, disturbed menstrual cycle and related ailments, repeated abortions or miscarriages, still-birth, diseases related to uterus, fallopian tubes, ovaries and vagina. As such, Mars in 5th is responsible (as Saturn too is) with <u>surgical treatment</u> of diseases and ailments concerning the procreational apparatus in the female body.

If Mars is in a damaging position in the *Dwadashansha-chart* and is anyway linked with Saturn or Rahu or Uranus in the basic Birth-chart, it can cause cancer of the uterus or adjoining area in the female body. Mars can give burn injury, cut injury, skin ailment in the region below navel point leading to the area below buttocks.

At the same time, Mars in 5th gives annoyance, anger, which are not considered good qualities but which help a person in achieving success in a fight, battle etc. It is very rarely that a man having Mars in the 5th house suffers any kind of, partial or complete, impotency, notwithstanding the position of Venus in the Birth-chart or Navamsha-chart.

With Mars in 5th, these men and women are generally good in management and administration, though expertise in marketing depends to a great extent on position and strength of Jupiter.

Another point worth note is that Mars gives good or bad results of its position quite often during its mahadasa or its sub-period, though degree of good or bad results depends on relationship between Mars and lord of the mahadasa.

It is also important that Mars gives definite results of its position in the Yearly-chart (*Varshphal*=annual progressive-chart). For Yearly-chart calculations, please depend more on manually-constructed charts of an expert astrologer, rather than on a computer system, because a majority of the computer calculations are much below the accuracy levels required for such detailed study of an Yearly-chart.

Mars in 5th house sometimes makes people mischief-mongers, specially in political or social arena, all the moreso if Gemini, Leo, Sagittarius or Pisces is in the 5th House.

Mars and Sun or Moon in the 5th House

The results of these two combinations have been discussed earlier under Sun and Moon's respective positions in the 5th House.

Mars and Mercury in the 5th House

Persons who have Mars and Mercury combination in the 5th house attain high position in the class, secure high percentage in final exams, and at the same time, they excel in some activity related to sports and games (though not equally as high as in academics).

Some of these people learn foreign languages, take to writing, including on history of wars, battles, struggles between races, communities, and societies. These people are impressive orators, moreso where they have on hand a hot subject.

They make good teachers too, but some among them are violent to the children and some of the students beaten by them even suffer long-term physical injuries.

These individuals are unable to take quick decisions whether a pregnancy should be continued or terminated medically. In administrative matters, they are rather lenient and forgiving, particularly if the offence or fault is minor in nature or for vendetta.

Mars and Jupiter in the 5th House

These individuals make very learned judges, lawyers, jurists, advocates, chartered or works and cost accountants, managers in business field, heads of any social or community-body. They have a touch of irritation and anger, and on occasions they might lose their calm but they keep their approach judicious and as far as possible, impartial too.

These individuals make efficient selectors of candidates for any kind of civil or defence jobs. They make good court-martial judges and prosecutors, bankers, treasurers, insurance executives, arbitrators and envoys. These people are experts in preparation of a budget for a country, state, business house industrial concern, but they are not successful in controlling fund-raisers for one cause or the other. They make trustworthy friends and guardians of youngsters.

Mars and Venus in the 5th House

The individuals with Mars and Venus combination in the 5th house have a touch of romance in whatever they think or do during their adult-life. They make impressive poets, singers, musicians, and throw their romanticism about without restraint and restriction. Though they keep off same-sex tendencies, they are quite daring in making sexual contacts and friends. They prefer a touch of roughness in sex life, and, are often ardent and trustworthy lovers.

If Saturn or Rahu is linked in any manner with this

combination, these people may indulge in an incestuous affair too. Even females are bold and take initiative into dragging young and innocent boys into their love-net. These people naturally go in for quick medical termination of conceptions. Extra-marital affair is no taboo for them. If they are in singing, music, or in the field of acting in films or on stage, they are often jealous of competitors, and do not hesitate to harm them. These are the people who lead others into prostitution and brothels, rather fearlessly. Whether their any action or deed is good or bad, they are always keen to achieve success in it by any method whatsoever.

Mars and Saturn in the 5th House

The individuals with Mars and Saturn together in the 5th house make expert spies, defence strategists, managers of forces on battlefields, trainers in use of weapons and ordnance items.

They have a combination of both, anger and stubborn nature, which suits defence forces and police duties. They make successful investigators and intelligence-collectors, or informers in any and every field. They are often violent and come to blows even on minor provocation. They prove successful managers of industries, big farms, mines, purification of minerals, placement services, manpower suppliers within and outside their country. They indulge in making false documents, medical and examination certificates, passports, driving licenses, permits for routes of passenger buses and goods vehicles.

They produce patent witnesses in any type of case before a legal forum. They stand guarantees, sureties and giving securities of false nature, which turn to a 'naught' (invalid) when the authorities want to take action on basis of that guarantee or surety or security.

Some of them maintain gangs of bad characters to recover debts for their clients on a heavy consideration. They come forward to buy or sell disputed properties and use their gangs to vacate or occupy such properties. They are good pirates, kidnappers and hijackers.

One praiseworthy quality in them is that they are the first people to come forward for social service at time of floods, fire, epidemic, draught, famine, earth-quack, tornado, storm, or any kind of natural or men-made calamity. In doing so they do not hesitate to endanger their limb or life.

Mars and Rahu in the 5th House

The first impact of Mars and Rahu in the 5th house is that it normally gives loss of (one or more) pregnancy, unless the stars of the spouse are very protective in this regard.

In childhood, these people are given to mischief in school, on playground and in neighbourhood too. They are firm in their administrative or management decisions. If their statements are recorded or they are in the witness box, they falter in their versions, sometimes leading to an impression that they are giving cock and bull stories. They bring falsehood in their date of birth and other details pertaining to their family and education etc. They call their falsehood as "cleverness", and often feel proud of their wisdom in this behalf.

They generally do not hesitate in deriving benefit of work done by others, but when a blame-worthy development comes up, they try to put the blame on someone else even for their own work.

One important role of Rahu and Mars combination is that the individual has weak grasp in studies, and this adversely affects his or her educational progress later on in life. Further impact is that these individuals try to steal knowledgeable work of others, and try their best to deprive the original workers of the credit for their good work. These individuals have no hesitation even in blackmailing the original workers of intelligence and wisdom for stealing credit of their work.

Mars and Ketu in the 5th House

When in combination with Mars in the 5th house, Ketu too gives results somewhat similar to Rahu and Mars in the 5th house, but in Ketu and Mars combination, the individuals are less false and a little away from the field of lies and cheating etc.

Ketu is not particular in giving loss of pregnancy to a female as Rahu is, because Ketu bears some qualities similar to Mercury. Ketu and Mars together give better account of the individual in management and administration.

But whether it is Rahu or Ketu with Mars in the 5th house, parents should pay full attention to their child's 'grasp power' in studies between the age of 5 and 15 years. Weak grasp power would always mean weak foundation of the child's education. Such children often avoid or evade written work and try to copy from the work of fellow students. They are vulnerable to unfair means in examinations, even if they do not get detected, and where real knowledge is concerned, they have minus results on their credit side.

Mars in the 6th House

This is one of the most helpful positions of Mars, giving good health, desire and capacity to work, keen to prove helpful to people around.

These individuals are fearless, daring, dashing, and brave too. They have a special kind of attachment to their property, but they hesitate to usurp or encroach upon property belonging to others. They do not withdraw from helping the spouse in domestic cores. They are very particular about their health and physical strength.

Some of them develop strained relations with mother's brother or sister, at least when in the Birth-chart, Aquarius, Taurus or Libra is in the 4th house. They often keep an eye on the worldly possessions of the spouse, without any intention to smart it.

If Sun is in the 9th or 10th house or a waning Moon is in the 7th or 9th house, these individuals have a chance of inheriting property from one of the maternal grandparents; it can be even a very valuable gift of assets. This factor too becomes a basis for strained relations with mother's brother or sister.

If Moon is in the 5th house, these people entertain worries internally and it adversely affects their efficiency in work. If Jupiter is in the 3rd, 8th or 12th house, there are chances of these individuals losing a battle in civil litigation, in spite of their over-confidence to win the case.

These people rise to position of power by their own effort, at least when Sun is in 3rd, 10th or 11th, or in the 6th itself. Otherwise they help others to rise to position of power, by election or by clout or by bout or even by violence. They normally have a religious bent of mind, but one cannot make them do a wrong thing under fear of religion or faith or cult.

Mars and Sun or Moon in the 6th House

These combination have been discussed under Sun and Moon with Mars in the 6th House respectively.

Mars and Mercury in the 6th House

It is a funny combination indeed of Mars and Mercury in the 6th house!

The individual should be careful in signing any formal documents whatever one's profession, vocation or calling, because the individual might land self into trouble, misunderstanding, confrontation, litigation and embarrassment etc. These individuals are often befooled by signing papers without reading or understanding them, merely out of 'over-trust' in the other people and then they get caught in a trap. Even while giving oral statement or evidence, they must think carefully before uttering their answer and should keep mental note of what they stated earlier, because often these people are led into contradictions created through confusion by the cross examination or by the interrogator.

They must keep their important documents and papers with care and should carry them with caution, as sometimes they lose them along with their money or brief case.

If they are in teaching or preaching line, they mustn't get violent, or romantic, lest they get beaten up. Students and scholars with this combination have to work very hard for success in studies and research.

Mars and Jupiter in the 6th House

This is another difficult combination equally comparable to that of Mars and Mercury in the 6th house.

These people often suffer losses in lending money, speculation in shares, careless operation of their safety vaults, loss of jewellery or stray ornaments by self or women in the household. They suffer theft by own domestic help, pilferage by employees and embezzlement by cashiers, accountant, buyers and sellers of goods and similar acts by godown-keepers.

They are vulnerable to diabetes, asthma, kidney trouble after the age of 47 years, in some cases earlier too. Often own mother's brother or sister tries to cheat or exploit them. If they stand for any elective office, their own workers cheat them money-wise and also vote-wise by playing double game of secretly helping their opposite candidate. These people blurt out secret and confidential matters under threat or temptation of any kind, and subsequently try to make amends.

Sometimes loopholes occur in their legal documents pertaining to property may it be a sale-deed or gift-letter or will or family-settlement, or lease-deed or grant by an authority.

Mars and Venus in the 6th House

The point is that Mercury, Jupiter and Venus are soft planets and they are harmful in the 6th house pertaining to health, reputation and enemies.

Thus Mars and Venus combination in the 6th house creates enmity on account of opposite sex, whether the individual is at fault or not. In some cases of sexual contacts in a loose manner, this combination can lead to venereal diseases and ultimately to some complaint nearer to AIDS.

This combination can give embarrassment through extra-marital affair of self or spouse, or one of the two lovers. It can give health problems by wrong medication or self-medication without possessing due knowledge of medicine. It can put a person in the company of drunks, and then the person may suffer the consequences thereof. It might lead a person to sex orgies and trouble later on. These people take pride in boasting and bragging about their contacts and connections with opposite sex and thus get into the maze of jealousy and adversaries. They do not hesitate to take resort to male and female prostitutes, married or not married. There are chances of their having incestuous relations with a member of the maternal family, and consequential repercussions in the family circle. They tend to give costly gifts to their friends of the opposite sex with no consideration of their own financial status to do so.

Mars and Saturn in the 6th House

The combination of Mars and Saturn in the 6th house proves very helpful to all individuals, in spite of the fact that Mars and Saturn are opposed to each other, and very effective too because both are strong and influential stars.

These two stars in the 6th house help the individual to wipe out any enemies, opponents and adversaries. The individual gets helped in any competition, academic or athletic activity or competition. Further the individual proves successful in police or combatant forces on defence or semi-defence side or in any strategy concerning police and defence.

Even if the individual is in mere ranks in the police or defence forces, she or he proves efficient, brave and bold in any act involving risk to life or limb. Most of them are fearless with regard to personal risks and dangers, provided Moon is not in the 8th, 12th or the 6th house itself. The individual proves successful and useful in any assignment relating to collection of secret information or as defence attaché' in any embassy in a foreign country.

These individuals come to own property both by inheritance and by own effort and earnings. Sometimes they are brought up and educated in maternal family, though later on they get quite aloof from that family. Even a big injury, wound or fracture caused to an individual with this combination in the 6th house gets cured or healed easily and quickly. Similar is the case with regard to any fracture to a bone of the body, which gets back to normal position, thoroughly, slowly and steadily.

They are very loving and caring for the spouse and in the same breath quite critical, and mildly violent towards the spouse, which is the result of two adversary stars in the 6th house. The husband and wife or lovers threaten separation and divorce, but it rarely happens. No doubt physical separation owing to circumstances or because of legal action or even divorce can take place if Venus or Jupiter or Moon too is in the 6th house, or if Jupiter is in the 8th or the 12th house. In this particular case, *drishti* would not prove really harmful, because *drishti* can cause real harm only when it is cast directly from the 7th position. It has already been clarified here that Jupiter in the 12th house (thereby casting direct *drishti*) can cause divorce. In so far as Venus is concerned, from the 12th house Venus too has direct *drishti* on the 6th house. However the most that Venus can do is to give a rival to the husband or wife, and chances of divorce are not so strongly created by Venus as can force Mars and Saturn combination to cause the divorce.

These individuals prove very serviceful to ill and sick persons whether they are mutually related to each other by blood or not.

Mars and Rahu in the 6th House

Combination Mars and Rahu in the 6th house is another favourable thing for the individuals, though not so forceful as Mars and Saturn there.

These individuals do not indulge in leg pulling or giving threats of separation and divorce to their spouse. On the other hand they are very helpful and caring towards their spouse.

These individuals are very rough towards their enemies, opponents and adversaries, but unless the enemies, opponents, and adversaries hurt them mentally or physically or financially and rather vigorously, these individuals do not turn ruthless or cruel to them.

These individuals come to own property by effort and earnings of self, irrespective of the fact whether they inherit any property from parents or grandparents or not. They in fact do not look forward to gain of any immoveable asset by gift from some source or the other.

These people are helpful, social and charitable to one and all without any selfish motives and intentions. They can safely be trusted in regard to opposite sex.

Even if they have strained relations with mother's paternal family, they do not exhibit strain in relations, and observe quite formal "give and take relations" normally.

They try to use unfair means in exams but only to a limited extent and normally do not get detected.

Mars and Ketu in the 6th House

This combination of Mars and Ketu in the 6th house leads the individuals to tell lies and fails to be trusted.

They try to use unfair means in exams and get detected, if not earlier, at the stage of evaluation of the answer books. They try to be brave and bold, but their inner timidity and cowardice gets revealed, if not sooner, then later.

They try piracy in literary field but there too they get caught and criticised openly, even broadly. They are poor in studies and have to work very hard for keeping pace with fellow students. In research work, these scholars have to rewrite their chapters of thesis often and even then the work fails to create a big impression of their work.

In matters of police work, intelligence and investigations, and defence strategy, they are good at table work but second-class in executive work and third rate in responsibilities and duties at or relating to a battlefield.

They are always nice and tolerant to their spouse, and extend help in indoor and outdoor chores and associate them in social activities and contacts etc. The individuals do not welcome any kind of domination of self on spouse or of spouse on self.

MARS IN THE 7ᵀᴴ HOUSE

This is one of those difficult positions of Mars of which learned astrologers are afraid to predict in the matter of adversely affecting the marriage prospects, and after marriage, the married life itself.

This (and the 8th house) position of Mars positively harms, damages, injures, and sometimes destroys the marriage and married life of the individual. Mars in the 7th house is bound to give quarrel-some and fault-finding nature, and since 'spouse' is the first element ruled by the 7th house, spouse becomes the first target or participant in quarrels, disharmony and maladjustment between the married couple or two lovers. One of the main remedies to meet this situation is to find a matrimonial match having Mars in the 7th or the 8th house. Experience of several generations of astrological practical knowledge and practice indicates that no other remedy is workable to wipe off the harmful effect of Mars in the 7th house on marriage and married life.

A person with Mars in the 7th house is a hard bargainer in business deal or even in minor transactions, provided that Jupiter is also in a benefit-giving house. These people are good fighters, but not very competent or efficient strategists in large-scale fights, battles or a war. If properly guided or properly induced they give an outstanding account of themselves in matters related to ordnance and weaponry. Some of them suffer from ailments connected with blood system (including menstrual cycle in women), functioning of the heart. Mars in the 7th house also causes skin ailment, headache, tuberculosis and ailments linked to extreme anger, and any minor or major ailment of the genital parts.

Mars in 7th house and Jupiter in 6th, 8th or 12th house are very likely to drag the individual into litigation on civil matter or into a criminal charge. In other words Mars itself generates such disputes and quarrels (specially related to women, wine and wealth, including property) as may lead the individual to a legal forum. Further because it is related to criminal acts or association with criminals and connection with contrabands, it might lead to financial loss, penalty, fine and a jail term too.

If Mars is in a cardinal Sign, it might lead an individual

to take domicile in another country, state, county or district. It becomes all the more imperative if Moon or Venus is in the 9th, 10th or 11th house. If lord of the 7th house is in the 8th, 3rd or 4th house, the individual would acquire immovable property in another country.

Separation with spouse owing to circumstances, parental pressure, mal-adjustment is also a destiny created by Mars in the 7th house. Depending on mahadasa and sub-period of Mars or Saturn or influence of Saturn or Rahu (by transit movement) with the 7th house or in the 7th house itself and Mars therein, the separation is very likely to last a long term.

As already stated above, Mars in the 7th house can lead to divorce, moreso if Mars' own mahadasa or sub-period intervenes within 10 years of the marriage. It can lead to beating, torture, violence or even loss of limb or life at the hands of the spouse or relations thereof. Not only in India, but in developed and undeveloped and semi-developed countries too, cases of 'marital violence' are not rare, whether they get reported or not, or go before a court of law or not

One typical effect of Mars in breaking a marriage is by fatal accident too. There have been cases where the married life worked extremely lovely and well, but suddenly an accidental death snatched one partner in married life. The point to be noted is that Mars rarely spares anyone from its adverse effect on the married life, unless countermanding stars are available in the Birth-chart of the spouse. Some astrologers suggest remedy for removing the harmful effect of Mars on married life, but experience proved that the remedy could not remove the wicked effect of Mars on married life.

And married life is such a matter that divorce or death of one of the partner naturally affects the other partner too in marriage. No doubt in may countries now second and third marriages are rampant and a common feature. The evil effect of Mars on marriage and married life has been described here in detail. It is for the readers and affected persons to take guidance from the paragraphs above or not.

The above impact of Mars in the 7th house takes us to the question as to when this torture or separation or violence of the extreme type can occur. For this purpose, one must study

(a) the Yearly-chart (annual *progressive* chart);
(b) a comparative study of the Yearly-chart with the Birth-chart
(c) these two elements should be read with mahadasa and sub-period.
(d) The transit position of Mars, Jupiter, Saturn and Rahu during the relevant year of age for which the Yearly-chart has been drawn.
(e) One important element known to very few learned astrologers even in India is the '*Tripataka-chart*' (crossroads chart) relating to the Yearly-chart under study.

If the planetary position in the Yearly-chart and its crossroad-chart have very harmful position of Mars (and/or Saturn or Rahu), and the mahadasa or sub-period (antardasa) are also of damaging stars, the astrologer should caution the person consulting him or her about disturbance to married life. However if the husband is against the wife, and the husband is consulting the astrologer, any such hint from the astrologer about planets harmful to the wife might encourage the husband to torture or hurt her all the more. The same position can be read otherwise too from the wife's side towards the harm to the husband. Cases of wife or beloved hurting the husband or the lover are also not rare under influence of Mars in the 7th House. The substance is that the astrologer should not put hints in the mind of the individual or the spouse that might lead to further deterioration to their married life.

It is indeed a duty and responsibility of the astrologer, who prepares the detailed horoscope of any individual to indicate in advance the risky periods to married life in the case of the individuals who have Mars in the 7th(or the 8th) house.

An individual with Mars in 7th house and Rahu or Venus in 8th house or Saturn and/or Venus in 12th house should avoid, as far as possible to have unrestricted sexual relations with any member of the opposed sex, unless both are officially and legally married husband and wife.

Now with tremendous progress in science, one very big problem has cropped up. About 90% of the population get their horoscopes made by computer system. A computer cannot give such detailed and minute study of the Mars in the 7th (or the 8th) house as a learned, experienced and unbiased astrologer can give. This position of planets applies to extra-marital affairs too.

Normally it happens that individuals with Mars in the 7th house, whether they know this fact or not, indulge in extra-marital relationship, and Mars is bound to adversely affect that relationship as well.

Mars and Sun in the 7th House

In combination of Mars and Sun in the 7th house, Sun becomes just a supporter of Mars in every respect, irrespective of the fact whether Mars is giving good results or bad results.

The only important point is that Sun brings the government machinery to the help and rescue of the spouse. In other words whosoever between husband and wife is the sufferer at the hands of the other, provided the matter is brought to the notice of the government machinery and in some countries the government machinery operates even on getting information about torture from other sources.

If either is in political field, some kind of honour or power is bestowed by this combination on one of the couple.

However, Mars and Sun together directly rule blood system and skin, they can cause serious problems to either blood system or the skin, all the more so if either of the two stars has its mahadasa or the sub-period. If it is mahadasa of one and sub-period of the other, some kind of ailment related to blood system and skin is very much likely. This guidance is in addition to what has been stated under predictions about Sun in the 7th house in the relevant chapter earlier.

Mars and Moon in the 7th House

As already stated under predictions about combination of Moon and Mars in the 7th house in the relevant chapter on Moon (earlier), it may be noted that these two together can give mental torture too to the spouse, besides physical or other trouble and torture. Though a soft planet, Moon is unable, as has been observed in practical experience, to reduce the cruel attitude and impact of Mars in 7th house on the spouse.

Mars and Mercury in the 7th House

The combination of Mars and Mercury in the 7th house helps in giving a touch of intelligence and wisdom to the cruel spouse, thus reducing the volume of anger, torture, violence etc in married life. It also gives an additional opportunity to the spouse to improve educational qualifications of self, and increase capacity for independent living in case of eventual separation or divorce.

Sometimes, this combination makes the individual a competent orator, teacher, writer, journalist, publisher, or bookseller. No doubt there can be a touch of irritation in speech, of violence in writing, of reporting more on the criminal side, of publishing books or literature with ample quantum of violent narration in them, or selling books of this nature. In simple words, both Mars and Mercury would have equal say in the nature of the individual and in her or his approach to life as such.

Mars and Jupiter in the 7th House

The combination of Mars and Jupiter in the 7th house is no doubt able to reduce, to some extent at least, the violent effect of Mars in the nature and actions of the individual, though not to full extent.

Finding Jupiter in the 7th house with Mars should not lead to a presumption that Mars has stopped working. Mars works in reduced degree, and further if the individual is having any criminal or violent intents, he or she would operate in a manner as to avoid the law, because Jupiter rules the law. This combination needs special attention while matching horoscopes for marriage purposes, because Jupiter does not totally mitigate the influence of Mars, though some less knowledgeable astrologers presume so, and naturally guide the consulting people accordingly. Unfortunately some books on astrology also lay down that conjunction of Jupiter with Mars in the 7th house totally mitigates the evil influence of Mars, but experience of several generations prove that it is not so. Mars would operate as and when it finds an opportunity when Mars is slightly outside the influence of Jupiter.

Mars actually finds this type of opportunity when Jupiter is in the 6th, 8th, 12th or 2nd house by transit, or Jupiter is having its sub-period in Mars mahadasa or Mars is having its sub-period in Jupiter mahadasa.

Other results of this combination are that the individual gains knowledge of law, sometimes develops expertise in civil, criminal, mercantile law, and practical application thereof. Otherwise too, these persons are good in trading, marketing, speculation in landed property, buying disputed properties, getting them vacated by temptation or threats or even actual violent actions, and then either using them or selling them with enormous profits. If in the profession of accountancy or business management, these individuals have no hesitation in giving and taking illegal gratifications, in kind or in cash. They make good arbitrators in disputes of boundary, river waters, trade practices, monopoly and patent issues in commerce, and in some rare instances, in joint family disputes relating to division of assets. If Mars has its Sign in the 11th house, it is likely that in matters of arbitration these individuals would not always prove above board.

Mars and Venus in the 7th House

The combination of Mars and Venus in the 7th house does not normally reduce to any noticeable extent the evil influence of Mars there.

This combination however diverts the bone of contention from every thing else to extra-marital relationship of one of the marriage-partners (sometimes of both). In some cases extra sexual or cohabitation demands of one partner remain unfulfilled by the other partner for various reasons including (a) incompetence for cohabitation, (b) friendship with someone else of the opposite sex of one of the couple before marriage and its impact on the married life leading to avoidance of sex, (c) intended separation and sometimes ultimate divorce under any excuse whatsoever, (d) so much physical violence and mental harassment to the wife that it may ultimately lead to the death of the wife by some means or the other, very common in India and few adjoining countries.

These individuals make successful importers or exporters, dealers in perfumes, electricals and electronics, dealers in white items like ghee, sugar, medicines, wines and alcohols. Some of these individuals indulge in unauthorised selling of property of spouse or of other relations, or friends, or property of an owner residing away from that particular town.

In countries or societies where laws permit, these individuals indulge in more than one marriage, or keep paramour(s), mistress(s), or indulge in casual sexual affairs. Often they are liked and loved by the opposite sex for their innovation and variety in actual sexual acts.

This combination prompts a person for domicile or settlement in another country, state or county etc, moreso after marriage or as a condition of marriage or on simple account of marriage. For example, a person in the US marrying a resident of Paris as a consequence of which there is shifting of residence by one of the partners to marriage.

Mars and Saturn in the 7th House

The combination of Mars and Saturn in the 7th house is positively a difficult combination initially for fixing a marriage partner, then for continuance of the marriage.

Many astrologers labour under the wrong impression that by Saturn being with Mars, the malefic (or evil) impact of Mars is wiped out or at least reduced to minimum.

Practical experience of several generations has shown it to be otherwise. The evil impact of Mars on marriage and married life is doubled by conjunction of Saturn with it in the 7th house.

If Venus and/or Jupiter be placed in 6th, 8th, 12th house or one in the 12th house and the other in the 2nd house, often the marriage itself becomes a much sought after event in life for repeated years under repeated efforts of self and others in the family or by the friends. And a formal marriage doesn't oblige the individual.

A lady with Saturn and Mars in the 7th house belonging to a rich family and well employed in the All India Radio could not get married till the age of 45 years, and then gave up the idea under advice of the senior author. This was in 1964. In another case, a girl with Mars in 7th and Saturn in 4th House is still awaiting marriage at the age of 42 years. A young man with Mars and Saturn in 7th house in Scorpio and Venus in 8th house (as lord of Ascendant) has had three official marriages so far, and two full-fledged affairs; he is not yet 36 years old.

In cases of the type described above, if however marriage takes place, maladjustment soon creeps into the life of both or one of the partners. It is by quarrels, obstinacy, intended separate living, avoidance of cohabitation, extra marital affair, interference of the family, paucity of means of livelihood, intended miserliness of one towards the other partner in marriage. It can happen even in the case of a man and woman living together as husband and wife without formal or legal marriage.

In addition to Mars and Saturn together in the 7th house, if Venus is in 4th, 5th, 6th, or 12th house, a *paramour* or mistress is a normal thing in life of the individual. Beatings, violence, injury to limb, loss of life is a common occurrence in this type of marriages.

But these individuals make experts in police and defence services. In criminal groups they are able to extract, by threats and actual torture, information about hidden money and jewellery etc. These individuals prove expert interrogators with expertise in use of third degree methods, and in many a new method often now depicted in films the world-over. They make efficient commanders, leaders or supervisors in arms, ammunitions, ordnance matters, weaponry, defence and border security strategists, defence intelligence, and revenue intelligence. They excel in duels and personal fights, wrestling, and though very rarely in running races, but positively in sports and games.

Mars and Rahu in the 7th House

The combination of Mars and Rahu in the 7th house makes the married life run or drag its feet in spite of all ill treatments, tortures and mal-adjustments in married life.

These individuals allow the married life to run or drag its feet for sake of maintaining their self-respect and sense of ego. They break but do not bend. They are willing to die, but do not become dead duck or dead weight or dead wood under any circumstance or pressure of the family or friends of either of the two. In other words they keep the marriage running.

However Rahu is unable to fight the evil impact of Mars on married life, on the other hand it enhances it to a certain extent. Even after ill-treatment, the ill-treating partner dramatises own innocence, not hesitating even to create a shadow of doubt regarding bad-nature or bad-character of the partner under ill treatment, more like adding insult to injury. Mars and Rahu in 7th house give sharp sense of ego, which encourages hiding, (from relations and others), the maladjustment or even torture in married life, or love life.

These individuals are good at indulging in shady deals and transactions in business, frauds and forgery, false evidence, pleadings of innocence, cheating by double deals and duplicate sales of property and goods. They are able to keep their extra-marital affairs or casual strayings as guarded secrets, and never hesitate to put up false excuses, and shout their purity and innocence in moral character from housetops!

Mars and Ketu in the 7th House

In the Mars and Ketu combination in the 7th house, the innocent Ketu is unable to reduce the evil effect of Mars on marriage and married life, though it imports occasional understanding and wisdom between the husband and wife.

It sometimes creates a desire for unnatural methods of cohabitation, extra-marital relationships, and a desire for such variations in sex life as are not considered socially acceptable.

In business matters and trade dealings, the trend and tendency of the individual are the same as created by Mars and Rahu or Mars and Saturn in the 7th house.

MARS IN THE 8TH HOUSE

This is one of the most ticklish and risky positions of Mars for the individual, as well as for the spouse. It adversely affects mutual relationship, companionship, happiness, health, continuity, or conclusion of a marriage. Conclusion can be by an injury or illness, Tuberculosis, venereal disease, AIDS, skin ailment, blood disorders, heart ailment, harmful results of stunt acting, risk of falling from horse, camel, elephant, buffalo, or any height; risk of animal-bite, snake-bite, rabies, injury to genital parts or anus, by undertaking any job or work or action or responsibility involving physical risk. Risk to married life can be from any kind of legal action, possessing real estate more than one's real needs; having various sources of income; success or failure of surgical or any other kind of instrumental treatment to self or to spouse by non-specialist in the required discipline of surgery.

However, if saviour stars are also effective in the horoscope, specially Sun, Saturn and Rahu, they can save the individual or the spouse from above mentioned diseases or risk to the person. Therefore the whole matter needs very expert, careful and cautious examination of the stars in full details. It would be foolish on part of the astrologer to give positive-type predictions on basis of haphazard study or calculations.

In one sentence it can be stated that this position of Mars is always favourable for income and earnings but injurious to health, marriage, or love, irrespective of the Sign in the 8th house. It is incorrect to believe that Mars is harmless if it is in its exaltation or a Sign owned by Mars itself or in *Vargottam* position. No, the effect of Mars in the 8th house is unconditional, the only difference is of degree or percentage of results depending on the Sign in the

8th house, lord of the 8th house, mutual relationship between Mars and the lord of the 8th house. It is therefore essential to keep the immediately preceding paragraph in mind before reaching any conclusion in this regard.

It is also advisable for an individual having Mars in the 8th house, that his or her matrimonial match must necessarily have Mars in the 7th or the 8th house; nothing short of it may work.

Please note carefully that some astrologers and *tantriks* suggest *puja* and *yantra* as a remedy in cases where one of the matrimonial match (boy or girl) has Mars in the 7th or 8th and the other doesn't have it. Practical experience shows that these remedies only go to postpone, or in some rare case, reduce to some extent the adverse results of this position of Mars. The adverse result does not get mitigated or wiped out totally. Even an excellent tally of *gunas* (points matching system based on a total tally of 36) would not help.

Another problem facing unsuspecting parents is that often parents of a boy or girl having Mars in 7th or 8th house either plead ignorance about remembering the date of birth and time of birth of the boy or the girl, or give a manipulated date or time of birth. The presumption is that the non-Mangali match alone would suffer the adverse effect of the Mangali boy or girl in question. In reality it is not so. The primary function of Mars <u>in these positions</u> is to disturb, damage, or destroy the co-habital union of two people, depending upon its degree and combinations. Thus the consequence can fall on either of the two persons in the marriage, or sometimes on both of them.

In one case recently, the girl had Mars in her 8th, while the boy did not have any adverse influence of Mars in his Birth-chart. Both were killed in a road accident. It later transpired that at the time of marriage negotiations, the parents of the girl had manipulated the time of her birth by 2 hrs and 45 minutes. That changed the ascendant and consequentially the entire Birth-chart of the girl. There are many such cases where a person with Mars in 7th or 8th met with an accident and died, whereby the marriage got destroyed. In many a case, parents were guilty of manipulating the year or date and time of birth to hide the Mars' presence in the 7th or the 8th house.

Sometimes the parents change the year of birth presuming that the position of stars would remain the same as that in the correct year of birth. It is not so. The Birth-chart of a person born, say on 12 Oct. 1926 and 12 Oct. 1927 would be very different, though the Ascendant and Sun's position would be the same in 1926 and 1927, provided the date, month and time of birth have not been altered. A learned astrologer can detect such manipulations!

The other results of Mars are discussed below in the process of discussing other stars in the 8th house with Mars.

Mars and Sun or Moon in the 8th House

These two combinations have been discussed in earlier chapters on Sun and Moon with Mars respectively under Sun in the 8th house and Moon in the 8th house.

Mars and Mercury in the 8th House

This combination of Mars and Mercury in the 8th house has got special adverse effect on the grasping power of the child in school, thereby laying a weak foundation for higher education. If such children make a grade at their school finals by private tuitions, guidebooks and unfair means, the lack of real knowledge works against them in later life. This weakness in grasping power becomes all the more problematic if Mercury is lord of the 1st, 3rd or 5th house. The 8th house is directly injurious to both 1st and 3rd houses, and it is injurious to the 5th house owned by Mercury because 5th house rules education. These individuals are either not expert in the matter of accounts, or they are negligent, in spite of their knowledge and expertise in upkeep of and promptness in keeping accounts, as a consequence of which they or their employers suffer losses.

These individuals are careless in attentively reading and understanding any formal or legally binding documents before signing, and as a consequence suffer loss of money, or prestige, or assets. They are also careless in observing or subsequently checking the weight of items being bought, and ultimately suffer loss in terms of money. They do not take seriously the teachers, who give helpful and friendly guidance to their pupils. On the other hand some greedy teachers try to help their tutored pupils by unfair means or by approaching fellow teachers and examiners. Students under this combination indulge in unfair means even at university level; and do not hesitate to pirate matter for their doctorate degree. In professional level, in literary or research or journalistic workshops these individuals depend more on piracy of material written by experts rather than acquiring knowledge themselves and then writing their own original matter.

Mars and Jupiter in the 8th House

This combination of Mars and Jupiter in the 8th house is as confusing as that of Mars with Mercury. In so far as young students are concerned, it gives them poor memory, which they try to make up by copying, unfair means, and approaches. Consequences are the same, weak foundation and half-baked knowledge. But this deficiency can be improved in students of young age by proper guidance and practice.

These individuals suffer losses in shares and stocks, in non-recovery or partial recovery or piecemeal recovery of their dues and deposits; and sometimes loss of bullion or gold ornaments or jewellery or precious stones by theft or own carelessness. These individuals are careless about their accounts, and suffer losses by embezzlement, wrong invoices, pilferage from godowns and of goods in transit.

They get cheated in candidature for elective offices of profit; sometimes they themselves surrender their candidature for a price in cash or kind. The main point is that these individuals do not reach the elective office of profit.

Mars and Jupiter together tend to give trouble to the respiratory system, complaints of diabetes and kidney; the main problem being that this combination works adversely with surgical or instrumental treatment of any of these physical ailments or troubles.

Mars and Venus in the 8th House

On one hand this combination makes a person master in the knowledge (theory and practice) of love, romance and all matters related thereto; on the other it gives an aptitude or inclination for more than one relationship with the opposite sex. The person knows artistic skills or musical or dramatic acts or acting including stunt acts & actions as also dance-oriented skills to attract first the attention and ultimately the liking and love of the opposite sex. Sometimes these very tendencies and skills kill the happiness in married life. If these people do not like a certain person of the same sex or opposite sex, they talk against the person and get rid of him or her from their inner circle of friends and acquaintances. Sometimes the same kind of treatment happens to them as well. They get paid in their own coin!

At the same time, this combination leads to diseases related to sex, including heat element in blood with outward manifestation on skin, all the more so if Mars or Venus happens to own the 6th, 8th or the 12th house or even the 2nd house. When 2nd house is owned by Mars or Venus the individual transmits own complaint of sex-oriented trouble to the spouse, or the partner in love or to those who indulged with that person in cohabitation.

The notable point of this combination is that these individuals can be used to influence persons in power or persons of importance. Women with this combination may be found being used *(willingly or unwillingly)* in spying work or assistance in it, as also in influencing politicians and persons in authority. Such individuals can be planted on politicians, persons in power to blackmail them for ulterior motives, because these women have a charming personality and know the art of winning over people by suggestive talks, voice and gestures.

These individuals are fond of good things in life, fashionable style of clothes and living, perfumes, flowers, decorated (well-appointed) drawing-rooms, and bedrooms. If another soft star is in the 12th house or the 2nd house, these individuals become fond of drinks, more or less on a regular basis.

They rarely take risk in shares and stocks or lending money

or jewellery to others. They are quite *civilised* in their refusals in such matters. In their romantic approach, they do not distinguish much between permitted and prohibited degrees of relations. They give impressive gifts but not very costly ones, unless Jupiter is in the 6th or the 12th house.

These individuals shouldn't take risk with water, fire, acids, electricity, poisonous items and should avoid smoking in bed.

Mars and Saturn in the 8th House

This combination of Mars and Saturn in the 8th house makes an individual brave, bold, daring, fearless to physical risks, knowledgeable in handling arms, ammunition, and weaponry. They are generally found very fit and efficient for service in combatant forces, armed police, ordnance factories, trainers to defence and police personnel, commanders of troops, leaders in charting strategy for wars and battles, for border security, or internal security.

They are given to anger and stubbornness. They may not indicate disobedience to an order or command face to face, but they often stick to their line of thinking and self-arrived conclusions.

They make expert dacoits, robbers, smugglers, and dealers in contraband goods, arms, ammunition, and weaponry. Some of them manufacture unlicensed weapons, while some others undertake sale and distribution of such weapons.

These individuals are vulnerable to oft-repeated injuries from the very childhood, but they keep on growing physically and habit-wise as well as nature-wise on the lines mentioned above. They rarely regret whether they have injured others or themselves, taking injuries as normal event in life. Artists and performers in stunt films and circus establishments generally belong to this combination in their 8th house. Jokers in circus would however go under Mars with Mercury or Mars with Venus combination in the 8th.

They are vulnerable to disturbed digestive system, and in spite of being in the defence forces or police-outfits, they become fat, moreso around the belly and waist. In the case of women, the fat is generally around hips and bottom too. These individuals suffer, in advanced years of age, from rheumatism, arthritis, sciatica, and allied ailments. Fractures of bones are also caused by this combination when any of these two planets is running its sub-period or a harmful placement in the Yearly-chart or in transit in the 2nd, 8th or the 12th house.

It has to be remembered that Saturn is lord of the entire bone frame in human body, with special impact on legs, waistline, spinal cord and skull. When it is in a harmful placement in the Yearly-chart or is running its sub-period, or is in transit over the 2nd, 8th or the 12th house, it would not hesitate to cause injury (minor or major) to any of these parts in the body.

And the last but most important function attributed to this combination is that they can cause termination of the pregnancy at any stage on slightest lapse or pretext. Women having this combination in their 8th house must avoid cohabitation with their male partner, at least after the completion of the 5th month of the pregnancy. Young kids, from infancy to adulthood, have the risk of repeated falls, minor injuries but sometimes leading to bone-fracture too.

Mars and Rahu in the 8th House

This combination of Mars and Rahu in the 8th house invariably gives obesity to the individual, irrespective of digestive problems.

In spite of strong physique, these individuals suffer a kind of fear complex internally, though outwardly they brag and boast about their boldness and brave nature. Even ordinary fever or minor injury makes them exhibit great pain than actuality. They are often secretive in their acts, actions and ambitions, and at the same time, they suspect intentions and motives of others (reflection of mind of self)! They are impostors; if they indulge in drinks or any kind of misdeeds, they would pose to be pious and prohibitionist. They are able to keep a guarded secret of their extra-marital affair or a love affair or even casual relationship with opposite sex.

They get wildly angry, and if the sufferer indicates even

a mild reaction, sometimes in the same breath they show an outward sympathy and sorrowful regret.

They may have tendency cold-blooded murders or some other similar barbaric act, action or crime.

They may have tendency or desire for unconventional sex.

Mars and Ketu in the 8th House

The combination of Mars and Ketu in the 8th house gives the same results as that of Mars and Rahu, but in a reduced degree of effect. But they are rarely rash and rough towards others in their behaviour.

MARS IN THE 9TH HOUSE

This position of Mars is difficult to analyse. However, three points deserve special attention:

(a) It disturbs the inheritance rights of the person. The individual doesn't get possession of full share in ancestral property. Other claimants, whether they are right or wrong, pull the leg of or get over, or overtake the rightful claimant. Quarrels, fights, civil and criminal litigation takes place quite often, drag on for years, sometimes from one to another generation. Even real brothers, real sisters, first cousins become enemies of one another. Sometimes, out of mere disgust or because of having earned assets and property by own effort, the right claimant surrenders own rights and claims willingly or unwillingly to keep the evil of litigation, quarrels, and fights away from the family. These vents happen even in such cases as have distinctly worded written will, or written settlement of family property and assets, because greed of human being for money, material and property is at the root of this evil. Disaster and murders are not uncommon in these disputes. For gain or for mere fun, neighbours and unconcerned relations too side with one party or the other in these disputes. It is advisable that when a parent finds Mars in the 9th house of a progeny, the parent shouldn't build houses for joint living of the progeny, shouldn't establish business and industry in joint names or joint ownership of the progeny. The parent should watch out for greedy uncles, aunts and cousins, nephews and nieces of such progeny with Mars in the 9th house, and keep them away from own progeny's inheritance.

(b) The additional evil of Mars in the 9th house is that if there are debts and liabilities in inheritance, the individual is burdened with much greater load thereof than the normal share of the individuals. Efforts of the spouse can protect the individual against burden of extra liability to a certain extent.

(c) Even while deciding marriage with a person (boy or girl) with Mars in the 9th house, the scope for quarrel and dispute over assets and property matters should be looked into by the parents or guardians on both sides, at least secretly. The reason is that a person with Mars in the 9th house is often at a big or small loss in matters of succession and inheritance.

In this particular matter, the individual has also to be blamed to a certain extent as he or she becomes intimate with and serviceful to the source of inheritance. Sometimes allegations fly openly that the dying person has given cash or jewellery in a hidden manner to the individual, depriving others of their due share.

First, it is always better to keep the relationship and services rendered to the source of inheritance open to other claimants. Secondly, when the source of inheritance is on death-bed as it were, it is better (and wise) to inform all other heirs and claimants, leaving no basis for suspicion and subsequent allegations or legal battles.

This question becomes all the more important where a person comes by adoption from one family to another family or by way of son-in-law domiciled in the family of the wife (known as *"ghar jamai"* in North India). It has to be so because often other relatives of the adopting parent(s) consider that their rights are crushed by the adoption of the son-in-law as a son, heir, and successor. Whether right or wrong, such relatives are very much looking forward to inheriting the assets of the person concerned.

So they try to create problems and trouble for the adopted child or the child-in-law.

Joint properties or joint business or joint industrial ventures between brothers or between cousins also constitute bones of dispute between the brothers, sisters, and cousins.

Even when the question discussed above is not there, often the relationship between the individual and uncles or aunts or cousins or nephews and nieces get strained for not any concrete reason or rhyme. This strain in relations can spring up between real brothers or between real brothers and sisters as also their respective spouses. Sometimes, these people get divided into groups; and (though quite a rarity) sometimes the entire group gangs-up against a particular individual with Mars in the 9th. Efforts of violence towards that individual are not also ruled out.

Whether of own volition, or per force, (which again is quite a rare occurrence but still possible), an individual with Mars in the 9th house gets pulled into prohibited degree relationship with a member of the opposite sex within the family of self or spouse. Consequences of this type of relationship are better guessed than described.

Then other less important effect of Mars in the 9th is that the person comes up on the administrative or management body of a religious, social, charitable, political, educational, medical formation. Depending on association of Mars with other evil stars, sometimes the individual suffers from defamation for misuse of funds or misuse of powers or misappropriation of resources of the establishment, not so much by acts of omission or commission of the individual, but more for the faults of others working there.

Mars in the 9th house helps an individual to come in contact with persons in power and authority, and thereby leading the individual towards any responsible position in politics or administration or membership of organisation considered as office of profit.

Mars and Sun in the 9th House

These two combinations have been discussed in chapters on Sun in 9th house. It may be added that Sun and Mars in 9th house take a person towards people in power in government and politics, and in any family disputes, the individual seeks help and support from government personages. It may be further added that any individual with this combination does entertain at least an idea (if not implemented in practical action) of romantic inclination towards a person of the opposite sex in an incestuous relationship.

For more on Mars and Sun combination in the 9th house, please see the earlier chapter on Sun in the 9th house.

Mars and Moon in the 9th House

If Moon is in 9th house with Mars, the individual puts the romantic inclination of an incestuous relationship into action by taking some concrete step. But in such cases, the actual result would depend to a great extent on the placement of Venus in the Birth-chart and mutual relationship of that Venus with this combination in the 9th house.

For more details, please refer to the earlier chapter on Moon and Mars combinations.

Mars and Mercury in the 9th House

This combination of Mars and Mercury in the 9th house permits intelligence, wisdom, and good morals to prevail upon the individual and helps to check thoughts regarding such unconventional relationship.

This combination further gives the individual a position of prestige in the running of an educational, literary, or journalistic body. It leads the person towards being a writer, poet, journalist, critic, priest or preacher of religion and devotion to God Almighty. Mercury leads a person more towards reading and reciting religious scriptures and less towards meditation etc.

Mars and Jupiter in the 9th House

The combination of Mars and Jupiter in the 9th house grants the individual, at least some relief, from the wicked and wrongful claims of others on the individual's material interests, assets and property due to him or her from ancestors, natural or adoptive parents or by any kind of inheritance or gift etc.

This combination can give the individual adequate insight and knowledge in law or economics or systematic account-keeping, history or political science, and if Jupiter is lord of the 5th, 10th or 11th house, this combination would give the individual proper education in any of the disciplines mentioned here.

This combination is also capable of giving the individual suitable post, job, or profession in judiciary or other openings connected with these disciplines of formal education. If Mercury is in any manner associated with this combination, the individual might become an author of stray articles or full-fledged books on subjects of his/ her education, study, or practical experience.

These individuals are very religious in thought, and sometimes in action too. These individuals, in spite of being well read and learned, feel more inclined towards meditation, or collective and mass prayers.

Mars and Venus in the 9th House

The combination of Mars and Venus in the 9th house gives the individual an interest in music (both vocal and instrumental), poetry (own composition and reading that of others), painting, photography.

Additional lines of activity for these individuals is distillery, running prostitution (involving both males and females), manufacture and marketing of alcohols, perfumes, trading in musical instruments, running passport rackets and illegally despatching humans (adults and young kids) to other countries and states.

Further line of activity for them can be arranging matrimonial matches for brothers and sisters of self and of spouse or of friends, loudly raising issues in public, in politics and in legislature pertaining to women.

They give a good account of themselves in medical practice, trading in herbals and medicinal raw material, end-product medicines. They attain success in import and export business too, in spite of tendency of lethargy and delayed functioning. Normally they get a good name in whatever career they follow.

On the drawback side is the indulgence of these individuals into romantic relationship with own students, disciples, and members of the opposite sex within prohibited degrees. In spite of this element in their character, they are able to keep a good face in the public, though not within the family circles because the 9th house concerns name and fame also.

Mars and Saturn in the 9th House

This combination of Mars and Saturn in the 9th house puts a hurdle on the rights and claims of the individual on rightful inheritance, succession and possession of assets and properties etc., including ancestral business and industrial interests.

These two stars together create scope for direct confrontation or conflict with uncle(s), aunt(s), cousin(s), nephew(s), niece(s), and spouses of brother(s) and sister(s). The individual should desist from dragging matters to physical violence. It is better to examine the position of Jupiter in the Birth-chart vis-à-vis mahadasa and sub-period as also transit of long term stars (Jupiter, Rahu, Saturn), at the critical point of time related to actual inheritance and then take the matter to a legal forum. If Jupiter is helpful in Birth-chart and in its Navamsha too, the chances are strong for the individual to enjoy own rights and claims fully, getting out of the traps laid by the above-mentioned relations.

Further, in the case of confrontation, the individual must keep off even mere thought of physical relationship within prohibited degrees of relations. Otherwise it would create more enemies than the individual's capacity to face and fight with.

The individual must always keep an eye on one's reputation, prestige, and popularity in public, as Mars and Saturn combination is positively out to damage it.

In the childhood and adolescent years, the individual should not indulge in beating any person, younger or elder, because the individual is likely to be blamed for a serious hurt or injury.

During adult age, it is always better for these individuals to keep away from confrontation and controversy with neighbours, with near relations, within caste and community, and in trade union arena. These people are apt to threaten and blackmail employers of large contingents of labour, the ultimate result of which can be a violent attack on their reputation in public or on their person itself, with attackers remaining undetected.

Those individuals who are working on intelligence or spying jobs must keep the work-address and home-address of their spouse and kids as much secret as possible, if necessary hiring a new residence for them at the cost of the employer so long as they are posted to that specific job.

Mars and Rahu in the 9th House

This combination of Mars and Rahu in the 9th house doesn't make much change in the effect and influence of Mars in the 9th house, except that the person earns a bad name easily and quickly for any misdeed in which the individual is involved. Sometimes the individual's name is dragged even without his or her involvement.

In so far as near relations and friends are concerned, they might give the individual a bad name even on shadow of suspicion, without solid basis for allegation against him or her.

So far as ancestral property and inheritance matters are concerned, the non-entitled person would put up only shadow hurdles and if the rightful individual puts forth a strong defence, he or she would suffer only minor loss, reduction, or deficiency.

In political field, these individuals have to struggle hard for their right position in the party, and as far as possible, they shouldn't give up the parent party and shouldn't try to float a new party, as they would not much succeed in such an endeavour.

Mars and Ketu in the 9th House

Mars and Ketu combination in the 9th would give results similar to that of Mars with Rahu described in the preceding paragraph, no doubt in a reduced degree.

Mars in the 10th House

All ancient and modern *acharyas* are unanimous in the opinion that Mars gives best result in the 10th house. Even *Abdur-Rahim-Khaan-a-khaana*, who was one of the important Ministers of the *Mughal Emperor Akbar* has laid down that success would touch the feet of the person with Mars in the 10th house. *Abdur-Rahim-Khan-a-khaanaa* was himself a very learned and experienced astrologer who authored some 4 or 5 books on astrology, though only one or two are available now.

No doubt it gives success. One condition is that Mars' own Rasi (Aries or Scorpio) shouldn't be in the 10th house. Secondly it gives better or full results if Mars is alone in the 10th house. Presence of other stars with Mars reduces the promised effect of Mars in the 10th house. Third important point is that Saturn, Rahu or Sun or Jupiter shouldn't be in the 12th house, nor Mars should be in the 12th or 2nd house in the Navamsha-chart of that male individual, or in the 12th or 2nd house in the Trinshansha of that female individual.

Another important factor is relationship of Mars with its house lord. Suppose it is Saturn's Sign (Rasi) in the 10th house, and Saturn is occupying the 5th, 9th or 7th house or casting its direct aspect from the 4th house, than Saturn would reduce the effectivity of Mars in the 10th house.

Yet another hurdle in the full effectivity of Mars is Jupiter in the 8th or 6th house. It doesn't make much difference in the effectivity of Mars being in its Sign of exaltation or *Vargottam*. No doubt Mars gives better results if it is in Leo and alone in the 10th house. Therefore an astrologer must study these points correctly and carefully so as not to make the individual jump with joy on simply finding Mars in the 10th house.

Subject to the above constraints, it can be said with confidence that Mars gives the best results in matters of career, profession, and gives very good results in matters of business. In so far as results in regard to industrial ventures are concerned, the results depend on other important factors, viz., what items the industry produces. Whether it produces capital goods, or just consumption goods, and what is the placement of Saturn in the Birth-chart and what is the mutual relationship between Saturn and Mars. It has to be kept in mind that Saturn has basic and primary concern with every kind of industrial venture. Mars generally helps in manufacture of electrical and electronic goods of all kind including computers, radios, televisions, and equipment allied to all these items.

It can however be safely predicted that Mars would give very brilliant results and rise to the individuals in matters of service (job) in any and every field, and also in political career of the individual. It gives outstanding success in speculation in property of any kind, and also in brokerage or middleman's business in property transactions.

Because this position of Mars is extremely helpful in trade or industry related to electricals, electronics, computers, so much so that it helps in matters of service also in any of these trades.

So far in respect of any planet and any house in the horoscope, the effect of ownership of wicked houses, that is 3rd, 6th, 8th, and sometimes the 12th house too has neither been mentioned nor discussed in this book. It is so because experience of over 66 years of the chief author has indicated that ownership of wicked houses doesn't deserve special and much detailed discussion, because simple ownership of a wicked house does not matter in giving results. Some ancient authors and their blind followers take the 11th house also as a wicked house, but it is not wicked, as other houses also are not, because how can a house of income (which the 11th house is) can be a wicked house!

But in case of Mars in the 10th house, it does matter, because some cases have come to notice where Mars happens to be in Gemini in the 10th house, thus owning the 3rd and the 8th house. This Mars has not been able to show any worth-mentioning results to the individuals in the matter of their service or career as such; no doubt these individuals tried to push up others to front line. No doubt it has been noticed that individuals having Gemini in the 10th house and Mars in the 4th house enjoyed great success in career and in acquiring property by own effort and earnings.

Mars in the 10th in Gemini could not give any political activity also to the individuals because Mercury owns Gemini, which is an enemy of Mars.

What other planetary positions to an extent adversely affect the position of Mars in the 10th house? Combust Moon in 9th house, because of 12th position from Mars in 10th house proved a hurdle for results of Mars in the 10th house. Similarly other stars like Sun, Mercury, Saturn or Rahu in the 9th house also reduce the effectivity of Mars in the 10th house. Normally Mercury in the 9th house, which is house of good fortune, should prove helpful, particularly because Mars and Mercury develop friendly relations at the time of birth being in 2:12 positions from each other.

Therefore, very plainly, one shouldn't blindly believe that Mars in 10th is an easy ladder of success and of no looking back.

It is the appropriate place to make it clear that some astrologers in South India take the 9th house as the house ruling 'father', while by correct consideration the 10th house rules 'father'. The 9th house is concerned no doubt with an individual succeeding to the assets, property, possessions, sometimes post of power, trade and industry owned by the father. It can be called direct inheritance. Since these items constitute means of livelihood, the South India's learned astrological scholars linked it with entire aspect of father. This theory is not quite appealing, going by ancient scriptures as well as our experience of several generations. <u>The 4th house rules mother and, the 7th house from 4th House is naturally the 10th house, which is of the spouse (husband) of mother.</u>

Once it is established beyond reasonable confusion that the 10th house rules father and all matters relating to father, *(excluding the element of succession and inheritance)*, we can go ahead with discussing the relationship between the individual and the father. The questions of father's health, his prosperity or poverty can also be discussed on basis of the 10th house. But primarily, *it must be remembered that an individual is ruled by his own stars*, and the influence of stars of others can have implications between 5 to 20 percent only.

In relationship between father and son (natural or adopted), much would depend on other stars in the 10th house and position of 10th lord in the Birth chart vis-à-vis its attitude towards the 10th house. This point is discussed in the following paragraphs while discussing position of other stars in the 10th house. Mars alone in the 10th house, whatever the Rasi in the 10th house keeps normally cordial relations between father and the son. It is so irrespective of the fact whether son is in the same profession, vocation, business or industrial ventures started and managed by the father, or whether the son has drifted apart from the father's main source of earning, and livelihood. It is also immaterial whether son is having a separate residence owing to his work, in the same town or in a different town or state or even in a different country.

In this entire context wherever the term 'son' has been used, it may please be taken as including the 'daughter' too.

However, if there is lack of cordial relationship between Mars and lord of the 10th house or both have 6:8 positions in the Birth chart, relations would be more formal between father and progeny. However the relations would not be on the border of alienation, boredom, or enmity, unless the spouse of both (father and son) have an upper hand on their husbands and both women have strained relations.

Normally a person with Mars in the 10th house doesn't suffer lack of love, care, and proper maintenance in the childhood and in adolescence. Similarly the father does get normal help, support and service from the son. In deciding father-son relationship it is always worth the trouble to examine the stars of the wives of both of them. Much would depend on the horoscopes of the son's mother and wife.

In case of daughters, in present day world, they get such education as can lead them to self-earning capacity and competence, and there is not much trouble within the family during the lifetime of the father. But after that, the relationship among progeny of the father would depend on stars of every individual.

Mars and Sun or Moon in the 10th House

For more discussions about Sun and Mars in the 10th house, and Moon and Mars in the 10th House, please refer the relevant earlier chapters relating to Sun and Moon.

Mars and Mercury in the 10th House

Note carefully that the combination of every other planet with Mars in the 10th house is very important, and warrants deep study.

Mars and Mercury together can make a person outstanding writer, orator, teacher, journalist, drafts-person, astrologer, palmist, soothsayer, *mantrik, tantrik*, ghost-writer on behalf of others, outstanding examiner of documents, hand-writing specialist, investigator of forged documents, guide to others in writing their applications / petitions / representations / appeals / notifications and copywriters for advertising. Their intelligence, wisdom and experience get recognition and appreciation wherever they work or for whomsoever they work. Sometimes they write poetry, stories, novels, *maha-kavya* (epic poetry) of eternal value. There have been individuals who wrote more for self-satisfaction rather than for the public reading, though ultimately it reaches the public, like the epic *Ramcharitmanas* of *Goswami Tulsidas*, which he claimed he wrote only for satisfaction of self.

On the wrong side, these persons indulge in piracy of others work, get expertise in forgery of documents, false signatures, mischievously changing part or full text of any important document, showing a new document as an old one. Some of these cheap cheats adopt names of ancient authors, poets so as to misguide people as if they too are as important as those authors and poets of the ancient times.

Mars and Jupiter in the 10th House

The combination of Mars and Jupiter in the 10th house produces experts in law, jurisprudence, legislation, economics, accounts, business management of trade and business, or experts on commerce.

Individuals holding important assignments in the

ambassadorial field are generally born under this combination. In India, some top-jurists and draftsman of law, or commentators on law had this combination in the 10th house, one of them being *Dr. Durga Dass Basu*, who wrote the famous four-volume commentary on the Constitution of India. Combination of these two planets makes very expert producers of statutes. For example, *Dr Bhimrao Ramaji Ambedkar* (one of the original authors of India's written constitution) had no correct Birth-chart but it is presumed that he had this type of combination in his 10th house. It is actually unfortunate in our country that we do not have any record of the Birth charts of eminent jurists and judges. It needs special effort to make a compilation of the *correct* Birth-charts of these eminent persons. Many members of legislator in every country have this combination in the 10th house. This combination makes efficient taxation officers and also experts, advocates and lawyers on taxation side.

It is noteworthy that in any country having proper and regular constitutional and legal system of government, there have been such judges of the supreme courts and high courts as have given judgements forming a part of the statute book or making important changes and amendments in the statute books. They had Mars and Jupiter in the 10th house.

On the wrong side, this combination makes supporters of crime and criminals in the shape of advocates and legal counsels, corrupt judges and magistrates, corrupt accountants, corrupt taxation officers, agents in the corridors of power, corrupt customs clearance agents, corrupt brokers in shares and stocks.

Then this combination gives the society leading corrupt Parliamentarians, Legislators, Dictators and Rulers, jewellers, ornament-artists, bullion merchants, money lenders, agents between borrowers and banks, clever or efficient bankers, insurers, brokers and agents in the field of insurance of human life and of goods and property etc.

Mars and Venus in the 10th House

This combination of Mars and Venus in the 10th house gives the society expert physicians and surgeons, radiologists, pathologists, orthopaedic and optical surgeons, heart surgeons, cardiologists, neurologists, and also those who write important books on these subjects.

This combination also gives experts in marine battles, sexologists, women politicians, heroines and actresses, seamen, smugglers by marine routes, spurious drug manufacturers and traders. The society also gets from this combination alcohol manufacturers and merchants, perfumers, florists, teachers in any of these professions and arts, dancers of the fiery *'tandava-nritya'* types, experts in instrumental music, irrigation and water resources engineers, ingenious water explorers, and other allied professions.

These persons are fond of making friendship with the opposite sex at place of work or in the field of work, including with colleagues, disciples or teachers. They normally do so without hitch or hesitation of morality and without botheration about disapproval by the family of self or of the spouse or friends or the society as such. These people often appear at their place of work in such costume, makeup as would immediately attract the attention of the person opposite them or looking at them, because they are often keen to create a first glance impression.

These are the people who scandalise the political arena. They are often senseless or violent when heavily drunk, irrespective of their status in society or their profession, job or vocation or calling.

Mars and Saturn in the 10th House

The combination of Mars and Saturn in the 10th house is an important one, and controversial too!

Both are very strong stars in their own right and valour. They give top class efficiency on one hand, and indulgence in confrontation and conflict or controversy on the other.

Individuals with this combination make top class orthopaedic surgeons, engineers, technicians, ordnance manufacturers, expert in defence and war strategy, fighters, experts in strategy relating to battles whatever their rank. They make expert band masters, owners of big and small industries or factories, transporters on large scale by heavy vehicles. They are successful electrical contractors in hill regions and high-rise buildings, experts in satellite engineering and techniques, explorers in wireless communications, experts in satellite communications including radio and television technology.

On the other hand, some individuals with this combination may turn out to be plunderers, dacoits and robbers by gang-system. They normally do not operate as a single person. Some others take to trading in contrabands including arms and ammunition, experts in replacing arms used in crimes, from police and court custody, efficient police and army personnel.

These are bold and brave people who indulge in booth-capturing of any kind, and any level of elections as also blocking voters from exercise of their right, creating violence with or without reason or rhyme, creating trouble in processions and demonstrations. They are expert in clandestine transport of arms and ammunition, and do not hesitate in acting as hired murderers and *goondas* (hooligans, or goons).

One important point to bear in mind about this combination is that Mars with Saturn combine often create ground for differences between father and son (whether natural or adopted one). Further this combination, during mahadasa of one and sub-period of the other, adversely affects the health or finances of the father or the mother, so much so that if the father's or the mother's own stars are not quite protective, chances get created for surgical treatment of one of them. And in a financial situation like the father (or the mother) sometimes go totally short of ready cash, and are unable to raise cash, even through offer of sale of their immoveable assets, for day-to-day and routine expenses, at that time these individuals provide ready help.

After becoming adult, generally these people stay away or separately from one or both of the parents by mutual agreement or disagreement.

It is also noticed that paternal or maternal grandparents or natural parents of these people sometimes go in for two marriages or develop extra-marital relationship, which in some cases adversely affects the upbringing of the individual in childhood and adolescence years in growth and sometimes in education too.

Mars and Rahu in the 10th House

Mars and Rahu's combination in the 10th house is yet another factor which diminishes to a certain extent the influence and working of Mars in the 10th house.

Rahu being a shadow planet, Mars manages to recover its influence and work-strength soon. Rahu no doubt creates occasional hurdles in the efficient functioning and progress of such individuals as are in service or in politics as profession or means of profit. These two stars together sometimes create disagreement between father and son/child. Whether these disagreements lead to any undesirable consequences depends on the lords of the 1st and 10th houses and their inter-relationship as well as their relationship independently with Mars and Rahu in the 10th house.

Further, in a battlefield or in a fight, this combination creates a touch of fear or withdrawal in the mind of the individual, midway during the battle. Normally Mars is a bold, dashing, daring and fearless star, but Rahu sometimes diminishes this quality in the individual concerned. These individuals apt to be dragged by others into corrupt practices, though normally, on their own they are not inclined to indulge in corruption.

Mars and Ketu in the 10th House

The combination of Mars and Ketu in the 10th house would act somewhat on the lines of combination of Mars and Mercury in the 10th house. It is so because Ketu has got qualities and effect somewhat similar to Mercury, and therefore readers may read in the above paragraphs observations given under combination of Mars and Mercury in the 10th house. The only difference in Mars and Ketu combination in the 10th house is that being a shadow planet, Ketu is not able to exert its effect to the extent Mercury can.

Mars in the 11th House

This is one of the most, beneficial positions of Mars in any horoscope, notwithstanding the Rasi in the 11th house.

Though Mars in 11th house with direct *drishti* on the 5th house, which rules education, naturally creates some untenable and inconvenient phases in school and post-school education. No doubt, Mars in the 11th house assures full results for an individual's effort towards earning an income or livelihood for self and the family. In some cases, when Mars occupies its own Rasi (Aries or Scorpio), or Rasi of its exaltation (Capricorn), or Leo or Sagittarius or Pisces, it is capable of giving unearned income to the individual. It helps in succeeding to property and assets, other than the ancestral or parental one, through adoption or gift. It is more or less sure that Mars in the 11th house makes the individual owner of one or the other immoveable asset, property etc., by fair or foul means, so much so that the individual might encroach upon someone else's property and subsequently manage to get it regularised. In some cases the individual buys a property by his or her own earnings or savings. Yet in some other cases, the individual, whether a man or a woman, gains ownership of property by marriage, which can be joint ownership or independent ownership.

If Sun is also favourable by its position in 3rd, 4th, 6th, 8th, 10th or 11th house itself, the individual has bright chances of selection to a high-ranking cadre under the government or in any public sector formation. Otherwise the individual gains a position of power in politics.

Mars in the 11th house in not concerned with fair or foul means in earning income. Income from any source or by any means is always income, nothing else! One of the sources can be bribery too owing to holding a position of public dealing or position of power. It can also be liaison work in corridors of power.

If Mars is in its own Rasi, Aries or Capricorn, the individual is unhesitant in use of cunningness, tricks, falsehood, force and violence in achieving one's ends. The individual would not hesitate even to hurt the feelings of mother (real or adoptive), elder brother, or elder sister for success in aims, ambitions, and intentions. The individual, whether man or woman, would have no hitch in usurping assets of the elder brother or sister of self or the spouse.

This position of Mars indicates the individual's relations with spouse of son or daughter with regard to their upbringing, education, career, and settlement in source of earning. It is Mars alone that has full 60 degree *drishti* on the 5th house. This is a very important point while determining the individual's relations with own progeny and their spouses.

Mars in the 11th house casts full *drishti* on the 5th house, irrespective of the difference in degrees. The 5th house rules begetting children. Mars does favour, and disfavour, in the same breath in this regard. It grants a male child as heir and successor, which a majority public (at least in India) is desirous of at all cost. And the same Mars causes natural or man-made loss of one or more pregnancies. However this matter equally depends on the stars of the spouse too. In so far as the number of progeny is concerned, it too depends on the stars of both husband and wife. But family planning and laws of the land too interfere in regard to number of progeny.

Because 5th house also concerns competence for education and management capacity, this position of Mars directly affects favourably or unfavourably the educational and management capacity of the individual depending upon position of others stars associated with the 5th house.

Mars in the 11th house sometimes gives an individual property more than real needs, and thereby generates income for the individual. It also encourages the father of the individual to overspend on the individual beyond the capacity of the father. It is likely that the father does so for the individual's education or marriage prospects with a very suitable match or settlement in source of income.

Mars and Sun or Moon in the 11th House

Results of these two combinations have already been discussed in chapters relating to Sun and Moon respectively.

Mars and Mercury in the 11th House

This combination makes the individual a forceful teacher (at school and university level), writer, poet, publisher, bookseller, impressive orator, a person with recognised intelligence, wisdom and experience. It is a different matter, depending on several other factors whether the individual puts these talents and qualities to good use or bad use.

The person always keeps a mental account of purchases, sales, deals, transactions as also of cash spent and actual cash in hand; they are put on record later on, as the situation prevailing may be. Some of the successful and famous writers and scientists have this combination in their 10th or 11th house.

Mars and Jupiter in the 11th House

The combination Mars and Jupiter in the 11th house is capable of making the individual a very capable jurist, lawyer, law-maker, advocate, economist, qualified accountant, business manager, company secretary, negotiator, envoy and ambassador.

If both stars are strong enough in Navamsha too, sometimes the individual stands chances of reaching a peak internationally, like the United Nations, or its allied bodies, or other commonwealth organisations. Advocates given to cross-examine or argue cases hitting below the belt of the person in the witness box or even individuals with this quality generally have this combination in their 11th house. Often honest, straightforward but truth-searching advocates (on the lines of *Sherlock Holmes*, the imaginary detective character by *Sir Arthur Conan Doyle*) are born under this combination in the 11th house. Professors and writers on economics, accounts finesse and finance management, bankers, insurers with diehard views leading to refusal of requests and rejection of claims are also gifted with presence of Mars and Jupiter in the 11th house.

Mars and Venus in the 11th House

The combination of Mars and Venus in the 11th house is considered by beginners in the field of astrology as a clumsy combination, because it leads a person to lack of morality in character.

No doubt, Mars and Venus give an individual freedom of thought about (and sometimes actual indulgence too in) male-female relationship. It does not necessarily mean that it is so always, and in the case of anyone having this combination in the 11th house. Rare cases are always there for every star in any of the 12 houses and also about any combination of two or more stars in any of the 12 houses. That would not always mean 'characterlessness'.

Debauchery actually depends on several other factors including (a) position of Moon and Saturn in the horoscope, (b) position of Moon, Venus, Mars and Saturn in Navamsha-chart in case of males and Trinshansha-chart in case of females, (c) which planet is the lord of the 7th house, (d) where is that lord of the 7th house placed, (e) which stars are occupying the 7th house, 9th and 12th houses, and (f) what is the position of the 'kaaraka' star for the 7th house at the time of birth in the Birth-chart. A collective examination of these six elements would give a correct idea whether the individual would develop any kind of debauchery or not. Even for possessing expert knowledge about "sex" on the lines of Vatsyayana (author of "Kamasutra"), examination of these six points, and in addition examination of position of Mercury and its relationship with the 7th house is unavoidable.

Mars and Venus together in the 11th house have produced some very renowned vocal and instrumental musicians, actors, actresses, producers of films, serials and episodes, owners of cinema houses, distributors of films. In fact very few expert and well-known gynaecologists, experts on venereal diseases, also experts on the disease known as AIDs, experts on treatment of cancer and its allied ailments, experts on sugar and chemicals technology, scientists on pharmaceuticals and pharmacology, experts on herbals and their effect on human body would be found without combination of Mars and Venus in the 11th house or in any other house in the Birth-chart or the Navamsha-chart (of both males and females).

In connection with this combination it should always be remembered that when any two stars are in combination in any house of the Birth-chart or Navamsha-chart, that combination is capable of giving good or bad results depending on many other factors in the horoscope. There are planets like Saturn and Mars that often give good and bad results simultaneously, like a father slapping his child and then immediately giving a chocolate, almost in the same breath.

Mars and Saturn in the 11th House

The combination of Mars and Saturn in the 11th house is taken by some semi-experienced or less experienced astrologers as a mischief generating combination. This is because the 11th house is the house of fair and unfair, earned and unearned income or money, and these two hard planets are taken as dishonest, revengeful and mischief-maker stars in 11th house, specially.

The first important point is that it is not always so. No doubt, these stars together in the 11th house grant, at least in some cases, property, assets, transport vehicles, industrial units, electrical appliances, telecommunication equipment, electrical and electronic items. In very rare cases, some stray individuals under the leadership of or on inspiration from a man or woman with this combination in the 11th house may indulge in looting petrol pumps, banks, bank customers, cooking gas agencies, and road or train passengers.

However this combination of Mars and Saturn, in 11th or any other beneficial house for these two stars to function, which makes the individuals either high class engineers or technocrats, or scientists, or experts in every technical or electrical or electronic trades, or experts in locating mines and minerals. This combination gives to the society a few very skilled or expert labourers and their supervisors working in deeply dug mines other industries, construction of roads and bridges and their maintenance. Architects and engineers expert on digging and laying of foundations for big machinery plants and multi-storied buildings, big job builders and colonisers, combatant or fighter pilots of air defence, war strategists, battle-commanders, fighters, wrestlers, cavaliers, swordsmen and sword dancers too have, very often, this combination in their 11th house.

Now the point is that in these professions too, there are experts and quacks, good-natured as well as evil-intentioned people. Experience of several years would guide an astrologer about predictions for combination of Mars and Saturn, particularly with regard to good and bad effects thereof.

One thing is certain. Normally these people are not given to any hard and fast scruples; money is their motto, money is their master. This greed for money sometimes adversely affects the education or even married life of their children, no doubt, depending on the stars of the children themselves.

As a normal rule, these individuals have robust or strong body and they enjoy good health, and take disadvantage of their physical strength to threaten and terrorise others, particularly those weaker to them. At the same time they are bold and brave and do not give unto threat easily, they face or even challenge the threat giver.

Mars and Rahu in the 11th House

In this combination of Mars and Rahu in the 11th house, the shadow planet Rahu often doesn't have much say if Rahu's influence gets opposed to the influence of Mars.

Rahu just helps and supports Mars in generating as much money as possible, without consideration of fair and unfair means; the end-product money is the concern for individuals with this combination.

These people prove to be good fighters, bullies; at the same time they have sense of fear hidden in their inner self, and when they realise that the threat is real and stronger, they do not hesitate to surrender/ yield.

For illegal activity and action, if they get into the trap of law and Order, they quickly confess their guilt, and if there are co-accused, they do not hesitate to become an 'approver'.

Mars and Ketu in the 11th House

The combination of Mars and Ketu in the 11th house makes Ketu often support and help Mars in whatever Mars is doing in the life of the individual. Ketu surrenders even its own power to Mars and does not land its conclusions on Mars. Though not exactly a follower, it is just one-step backward companion or even a follower of Mars in all good and bad acts.

Mars in the 12th House

This position of Mars is of *general caution for an individual* in matters of behaviour, conduct in private and in public life, expenditure, wrong actions like taking or giving bribes or gratification of any kind. Social offences, criminal acts, penalty and punishment including imprisonment (i.e. jail sentence with or without hard labour), cruelty to own progeny, medical termination of pregnancy adversely affecting the health of the spouse are some of the results which can easily be attributed to Mars in the 12th house.

Mars in 12th can lead an individual to seek premature retirement from service owing to personal circumstances or pressure from the employers, or dismissal from service. Any kind of loss in business, loss by fire and electricity is also caused by Mars in the 12th house. It can cause losses by domestic help and other regular employees, physical attack by own people or by outsiders including opponents, adversaries, thieves, robbers, and dacoits. Man-made disaster to factory or electricity generation and distribution system can be attributed to Mars in the 12th.

The individual might be accused of involvement in acts of theft, dacoity, robbery, smuggling, trading in contraband goods, sheltering criminals, addiction to drinks and other intoxicating drugs or dealing in these drugs. Economic drainage as a consequence of these activities, besides adverse effect of bad habits on married life or wider family life or social life can easily be included in the unfavourable effects of Mars in the 12th house. These results adversely affect the working capacity of the individual.

Certain individuals may have to face enquiries or survey or investigations against their acts of commission and omission. Some individuals suffer heavy losses in betting at the racecourse, gambling, card-games, speculation, and losses for any other reasons. This position of Mars many a time leads to sale of property or other assets to cover up losses and for settlement of debts or sale of one property to acquire another property. Loss of property by encroachment, division in joint family, for education or medical treatment of progeny, for payment of alimony (periodically or in a lump sum settlement) may be included in the results of Mars in the 12th house. Another source of loss of cash or property can be under order of a forum of law, any other empowered department of the government, or even local government or by social and communal formations.

On the favourable side, Mars in the 12th house leads an individual to give substantial help in cash or kind by way of donation or gift to any social, charitable, educational or medical cause. It could be donation of property or premises too.

Dismissals from service, and even death-sentence also fall under the results of Mars in the 12th house.

Renouncement from active family life by acceptance of '*sannyaas*' or by leading a secluded life is also covered by this position of Mars. At the same, returning to and resumption of normal family life after acceptance of '*sannyaas*' also are results of Mars in the 12th house, if a soft planet too is in the 12th house with Mars within 10 degrees.

Putting one's own self into the background for advancement of the spouse falls within the influence of Mars in the 12th house.

Mars can cause disturbed menstrual cycle to ladies or other blood-system-disorder to either of the two sexes, but this position of Mars in isolation normally doesn't lead to actual heart attack, in spite of angina ailment.

It may also be noted that this position of Mars is counted among Defects of Mars for marriage and married life, but it is considered as one of the soft-type defects *(Mangal Dosh)*.

One of the important impact of Mars in the 12th house is that it gives bleeding injuries to the individual often upto the age of 12 years, in some cases extended to the age of 24 years.

Further, minor or major surgical operation is also caused by Mars in the 12th house, moreso in the case of females, which will include caesarean delivery of child or clearance of pregnancy in advanced stage thereof.

Mars and Sun in the 12th House

The combination of these two stars in the 12th house is likely to bring an individual in government service or in the service of any undertaking or organisation or local body connected with central or provincial government or in a corporate body or company within the ownership of any government or in any legislature or advisory body or *panchayat*.

Then while functioning in that capacity, these stars hit the individual with an enquiry or investigation or any other kind of trouble; then bring a situation of penalty, punishment, demotion, degradation or dismissal or institution of a criminal charge and consequential results which might include even imprisonment. Sometimes depending on other protective stars, the individual might be asked to resign, just to save the face of the employer and the employee. In certain hard cases, the punishment comes at the fag end of the career, forfeiting all retirement benefits. In this connection it is better to find out the lord of the 12th house and its relationship with the 12th house as also with Sun and Mars sitting there. The degree of suffering, loss or insult might depend on the lord of the 12th house and its relations with Sun and Mars in the 12th house.

Some of these individuals are bold and brave to sacrifice their interests, physical safety and financial status or goodwill to help a person in distress (often on account of governmental action). This is the bright side of this combination.

These individuals are vulnerable to ailment and disease related to eyes, blood system, skin, headache, and migraine. Because this combination in the 12th house can cause sex-oriented disease too, it is always better to stay restricted to one's spouse only.

Another result of this combination in the 12th house is drop in ownership of property, as stated above, by sale, gift, partition in joint family, dispute within the wider family, governmental action, enemy action, change in boundaries between countries, provinces, counties, municipal bodies, *panchayats*, etc.

Mars and Moon in the 12th House

This combination of Mars and Moon gives wicked, vulgar, damaging and sometime violent thoughts. The question that arises next is whether these thoughts find an expression into actual action or practice. It would depend on the lord of the 12th house, and whether that Lord has friendly or non-friendly relation with the House and these two stars there.

Normally these individuals are at two extremes, viz., either honest, truthful in words and action, straightforward and noble in conduct and character. Or they are expert liars, corrupt as an instinct, tendency to find fault with others, deceitful, taking advantage of thoughts and writings or initiatives of others. They do not hesitate to function as hired witnesses, luggage lifters, indulge in food poisoning, agents of mischief mongers, smugglers and dealers in contraband. However, they are clever enough to always keep a way out for themselves to escape any trouble including that with law and order.

They manipulate bills, memos of sale and purchase, can indulge in high-level over-invoicing and under-invoicing, and cheating innocents, foreigners, etc.

If the combination is in a watery Sign like Cancer, Capricorn, Aquarius, or Pisces, these individuals make good commanders in navy, navigators, swimmers, giving effective medical treatment by water, and some of them prove as real saviours of persons drowning in deep waters.

This combination also makes some individuals importers and exporters of weaponry across the seas, real or hired competitors in the trade of garments, long cloth, medicines, sugar, ghee, cotton, silverware, and pure silver, particularly if either Mars or Moon also owns the 2nd, 10th or 11th house.

Mars and Mercury in the 12th House

Combination of Mars and Mercury in the 12th house produces pirates in the field of literature, journalism, films, episodes, serials, stories, songs, *ghazals*, mottos, emblems etc.

These people imitate the style of speaking and lecturing of the successful personalities. Students are given to use of unfair means in exams and to depend upon approaches and recommendations, or bribes. These persons, without hesitation or hitch, use the material, notes, drafts, reports prepared by intelligent subordinates or by colleagues whose work gets routed through them, as if it had been produced by the individuals themselves.

If the combination is in a Sign owned by Mercury, Jupiter or Venus, these individuals are forceful orators, and capable of giving speeches impressing the audience. These persons have sharp memory if the combination is in Gemini, Libra, or Pisces.

When these people intend to do good work or social service, they do it with full responsibility and commitment, but they cannot stand interference or criticism of their actions, and do not hesitate to use violent language, though they do not indulge in actual violence. If provoked to charity or generosity, they give away their work of labour to others without any hitch or reservation or restriction (it relates to literary work only, which includes ghost writing too).

Mars and Jupiter in the 12th House

The combination of Mars and Jupiter in the 12th house is rather a risky one, in spite of the fact that both are friends to each other.

Some results of this combination are trouble with law and order, irrespective of the fact whether the individual is at fault or not or whether one has committed any offence or crime or not. This individual does not hesitate giving false evidence, making false statement, indulging in production or submission of forged or false documents, or issuing misguiding documents. Some of them have no hesitation in impersonation for pushing forward interest of self or of others for a consideration or in use of stolen documents intently.

They have no hesitation violating any law, rules or regulations of the land or of the civic system, or disturbing the peace and mutual understanding in the neighbourhood, crossing family restrictions, or violating international restraints or customs constraints. They are seldom afraid of penalty, fines, punishment, imprisonment, beatings, and even third degree methods, no matter what the Rasi in the 12th house be. They are certainly afraid of capital punishment and would use all laws and lawyers to escape it by any means including pressure tactics, clemency petitions, agitation, and demonstration.

Normally these persons have enough monetary resources at their disposal, otherwise they know means and methods to obtain money and other assets in their hour of need. They have no hitch to 'beg, borrow or steal', because they have a single track of mind and are single minded towards achievement of their aim or ambition. No means are unfair for them.

But depending on the relationship between Mars and Jupiter on one side and the 12th house lord on the other, they can be very generous, charitable, sacrificial in helping others. They would not mind, if the 12th house is in Gemini, Pisces, Virgo, Cancer, or Scorpio, to spend their last bit of money or wealth for the benefit of others, provided they feel convinced about the need of the sufferer(s). They entertain no fear in full use of their physical power, strength and prowess to rescue any person(s) in distress, calamity or disaster, be it caused by human beings, by animals or by nature's fury, or earthquake or land-slide.

These individuals make expert lawyers on criminal side, or taxation side. Some of the lawmakers have this combination in their 12th house, but their law-drafts suffer from lacuna of mercy and sympathy towards humans. They are straightforward but harsh. Their arguments and judgements survive as readable material for many years, even over centuries. The saints *Yajnavalkya and Manu* (the two great lawgivers of ancient India, authors of *Smritis*, that is Rule-books by their names) must have had this combination in their 12th house, (just a guess; the Birth chart of either of the two are not known!), because their prescriptions of punishment are harsh and hard. The British-India laws and present independent

India's laws have drawn freely from these two most important law-makers of ancient India.

Mars and Venus in the 12th House

Combination of Mars and Venus in the 12th house is an interesting one indeed!

The individual is generally fond of love, romance, sex, could show an inclination towards rough/violent attitude in matters of love and sex, artful, artistic, sophisticated, colourful, extrovert; a bit of a narcissist. No one now knows but scholars presume that *Vatsyayan* (author of *Kama-Sutra*, the Hindu book on sex and lovemaking), could have had this combination in the 12th house, if not in the 5th or the 11th house. In addition he might have had Mercury as lord of the 5th, 11th or 12th house or direct *drishti* of Mercury from the 6th or 5th house, and if none of the these, then perhaps a *Trikona* or *Kendra* relationship with Mars and Venus in the 11th or the 12th house.

With three wives, it is likely that *King Dashrath* (father of *Lord Rama*, the hero of *Ramayan*) also had this combination in the 12th. At least *Keechak* (brother of wife of *King Viraat*) and *Jayadrath* (*Duryodhana's* sister's husband) must have had this combination in their 12th house, otherwise *Keechak* would not have tried to entice *Draupadi*, and *Jayadrath* would not have made an attempt to kidnap *Draupadi, both* with immoral intents.

Individuals having this combination in the 12th are fond of luxury, style, pomp, and show in their living, extra decoration of at least their bedroom. They like paintings on walls, statues on pedestals, fashionable light arrangements, fine and latest-fashion-wardrobe, best quality perfumery and flowers.

How would this prediction reflect on a poor man, labourer, gardener, farm-worker, mason, or others without resources and means? Even they, persons with less means of a luxurious living, stay unusually clean by body and clothes, with whatever little they wear or have. So far as love, romance, and sex are concerned, they can be equally matching in their thoughts, actions and style at their social level, because it doesn't involve money.

This combination can make an individual expert in music (vocal or instrumental), art of acting and dancing, art of architect and sculptor, painting, drawing (including mechanical or electrical sketches and landscapes), in preparation of perfumes, flower decoration, medicines, alcohol, liquors, different kinds of drinks, and intoxicating drugs. If they take to drinks or any other kind of intoxication, they are often violent, hurt themselves or others, specially the opposite sex. They would go to any extent for their pleasure, of whatever kind it is.

Because this combination takes place in the 8th *position* from the 5th house, these individuals have no hesitation resorting to medical termination of pregnancy, or being cruel to their own progeny, or to their step-children. Step-mother or step-father's ill treating and beating step-children may have this combination in their 12th house. Cases are not unheard of in every country individuals have killed, murdered, or led to the murder of own progeny or that of others.

On the softer side, these individuals make sacrifices of any and every kind for sake of their lover or beloved. They have no reservation in giving their disciples and students best of their knowledge of fine arts, medicines, and of everything; however at the same time they are very harsh in treatment of mistakes and lapses on part of disciples and students. Some of these teachers and Gurus do not hesitate in making romantic advances towards their students and disciples.

Another important point about this combination is that it is in the 6th position from the 7th house, which concerns marriage, married life, and relations with spouse. These individuals do not hesitate in extra-marital, casual, or full-time affair(s), taking a mistress, paramour, lover, or having a second spouse during the lifetime of the first one, and they do so in the style of acting as adversary to their first spouse.

Mars and Saturn in the 12th House

Combination of these two hard stars in a difficult house could lead an individual to use of violence, threats, indulgence, or involvement in unlawful acts of commission and omission.

Crime is no big thing for them. They are harsh, and hard towards younger generation, including their own children. They do not bother about money, whether their own or of others, and they have the same attitude towards life and limb of their own and that of others. They neither bother nor worry when they are sentenced to hard-labour imprisonment or capital punishment.

They are somewhat harsh, but in the same breath, they can risk their own life out of kindness and mercy and sympathy for others, may it be even for animals. For this purpose they do not mind any kind of expenditure, notwithstanding whether the money is their own or of others or of the common public. Some of the extravagant Ministers, politicians and bureaucrats, even in the lower strata of establishment, have this combination in their 12th house.

They suffer one kind or the other of penalty, fine, punishment, imprisonment, searches by investigating agencies of taxation, police, or spying outfit. They make expert commanders or supervisors or administrators of spy-ring or any kind of intelligence outfit in the field of commerce, police, defence and matrimony, also officers and commanders of combatant forces and armed police force.

Quite often, these people have serious trouble in their service career and have to change jobs often or have to take premature retirement or have to resign from job or are dismissed from service. Sometimes they lose even their retirement benefits. They make expert controllers or masters over labour force. They prove skilled strategists in war matters.

They gain expertise in electrical and electronic trades, *though without the helpful association of Jupiter* they do not prove so successful in marketing, nor they are very good in recovery of dues. Thus they suffer losses if financial management is left to them entirely.

These two stars together do have a damaging effect on married life of the individuals, more often owing to pressure from the family of the bridegroom or the bride. These persons are often hard-taskmasters and have a tendency of fault finding, giving pinpricks over petty matters, harassing, torturing, beating or proving cruel to the spouse. If a third angle develops in the married life on part of either the husband or the wife, matters go beyond endurance and tolerance, and passage to separation or divorce opens up, though sometimes slowly on account of Saturn's presence with Mars in the 12th house.

These stars also create hurdles and obstacles in trouble-free enjoyment of the ancestral property and assets, which includes that received in adoption, gifted by a near relation or by outsiders. This combine of Mars and Saturn can cause losses in business, contract works, speculation in shares and stocks, betting at horse races, betting of any other kind, gambling, card games, in kitty parties, in savings groups, loss of deposits with private parties including flimsy finance companies.

Mars and Saturn in the 12th house are capable of causing injury to own progeny or other members of family in any kind of accident, fire, firing, violent clashes within family. It could also be between two families, two groups, or in gang-wars, or in struggle for control over an area of crime, smuggling, contraband trading, and other kind of criminal activity or gaining control over a gang or group of criminals.

Mars and Rahu in the 12th House

The combination of Mars and Rahu in the 12th house gives more or less the same results as Mars and Saturn together in the 12th house, the difference being only in *degree* and *intensity* of results.

One major, somewhat adverse impact of these two stars is on the vitality in the bedroom or 'sexual-desire' of one of the partners in marriage or love affair, resulting in adverse impact on the mental faculty of the dissatisfied partner. In some cases this situation results in entry of a third angle between the two which can lead to a gradual drop in the mutual physical relationship between the two partners in marriage or love. There are several other reasons for the development of this situation between the two partners, and it is virtually impossible to enumerate them all. It can be an actual low-vitality or less desire or low physical capacity in the one of the partner. Also, there could be (misplaced) guidance by some of the elders in the family or friends, implying that physical relationship outside moderation could be harmful to the health of either of them. It can be religious feelings, or teachings ingrained in one of the partners, which may be proving detrimental to the other partner. Delicate health of the female, or pressure of upbringing of the young children, low monetary resources, even lack of children could be a possible cause in such matters.

The loss element has also to be considered because the 12th house is chiefly concerned with loss of money (or loss of prestige), loss of job, loss of means of livelihood. The individual sometimes shows losses to the family, to the outsiders, to creditors and lastly to the taxation system, at a much higher level than that actually suffered by the individual, or sometimes no loss suffered at all. Almost all small and medium business people are doing this everywhere. It is presumed that business cannot survive without showing exaggerated and inflated losses, considering the very high share of the income-pie our own government demands on all fronts, from its citizens.

These individuals quite often gain expertise in cheating others for personal gains, or for giving benefit to someone else, or only for sake of malicious satisfaction. There is a saying in English language, "hunter hunted". In the same fashion these individuals get cheated while trying to cheat others.

If in private service, these individuals sometimes conspire with their employers for flimsy dismissal from service to gain the benefit of unemployment allowance or other benefit from the government or undertaking some clandestine business or criminal activity on behalf of the employer.

These individuals change their jobs more often than normal, on their own accord, or under pressure of the employer, or actual and factual dismissal from job. If in defence forces or armed police service, these individuals seek premature retirement to seek civilian job or starting some career on their own.

This is the type of individuals who make their escape good from police custody, or while on bail, or from any jail etc.

They sometimes extend help to others too for escaping from police or judicial custody or from jail etc. If this combination is in Aries, Cancer, Libra or Capricorn in the 12th house, normally they manage their escape while in movement, or from courtroom, or from hospital, etc. If these individuals are punished with fine or financial penalty, they manage in later course of time to evade payment of instalments of the fine or penalty.

These individuals often try to get best benefit for self in any partition of the joint family or division of assets in joint business or partnership in profession. In any case of violent quarrel or fighting, they often are successful in exaggerating their injuries or sufferings and physical hurts.

Mars and Ketu in the 12th House

Ketu sitting in 12th house with Mars reduces the degree and intensity of adverse results of Mars on the individual or his family.

Losses suffered get recouped. Fine or financial penalty sometimes gets pardoned or waived. The individual has hitch and hesitation in deriving undue benefits from parting of ways in joint family or joint business.

This combination makes a person vulnerable to piles, bad stomach, untimely anger, and temporary suffering from skin trouble. These persons should, as far as possible, avoid any kind of unnatural or unhygienic physical relations, as might lead to physical and mental complaints. If these individuals indulge in child beating, the consequences might be risky for the child itself as well as for the individual. These individuals often try to keep accounts by memory and then record them periodically. This will involve risk of loss to them, as they would not often be able to countermand the false claims by the opposite party. It is better for them to be prompt and regular in jotting of accounts, final entry into regular books can be done periodically thereafter.

MERCURY IN THE 12 HOUSES

MERCURY IN GENERAL

The first thing to remember about Mercury is that it is the lord of intelligence, wisdom, experience and application of mind to studies. Thus both formal and self-acquired education depend to a great extent upon Mercury, whatever the subject or discipline of the study. Mercury directly rules teaching, astrology, astronomy, mathematics, journalism, talent for writing books and poetry, any kind of literary work or composition, paper and stationery, science and games of numbers, combinations in games of cards, but it certainly does not rule quack practices in the field of future-telling.

Mercury is a swift moving planet, next only to Moon. It always moves in the vicinity of Sun, and therefore, in the sky, it is rarely visible to the naked eye. Mercury also rules witticism, and sharpness of mind that rules the thinking process. Most important of all, it rules the physical mechanism of speech in the body. While dealing with any defect in speech, one should first of all think of remedy for Mercury. Where deficiency in intelligence and application of one's mind to studies is concerned, only worship of *Goddess Saraswati* will help, whether one's faith or religion permits this type of worship or not.

(a) Education has three main ingredients:

(b) grasp (understanding),

(c) memory (retention), and

(d) capacity for subsequent reproduction from memory (expressing what one learned and remembers).

It is important to understand astrologically that Mercury rules two ingredients, viz. 'grasp' and 'reproduction', while *Jupiter rules 'memory'*. Some persons may have a slow grasp of concepts and fundamentals, but have a good memory for retaining whatever has been learnt and understood. Some may have a good understanding (grasp), but poor memory retention. As is true for any other field, try to search for an experienced, learned scholar in astrological and spiritual field, for any serious consultation and guidance. Quacks, half-baked learners, free-lance experimenters are just out to learn at your expense. They hardly prove helpful, and by putting wrong ideas in your head, they may make things worse.

MERCURY IN THE 1ST HOUSE

Mercury in the 1st house makes an individual highly intelligent. It gives the individual rich power of imagination, analysis, argument, power of oration, capacity for being a successful teacher, writer, poet, journalist, priest, preacher of religion. She or he can be an impressive public speaker, radio-announcer, and newsreader on electronic media, music-composer, songwriter, clerk or clergy.

Normally the individual has good handwriting, and sometimes she or he is an expert in analysis of handwriting including examiner of forged documents or any kind of fraud pertaining to documents.

Most of the great writers, poets and speakers have Mercury in the 1st house, or at least Mercury is the lord of the 1st house. Individuals become all the more sharp in intelligence, writing, teaching and witticism if they have Mercury in the 1st House in Gemini or Virgo. It has to be remembered that Mercury is ascending towards its highest point in *exaltation* upto 15th degree of Virgo, and thereafter it is considered as occupying its own Sign from 16th to the 30th degree. In spite of high level of intelligence, wisdom or experience, an individual with Mercury in the 1st house is vulnerable to cheating by others.

These individuals do not themselves use unfair means in examinations, but allow or help others to use unfair means. But individuals with Mercury in the 1st house often get cheated by their publishers, by editors, and co-writers; in a sense they are easy victims of piracy in the written matter. Sometimes, in spite of being intelligent, they have to manage their education by own effort, say by undertaking tuitions, or some other part-time means of earning while learning. They are always keen to help others in receiving education, either by coaching them or giving scholarships or other kind of encouragement and help. One problem with some of them is they cannot teach dullards and duffers; they lose their patience rather quickly. Neither they resort to flattery easily, nor do they easily stand flattery towards them. They are frank, outspoken and blunt to the extent of hurting the feelings of others. In the field of literature, they prove to be honest but bitter critics. These persons make very efficient and successful research scholars.

Mercury and Sun, Moon or Mars in the 1st House

Combination of Mercury in the 1st house with these three planets has been discussed in earlier chapters.

Mercury and Jupiter in the 1st House

It has been stated above that Mercury is the lord of *intelligence* and Jupiter is the lord of *memory*. These two stars in combination in the 1st house help the individual to receive a high degree of education.

These individuals reach top position in their class, and obtain high percentage of marks, and equally high achievement in post-secondary education. They give an outstanding record of themselves in research work. They are successful in all those subjects or disciplines that have been listed under Mercury and Jupiter individually. They make very efficient law-makers, parliamentarians, legislators, judges, lawyers, advocates, authors on the subjects of economy, accounts, education, journalism, business management, codes of conduct and ethics, laws, treatises on religion and faith, preachers, priests, propagandists, proclaimers, lecturers, readers, professors, journalists and critics.

One major defect in these individuals is that they are sometimes open for buying by others, though they are not basically corrupt, specially if there is no hard planet like Mars, Saturn, Rahu, Sun in the 3rd or the 11th house.

Mercury and Venus in the 1st House

Combination of Mercury and Venus in the 1st house often produces poet–laureate, poetess, court-poet, individual given to poetic justice, free-lance song-writer for films and allied fields, *ghazal*-writer and *ghazal*-singer, or other category of singer, composer of music and tunes.

Pirates of music and songs also fall under this combine. In the modern world, the composers and singers of playback music in films also come under this category.

These persons make emotional lovers, and very artistic partners in the bedroom. Most of the poets of the romanticism era in Sanskrit, Hindi, Persian, Urdu, and other languages in India, as well as those in Europe must have had this combination in their 1st, 5th or 9th houses or in these houses in their Navamsha-charts. Women, who directly or indirectly encouraged their lovers or husbands to write some kind of romance literature, romantic poetry that became classics or best-sellers, must have had this combination in their 1st, 5th or 7th house in the Birth-chart or in their Trinshansha-chart.

These individuals are fond of perfumes, flowers, good garments, decorated houses, or at least their bedroom. Luxury and comfort are the aim and ambition of these individuals. These people are capable of talking, discussing or writing a lot about romanticism, love, lovemaking, and different kinds of sensual pleasures.

Mercury and Saturn in the 1st House

The individuals with Mercury and Saturn combination in the 1st house are intellectually obstinate, and they know how to convince others with their analysis, elucidation and arguments.

Physically they are not strong built, but they have such strong willpower that makes them bold and daring to pick up a fight with persons stronger to them. They do not take their defeat easily, nor do they forget it. They are revengeful, though not to the extent of hurting below the belt. They are always open to pardon a wrong done to them, but do not easily pardon a wrong done to women or to helpless or destitute people. They are honest to their duty, responsibility and conscience; generally honest in money dealings too, but become difficult when anyone tries to be dishonest with them.

They take to writing late in life, but when they do write they are very much correct to the point and stick to the core of their subject. They are not given to flattery.

They are honest critics and often suffer consequences of their honesty. They have parental care and affection for subordinates, but they are hard-task masters at the same time. They come in contact with all categories of people; from poorest among the poor, and richest among the rich, most powerful and authoritative people; but they neither misuse their contacts nor brag about them nor allow themselves to be misused by such high-class contacts.

They generally keep away from any civic offence or severe or simple type of crime. But at the same time they prove to be efficient information gatherers, investigators and invigilators. They neither use unfair means to achieve any desired result, nor extend support to anyone using unfair means.

These persons are rather individualistic in nature, a friend to all but intimate with none. They talk a lot but rarely give out their inner secrets, whether official or private.

They have often to struggle for their education, and quite often they have to manage it themselves by self-help.

Such persons often start their career by service, and there too they have to struggle hard for promotion, rise in rank, full emoluments, etc.

Mercury and Rahu in the 1st House

The individuals with Mercury and Rahu combination in the 1st house are given to sharp sense of self-respect and ego.

Whether male or female, they are unable to control their tears on being insulted or when faced with failure. But at the same time, they are very sensitive to the sufferings of others, and they try their best to help the sufferers.

Rahu in the 1st house often puts hurdles and obstacles in higher education, and sometimes these people do not get admission into a discipline or subject of their choice and have to go in for some inferior course of study. In examinations, they neither suffer failure nor get a very high level of percentage, because they might often be earning while learning. In matters of career too, they often ride two horses at one and the same time, and therefore do not achieve great heights in either of the two lines of their career.

If Saturn or Sun get associated in any manner with this combination of Mercury & Rahu, these people get married to a spouse, who is self-centred, easy-going, quarrelsome and fault-finding type. These individuals often have to attend to their spouse, to keep the peace, and to keep the marriage.

Because of their high sense of *ego*, they often stay honest and responsible to their assignment or undertaken task. They do not beg or steal, and borrowing is also very rare trait as their ego always stands in their way. Because of their sharp-ego, they are generally liked by ladies and gents, instead of being hated, owing to Mercury always staying on the top in their sense of ego. In other words, they have a touch of intelligence and wisdom in their ego, and people coming in contact with them do like them for this reason. Additional point for common people liking these individuals is that they benefit from the sensible and time-befitting counsel of these individuals.

Mercury and Ketu in the 1st House

This individual is *twice* as intelligent as the average person.

In some cases they are unable to put their intelligence and wisdom to their own best advantage, though others may derive full benefit from their wisdom. They are simple and unassuming. They are not much bothered about their dress-sense, their upkeep of personality, nor they are very decorative towards their house, residence or surroundings. They are single-minded towards their aims and ambitions.

They want to be known for their wisdom and experience at any gathering, group of people, meeting or conference; and if they are doubtful about their recognition there, they avoid going there. Here, contrary to the effects of Rahu and Mercury, it is not actually their ego; it is their sense of respect for "pure knowledge and wisdom", which is more important to them. It is more important than recognition of even God. Thus, they are always very respectful towards others possessing knowledge and wisdom. In this 'sense of respect', they are not influenced by titles, fancy degrees, or decorations. They can said to be in the service of people, though not so much physically as intellectually. They get respect from learned people, and those who know the worth of wisdom. Neither they stand fools, nor fools stand them.

MERCURY IN THE 2ND HOUSE

Mercury rules literature, poetry, writing, lecturing, preaching, priest-hood, journalism, account keeping, copy-writing, copying manuscripts, trading in stationery and all kinds of paper, printing on paper or on cloth.

Mercury is further directly concerned with architectural drawings, mechanical drawings, drawings connected with ordnance and weapons, any other kinds of drawings, cartoons, caricatures, taking and giving autographs, writing of stories, dialogues and songs for films and allied areas like TV-serials, episodes etc.

Mercury encourages the individual for writing descriptions of photographs, paintings, functioning as examiner of written tests, conducting interviews and viva-voce, written submissions in courts of law or any legal forum, in taxation offices. And on top of all, Mercury is directly concerned with *piracy* of literature or any other material on any of the above mentioned subjects.

The 2nd house pertains to *collection*s, to *accumulation and accounting* of wealth of any kind and in any shape. Thus Mercury in the 2nd house gives accumulation of any or many of the items and elements mentioned above and also gaining wealth from those sources.

Second house being concerned with collection of any of the above items, it also points to building a library of own or managing the library of any office, institution, school or college or university, and thus includes the job of librarian. Many learned scholars are fond of collecting books and literature, magazines etc. on all subjects, including account keeping.

Depending upon Mercury's association with other planets, preparation of or making use of forged documents or examination of forged documents is also the domain of Mercury.

However, note that *making false statements, denying any statement once made, giving false evidence,* fallacy, perfidy, perjury are also *qualities of Mercury.* These are being mentioned under the 2nd house, because when any kind of gain or benefit or profit or advantage is connected with indulging in any of these acts, the 2nd house becomes relevant. Professional witnesses in courts or connected with searches and seizures by any agency of government fall under Mercury's position in the 2nd house. Suppliers of *ante*dated stamp papers or forged documents or forged signatures for any kind of gain or advantage are also covered by Mercury in the 2nd house.

This shouldn't mean that Mercury has a wicked position in the 2nd house. No, just the contrary. Mercury is a soft planet and always very helpful in gaining knowledge and experience by reading and writing. But it *can* give malicious results too, moreso when in the company of hard planet or when the lord of the 2nd house is connected with any act of malice or falsehood

Mercury and Sun, Moon or Mars in the 2nd House

Combination of Mercury in the 2nd house with these three planets has been discussed in earlier chapters.

Mercury and Jupiter in the 2nd House

Combination of Mercury and Jupiter in the 2nd house is a beneficial one, and it gives to the individual intelligence, wisdom, experience and capacity to derive benefit of these two soft stars in the 2nd house.

The benefit can be derived by the individual from writing books, journalism, teaching, writing textbooks, public speaking, preaching, priesthood, teaching law. Other sources of deriving benefit can be working as a lawyer, advocate, solicitor, attorney, legal representative, envoy, representative at one of the United Nations formations or its allied organisations, like working with the World Bank or International Monetary Fund or any such banking group of allied nations, like the European Union.

These two soft stars in the 2nd house are also connected with banks, insurance companies, brokerage, in shares and stocks or in bullion business, or also with agent to money lending system.

Mercury and Jupiter in the 2nd house also produce stock market broker, bullion market broker, moneylender, broker in banking and insurance markets, speculator in bullion, custodian of valuable items on behalf of others, owner of or manager of Safe Deposit Vault. It also produces bookseller, publisher, copyright agent, indenting agent for books and periodicals, writer of notes on textbooks, manager of all levels of educational institutions, secretary, stenographer, running a placement service for clerks, typists, stenographers, secretarial staff, mediator in legal cases, court counsel in marriage disputes, accounts-expert including expertise in 'number two' accounts (hidden accounts, black-money accounts, laundered accounts), arbitrator or evaluator of assets.

These individuals are fond of collecting books by way of personal library or functioning as a librarian, curator of museum, collector of rare law books, accounts books, books on economy, literature, poetry, epics, ancient books, and manuscripts, coins (numismatics).

Sometimes, specially if Jupiter is lord of the 9th or 11th house, these individuals try to make big money from their valuable collections. These individuals rarely suffer losses in their money dealings, but if the spouse deals in speculative-type business in shares, losses descend on the couple.

If Mars also joins this combination in the 2nd house, these individuals might fall victim to con-men, con-women, and cheats, and ultimately lose a part of their earnings and savings.

Some readers might wonder why we have enumerated *subjects of profession*, career, or calling under the 2nd *house* which ought to have been covered under the 10th house. The reason is simple. The 2nd house concerns wealth and collection, and subjects enumerated above are main sources of accumulation of wealth, which Mercury and Jupiter combine are capable of granting to the individual.

Mercury and Venus in the 2nd House

The combination of Mercury and Venus in the 2nd house is another favourable combination in the 2nd house.

These two are good friends! This combination suggests a person will be fond of good style and standard of living, decoration of house and office, (even of factory), perfumes, fresh flowers, high style and most modern clothes and costumes, impressive dresses whatever their design and fashion. The person will also be fond of books and literature on fine arts, drama, films, serials, episodes, songs, music, musical instruments, illustrated and other kind of books and literature on sex, romance, pleasure, enjoyment, magnificent buildings, temples, gardens, parks, paintings and photos of high class and low class film personalities, exhibiting imported items of household and luxurious living, drawings and caricatures of well-known artists, cartoons, paintings on paper and cloth, photos of gods and goddesses, photos & paintings of ancestors, even of non-ancestors claimed as ancestors or lineage just for creating an impression.

Some of them could not only be inclined towards pornographic literature, photos, graphics, but also of peeping through keyholes, bathing areas, riversides, sea-beaches, by the banks of ponds and lakes. Some of them may indulge in extra-marital affair, and if, for some reason or the other, they cannot or do not want to, they satisfy themselves by a platonic affair. They can be seen talking intimately to spouses of others at clubs, in offices of political parties, at social gatherings, in cinema houses, at airports and railway stations, in trains and buses, and at religious gatherings.

Mercury and Saturn in the 2nd House

Combination of Mercury and Saturn in the 2nd house could said to be a *mischievous* combination of the 2nd house, because Mercury rules intelligence, wisdom, experience and insight, while Saturn rules mischief, undue advantages, bluffing, exploitation, and in certain given situations social and civic offences and sometimes even crimes of serious nature. This combination in certain cases works against the interests of the spouse or against the spouse itself.

This combine leads to false statements, false evidence, false reporting, mischief by police officials in registration or non-registration of crimes and complaints, false entries in police records which may have legal importance or implications. Any kind of forgery of documents, preparation of forged sale-deeds, mortgage documents, transfer-deeds, wills or family settlement papers, power-of-attorney, forged passports, false certificates of every kind, including those in matters of customs and immigration, domicile, residence, parentage, caste and community, are also creation of this combination. Mercury gets subdued under influence of Saturn and then both indulge in production of patent witnesses in court of law, including at search-and-seizure operations.

On the bright side, these individuals are often ready to help persons in need of financial support or moral support, muscle support, security, surety or guarantee of any and every kind.

This combination becomes responsible for giving pain in joints and bones, injury to bone(s) of the spouse too, moreso when Saturn is unfavourable in the yearly progressive chart or in mahadasa or antardasa or in transit movement. In so far as mahadasa and antardasa is concerned, it is more effective during Mercury mahadasa and Saturn antardasa or vice versa. This combination sometimes, correctly or incorrectly, gives suspicion to the individual about the character of the spouse or vice versa. Another disadvantage of this combination is that the family of the spouse interferes in the married life of this couple, or indulges in their exploitation of some kind or the other. No doubt, sometimes the individual may want, on own volition, to prove helpful to the family of the spouse. If the 7th house is stronger than the 2nd house, the spouse helps own family secretly.

Mercury and Rahu in the 2nd House

Usually, some students of astrology believe that in a reduced degree, the combination of Mercury and Rahu in the 2nd house gives the same results as Mercury and Saturn in that house, but in reality, it is not so.

    This combine gives a good accumulation of wealth in the hands of the individual, both by accounted and unaccounted means and methods. The individual often has a very accurate memory of all incoming and outgoing money, of all monetary deals and dealings, and secretly everything is jotted down sooner or later. The individual promises bigger help, donations, contributions for religious, charitable or educational purposes, but in fact, gives much less under excuses and pleadings.

    These individuals do not indulge in too many and too much of false behaviour or false acts and actions, but, if at all they do commit such an act, they are able to conceal it tactfully and successfully. This applies to their general character, including extra-marital affair, if any. *Spouses* of such individuals must always stay alert about their body-weight, because it is usually the spouse's extra body flab that leads such individuals to an extra-marital relationship.

    These individuals normally refuse to give loans without secure security, but if they give a loan, they are strict and punctual about recovery.

Mercury and Ketu in the 2nd House

The common astrological belief is that Ketu has to some extent, the attributes of Mercury and so this combination would rather double the results of Mercury in the 2nd house. It is not so always.

    In this position Ketu acts as a counterpart of Rahu, which it actually and indeed is, and gives results parallel to that of Rahu with Mercury.

    In rare cases, it may give a shadow of suspicion on the morality of the spouse. *Depending* on the Rasi in the 2nd house and relationship of Mercury with Ketu with the lord of the 2nd house, the suspicion may be short-lived and may not persist for a long time. If it is Taurus, Leo or Scorpio, or even Aquarius in the 2nd house and its lord is in 7th or 9th or 12th house, the suspicion persists for long time.

This combine gives a liking for unnatural or unconventional sexual union, either with own spouse, or with someone else.

It also gives a fondness for dabbling in shares and stocks, encouraged by initial gains; the net result is always on the gain-side, if Mars is not in the 2nd or the 8th house.

MERCURY IN THE 3RD HOUSE

Mercury being the lord of education, affects rather adversely such students as those who make excuses in studies, get lower grades, and failures.

These results are all the more inferior if Aries, Cancer or Capricorn is in the 3rd house. Mercury here positively gives a tendency for lethargy but very convincing arguments or reasoning for non-working, working in piecemeal manner, working with diverted attention and half-heartedly. These individuals are generally fond of reading books, periodicals, or even text-books reclining on a couch, sofa, arm-chair or even lying in bed.

These individuals are quite attached and affectionate to brothers and sisters, but when call comes for help or support or assistance of any kind, the response is often late, when more or less it becomes unwanted.

These individuals are good in making excuses and stories of any kind for lapse or failure, and often quite convincingly too. However they have neat and sturdy handwriting, they somehow gain command on language and expression, even on writing speeches and songs infusing bravery and boldness, though they themselves are not good at physical fighting, irrespective of their physical built. They generally avoid working long hours at a stretch, but they see to it that they complete the assigned or undertaken job or work within the anticipated time limit. These individuals have no hesitation in cutting cheap jokes and having light (sometimes bordering on erotic or vulgar) talks.

Mercury and Sun, Moon or Mars in the 3rd House

Combination of Mercury in the 3rd house with these three planets has been discussed in earlier chapters, under the relevant sub-heading.

Mercury and Jupiter in the 3rd House

The combination of Mercury and Jupiter in the 3rd house often makes the individual agreeable and eager to extend a helping hand in any matter, financial, physical or moral, to brother, sister, brother-in-law or sister-in-law, cousin and cousin-in-law; also to uncle and aunt on the side of self or the spouse.

If any of these relations mentioned here have any quarrel or litigation with any outsider, the individual tries to be helpful there too. However, if the quarrel or litigation is between or among own relations, the individual hesitates to take sides and tries to stand aloof.

On the other hand, if the litigation is between the individual and any of the relations, the individual puts in a big and non-compromising fight, whether in a legal forum or outside. Whether the individual is a lawyer or not, he or she exhibit wisdom and legal study to put in a real and substantial fight. Even in verbal dual, the individual would excel others in discussions and arguments.

At the same time, these individuals are helpful, physically and financially, towards sufferers without any hitch of caste, creed, religion, colour, culture, etc. They are perfect in performing their religious and social duty, and responsibility.

If these individuals stand for any prestigious election, they must have their 'favourable hard stars in real helpful positions' examined thoroughly, otherwise Mercury & Jupiter combination in the 3rd house might let the individual down.

Mercury and Venus in the 3rd House

Mercury and Venus are two intimate friends, and normally they are in close vicinity of Sun. Being in the same house, they have to be treated as 'temporary' enemies to each other. When stars are together in the same house they are treated as enemies to each other in Indian astrology, though the enmity gets reduced by being in *Kendra* (square) to each other. But the experience of authors doesn't show any diehard enmity between Mercury and Venus. They function more as friends, both being soft stars, astrologically speaking.

These individuals love, and in response are loved by their brothers, sisters, cousins and their spouses, and also by uncles and aunts, by close relations of mother, though sometimes paternal relations entertain a grudge against them with or without cause. They unhesitatingly indulge in romantic dialogue and jokes with people in their age range, sometimes with uncles and aunts too or their spouses, female friends of wife or male friends of husband. This romantic dialogue introduction sometimes leads ultimately to romantic involvement, or in physical relations, (without consideration of the closeness in relations).

These individuals are neither hard workers themselves nor hard task masters; on the other hand they are always willing to extend any kind of help to their employees, aides, assistants and consultants.

If the responsibility of upbringing younger brother(s) or sister(s) descends on these individuals, they are very careful and alert in discharging that responsibility in a satisfactory manner. They would go to the extent of themselves going without food, but see to it that the ward under their care gets proper feeding.

Mercury and Saturn in the 3rd House

The individuals with Mercury and Saturn combination in the 3rd house exhibit boldness and bravery, hard-work, fulfilment of duties and responsibilities, with a touch of wisdom and experience.

Sometimes they are vulgar in their approach to human beings and matters related thereto; but at the same time chivalrous too in their behaviour, conduct, and attitude. They are nice and affectionate to brother(s) and sister(s) so long as they are responsive. But the moment these individuals find deceit, cheating, cunningness, treachery in behaviour and attitude from any brother or sister (of self or spouse), these individuals become ruthless in return, and would have no hesitation in usurping their rights, possessions, even titles.

If these individuals find adverse attitude or behaviour on part of the mother, step-mother, or adopting mother, they would, without any hitch, express annoyance to her also. Employees of these individuals work hard but do not stand rough treatment or false accusation by the employer.

Mercury and Rahu in the 3rd House

In a reduced manner, the combination of Mercury and Rahu in the 3rd house is likely to give any or all of those results as have been described for Mercury and Saturn combine in the 3rd house.

Being a shadow planet, Rahu when alone in any house does *not* give its full results. But in the company of any solid planet, it becomes fully effective.

Mercury and Ketu in the 3rd House

Though Ketu usually gives results somewhat similar to Mercury, in the 3rd house, even though with Mercury, it makes the individual a hard working person, committed to aims and ambitions adopted, or any work entrusted to or any assignment handed over or any responsibility undertaken.

MERCURY IN THE 4TH HOUSE

This is normally a very favourable position for Mercury for domestic happiness, affection and care *from* mother, affection, respect and care *for* mother.

Mother of the individual supports, helps and guides the individual towards good education, formation of good habits and developing capacity for walking long distances, for education and experience. She also helps and guides the individual to learn caring and affection for the general family resulting in domestic happiness, generous and sympathetic attitude towards all those who come in contact with the individual. Mother further teaches the individual, whether boy or girl, commitment and devotion towards one's assigned or undertaken work, source of income, sense of being useful to the common man.

These individuals often try to acquire property by own earnings, moral, physical and financial support towards construction and establishment of educational, medical, social-utility institutions and works. They have natural instinct to help and guide students, disciples, juniors, as also friends and acquaintances, to help sick and suffering masses without any fear of epidemics and infectious diseases. They have a fondness for various kinds of means of communication and transport.

If not capable of owning a vehicle, these individuals get a lift from others even without asking, and rarely suffer inconvenience for not owning a vehicle.

One specific point noticed about these individuals is that they do not normally prefer to go into adoption, and if they are given into adoption during their infancy or childhood, they try to revert to their natural parental family, not for any greed, just for sake of originality of belonging.

In general, no bad or adverse results have been observed for Mercury in the 4th house, whatever be the Rasi in the 4th house. To top it, Mercury in the 4th house gives a child quick grasp of what is taught at home or in school, and it stands in good stead in later life.

The lines of career, profession or calling that have been enumerated under the 1st and 2nd houses above suit the individuals very well with Mercury in the 4th house.

Mercury and Sun, Moon or Mars in the 4th House

Combination of Mercury in the 4th house with these three planets has been discussed in earlier chapters, under the relevant sub-heading.

Mercury and Jupiter in the 4th House

This is one of the most favourable combinations of Mercury and Jupiter in the 4th house and is very favourable for any individual for various reasons.

Firstly because both are soft planets, and secondly because they have direct aspect (*drishti*) on the 10th house which rules profession, career, calling and source of income. We have already studied that 4th house concerns many important matters in the life of a human being.

The first is feeding immediately after being born. These two stars assure the newly born enough and proper natural breast-feeding. If the mother hasn't enough for breast feeding or is unable for one reason or the other, often 'feeding' by foster mother is arranged, either by employment or by a search in the near relations, or even among neighbours. *That is most important because cases have been noticed where the infant missed mother's natural breast feeding (and affection) in infancy, with the result that the individual, subconsciously, felt something missing in life, and it directly affected the psychology and attitude to people and situations. These two soft stars in the 4th house assure the individual of natural feed, food, love and affection in infancy and childhood, thus helping him or her to grow into a normal, competent and capable person.*

Then 4th house concerns inheritance, whether it is of moveable and immoveable assets or of proper upbringing including maternal care for initial education. In this case that is also assured.

These two soft stars make the person very charitable, generous, helpful and public service oriented individual. If these individuals have no money or resources of their own, they try their best to get resources from donations and contributions in cash or kind or even physical service to the cause. Thereby they try to build-up and run educational, medical, shelter-providing institutions and orphanages, widow-homes, homes for old and destitute persons, without reservation of caste, creed or community or colour.

Whether fully competent or not, stars help them to

earn a big name and reputation as writer, poet, teacher, priest, literary figure, lawyer, advocate, jurist, judge of lower and higher court, legislator, business manager, economist, journalist, expert accountant, etc.

These individuals often try to stay above-board in matters of corruption and dishonest practices, bribery, or illegal gratification of any kind.

These individuals will usually never find themselves in want of a roof over their head and a means of transport; On the other hand they get decent home for residence, office, shop, or for any other work. Conveyance is afforded by self or provided by the employers. If the 4th is a Rasi owned by soft planet, these individuals come to own more than one property and conveyance of the most modern type.

Otherwise, if Aries, Leo, Sagittarius or Capricorn is in the 4th house occupied by these two soft planets, chances are strong for the individual to go into adoption and become rich thereby, or acquiring immoveable assets as gift ('*daan*', or dowry).

These individuals always have a dependable group of friends, and they remain popular in their friends' circle. They are always willing to help or support relations, friends, and also domestic helps; in turn they get suitable response when they stand in need of help or assistance. In case of these individuals the employer-employee relations are cordial and loyal.

Mercury and Venus in the 4th House

In regard to Mercury and Venus combination in the 4th house, the remarks under first paragraph of this chapter relating to Mercury alone in the 4th house may please be read again.

Those results apply in this case too to a good extent. These individuals are often fond of *decorated* residence with modern comforts and facilities, for which they may not hesitate in changing their residence, office, or work place often. Even a slight improvement in their financial status leads them to it. They wear noticeably fashionable clothes and often own an up-to-date wardrobe.

They are open-minded and liberal in their relations with the opposite sex and don't hesitate in either exchanging or even one-sided banter of light jokes and anecdotes. Some of them use this tendency and liberality for making friendship and sexual advances, and if Taurus, Virgo, Gemini, or Pisces is in the 4th house, they may not bother to distinguish between prohibited relationship as opposed to a romantic relation. They get noticed rather quickly for this kind of behaviour and approach. For their pursuit, these individuals make liberal use of flowers, perfumes, items of presents, gifts, offers of help and assistance, offer of company, care and custody too.

They often possess remarkable knowledge about fabrics, clothes, garments, perfumes, and items of fashion and decoration. They do not hesitate in volunteering help and service to obtain them for friends, specially of the opposite sex (sometimes with the hidden motive of romance), including domestic servants and other employees of self or neighbours.

These individuals are good actors, actresses, musicians, painters, and propagandist of *"Shakti-cult"* with honest or hidden selfish motives. Sometimes, in association with some individuals, they work for public service, common-good and social work, which seem, though not always, to carry hidden indecent motives and nuisances.

Mercury and Saturn the in 4th House

The combination of Mercury and Saturn in the 4th house needs careful study.

Intentions and motives of these individuals are neither noticeable nor judge-able on the face or surface of their personal appearance. Mercury gives them the intelligence, wisdom and experience, while Saturn gives them the wilful, wild, wrong intentions in any and every matter where they see their interests.

If the combination is in Taurus, Gemini, Virgo, Scorpio, or Pisces, the individuals will rarely wear dual personality. If it is Aries, Leo, Capricorn, Sagittarius, or Aquarius in the 4th house, they are dependable friends as well as revengeful to wrong-doers, but sometimes even without cause or provocation. If they take to a cause, they are very able fighters, whether it is a court of law or legislature or '*panchayat*' or communal gathering or even on a battlefield. They would go to any extent to achieve their aim or ambition. They never mind hitting below the belt, because they have nothing else than their self-interest in view.

They are not given to change their residence, job or career easily and often. They stick to where they are. They make intelligent but unreliable trade unionists or leaders of farmers and cultivators and of the agricultural labour.

If Pisces, Aries, or Cancer, or Leo is in the 4th house, these individuals sometimes suffer separation from their real mother in their childhood for one reason or the other. It could be illness of the mother, for purpose of education (boarding school, etc), divorce between parents, adoption by others, upbringing by relatives other than natural parents (maternal or paternal grandparents or relations of one of the parents). This separation from the natural mother anytime before the age of 19 years adversely affects the mentality and attitude of these individuals. Some of the adverse traits flow from separation from mother in childhood or at adolescence.

If the stars of the mother or the father are adverse, sometimes the separation from mother might be caused by death of the mother before the age of 19 years of the individual.

These individuals should always be careful about their digestive system, and should watch out against injury or accident by means of transport, train, aeroplane, etc. They have chances of danger from militants, highway robbers, and hijackers, specially if Saturn's mahadasa or antardasa or the 7-1/2 years bad transit is in progress (called the Sani *Saadhe-saati,* in common parlance). Means of transport might be stolen.

In the context of this combination, in some rare cases, the adopting mother, (or even the natural mother) tries to deprive this child of its ancestral assets and claims. On the other hand, this individual might also try to deprive the mother of her rightful assets and means of livelihood. But before giving any prediction in this behalf <u>the astrologer must be sure of his study</u> and experience on this matter, because a slip on part of the astrologer might poison the relationship between mother and progeny.

It is observed that under this combination mother and spouse of an individual do not see eye-to-eye, whatever be the outer behaviour towards each other.

Mercury and Rahu in the 4th House

Combination of Mercury and Rahu in the 4th house is likely to give, in a lesser degree, the same results as by Mercury and Saturn combine in the 4th house; though the results would neither be wild, nor so severe as in Rahu's case.

Mother of such an individual often maintains a deep sense of self-respect, whether she is educated or not. At the same time, progeny also takes care that the mother's ego is respected by all concerned. This combination gives a bit bulky or fattish body to the mother, but only to the natural mother, not to the adopting mother. Another point is that mother of the individual develops a strong sense of understanding and appreciating the nature and psychology of the persons she comes in contact. In other words, she is a good (and rather accurate) judge of human nature. Because of her own sense of ego, she would not try to deprive any person of his or her rightful assets, or possessions. However, mother of this individual may be in the habit of carrying and spreading tales, real or imaginary.

This combination can lead to minor accidents involving the means of transport being used by the individual, but normally the individual doesn't suffer any serious injury as such. Chances of theft of means of transport are not ruled out, but in due course it gets detected.

Mercury and Ketu in the 4th House

Combination of Mercury and Ketu in the 4th house gives the individual a mother, who is kind-hearted, open-minded and generous.

The natural mother of the individual is kind-hearted towards the needy, and she has an eye to realise, recognise and understand the needs and difficulties of others. Because of her correct sense of judgement, whether she has had formal education or not, she does not get impressed by false and manufactured stories of need and difficulty. She is usually quite intelligent.

The mother is always awake to the need of education for own progeny, as also for the children of others, and whatever help she is able to extend for education of those in close contact with her, she would not hesitate to give it. Her progeny is always respectful towards her, and all elderly ladies.

This combination generally doesn't cause accidents of vehicles, and, if rarely it does, the individual escapes unhurt or with just minor bruises.

These individuals are generous and helpful to common man without any reservation. They are keen to help the cause of education, medical facilities, providing shelter to the homeless and rescue-homes for orphans and widows, as also the destitute.

MERCURY IN THE 5TH HOUSE

This is one of the important houses for Mercury; <u>it can be said that Mercury and Jupiter function as the real masters of this house</u>. The 5th house concerns intelligence, education, capacity and training for management, pregnancy, progeny, expertise, mental smartness, safe-and-smooth or difficult-and-painful childbirth, and upbringing of the progeny upto the age of 13 years.

Mercury rules intelligence, and wisdom, learning, experience, education, capacity to grasp, imagination, guess-work, threading the missing links, analysis, collection of information and statistics. Thus it will be seen that *5th house and Mercury are made for each other*. Always consider the placement of Mercury in any Birth-chart and its relationship with the 5th house, and at the same time, consider the *Saptamansh* chart also, irrespective whether it is the horoscope of a male or female.

However, the fact be remembered that memory is basically ruled by Jupiter, but Mercury too is directly connected with memory in the sense that if a matter has not been grasped, it hasn't gone into the mind, and so there is no question whatsoever of memory. Qualities like writing, speaking, literature, journalistic reporting, editing, translation, and oratorship are all ruled by Mercury, and Mercury alone.

Even knowledge of any future-telling sciences, including astrology and palmistry, are the domains of Mercury. No one can become a good and impressive speaker, whether in private conversation or public speaking, without the favourability of Mercury. It has been observed that it is immaterial what Rasi is in the 5th house; Mercury's mere presence is enough to make a person exceptionally intelligent and capable of grasping a matter or a situation in the first instance itself.

If Aries, Gemini, Leo, Virgo, Libra, Sagittarius or Pisces be in the 5th house, the person could become a writer, poet, journalist, professor, teacher, preacher, priest without any restriction of religion, faith or cult.

However, Mercury is not very effective in so far as *drishti* (aspecting) is concerned. From 5th house, Mercury would have direct *drishti* on the 11th house, which concerns income. Mercury would not influence the 11th house to any great extent in spite of its direct *drishti* on the 11th house from the 5th house. One can often find learned scholars, authors, poets, editors, dialogue-writers for films, professors, teachers, priests and preachers in rather tight or hand-to-mouth financial position, often depending on others for financial help, for medical treatment and marriages in family. Though, in modern times things have changed, but in not so distant past, there was a common saying – where there is wealth, there is not much of education, and where there is vast education, there's not of much wealth!

Mercury and Sun, Moon or Mars in the 5th House

Combination of Mercury in the 5th house with these three planets has been discussed in earlier chapters, under the relevant sub-heading.

Mercury and Jupiter in the 5th House

In so far as combination of Mercury with Jupiter in the 5th house is concerned, Jupiter being the lord of money and wealth, helps the individual to have enough income.

In the preceding paragraphs it has been clarified that though Mercury has direct *drishti* on the 11th house, it doesn't help much in matters of income and wealth. Jupiter joining Mercury in the 5th house changes the situation, because Jupiter's direct *drishti* on the 11th house of income would generate enough income in the hands of the individual or her/his spouse. And then normally the individual would not feel paucity for funds for maintenance of the family, for education and marriages of the progeny, for medical needs etc.

Because Jupiter is often success-minded, these individuals do not hesitate in using all means and approaches available to them for fulfilment of their aims and ambitions relating to positions of power, such as judgeship, job of envoy and ambassador, membership of Parliament or of the Legislature.

Appointment on the Cabinet, appointment to any statutory or constitutional formation, professorship, editorship, and all appointment to such posts as have been mentioned above also become within the reach of the individual, because the required educational background had already been provided by Mercury in the 5th house.

Mercury and Jupiter, though normally not very friendly to each other, can work wonders in the 5th house, no doubt if there is no backfiring by any hard planet like Mars, Saturn and Rahu. The 5th house is the one house in any chart where Mercury and Jupiter forget their enmity.

Mercury and Venus in the 5th House

Where the combination of Mercury and Venus in the 5th house is concerned, it has to be remembered that the *5th house rules the mind*, and Venus rules, among other things, romance, love-talks, jokes and anecdotes bordering on the erotic; sometimes downright vulgar.

Thus, with Venus in the 5th house, expect all these qualities. This is the lighter side of the matter. The serious side of this combination is that these individuals could be poets, singers, musicians, medical persons, perfume manufacturers or researchers, fashion designers, garment manufacturers, tailors of high class apparel, architects, landscape designers, pharmaceutical manufacturers, producers or directors of films, serials, episodes; designers of posters and publicity material. Some of them may become educated actors and actresses, duplicates for actors & actresses, dancer, danseuse, songwriters or music-composers, and all these of a high calibre.

It has to be repeated that Mercury is lord of imagination, thinking, guesswork, intelligence, originality, while Venus is master of all fine arts. When these two are together in the house of creativity, wonders naturally work. Because Venus rules love, romance, and sex also, it cannot be helped if these matters also figure in the personality of these individuals. However these individuals normally would not hurt the feelings of others, *except* when they turn critic of the persons performing any of the above activities. A touch of bitterness, or even under-the-surface damage could seep into the criticism, because Aries, Leo, Scorpio, Sagittarius or Aquarius in the 5th house gives rise to personal jealousy or enmity into the criticism. Sometimes it may happen that this individual wishes to support an adversary or competitor of the said writer, poet or artist, and therefore indulges in damaging or destructive criticism of her or his competitor.

Another important point relating to this combination in the 5th house is that it can lead young children, adolescents (boys and girls alike) towards romantic literature, magazines, print-media, video-TV media, whereby they get wrong ideas and impressions, and misleading guidance. Then they want to experiment on those ideas or proceed in the direction of guidance thus received in their young minds. The ultimate result is getting involved in romance and love at an unripe age and immature stage.

The consequences could be socially and personally disastrous, particularly for girls. Educational progress may get dumped. Girls may land into conception, because 5th house rules conception, pregnancy, and ultimately to childbearing. To avoid social stigma, quacks and low-level medical practitioners are usually sought to unburden such conceptions. Sometimes these developments may lead to serious situations. One of the results is temporary or permanent damage to the girl's reproductive organs. Second adverse result can be strain and bitterness in relations between girl and boy, escalating to situations between the parents, or families on both sides.

Co-education school or not, summer camp or not, outstation exams and tests or not, competitive gatherings or not, television or no television, the sum total of this discussion is that if the parents find their child has Mercury and Venus in the 5th house, they should keep a (discreet) vigil on the adolescent. The parents should give guidance in advance so that the adolescent stays on guard of course, and does not fall into an avoidable risk.

Children with this combination in 5th house, <u>have to be emotionally and sexually protected in their growing years</u>, from near relations, teachers and tutors, friends of the same sex but with immoral leanings or character, even teachers in the art of dance and music, or any other fine-arts branch. However, it doesn't mean that such youngsters who do not have this combination in the 5th house may not go in the wrong direction. There *are* several other planetary influences in the horoscope that could lead youngsters, as also grown ups, to deviate.

Mercury and Saturn in the 5th House

Combination of Mercury and Saturn in the 5th house can be defined in one phrase: "mind and mischief".

Mercury is entire mind (the process of thinking), and Saturn is all mischief. It gives all kinds of wrong, mischievous, offensive, criminal-like ideas, and if the owner of the Rasi in the 5th house be Sun, or Mars, or Saturn, the ideas go to the extent of experimentation or implementation on regular basis.

The first question that arises in this context is about the educational progress of the youngsters with this combination in the 5th house. As said earlier, Mercury is the sole Lord of grasp-

power of students, while Saturn is the slowest moving planet among the main nine planets. Herschel, Neptune, and Pluto are not believed to affect individuals so very directly as, (a) they are too far removed from Earth, and (b) they are extremely slow moving to be of major significance in one's lifetime.

The conclusion is that the student would need repetition of the subject taught for correct and long-lasting grasp. If those responsible for teaching (parents and teachers) miss this point, the child could go ahead with a wrong or weak foundation. And she or he would ultimately face either failure, or resort to unfair means, like approaching the examiners, recommendations; some may resort to threats and in extreme cases even violence (depending on position of other stars), to the paper-setters, examiners, for success and promotion.

Check on the transit position of Saturn. When it is in the 4th, 8th, 9th or the 12th house from the Ascendant, the result of the examinations would be disappointing. When Saturn is in the 1st, 3rd, 6th, 10th or the 11th house, the result would be above expectation. If Saturn is in 5th house itself by transit, expect either very inferior results (may be failure too) or student may be admonished for very inferior performance. There is also a remote chance of the student being detected using unfair means at the exam. The result would be the same on Saturn being in the above mentioned positions in the Yearly-chart (*Varshphal*).

For students in science, engineering, or any technical discipline, the influence of Saturn by transit differs. The student would do extremely well if Saturn is in 1st, 2nd, 3rd, 5th, 6th, 8th, 10th or 11th house by transit from the Ascendant or in the Yearly-chart.

While in career, individuals with this combination in 5th house would prove to be efficient and competent technocrats, scientific executives, engineers, builders, ordnance experts, war strategists, spies and intelligence experts. On the adverse side, such the individuals could be successful terrorists, leaders of Mafia or smuggler-gangs, guides to thieves, robbers and dacoits, saboteurs (as friend or as enemy), referees in sports and games. They make efficient teachers of science, engineering, any technical subject, mining, geological survey, and defence strategy.

These individuals take their time in thinking and planning any strategy, but once they decide on, or conclude a plan of action, they stick to it and successfully implement it. They are often competent managers of labour and *subordinate* technical staff, and if there is any labour problem, they prove successful trouble-shooters, if left alone to handle matters.

Then comes the question of pregnancy. By even the slightest lapse, Saturn can cause loss of pregnancy, all the more so if it is in 4th, 7th, 8th, 11th or the 12th house by transit from the Ascendant, or in the Yearly-chart. But at the same time, remember that **Saturn is considered a female planet** in astrology, and if the embryo in the womb is a female child, the loss of pregnancy is not so imminent, so quick, or so easy.

Mercury and Rahu in the 5th House

The combination of Mercury and Rahu in the 5th house gives mischief, without any noticeable or mentionable harm or damage or injury; it is more of fun and mockery type.

However Rahu is quicker than Saturn in causing loss of pregnancy without consideration of it being a male or female embryo in the womb.

This combination leads a child and adolescent to evade own studies including homework and depending more on copying from the work of other students. They depend less on memory and more on reference to books and notebooks, as also on "guide books" instead of textbooks, and on "guess question papers". But a failure or very poor result even once opens the eyes of the students, they become more careful and studious the next year, and then in the years that follow. This combination has no distinction of what Rasi is in the 5th house.

In management matters, these individuals take often resort to divide and rule, and planting spies or stationing one group of workers against the other. They often believe in hearsay, and at the same time are fond of carrying tales and stories.

Recall that Rahu is lord of 'ego' and when intelligence, wisdom, educational qualification experience is under challenge, these individuals rise to the challenge, face it and try their best to prove their worth.

They prove good advisers to rulers and politicians, but if they themselves become rulers or politicians in power, they look to others for advice and guidance. One can find, by sheer observation, well educated and experienced leaders in politics and on seats of power behaving and acting like fools and idiots unless they have the advice and guidance of some 'wise person(s)'.

Mercury and Ketu in the 5th House

As regards combination of Mercury and Ketu in the 5th house it has been repeatedly said above in relevant context that Ketu behaves more or less like Mercury.

Therefore these two together mean that the individual is intelligent, clear-headed and has strong common-sense approach. These individuals are very good in studies and games both, though not so well in dramatics and stage performance. This combination can also cause loss of pregnancy but only on any serious lapse on part of the pregnant woman. These individuals are more theoretical than practical, unless they are under direct *drishti* from the 11th house of Sun, Mars, or Saturn or they have Herschel in the 11th house from the Ascendant. An individual having Sun, Jupiter, Saturn or Rahu in the 1st house would not often need advice and guidance from others, but would, if she or he is agreeable to guidance and advise of others, would implement, without reservation, the schemes, decisions and plans of others too.

This individual becomes sad often, and even boys and men are given to shedding tears on minor matters of failure, sorrow, grief or loss of men, or material.

MERCURY IN THE 6TH HOUSE

In dealing with influence of Mercury in any house, remember that Mercury is an <u>innocent</u>, <u>non-harming</u>, <u>non-violent</u> planet. It doesn't indulge in any harmful activity, at the most it *helps* blackmail, forgery, and threats by spoken and written word.

In ancient times, there was a saying that an educated enemy is better than a foolish friend. This saying applies in its totality to the effect of Mercury in the 6th house. This house rules mainly enemies, opponents, adversaries, competitors, also illnesses and diseases.

In so far as illness is concerned, Mercury in the 6th house adversely affects the intelligence, wisdom, thinking faculties of an individual. And if Mercury in the 6th house has the association of Moon in the 6th, 8th or the 12th house from the Ascendant, Mercury can help Moon in causing touch of fickle-mindedness, indecisiveness and a not-so sharp memory.

If Moon is extra harmful being in waning trend or under pressure of hard planets, then this association between Mercury and Moon might lead the individual to partial insanity. Full insanity would depend upon Navamsha and *Saptansha* charts too, as also family history for the last at least three generations of ancestors, or physical or sexual association with an insane person for quite some time. It has been observed that in case of partial or complete insanity or loss of memory by any accident, hard beatings, illness caused by association between Mercury and Moon, the remedy for recovery lies in medical treatment. Religious and spiritual remedy should be undertaken first for Moon and then, when signs of recovery start appearing in the individual, similar remedy should be undertaken for Mercury too, along with that of Moon.

Mercury does not cause death, even if brain haemorrhage has taken place for any reason whatsoever. Mercury helps the cause of an individual slipping into coma, but if other stars responsible or capable of causing death are not interfering, it might be hoped that the patient would fully or partially recover from the state of coma. Mercury is responsible to a certain extent for eccentricity or delirium before actual death, but even then Mercury doesn't cause the death.

Then comes the question of education, studies, and students. Firstly, the students do not pay enough and un-diverted attention to their studies. They are not hard working; do not attend to their homework or written work fully and properly; depend more on copying from the work of other students. When they take resort to copying and other unfair means in the examination, they get caught, and get punished also, unless they have background support of money or influence.

Mercury in 6th house is capable of giving differences of opinion with mother's paternal family, and if Mercury is in Pisces, Taurus, Leo, or Aquarius, the differences might lead to actual enmity. If Mercury happens to be lord of the 3rd or the 12th house, the maternal family might cause loss of ancestral assets of the individual.

Mercury is lord of written word too, which means that the individual takes extra interest in preparation of petitions, writs, appeals, representations, applications, statements for others or on behalf of self or spouse, required for submission before any court, legal-forum, taxation-authority, police or investigating agency etc. The individual might introduce considerable falsehood or bitterness in such written word; indulge even in forgery knowingly and intentionally. And if the individual loses his or her plea, it is taken as a big defeat and loss of face. In rare cases, the defeated individual takes resort to writing anonymous letters with false or true allegations against the person responsible for his or her defeat or failure.

These individuals have faith in spiritual powers and influences and troubles caused by them, with the result that they either take resort to *mantra, yantra and tantra* themselves, or go to such experts or quacks who claim efficiency in such matters etc. Further, these individuals are sometimes highbrow and consider themselves as master of all knowledge and take resort to mantra, tantra etc. without introduction to it by a '*guru*' (a teacher and a practical guide combined), which tendency quite often ends in harm to them. It is often so in any '*upasana*' (religious remedy) related to *Goddess Durga* or *Bhairava* or any *Yakshini*. Unfortunately, these individuals think that all the knowledge is given in the books and therefore there is no need for a '*guru*', which is not a correct.

Another weak point of persons with Mercury in 6th house is that they are not prompt and regular in keeping accounts, for self as well as for their business, venture, self employment; even when they are employed on accounts-keeping, often they try to manufacture accounts from memory, and mistakes creep in, damaging the system.

Mercury and Sun, Moon or Mars in the 6th House

Combination of Mercury in the 6th house with these three planets has been discussed in earlier chapters, under the relevant sub-heading.

Mercury and Jupiter in the 6th House

The combination between Mercury and Jupiter in the 6th house is a quite risky one, because both are soft stars.

Jupiter is lord of legal troubles, and Mercury rules spoken and written word, including any undertaking, agreement, contract, complaint, false or true allegations. These two stars in the 6th house now and then prove a source of worry, quarrels, disputes, illness, litigation, contempt, and defamation.

Further these two stars are responsible for loss in speculation, litigation, sometimes in criminal charges against the individual, and then loss of hard cash, jewellery, gold items, bullion and other valuable assets by theft, robbery, dacoity, pilferage, embezzlement, snatching of purse or brief case. It is rather difficult to enumerate all means and methods by which losses are caused to the individual.

Losses can be caused also by seizures and searches by the income-tax, customs, central-excise, sales-tax, and revenue recovery outfits of the government. Bribe giving can be another source of a substantial loss of money or costly items, because often in modern times, bribe-receivers refuse to accept hard cash, and want the bribe in the shape of precious stones and jewellery or other costly items.

These two stars are quite capable of getting an enquiry or investigations started against the individual, irrespective of the fact whether there are any substantial grounds or not for such an action as mentioned here.

Then often, at the start of detailed investigations into the conduct of the individual, he or she is suspended from service. In case the individual is in business or industry, his or her bank accounts and bank lockers are put under seizure, thereby preventing the individual or his or her family from operating them. Naturally when such developments take place as mentioned here, the individual and family suffer all kinds of financial hardships, as also loss of face in society.

In cases where the end-result of investigations is dismissal from public service or filing of a criminal complaint against the individual in a court of law, the sufferings of the individual and his or her family are just imaginable.

Combination of Mercury and Jupiter is also capable of bringing troubles and wild charges from the maternal family at the door of the individual. These troubles or wild charges can include allegations of forgery or fraud or embezzlement of mother's personal belongings gifted by her paternal family.

If the individual is holding any position of power or political office of profit, allegations of favouritism and undesirable patronage are likely to be levelled against him or her. There can be allegations of mismanagement of public, charitable, religious or social-cause funds.

A rather <u>unusual</u> effect of this combination can be a *challenge* to the individual for a physical fight, duel, or bout by a rival, competitor, or adversary. It can be an attack on the person of the individual, but in no case it would be dangerous in nature; just to frighten the individual.

Students with this combination need a lot of effort for studies and all the more so if they go in for research in any subject, and should avoid, at all cost, use of unfair means in examinations as otherwise severe punishment might await them. Arts and Commerce would suit these students better than science, engineering and medical studies. They normally need systematic remedy for improvement in grasp and memory. Dropouts from school or from early years in college have this combination in the 6th house in *Janma-Lagna* (Ascendant) or Navamsha or Saptamansh.

Whether the individual is a student or is in career, it is always safe, favourable, and profitable for him or her to offer prayers to *Lord Ganesh* and *Goddess Saraswati*. The individual should not avoid these prayers because of his or her religion or faith or cult being different than Hinduism. He or she should pray every day even if he or she is an atheist. These prayers would positively improve the individual's grasp of a subject matter and also memory.

Sometimes the individual is fond of indulging in making other people quarrel with each other, whether they are husband and wife or father and son or uncle and nephew, or good friends or colleagues and co-workers. If the individual happens to be in legal profession, he or she instigates and encourages people into litigation, often for personal interest or gains. Otherwise too, he or she doesn't fail to offer own services as an intermediary and mediator, arbitrator, social consultant, matrimonial dispute guide and settler of any other kind of dispute or quarrel. The individual often has an eye as to what is there in it for him or her.

These individuals have the boon of knowledge, but they use it more for destructive purpose than for a constructive one. The only good point about them is that they can easily induce and influence others to give donations, contributions, charitable gifts or physical help to the needy persons, sometimes with selfish motive and sometimes selflessly.

These individuals should always stay preventive against cough, cold, bad throat, complaints of the respiratory system, kidney, liver, thyroid. They should avoid over-consumption of ice-cream, cold-beer, cold-beverages, even ice-cold water or curd, and soft drinks.

Mercury and Venus in the 6th House

The combination of Mercury and Venus is yet another pair of soft stars in the 6th house.

They generally have the same good and bad qualities as have been described in the immediately preceding paragraphs above while discussing the results of Mercury and Jupiter combination in the 6th house.

The main difference lies in the mode and manner of mischief, which many a time revolves around the opposite sex, sexual pursuits, medicines, and medical treatment. In certain cases, particularly Mercury or Venus owning the 7th or the 12th house, the mischief or malefic deed might even include trade in women or of young kids for prostitution or slavery or for murderous games and sports. It could be mere source of appeasement of some powerful person or any in authority or in a position to harm the individual.

These individuals often try to function as marriage-makers, marriage brokers, matrimonial trouble-shooters, mediators between husband and wife, but more often than not they do not miss their own motives in so doing.

Whether the individual is a boy or a girl, he or she should go in for own marriage between the age of 18 and 24 at the most, because lack of sexual satisfaction is likely to cause him or her neurological complaints, or partial fickle-mindedness, unlinked thinking, meaningless ideas, hollow and vague thoughts.

These individuals should always stay preventive against sex-oriented ailments and sex-transmitted diseases, including AIDS. It is always in their interest not to have extra marital physical relations or pre-marriage sex with anyone. Girls with this combination are easy sexual victim to teachers, tutors, medical men, spiritual Gurus, maternal uncles and cousins, naval personnel, beauticians, masseurs, florists, musicians, singers, music teachers, dancers and dance teachers. These girls are easily vulnerable to conception, which though cleared, sometimes has a bad bearing on the married life, or temporary or permanent physical damage, including adversely affecting the future fertility.

Generally these girls are tempted by abovementioned type of men through praise of their personality, face, bust, belly and upper portion of legs, with which the 6th house and Venus are directly concerned.

The bright side of this combination in the 6th house is that these individuals make good nursing and medical attendants, conscious to their duty and responsibility. They are good musicians, dancers, teachers, or preachers of all kinds of fine arts, singers, and experts in first aid.

These individuals should stay preventive against risk from water, risk in water and food poisoning. They should check freshness and purity of what they eat and drink, specially during mahadasa or antardasa of Mercury in Venus or Venus in Mercury, or when Mercury or Venus be in the 6th, 8th or 12th house in the Yearly-chart. They are vulnerable easily to poisoning by others.

Mercury and Saturn in the 6th House

In combination of Mercury and Saturn in the 6th house, Saturn is a very strong star moreso in the 3rd, 6th and 11th houses, and no other star, soft or hard, can hold ground against the influence of Saturn there.

This rule applies to Mercury, all the more so because basically Mercury is a friend of Saturn in permanent relationship, and Mercury is a kind of mediator between Sun, Moon, Mars and Jupiter on one side, and Venus, Saturn, Rahu and Ketu on the other side.

Saturn removes all difficulties, suppresses all opposition and enemies or adversaries. Saturn tries its best to give a quick recovery from illness or disease. Saturn encourages the individual to proceed on one's pursuits, aims and ambitions.

The difficult situation is that Saturn cannot remove the problems of the individual created by Mercury in her or his studies, education, research, literary pursuits, teaching, journalism, all activities attributable to Mercury. However Saturn's combination with Mercury encourages the person to work hard and with attention, concentration and devotion. This makes good the deficiency in proper grasp and memory.

The individual makes very useful suggestions in defence strategy, ordnance matters, weaponry, but the one problem that comes in the way of the individual is that some other people take benefit of the individual's work, sometimes the credit also!

Another good effect of Mercury and Saturn in the 6th house is that the individual becomes a good leader of student-unions in school, college, university and any other educational institution. If the individual has, besides having Mercury and Saturn in the 6th house, favourable influence of Sun and/or Jupiter, he or she can develop in due course into an important trade union leader, and later on into a politician and a legislator, parliamentarian or a senator.

The adverse effect is that the individual becomes a bully in school, college, and hostel etc indulging in intimidating weaker students, as also exploiting them in whatever manner it is possible, including extracting money from them. An individual having bad influence of Mars or Venus in the Birth-chart, would turn into a sexual bully too, or a member of the *'goonda-gang'*.

Mercury and Rahu in the 6th House

Combination of Mercury and Rahu in the 6th house would give results somewhat similar to Mercury and Saturn in the 6th house, though on a very reduced scale.

As already stated more than once, Rahu is a shadow planet and so its results, whether alone or with a soft planet, are neither so powerful nor so solid, as that of Mars or Saturn, alone or with some other star. However in this particular house, Rahu removes to a good extent the deficiency is grasp and memory of the individual. It also helps in quick recovery of any brain ailment or mental disturbance of the individual. It helps the individual in winning over any adversary, opponent and even an enemy.

Rahu in the 6th house (notwithstanding Mercury's presence in the 6th house) gives the individual a compromising attitude with a touch of forgiveness, though not forgetfulness. In case the individual is likely to suffer any setback from the paternal family of the mother, this combination would protect the individual from that possibility too. In addition, the individual is able to exercise control over wasteful expenditure by the spouse and to an extent by the general family too.

Mercury and Ketu in the 6th House

Combination of Mercury and Ketu in the 6th house is of a bit difficult type, because as already explained, Ketu follows the result-pattern of Mercury in this particular house too.

It means that the individual would have to exert very much to keep grasp in studies at the required standard. Parents and guardians of such a child should always try to understand the planetary weakness of the child and should help it at personal level, instead of being rough, harsh and wild with anger on the child. After all Ketu has a touch of a hard planet and therefore it would help improving the grasping faculty of the youngster in studies, and capacity for memory would have to be inculcated in the child by parents and teachers or tutors.

In later life, Ketu helps the individual to adjust with colleagues and co-workers as also employees and subordinates or superiors and bosses by bestowing adjustment capacity on the individual. Ketu's combination helps in recovery of any illness or disease. Ketu too is a shadow planet and not so effective as Rahu is, because Rahu is the head, and Ketu is the torso.

Ketu no doubt proves helpful in its own limited way. The difference in effectiveness of Rahu and Ketu, which can be judged from the fact that Rahu mahadasa runs for 18 years while Ketu's mahadasa runs for 7 years only. But this theory shouldn't be applied in the case of Mars. Its mahadasa period is also of 7 years only. The reason is that Mars is a very hard planet and the only planet to stand in comparison to Saturn, and also against Saturn.

MERCURY IN THE 7TH HOUSE

It is one of the best positions for Mercury. We already know that the 7th house rules marriage, married life, opposite sex partner in life.

The 7th house concerns many other elements too, which have been detailed earlier. The subjects concerning the 7th house chiefly concern love affair, and the beloved or the lover, sexual tendency and sexual capacity or lack of sexual capacity (partial and complete, curable or incurable). The 7th house also concerns buying and selling, confrontation, quarrel, fight, settlement in a foreign land, wound or injury at the hands of or at the instance of competitor, opponent, adversary, and enemy.

The success or failure of a marriage (failure includes separation by circumstances, separation because of maladjustment, divorce, death, due to a third person angle in the married life, or due to character-angle of the spouse) are ruled by 7th house. Similarly, lower abdomen, genital area (and any injury to it or any defect or deficiency thereof), sex-related diseases are the domain of the 7th house. Also, encouraging the spouse towards immorality for any kind for personal benefit, or because of deficiency in self, marriage of convenience, contract marriage for a fixed period, taking a mistress or paramour, spouse encouraging or leading the marriage partner towards illegal sexual relations with others are other subjects of the 7th house.

Further litigation, natural or developed tendency towards illegal activity, criminal tendency are also ruled by the 7th house. This enumeration of subjects under the fold of the 7th house is repeated for sake of immediate attention and to serve as a reminder.

When Mercury is alone in the 7th house, it normally gives normally good and beneficial results. Mercury could give, in some rare cases, harmful results when any planet has direct *drishti* on Mercury from the 12th house.

The only bad effect of Mercury in 7th house is that if it is in a Rasi owned by Mars or Saturn (and sometimes the one owned by Sun too), it gives the individual a tendency to blackmail others by writing anonymous letters. Mercury does this to harm a person, or even to favour of a person. The individual might indulge in making bogus-telephone calls, or sending mischievous message on e-mail. If a woman has Cancer in the 7th house (apart from the Rasis mentioned above), she might indulge in some type of blackmail for one reason or the other.

Normally, Mercury in the 7th house gives a person an educated life partner or a friend of the opposite sex. If the partner is not educated, she or he would be intelligent, worldly wise and would have or develop very good understanding of human nature.

The spouse might be a writer, poet, journalist, astrologer or palmist or in any other profession or career mentioned under Mercury's attributes.

Mercury and Sun, Moon or Mars in the 7th House

Combination of Mercury in the 7th house with these three planets has been discussed in earlier chapters, under the relevant sub-heading.

Mercury and Jupiter in the 7th House

The combination of Mercury and Jupiter in the 7th house makes the individuals themselves or their spouses literary persons, jurists, advocates, lawyers, solicitors, judges (at lower and higher levels), expert legislators or accountants/ economists, business managers/ bankers/ insurers, booksellers and publishers, print media tycoons.

When in the field of literature or law, some of them become very famous because of their writings, judgements, arguments before any legal forum, speeches in Parliament or Legislative bodies, introduction and framing of laws with social background, beneficial to the common public. They become very expert teachers, professors in literature, poetry, law, economics, accountancy, business management, commentators on any of these subjects. These attributes could be found in the individual or in the spouse or a friend of the opposite sex substituting for spouse.

On the unfavourable side, these individuals become, (some of them only, and that too in some combinations only), writers, publishers, and sellers of pornographic literature. However, quite a good number of these individuals write and get published damaging comments and criticism on commendable pieces of literature.

They rarely hesitate in favouring criminals and wrong-doers in a court of law or before any other legal forum fully knowing the truth in the matter. They leak out economic and commercial information to the competitors of the firms, companies, parties or persons for whom they might be working.

These individuals tend to exploit their clients by extracting exorbitant fees and other 'cuts' in the resultant gains in law cases or taxation matters. For example in the US (and some other western countries), the advocates, lawyers, solicitors officially claim one-third of the compensation or claim allowed to any victim of accident or from the victim's next of kin, in case of death of the victim by accident or attack.

These individuals do not hesitate in producing false evidence and converting truthful witnesses into hostile witnesses, and thereby extracting extra (and large) gains for themselves. They have only one aim in view: to win the case for their client, and then extract as much gains from the client as becomes possible.

Mercury and Venus in the 7th House

This combination of Mercury and Venus in the 7th house is a boon for gentle individuals, but it can prove to be a nuisance for others when in the Birth-chart of a rascal.

This combination brings a very charming, very beautiful spouse. It could prove a threat too, as the ancients used to say:

> *A father who leaves behind debts, is like an enemy;*
> *A mother who is of loose morals, is like an enemy;*
> *A son who remains an uneducated fool is an enemy; and*
> *A wife beautiful beyond compare, is like an enemy.*

(Ancient Hindu saying)

[In traditional male-dominated societies, handsome husband was not considered such a threat to the wife, as an extraordinarily beautiful wife was to the husband (and his peace of mind)!] Most of us know from Indian history the example of Queen *Padmini* of *Chittaurgarh* and the Emperor *Allauddin Khilji*, and the history of civilisation is replete with many more known and unknown such examples. However, modern and culturally evolved societies respect the privilege of a woman to be beautiful or attractive in her own right, without the male wanting to 'kidnap' her to own her, possess her. But the undercurrent of the <u>feeling</u> (*wanting to somehow associate with such a beautiful woman such as this*) may still exist even today! Therefore, perhaps, most developed countries have some law or the other against 'harassment of women'.]

The spouse can be a highly educated individual, a medical person, a top musician, a well-known dancer or an actor or actress. The spouse can also be an expert in any fine art like architecture, sculpture, designing, colouring, painting, expert in use of herbals, and an expert in knowledge and use of *mantras* for the benefit of the common public.

One aspect is sure –the spouse would be intelligent and worldly wise. However, sometimes this combination can make one (out of the couple) an addict of alcohol or any other drug or some vice-like habit, and the life of the other partner becomes a hell of suffering. If both the partners become addict, which is likely because of this combination in the 7th house, the life for the child(ren) can become a hell!

These individuals generally are kind, generous, charitable, and soft-hearted so long as they are not affected adversely by hard planets casting direct *drishti* on this combination. If however Mars, Saturn, or Rahu join this combination in the 7th house, character and health of the spouse becomes a subject of minute observation and care. If Moon joins Mercury with Venus in the 7th house, the spouse might develop platonic love but would hesitate to indulge in physical connection with a third person, by way of extra marital affair.

These individuals prove good medical persons. But even being a doctor, *hakim* or *vaidya*, the individual must avoid, as far as possible, self-medication without consulting another physician. If Mars or Saturn is also in the 7th house, and if the individual is a surgeon, radiologist, or pathologist, she or he is dependable for others. However he or she should avoid performing any major surgery on spouse or mother of self. In case, Mars or Saturn or Mercury or Venus is lord of the 5th house, the individual shouldn't perform any major surgery on own children.

Mercury and Saturn in the 7th House

The combination of Mercury and Saturn in the 7th house would give to the individual a stubborn, hard-headed but intelligent, clever (sometimes cunning), and educated spouse.

This combination sometimes delays the marriage, or leads the marriage to a separation (circumstantial or intentional), which can be for short or long period depending upon the mahadasa running at that time, or even divorce if the family of either of the two (i.e. husband and wife) is interfering in married life of the couple. It is always advisable to match the Birth-charts of the boy and the girl before marriage and find a counter influence in the horoscope of the opposite partner for marriage. Otherwise the person with this combination in the 7th house should be advised to adopt compromising and adjusting attitude towards the spouse and the family of the spouse.

Other times even an intelligent and/or educated spouse becomes so hard-hearted or hard-headed or hard-boiled that she or he doesn't want to see any reason and consequences. Sometimes the spouse develops a feeling that the other partner in marriage is not lucky for her or for him, which feeling is not correct always, but once it takes origin in the mind of one of the two, it becomes rather difficult to uproot it.

Another point of differences between the husband and wife is the interference in their affairs by a member of the family of the spouse. Money management is third point of differences between the two. After marriage, the spouse develops a potbelly, (normally as a sign of prosperity in the case of men), and in the case of women, mostly on account of child bearing. Then the other partner becomes critical, causing annoyance to the 'potbellied' partner. It is generally noticed that persons with this combination in the 7th house do not have complexion matching to each other, which often happens in inter-religion, inter-provincial, inter-continental marriages, though in most cases it doesn't affect the harmony between the two.

One more important point about these individuals is that some of them are quite open to extra-marital relationships, and if it actually happens, they are capable of keeping it a guarded secret. If Venus is in combination with the Mercury+Saturn combination or has exchange of direct *drishti* on these two from the Ascendant (Janma-Lagna), the couple might willingly indulge in group-sex situations or swapping.

Another effect of these three stars, Mercury, Venus and Saturn joining hands in the 7th house is that husband and wife both carry on extra-marital relations <u>within the knowledge of each other</u>. In rare cases, this kind of relationship leads to ailment or disease of the genitals, or sexually transmitted disease.

The individual with Mercury and Saturn in the 7th house often proves a good support in any quarrel, dispute, fight, confrontation, electioneering, influencing the labour and peasant class, and producing or helping in production of black-mail-type literature. They prove efficient trade union leader or leader of the peasant and agricultural labour class. If these individuals take to smuggling of arms, goods and drugs, it is difficult to detect their involvement, and even if detected, it is difficult to bring them to book to the extent of punishment. It is difficult to get confession from them. However, because of their quality of strong head, these individuals often prove to be very intelligent (on account of Mercury) and dependable friend (on account of Saturn).

These individuals prove to be efficient officers for collecting intelligence, conducting investigations and interrogating criminals. A coin always has two sides, and this paragraph and the preceding one are the two sides of this combination in the 7th house. These persons are successful defence strategists in all matters, but specially in matters relating to deployment of forces, fixation of time and place for conducting attacks or taking offensive or defensive measures, designing weaponry and ordnance items, arms, ammunition.

Mercury and Rahu in the 7th House

It is in the matter of this combination of Mercury and Rahu in the 7th house that Rahu <u>does not</u> function on the pattern of Saturn in the 7th house.

First of all, Rahu doesn't destroy the marriage by separation, divorce, or death. No doubt it gives fattish personality to the spouse, and a touch of very sharp sense of ego or self-respect. This combination gives capacity for finding fault with others within the family periphery or even outside. It also gives a touch of suspicion on the character of the individual by the spouse, but the latter doesn't stretch it to the extent of a showdown or break-up. Further it gives capacity for dubious deals in business, falsehood in oral transaction of cash or delivery of goods when the outgo is in repeated consignments.

It also gives the individual tendency towards smuggling, helping criminals and trading in contraband goods and drugs. But the individuals carry on their operations in a manner to keep off the front line, so that in case of trouble they remain aloof, and escape the trap of legal action.

Similarly if there is dispute within the family or between the family of self and the spouse, they pose to be aloof and if they have to take sides, they do in a clandestine manner. That is always the advantage of a shadow planet –the shadow evaporates the moment the light is off. The same law applies in respect of any quarrel, dispute or even litigation. In matters of civil or consumer litigation or any claim, they try to put forth the matter through others in the shape of a public interest litigation.

Because of fatty body, at least, around waistline and thighs, Rahu gives these trouble in walking, running, also ailment like rheumatism, arthritis, sometimes even cirrhosis. But generally diseases attributable to Mercury and Rahu combination are curable with the help of strong willpower of the individual, by exercise, and by medical treatment.

Mercury and Ketu in the 7th House

Though it is rare but the combination of Mercury and Ketu in the 7th house gives, in a less degree, the same results as those of Mercury and Rahu combination.

The only difference in Mercury and Ketu combine is that these individuals are of timid nature, entertain fear of law and order and, therefore as far as possible, do not indulge in any unlawful activity or business directly or through others. Secondly, Ketu normally doesn't cause diseases mentioned in the above paragraphs dealing with Mercury and Rahu combine in the 7th house.

MERCURY IN THE 8TH HOUSE

It is a difficult position for Mercury to be in the 8th house, irrespective of the Rasi in the 8th house.

Firstly, the individual has dull intelligence, even if it is sharp, the individual avoids its full application, avoids written work and homework, depend on work and guidance of fellow students, if need be, by exhibiting a tendency of a snob or a bully. This speciality applies also to teachers, tutors, journalists, petition writers, written work on the desk of advocates, solicitors, accountants, story and dialogue writers in the film line.

The written work of these persons becomes more or less stereo-typed, copy or a repetition of past work of others or themselves, and they do not hesitate to indulge in piracy, even openly. If they are typists, stenographers, clerks and juniors assigned to drafting or copying, they do not hesitate to keep work pending and going in arrears unless someone is rigidly supervising their work.

If these people have a speaking job like that of teachers, professors, lawyers, advocates, taxation representatives, they generally try to be brief in their submissions and arguments, teachings and lectures, even if some salient and important points get left out.

These individuals do not hesitate in suppressing a matter by destroying material written evidence, replacing genuine papers, documents by false or forged or fictitious ones, at the same time denying their earlier written or oral statements or submissions or evidence. If Mercury is lord of the 1st, 10th or 11th house, they indulge in wrong actions for personal gains and motives.

However, one thing may be noted. Mercury is easily remediable, provided there is regularity in the remedy on part of the individual. Mercury in 8th house, specially if it is lord of the 2nd house, is capable of giving the individual stammering, faulty style of speaking, stuttering, mumbling, etc., and sometimes even partial or complete dumbness. Some people get this defect in speech from birth, while some others develop it in early childhood; still others get it as a result of nervousness and hesitation in putting forth one's lesson in school. Then it prevails in debates in college or university, and then in full adulthood, a result of copying someone else, at least because of inferiority complex. Using a word or phrase repeatedly, without reference or relevance in talks is also a result of Mercury in the 8th house.

The only other trouble Mercury in 8th house can give is biting (physical injury) by a rabid dog, fox, jackal, camel etc. Another point: while driving any vehicle (auto or non-auto) these individuals make a mistake in judging the movements of other vehicles or pedestrians on the road, and might cause an accident if the person walking or the driver opposite, or behind is not rather watchful.

Mercury and Sun in the 8th House

We would have to discuss this combination of Mercury and Sun in the 8th house in addition to what has been stated in earlier chapters on Sun, because <u>Mercury</u> in the 8th house normally <u>becomes inactive</u> and allows the other star to rule the roost.

Thus this combination would give the individual capacity to stand for and win a seat in legislature, parliament, senate, local body, any elective office as in the USA, or at district or county level. The individual might get selected for an appointment in any administrative establishment (like the IAS in India) or in such government or semi-government service as is open only to a written test and/or an interview.

In case of any ailment or disease or injury, these individuals make a lot of noise by crying, shouting, and overstating the sufferings. This combination gives complaints of the blood system, headache, skin ailment, a bleeding injury, weak eyesight specially for reading and writing. It is always better that eyesight of children with this combination is tested at an early age and if necessary or medically advised, remedial steps be taken forthwith.

These people generally prove very efficient and successful ghost-writers of speeches for politicians and people in power. They generally become successful, by use of fair and foul means, at competitive examination for entry into service, and later on in getting promotions. These people often have a godfather for their help and support. They prove to be able administrators, moreso by issuing written orders for every important and unimportant matter.

If these individuals have to announce punishment to any person, and that person revolts or attacks them verbally or physically, they cannot stand the situation.

Mercury and Moon in the 8th House

The combination of Mercury and Moon in the 8th house is yet another tricky combination in the 8th house.

From the very early childhood these individuals should be observed for non-development of intelligence, defect in speech, unsound or deranged mind, unsteady development of limbs or minor parts of body. Parental observation should include any touch or indirect indication of neurological trouble, sometimes being on the verge of partial insanity and polio trouble.

In later life these individuals are vulnerable to food poisoning, sinking, drowning, injury on the head adversely affecting the brain, concussion of the brain, incoherent talks and similar other troubles of the body and brains.

These individuals are not very dependable for jobs of secrecy, whether lawful or unlawful, because they would unfold the whole plan under pressure, fear, torture or temptation. Further, these individuals should avoid taking risk with water (both flowing and stationary) as well as high waters, and there is always risk for themselves and others too if they function as boatmen, sailors and navigators. They are vulnerable to nausea in any kind of journeys. In case of females long journeys should be avoided between 6th and 9th months of pregnancy.

Mercury and Mars in the 8th House

With regard to Mercury and Mars combination in the 8th house, it is normally presumed, and rather correctly too, that this combination would give results somewhat similar to Sun and Mercury combination in the 8th house.

The story is a little different in regard to Mercury and Mars combine in the 8th house. These individuals can get elected to political offices. However they find it rather difficult to get selected for posts where written competitive test is compulsory, because their pressure tactics often do not work there.

These individuals do extremely well in formulating defence strategies, producing written rules, regulations, and guidelines for defence forces, armed police, and para-military troops. They are efficient in designing and manufacturing of ordnance and weaponry, training of personnel in use of weaponry and also in offensive/ defensive measures, combat fighting, etc. They give very useful advice with regard to deployment of troops in peacetime and on battlefields in emergency of war and similar other jobs. But these individuals do not prove successful spies and intelligence agents, though they might assist in subversive activities in enemy territories, using third degree methods on spies and intelligence agents.

These individuals are open to black-marketing in police and defence stores or receiving gratifications for approving supplies for defence and police.

In so far as health is concerned, this combination leads to serious complaints of the blood system in both males and females, headache, complaints of the eyesight, brain injury or injury to an eye adversely affecting the eyesight. They are at the same time vulnerable to sexually transmitted diseases, injury to inner and outer genitals, and other inner and outer parts of body connected therewith. Care has to be taken with regard to any bleeding injury going septic and sometimes even risky to life itself for these individuals.

Extra care is needed to their injury anywhere between the neck and the waistline, injury by fire or acids or inflammables, electric-shock, any other kind of burn injury, disorders of the blood pressure and heart trouble. They are open to suffer from malfunctioning of one or both kidneys or their total failure, wrong surgical treatment of any part of the body, including unnecessary forceps or caesarean delivery of child, where women are concerned.

On top of all, this combination can bring failure of marriage, which first starts with exchange of heated arguments and fights orally or in writing. Sometimes filthy allegations are bounced in courts of law while fighting a case of legal separation, divorce, maintenance, compensation, or child-custody and other damages etc.

It is always advisable to have an advance check up of the Birth-charts of the boy and the girl in case either of the two has this combination in the 8th house. If it so, go ahead with the marriage only if both the Birth-charts have parallel position of stars, or otherwise if the other Birth chart has countermanding influences against this combination in the 8th house.

Mercury and Jupiter in the 8th House

Normally the combination of Mercury and Jupiter in the 8th house, two soft planets, do not show favourable results in the 8th house.

They create more problems and trouble for the individual, including problems of health and mutual adjustment with the wider family of self and spouse. This combination is often inclined to give financial losses in money lending, share market, *'benami'* transactions and investments, theft of cash and jewellery.

These two stars are capable of subjecting the individual and/or her or his family to search, survey and seizure operations by the taxation agencies. In these searches written accounts, other documents and papers of incriminating nature get into the hands of the taxation authorities. It might ultimately lead to fines, penalties, and heavy taxation with implications for the following years too. Sometimes the searches might lead to confiscation of moveable (and immoveable) assets, if the individual is unable to pay the demands relevant to revised taxation. In cases where an individual escapes extra fine and penalty etc., she or he has to suffer loss of hard cash paid as bribes to the taxation officials.

Under this combination, several cases have been noticed where thefts took place from safety deposit vaults in banks and private operators of safety vaults. Sometimes differences occur between husband and wife on overall control and management of money, leading to rather serious consequences in mutual relationship.

Problems of cough, cold, bad throat, tonsil trouble in childhood, complaints of the respiratory system including asthma and allied complaints, preliminary complaints of liver and kidney are liable to be given by this combination in the 8th house. On top of all this, diabetes too is possible.

Problems related to litigation are also the concern of these two soft planets in the 8th house. Even learned and experienced individuals lose their own litigation in civil courts and other legal forum. It is generally advisable for individuals to settle disputes outside the courts by mutual compromise or at the most by mutually appointed arbitrators. Loss of face and litigation both are often evident in matrimonial cases, generally the party taking the initiative loses the case and is sometimes burdened with cost of litigation and/ or compensation or maintenance or one-time lump sum compromise.

It is advisable to have the birth stars checked up by an expert and unbiased astrologer before entering into litigation, and irrespective of the fact whether the individual is the defendant or the respondent, a learned and trustworthy lawyer should be engaged. There have been several cases where the advocate or the lawyer of one party was won over or 'bought' by the opposite party.

While borrowing money the individuals must have proper and correct estimate of their repayment capacity without depending upon expectations and guesswork of arrival of money. Expected money may arrive, may not arrive in time, or may not arrive at all, and there may be loss of assets to the borrower. Even bank-loans and institutional-loans prove difficult to clear off and the assets mortgaged go haywire. No doubt, if Mars is in a very favourable position in the Birth-chart or the Navamsha, it is likely that property might not be lost in repayment of the loans. Some way out might be reached.

These individuals should avoid carrying heavy cash or costly jewellery on their person, specially when Jupiter is in a damaging transit or harmful placement in the Yearly-chart or by way of mahadasa / antardasa mutually of Jupiter and Mercury.

These individuals should stay alert about their duplicate (number two) accounts books, notes and small slips, and as far as possible should employ only very trustworthy employees in the maintenance of accounts, and shouldn't annoy them. There have been several cases where the accounts-staff gave away their employers to taxation agencies, or to thugs and robbers.

Further these individuals shouldn't be tempted in buying gold-bullion or ornaments from unknown and semi-known persons, and shouldn't entrust their costly items to fake *mantriks* and *tantriks* (spiritual saviours), whatever the stories of success being recounted.

The bright side of this combination is that these individuals make good experts in medical jurisprudence as also teachers of this difficult, non-interesting subject. But when in the witness box, they need a pushing by others to gather courage to give correct, and corroborative evidence.

Mercury and Venus in the 8th House

The combination of Mercury and Venus too in the 8th house needs careful study.

Even in the normal course, Venus is a double-edged star when in the 8th house, and Mercury being its mutual intimate friend, Mercury often surrenders to wishes, wants and whims of Venus in the 8th house. This combination can give excess desire for sex (though excess desire does not necessarily mean a proportionate capacity for it). The actual body-capacity might be less than the desire or the want. It applies more to males than to females. If the females have an excess desire, they do carry the capacity too for it. Much depends upon what houses are owned by Venus in the Birth-chart, what is its strength and what hard stars are casting full *drishti* on this combine, which factors decide the individual's capacity too.

However, these individuals like too much talks of lighter nature and sexy gossips, which can be classed as either romantic or erotic. Some males lack capacity for giving full satisfaction to the partner in bed but do not hesitate to boast about their capacity and capability. They are often in search of stimulating literature and medicines.

No doubt if Aries, Taurus, Sagittarius, or Aquarius is in the 8th house, these males do possess the capacity and capability to fully satisfy the partner in the bed.

If it is Aries and Aquarius, these males do not hesitate in being rash, rough, or arrogant with the opposite sex, even going to the extent of forced or playful fantasy of non-consensual sex, but certainly not amounting to rape. For a situation of rape (or forced sex, without-consent sex), either Mars or Saturn also has to be present in the 8th house or in the 2nd house with full *drishti* on Venus (and Mercury) in the 8th house.

These individuals, both male and females, are easy addicts to drinks and/or use of intoxicating drugs. They know the disadvantages and damage to health and intellectual faculties, but often are unable to drop the addiction, once formed.

The brilliant side of this combination in the 8th house is that these individuals make very efficient medical personnel, specially on the medicine side as also in teaching in medical schools or colleges. Some of them have been able to write very useful books on medical sciences. They prove efficient doctors for curing sexually transmitted diseases including AIDs. Perhaps, as the author of *Kama-Sutra, Vatsyayan* may have had this combination in his 5th or 8th house, because he exposed such efficient knowledge on the sex act in his immortal treatise.

This combination gives health complaints of cough, cold, bad-throat and congestion in the chest region and ache in the groins but without acute pain or serious trouble in the bones, which is the domain of Saturn. These individuals are fond of taking medicines and at the same time not observing the restrictions attaching to the medicines. Also they are not regular in taking medicines, and often leave the course of treatment halfway, once the recovery-progress is visible.

They are fond of, and choosy about what they wear more for impressing others and specially the opposite sex, but they are not very careful for the upkeep of the clothes and garments after use.

Mercury and Saturn in the 8th House

The combination of Mercury and Saturn in the 8th house is a combination between two friends in the permanent relationship among the stars.

However, though a friend of Saturn, Mercury is not very effective in the 8th house when in conjunction with Saturn. These individuals make good leaders of trade-union, labour-class, staff-associations, and they are clever in talking talent and pushing forth their points of arguments and claims, thinking themselves to be top intellectuals, without duly listening to the opposite party or the opposite point of view.

They do not hesitate in putting forth exorbitant claims or even false claims, in leading shouting brigades in the offices, factories, and residence of the employers or competitive trade unions and staff associations. They are arrogant and rather over-confident in their approach to men and matters.

And Saturn is sure to give much higher income, savings and large-scale investments to the individual, which even Mercury is unable to touch or harm in any way. Soft stars in the 8th house are normally unfavourable to savings and investments, though not so much to regular income. But when in combination with Saturn, particularly in the 8th house, soft stars become, more or less, ineffective.

They can receive injury, and can inflict injury, without any restraint whatsoever in their attitude.

But these very minus qualities make a very useful quality when these individuals are employed in defence services, intelligence and spying jobs, armed police forces, anti-militant activities, because they know both sides of the coin. They are able to formulate top class strategy for offence as well as for defence, and are of the type who can handle table work efficiently as well as fight or command on a battlefield.

If they are remarkable criminals, they prove to be efficient police officers, investigators of crimes and preparation of prosecution cases. They are good at use of arms and weapons, and they do not claim credit as an individual but share the credit or criticism with colleagues and subordinates also. Whether they are tall or short in height or thin-built or otherwise, they are able to run swiftly and chase suspected criminals very well.

On the health side, they might suffer blunt injury in a fight, in a fall from a height or even while walking on plain-land. They are very vulnerable to accidental injuries whether by vehicles or even while walking. The injury can be by a weapon, but generally not by a firearm unless Mars is also associated with this combination or casting direct *drishti* on Saturn (and Mercury). They are vulnerable to diseases like tuberculosis, cancer, gangrene; laceration, hernia, thrombosis, dyspepsia, arthritis, pain in joints and bones (specially in waist line, thighs, knees and calf), sciatica, elephantiasis, dystrophy and malfunctioning of muscles.

Unless Moon is also associated with this combination or Mercury and Saturn are under direct *drishti* of Moon from the 2nd house, these two stars together do not cause trouble of brains and neurology etc. However the individual might grow heavy abdomen and buttocks, whether other parts of the body are equally proportionate or not.

Whenever Saturn is in the 8th house by transit or in the 8th house in the Yearly-chart or its *saadhe-saati* (seven and a half year malefic transit from *Janma-Rasi*) is running, the individual must make it a habit to go for a walk for sake of a walk. Being a messenger planet, Saturn feels appeased by walking. Its evil effect reduces to a good extent. <u>It has been observed that a majority of sufferers of Saturn's evil influence do not keep regularity in walking, and instead seek other remedies, which are not so effective.</u>

It is also a fact that whenever Saturn is in the 8th house by transit, or in the 8th house in the Yearly-chart, or Saturn's mahadasa or antardasa is current under any star's mahadasa, Saturn gives a big rise in income, savings and investments.

Mercury and Rahu in the 8th House

In the combination of Mercury and Rahu in the 8th house, Mercury too is effective in the 8th house.

Rahu with Mercury brings obstacles in the education of the individual in childhood. And the education gets completed in phases and often by self-effort of the individual, moreso at post-school stage. These two stars are apt to give fatness to the individual, in some cases from the childhood itself and in other cases after the age of 36 years. The individuals always have excess feeling about their illness and injury, and they often cry and shout under pain overestimated by self.

However Rahu helps, like Saturn in the 8th, enhancement of income and earnings, as also savings by both earned and unearned income. These individuals are often successful in making unearned and unaccounted money and they are more careful about their chits of accounts, making them so rare and quickly destroyable that taxation agencies hardly reach upto these chits. They know better places for hiding their cash than even thieves and 'thugs'. They prefer to take their spouses into confidence in money matters, as also about investments, though often they do not seek their advice.

Females going into active participation or own independent business often achieve success because they keep an observant eye on profit angle and do not jump to risks under extra greed of higher profits. Females prove more helpful in earning unfair and unaccounted income, and they are capable to keep it a secret.

Rahu is a shadow planet and doesn't give any ailment, illness, or disease itself directly but provides the ground for health complaints, because of bad digestive system, extra fat, less exercise originating from laziness.

This combination can however give over-estimate of one's intelligence and wisdom, which can lead to semi-neurological troubles or ailment of the brains. Another problem with these individuals is that because of they over-estimate their qualities, they are over-ambitious and want to tread on difficult paths and plans, in unknown lands, among unhelpful people. Success depends on positions of other stars in the Birth-chart, read with mahadasa and antardasa, as also transit of Saturn.

Mercury and Ketu in the 8th House

The combination of Mercury and Ketu in the 8th house is generally inclined to cause damage to the educational progress of the individual because both are soft stars with common type of effect in the 8th house.

These stars give some unusual trends and traits in sexual activity too, which is often disliked by the partner of the opposite sex. It applies to both males and females. Ketu with Mercury combination normally doesn't cause fatness of the body but gives piles trouble, and, therefore the individual could minimise the intake of spicy food.

Bisexuals, and transsexuals (eunuchs) would generally have this combination in their 8th house; Ketu helps in enhancement of earnings, but generally in 'earned' income only.

MERCURY IN THE 9TH HOUSE

Occupying the 9th house is yet another favourable position of Mercury, irrespective of the Rasi in the 9th house.

The individual is intelligent, wise in reality, has good grasp on what is taught, has impressionable recitation power, has good handwriting, can write fast and clean (even without knowledge of shorthand). The individual is good at typing and in use of computer.

She or he has poetic talent or at least appreciation for poetry and songs of all kinds, has capacity for writing novels, stories, religious books, guide books, books of theory and practice of any science or branch of knowledge. She or he can deliver talks and lectures on religion, social services, and any general subject of public interest. The individual is good at teaching at school, college or university level, doing and guiding research work, examining authenticity of books and old manuscripts and documents. The individual sometimes is capable of preaching and leading religious faiths or cult, and guiding the community towards cultured life.

These individuals are normally honest, truthful, trustworthy, and reliable in all matters including money and accounts. They are soft and noble unless Aries, Leo, Scorpio, Sagittarius, or Aquarius is in the 9th house.

They are good at writing petitions, representations, wills, deeds, and documents of family settlement. However they often fumble in the witness box, because they go into unwanted details, and talk or argue more than needed, make mistakes therein unintentionally slipping into self-contradictions and thereby irritating own side and pleasing the opposite side. These individuals prove helpful in the education of brothers, sisters, and/or cousins and their spouses and progeny, and in return normally do not take any undue advantage from them.

Mercury and Sun, Moon or Mars in the 9th House

Combination of Mercury in the 9th house with these three planets has been discussed in earlier chapters, under the relevant sub-heading.

Mercury and Jupiter in the 9th House

The combination of Mercury and Jupiter in the 9th house, the house that rules fortune, devotion to one's duty (religious, cultural, social and to the public) generally gives favourable results only.

These two soft stars, though having feelings of enmity towards each other, are always beneficial to the individual concerned. The results described in the above paragraph relating to Mercury's position in the 9th house apply totality to this combination.

In addition, these individuals make expert and efficient lawyers, advocates, solicitors, judges, qualified or experienced accountants, taxation exponents and consultants, counsellor in business management, teachers of any and all non-technical subjects and disciplines. They are normally very balanced in thought, words, and action, impartial and unapproachable where matters of justice and arbitration are concerned.

Some of these individuals are efficient authors on literature concerning law, justice, accounts, economy, teaching, journalism, religions and spiritualism. They are no doubt good journalist and publishers too.

If these two soft planets fall under direct *drishti* (aspect) of Mars or Saturn from the 3rd house, they indulge in conversion of faith of others by methods of temptation, threats, and force. Fundamentalists belonging to any religion are likely to have this combination in 9th house, with one or two hard planets in the 6th, 3rd or 12th (not in the 8th) house. They normally do not indulge in violence themselves but instigate and guide others to do so under garb of religious activity; and they are always diehards.

Other attributes of this combine in 9th house is that these individuals take leading part in all kind of public service and public utility institutions, formations, non-government organisations (NGO), including building and running schools, colleges, hospitals, old-age homes, orphanages, night shelters for poor. If there is a watery Sign (Cancer, Capricorn or Pisces) in the 9th house, they take active interest in creating irrigation facilities and drinking water resources. They are good at collection of donations, contributions, charity funds and enlistment of voluntary services towards these causes.

A point to note: if Mars or Saturn get directly associated with this combine, these individuals do not hesitate in malpractices in the course of management of social, educational, religious and charitable institutions and organisations, and sometimes in embezzlement of public funds.

And if Venus is in association with Mercury and Jupiter combine in the 9th house, these individuals do not hesitate to derive romantic and sexual gratification during the course of their function for such public utility services; the older such individuals are in age, the more mischief-minded they are.

[As per Hindu culture and mythology, these individuals may generally be inclined towards the male powers, i.e. worshipping *Lord Vishnu*, *Ganesh*, *Shiva* and *Kuber* (the last one because they desire more and more wealth, much beyond monetary requirements of self and the family)].

Mercury and Venus in the 9th House

One special attribute of the combination of Mercury and Venus in the 9th house has been discussed in the immediately preceding paragraph, in rather brief.

These individuals are romantic and sex-oriented in talks and actions, and entertain no hesitation in making advances towards own student, disciple, sister-in-law or brother-in-law in near or distant relationship; also towards teacher, tutor, *guru*, religious or cultural leader, socialite, politician, even towards an uncle or aunt or a cousin, nephew or niece.

These attributes and trends are visible more in efficient doctors (specially physicians), teachers of medical sciences of every system, famous actors and actresses, musicians, exponents of any of the fine arts (including painting, photography, designing, dancing, music, sculpture, film-making). These trends are equally noticeable in experts in use of chemicals and forensic side of medical science, scholars and researchers for doctorate degrees, their guides and teachers, because Mercury and Venus are particularly responsible in the 9th house for influencing all these categories of individuals, towards extra-marital relationship or an affair with anyone and whosoever comes in intimate contact with them!

Whatever be their good and bad qualities, these individuals are often competent, efficient, and to an extent expert too, in their speciality of knowledge and thereby they become famous (sometimes fame mixed with notoriety for above mentioned negative attributes).

Health-wise, these two planets in the 9th house do not offer any adverse effect, except that these males do not possess as much capacity or vitality in bed as per their bragging.

[As per Hindu culture, such individuals could be inclined towards the female powers, i.e. they could be worshippers of *Saraswati*, *Laxmi*, the soft side of *Goddess Durga* and *Chandi*, or *Parvati*. For romantic purposes, they may worship *Indrani*.]

Mercury and Saturn in the 9th House

Imagine the results that can be caused into the life of an individual by this combination of Mercury and Saturn in the 9th house, which happens to be a mixture of intelligence and mischief.

That is the main attribute of these two stars in the 9th house. Basically, these two have a friendly relationship with each other and so even if they stab in the back, they do so under the disguise of friendship. They often have an eye on public utility money, and have no hesitation in its embezzlement without even a remote consideration for the purpose for which the money was meant.

On the other hand, these individuals are nice and helpful to their employees, subordinates and workers, and at the same time they are selfish, given to exploitation, misuse without consideration for the safety or well being or financial 'near-poor' condition of the employee, subordinates and worker.

Similarly these individuals have no hesitation in piracy and plagiarism of ideas, thoughts, and language of literary or scientific work of any one and of every kind, so much so that they do not spare even published works and famous authors and poets known for centuries. They have no hitch in plagiarism of work of their students, disciples, subordinates, employees and workers, and by a little effort a student of astrology can come across many examples of this type. They adopt names, surnames, or pen names of ancient authors and poets just to steal their fame.

The same shamelessness applies in their lack of morality in conduct towards near and distant relations of self and the spouse, even towards students, disciples, followers, workers, subordinates, employees. Criticism and infamy often fail to bring improvement in their habits and attitude.

However, they prove to be very good in collecting crowds and followers for political campaigns, electioneering, social and religious gatherings and at quite a low cost.

These individuals try to exploit bigger share in inheritance of property and assets at the disadvantage of other claimants, but normally they themselves suffer in the end. They have no hitch in producing in evidence, forged letters, papers, documents, and wills for their selfish purposes. For such motives, they may try to have Birth-chart or birth-data of other claimants, have it checked with their own current stars, and may try to strike when the stars of these individuals have an upper hand on the stars of the other claimants. These individuals keep their own affairs a guarded secret and are often on the lookout for knowing the secrets of others.

[As per Hindu culture and mythological beliefs, these individuals may be more inclined towards the female powers, in their hour of need. They may be staunch worshippers of Goddesses like *Durga, Kali, Bhairavi, Yakshini, Pishaachini*, sometimes also of *Saraswati,* and *Laxmi* (only rarely, and that too temporarily under pressure of immediate need for higher education, success at exams, tests, viva voce, or for meeting immediate requirements of money.]

Mercury and Rahu in the 9th House

This combination gives results somewhat parallel to Mercury and Saturn combine in the 9th house, the only difference is that Rahu being a shadow planet doesn't give severe or furious or damaging results to the individual or to others at the hands of the individual.

At the same time, it is also true that this combine is unable to give beneficial results too pertaining to the 9th house, such as relate to labour force, followers, workers, slogan shouters for gathering masses at public meetings, processions, rallies, electioneering, demonstrations, '*dharnas*' and other similar activities.

Another peculiarity of this combination is that misdeeds of the individual in management of educational, social, religious, charitable organisations, formations or establishments get revealed to the opponents and adversaries concerned and through them to common public of the area or region. Pretty often the misdeeds of these individuals get exposed through the media too.

These individuals are usually fans of people in power, whether they get any material gain from them or not.

They sometimes harbour romantic attitude towards persons of opposite sex in close or distant relations, but normally avoid going beyond light talks. On the other hand, they seek listeners in the opposite sex for their boasting, and tales of woes and worries.

[In Hindu culture and belief, these individuals may be worshippers of Goddesses like *Durga*, *Kali*, *Kaatyayani*, *Chandi*, *Bhawani*, *Bhairavi*, but rarely of *Laxmi* or *Saraswati*.]

Mercury and Ketu in the 9th House

What has been stated above about Mercury being alone in the 9th house also totally applies to the combination of Mercury and Ketu in the 9th house.

They are often sincere to their duties and responsibilities, and true to their word. In the usual course of events they do not have the tendency to cheat others or indulge in piracy and plagiarism unless Mars, Saturn or Rahu gets associated with this combination. Though they try to help cousins, nephews, nieces and other near and distant relations, they generally do not try to take any due or undue advantage from them, neither immediately nor in later life.

If they undertake to original writing or reviewing a literary work or art performance or go in for being a critic, they are generally fair and balanced in their views, and make it a point to first study well and then start writing. In other words, they avoid indulging in exposition of half-baked knowledge.

[As per the Hindu cultural beliefs, these individuals could be inclined towards both male and female powers –worshippers of both *Saraswati* on the one hand and *Vishnu*, *Shiva*, *Ganesh* or *Indra* on the other.]

Mercury in the 10th House

This is one of the best positions in any Birth-chart for Mercury, irrespective of the Rasi in the 10th house.

The individual is soft, knowledgeable, experienced, sober even in criticism, docile, thinker, writer, poet, professional in any future-telling science, teacher, professor, researcher, journalist, editor of literature, efficient translator. If the individual becomes a commentary-writer, she or he does the job like *Mallinath* in Sanskrit literature. If she or he writes on grammar, her or his work can stand comparison to grammarian like *Paniniya* in Sanskrit, or *Kamata Prasad Guru* in Hindi grammar and literature, or like *Nesfield* and *P.C.Wren* were for English grammar.

The individual proves an efficient orator, priest, preacher of religious knowledge or any faith and cult, '*katha-vachak*' (recitation and explaining religious scriptures), narrator of old and new stories, prompter at stage or theatre, writer of explanatory notes and guide books for school and college text books. He or she proves a successful manager of school, college or any educational institute, vice-chancellor or principal or registrar or professor or lecturer.

If the individual is entrusted to function as an *imam* in mosque, padre in church, *granthi* in *gurudwara*, monk in Buddha *math*, head or subordinate priest in temple, trustee of educational or religious formation or organisation, or as adviser to top persons in authority, or as a court jester, or in any other job or on any post, in that job too she or he would prove fully efficient and successful.

These persons are often gifted with maternal intelligence (it is not relevant whether mother is educated or not, because many a mother are very intelligent in their own right even without formal education). It is so because from 10th house Mercury has direct and full *drishti* on the 4th house, which rules, besides other aspects, mother too.

Further, because of this direct *drishti*, these individuals enjoy facility of conveyance and roof over the head whether they themselves own any vehicle or roof of their own or not.

These individuals are normally straight-forward in approach and outspoken, have a loud voice, a minute observation, expert in calculations and mathematics, have competent command on '*mantras*'. As far as possible they avoid indulging in '*tantrik*' system (black-magic kind of systems), though they are good at suggesting making of gold or silver or copper and steel '*yantras*' (talismans) and also the method of worshipping the '*yantras*'. In spite of their knowledge of the religious scriptures and connected means and methods, they normally avoid officiating as a priest at any marriage or sacred thread ceremony, first hair-cut ceremony (known as '*mundan*' in Hindu society), nor as a priest at last rites.

As writers, they get cheated, but as publishers they are, to a great extent, honest in their dealings.

Left to them, these individuals do not indulge in making forged documents or any other kind of fraud.

Mercury and Sun, Moon or Mars in the 10th House

Combination of Mercury in the 9th house with these three planets has been discussed in earlier chapters, under the relevant sub-heading.

Mercury and Jupiter in the 10th House

Combination of Mercury and Jupiter in the 10th house produces individuals, who are outstanding, competent and efficient advocates, judges of lower and higher or possibly highest courts upto the level of the International Court of Justice (at the Hague), members of judicial tribunals or of special courts, commissioners of enquiry and investigation or public prosecutors.

Professors in law colleges, draftsmen in government law departments, public undertakings and local bodies, also constitutional experts, leading accountants, solicitors, jurists, writers on law, commentators on judgements, legislators, parliamentarians, municipal leaders, important appointees in public sector, in banks and insurance field are also produced by this combination in the 10th house.

Similarly, writers and producers of literature, publishers and booksellers of repute, chiefs of *'panchayat'* bodies in rural and semi-rural areas, money lenders, jewellers, bullion merchants, traders in precious stones, stock exchange brokers and experts, brokers in the corridors of power are also product of this very combination in the 10th house. There is no limit to this counting, it has to be mentioned that expert negotiators between nations and countries, arbitrators, surveyors and valuers of jewellery and precious stones, guides in the matter of embezzlement, investigators in matters of fraud, forgery and embezzlement, and all other similar investigations into incomes and earnings normally have the combination of Mercury and Jupiter in the 10th house.

Even if located in a Rasi owned by hard or cruel planet, these two *basically soft* stars keep the individuals stay aloof of wrong deeds, though sometimes they do not mind giving guidance or expert advice in socially incorrect actions. They are always respectful to elders, teachers (of any age), Gurus, leaders of community, and preachers of religious matters or of ethics and culture etc. But at the same time they do not hesitate to disobey orders, which they deem as wrong, or unwarranted or unnecessary.

Mercury and Venus in the 10th House

Combination of Mercury and Venus in the 10th house produces both categories of individuals, that is literary and medical and fine arts experts.

These categories include story writers for films and serials, directors in films and any visual subject, photographers, actors, actresses, musicians, singers, dancers, background prompters of dialogues.

The category on the medical side would include professors in medical institutions of any and every system, physicians, writers of medical books and of research articles on medical subjects.

This combination of Mercury and Venus produces also consultants to importers/ exporters, customs officers, writers of books, booklets, pamphlets and leaflets on customs, customs clearing agents, examiners of drugs, alcohols, narcotics, medicinal herbs and substances.

Acrobat and *'nat'* (local entertainers of rural the India), magician, *'tantrik'* (practitioners of *tantra*), *'mantrik'* (those who enchant or recite the sacred *vedic* and classical Sanskrit verses), people teaching and indulging in black magic, often have this combination in their 10th house.

Though Venus is a soft planet, being the *guru of demons*, it wouldn't hesitate in indulging in wrong deeds connected or concerned with any of the professions and the branches of knowledge mentioned above. They would have no reservation in giving their good and bad knowledge to their disciples, though they can neither be classed as greedy, nor as money-minded.

Further, individuals with this combination in the 10th house have no scruples in indulging in romantic or immoral relations with their subordinates, superiors, students, teachers, disciples, followers, associates in political or literary or medical or films field. They are very impressive talkers, and win over people by their talks.

They are successful owners of placement services and labour suppliers in the limited field of hospitals, nursing homes, sanatoriums, junior actors/actresses/extras for the films and show business). They do not hesitate in supplying girls and boys to big hotels, motels and private commercial guest-houses for escort service or for plainly sexual purposes.

Mercury and Saturn in the 10th House

Combination of Mercury and Saturn in the 10th house produces intelligent strategists for fights, battles, and war.

This combination also produces planners and designers for arms, ammunition and ordnance equipment, including guides to the manufacturers of these items.

They are often true to their word and devoted to their undertaking, but at the same time stubborn in their line of thinking and action. They avoid indulging in 'double dealing'; they are straightforward and if they decide to desert or dissociate from any person or formation or organisation, they often indicate their intentions in advance. These individuals often need tactful handling or dealing with. They make very good trade-union leaders, particularly of agricultural labour, industrial workers, and the lower-class employees in big hotels, big hospitals, and equally big nursing homes. For solution of disputes, these individuals generally think in terms of labour strike and going on (sometimes false) fasts unto death.

These individuals make intelligent and dependable spies, and intelligence *operatives* but not equally expert in enquiries, investigations, or interrogation.

Another important influence of this combination in the 10th house is that the individuals get into differences with father or grandfather or adopting father on both justified, and unjustified grounds. These differences may sometimes, on a very small percentage, lead to parting of ways between them, specially if matters relate to property, assets, use and utility of money in the hands of one of them –whether father, grandfather, son, or grandson. Either side does not hesitate in writing notes and letters to, or even serving legal notice on the other party. Sometimes to avoid taxation or any kind of attachment of the property for recovery of loans, fines and penalty etc., artificial dispute is also planned between child and father or grandfather, as the need be.

It is often observed that for purpose of a good education, these individuals in their childhood and early youth have to stay away from father; though cases are not rare that either of the two could also desert the other owing to some differences or different reasons. Therefore the question of <u>separation between father/ grandfather and the progeny</u> should be examined carefully. If the stars indicate separation by death, the horoscopes of both the persons must be examined before giving even any casual and indirect hint of the impending event. In all these cases where the term 'son' is used, it applies to both sexes equally –daughter *and* son.

And then the question for serious consideration (in the case of individuals in public or private service) relates to their differences with the superiors or employers. Quite often these individuals consider themselves as more intelligent, or more experienced, or cleverer than their superiors and employers, and this opens the floodgates of confrontation and conflict, sometimes resulting in departure of the employee to seek job elsewhere.

And yet another point for individuals in this connection is that they, (in less cases now and many cases a few decades ago) suffered beatings or corporal punishment at the hands of their father, mother, guardian, adopting father, teacher and tutor for progress in education. These supervisory-people in matters of education did not go by the capacity of the learner, but by their own estimates, and expectations. Often it happens that what the father, teacher or tutor could not achieve himself or herself, he or she expects fulfilment of such ambition from the youngster under his or her care and coaching.

Mercury and Rahu in the 10th House

The individuals with Mercury and Rahu combination in the 10th house are best suited for spying and piracy, whatever kind of job and whatever the field for these activities.

These individuals are very intelligent, and they prove an asset to crime-oriented politicians, and at the same time, these individuals do not hesitate to blackmail anyone (for personal gains) even their employers, patrons, financiers, and gurus-cum-torch-bearers in the art of spying and piracy. They are honest to themselves and to their own aims and ambitions.

Normally they avoid indulging in any violence, and if they get cornered in any situation warranting indulgence in crime or violence, they use their wisdom and talent or seek help and assistance of hardcore-criminals. However if the situation is such as does not allow them margin of time and space for seeking help from others, they try outright to buy their safety and liberty. If that too doesn't work, they surrender to the situation or the person opposite. They might possess weapons used in violence but they prefer not to use them, whether they are expert in their use or not.

This combination generally produces quacks in any and every profession, be it medical or advocacy or running an agency of public utility or any profession which brings them into close contact with the common public. They are good at fraud and forgery, adopting methods of impersonation, wearing different costumes and disguises, posing as a person of power and position. If ever caught in an act of defamation or contempt or fraud or forgery, they quickly admit their offence and try to get out of the trap of law.

If they are in the teaching line, they teach less and tutor their pupil in use of unfair means, mischievous methods of clearing the exam or threatening the invigilators, examiners and valuers of answer books.

They are good at selling fake currency notes, duplicates as originals of master-painters or sculptors, or selling items made of camel-bones or crocodile-bones as genuine ivory, polished gold items of silver or little gold as of pure silver or gold or selling chemicals of precious stones as genuine precious stones.

The main point is that Mercury gives these individuals intelligence and makes them clever, and Rahu grants them success in dubious activity. It has to be noted in this context that so long as they are loyal to their master or employer, they prove a real asset; once they give up their loyalty, they can even prove to be a danger.

Mercury and Ketu in the 10th House

It has been repeated time and again that Ketu, whether alone or in combination with Mercury (in the 10th house) gives results parallel to Mercury.

Therefore when they are together in the 10th house, take it that favourable results of Mercury are doubled. Ketu avoids, unlike Rahu, to indulge in mischief or misdeed of any kind for benefit to self or others. Ordinary use of un-approvable means to derive some 'side-benefit' is always a different matter for most of the human beings, and thus individuals with this combine in the 10th house are no exception to the rule.

MERCURY IN THE 11ᵀᴴ HOUSE

There is not much difference in results of Mercury in the 10th house and in the 11th house, except that Mercury has got direct and full *drishti* on the 5th house which rules, besides other things, education learning, intellectual talent and managerial capacity, competence and capability of the individual. Mercury also rules progeny, its upbringing, education, marriage, and settlement in career in later life.

Mercury in 11th house gifts the individual with high level of intelligence, continuous or broken but linked educational fulfilment, wisdom for management, and modest skill, capacity and competence for sex, pregnancy and begetting progeny, though it guarantees progeny if there be no physical deficiency in the spouse.

All other superior or inferior results of Mercury in the 10th house apply, *mutatis mutandis*, to the 11th house also.

Mercury and Sun, Moon or Mars the in 11ᵗʰ House

Combination of Mercury in the 11th house with these three planets has been discussed in earlier chapters, under the relevant sub-heading.

Mercury and Jupiter in the 11ᵗʰ House

For combination of Mercury and Jupiter in the 11th house, virtually all results mentioned under Mercury and Jupiter combine in the 10th house apply.

Here in the 11th house, these two stars would give most of the results in terms of cash and other money or other assets, though not the same strong results in terms of power and position. Be it the position of power in the field of law, economics, accounts, taxation, membership of local bodies and legislature including the parliament or the senate, such forceful results may not be expected as are possible to get through these very two stars together in the 10th house.

These two stars open a vast scope for writing books, articles, notes, comments on any subject relating to law, literature, economics, accounts, business management, journalism, criticism of books and other literature, arbitration and all other allied subjects. These two stars in combination give satisfactory earnings from writing or teaching or lectures on these subjects. The individual hardly experiences any kind of paucity of funds even upto old age, except if the individual becomes a full-fledged speculator in shares, or real estate, or jewellery, or other similar assets.

These individuals are not outwardly very sexy persons but they do not lack in the normal and average capacity and competence for sex. Generally their progeny is also intelligent and if arrangements, facilities exist, the children receive good education too.

Mercury and Venus in the 11th House

This combination of Mercury and Venus in the 11th house is rather a complicated one.

Though the 11th house rules the income, the planets occupying this house have two other important functions: firstly the 11th house is 8th position from the 4th house; second, a planet occupying the 11th house has direct and full *drishti* on the 5th house.

Thus, this house has a telling influence over mother, education of self, and later-on upbringing, education, formation of habits, marriage and career of the children. As we already know, Mercury is the lord of intelligence while Venus rules sex, romance, and all good things in life, luxury, and fine arts.

These two together are capable of making the individual a great artist, actor, musician, medical personality, importer/exporter, a renowned teacher in the field of fine arts and medical sciences. The Mercury and Venus combine also help an individual to become a dancer, writer in any field of fine arts, medical sciences, poet, composer of songs, director of films and television episodes and serials. And these lines of activity would ensure satisfactory income for the individual.

On the wrong side, this duo helps the individual to become a free-lancer in matters of romance and sex, casual relationship and friendship with the opposite sex without much restriction or restraints, including those of an incestuous nature.

Another impact of this combination is that the individual indulges in misuse of knowledge, experience, and reputation for immoral purposes. This misuse can be in the shape of making money by unfair and 'illogical' means, besides what has been stated in the immediately preceding paragraph.

If Mars or Saturn is in the 6th or 12th house, the individual might even indulge in smuggling, trade in drugs, narcotics and contraband goods, trade in humans (such trade includes kidnapping young children for carrying smuggled and contraband goods, even maiming young children for begging, kidnapping girls and young women for ultimately putting them into prostitution, indulging in mock marriage for exploitation in terms of money or for immoral trade purposes).

It may however to be noted that the progeny of these individuals is often intelligent and takes keen interest in learning one of the fine arts, or depending on their own stars at Birth. They can make renowned medical experts, actors or actresses, musicians, dancers, exporters and importers, without any relationship to the good or bad habits of the parents.

Mercury and Saturn in the 11th House

Since Saturn is always a benefactor in the 11th house, normally the combination of Mercury and Saturn in this house makes Saturn give up some of its wicked characteristics.

The effect of Saturn concerns mainly to generate money by whatever (intelligent or unintelligent) means possible. In real terms, this is actually the effect of Mercury being there. However, in spite of Mercury's influence through the combination, owing to the nature of Saturn and being in the 11th house, such individual would not hesitate to exploit even own mother, or children, or both for personal gains.

One point may be noted. Hardly any of these individuals are dud, or dull, or down-spirited. They do not mind or hesitate deceiving people for personal gain, however they would never do so for mere fun. If they see no gain, they would give up.

Because of association with Mercury casting full *drishti* on the 5th house from the 11th house (no doubt with Saturn too), Saturn pays full attention and creates enough financial resources to give good education to the progeny. "Beg, borrow or steal" is the motto of these individuals where money for progeny's education is concerned.

These individuals become good engineers, researchers, scientists, builders, contractors, colonisers, owners of petrol/gas filling stations, dealers in lubricating oils, dealers in machines and machinery spare parts, dealers in any kind of weapons, arms and ammunition as also in ordnance equipment. They prove competent strategists with regard to planning for battles, war, and formation and posting of troops in peacetime, and wartime as well.

Some of them come to own placement services, or leading gangs to smuggle human power from one country to another, possessing vast and verifiable knowledge of geography with minutest details of any particular area or spot or region, and also surveyors for purposes of geography. Some other individuals with combination of Mercury and Saturn in the 11th house become dealers in iron and steel, examiners of soil, experts in measurement of land and landscape, possessing expert knowledge of anthropology. A few others become experts in knowledge and use of various kinds of stone, owners of brick and/or ceramic kilns, or experts in installing big factories, furnaces, and/or running them as big or small industrialists.

They often function with a smile and are rarely rude, harsh or discourteous, even when they cheat or deceive or rob a person of his or her knowledge or of assets of any and every kind.

Where the question of progeny is concerned, they are quick in taking decisions about medical termination of pregnancy; sometimes pregnancy is lost by natural causes too.

Whether these individuals are well educated or not, they

always insist on giving good education to their progeny and would go to any extent, fair or foul or even violent method to make their progeny serious and successful in studies. They generally prefer their children to go in for engineering, pure sciences, surgery, ornithology, orthopaedics, orthodontics, optometry, ophthalmology, oceanography and allied subjects. It is a different thing whether the particular child goes into any of these lines or not, because upto 90% would depend on the birth stars of the individual child.

These individuals are very good at management, particularly that involves control over labour (personnel & industrial relations), knowledge of science, engineering and technology. Because they are often destined to earn big money, they are wise in making full use of their knowledge, experience, and expertise. Their industrial ventures generally run profitably because they know how to make best use of skilled and unskilled labour and also of technocrats and engineers etc.

Mercury and Rahu in the 11th House

This combination of Mercury and Rahu in the 11th house assures the individual of good income, whatever the means and methods of income or earnings.

Sometimes a hollow superficiality, as also certain swankness enters into the personality of these individuals. But these methods do achieve success in generating big money.

They are keen to give a good education to their children, provide money and tutorial facility for the purpose, but generally take no personal interest in their educational progress. They are more concerned with their clubs, get-together-of-friends and colleagues, and other extra-curricular activities. They do not mind indulging into unfair means and illegal activities to make money, and they are not much afraid of the law and order system of this or that country.

There are greater chances for loss of one or more pregnancy by natural, or medical causes.

They sometimes fall out with their mother or their children on matters relating to money and assets.

Mercury and Ketu in the 11th House

Results of the combination of Mercury and Ketu in the 11th house are similar to that of Rahu and Mercury combined in that house.

It is so because in this particular house Ketu gives results similar to that of Rahu. The only difference is that Ketu creates a sense of fear in the minds of the individuals in matters relating to unfair and illegal activity for gain of money and assets.

MERCURY IN THE 12TH HOUSE

As with all other planets in the 12th house, Mercury too in the 12th house needs special attention while assessing a Birth-chart, Yearly-chart, monthly-chart or a 2.5 days Hora-chart or even a question-chart.

Firstly, the 12th house relates to spending, losses, trouble with govt. agencies, penalty, punishment, disputes within the family, problems regarding to children or with children or from children. Secondly –problems, trouble, harassment, torture an/or losses may be given by enemies, opponents, adversaries, because Mercury has direct and full *drishti* on the 6th house. The 5th house relating to children, and also to education of the individual is adversely affected because of Mercury occupying the 8th position from the 5th house.

The preliminary disadvantage caused to the individual is about education. The individual is either poor in grasp when anything is taught or needs repetition of teaching. Problem of below standard intelligence could also be there. In some cases it could be lack of educational facilities specially for higher studies, and last of all, there could be financial paucity for primary, secondary or higher education or lack of facilities of such education as is desired for the individual. For example, in the 1920's, 30's and 40's, there were no facilities for learning any science subjects in any high school in four or five princely states of upper Central India and Lower Rajputana within a radius of 70 miles (112 km). As a result, there was no student from that region in those years from engineering or medical or any other education with science as the basis.

Then comes the question of keeping of accounts if the individual is in own business or associated with any kind of account work of business run by employers. The individual is neither prompt nor regular in jotting down accounts as soon as any transaction in cash or goods takes place; the tendency is to note down the accounts later on by memory, and thus there remains scope for mistakes and lapses.

The third question coming up is about the education of the children, and the same problems might be there which have been discussed in the preceding paragraphs relating to the education of the individual. In modern times, it is a misfortune for the children as well as the parents, if the progeny, (even one of them), remains uneducated or less educated. This or other causes often lead to differences between the progeny and the parents. And if hard or cruel stars get associated with the 12th house and Mercury is no doubt therein, these differences take the shape of a dispute.

The fourth question is about dispute, trouble, problems that might be created by mistakes, lapses, fraud, forgery in matters of documents, deeds, any kind of important papers, oral and written statements. Another source of worry or problem for the individual could be any evidence he or she might have given, against which a charge of perjury has cropped up.

Then comes the question of piracy of written or published works of others, wrong oral or written commitments, wrong reporting in journalism, critical or defamatory editorials of articles in print media, and biased criticism of books and other material in print media. Disputes related to royalty, using false documents in support of individual's case or in contradiction of the opposite party's case, and all other similar subjects too fall within the domain of Mercury in the 12th house.

Mistakes in drafting legal documents also crop up owing to Mercury in the 12th house, and the individual has to indirectly suffer the consequences.

Mistakes in filling of any kind of taxation returns or nomination papers for any election also fall within the control-arena of Mercury in the 12th house. Naturally, the consequences follow bringing disadvantage to the individual.

Problems cropping from spoken or written word or withholding written or spoken word at the right moment or opportunity are also consequences caused by Mercury in the 12th house, and this aspect ultimately gives rise to enmity, confrontation, conflict, opposition, dispute and sometimes legal action too.

It is always better to have detailed examination of Mercury's position in the 12th house on the basis of the Bhava-Chalitam (i.e. chart of fixation of planetary positions in the twelve houses). And Navamsha, and in addition Trinshansha-chart in the case of females need to be examined as soon in childhood as possible. If Mercury is found harmful in both Bhava-Chalitam and Navamsha/ Trinshansha, remedial steps should be suggested as and when considered necessary by the astrologer examining the horoscope. It may be noted that Mercury's bad influence is always remediable, the only question being that of the astrologer's expertise in suggesting the remedy and the client's seriousness, promptness and regularity in implementing the suggested remedy.

Mercury and Sun in the 12th House

Besides other points discussed in earlier chapters relating to Sun (relevant to 12th house position), it has to be borne in mind that Sun and Mercury combination in the 12th house might bring trouble from government or the law and order machinery or disputes between private parties. Generally the individual is the sufferer in the end. It is therefore always better to remain on one's guard and, as far as possible and feasible avoid creation of such circumstances as would bring trouble for the individual. Compensation, payment of damages and costs, penalty, punishment including even simple imprisonment are some of the consequences that follow the developments of this type.

Mercury and Moon in the 12th House

In the case of combination of Mercury and Moon in the 12th house, the individual would need guidance and safeguard against deficiency of intelligence, fickle-mindedness, uncertainty in thought and action, less application of mind to studies during age of education.

If the 12th house has Aries or Scorpio, and if its lord Mars is in the 5th or the 7th house, the individual might suffer, during mahadasa of Moon, Mars or Mercury or Saturn's *Saadhe-saati* from partial mental disorder, partial loss of memory. If Navamsha-chart too is under damaging influence of both Moon and Mars, partial insanity is not ruled out. Neurological disorders are also caused by this combination of these two soft stars (though father and son in astrology) in the 12th house.

Another result of Moon **and** Mercury in the 12th house is that the progeny do not want to pay due attention to studies and to an extent disobey the guidance of the parents.

If Saturn's Rasi is in the 12th house, and Saturn is in the 5th, 8th or 12th house itself, the individual is likely to suffer by or before the age of 23 years a head injury, which might ultimately result in epilepsy or similar kind of neurological ailment.

Further these individuals should stay careful while swimming or crossing canal, river, rivulet, *nala*, and should never take risk with sea, gulf or ocean, irrespective of whether they know swimming or not. Also these individuals have to be careful against food-poisoning, either by own mistake or by unintentional mistake of others or by malafide or malice of others.

If this combine suffers from evil influence of Venus (being in the 6th, 8th or 12th house itself), the individual should avoid regular intake of drugs or drinks or any narcotics, because this habit would lead to mental disorder and adversely affect the memory.

If Rahu too joins this combination in the 12th house, the individual suffers from false sense of ego, and feels insulted at the slightest provocation.

Mercury and Mars in the 12th House

Individuals having Mercury and Mars combination in the 12th house generally suffer from sharp anger, which though lasts for a short-while, hurts the feelings and emotions of others. And this anger descending upon children in school or college adversely affects their capacity and capability to grasp what is taught to them.

In case of fire breaking out, these individuals are often unable to render any physical help or assistance in putting off the fire, but they certainly make a lot of noise to others for extinguishing the fire (small or big).

These persons shouldn't sit long hours for studies or writing or even reading at a stretch, as that would make them suffer from headache, or pain in eyes.

Mercury and Jupiter in the 12th House

Combination of Mercury and Jupiter in the 12th house is very likely to give trouble with law and taxation, trouble with the society and with neighbourhood.

Litigation and often unwarranted expenditure in litigation with sometimes defeat in it are other attributes of these two soft stars in 12th house. Survey or searches or raids at every premises of the individual by investigating agencies of any department of the govt. are also caused by these two stars in the 12th house. Penalty and punishment including jail sentence can also be the other outcome.

Parents are normally not satisfied by the educational progress of the progeny, and they subject the progeny to criticism, financial torture, beatings and any other kind of violent-treatment. Sometimes because of family circumstances the individuals suffer money difficulties in school and college and have to manage affairs of education by own work like tuitions, part-time or night jobs, night errands etc.

On one hand these two soft stars compel an individual to spend on gifts, gratification, bribes, favours, and on the other hand, the same actions bring further trouble for them.

Expenditure on second wife (during life of the first one) or a mistress, concubine, second husband, paramour, sexual friend of the opposite sex is also caused by Jupiter and Mercury in the 12th house.

Loss in shares, or any other kind of speculation, or business, or loss in self-employment, or loss in writing and publication of books including loss of royalty, or loss in profession, or loss owing to any guarantee or security or surety or pledge, is normally caused by these two soft stars in the 12th house. Loss in insurance or bond or assurance can also be caused by these two in the 12th house.

Expenditure on charitable, social, public welfare-cum-utility matters, educational or medical help to others also falls under the domain of these two. Similarly spending on wasteful purposes including on useless costly entertainment, social gatherings, drinking, drugs, intoxicants are other results of these two in the 12th house.

Expenditure on buying freedom from any bond or contract or agreement is caused by these soft stars in the 12th house. Losses caused to individuals by bankers and insurers or losses suffered by bankers and insurers are a result of Jupiter & Mercury in the 12th house.

These two are capable of dragging an individual into enquiry and investigations by any government agency, whether the individual is in the employment of the public services or not. Similarly, any feud, rift, or dispute within the parental family, or with the family of the spouse, is generally caused by these two stars.

Demand and payment of ransom money to blackmailers and kidnappers or refusal to pay it and consequences thereof are initially governed by these two stars, though if the consequences are physical torture or death, hard planets have to figure in into the picture either by joining the company of these two stars in the 12th house, or by 6:8 relationship with these two stars from the 5th or the 7th house or by direct and full *drishti* on the 12th house (including Mercury and Jupiter already there), which is possible from the 6th house only. Blackmail can be by method of written word or spoken word on telephone, by any other means or method.

All kinds of problems relating to taking or giving loans are caused by Jupiter and Mercury in the 12th house. It includes false documents, forged documents, signatures obtained under duress or torture or pressure or blackmail, and finally litigation.

Infringement of copyright is caused by these soft stars in the 12th house. Likewise any kind of arbitration in any dispute of legal nature or otherwise is the result by Jupiter and Mercury in the 12th house.

And fame or notoriety, honour, dishonour, setback to economic status, setback to social status, condemnation, loss of reputation for good deeds or evil actions or association with unsocial elements are also caused by Jupiter and Mercury in the 12th house. Money and effort spent on regaining lost reputation and honour are also controlled by these two stars.

Physical ailments like diabetes, asthma, kidney trouble, lever ailment, and childhood diseases like diphtheria and tonsillitis are normally caused by these two soft stars in the 12th house.

Mercury and Venus in the 12th House

Combination of Mercury and Venus in the 12th house is capable of giving losses and heavy (rather unwarranted) expenditure on luxury, romance, on friends of opposite sex, on study of specialised subjects in literature and different kinds of medicinal systems.

The combination can give heavy spending on clothes/ wardrobe/ garments, on collection of medicinal herbs, imported items, on drinks and collection of various kinds of wines and liquors too. Then other items of expenditure caused by these two soft stars is dance and music parties, on help to educational and medical institutions as also help to individual students in pure sciences and medical courses of study as also those studying music, dance or any other fine art.

Other subjects of domain of Mercury and Venus in the 12th house are gardening and collection of various kinds of flowers and plants from different parts of the country and from foreign countries, on paintings, on various kinds of musical instruments, on study of music and dancing, on running institutions for teaching music and dancing.

Sometimes these individuals maintain spouse-type relations with a member of the opposite sex or a homosexual relationship. It would naturally include spending on flatterers and courtiers, on teachers of one or more fine arts and their families (more so after the demise of the teacher). It can also be on collection of currency of foreign countries, on collection of piece de art, on helping and encouraging painters. The field of expenditure might include promotion of any branch of the fine arts and learning. Spending beyond capacity is also caused by there two soft stars in the 12th house.

However the losses or heavy expenditure given by these two stars can be of tolerable nature, so long as these two are alone in the 12th house. But if they get joined by or associated with by direct and full *drishti* by hard planets, the losses can be of intolerable nature.

Losses become more serious in the trade of chemists, importers, exporters, dealers in cloth or garments or fashionable apparel, items of fashion, luxury and decoration, drinks, music and dance parties.

Heavy expenditure of non-bearable type on supporting mistress, concubine, paramour, spouse-type friend of the opposite sex, on medical treatment of self or spouse or any other member of the family, moreso on own progeny is not so much open to criticism.

Sometimes theft of valuable books, music instruments, items of luxury, fashion and decoration, of radio, TV or computer, etc. can also give huge losses. Children going on wrong path can be a source of big outgo of money and also prestige of the family, even if it is not affordable by the parents.

Some of these individuals feel tempted to write or publish and sell pornographic literature and photos connected therewith.

An important point to remember is that these two soft planets do not cause demise of any individual, and if the individual lives a regular and non-intoxicant life, with restraint in sex matters with spouse only, these two stars do not cause any serious illness too. They normally do not lead to rigorous imprisonment. If these stars cause any imprisonment, it is always simple one and of limited period.

Mercury and Saturn in the 12th House

Combination of Mercury and Saturn in the 12th house often creates a difficult situation, because Saturn whether alone or with any planet always does so in the 12th house.

This combination adversely affects the individual's relations with immediate and wider family, even if the individual spends wastefully, it doesn't undo the rift within family, specially with paternal and maternal uncles.

This combination is capable of giving governmental action and punishment or penalty linked with it. Trouble or problems might crop up with or from labour as also trade-union leaders, so much so that labour might indulge in damaging machinery and production line. It would naturally cause heavy burden over the individual. Firstly, by zero production in the factory. Secondly by losing market to competitors and other manufacturers. Thirdly, the loss can be caused by way of compensation to any skilled or unskilled labour for any injury, or to the labourer's family in the event of his or her death.

Compensation may have to be paid for an accident on the road or heavy spending on treatment of self for injuries sustained in a fall or accident on the road or with any vehicle. These individuals must always be careful about accuracy and honesty in their accounts, whether these accounts relate to their own affairs or the affairs of their employers or clients and customers.

Normally owning an industrial unit rarely suits these individuals unless they enter into a partnership with spouse having a favourable position of Saturn for industrial venture or partnership with a friend having profit-giving position of Saturn.

These individuals should, as far as possible and convenient to them economically and prestige-wise, take a stand of compromise in any rift or dispute within the family, with labour or with trade unions, even if a little extra money has to be risked in doing so. If arbitration or litigation gets involved, the individual should prepare (or get prepared) a brief very logically so as to convince the arbitrator(s) or the judges of the genuineness of the case of the individual.

Remember that Saturn can give the individual severe punishment for acts of commission and omission. In the event of indications that the individual might have to undergo punishment of imprisonment, it is always better to simultaneously examine the positions of Mars, Jupiter and Rahu from all angles, including mahadasa, antardasa and Yearly-charts for the relevant years. If the main period or sub-period is of Saturn, Mars or Rahu, punishment is likely to be upheld in appeal too. It should not however mean that combination of Saturn with Mercury invariably gives bad results. No, it is not so.

This combination gives liberal and generous attitude towards paternal and maternal uncles and aunts, nephews and nieces, notwithstanding their response towards the individual.

Saturn and Mercury in the 12th house give the individual an attitude of help and assistance towards the poor, and downtrodden, towards spouse of an enemy or opponent or adversary or competitor, who might have suffered destructive loss in business or industry or might have met with death.

These individuals do not hesitate to attend even menial jobs in a voluntary capacity in hospitals and at the time of natural calamities like floods, draught, famine, storm, cyclone, landslides, earthquake, hailstorm causing disaster to the common public, communal violence etc. On occasions such as these, these individuals would give all kind of help and assistance without reservation or restraint relating to their own resources vis-à-vis colour, caste, or creed of the sufferers. They do not hesitate to take personal risk in rendering service to the sufferers. At the same time they do not stand exploitation by clever, greedy and cunning persons in this behalf.

Mercury and Rahu in the 12th House

This combination of Mercury and Rahu in the 12th house gives an inclination for offensive and criminal activity, but because this combine gives a strong sense of consequences, an internal sense of hesitation and fear overpowers them and this hesitation saves them from actual indulgence in offensive or criminal act.

No doubt they provoke and excite others to indulge in such acts of offence and crime as these individuals had in their mind.

This provocation can take any shape, oral talks, public speech, writing, printing and distributing pamphlets or leaflets, booklets, exhibition of big posters, appearance on visual media. As far as possible, they would avoid being present at the spot and at the time of occurrence.

These individuals are always good at over-invoicing and under-invoicing, manipulation including preparation and presentation of false account papers, made-up documents, forged wills of deceased persons, false or forcibly signed promissory notes or guarantees and undertakings. But they avoid writing any such false papers or accounts or any other document in their own hand, because they are afraid of even slightest legal action against them. They do not hesitate in giving false evidence so long as they are sure that they would not have to face legal charge of perjury.

They are afraid of extra body weight, and more afraid of any disease between chest and chin. They are often suspicious of their own domestic servants and personal attendants, particularly during a travel or tour. They prefer to stay with friends instead of hotels, not for fear of bills of the hotels but for fear of any physical attack on their person.

These individuals should stay preventive against headache, migraine, swelling in eye region or ears, injury to left eye or left ear, and –a somewhat rare occurrence but piles trouble too.

Mercury and Ketu in the 12th House

The combination of Mercury and Ketu in the 12th house gives intelligence and wisdom to the individual, but often these qualities function *after* the event.

The individual intends physical harm to none, though her or his actions might hurt the feelings of others, and because those actions or utterances originate from thoughtlessness, the individual is unable at the moment to distinguish between dear ones and distant ones, or between detractors and adversaries.

This individual becomes an easy victim of piles (haemorrhoids) troubles and therefore they must eat less of spicy or hot food. Parents should check in infancy itself that the child has no problem with hearing, and also that the child's grasping power for education is functioning normally. If any deficiency is detected, medical, or other remedies should be taken care in the childhood itself.

The main point attributable to this combination is that the individual develops a tendency to think and plan misconduct, mischief, and malafide deeds, but unless under pressure from other hard-planets like Mars, Saturn, Uranus or Neptune, the individual doesn't indulge into actual action.

Thus the effect of Mercury alone in all the 12 houses as also in combination with other stars in each of the 12 houses, in brief, is here for general guidance.

JUPITER IN THE 12 HOUSES

JUPITER IN GENERAL

Jupiter in the 1st House (i.e. the *Lagna* or Ascendant) takes charge of memory, wisdom, experience, capacity for accountability for money and actions linked thereto. Jupiter in the 1st house further gives maturity in thought and also in action, good understanding of common law (irrespective of whether one has studied law or not), wide knowledge of business management, shrewdness in thought and talk.

It favours the individual also with clarity in written and spoken word (provided Mercury too is favourably seated in the Birth-chart), as also in theory and practice of economics. If the individual wants to go into teaching law, economics, accounts, business management, in these subjects too, Jupiter grants expertise to the individual.

If the individual enters the field of politics, through election or nomination, there too she or he functions efficiently as a parliamentarian or legislator or member of county council or member of *panchayat* and *zila parishad* etc.

If the individual is interested in buying and selling of shares as speculation or as long-term holding, or functioning as a broker in stock market, or as a promoter for loan seekers and arranging loans from banks and financial institutions, there too she or he proves successful, without much scope for major loss.

Jupiter rules pure gold, bullion, ornaments made of gold, jewellery, precious stones and often gains good profits in purchasing and selling these items.

Because planet Jupiter is envisioned as a 'person of advanced age', the individual can rest assured of getting comfortable and convenient living, though in matters of old age; so is Saturn similarly helpful. At the same time the 5^{th,} 12^{th,} houses, and Mars play an important role relating to comfort or discomfort from progeny and youngsters in the old age.

Jupiter is deemed to be the *guru* (teacher or preacher) of the all the gods & deities (the whole universe), but unfortunately its good effect gets marred by conjunction with Sun, Mars, Saturn, or Rahu, or even by direct *drishti* of any of them. Normally, it is presumed that Jupiter alone does not become '*maarak*' planet ('a killer' planet like Mars), unless it is under influence of hard or 'cruel' planets.

However disease-wise it can cause diabetes, asthma, kidney trouble, and liver ailment.

Jupiter normally takes 12½ months in its movement (transit) from one Rasi to another; its share in the Vimshottari mahadasa is of 16 years out of a total of 120 years. Its mahadasa is preceded by Rahu's and followed by Saturn's. It owns Sagittarius and Pisces, of which first Rasi is considered a rather hard one, while the other Rasi is considered a soft one.

Jupiter in the Lagna or the 1st house is a controversial subject as some ancients consider it is favourable with regard to money, jewellery, success in business, while some others consider it as adversely affecting these very subjects.

The memory element in a student, forgetfulness in keeping accounts by memory and jotting them down after substantial delay (from a few hours to 9 ½ days) are other attributes of Jupiter. Experience shows that both impressions about Jupiter are correct and well-founded.

JUPITER IN THE 1ST HOUSE

Jupiter in the 1st house gives maturity of thought and action, and makes an individual, as already stated above, an efficient and good-natured legislator, parliamentarian, or a minister in the cabinet or an able adviser to a king or ruler or emperor. It is a fact that in ancient times, while appointing a person as a minister or adviser or in any other important capacity in the court or *darbar*, the king or the ruler or the Emperor used to get the position of Jupiter examined in the Birth-chart of the individual concerned.

With Jupiter in the 1st house, an individual would prove to be a good treasurer, cashier, banker, insurer, accountant, lawyer, law-maker, judge, jurist, advocate, solicitor, economist, teacher or professor in economics, statistics, accounts, law, business management, and other such subjects as have been mentioned above.

Jupiter and Sun, Moon, Mars or Mercury in the 1st House

Respective chapters on Sun, Moon, Mars, and Mercury under the relevant sub-headings for the 1st house may please be referred to for results of these four combinations with Jupiter in the 1st house.

Jupiter and Venus in the 1st House

Combination of Jupiter and Venus in the 1st house allows Jupiter to retain its all influences, because Venus is a soft planet, and because of enmity between Jupiter and Venus, Jupiter normally has a slightly upper hand over Venus. It is so also because Jupiter considered as *guru of deities* (the good), while, Venus is treated as *guru of the demons* (the evil), and the good has an upper hand over the evil.

In spite of Jupiter's maturity in thought and action, its conjunction with Venus gives an individual romantic touch in nature, habits, inclinations, and personality, thereby opening scope for earning a bad name. Being a teacher or preacher or priest, whatever be the field of teaching and instruction, romanticism is a natural instinct, and it is positively difficult (if not impossible) for most of the people to earn complete control over feelings of romanticism. This is the dark side of this combination though in a sense it is just a routine

The bright side is that these individuals make very efficient teachers as also exponents and makers in the field of law (specially laws relating to marriage, divorce, alimony, maintenance, etc.). These individuals are good both at teaching and learning dance, instrumental and vocal music, economics relating to films and fine arts, sculpture, painting, interior decoration, modelling, acting on stage. They are good also at acting in films, episodes, and serials.

Some of these individuals have expert knowledge of gems and jewels including precious and semi-precious stones.

If these individuals take to designing of various-purpose buildings (including according to the *Vaastu Sastra*), they give a better account of themselves as compared to others in the same profession.

They do not mind using damsels and danseuses in spying and collecting strategic 'intelligence' about enemies and opponents. Some others among these individuals are experts in colour printing on paper, cloth, walls, and on roofs, as also painting of motifs in caves and on buildings, as even now are found in the caves of *Ajanta* and *Ellora* near Mumbai.

They excel in marketing of perfumery in different countries and working the economics relating thereto; also the art of over-invoicing and under-invoicing in import-export trade, and winning the favour of customs officers at barriers and borders of different countries.

Jupiter and Saturn in the 1st House

The combination of Jupiter and Saturn (in the 1st house) is in reality a combination of law-abiding and law-breaking stars together in one house.

Together these two stars influence the thinking, planning, implementing the plans, and these two are capable of giving immense success or sure trouble in pursuits of livelihood and income. The individual is generally rigid in business deals and transactions, with no hesitation in use of falsehood in buying and selling or in taking and giving bribes, in profiteering, in hoarding with an eye on higher profits later on owing to deficit supply.

These individuals happen to be good at collation and co-ordination of wrong statistics in economic matters as well as in index figures relating to labour and low-level population, mischievous provisions in laws relating to or affecting adversely the labour class and low-level agriculturists.

If the individual is working in police-force on the civil or the defence side, or in any investigating agency, he or she might implicate innocent people into clutches of law and crime, and thereby spare the real culprits just for considerations of gratification, or under any other obligation, influence or pressure.

The individual is likely to have self-acquired knowledge of law or has the backing of anyone in the legal profession or in the police outfit or in any investigating agency, and thus indulges in unlawful and illegal activities including heinous crimes.

On the bright side of this combination, these individuals prove competent judges hearing cases relating to labour, juvenile criminals, anti-national and anti-social criminals. Also these individuals prove efficient economists relating to defence matters including strategy relating to war, battles, and border skirmishes.

Jupiter and Rahu in the 1st House

The combination of Jupiter and Rahu in the 1st house gives an individual a mixture of knowledge, experience, sharp sense of self-respect bordering on fantastic ego, and sometimes a fattish body, though not ugly in appearance.

He or she is just opposite of 'jack of all trades, master of none'. No. Whatever subject the individual catches up for study, he or she makes best effort to master that branch of knowledge. If he or she gets associated with any investigative or intelligence agency in the government or private sector, he or she exhibits efficiency in minute observation, deep study of events and developments, and reproduction in reports of what has been seen, observed and studied.

By chance, if this type of individuals go on the path of illegal activity and crime, it becomes very difficult to apprehend them, sometimes to the extent that only death brings an end to their nefarious activity. They are good at shadowing any person or group of persons and collecting useful and dependable information about their activity, but these individuals do not prefer to become a regular employee or part of any spying outfit. They have less command on language but accuracy about facts, figures, and developments. Whether on right path or wrong one, they are often dependable in their conduct and promises.

Jupiter and Ketu in the 1st House

The individuals having the combination of Jupiter and Ketu in the 1st house do have some attributes of Rahu and Jupiter in the 1st house as mentioned in the preceding paragraph.

The only difference is that they are general in observation (that is not minute and precise), verbose in their style of reporting, and sometimes they depend on hearsay stories, like some of the easy-chair intelligence officers in air-conditioned offices! They are intelligent but not intelligence-oriented in the sense of collecting secret information. In investigation matters, these individuals are routine and superfluous in their work.

They are 'no good' in field-work or executive jobs, but good at table work, in coordinating statistics, preparing impressive and convincing reports, even if the facts and figures are hollow and good for nothing.

JUPITER IN THE 2ND HOUSE

Recall that Jupiter is the master of wealth, ornaments, jewellery, cash, valuables and also of moveable assets, and the 2nd house concerns wealth, savings, ploughing-back of profits.

The 2nd house also concerns ornaments, jewellery, moveable assets; thus it is clear that Jupiter in the 2nd house is one of the best benefit-giving star with regard to all these matters. This is the best position for Jupiter. Money-lending, business in gold ornaments, jewellery, precious stones, costly paintings, valuable statues of gold and silver, and ancient items of these categories may constitute the main source of livelihood.

In case of professions concerning law, accounts, economic advice or teaching any of these subjects, service concerning judiciary or economics or accountancy, adjudication, arbitration, survey or valuation of moveable and immovable assets including property or practice as chartered-accountant or costs & works accountant constitute the source of livelihood of the individual, great success is promised by Jupiter in the 2nd house.

Similarly, employment with income-tax, sales-tax, central

excise or state excise, bank, currency control including trading or supervising trade in foreign exchange, service in a currency printing press and circulation of currency and coins, control over banking system, life insurance and general insurance, financing or import/ export of films would give outstanding success to the individual.

If the individual is in the trade of items of fine arts, or in the trade of buying and selling books on law, business, accounts and economics, success is assured there too. To an extent, envoys, ambassadors and consular services are also within the domain of Jupiter, and thus affected by its position in the 2nd house.

Whatever the Rasi in the 2nd house, Jupiter in 2nd house generally gives beneficial results, moreso during its mahadasa or antardasa under Sun, Moon, Mercury and Venus. Fairness or unfairness in dealings and transactions or trading depends on the Rasi in the 2nd house. In case it is a Rasi owned by Jupiter itself or owned by Sun, Moon, Mercury or Venus, the individual maintains fairness in accumulation of wealth and assets. In case Mars or Saturn owns the Rasi, the method and means can have a touch of unfairness. Sudden windfall by lottery, betting at horse races, speculation in shares or gambling have direct concern with Jupiter in the 2nd house. This type of income is considered by some people as fair, while some criticise such income as unfair, because one gets this money by making thousands of people poor, be it by one rupee or thousands of rupees. Ethics is not the concern here and so this ethical fineness of distinction or differentiation between fair and unfair be left out.

Jupiter and Sun, Moon, Mars or Mercury in the 2nd House

Respective chapters on Sun, Moon, Mars, and Mercury under the relevant sub-headings for 2nd house may please be referred to.

Jupiter and Venus in the 2nd House

The combination of Jupiter and Venus in the 2nd house is capable of giving the individual wealth, beauty, comfort, luxury, sophistication and outer show 'get-together' whatever the means of livelihood of the individual.

If the individual cannot afford it on own resources, he or she tries to enjoy it with the help of, or at the cost of—friends, employers, and spouse. In some rare cases, even the character or moral values are put at stake for attaining and obtaining luxury, fashionable possessions, social-status and show in society. Minute observation would bring many an example to notice. Sometimes, if resources are ample, these individuals buy romantic pleasure and enjoyment by their money and other resources, and they get easily a good number of flatterers, followers, courtiers, and courtesans.

However if Mars, Saturn or Rahu get directly associated with this combination, loss of money, loss of face, loss of health and some illness or disease cannot be ruled out.

One 'dark' observation about this combination: these individuals may sometimes have a tendency or urge to share the spouse with another person for fulfilment of lust, or for wealth, or favour, or worldly possessions. But before uttering this type of prediction, the astrologer must carefully and minutely study the Navamsha and Trinshansha-charts, as also the position and relationship of Mars and Venus, and the *karaka* star for the 7th house at birth of the individual. Sometimes it is beneficial for the astrologer to include study of the 9th and 12th houses which rule friendship with opposite sex outside the framework of marriage.

Jupiter and Saturn in the 2nd House

Combination of Jupiter and Saturn in the 2nd house gives cunningness and desire to possess riches and items of luxury and comfort, irrespective of the fact whether the individual could afford them or not.

Since cunningness is there, some success is achieved in pursuit of this desire's fulfilment. The saying, *"slow and steady wins the race"* applies to this combination.

Quite often, though not openly admitted, violent attitude and behaviour peeps into the married life of an individual with this combination in the 2nd house. And if by chance Mars or Rahu be in the 7th or 8th house, the violence can be physical also leading to disaster to the marriage and married life by permanent separation, divorce, death, or arrival of a third angle in the married life. Since it is a delicate subject, careless or casual study by the astrologer can ruin an individual's married life. Therefore, utmost care and caution be observed before giving any prediction of the type discussed here.

It is also likely that an individual becomes rich or well-possessed from the sources of the spouse, and then tries to get rid of the spouse. And because of Jupiter in the 2nd house, the individual might be successful in going scot-free from the clutches of law.

Jupiter and Rahu in the 2nd House

Long experience shows combination or no combination, Rahu in the 2nd house, invariably makes an individual richer, and if Jupiter with control over wealth and possessions joins hands with Rahu in the 2nd house, undoubtedly the person becomes richer than what the status was in childhood.

Rahu is not concerned much with means and methods of becoming rich. Ethics are more in the region of Jupiter. Rahu (following the pattern of Saturn) is not much concerned with ethics, morals, or honesty of purpose.

The only other result Rahu can give in the 2nd house is a smokescreen suspicion on the character of the spouse, whether such suspicion is justified or not. Rahu also gives extra weight to the physique of the spouse unless extra care is taken to keep the physical fatness under control throughout. Generally lapse means loss, but in this case lapse means addition of a few pounds to the body weight. However Rahu doesn't cause any ugliness to physical appearance, except towards an advanced age.

Another result of this combination in the 2nd house is sometimes complaint of diabetes or asthma or kidney ailment to the spouse, but it happens only if the stars of the spouse too are inclined to give this type of ailment. Remember that every individual is ruled by his or her own stars, and stars of others affect only to a very limited extent.

Jupiter and Ketu in the 2nd House

The combination of Jupiter and Ketu in the 2nd house gives more or less the same results as are given by Rahu and Jupiter combine in the 2nd house.

This combination gives good results in regard to wealth, savings, plough-back of profits, worldly possessions. However this combination is likely to give the same ailments or complaints of health as are given by Jupiter and Rahu combine.

But this combination doesn't give extra fat to the body of the spouse. On the contrary, Jupiter and Ketu in the 2nd give a presentable personality to the person concerned and sometimes to the spouse too.

The individual realises quite early that the suspicion on the character of the spouse was ill informed, ill guessed and ill founded.

JUPITER IN THE 3RD HOUSE

Jupiter plays tricks in this house, and warrants special attention in the case of students and people engaged in physical labour as source of livelihood.

Students initially pose weakness of memory as an excuse and then it becomes the real default in their studies. Then there are some students who know their answers in the exams but are unable to answer all (desired) questions as they do not write fast.

For adults, this position of Jupiter gives a tendency for calculated work; this much work only for that much result; the calculations often prove wrong and, therefore, sometimes unproductive too.

In calculated work the problem is that the calculation of time, energy, and labour might not always correspond to the volume of work, and the work doesn't get completed in time, and fully. It matters little when the work is being done for any government or public-sector undertaking, but it matters when the individual is working for any private sector company or a single employer. It matters also when it is self-employment job, because in plain words, the factor of time and effort counts there too. Readers might not be unaware about government and public-sector contracts earmarked for completion within say 2 years and they continue dragging feet for 12 to 20 years. The cost of the work in the meantime multiplies 20 to 40 times, whether justified or not, just by drop in the economic graph.

Jupiter affects, rather adversely, the relationship with brothers and sisters of self, and also of the spouse when it is in the 3rd house (which means directly aspecting the 9th house). If Jupiter is in the 3rd house in Pisces, Cancer, Leo, or Scorpio, the relationship with brothers or sisters of self and spouse are sweet and mutually helpful to one another. However if Jupiter is in Aries, Gemini, Libra, Sagittarius or in Capricorn or Aquarius, the relationship often is on the basis of 'give and take', with no relation to the financial status of the persons concerned.

Because Jupiter has, from the 3rd house, angular full *drishti* on the 6th and 7th houses, developments between the individual and his or her brothers and sisters adversely affect the mutual relationship between the husband and wife.

Jupiter in the 3rd house makes an individual quite ambitious and often boasts of own capacities and capabilities, and also of contacts, influence and approaches, which often prove a hollow claim. It has been mentioned above that these individuals are calculative workers, while calculation with regard to quantum and quality of work (assigned or undertaken) do not go hand in hand with ambition. Therefore while predicting about anyone's ambition, the astrologer must keep in mind that Jupiter in the 3rd house might not prove helpful in achieving one's ambitions or aims in life. In a sense, Jupiter alone in 3rd doesn't make a person hardworking or brave.

Jupiter in 3rd has direct full *drishti* on the 9th house, these individuals, at least some of them, show great devotion and enthusiasm in pursuing religious and charitable programs. It is a different matter whether they do so with selfless sense of duty and responsibility or with ulterior motives. In some rare cases, Jupiter's direct *drishti* on the 9th house from the 3rd house brings sudden good luck to the individual, specially when Jupiter is in favourable transit or has its own mahadasa or antardasa.

Jupiter alone doesn't normally give rude, crude, and cruel attitude to the individual, who might, under pressure of Mars, Saturn or Rahu from 3rd, 8th or 9th house, connive in crude and cruel behaviour or actions of others.

Jupiter and Sun, Moon, Mar or Mercury in the 3rd House

Respective chapters in Sun, Moon, Mars, and Mercury under the relevant sub-headings for 3rd house may please be referred to.

Jupiter and Venus in the 3rd House

The combination of Jupiter and Venus in the 2nd house gives good and bad results, both at the extremes.

It makes an individual very soft hearted, sometimes expert in medical jurisprudence or in forensic medical interpretation, a good judge and critic of fine arts like dance, instrumental and vocal music, paintings, landscape designing, architecture, sculpture, knitting, needle work, acting, etc.

These individuals in some cases become expert consultants in matters concerning imports, exports, and legal matters related therewith. They make expert advocates fighting the litigation on behalf of smugglers, brothel owners, kidnappers for ransom, but positively not for terrorists.

They are generally helpful and accommodating for brothers and sisters of self and spouse, as also their spouses.

But on the wrong side, these individuals have little hitch or hesitation to indulge in romanticism with persons falling in a category equivalent to that of a brother or sister or brother-in-law or sister-in-law, or even uncle and aunt. In matters of romanticism they have no distinction between ordinary places and places of religion, like temple, church, mosque, Buddhist *math*, Jain *upashraya* or *chaitya*, or holy places of religious pilgrimage. They have no reservation enticing a person of the opposite sex while running or managing orphanage, widow homes, *nari-niketans*, hostels for students, shelters or homes for poor, ashrams, residential part of mosque/ church/ *math/ chaitya/ upashraya.*

Cases are not unknown where this type of individuals with Jupiter and Venus in the 3rd house, led their brother/ sister/ cousin/ nephew/ niece on the path of drinks and drugs as also of romanticism.

Jupiter and Saturn in the 3rd House

The combination of Jupiter and Saturn in the 3rd house gives the individuals expertise in strategy in matters of conflict, confrontation, fight, battles, war, skirmishes on border region.

This combination also gives expertise in manufacture of arms, ammunition, weaponry, ordnance items of larger size, machinery parts, spare parts for arms and weaponry, maps and surveys of areas important from offence and defence point of view.

They would go out of their way to help or harm their own kith and kin, brethren of every and all category, and would not hesitate to introduce violence in personal quarrels or family disputes including matters related to inheritance and succession.

They have no reservation in embezzling funds of social, religious, and charitable formation, including religious and educational places. For sake of power and position, they may indulge in underground tactics including threats of violence and actual violence too. But they are hard working, daring, brave, bold, and courageous and encourage or help others to become likewise.

Jupiter and Rahu in the 3rd House

The combination of Jupiter and Rahu in the 3rd house carries all the good attributes of Jupiter and Saturn combination in the 3rd house. However, it doesn't carry the bad, harmful, and violent points mentioned therein.

These individuals are bold and brave, if not on a battlefield, at least on the back-lines of the fighting forces. They give valuable suggestions for strategy of fighting, and if in anyway they are put on broadcasting or giving command, warnings, and threats on the loudspeakers, they excel in boastful broadcast carrying effective results.

They do not mind usurping any dues or shares due to brothers/ sisters/ cousins/ nephews/ nieces, but they would not descend to utter dishonesty or violence in that process. They often do so with a sweet sting. They are good at fighting cases in legal forums, at conference tables and in negotiation parleys. Some of them prove economic wizards, and carry the capacity and quality of convincing about their views even to the hardcore on economic and commercial front.

They try to help and assist others so long as their own assets or interests are neither harmed nor hurt in any manner.

Whether they work hard or not, they often create an impression that they work hard, and it carries conviction with one and all.

They have romantic ideas even towards near relations, but they keep themselves restricted to oral talks and casual physical touch, like the one gets anywhere in a crowd.

Jupiter and Ketu in the 3rd House

Under the combination of Jupiter and Ketu in the 3rd house, the individuals carry a touch of bitterness in their written or spoken word.

Otherwise these individuals are normally soft and smooth in their conduct and behaviour. They possess much higher intelligence, wisdom, experience, and simplicity and never miss a chance to put any of these qualities to timely use. They have the capacity, knowledge, and talent for writing, but their intentions are generally coated with lethargy and tendency to put off today's work on tomorrow, and that tomorrow hardly comes in their life.

The difference between Jupiter and Rahu combination and Jupiter and Ketu combination in the 3rd is that individuals with the latter combination would not mind hurting or harming their own assets and interests in the process of helping and assisting others, even semi-known persons or unknown persons. They need to be convinced about the need and necessity of the person approaching them for help or support.

JUPITER IN THE 4ᵀᴴ HOUSE

This 4th house is one of the most advantageous positions of Jupiter, because this house concerns mother, breast feeding in infancy, food in later life, shelter or home i.e. residence.

The 4th house rules also means of transport, heart, right shoulder, right-side ribs, right breast/ chest, digestive system vis-à-vis stomach, respiratory system, medical treatment and its success or failure. It further concerns ownership of property, co-operation and contribution in construction of social and charitable buildings like schools, colleges, dispensaries, hospitals, shelter homes for poor and old-age persons, shelters for orphans or *nari-niketans*.

The individual has chances of being adopted by someone in better financial status than the natural parents. Jupiter also dominates ownership of bullion, ornaments and jewellery, timber and wood-work decoration of premises in the 4th house.

One major function of the 4th house is domestic happiness, and Jupiter often ensures that domestic harmony is maintained at all costs. In case of interference in it by association of hard planets, Jupiter becomes helpless and surrenders to the influence of hard planets as Jupiter is (astrologically) an aged planet, less competent to struggle or conflict.

Thus, it is noteworthy that all "life giving" elements are the subject matter of the 4th house, including failure of functioning of the heart or the respiratory system which prove fatal to human life. These days, trade-union leaders and political slogan-mongers shout from roof-tops that every human needs '*roti, kapada aur makkan*' (food, cloth and roof over the head), and all these three important elements for human life are governed by the 4th house. Jupiter in the 4th house, whatever Rasi be there, is in rather the best position to help in acquiring or getting these basic needs.

Jupiter has, from the 4th house, direct *drishti* on the 10th house, which rules sources of livelihood for every human being.

Thus Jupiter in 4th house influences the means of livelihood too. Jupiter even in debilitated position in the 4th house proves helpful and advantageous, though the channels and means of its giving the results of the 4th house might not be of such high standard or purely satisfactory ones.

So far as students, scholars, researchers, qualified accountants, judges, jurists, lawyers and economists are concerned, Jupiter gives them high-class proficiency, and because Jupiter has higher than normal *drishti* on the 12th house, Jupiter keeps a scope to adversely affect the name and fame to the individual concerned. Relationship with natural mother or adopting mother or foster mother depend to a great extent on association of other stars with the 4th house and Jupiter sitting therein, but so far Jupiter is concerned, the relationship is normally cordial, sweet and affectionate.

Jupiter and Sun, Moon, Mars or Mercury in the 4th House

Respective chapters Sun, Moon, Mars, and Mercury under the relevant sub-headings for 4th house may please be referred to.

Jupiter and Venus in the 4th House

Combination of Jupiter and Venus in the 4th house is helpful for all such matters as are controlled by the 4th house.

The individual pays greater attention to render public utility services and tries to provide premises and equipment for the purpose of medical facilities to the common man. Sometimes greed functioning in the mind of self, spouse, or friends prompts the individual to start expensive nursing homes only within the reach of very rich people. Some of these individuals make knowledgeable and efficient experts in medical jurisprudence presently renamed as forensic medicine. These individuals become very successful in import/ export business, as chemists and druggists, as physicians, *vaidyas*, *hakims*, acupuncturists, healers by use of *tantras* and *yantras*.

One weak point with these individuals is that they are romantic in their behaviour and attitude towards the opposite sex, without much distinction between near-relations or common persons, as also between agreeable and non-agreeable ones.

They know the art of under-invoicing and over-invoicing without much risk of apprehension.

These individuals are always very keen to decorate their premises (residential and work premises) with paintings, murals, colour effects, beauty-oriented curtains and window-panes, and artistic doors. Otherwise too they are fond of making huge investments in master-paintings not only for personal use but for profits too, and in the process they do not have hitch or hesitation to buy and sell seconds (copies) of master paintings and miniatures as original masterpieces.

Some of them become heavy built by the time they reach early 40's of their age. They are fair complexioned and have smooth and soft skin. Females are generally keen to pull on their youth appearance upto declining years by appropriate make-up techniques and plastic surgery.

This combination of Jupiter and Venus gives repeated long journeys including to foreign lands, and if the stars of other members of the immediate family are helpful, they succeed in settling in a foreign land.

These individuals make successful matrimonial agents, negotiators for compromise between husband and wife on break off path, and they make efficient lawyers and judges in separation and divorce cases of marriages.

Jupiter and Saturn in the 4th House

This tricky combination of Jupiter and Saturn in the 4th house, makes a mixture of fair deal and justified approach to all matters relating to domestic affairs, while Saturn is inclined to give "self interest" the top position in the list of priorities.

These individuals do not mind in over-riding the interests of all others, including those of the natural mother, adopting mother, and foster mother. When these individuals get associated with any social, charitable, religious formation, they render best possible physical service to that formation but at the same time keep a wilful eye on finding monetary or other advantages from that source for self or for own near and dear ones.

In domestic matters too, if they do not go violent, at least they do not hesitate to give threats of violence. They eat well without differentiating between suitable and unsuitable food for their health and physique. Most of them become pot-bellied with or without proportion to other parts of the body. Many of them are prone to accidental injury to themselves by bad/careless driving, or while crossing a road, or by fall on any slippery floor inside or outside the house.

If they are the cause of injury to others, they always try to get out of the situation, by even putting the blame on their chauffeurs, drivers, other servants, or even on passers-by. They are often afraid of the law and order system and therefore search any means to stay out of that, by hook or crook.

Some of them are rude to their mother, neglecting her comforts, her health and even her maintenance, and some others have malafide intentions of depriving the mother of her personal possessions. If these individuals go into adoption by others (whether blood or near relations or not), they are less sincere to their adopting parents and have intentions of exploiting them for personal gains.

This combination generously grants extra body weight to females, who then face fluctuating problems in respiratory system too. Such fat females should have proper medical check-up before going in for child bearing, and also during pregnancy and at the time of delivery of the child.

However unless Mars gets associated with this combination from 1st or 8th or 9th or 12th house, these individuals have no obvious fear of developing heart trouble, in spite of the blood pressure complaints they suffer.

These individuals are neither kind employers, nor dutiful and loyal employees. They often have their eye on extra gains and benefits from the job with efforts for a change for better without the knowledge of and causing inconvenience to the current employer. It is so because Saturn has direct *drishti* on the 10th house, and no Rasi (whosoever its owner) can be friendly to both Jupiter and Saturn the same time.

Whether male or female, these individuals do not bother about neatness, cleanliness, and order/ systematic arrangement within their residence or office, though they always try to fill it up with all kinds of comfort-giving equipment and decorative items. And even in that untidy atmosphere they are able to work better.

Jupiter and Rahu in the 4th House

With combination of Jupiter and Rahu in the 4th house, one point is sure: hardly any person has lean and thin body with this combination in the 4th house.

Complaints of digestive system are a regular feature with them. Where self-interest is involved, they do not distinguish much between a truth and a lie, or patent falsehood. They are trustworthy so long as their selfish motives are not involved in the matter. If others keep their residence and office neat, clean, and in order, they like it but do not appreciate the effort of the other person. If they have to bring some order and system in their style of living/ working, they do it once on a blue moon.

They suspect intentions of others easily and quickly, and in the same tone, they too suffer from suspicion of others about their own intentions, though not in a 'give and take' system with them.

Their body weight generally leads to pain in the waistline, and sometimes leads, at least in their 50' and 60's of age, to arthritis, hernia, and physical complaints associated therewith, rheumatism, insomnia, sciatica, etc.

If these individuals are driving an auto-vehicle in the night, they themselves and others with them should be careful that they do not go drowsy while driving.

They do try to get undue benefits from mother and other near relations, but they avoid rudeness and pressure in getting what they want.

In social, charitable, and religious formations and groups, they make louder noise than much of real financial or physical service rendered by them actually. They are often in the habit of making a show of hard work and they do not hesitate to take credit by pirating work of others, whether in school, college, university or teaching line or journalism or legal practice and medical functioning, or anywhere else.

Jupiter and Ketu in the 4th House

Whether in combination with Jupiter in the 4th house, or alone in the 4th house, Ketu is normally a subdued star and does not make any great show of its own capacities, abilities and capabilities.

In matters of inheritance, the individual accepts what is his or her due and what is offered, and tries to obtain progress and greater success by making that inheritance as a starting foundation or base. Others describe the individual as moody and self-centred in his or her thoughts and plans. The individual's behaviour and conduct is normally that of a modern-day gentleman/ woman.

They are secretive and better qualified to work as a spy or in intelligence agencies or in commercial information services. They are often routine and middle-levelled if they go into their own business or industry, but they do better in such self-employment that doesn't need large monetary investment.

They have to be extra careful about their digestive system and to prevent asthma, diabetes, and rheumatism ailments, particularly after the age of 42 years.

JUPITER IN THE 5TH HOUSE

This is yet another very favourable placement for Jupiter. Very good memory, rich experience, vast general knowledge, maturity of mind and robust common sense are some of the gifts which Jupiter bestows upon these individuals, whether they are educated highly or not.

The second gift that Jupiter grants to these individuals is that of sensible progeny, whether male or female.

Education-wise and profession-wise, these individuals make efficient and knowledgeable lawyers, parliamentarians, senators, legislators, economists, constitutional *pandits*, qualified expert accountants, taxation experts, teachers, professors, editors (neither reporters nor for outdoor work in journalism).

Normally they think good of all, and bad of none. Even in childhood and school life they give all kind of help in studies to others deserving children and students. They make trustworthy private tutors. Their language enjoys flow and simple construction, one doesn't have to consult the dictionary often while going through matter written by them.

In their own household management and business matters they are very good economists theory-wise, but they need the guidance and assistance of others, particularly of juniors and youngsters, to be practically successful in it.

They are kind and generous to their employees, subordinates, and domestic help. Sometimes they have to suffer harm and damages by this attitude. They are liberal and tolerant towards their progeny. This tenderness on their part towards progeny sometimes proves a hurdle in high standard of educational rise of their children.

They are noble writers often cheated by their publishers. The modesty and simplicity of these individuals are generally misunderstood by such people as are out there to exploit them. As lawyers, cheats and criminals do not find a mutual suitability with them, though straightforward litigants prefer them.

Generally judges in higher courts and supreme courts as also at the International Court at The Hague should have Jupiter in the 5th, 9th or 10th house. Top economists and some of the finance ministers in different countries, who have been successful on their own, must have had Jupiter in 5th, 9th or 10th house. Good and outwardly honest ministers in council of ministers also have Jupiter in the 5th, 9th or 10th house.

However, an important point to note is that because Jupiter in the 5th house is in 11th position from the 7th house which rules spouse, spouses of some of these judges, economists and ministers may not be above board in matters of integrity and honesty. The spouse is not upto mark in maintenance of confidentiality and secrecy pertaining to the work of their husbands or wives in high positions.

On the negative side, these individuals are generally failures in judging the economic and financial position of the enemy or competitor countries, commercial houses, business adversaries and opponents in litigation. Some of them are unable to maintain the integrity and honesty of their subordinates and juniors or even co-workers, whatever their field of activity and work.

If Jupiter is in Gemini, Libra or Aquarius, it is likely to cause hernia trouble to the individual either before the age of 19 or after the age of 48 years.

Jupiter and Sun, Moon, Mars or Mercury in the 5th House

Respective chapters Sun, Moon, Mars, and Mercury under the relevant sub-headings for 5th house may please be referred to.

Jupiter and Venus in the 5th House

Even a gentleman can earn a bad name in bad or dubious company. Combination of Jupiter and Venus in the 5th house is no exception to this rule.

Venus (master of lust, romanticism, high quality medical knowledge, fashion, luxury, comfort, decoration, beauty, tenderness) is at its best in this first *trikona* (5th house), particularly in the company of Jupiter, which is old in age and vulnerable to influence of Venus. It can be anything,—thought, talk or actual action, behaviour and conduct. A good number of well educated physicians, *vaidyas, hakims* and spiritual healers have this combination in the 5th house, with the result that they too are not free from this malice.

Some of the individuals given to incestuous behaviour get their foundation from this combination, moreso if Mars is in 3rd, 7th, 9th, or 11th house (but not in the 1st house).

Females have special lustful attraction towards son-in-law

while males have a lustful eye on the daughter-in-law. Same is the case towards their pupils, students, disciples, junior doctors, nurses, compounders, juniors of opposite sex in parliament, senate, legislature and county councils, or even in courts consisting of many male and females judges, like higher courts and supreme courts. Physicians with these combinations have faced charges of molestation (and even rape) of their patients and attendants on patients.

While studying this type of horoscopes, special attention has to be paid to Navamsha-chart of males and Trinshansha-chart of females, and also position of Moon and Mars in Birth-chart and Navamsha/ Trinshansha-charts.

If Moon is in 6th, 8th or 12th house, these individuals would get into a typical mental anxiety, or agitational attitude, or even mental disorder under pressure of physical needs pertaining to the 7th house, which concerns sex. This impact of Moon is so serious that Moon in 6th, 8th or 12th house, and Jupiter and Venus combine in the 5th house, might lead to neurological problems to the individual, sometimes leading to epileptic behaviour, or partial disorientation of the mental faculties, etc.

Some astrologers may not agree with theory of partial disorientation because Jupiter in 5th house would rather prevent it, but experience shows that under influence of Venue and Moon, Jupiter becomes rather helpless in preventing mental disorders etc. No doubt this is a delicate point and the astrologer should very carefully study the planetary positions in the Bhava-Chalitam as also in Navamsha and Trinshansha-charts of males and females respectively. <u>If the astrologer is not confident of his study on this topic, he or she should avoid giving any prediction in this regard.</u>

This is the stage where influence of mahadasa and antardasa also assume prominent importance. If the mahadasa or antardasa of Venus or Moon prevails at a time when the individual is in prime of youth, if physically healthy and without relief for cohabitation with opposite sex, chances of mental-disorientation become more possible.

A workable remedy is either to get the individual married,

or allow the person non-official relationship/partner of the opposite sex. In several cases, this type of a practical approach has worked well and given the desired results.

Jupiter and Saturn in the 5th House

The most important result of this combination of Jupiter and Saturn in the 5th house is that it adversely affects the standard of achievement of the student at least upto completion of the 17th year of age.

It is so because in spite of good memory, the individual's effort for study is steady but slow, and some other hurdles enter into the individual's life in educational progress that are often outside the command of the individual. This problem can get solved, at least to a great extent, if the individual has great strength of determination, will-power, and serious effort to get over the hurdles.

In case the individual himself or herself is unable to develop these helpful qualities for desired level of educational progress, the elders in the family, teachers and tutors can help in this behalf. If prompted, the fellow students of the individual can also help him or her in good progress of studies.

When still students, these individuals intend to play mischief with other students and some times with teachers, which would depend much on the company and cooperation of other students of similar tendencies.

Another point is that these individuals, step by step, become very obstinate and rigid in their attitude and approach to normal events and developments in life of themselves as also in the life of others near and dear to them. They often presume that their own thinking is more correct than that of others around them. This creates problems in the thinking and working process of others.

These individuals generally develop differences of opinion with their spouse over the question of when to have a pregnancy, and if by chance a pregnancy takes place outside their plan and programme, they thrust their decision of getting it cleared over the spouse, irrespective of the medical opinion in the matter.

They are often hard-task masters and harsh to their subordinates and employees including domestic help. In cases of ill-treatment and violence to the domestic help, it can easily be found that Saturn had an association with another hard star in the 4th or 5th or the 9th house. Where the individual proves dishonest in paying the settled emoluments of the employee or domestic help, take it that Herschel, Mars or Rahu is in the 12th house with another star with it, having 6:8 relationship with 5th house.

They often try to prevail upon the expert opinion of their qualified accountants and taxation advisers, and if these individuals themselves appear in person before a taxation authority they try to stick to their own version and their own stand, whether it is correct and convincing, or not.

In other words, to an extent, they can be classed as strong-headed individuals. It has been observed that if these individuals are in legal profession, they continue harping their own line of argument whether it is convincing or not, to the authorities. If they themselves are on the bench and positioned to decide a case, they are stubborn in following their own line of thinking, whether correct or not, and they are not bothered whether their judgement/ decision/ assessment would stand or not stand its ground in appeal.

If by chance these individuals are examiners entrusted with valuation of the answer books or judging a candidate's worth at viva voce/ clinicals, etc., they are so rigid in their approach that they stick to their line of thinking even if they are on a wrong track. Several such cases have come into observation where their assessment of a candidate's worth has been later over-ruled by greater experts on the subject.

Women with this combination in the 5th house have to guard their pregnancy in 2nd, 4th, 5th, and 8th months, and should be prepared for longer than normal labour pains.

Jupiter and Rahu in the 5th House

In case of combination of Jupiter and Rahu in the 5th house, whether these individuals are examiners or examinees, litigants, advocates, or judges, their sense of ego often prevails over them in their decisions and judgements or assessment.

If the person standing opposite or in front of them, satisfies their ego, he or she normally gets the maximum of the desired results.

Females having this combination in the 5th house often suffer, by natural causes or causes beyond their control, loss of pregnancy at earlier stages. In case the pregnancy reaches the stage of complete para, there are problems at the time of delivery owing to delayed labours, and sometimes post-natal problems also need instant attention/remedy. If Mars or Saturn joins this combination in the 5th, or is in the 8th house in the Yearly-chart, loss of pregnancy becomes extra possible, and surgery might be needed in clearing the embryo or foetus. Though less often, but this type of result might take place even if the husband has this combination in the 5th house, and chances become more strong if the above mentioned influence of Mars or Saturn gets added to the situation. However, this is again a delicate subject and the astrologer must use his full experience and expertise before giving prediction on this point. Prediction such as these mustn't create a sense of fear in the couple or specially the wife, because if nothing else, this fear itself may sometimes lead to the loss of pregnancy.

In student life, these individuals are often given to mischief with fellow students and sometimes towards the teachers too. They often try to influence the teachers or examiners to get results better than their actual performance. Here too, their ego works to show by fair or foul means that they are better than fellow students.

When arguing a case before any legal forum or taxation authority, these individuals keep beating around the bush, and often miss the main point of their case, unless someone else draws their attention to the main point. However if Mercury is in any way associated with this combination, these individuals become quick to grasp and make amends in their attitude and approach, whether they are arguing or deciding or judging a point.

These individuals are easy to suspect the conduct, character, and honesty of others, but at the same time under influence of Jupiter in the same house, they are quick to understand the correct situation and make amends.

They have no hesitation in working less and pirating the credit of another's work, particularly in the field of law, accounts, economics, editorials, and literature of any kind.

Jupiter and Ketu in the 5th House

As in the 4th house, in the 5th house too, the combination of Jupiter and Ketu is more or less a supporter of Jupiter's results.

It doesn't often interfere with Jupiter's functions in the 5th house, except that it gives bright colour to those actions and functions. It gives a mischievous thinking but rarely the actual mischief. Similarly it disturbs the pregnancy at earlier stages but neither very often nor very seriously, rather easily correctable/curable by medical remedy. They do more reading, including general reading and less written work in school and post-school studies or higher education. These individuals make good and hard working researchers. They have a tendency for accuracy and do not pirate work of others without giving credit to the original thinker, author, creator, or inventor.

These individuals are more inclined towards honesty and integrity, both theoretically and practically.

Ketu doesn't lead to fatness and heavy body weight in earlier or later stages of life.

JUPITER IN THE 6TH HOUSE

Jupiter in the 6th house is a difficult position for the individual with regard to recovery of loans, tracing lost items of jewellery, gold, cash, earning profits in speculation of any and every kind.

The individual is generally a loser ultimately in card-games or at horse-races or in other kinds of betting, and even in cases in courts of law or in taxation matters, moreso if a problem takes origin.

Sometimes asthma, diabetes, and kidney problems also peep into the life of the person, moreso if Jupiter is owner of 6th, 8th or 12th house. Males or females with Jupiter in the 6th house must *not* travel with heavy cash on person, and must *not* operate bank-lockers or safe-deposit vaults so very often; over-confidence about such matters or negligence can lead to undesirable results.

In matters of litigation, caution should be taken that the individual's lawyer/ advocate is not won over by the opposite party by any means or in any manner. He or she should try to be present at the time of hearing, just to observe, whether the presiding officer or his/her colleagues on the Bench is showing any inclination in favour of the opposite party outside the norms of judicial impartiality. The power, resources and influences of the opposite party, adversary or opponent shouldn't be under-estimated.

In matters of taxation, it is always better not to annoy the officer assessing the individual's case or hearing and deciding the appeal or revision or review petition. At the same time the individual should not be mislaid by the chartered accountant or taxation adviser about demands of large bribes by the assessing officers and appellate authorities, as the CA or the adviser would very often keep own share in view in fixing the amount of bribe. Further these individuals sometimes suffer from second thoughts after submission of the return, appeal, review petition, representation, etc.

Jupiter and Sun, Moon, Mars or Mercury in the 6th House

Respective chapters on Sun, Moon, Mars, and Mercury under the relevant sub-headings for 6th house may please be referred to.

Jupiter and Venus in the 6th House

Combination of Jupiter and Venus in the 6th house is capable of giving physical ailment, specially asthma, diabetes, lever, loss of vitality, harmful fluctuation in body weight, hernia, inflammation in the middle part of the body.

It can also give differences with spouse, misunderstanding

with friend of the opposite sex, bad name on account of company with persons considered undesirable by family and society.

Sometimes during the mahadasa or antardasa is of Jupiter or Venus, the individual finds that mother is not very much cooperative with the individual. Spouse makes complaints of paucity of funds, whether it is actually so or not. Children of marriageable age face problems with their friends of the opposite sex, in case they have any.

For importers/ exporters, recovery of dues gets stuck or delayed causing imbalance in managing further business. Medical persons including *vaidyas* and *hakims* face charges (of dissatisfaction from the patients), and as a consequence, the fees or service charges or examination charges or nursing-home charges become over-due.

Actors, actresses, musicians, directors, cameramen, stunt-persons, extras do not get their full payments from their producers, directors, placement agencies. Architects either get complaints from the clients or payments get stuck up on charges of bad/ shoddy work.

Medical treatment doesn't show favourable effects instantly; different medical persons give different opinions about the disease as well as treatment prescribed.

The only favourable effect of this combination is that brothers/ sisters and their spouses, whether of self or of husband, are always in touch to extend help and assistance in any hour of need, and they do not grudge or grumble it, specially if the need relates to any illness.

Jupiter and Saturn in the 6th House

In the combination of Jupiter and Saturn in 6th house, Saturn being the stronger planet, it is fully capable of serving as an antidote and remedy to most of the evil effect of Jupiter in the 6th house.

<u>The 6th house is one of the most favourable houses for Saturn, whether alone or with other planets, because Saturn is capable of overriding the influence of other planets</u>, and no other

star (except Mars to an extent) is capable of adversely influencing the effect of Saturn in the 6th house.

Jupiter is often able to have its 'say' in matters pertaining to non-recovery of loan, loss in shares and stocks, defeat in civil or property or marriage litigation, and loss of money by carelessness. But in the event of any loss of this type, Saturn provides chances of recovery and revival, thereby making good the loss.

The *first* strongly favourable point of this combination is that Saturn protects the individual from any such disease/ ailment/ injury/ illness as is likely attributable to Jupiter's position in the 6th house.

The *second* favourable effect is that Saturn protects the individual against being dragged into any criminal charge.

The *third* favourable result is that Saturn helps against sabotage and mischief in any election, which the individual himself might be fighting.

The *fourth* favour likely to be granted by Saturn is that enemies aren't able to override the interests of the individual.

The *fifth* advantage is that Saturn keeps the labour contented and under control, and trade-union leaders are often unable to create trouble in the factory, manufacturing-unit, or hotel, or restaurant, or large marketing-outfit.

The *sixth* gift from Saturn is in the shape of buying good and genuine machinery, and spare-parts at reasonable price without middleman's mischief.

Saturn is capable of instigating the individual to engage miscreants for recovery of money from defaulters. However special attention should be paid that this type of effort may not misfire, because Jupiter is also in the 6th house and it can lead to misfire and new problems for the individual, instead of getting the dues recovered.

The same point is applicable to individuals engaging detective agencies for collecting information about the opposite party in matrimonial litigation. Similarly, a commercial unit engaging detective agencies to collect secrets-of-success of a competitive commercial unit can also misfire. Therefore in all these matters, the individuals should weigh in proper perspective the pros and cons of engaging the secret service agencies, and unless unavoidable, should drop the idea.

Jupiter and Rahu in the 6th House

This combination of Jupiter and Rahu in the 6th house would give more or less the same results as those discussed above about Jupiter and Saturn combination in the 6th house.

Remember that Rahu is a shadow planet, and therefore not capable of giving as 'solid' results as Saturn can. Also, Rahu is not capable of exercising such strong and undefeatable control over Jupiter as Saturn can. Thus an over-reliance on Rahu against Jupiter would not help. It is advisable for such individuals to always weigh the balancing effect in proper perspective, and only then become active or start any activity.

In this context it is better to determine the Jupiter's strength, and also Jupiter's relationship with the lord of the 6th house. In case the lord of the 6th house is Sun, Moon, Mars or Jupiter itself, Rahu would not be of much help. However if the 6th house is owned by Mercury, Venus or Saturn, Rahu would be able to exercise control over troubles created by Jupiter, whatever the field and scope of the trouble.

However, again bear in mind that if any matter relates to character and conduct of the husband or wife or friend of the opposite sex of either of them, Rahu would give a fillip to the suspicion instead of wiping it off. In fact, Rahu would make matters further worse by pulling in money allegations in the matter. No doubt Rahu helps and rather protects the individual in all other matters outside the arena of matrimonial disputes and quarrels.

Jupiter and Ketu in the 6th House

In this combination, Ketu is not very much capable of controlling or countermanding the ill or evil effect of Jupiter in the 6th house.

It provides protection to a limited extent. And if Jupiter is in its own Rasi or a Rasi owned by Sun, or Moon, or Mars, Ketu would be all the less important, less strong, to provide protection to the individual. No doubt, Ketu would provide protection in the matter of illness, ailments, or disease and if Ketu is unable to prevent it, at least it will help in quick recovery

If the individual is a writer, poet or journalist, he/ she has to stay alert not to pirate material, and avoid unnecessary criticism of any living or dead person as it might lead to defamation or conflict or contradictions, and sometimes ultimately to litigation and damages.

JUPITER IN THE 7TH HOUSE

The 7th house is yet another house wherein Jupiter showers favours on the individual in money matters, in income, in earnings, in enhancing prestige and power, granting success in love affair, in getting a suitable matrimonial match, also in giving success in buying and selling. Jupiter helps in marriage at the right or desired age.

Jupiter gives capacity to gain an upper hand over enemies or adversaries and opponents. If it is in a watery Sign, Jupiter helps in migration of the individual to another country or a town by sea-coast, and successfully settling there.

Jupiter is also helpful in matters relating to elections, litigation on the civil side (but not on the criminal side), in matrimonial disputes, in matters of arbitration, in managing the property and assets and even business or office affairs of the spouse. It helps in quick recovery from physical injuries, provided it was a bleeding injury. It also helps in securing loans from banking and other similar financing institutions for any kind of business venture or enterprise.

The individual can, himself or herself, become a successful banker or insurer. Jupiter in the 7th house provides scope for money lending against mortgage of gold and jewellery, or earning a livelihood from running hotel, motel, restaurant, furniture and furnishing trade. <u>Some readers might question how the 7th house is concerned with livelihood.</u> The answer is that 7th house directly and importantly concerns buying and selling of goods for business and the gains therefrom.

One unique point regarding Jupiter in the 7th house. These individuals have remarkably good memory and they are able to express their thoughts and ideas very clearly and impressively in writing but often it is seen that they are not very impressive speakers.

If readers minutely study, they would find that some of the judges on the benches of higher and lower courts may have Jupiter in the 7th house and they preferred service in judiciary instead of functioning as a lawyer because they considered themselves less proficient in speaking. Same is the case with some chartered accountants, who prefer to prepare returns, representations, notes for submission and appeals but send their colleagues and juniors to argue the cases before taxation authorities. Cases are not rare where a great author is not so impressive while speaking in public. Some actors and actresses are good in acting, but not equally good in dialogue-delivery.

Readers might question why this is so. The answer is like this: the 2nd house rules the capacity and capability or competence for the spoken word, and the 7th house is in 6th position from the 2nd house, impact of which has been given above in preceding paragraphs. However, it may also be noted that these individuals have very correct and minute observation of any event or happening and they can stand any kind of cross-examination when standing in the witness box of any legal forum.

One major advantage of Jupiter in the 7th house is that whenever there is any problem, which might involve besides other things, a monetary angle, the family of the spouse comes forward to extend monetary help and all other kind of support to the individual. In some cases, a male having Jupiter in the 7th house would find his wife, in case of emergency, coming forward to help him from her petty savings collected over the vast period of married life. And cases are not rare, at least in South Asian countries, where the wife sold her jewellery to help the husband monetarily.

Jupiter and Sun, Moon, Mars or Mercury in the 7th House

Respective chapters Sun, Moon, Mars, and Mercury under the relevant sub-headings for 7th house may please be referred to.

Jupiter and Venus in the 7th House

There is a saying in Hindi: "*sone pe suhaga*" which means 'that which is even better than gold'. This combination Jupiter and Venus in the 7th house is very likely to give the individual a spouse with presentable personality/ features/ fair complexion (going by the local climate), sensible and cooperative person adjusting with the circumstances.

In short, sweet natured and loveable spouse! What more a person might want, whether it is a man or a woman. However, no hard planet like Saturn, Mars, Rahu or Herschel should be in the 7th or the 1st house. Saturn, Mars or Rahu can bring problems in married life from the 8th house, and sometimes from the 2nd house too, which house is responsible for the health of the spouse. The question might arise as to why from the 2nd house. It is so because the 2nd house is in the 8th position from the 7th house, and 8th position is always deemed as damaging.

Saturn alone even in the 6th house would cast evil *drishti* on the 7th house and thus disturb the married life. It may also be noted that whatever the Rasi in the 7th house, in case it is owned by either Jupiter or Venus or a friend of either of the two, the damage to the married life would be short-lived or manageable.

Normally, this combination, though rarely found in horoscopes, gives satisfaction to the couple with regard to every important matter in life including money, wealth, source of livelihood, love and affection between the two in the bedroom, comfortable standard of lifestyle, sweet-natured friends.

This combination normally helps in business matters too, specially business relating to medicines, herbals, cloth, garments, sugar, ghee, running and/or managing hotels, motels, and restaurants.

Import/ export trading, perfumery, bullion, gold and silver utensils, precious stones, jewellery, gold and silver ornaments, wooden items of decoration, drapery, cotton, cotton-seeds, hospital equipment etc. also give highly profitable results to the individual. Sometimes it becomes profitable to the married couple or friends of opposite sex if both, husband and wife, actively associate with the business or function in legal or medical profession (including running hospital, dispensary, clinic and nursing home etc). It has already been discussed above as to how the 7th house concerns and helps in livelihood matters.

Another important point is that either the husband or the wife or both might have livelihood from medical career or career in law and justice.

The disadvantage of this combination is that big success at initial stage makes an individual very bold with self-confidence and leads to illegal, non-commercial activities. In case lethargy gets combined in the career or source of livelihood of these individuals, the results are often disadvantageous. This ultimately leads to run down of the graph of profits and invested capital unless spouse comes to active help and rescue. One of the best remedies to this situation is to keep the spouse in touch with progress or downward trend in the source of livelihood, in case the spouse is not actively associated with it. It is all the more beneficial to keep getting, from time to time, guidance from the spouse in this behalf, without bothering about the education, experience and capacity of the spouse in these matters.

Jupiter and Saturn in the 7th House

It is repeated again that Jupiter and Saturn in combination in the 7th house, considered old in age astrologically speaking, come face to face with each other wanting to harm and hurt the influence of the other.

Jupiter wants the marriage to be a success, and the married life to be a soft, sweet and smooth run of life, while Saturn makes the spouse a stubborn person, fault finding, sometimes abusive or bordering on physical violence towards each other. Jupiter wants to give maturity of mind to the spouse; Saturn wants the spouse to behave in a fickle minded manner, uncertain and unpredictable in attitude and behaviour.

If this is the case, much depends on the Rasi in the 7th house and its lord, and the relationship of the lord of the 7th house with the 7th house itself and also with Jupiter and Saturn there. If the Rasi is owned by Jupiter itself or by Sun/ Moon/ Mars, the marriage is likely to work with greater percentage of softness, sweetness and smoothness. If the Rasi in the 7th house is owned by Mercury/ Venus or Saturn itself, the married life would just drag its feet. In case the 5th or the 11th house is also owned by Mercury/ Venus or Saturn, the roughness in married life of the couple would adversely affect their progeny too, to some extent at least.

The individual is not very stable, and not straightforward in money dealings, business matters and paying due taxes of the government, as well as of the local bodies like municipality etc. It is always better to have written agreements/ contracts/ undertakings with this type of individual, but the problem is how would the other party know initially what type of horoscope and mentality the individual has! Thus those who deal with such individual would become wiser only *after* some experience.

If this individual is involved in any litigation relating to marriage or business or taxation, he or she would often try to gain ground by mischievous representations and pleadings, and even producing false or forged documents, or tutored witnesses.

These individuals give loans easily, but on very hard terms and are rough or even cruel in recovery of the loan, and its interest on due dates. However if these individuals take loans, they are always late in repayment and make excuses in payment of interest and even sometimes in payment of the original amount borrowed.

These individuals are trustworthy if money matters are not involved; they may dare taking risk for the help and support of a friend, well-wisher, superior or senior colleague or the employer. In the normal course they can be trusted in matters related to moral character and conduct, but if Venus gets associated with Saturn by *drishti* or exchange of houses, it is better not to put their moral character and conduct to any real test.

Where extra-marital affair or any affair with physical closeness is involved, it is always better to use preventive measures against AIDS and allied diseases, because if by chance Mars also gets associated with this combination, the risk of contacting infectious disease are often there. Rahu's association with this combination in the 7th house can also give some disease arising out of unprotected sexual union, but because Rahu is a shadow planet, the disease gets totally cured easily and quickly.

If any cut/ blood injury gets at or near the genital organs or near the anus, immediate medical treatment is unavoidable, as otherwise it has the potential to become septic.

Jupiter and Rahu in the 7th House

The first and foremost effect of this combination of Jupiter and Rahu in the 7th house is that the spouse would have a sharp sense of ego of personality, education or status in society or of wealth leading to bragging and boastful utterances. These utterances can be anywhere and everywhere, before the marriage partner, or before friend of the opposite sex in love.

These individuals generally put on weight below the navel point upto genitals, and upper thighs near the thigh-joints. Some of them, *depending on position of Venus and its relationship with the 7th house,* and of-course with these two planets sitting in 7th house, *may* go weak in sexual capacity within 9 to 16 years of marriage. The experienced astrologer keeps an eye on this point while matching horoscopes of the boy and the girl for marriage purposes.

These individuals are dependable in the normal course, unless Mars or Saturn is in the 2nd or the 12th house. They do not indulge in forgery of documents, presentation of false papers, producing tutored witnesses and the like in any litigation.

Rahu is said to be more effective in the case of females when in the 7th house, and therefore the husband and the members of the husband's family should always be mindful to respect their sense of self-respect and ego of a *'bahu'* (daughter-in-law). It is also established by experience that if this type of lady participates actively in management of any business, industrial venture, school, hospital, nursing home, hotel, motel, restaurant or money lending house or jewellery shop, she gives very good account of her working. Unless some outside pressure is there, she stays honest and above-board even in dealings with customers and buyers. If she herself or her husband is a candidate for any elective office, she takes care that promises made to voters on behalf of self, or the spouse, are fulfilled to the extent possible.

Chances of loss of pregnancy are there in the case of these females in the 3rd and 5th month during hastily climbing a staircase, or hill / hillock, or lift any heavy weight, or indulge in jogging, or do not keep off sex in the husband-wife relationship.

Jupiter and Ketu in the 7th House

In this particular house, combination of Jupiter and Ketu in the 7th house gives 50% results of Rahu and Jupiter combination, and 50% results of Mercury and Jupiter combination in the same 7th house.

The spouse is in all probability an educated person given to clear thinking and quick workable and practical decisions, and keeps gathering experience from every event and development in life of self and those around both husband and wife. And the individual doesn't store that experience in a dark cell of the mind, but often puts it to practical use.

The individual is not given to putting on much weight around and below the naval point, rather maintains a presentable figure. The individual is fond of flowers, fragrance-giving items including perfumery, and normally doesn't suffer from bad odour. The individual has fondness for literature, is a regular reader of whatever is available, and has the tendency to write articles, short poems, stories, and if nothing else letters to relations and friends.

These individuals are always very practical in management of household, office, factory, hospital, school, but not in management of hotel, restaurant etc. They would not like to handle business in furniture, drapery and furnishing material as well as interior decoration.

JUPITER IN THE 8TH HOUSE

This is also an important placement for Jupiter, because it determines loss of money, losses in share and stock speculation, diseases like asthma, diabetes and kidney trouble.

Jupiter in the 8th house also determines whether the individual would have an easy and peaceful death with contentment in past life. Otherwise he or she would have death after prolonged illness or severe sufferings even for a short period or death in mental worries and dissatisfied aims and ambitions and incomplete tasks left behind. Another worry would be whether the death would cause any financial problem/ struggle/ dispute to the spouse or mistress or paramour or friend of the opposite sex in love who is left behind.

The ancient *acharyas* have laid considerable importance in this regard on the *Dreshkana-chart* (one-third divisional part of the Ascendant/ Lagna) in the 8th house, as the 8th house is connected with death.

The question can arise as to why this point relating to *Dreshkana* is being discussed with reference to Jupiter's position in the 8th house and not earlier. The ancient *acharyas* have attached importance to both Jupiter and Dreshkana in the 8th house for determining whether the death of the individual would be a contented person's death with a peaceful mind or it would be a death of a uncontented person in a disturbed and worried state of mind.

Each Rasi has three Dreshkanas. **The Dreshkana effect is discussed below Rasi-wise for easy and clear understanding**:

(1) If it is the 1st Dreshkana of (Mesh) **Aries** in the 8th house, the death would be caused by liver or kidney trouble. Death would come after quite long struggle with illness and medical treatment.

(2) If it is the 2nd Dreshkana of Aries, the death would be by drowning, by water, by any disease caused by water, on a sailing ship or sinking of the ship, by floods, by landslide or by snowfall, or storm, or cyclone etc.

(3) If the 3rd Dreshkana of Aries, the death might be caused by landslide, falling in a ditch, well, canal or on the banks of a flowing or dry river, or by falling from a height of any kind.

(4) If it is the 1st Dreshkana of **Taurus**, the death would be caused by fall from a horse/ camel/ elephant or by dog bite, jackal bite or by an attack by a wild animal like lion, tiger, panther, wolf.

(5) If it is the 2nd Dreshkana of Taurus, the death would be caused by fire, electrical shock, acid, poison, cough, cold, bronchitis, or congestion of the chest.

(6) If it is the 3rd Dreshkana of Taurus, the death might be caused by debris of a house, volcano, earthquake, falling or jumping-off or by being thrown from the roof of a house or multi storied building, or by an attack by a wild animal, or rabies.

(7) If it is the 1st Dreshkana of **Gemini**, the death is likely to be caused by suffocation caused by smoke/ dust/ pollution, asthma trouble or obstruction in respiratory system or by body being overburdened by so much fatness that breathing becomes difficult.

(8) If it is the 2nd Dreshkana of Gemini, the death might be caused by high fever, malaria, cholera, tuberculosis, or similar allied illness.

(9) If it is the 3rd Dreshkana of Gemini, the death is likely by accident by vehicle, train, aeroplane, or being pushed from a high level by someone intentionally, or by landslide, or by falling into a ditch, stream, brook, valley from any kind of a vehicle.

(10) If it is the 1st Dreshkana of **Cancer** in the 8th house the death is caused by food poisoning, poisoning by someone else intentionally, injury by arrows, gun, fire, knife, or thorns, or sharp-weapon and bleeding caused thereby.

(11) If it is the 2nd Dreshkana of Cancer, the death is caused by piles, inflammation in intestines, serious kind of gynecological trouble, diarrhoea, or dysentery.

(12) If it is the 3rd Dreshkana of Cancer, the cause of death is likely to be failure of spleen, kidney or intestines, cholera or plague.

(13) If the 1st Dreshkana of **Leo** is in the 8th house, the cause of death may be plague, any epidemic, venereal disease or AIDS and allied trouble, or dyspepsia of serious kind.

(14) If the 8th house has 2nd Dreshkana of Leo, cause of death is likely to be congestion in chest, asthma, bronchitis, acute problem with respiratory system, and (rarely but sometimes possible) by drowning or being pushed in water, river or sea, or by poisonous liquor, wine, or any drinkable item.

(15) If it is the 3rd Dreshkana of Leo in the 8th house, the cause of death can be an injury by firearm, spear, arrow, knife or by a gunshot on a battlefield, or by vehicular accident, or poison in blood system by injection, or infection.

(16) If it is the 1st Dreshkana of **Virgo** in the 8th house, the death is likely by insanity, neurological trouble, brain hemorrhage, epilepsy, or some allied ailment.

(17) If it is the 2nd Dreshkana of Virgo in the 8th house, cause of death is likely to be a fall from a height, being killed on the ramparts of a fort or high-rise building, or a fall from a tree, hill, mountain.

(18) If the 3rd Dreshkana of Virgo is in the 8th house, the cause of death could be by an order of a king, ruler, chieftain, head of a tribe or criminal group or death sentence by a court of law.

(19) If the 1st Dreshkana of **Libra** is in the 8th house, the death is likely by a woman or connivance of a woman, mistress, paramour, or by spouse (wife or husband), or by being thrown down from a height, high-rise building, hill, or mountain. In any case it is a death planned by a human being(s).

(20) If the 2nd Dreshkana of Libra is in the 8th house, the death is likely to be caused by attack by a domestic or wild animal, by indigestion, by dyspepsia, dysentery, diarrhoea, i.e. any ailment of the abdomen and digestive system.

(21) If it is the 3rd Dreshkana of Libra in the 8th house, the cause of death would likely be snake-bite, attack by crocodile, pit-viper, python, biting by bees or any other insect in or near the water.

(22) If the 1st Dreshkana of **Scorpio** is in the 8th house, the cause of death could be poison or injury by a weapon or firearm, on battlefield or otherwise, or by poison gas, chemicals (being used these days in modern warfare).

(23) If the 2nd Dreshkana of Scorpio is in the 8th house, the death will be caused by lifting any heavy weight or big burden, abortion caused by lifting burden or abortion caused by forced or consented sex or by rape during pregnancy, by major fracture of waist-line or spine bone or of the back portion of the ribs.

(24) If the 3rd Dreshkana of Scorpio is in the 8th house, the cause of death could be attributed to serious injury by a large stone, rock falling on head or body, by landslide, by debris of a building or fall of a big machine or a railing or iron rail or big rod etc. on the head.

(25) If the 1st Dreshkana of **Sagittarius** is in the 8th house, death is likely by piles, after effect of a surgical operation or by infection caused by syringe. Death can even occur under general anaesthesia or on a surgical operation table.

(26) If the 2nd Dreshkana of Sagittarius is in the 8th house, death is likely on a battlefield, by explosion of any bomb or mine, by enemy action, by attack by dacoits, robbers, thieves, opponents, adversaries, terrorists.

(27) If the 3rd Dreshkana of Sagittarius is in the 8th House, the cause of death may be by crocodile, by eating poisonous fish, by attack from a group of tortoise, by drowning, by being pushed into water or river or sea etc., or by any poisonous watery substance entering into the stomach system.

(28) If it is the 1st Dreshkana of **Capricorn** in the 8th house, death may be predicted by an attack by lion, tiger, wild boar, monkeys, panther, wolf, wild buffalo or any four-

legged animal in anger, or even by scorpion bite or drinking a substance containing a dead poisonous creature.

(29) If the 2nd Dreshkana of Capricorn is in the 8th house, death be predicted by snake-bite, python attack, on account of bees, scorpion, or any such poisonous creature/insect.

(30) If the 3rd Dreshkana of Capricorn is in the 8th house; the cause of death may be thief, robber, dacoit, fire, firearm, electric-shock, electric short-circuit, any kind of fatal fever, malaria, tuberculosis or diphtheria specially in childhood.

(31) If the 1st Dreshkana of **Aquarius** is in the 8th house, death can be caused by wife, mistress, prostitute, concubine, paramour, husband, natural or adopted son or daughter, or by a sharp weapon or firearm injury on the abdomen or even a kick on abdomen/womb/stomach or on the testicles (for man).

(32) If the 2nd Dreshkana of Aquarius is in the 8th house; death can be caused by venereal diseases, AIDS and allied ailment, infection of any kind, septic wound, or poison consumed or injected into the blood system.

(33) If the 3rd Dreshkana of Aquarius is in the 8th house, the cause of death will be biting by any poisonous insect including snake, lizard, scorpion, python, or by any wound or injury going septic.

(34) If the 1st Dreshkana of **Pisces** is in the 8th house, the cause of death is likely to be diabetes, urinary disease, tuberculosis, pyrolesis, paralysis, dengue fever, or typhoid.

(35) If the 2nd Dreshkana of Pisces is in the 8th house, the death is likely by attack by an elephant, camel, horse, donkey, zebra, wolf, fox, cow, rabies, buffalo, or falling into water from a boat, steamer, sailing ship or by being pushed into water, river, canal or, by floods.

(36) If the 3rd Dreshkana of Pisces is in the 8th house, death may be predicted to occur by long-term disease, cholera, asthma, diabetes, kidney trouble, plague, any epidemic, any fatal fever or by food poisoning.

These are just astrological indications, <u>which can be used to verify past events</u>, and should not be taken as absolutely binding, hard-and-fast rules. Many more other factors would need to be checked before venturing any prediction.

Planets of husband and wife affect each other directly and closely. Therefore any indication of death to be predicted on basis of the horoscope of either husband or wife should not be given. The horoscopes of both husband and wife or mistress and paramour, must be studied in full and complete details, including mahadasa, antardasa and the Yearly-charts (and if possible monthly-charts too). Then, and only then, a prediction about death be put forth. As far as possible, **refrain from making predictions about the event of death**. Prediction about death should **never be made** from a casual study. Such predictions can affect the mental and emotional state of the person concerned, as well as those of relatives and friends.

Jupiter and Sun, Moon, Mars or Mercury in the 8th House

Respective chapters on Sun, Moon, Mars, and Mercury under the relevant sub-headings for 8th house may please be referred to.

Jupiter and Venus in the 8th House

The combination of two soft planets, Jupiter and Venus in the 8th house often proves risky, particularly to prestige, physical safety.

This combination is likely to cause illness, and because Jupiter is among long-term stars, the illness thus caused could be, some times, of long duration.

These two stars are more vitally concerned with sexual vitality, general vigour and strength, cough, cold, bronchitis, congestion of the chest region, sour throat, diabetes, complaints of the respiratory system, liver problem, mumps. quinsy, ranula, cyst of female breast, irregularity of digestive system socially caused by excess of drinking, excess consumption of sweet items, excess of sexual activity.

This combination could also cause disorder of the ovaries,

nausea, diseases transmitted through unprotected sexual union, pleurisy with effusion, jaundice, tumour in kidney, urethral abscess, pain in lungs caused by repeated complaint of cough and cold, etc.

Whenever these two stars are found together in any Birth-chart or in the Yearly-chart, it is always better to examine the Bhava-Chalitam and also the Navamsha-chart, irrespective of whether the horoscope is of a male or a female.

Whether an individual is actively involved or not, sometimes charges are levelled against her or him for lack-of-morals, debauchery (morally corrupt).

When Saturn or Mars or Rahu is in the 2nd house, or any of these three stars is in the 8th house itself, some of these individuals might be charged (be it on rumours) about being involved in trade in humans, kidnapping, running a call girl racket or private-home-prostitution racket, and similar other illegal activity.

Then there are chances of any of these allegations reaching the police or social workers, and consequences can follow.

Because both these soft stars have a direct *drishti* on the 2nd house, the expenses of getting out of the above-mentioned charge can be met out of the current income and the permanent savings/ assets remain more or less untouched.

Another caution needed about this combination is that the individual might suffer a loss of money or assets or prestige by cheating, exploitation in matters of money, jewellery, moveable assets by own spouse, by mistress, by concubine, by paramour, by friend of the opposite sex, by a call girl or by a male or female prostitute. An individual has to face the blackmail.

Then there is also the risk of loss of money in speculation, by embezzlement, by pilferage, by cheating on part of own advocate/ counsel/ accountant/ cashier, or customs agent.

Because these two stars can cause wrong medical treatment at the hands of a medical man or woman, because of extra greed for money in the mind of that medical man or woman, it is always necessary for the individual to stay alert in this respect, and if the need is felt to consulting another doctor, it should be done with out delay. Cases are very common in virtually all countries were a surgical operation or delivery of a child by unnecessary caesarean section has been thrust on the patient merely for gaining extra fees.

If any theft or robbery or dacoity takes place in the premises of these individuals or in a travel or outdoors, if not more, at least one woman or eunuch or medical man or a legal person with inside knowledge is likely to be involved in it.

These individuals should avoid giving loans to and making deposits with any persons during sub-period of Jupiter under Venus or of Venus under Jupiter or when Jupiter is in the 6th, 8th or 12th house by transit from the Janma-Lagna.

Jupiter and Saturn in the 8th House

Combination of Jupiter and Saturn in the 8th house is capable of operating both ways.

Saturn can function as a strong check on the unfavourable results likely to be caused by Jupiter in the 8th house. On the other hand, Saturn might join Jupiter in giving unfavourable results thereby making matters worse for the individual. Sometimes both results follow each other or take place simultaneously.

Where the question of bad results of this combination on health is concerned, the main trouble would be related to injury or fracture of any bone, injury to the skull, tooth trouble, pain in joints or the spinal chord or the waistline bone, pain in knees and in soles.

This combination also gives loss of general vigour and vitality, diseases caused by lack of nutritional diet or lack of two meals a day on account of abject poverty, revival of pain caused by any old injury or fracture, arthritis, sciatica, illness connected with genital organs. Gout, leprosy (provided Mars is in some way associated with this combination), pleurisy (dry or with effusion), inflammation of any inner or outer part or limb. Tuberculosis can also be attributed to this combination.

Further, cancer of any kind (again provided Mars is

somehow connected with these two stars in the 8th house), variation in formation or length or built-up of muscles of both hands or both legs of the individual is also caused by Jupiter and Saturn in the 8th house.

Because Jupiter rules the ribs and spinal chord, in any accidental fall or vehicular accident, chances are of injury to the ribs or the spinal chord. Sometimes Saturn gives gastric trouble, which could adversely affect the heart (specially if Mars also has any unfavourable impact on the heart region in some way), or the respiratory system, including bad throat. The trouble is controllable and curable, no doubt, with regular care and medical treatment.

On the favourable side, Saturn sitting with Jupiter quite often saves the individual from cheating, exploitation, theft, loss of jewellery or cash by any lapse on part of self or spouse, or from loss by speculation.

For this purpose it is always better to determine the strength of both the stars. When Saturn is more powerful than Jupiter, it would be able to provide full protection against evil effect of Jupiter. If Jupiter is stronger, Saturn would be able to provide partial protection, and it would necessitate extra alertness on part of the individual and spouse, to escape such losses.

However, this unfavourable effect of Saturn shouldn't be misunderstood. Saturn can still give an injury or fracture or any other physical trouble mentioned above and therefore preventive attitude is anyway necessary.

Another favourable impact of Saturn in 8th house with Jupiter is that Saturn gives good rapport between employer and the employees. The workers stay loyal and hard working in any election campaign.

In Industrial venture owned or managed by the individual, Saturn would take full care of the raw material and production, but marketing and recovery of dues would need special attention as it is the domain of Jupiter, which is naturally unfavourable in the 8th house.

Jupiter and Rahu in the 8th House

Combination of Jupiter and Rahu in the 8th house provides protection against loss of cash and jewellery, whatever the cause.

Investments made in the name of the spouse give expected returns. Stomach disorders and overweight of body are adverse gifts of this combination, but gases do not affect the heart region or the respiratory system. Sharp sense of ego is another impact of Rahu where spouse is concerned, but thereby Rahu doesn't disturb the married life to the extent of break-off between husband and wife. No doubt, families on either side do try to interfere in the matter, but if there are no differences between the couple over management of money, the families on both sides would not be able to make any visible adverse impact on the relationship of the two.

In matters of cash and stock management by the employees, it is advisable to keep strict vigil, and during election campaign too. Trustworthy persons should be put on supervision over the workers.

If there is even an iota of family history of piles on the either side, preventive measures are necessary on part of the individual. Further, Rahu would not protect the individual against touch of diabetes or asthma, which is the domain of Jupiter in the 8th house. The individual has to be self-careful about these ailments.

Jupiter and Ketu in the 8th House

Combination of Jupiter and Ketu in the 8th house is on the whole unable to provide any mentionable protection against unfavourable results of Jupiter in the 8th house.

On the other hand, it provides indirect assistance to Jupiter in causing loss of money or jewellery or moveable assets.

And Ketu is more powerful in causing piles or fistula trouble to the individual as compared to Rahu, and therefore greater prevention is needed on part of the individual, specially in the matter of diet and drinks. Ketu encourages the individual towards drinking alcohol or any other intoxicating intakes, which harm the general health sooner than later.

Ketu (with Jupiter in the 8th house) is unconcerned with mischief by employees in the matter of embezzlement and pilferage and also in the matter of cheating and double role by workers in any election campaign.

Ketu's remedy of wearing a genuine, high-quality 'cat's-eye' is always effective. Precious stone remedies for other planets, (Moon to Rahu) are also effective if the stone is genuine and of very high quality purity.

The senior author suggested to a cloth merchant in Khan Market (in New Delhi) to wear a 'cat's eye' because he was suffering losses and was always under debts. With three months, the losses stopped, profits started, and within 18 months, he was able to pay off all debts with interest. He had purchased that precious stone through the author for just ₹900/- in 1955. In 1975, the cloth-merchant's nephew offered him a sum of ₹90,000/- for the same 'cat's eye' because the nephew was running a harmful mahadasa of Ketu. The uncle just refused to part with the stone!

JUPITER IN THE 9TH HOUSE

This is one of the most favourable positions of Jupiter for the individual and in a limited sense for brothers and sisters of self and spouse. Good luck is often operative in moments of difficulty or trouble from taxation authorities, or from banking institutions, or from insurance companies.

If the individual is given to faith in God Almighty in any form or shape and is given to regular prayers, favourable results are often granted by the God Almighty, whatever the religion, faith or cult of the individual.

These individuals should never change their faith or religion, whatever the temptation and pressure, otherwise the good results of prayers would be lost, or at least become less effective.

The individual gains good name and praise for association with any non-government public service formation, as also with any religious and charitable institutions or with free-medical-aid-providing organisations so long as the individual stays real active in public service, honest to the purpose, and also to the funds of the organisation.

If Jupiter gets associated with any hard planet like Mars, Saturn, or Rahu in the 9th house, the individual might adopt dishonest ways and means in management of the religious or social service institution. If any of these hard planets cast their full *drishti* on Jupiter in the 9th house, the individual stays honest, but others working in or for the institution might indulge in any kind of dishonesty, and bring blame to the individual.

The individual stays honest and straightforward in matters of inheritance of ancestral assets and property vis-à-vis other claimants or heirs. However, if Mars or Saturn is in conjunction within 10 degrees with Jupiter, the individual has to suffer a setback in share of assets and property in favour of other claimants and heirs. In litigation or arbitration connected with this matter, it is the individual who suffers ultimately giving up some portion of the individual's due and legal share.

The individual is often of religious nature and does offer prayers or maintains meditation more or less regularly. Such as these individuals are rarely found to be atheist. If Jupiter is in a Rasi owned by Moon or Mercury or in Pisces, the individual is generally secretive about her or his mode, nature and text of prayers as also about the *'guru-mantra'* which she or he recites.

These individuals make balanced, fair-minded, and impartial judge, magistrate, arbitrator, valuer or assessor, so long as Jupiter is not under influence of any hard planet like Mars, Saturn or Rahu. If the individual is a qualified accountant or a taxation officer or subordinate in any taxation outfit, she or he always tries to stay above-board where integrity is concerned.

These individuals are often efficient in arguing or pleading a case or cause, when functioning as a lawyer, advocate, or solicitor. They are very public spirited at framing or drafting any law or rules and regulations.

But remember, though Jupiter gives such favourable results

in the 9th house, it surrenders its capability for good results to the influence of any hard planet. Further Jupiter allows that hard planet to have an upper hand in the 9th house, irrespective of what Rasi is in the 9th house.

Jupiter and Sun, Moon, Mars or Mercury in the 9th House

Respective chapters on Sun, Moon, Mars, and Mercury under the relevant sub-headings for 9th house may please be referred to.

Jupiter and Venus in the 9th House

Combination of Jupiter and Venus in the 9th house is always advantageous to the individual in matters related to inheritance, succession, victory at elections, in matters pertaining to religion, charity, public service, and also in relations with brothers and sisters of self and spouse, as also with uncles and aunts.

The individual is extra close and affectionate to these categories of relations, and if the response from the other side is positive, the relationship could acquire romantic affiliation too. But extra caution has to be observed before giving any such prediction as it might hurt delicate or sensitive feelings.

These two soft stars together make an individual an efficient doctor (moreso on the medicine side), advocate, lawyer, judge, jurist, parliamentarian, senator, legislator, actor, actress, musician, dancer, and perfume-seller.

And these persons are often liberal, charitable, helpful to others, irrespective of the fact whether they get paid for their services or not.

These individuals make it a point not to exploit or cheat their sisters, or progeny thereof. Instead they do their best to prove helpful to them. If the sister gets involved in matrimonial litigation, she gets help from these individuals. Sister too proves helpful and of physical assistance to the individual in an event of illness of himself or his wife or in the event of any death in the family.

[In the context of Hindu culture, such individuals may

generally be inclined towards female power (worshipping Hindu Goddess, say, *Saraswati, Parvati, Laxmi, Durga, Chandi, Bhawani, Indrani,* even *Yakshini* and *Pishachini,* in any form or shape, and they considering the Goddess as the most kind-hearted deity)].

Jupiter and Saturn in the 9th House

The individuals having Jupiter and Saturn combination in the 9th house are at two extremes, very serviceful physically, simultaneously serving hidden personal greed, whatever their profession, business or calling.

They prove successful as election agents, representatives at any meeting or conference or seminar, but their performance is below mark if they are at such meetings, conferences or seminars as a master, that is representing themselves.

These individuals often believe and have faith in lower-level of deities and in helping or harming others by black-magic performed by self or by professionals. They have neither hitch nor hesitation in indulging in good deeds as well as bad deeds; they can be both faithful friends and die-hard enemies. It is always better to behave and deal with these individuals with care and caution, even if they are blood relations. They believe in rough handling matters relating to inheritance and succession. If they go into adoption into another family, they try to have a footing in both the families, original and the adopting family.

They have no reservation in use of unfair and foul means for winning any election; they do not mind spoiling anyone's career, business, or profession by writing anonymous letters and complaints.

They are affectionate and helpful towards brothers and sisters of self and spouse, only so long as their personal interests do not come into clash with those of brothers and/or sisters. To the outsiders and the public they try to project their image as accommodating and helping their brothers and sisters.

But if situation arises, they do not mind indulging in violent attitude towards the situation and the person concerned.

Jupiter and Rahu in the 9th House

The combination of Jupiter and Rahu in the 9th house has the same attributes as those of Jupiter and Saturn in the 9th house, but in a reduced degree, more like a shadow or outer exposure instead of real thing.

Even if these individuals have romantic attitude towards near relations, they keep their feelings concealed in heart, and do not get exposed in reality and practice.

Their faith in God Almighty is often shaky depending upon helpful and harmful events and developments in their life, and they change their faith from one God or Goddess to another one depending upon events and developments in life. They go even to the extent of atheism. They do have trust in black magic, and as they themselves are unable to perform it, they take assistance from professionals. They try to harm others only to the extent of serving their self-interests, and never go to the extent of endangering anyone's life as such. That is the remarkable difference between Jupiter with Rahu in 9th house and Jupiter with Saturn in 9th house.

They do not mind use of unfair means in any election or securing any contract or very profitable business etc. However they use the unfair means to a limited extent and with effort to keep such unfairness a guarded secret.

Jupiter and Ketu in the 9th House

The combination of Jupiter and Ketu in the 9th house leads individuals to good deeds, provided there is no clash of personal interest.

They talk a lot, bragging and boasting or burdening others with sense of obligation, whether these individuals had done or not done anything real to help the other person. They are good at making false and hollow promises and assurances; they are best suited as assistants to or representatives of politicians in power and to high bureaucrats or as envoys and ambassadors.

They often try to project their own image as better they can. They do not hesitate in usurping credit due to others for any gentlemanly deed, writing, any work as an author or poet, any public service rendered by others. They may entertain indecent ideas in their mind but do not expose them under fear of earning a bad name.

As far as possible, these individuals create hurdles in adoption of children by childless couple or person, they put hurdles in cases of love marriage, but try to over-project matters relating to an arranged marriage.

They change their loyalty to any person or party or group, even to any state or nation as easily and quickly as they change their shirt.

JUPITER IN THE 10TH HOUSE

Most of the astrologers attach considerable importance to this position of Jupiter. But experience shows that this position is helpful to all those in the field of law, accounts, economics, taxation, banking, insurance, arbitration, business, trading and advising the business people.

It is helpful where the question of politics, elections to parliament, senate, legislative houses and to similar other houses is concerned. Jupiter helps an individual in achieving success as an envoy or ambassador, or junior official in embassies and consular offices.

<u>Jupiter needs the overriding help of Sun, Mars, Rahu or Moon in that order of precedence</u>. One going to a court of law or any legal forum would find many of the judges and advocates wearing yellow-sapphire rings, which is the prescribed stone for Jupiter. Check the Birth-chart with Navamsha-chart of any judge of the higher courts or top level lawyers, and advocates, or chartered accountants or costs & works accountants, and you should find that they have Jupiter is in the 4th, 5th, 9th or 10th house.

One peculiarity is that often these individuals want their progeny to follow in their profession or that of the mother, as is the case with the children of political leaders, not only in India but (to a less extent) in some other democracies too.

Because Jupiter has direct *drishti* on the 4th house, these individuals are often fond of owning properties, and presentable means of transport. If they actually indulge in charity, it is more for a show, a name and for fame, rather than towards any genuine urge to serve the masses.

The nature, habits, and general outlook of these individuals go in line with the mother and the maternal side of the family, even if they follow the profession or career in line with that of the father or a grandfather.

Some of these individuals make successful jewellers, goldsmiths, bullion-merchants, money-lenders (given to all fair, unfair and foul methods of mortgage and recovery). They have no hesitation in interfering in the affairs of others, even uninvited.

If elected to parliament, senate, house of commons, legislative house, they make valuable contribution to the proceedings as well as to law-making by that legislative body.

If they do not become a judge, lawyer or advocate, they make efficient staff of court. Otherwise they function as an assistant, clerk, *munshi,* or agent to advocates and lawyers, and also function as chartered accountants or costs & works accountants.

Jupiter and Sun, Moon, Mars or Mercury in the 10th House

Respective chapters on Sun, Moon, Mars, and Mercury under the relevant sub-headings for 10th house may please be referred to.

Jupiter and Venus in the 10th House

The combination of Jupiter and Venus in the 10th house is a rather mischievous one.

Though Jupiter and Venus are enemies to each other, they often co-operate in the 10th house. Jupiter would be able to give any or most of the results mentioned in the preceding paragraphs. But in the same breath Jupiter would yield ground to Venus to allow its own results too, like Venus gives the individual as romantic nature, behaviour and action, no doubt to a restricted extent. She or he makes efforts to attract attention of the opposite sex, and depending on response thereto, she or he then proceeds towards making advances, and then to commencement of a love affair.

These individuals have no hesitation in offering gifts in cash or kind for achieving their aim and ambition, whether it is service matter, business, profession or self-employment, or even love affair.

They make successful importers and exporters. Having business connections with foreigners, they indulge in '*hawala*' payments or unauthorised sale of foreign exchange earned in routine course of their work. They make good arbitrators. Females having this combination make successful and impressive envoys, ambassadors, lower-rank consular staff in embassies and high commissions, officers in World Bank, in Commonwealth Secretariat, in International Monetary Fund, United Nations and its other allied organisations.

Jupiter and Saturn in the 10th House

It often needs a lot of experience to predict about this combination of Jupiter and Saturn in the 10th house, because it can give extremely good results, and extremely bad results.

It is the speciality of Saturn, and Saturn alone (sometimes Mars too, and Rahu marginally), that it sometimes gives good results *and* bad results, *both at the same time.* As already mentioned earlier, in spite of Jupiter being the *guru of deities* (the universe), and consequently of the planets too, Jupiter nevertheless has less capacity to overrule or override the influence of the more powerful Saturn, whatever Rasi they may occupy jointly.

With the support of Saturn, Jupiter tries to attain and achieve the aims and ambitions for the individual by fair, unfair and foul means. Methods are immaterial, be it profession, job, promotion or permanency in job, business, industrial venture, placement services, self-employment or capturing and winning clients and customers for practice in law, taxation or accounts. It can be obtaining/ establishing dealership in petrol-filling station, kerosene/oil depot, agency in lubricants, dealership in bicycles and auto-vehicles, middleman in sale and purchase of sailing ships, and airplanes.

These individuals are often successful in working as liaison agents in corridors of power, as election agents, as an agent gathering proxy votes at general body meetings of commercial and industrial concerns, as helpers in use of unfair means in educational examinations of students. They are very useful as slogan shouters, as mob gathering agents for political rallies, as disturbing factors at meetings and rallies of opposite political parties or trade unions or farmers' formations.

These individuals can earn money and spend money in obtaining their end-product in view.

And on top of these fair and foul activities, they somehow manage to keep outside the dragnet of law and order or the trap laid by politicians in power. If they get caught, they often try (and sometimes are successful) to escape from the dragnet or the trap, even from law and order agencies.

Because of Jupiter's company, Saturn normally keeps off any kind of extreme violent activity, though they have no restraint in planning and activating violence by others, followers or hired-elements.

One important point is that these individuals are often afraid of their father, if not always, at least upto the age of attaining adulthood, but where management of money and finances are concerned, generally father and son will be in agreement. These individuals often secretly get money from their mother or any motherly woman or from first-uncles or aunt on either side, specially in childhood and in teens and even till their twenties.

Jupiter and Rahu in the 10th House

Alas, the combination of Jupiter and Rahu in the 10th house doesn't grant to the individual all good and bad qualities and activities that have been attributed to the Saturn and Jupiter combine in this house, and as detailed above paragraphs.

Rahu generally hampers the effectivity of Jupiter, and doesn't miss an opportunity to bring bad name, damage to the prestige, temporary failure of plans and schemes of the individual in any and almost all activities for earnings and income. If the individual is in judicial service or employed in a taxation outfit or holding a post of accountant in government or semi-government establishment, or in banking or insurance service, chances are that at least an enquiry would get conducted about the work and official conduct of the individual.

And if in the meantime, the individual comes under an unfavourable antardasa, with unfavourable transit of Jupiter, Saturn or Rahu or of retrograde Mars, the results of the enquiry would lead to further trouble including minor or major punishment or even legal prosecution.

Some students of astrology would be surprised to know that going by experience of several generations, the authors can say that Rahu is capable of <u>greater mischief</u> when with Jupiter in the 10th house as compared to even powerful Saturn and great Jupiter in 10th.

In the case of persons employed on flight services of aircrafts including pilots, this combination creates chances of accident, or chances of blame for any kind of mishap, including hijacking, or any other accident. However it is not so in the case of crew of a sailing ship, steamer or mechanised boat etc.

In case of relationship with father, Rahu is able sometimes in creating a gulf between father and son, and if nothing else, there is comparatively less communication directly between father and son when the son is between 18 and 36 years of age. It is also likely that sometimes the individual has to stand up on own for matters relating to education and marriage as also settlement in life, whatever the causes thereof.

Jupiter and Ketu in the 10th House

As in the 9th house, so in 10th house too, Jupiter and Ketu combination is more or less tilted in support of Jupiter.

Even if Ketu creates any controversy or conflict at the place of work of the individual, it is either short-lived and gets solved automatically, or any damage or harm or hurt created by Ketu is neither serious nor alarming. Ketu doesn't give any major differences with father either. Ketu is such an innocent star that doesn't deprive the individual of parental care (necessary for education and correct upbringing from childhood to adulthood). In brief, Ketu can be taken as non-interfering star in conjunction with Jupiter in the 10th house.

JUPITER IN THE 11TH HOUSE

Jupiter often prevails upon the individual to have only fair income, whether earned or unearned. It helps an individual in passing, no doubt with hard and continuous work, the chartered accountancy or similarly the costs and works accountancy, or likewise the company secretary's exam. It also helps entry into judicial service, but not directly at the higher level, and it very rarely helps an individual's elevation to the bench from the bar. It gives routine promotions.

In the professions of chartered accountant or cost & works accountant, it gives higher income but only by fair means, cutting no slice from the gratification money to be paid to the taxation or court officer.

One big favour that Jupiter grants from the 11th house is one or more male child(ren), and when grown up, good education to the progeny, provided the progeny's own stars are very helpful for the purpose. If other hard stars do not interfere with the 5th house, the progeny would normally learn and develop good qualities.

Jupiter in 11th house helps solving problems related to income-tax, sales-tax, excise-duty, and if Moon or Venus should be with it in the 11th house within 12 degrees, Jupiter helps solving cases in customs too. However, note that Jupiter generally helps in solving cases pertaining to *avoidance* of tax (staying legal but manipulating to pay less tax), and *not evasion* of taxes (going illegal by not paying the tax at-all). Further, Jupiter in 11th house doesn't help in matters of giving or receiving illegal gratification in cash, or jewellery, or in kind, unless Mars, Saturn or Rahu and sometimes Ketu (in place of Rahu) is with Jupiter in the 11th house.

Jupiter, to a very limited extent helps in recovery from minor illness of a temporary nature.

Jupiter and Sun, Moon, Mars or Mercury in the 11th House

Earlier chapters on Sun, Moon, Mars, and Mercury under the relevant sub-headings for 11th house may please be referred to.

Jupiter and Venus in the 11th House

Combination of these two soft planets, Jupiter and Venus, in the house of income with direct *drishti* on the 5th house helps in giving to the individual's children much better standard of living than what the individual had in his own childhood.

This combination also help in gaining the individual's child, (depending on the child's own stars), admission in a medical institution, in fashion designing school, in learning a beautician's work, in learning one of the fine arts like painting, music, dance, architecture, interior decoration, sculpture or landscape designing. The individual himself or herself might also learn any of these branches of knowledge. The individual might become a good teacher of any of these branches of knowledge mentioned here.

This combination helps the individual in solving problems with the customs department, and quite often the individual proves an expert chartered accountant or a lawyer or a successful agent in matrimonial matters, or as a customs clearing agent, importer or exporter, or an accountant, or advocate for importer or exporter.

On the wrong side, these individuals often help kidnappers/ procurers/ agents for procuring girls for functioning as call girls/ prostitutes, or helping rapists and other criminals who commit crimes against women. The help is all-encompassing, including influencing the police machinery as well as help in fighting legal cases in courts.

In case the individuals are in medical or nursing practice or even functioning as a midwife, these individuals indulge in conducting illegal abortions and medical termination of pregnancy at even an advanced stage by surgery, whether they have training and experience in surgery or not. Sometimes these individuals try their medical or nursing expertise or half-baked knowledge on own progeny, naturally with less success and utter failure.

Jupiter and Saturn in the 11th House

Saturn is concerned with generating income when it is in the 11th house, and when in combination with Jupiter in the 11th house, Saturn doesn't give up its natural effect of generating income by fair and unfair means.

Saturn has no consideration for fair or foul, its aim and ambition is income, arrival of money. On the better side, Saturn (with Jupiter in 11th house) gives the individual capacity, initiative, and capability for establishing and successfully running an industrial venture. Saturn grants capacity and capability to start and run a manufacturing unit, assembly-unit, processing from one stage to another, dealership in fuel, lubricants, machinery oil.

Saturn is directly concerned with dealership in machines and spare-parts, in kerosene oil, running placement service, running manpower (labour) supply outfit, providing guidance and protection to criminals. Saturn (even with Jupiter in the 11th house of income) demands and sometimes successfully receives substantial ransom in cash or kind for kidnapping conducted by the individual or through the individual.

Manufacture of arms and ammunition, black marketing of illegal arms and ammunition on small scale to individuals and groups of people and on large scale to terrorists outfits, even to nations and countries is also the domain of Saturn in the 11th house.

A serious point for consideration is that on account of Jupiter's presence in the 11th house with Saturn (within 15 degrees), these individuals manage often to go scot-free from all these nefarious and illegal activities because they are generally successful in getting connivance and making inroads in police and armed forces.

However, Saturn & Jupiter together protect an individual's investments, deposits and unsecured loans given, and from any major loss by theft, cheating, embezzlement, pilferage, etc. If Saturn gets the support of Mars from 3rd, 6th or 10th house, Saturn is capable of getting such dues recovered as have been considered 'bad debts'.

Jupiter and Rahu in the 11th House

Rahu's combination with Jupiter in the 11th house, unlike Saturn and Jupiter's combination there, doesn't bother itself with too much responsibility.

No doubt, Rahu with Jupiter there opens the floodgates for arrival and departure of money by unfair, foul, illegal means. Rahu instigates the individual to collect large funds under pretext of politics, labour leadership, fighting an election, fighting a public cause, representing the public before higher authorities, and to usurp a good portion of the money thus collected.

A *second* function that Rahu doesn't normally miss to perform is to give loss of one or more pregnancies to the spouse.

The *third* function that Rahu tries to perform, and sometimes with remarkable success, is disturbance in studies of the individual or progeny thereof, provided the progeny's own stars have scope for such disturbance in their educational progress, as Rahu wants to create.

One good that Rahu (with the help of Jupiter) in the 11th house bestows on the individual is quick recovery from short duration illnesses or diseases.

Further, with the help of Jupiter, Rahu protects an individual from loss of investments or deposits, and sometimes from bigger losses, like through theft, robbery etc.

Jupiter and Ketu in the 11th House

Normally, Ketu functions innocently when with Jupiter in the 11th house.

It helps in recovery of royalty money dues from publishers and booksellers, dues from litigants, dues from school or college or university for services rendered including examiner-ship, also dues from patients who received medical treatment (with no surgery of any kind) or fees for tests, etc.

Very rarely, perhaps only once or at the most twice and that too if other stars are also in the arena, Ketu could lead to loss of pregnancy. Ketu, with Jupiter in the 11th house, helps the children get a good grasp and good retention (memory) of what has been taught; though an offshoot effect could be is that children (at school level) avoid doing homework but may copy from the work of fellow-students.

One bad impact on children is that some children get into the habit of stealing books and exercise books of others, not from any monetary angle, but to cover missed lessons and neglected studies.

JUPITER IN THE 12TH HOUSE

Jupiter in the 12th house can lead to loss of money or of moveable assets by lapse on part of self, by carelessness, by misconduct of people around, by cheating, by embezzlement, by pilferage of goods.

Jupiter leads to loss by penalty, fine, or punishment, or by imposition of penal interest by action taken by any legal forum or taxation authorities. Jupiter might require the individual to pay compensation or ransom money in case of kidnapping of a near and dear one.

It is Jupiter, which requires the individual to pay alimony in matrimonial matters, and causes loss of money by losing a civil or matrimonial litigation (this being an important point).

Other minor causes of loss of money or goods by Jupiter in the 12th house is by loss of books and notes in school and college, by pocket being picked, or bag or baggage or luggage being snatched, or stolen, by loss in shares and stocks.

Still other means of loss can be by losing gold/ silver items, bullion, jewellery, ornaments, other household assets by theft, robbery, dacoity, or by mischief of the partner, or by losing finance in the individual's capacity of a sleeping partner.

There is no limit to describing sources of loss that can be caused by Jupiter in the 12th house. It can be by losing finance in films and fine arts, or by non-recovery of dues in the shape of cash or wages, royalty, compensation, or by rejection of claim on insurance company, by theft from a safe deposit vault.

There can be loss in business or industrial venture or manufacturing unit, or by forfeiture of pension or gratuity or provident fund or any kind of compensation or wages for work. There are many other minor means of loss of money or assets, but herein given are the main sources.

Jupiter in 12th house adversely affects the memory of an individual at educational stage. It can cause trouble with kidney, liver, respiratory system, sugar content in blood system, ovaries in a female.

Another source of unfavourable influence of Jupiter in 12th house is that the boss, superior authority or the employer indulges in taking credit in the name and under the signatures of the individual, without acknowledgement or any kind of compensation, just like cheating or a kind of piracy. Or it can be a trick of the employer to force the individual to continue in adverse service conditions of the employer, or even in harmful circumstances.

Further, it adversely affects the educational progress of the progeny, if the children's own stars are unfavourable in this regard.

In rare cases does Jupiter delays delivery of a child from the mother's womb or creates complications that might sometimes lead to a caesarean section. If Jupiter happens to be lord of the 5th house, it disturbs the normal weight of the child in the mother's womb, and necessitates extra 'post-delivery' care for the newly born.

Jupiter and Sun, Moon, Mars or Mercury in the 12th House

Earlier chapters on Sun, Moon, Mars, and Mercury under the relevant sub-headings for 12th house may please be referred to.

Jupiter and Venus in the 12th House

When it is the combination of Venus and Jupiter in the 12th house, it invariably helps Jupiter in giving full results of Jupiter's presence in the 12th house as have been mentioned in the preceding paragraphs.

However, Venus creates some mischief too, specially with relation to opposite sex, and if either of them is lord of the 1st or the 7th house, lapses might reach a law court or legal forum, or prior to it some police set-up!

If Saturn is also associated with these two soft stars in the 12th house, things might go to the extent of trade in humans, kidnapping of girls for immoral activity including smuggling, theft, pick-pocketing, prostitution, spying under cover of a romance-and –love-affair. These three stars might use girls, and / or wine and / or money for winning legislators from one side to another side.

In case, Mars too gets associated with these three stars either by combination, or by direct *drishti,* or by ownership of the 12th house, the individual gets involved or associated with smuggling and black-market sales of arms and ammunition or large-size weapons or ordnance stores. Wine and women become a fondness with some of these individuals, while some others supply both or either of the two for personal gains or deriving any or every kind of other benefits, from people in power or authority.

The favours sought by the individual indulging in the activity detailed in the immediately preceding paragraph can be promotion in job, securing an agency kind of work, getting a trade-contract concluded, effecting big sales like that of ships or aircrafts. It can also be a big deal in arms, ammunition, or ordnance supplies.

When Rahu is also present in the 12th house with Jupiter and Venus there, chances of a big penalty or simple imprisonment get developed for the individual. When Saturn or Mars or Uranus gets associated with these two soft stars in combination in the 12th house, the ultimate result for the individual can be confiscation of moveable or immovable assets or imprisonment with hard labour.

Some of these individuals do not hesitate in taking undue advantage or romantic liberty with their own subordinates, employees, students, workers at any level, disciples in fine arts (like acting, dance, music, painting, fashion designing), etc.

Jupiter and Saturn in the 12th House

Jupiter and Saturn together in the 12th house often bring disaster to the individual by way of complete financial ruin, penalties, and punishment in terms of fine of cash amount.

With punishment of imprisonment, if Mars also gets somehow associated with Jupiter and Saturn, it could mean loss of limb or life by God-given accident, or man-made mischief, or by judicial verdict. These two stars, Jupiter and Saturn, affect, by illness or accident, the left lung, left ribs, left ear, left side of the skull, left cheek, left jaw, left nostril, and left eye, all the moreso if Mars or Sun too is associated with this combination of Jupiter and Saturn.

Sometimes, these individuals suffer loss of money by paying ransom, protection money to the goons / *goondas* / police, by paying periodical help to terrorists, paying regular contribution to blackmailing politicians (in power), paying bribes without getting the job done by the bribe-taker. In some cases the near and distant relations of these individuals demand and receive financial help in exorbitant sums by half-truth and fabricated excuses of hardship and illness etc.

The progeny of these individuals also leads them to spend money in amounts beyond-capacity, for the progeny's own misdeeds or for partly justifiable demands, which are not directly connected or concerned with their education or with any extra-curricular activity, nor for games and sports or any kind of approvable hobby. However the children get the money, and render no actual accounts of spending it.

These two stars in the 12th house lead to wasteful but unavoidable expenditure on appeasement of labour, on other employees, on domestic help, on subordinates and menial staff. Further, many a time considerable money gets spent on fighting claims and demand of the labour or other organised staff in courts of law, or labour tribunal or other lower authorities or in arbitration awards etc.

Loss of money or of assets by theft, robbery, cheating, by betting at horse races, by other kind of betting or by gambling can be caused by Jupiter and Saturn combine in the 12th house.

Loss can also be on account of advocates, lawyers, chartered accountants, or other consultants, or on appeasement of middlemen, intermediaries in any kind of disputes and litigation.

Loss of money accompanied sometimes by loss of prestige can be caused by speculation in shares and stocks, by payment of advances for anticipated inventory or by act of under-invoicing / over-invoicing not going the expected way.

Furthermore, sometimes any of the above mentioned kind of losses may lead to sale of moveable or immovable assets or they might be sold by arbitration or by a court judgement.

In construction work, cheating, pilferage and theft at site or theft of raw material in transit, can cause substantial loss, or it can be on account of correcting defects or re-doing wrongly done construction, damage to the building or factory shed because of use of inferior material or malfunctioning of craftsmen.

Another source of loss can be from making changes in the design of the construction, making additions and alterations in any premises to suit the requirements of a prospective customer / client / tenant, and then at the 11th hour the changes are discarded / not-approved, and agreed terms and conditions are not honoured.

In all these matters of loss or damage or punishment becomes more eminent or imminent during main period of Jupiter, Venus, Saturn, Mars or Rahu with sub period too of one of these stars. The loss can be during transit of Saturn, or Jupiter, or Rahu, or retrograde Mars over the 12th house.

Jupiter and Rahu in the 12th House

Rahu and Jupiter combination in the 12th house indicates mischief, rather of minor nature, in both, financial matters and imposition of minor fines, penalties etc. on the individuals.

In student life, Rahu encourages use of unfair means in exams, harassing fellow students by tolerable mischief or jokes and acts. The combination leads to drop in attendance, taking resort to copying from the homework of fellow students, instead of attending studies at own home.

Loans given do not get recovered on due dates, nor in a lump-sum but in instalments, on irregular basis. Malafide intentions of the borrowers of money hover over repayment of loans given by the individual; at least attempts would made to avoid payment of interest or to lower the rate agreed.

One good point Rahu bestows upon the individual is that of putting up a bigger show at a low cost, as compared to other people. No doubt the individual might claim a higher cost with an eye on pocketing a part of the cost, but the good performance is often achieved at lower cost tan claimed.

Very strict vigilance and guidance is needed when the progeny of these individuals is at school level, otherwise the progeny's performance would not secure them admission in prestigious or desired college or institutions. Books are generally lost or torn or given away to others with lame excuse at home that they are lost. In case private tutors are engaged for these students, the tutors have to be rigid and strict, otherwise no 'better result' would be forthcoming.

The individual should watch health of the wife during pregnancy. If she is not inclined for its continuance, it is better to terminate it medically at the earliest possible stage. The more correct thing would be that these individuals should plan the pregnancy in consultation with wife, and when she doesn't agree with the husband's planning, the pregnancy must be avoided, instead of its medical termination.

These individuals function as expert cover agents in smuggling and black-market activity, also as custodian of contraband goods, but unless Saturn or Mars are associated with this combination, these individuals avoid direct indulgence in illegal activity of this type.

However they do not hesitate to function as middleman in transaction of bribes and illegal gratification in the shape of jewellery, assets, any other kind of favour or obligations to the persons in power or authority.

It may be noted that in cases of family history of piles, fistula or any allied trouble on either side of family, even upto grandparent's level, the individual is also likely to suffer from any of these diseases.

Jupiter and Ketu in the 12th House

This combination of Jupiter and Ketu in the 12th house would give more or less the same results as have been mentioned above with regard to Rahu and Jupiter combination in the 12th house.

The only major difference is that Ketu would induce an individual to indulge in piracy of literary work in journalism and book writing or story of a TV serial or of a full-length film.

Ketu is more competent in giving piles or fistula or allied trouble, whether the individual has a family history of this kind of complaints of health or not.

This combination can cause loss by theft, robbery, snatching, embezzlement, pilferage etc. And in contrast, the individual too might gain by indulging in similar type of activity or source, which Rahu's combination with Jupiter in the 12th house would normally not give to the individual, because of a sense of respect and prestige for self.

However, note that Ketu with Jupiter in the 12th house would have the same impact on students as that by Rahu and Jupiter combination in the 12th house. No doubt one major difference can be: Ketu and Jupiter combination would encourage an individual to indulge in minor theft, pilferage, blackmail, taking advantage by giving threats to physically weaker students, with all kind of mischievous intents and acts (as are now commonly shown by magazines of the developed countries of the West).

If Saturn, Mars, or Sun (in that order) be associated with this combination, the same individual will very likely indulge in illegal acts and activities as had been experimented during school days.

VENUS IN THE 12 HOUSES

VENUS IN GENERAL

Venus rules all nice, tender, soft, smooth, sweet, beautiful things in human life. It is also the lord of sexual relationship between males and females, though it has to be remembered that Venus has nothing to do with sodomy, or lesbian, or homosexuality tendencies. Very often students in astrology try to search this type of relationship under the influence of Venus. For example tenderness, smoothness, softness of human skin is the domain of Venus. But ailments and medical complaints related to skin are under Mars and Sun. Similarly friendship with opposite sex (may be of platonic type) is under control of Venus, but break-off of the friendship is caused by other stars. Sexuality in men and their ability to satisfy the female partner in bed is ruled by Venus, but partial or complete lack of capacity to satisfy a female depends collectively on Venus, Mars and Moon.

Individuals with favourable placement of Venus in Birthchart or Navamsha-chart achieve efficiency in fine arts such as music, acting, dance, paintings (generally of murals and portraits of persons). Venus gives liking for top class perfumery, jewellery (real or imitation), ornaments, high quality apparel according to or even beyond one's financial capacity.

Then comes the question of procreation. This is not the domain of Venus alone. It is the domain of Venus and Mars collectively, because Venus is lord of the semen in men (and that is why our ancients gave a common name to both Venus and semen as "SUKRA" in Sanskrit, Hindi, and other languages flowing from Sanskrit). Mars is the master of menstrual (blood) system in the females. While predicting about progeny, begetting children, as also sex of the child in the womb, a deep study of both Mars and Venus is needed. Venus would indicate if the semen of the man is fully competent to produce children or not. If it is semi-strong, conception would take place, but the pregnancy would not reach the stage of full para and delivery of a full-grown baby. Experience shows that there have been cases of 3 to 5 miscarriages of conceptions to certain females, and normally medical experts searched the problem mainly in the female's system, but when astrology suggested, the semen of the male was tested and found defective and weak in procreation.

Otherwise normally miscarriage or abortion is influenced by Mars, Saturn, Rahu and to a limited degree under influence of Sun and Ketu. There are several medical grounds and causes to determine the origin of the miscarriage or abortion, and astrology is guided in this respect by the medical science also. The ancient *acharyas* have dealt with, in great detail, all questions relating to:

(a) childlessness,

(b) getting only female issues,

(c) getting only male issues,

(d) loss of first pregnancy or repeated loss of pregnancy,

(e) still birth i.e. a dead baby being delivered after full para,

(f) death of a child within one year of birth.

And similar many other matters related to pregnancy and childbirth. Here only a mention has been made because all these subjects relate to VENUS in one way or the other, no doubt in association with, or under influence of other stars. However, **it should always be borne in mind** that all or any of these subjects should not be dealt with on the basis of birth stars of one-person only (i.e. of the husband or the wife alone). Very often it happens that people coming for consultation show Birth-chart and other details of horoscope of one person (husband or wife) only. Sometimes they even avoid showing the Birth-chart of the other partner and resisting it in such cases as this; it is better then to refuse to give any consultation or predictions.

Though two more questions are not directly relevant here, it is better to mention them just for general knowledge. The first is whether the child in the mother's womb is a male or a female. The medical science has no doubt now devised tests to declare the sex of the embryo in the womb, but astrologers should as far as possible avoid answering this question. In spite of very detailed and deep study of the birth stars of both husband and wife, high percentage of accuracy is never found in this type of predictions. Several instances have come to notice where even medical tests have failed badly to predict the sex of the embryo in the womb.

The second question relates to who of the two (husband and wife) would die first. Even if the astrologer is sure about the accuracy of the prediction, positively avoid it. It might give origin to rage and hatred towards the astrologer, as if the astrologer is the cause of earlier death of one of the two (husband or wife), besides the fear which such a thought implants in the mind of both.

Then another important question often posed to the astrologer is about the fidelity of the spouse. Even if the astrologer is sure in astrological study about the correct answer to this question, the answer might lead to suspicion in the mind of one partner in marriage/ love. It might develop into big bitterness between the husband and wife (or lovers), and sometimes leads to break off of the marriage/ love affair itself. Ancients have said that sometimes the dilemma before the astrologer is very great because TRUTH can be damaging or destructive.

Yet another question which confronts the astrologers is about the real father of the child when the woman has slept with more than one person during those 24 hours, or near about the period of conception. Sometimes the woman herself puts this question to the astrologer, and sometimes the husband or paramour of the lady confronts the astrologer with this question. It is better and safe to avoid direct or even indirect answer to this type of question. The answer even if correct, might damage or destroy the marriage or the life of the embryo in the womb.

All these general points have been mentioned here, because a majority of the astrologers, even experienced and learned ones, relate them to VENUS. While with some of these questions Venus has no connection or concern and to some other questions Venus has a minor role to play as compared to the influence of other stars.

VENUS IN THE 1ST HOUSE

Venus in the 1st house makes an individual sophisticated, given to neatness and cleanliness, a system and order to residence as well as to the personality of self. Venus in the 1st house gives love for fashionable loving, liking decoration of body and surroundings, fond of good clothes/ outer show of food (even if the food may be poor in quality). Other points related to Venus in the 1st house are romantic nature, free in talks, given to smiles and laughs (both loud and slow), pleasant personality (charming, handsome, beautiful) which might attract the attention of the opposite sex.

Venus makes an individual, on the whole generous by nature depending on financial background, liking for picnics and journeys to beautiful places, fond of music/ drama/ stage performances/ acting/ dancing, adopting some habits for sake of attracting attention of others, especially of the opposite sex.

They are given to high perfumery, fresh flowers with sharp fragrance, exhibitive, ornaments and jewellery (real or imitation or costume).

One should always be careful in behaviour towards these type of individuals because they might be bohemian in talks and in inter-personal behaviour. But at the same time, they might feel offended if the other person takes the same type of freedom in talks and behaviour towards them. It is the same case in earlier stages of romance, love-affair and marriage where these individuals are concerned.

One of the favourable points is that these individuals make efficient physicians, painters (including that of murals, portraits of persons), designers of apparel as well as landscape, interior decoration, sculptures and even furnishings and furniture. They gain good knowledge in use of herbals, cosmetics (puffs, powders, lipsticks included), and therefore they make very good fashion designers and beauticians.

As a bad influence of Venus in the 1st house, an individual might lead steps towards bad habits and bad company and even immoral activities. This is more often when Venus is in conjunction with Mars, Saturn, Rahu, or Herschel, all the more so if the conjunction is within 12 degrees at the most. Sometimes this type of conjunction with hard stars gives a leaning towards drinks, intoxication and bad habits connected therewith, romantic or casual sexual relationship with more than one person of the opposite sex.

It should also be borne in mind that Venus, when influencing any kind of romantic connection or love affair with any person of the opposite sex; does not normally allow the individual to be much bothered to distinguish between truth and falsehood.

Venus and Sun, Moon, Mars, Mercury or Jupiter in the 1st House

Respective chapters on Sun, Moon, Mars, Mercury and Jupiter under the relevant sub-headings for 1st house may please be referred to.

Venus and Saturn in the 1st House

Combination of Venus and Saturn in the 1st house needs very careful study, because though Venus is soft and Saturn is hard, both are strong stars and both insist upon giving full results of their presence in the 1st house.

The main effect of Venus in the 1st house is already discussed above in the preceding paragraphs. In addition, Saturn would give a touch of obstinacy, evil thoughts leading sometimes to evil actions and activity to self, or a tendency to give protection to persons indulging in immoral or illegal or antisocial activities. These individuals generally do not distinguish between fairness and unfairness or courtesy and harshness in business or any kind of deal or transaction.

This attitude goes to such an extent that they do not hesitate in treating a marriage proposal as a business transaction. The ultimate result is that their behaviour after marriage has a touch of taunt, criticism or torture towards the spouse, particularly in those cases where their all demands were not fulfilled. Because of this combination of Venus and Saturn, these gentlemen want in marriage, both, money and beauty in the wife. The ladies would want financially well-established husband as well as presentable personality of the husband. These individuals prefer to employ female staff or having subordinates of the opposite sex and do not hesitate, circumstances permitting, in making romantic advances towards them, because they do not have much fear of society or consideration of self respect and prestige. Besides, these individuals are fond of innovations and experiments in sexual relationship with the opposite sex.

On the favourable side, these individuals are often successful managers of labour, on production side of an industrial venture, transport, filling stations (petrol pumps), mechanical-outfits, repair workshops. They are very efficient and experienced engineers, technocrats, scientists, ordnance planners, and workers. They may also be agriculturists, owners of garden orchards, growers of fresh flowers and manufacturers of items for export trade, builders of nice looking flats and houses or other premises, employers of females for spying services or carriers of smuggled weapons and other contraband goods.

Some of them prove very efficient and successful surgeons, particularly on surgery of the middle part of the body of both males and females. If they find a case for surgery, which is beyond their expertise they either request another surgeon's cooperation or flatly refuse to perform the surgery. They are straightforward in this behalf.

These individuals make good of female power at election campaigns, in public meetings, conferences, rallies, processions and demonstration, pickets, trade union strikes and slogan shouting gangs.

However one important point is that in spite of all ambitions and aspirations, these individuals settle in life in a job or at the most in a business or self-employment. They hesitate to start an industrial venture or private practice in medical field, unless they are pushed to it by their spouse, or intimate friends.

They very rarely jump into active politics, because these individuals keep throwing pebbles into the water to guess the depth of water. Instead of getting down into the waters of politics, they keep sitting on the bank or coast.

Venus and Rahu in the 1st House

It has to be refreshed in mind that **Venus, Saturn, Rahu, and Ketu** belong to one group (the other group consists of Sun, Moon, Mars and Jupiter, while Mercury is friendly to both groups).

Therefore Saturn or Rahu or Ketu doesn't put hurdles in the normal functioning of Venus in the 1st house. Saturn, Rahu, or Ketu add their special results to those of Venus in the 1st house. For example, Rahu in the 1st house whether alone or in conjunction with Venus would give considerable sense of self-respect, ego based on beauty or personality or education or financial status or position of power.

If in any regular service, Rahu helps in getting promotion at due stage without being superseded.

If in self-employment, Rahu keeps up the prestige and rarely lets down an individual from the pedestal once occupied. In some rare cases, Rahu gives expert knowledge in *mantra-sastra*, in *yantra* science, in *tantrik* theory and practice, in religious scriptures, and sometimes (though rarely) in black magic. However, this type of knowledge of these individuals is not used by them for harming or hurting any individual or group of people, though they do use it for the benefit of members of their own family or for friends and outsiders personally known to them. They do so to satisfy their sense of 'ego'.

If in business, these individuals are on the whole straightforward and outspoken about their product as well as their motives of profitability.

These individuals do not hesitate to help others, and normally they do not expect any return from those obliged persons.

These individuals add to their weight after the marriage or around the age of 36 years whichever is earlier.

Venus and Ketu in the 1st House

Ketu with Venus in the 1st house, unlike Rahu, gives an individual touch of politeness, habits of neatness, cleanliness, system, order, fashion, decoration, presentability etc, which are normally the qualities of Venus.

The individual exhibits qualities of intelligence too; sometimes creativeness like writing and journalism, provided Mercury is in the 1st or the $2^{nd,}$ the 11th house. This combination gives clarity of thought and action, specially if the individual has anything to do with fine arts like, dance, drama, music, painting, photography, landscape designing, acting in or directing/ producing films, serials, episodes etc. It is very rarely that this combination gives any harmful or damaging or hurting results either to the individual or to the spouse.

In modern times, many an astrologer, without much practical experience of applied astrology, propagate the theory that Rahu and Ketu too have *drishti*, which is not at all acceptable by knowledge and experience of several generations. They are both shadow planets, visible only through solar and lunar eclipses. Therefore though Venus would cast direct *drishti* on the 7th house (which rules spouse, confrontation, conflict, quarrel), Ketu doesn't have any *drishti* on any house directly or indirectly whatsoever.

VENUS IN THE 2ND HOUSE

It is virtually normal for Venus to give decoration to residence or office premises, liking for a rich wardrobe whether the individual could afford it or not. It also gives a craze for silk and soft clothes and linen, tendency for use of multi-coloured items of daily use as well as items of rare use or simply for preservation. These individuals often want to have a collection of beautiful ornaments, jewellery, furniture and furnishings, garden around residence with plants giving multi-coloured flowers.

If affordable, the individual would try to have silverware and items of decoration including silver frames for pictures and paintings, even use of silver thread in apparel, extra use of silver in *puja* or prayer room including statues and silver talisman.

However a little snag in what has been said above is that the spouse is not agreeable to likes of the individual for decoration, pomp and show. This position of differences between husband and wife sometimes directly or indirectly affects the mutual love, adjustability and sexual understanding, now and then if it is a cardinal Sign (*char* Rasi) in the 2nd house, and on quite regular basis if a fixed Sign (*sthir* Rasi) is there.

Another conflict that Venus in the 2nd house creates, though rarely, is presence of a third angle in the married life. If Venus is associated with hard stars like Mars, Saturn, or Rahu in the 2nd, 7th or 8th house, the soft star like Venus too might play havoc with the married life, because Venus is ruler of married life as such, including sexual relations between husband and wife. With joint families virtually gone in most developed and developing countries, affording privacy to husband and wife with their own progeny, sex has come to play 80% influence in the secluded life of couples these days.

In all cases of this type the first salvo is fired by the individual, who has Venus in the 2nd house, because Venus is in 8th position from the 7th house, which rules marriage and married life.

Yet another point of differences between wife and husband or lovers is over the question of drinks or habit of intoxication in either of the two, which the other partner in life or love affair doesn't like or approve. Style of dress, upkeep of personality, presentability of face and figure too might receive, in mild tones only, critical remarks/ hints from one spouse to another.

Gains or no gains from the family of the spouse might, though very rarely, become a bone of contention between wife and husband, though this is not a matter to affect the marriage adversely.

There is sometimes general disagreement between the two about giving or receiving gifts from members of the immediate family, wider family and total outsiders, who want some favour in return for the gifts given. There are cases where the wife is more keen than the husband to receive gifts offered or given as means of gratification. These points do not create a big rift between the couple, but a sting remains in the mind of the non-agreeing spouse.

Venus and Sun, Moon, Mars, Mercury or Jupiter in the 2nd House

Respective chapters for Sun and Moon, for Mars, Mercury and Jupiter, under the relevant sub-headings for 2nd house may please be referred to for results of these combinations with Venus in the 2nd house.

Venus and Saturn in the 2nd House

In simple language, Saturn's presence with Venus in the 2nd house adds bitterness, harshness, criticism, and disapproval to all those points that have been detailed above for position of Venus, when alone, in the 2nd house. Further Saturn imports physical violence between the couple.

If by chance, Mars happens to be sitting in the 7th or 8th house in the Birth-chart of either of the couple; the combination would first import a third angle in the married life or love affair. Then it will gradually lead it towards separation or staying apart in the same premises or in different premises, and then towards complete break down or divorce.

Saturn is a very slow moving star and it prevails over its friend Venus and therefore the whole process of separation or formal break down between the wife and husband moves gradually. And if in between, some soft favourable stars intervene by mahadasa or antardasa or favourable position in the Yearly-chart, or Jupiter moves to a favourable transit for about 13 months, the run down of married life would stop temporarily or permanently depending on the stars of the spouse.

This combination would give, slow and steady, rise in savings, investments, and purchase of moveable and immovable assets. This effect would be higher in intensity and speed, if mahadasa or antardasa of Venus or Saturn runs during the prime years of earning by either of the couple. The money element would further rise if Saturn happens to transit over the 1st, 2nd, 3rd, 6th, 8th or 11th house in the Birth-chart of the individual.

One caution is necessary under this combination in the

2nd house: Too many easily breakable decorative items shouldn't be used or stored in the house. This is because Saturn would not hesitate to cause breakage of any or many of them, sometimes unintentionally, sometimes intentionally by the spouse, and it will give rise to further quarrel between the wife and the husband.

Whenever Saturn is in transit over the 1st, 2nd or 7th house of the individual, spouse has to take extra care to avoid a bone injury, especially to a leg or sprain on a foot.

Venus and Rahu in the 2nd House

This is one of the very favourable combinations in the 2nd house, in spite of some half-baked astrologers forming an inferior opinion about Rahu in the 2nd house.

The well-established fact is that Rahu in 2nd house always improves the financial status of an individual. But at the same time this principle also applies that unless Rahu (or for that matter Ketu) be accompanied by a solid star (Sun to Saturn), it is unable to give full results of its position. Thus Rahu with Venus make an individual richer in money, in worldly possession, besides giving all those benefits which have been described in opening paragraphs about Venus in 2nd house. Rahu and Venus together encourages the individual and spouse to lead a comfortable and luxurious life, the only condition being that Mars or Saturn must not be in the 12th house.

Further it is also a fact that Rahu doesn't adversely affect the married life or love affair in a manner in which Saturn in 2nd house does. Venus and Rahu in conjunction stand on equal status, and they are both friendly to each other. The maximum Rahu would do is to give casual bickering or jocular critical remarks, which do not harm the day to day run of married life.

Venus and Ketu in the 2nd House

Ketu, when with Venus in the 2nd house, positively gives financial benefits, but the quantum of the benefits in riches is smaller than those given by Rahu.

Ketu doesn't give any bickering or even minor quarrels in the married life, nor does it interfere with the benefits being given by Venus in the 2nd house. No doubt the individual or the spouse should stay alert to any ailment akin to piles and should make it a rule to reduce the consumption of red chillies to the minimum.

Ketu gives colour and variety to furnishings and furniture in residential or office or shop premises; even the tapestry is of different colours and designs. Ketu stands for variety and designs.

Venus in the 3rd House

With Venus in the 3rd house, it becomes a tendency of the individual to get all comforts, luxuries, and fashionable things without doing any work or much work and without exertion. The individual wants all comforts at the cost and labour of others, and doesn't hesitate to derive benefits from brothers and sisters of self as well as of the spouse. The individual wants health and good treatment for ailments either free of cost or at the cost of others.

The individual is withdrawn to a safe level when actual fighting is on the field, but comes forward to claim credit for the bravery and vigour employed by others. Whether the individual is beautiful, comely, good looking or not, whether has an impressive personality or not, she/ he dresses elegantly to put up a presentable, imposing impression on others, so that others might recognise and accept her/ his claims for work done by others.

If the individual is in a position to assist own brothers or sisters, the individual would not miss the opportunity to help financially or physically or morally, though the tendency of indicating the obligation at the same time or subsequently prevails very well.

If the individual possesses knowledge of medicine (any system), normally her or his treatment of patients would be result-oriented, but the physician or the *Vaidya* or the *Hakim* herself or himself would be lethargic in both, work and updating the knowledge.

These individuals tend to depend, in their advanced years of age, more on the grandchildren and their spouses, instead of on their children. They are quite generous and accommodating towards the grandchildren and their spouses.

Western astrology attaches great importance to Venus in the 3rd house, because according to it, Venus influences the means of livelihood and determines the source of income. Going by Indian system, this position of Venus adversely affects the work-capacity and capability of the individual.

It might lead the individual towards import, export trade and dealings with foreigners, but the scope of losing income is there because of sluggish trend of working. It is always better for these individuals to associate their children with their source of income, if it is possible to do so by education and inclination of the children themselves. Sometimes it might not even be possible, because of the profession, business or self-employment of both the parents or parent and the progeny might be poles apart, with no scope for link and coordination.

However, to this basic trend of lethargy of the individual, there are some exceptions that are given below while discussing conjunction of Venus with other stars in the 3rd house.

Venus and Sun, Moon, Mars, Mercury or Jupiter in the 3rd House

Reference is invited to the relevant chapters on each of these stars in the 3rd house, which contain sub-headings dealing with combination of Venus.

Venus and Saturn in the 3rd House

When Saturn and Venus are in combination in the 3rd house, Saturn though a friend of Venus, often overrides the influence of Venus, and Saturn virtually gives very favourable results in the 3rd house, because the 3rd house is one of the most favoured houses of Saturn.

Saturn over-turns the sluggishness of Venus, when they are together in the 3rd house. The individual normally becomes very hard working, taking best care of personal interests and of the results of effort. The individual gets given to continuous work till the end product is achieved, whether it is a job or service or contract or trade or profession or self-employment.

Saturn would positively influence the source of income of the individual, leading towards regular job or contractorship or working as a builder or coloniser or trading in oil-seeds, oil, oil-products, lubricants, machinery, machine parts, running industrial units or any other attribute within the domain of Saturn. Then the western system of astrology holds ground, because Saturn positively influences, when in the 3rd house, the means of livelihood of the individual.

The individual is capable of proving efficient and competent strategist in police, armed police, in combatant forces, in ordnance and weaponry planning and management, in intelligence outfit.

Spying activity related to commercial and industrial houses, smuggling and anti-smuggling establishments, terrorist activities lure the individual on account of Saturn (with Venus) in the 3rd house.

These individuals with Venus and Saturn in the 3rd prove successful in espionage and intelligence services of one nation against another when free hand is given for use of money, wine, and women. They normally have honesty of purpose, and do not indulge in double-dealing or crossing their loyalty from one nation or employer to another, even under the influence of money, wine, and women which, they too indulge in for trapping others. However they do not function against their belief and faith, and do not bother about being pulled up for insubordination or disobedience.

Because of Saturn in the 3rd house, the individual is generally helpful to brothers and sisters of self and spouse but not very affectionate or attached to them, or to other members of the immediate and wider family including uncles, aunts, and cousins. The individual is often financially and physically serviceful to near and dear ones as well as to others and outsiders, without any depth of emotional attachment.

If the individual is the eldest or pretty elder to brothers

and sisters, on account of Venus in the 3rd house, the individual takes active interest in getting their marriages fixed and helps out in marriage. Though the elders to the individual want to consider financial angles too, owing to Saturn's presence in the 3rd house, the individual doesn't show any involvement in this behalf.

These individuals normally have no hitch or hesitation in undertaking or doing any kind of manual labour, because they do not stand on ego or prestige.

Venus and Rahu in the 3rd House

Rahu with Venus in the 3rd house makes the individual regular and dedicated in work, though sometimes the individual cannot give up the temptation of taking credit or benefit for work done by others. The individual makes a greater show of help and assistance to brethren of self and spouse, though sometimes the actual help or assistance is less solid/ factual/ practical than boasted. It is the same position about bravery of these individuals, because instead of their own valour and action, they try to pirate the credit of others.

But they are always clever and mindful about their own interest, without much consideration for time, place, and occasion, and even by undercutting others. In young and youthful years they tend to change their field of activity and main means of livelihood, but between the age of 28 years and 32 years, they settle down on any one main activity or source of livelihood.

However these individuals are always alert about helping their progeny in matters of career and livelihood, and would go out of way to help even married daughters and sons.

Rahu does not very much interfere with the fineness of Venus bestowed qualities on the individual concerned.

Venus and Ketu in the 3rd House

In this particular combination, Ketu gives more or less the same results as those attributed to Rahu and Venus in the 3rd, the only difference being in degree.

Ketu doesn't deal in harshness, hard attitude, rough behaviour and dubious dealings. And Ketu is not able to do much for settlement in life and livelihood of the progeny of the individual.

These individuals always overestimate their ailment and illness or disease and become very nervous if left alone during any long-term illness.

VENUS IN THE 4TH HOUSE

Venus in the 4th house is capable of giving so many good things in life to the individual that sometimes the person is not left with any desire for more. An affectionate and caring mother and in later life very mutual loving relationship with mother. The individual's mother would be an impressive personality for her beauty and self-bearing. Venus in 4th gives a nice residence with most of the comforts including that of conveyance right from the early age. It also gives an enviable digestive system, and also availability of all kinds of tasty and nourishing food.

At the right age, Venus in the 4th house makes possible friendship with opposite sex with or without physical indulgence. It also gives ornaments and jewellery, and a well provided colourful wardrobe and chances of wide travels within and outside the country. It is possible that the individual sometimes, against the family tradition, indulges in drinks. But Venus in 4th house gives a healthy heart even upto advanced age and popularity among members of wider family, distant relations and friends.

It gives comfortable relationship with father of the spouse, though women must keep a respectable distance from the father-in-law lest it is misunderstood, even without any touch of vice in it. The individual gets love, affection, and gifts from grandparents every now and then.

It has been observed that Venus would give most of the above results even when occupying an unfavourable Rasi, or a Rasi owned by an enemy of Venus.

Venus and Sun, Moon, Mars, Mercury or Jupiter in the 4th House

Please see the relevant chapters earlier on each of these five planets, which contain sub-headings dealing with combination of Venus with each of these five stars in the 4th house.

Venus and Saturn in the 4th House

This combination of Venus and Saturn in the 4th house is like an iron nail at the centre of a gold plate. Saturn would obstruct many of the good results of Venus in the 4th house detailed above.

This combination generally gives a poor digestive system. Bitterness in relationship with one of the natural parents, sometimes loss of a parent before the age of 20 years. The individual upbringing could be by grandparents owing to difficult circumstances of natural parents or death of one of the natural parents at a very tender age of the individual. Minor and major accidents on the road or on train or in water or in air travel. Sometimes pain in ribs and upper abdomen, specially when Saturn is, by transit, in the 4th, 8th, 11th or 12th house, or Saturn has its antardasa under Venus or vice versa.

This combination is capable of giving trouble of gaseous reflux disturbing the normal functioning of the heart, but not totally upsetting it as such. It can give a bit out of proportion appearance to middle part of the body of the individual (moreso in the case of women). If Mars is also associated with this combination, trouble could be there for women at the time of delivery of child. Saturn is concerned with delivery by forceps while Mars causes caesarean section. Any blunt injury (without bleeding) is likely to be caused by Saturn with Venus in the 4th house to any individual during Saturn's transit over the 4th, 8th or 11th house or during Saturn's antardasa in Venus or vice versa. Chances of blunt injury (without bleeding and without miscarriage or abortion) to some pregnant woman between 4th and 7th month of pregnancy.

Saturn in the 4th house with Venus often creates problems in due inheritance from parents, problems in source of livelihood. It can give labour problems in industrial enterprise, also sudden and unexpected break-down of a main or major machine in any production or manufacturing unit, trouble from customs people in import or export business.

During Saturn's harmful transit, an individual might get stranded on road due to trouble with conveyance or mode of transport. Accidents are a common feature with Saturn, and if the individual gets spared, the vehicle does not. The question of compensation too sometimes figures if Jupiter is during that period in harmful transit in 6th or 8th or 12th house or is in harmful antardasa under mahadasa of Venus or Saturn.

Apart from differences with natural or adopting mother, this combination is capable of giving trouble between the individual and parents of the spouse. Untimely and undue demands for money from progeny or the individual will be dragged into problems of married life of the progeny.

The main impact is that the 4th house rules comfort in life, which even Venus intends to give, but Saturn driven by its very nature, disturbs that comfort in life of the individual.

One matter in which individuals with this combination should stay alert is about residential premises. One might be dislodged from it for various and varied reasons. The house or cottage might suffer large damages owing to wind, storm, heavy rains (not floods), snowstorm, landslides in hills and mountains, earthquake (volcano only if Mars too is associated with this combination). It can be owing to indebtedness or disinheritance by some formal Will or it can be from employer-owned residence on end of the job.

Venus and Rahu in the 4th House

Rahu and Venus combination in the 4th house normally doesn't create all the above given troubles, but it does give, now and then, shadow and solvable problems in routine life of the individual.

This would include occasional differences with mother or grandparents, extra weight than prescribed medical limits, repeated problems of digestive system, but not such as would warrant serious medical treatment, and disturbed sleep now and then.

It also gives the usual type of problems from subordinates and employees (which might include embezzlement and pilferage too), pressure on heart by gases in stomach but not leading to heart attack (unless Rahu gets direct support from Mars in the 4th, 8th or 11th house). Rahu is capable of disturbing pregnancy, sometimes leading to miscarriage or abortion. It is often so on account cohabitation between the couple, specially during the first 4 months of the pregnancy (in this matter, the influence of Rahu exceeds that of Saturn).

This combination does give some minor problems in inheritance from parents (natural or adopting), but if other stars are not interfering in the matter, the problems are of solvable nature. Rahu can give problem from conveyance or mode of transport on road, but the individual might not get stranded on road. Help or lift might become available.

Saturn's combination with Venus in the 4th house doesn't normally adversely affect the reputation or prestige of the individual. But Rahu and Venus combine in the 4th house does adversely affect the reputation or prestige, quite often from relationship with opposite sex, which might be pure and platonic but would be misinterpreted or misrepresented by persons opposed to the individual. Therefore individuals with Rahu with Venus in the 4th house must always stay alert about their reputation and good name, and it is more applicable in the case of women and unmarried girls.

Another special feature of Rahu with Venus in the 4th house is that unsecured loans given to the opposite sex do not get recovered. The recovery is never in time, never in lump sum and often not the full amount given. Same fate can be of deposits made with private parties or dubious companies.

This combination can give trouble in the matter of residence either by damage to it demanding huge repairs or trouble from other claimants from within the family. Sudden change of residence could also be due to an eviction order passed by a court or competent authority owing to indebtedness or other reasons, or end of the job in case of residence provided by the employer.

Venus and Ketu in the 4th House

In 4th house, Ketu in conjunction with Venus gives results neither of Saturn nor those of Rahu. It simply supports Venus in leading a comfortable life, having affectionate relations with mother, no pain in ribs or upper abdomen, no pressure on heart in spite of mild digestive trouble now and then.

Further, this combination does not give any major or serious trouble with or from conveyance or mode of transport. The individual doesn't suffer for want of suitable residence as per status of the family, nor does it lead to eviction from the residence for reasons discussed in the preceding paragraphs under Venus with Saturn or Venus with Rahu combine in the 4th house.

Individuals with this combination are fond of decorating their residence and office by painting it in different colours, and furnishing it with colourful designs, even the furniture therein wears a decorative look.

In their wardrobe too, these individuals have different patterns, different designs, and different colours with regard to their under-clothes and outer apparel. They are fond of loud perfumes and wearing fresh flowers to look attractive (moreso in the case of females, including young girls).

These individuals join dance and music or painting or acting classes, if Mercury too is helpful, they complete the course of study, if Mercury is unhelpful, they leave the course of study in between.

VENUS IN THE 5TH HOUSE

Venus in the 5th house gives either expertise in one or more branches of fine arts, or an interest in music, dance, acting, painting, embroidery, knitting, interior decoration, landscape designing, making of murals. It gives expert knowledge of various colours befitting use, textile designing, making of various kinds/ designs of ready-made garments and apparel, sophistication about furniture and furnishings, choice of linen.

It also give deep knowledge and understanding about all or many kinds of wines, liquors and alcohols as also other items of intoxication like *bhang, ganja*, heroine and other drugs.

Venus in the 5th house produces efficient and competent physicians, provided it is favourably placed in the Navamsha-chart also and has the support of Moon from a favourable house, and these two stars do not have 6:8 relationship between them.

There are many instances of youngsters not getting admission in Medical courses initially itself because out of Venus and Moon, one was favourably placed and the other was not. But Venus alone does help making a person an expert *Hakim, Vaidya* etc in indigenous system of medicine, and all the moreso if the individual has family background of profession in medicine.

On the minus side, Venus in the 5th house makes an individual, by very nature, romantic. Because of other stars, if the individual doesn't have cheap demeanour in romanticism, at least the individual has a touch of flirtatiousness in nature.

One typical point that is normally lost sight of by some astrologers is that individuals with Venus in the 5th house are sensible in use of alcohol and except on rare occasions, do not get drunk. In matters of romanticism too, they observe a restraint according to the response of the person opposite. In other words they are not diehards in such activities.

No doubt, physicians, singers, musicians, actors, actresses are rather free in behaviour with their colleagues, disciples and subordinates. If it couldn't be helped in ancient times, how can it be helped in modern times of close contacts between men and women right from childhood in coeducation schools, and at places of work.

As has already been stated, these individuals are given to comfort, luxury, fashion, exhibitionism, show and glamour, whatever educational background and means of livelihood.

And it is not surprising that some of these individuals when in deep love do not bother or mind setback to their profession, career, job, means of livelihood, nor they pay attention to reputation or loss thereof.

Depending on the Rasi in the 7th house and 12th house and positions of their lords and their relationship with Venus, these individuals sometimes have physical relationship with more than one person of the opposite sex.

Some astrologers hold that Venus in the 5th house gives more daughters to an individual, but experience doesn't confirm it. It much depends on the Rasi in the 5th house, its lord, and relations of that lord with Venus. And one most IMPORTANT point in this regard is that getting a male child or a female one depends on the stars of both husband and wife or lover and beloved. There are instances where a wife had stars for getting more daughters than sons, and the couple had 7 sons and one daughter because of force and strength of the stars of the husband. Vice versa of this example is also amply correct and confirmed by actual experience.

Any astrologer rarely goes correct about the sex of the child to be conceived or already conceived. However, medical science has developed methods to determine the sex of an unborn child and it is most unfortunate that, at least in India, if it is female embryo, some women go in for medical termination of the pregnancy. These are the advantages and disadvantages of scientific research and development of knowledge in the world!

Venus and Sun, Moon, Mars, Mercury or Jupiter in the 5th House

Reference is invited to the relevant chapters earlier relating to each of these stars in the 5th house, which contain sub-headings dealing with combination of Venus with each of these five planets in the 5th house.

Venus and Saturn in the 5th House

Combination of Venus and Saturn in the 5th house is really a risky one and it can give loss of pregnancy or loss of a child after birth.

It can give a bad name to the individual for romantic nature, it can give bad name for drunkenness, and it can give a bad name for matters related to character. It can also give a bad name for partial or full loss of or damage to means of livelihood and it can give lack of neatness, cleanliness, system, and order in the very temperament of an individual.

Generally individuals with this combination remain confused about choice of a matrimonial match, and in the process sometimes make a wrong choice. There are several instances like that.

In general, Saturn's influence over Venus in the 5th house gives an individual confused thinking, delayed decision-making so much so that the individual sometimes misses the bus in life.

Hardly an individual can be found who has this combination in the 5th house and who doesn't have a hard touch of obstinacy, rigid attitude, stubborn trend of mind and action. The individual often takes it that the line of thought and action adopted by her or him is correct and that is the only possible line of action. She or he is rigid in administration and management matters too and imports violence in recovery of money.

However these individuals are experts at designing arms, weaponry and other items of Ordnance. They are good in espionage especially if they are of the fair sex, because they can tempt a person of the opposite sex to extract information without falling from grace themselves.

Where the question of relationship with progeny is concerned, these individuals are often harsh and hard with their children, at least upto the age of 18 years, and sometimes their strictness is overbearing. They try to dominate the children about line or course of study or branch of education to pursue. These individuals do not hesitate to give physical beating, punishment, or torture to children of own or of others. They are at two extremes, either they want their kids to be very fashionable or they are pretty miserly towards education and needs of the children.

Similarly, in matters of comfort, luxury, fashion, and decoration too, these individuals are at extremes, either extra liberal or extra miserly.

Because of tendency of delayed decisions, they sometimes decide late in the day on medical termination of pregnancy and do not hesitate to compel the gynaecological expert to do so if necessary, by surgery. This might involve risk to the capacity of future procreation for the female in the family way, or even to her life.

These individuals carry in their mind very conservative estimate of their income; they are not liberal towards others in money matters. This tendency sometimes harms their prospects at elections or getting promotion in job, or getting favours in matters of business/ industry etc. If they pay a gratification in cash or kind, they are very often keen to get full return on it. This spoils the game as well as relationship for future.

In the case of this combination of Venus and Saturn, special attention should be paid to transit of Saturn as also mahadasa of one and antardasa of another, because the above mentioned results would necessarily affect the individual during that period.

One matter that deserves attention towards this combination is that greater attention would be needed towards formal education of these individuals, at least at school level or upto the end of the 17th year of age, whichever is later.

Venus and Rahu in the 5th House

The main concern of Venus and Rahu combine in the 5th house is to give loss of pregnancy by natural or medical means.

If the progeny's own stars are also unhelpful for a particular year during the school education, chances are strong for loss of one year of the child by failure or change of school or change of town or for any other reason.

However Rahu doesn't unnecessarily interfere with habits of the individual relating to neatness, cleanliness, system, and order in life at home and at work place. But Rahu does divert attention of the individual between the age of 10 and 11 years from studies towards one or more branches of fine arts, moreso if the young person gets into bad company.

Rahu gives, even to adults with education and experience, a touch of sharp ego, particularly on basis of knowledge and learning of the individual. And this ego costs them sometimes a heavy price, with regard to relationship with own progeny.

This sense of ego is sharp in physicians, musicians, singers, actors, actresses, painters, photographers, chemists and druggists, consultants in the import/ export trade, designers and fashion-makers, as also administrators and managers, and teachers in any of these lines.

Venus and Ketu in the 5th House

As already stated, Ketu, when in combination with Venus in the 5th house, normally doesn't interfere much with functioning of Venus.

On the other hand Ketu supports and supplements the functions of Venus. Thus this combination provides to the individual good chances for developing writing skill, public-speaking and teaching talent. Besides other advantages of Venus in the 5th house like romantic ideas and actions, nurturing and preparing one or two of the progeny for medical/ music/ fine arts courses of study get full support from Ketu. Sometimes for the individual pursuing fine arts like music, dance, painting, acting, sculpture, architecture, photography, there is extra support from Ketu.

The only minus point which Ketu might impose, though only in rare cases, is the loss of pregnancy at earlier stages, moreso if at that given time the spouse also has stars leading to loss of pregnancy. If the spouse has stars stronger for pregnancy going a full term, Ketu's presence with Venus would create a fear but not actually cause the loss of pregnancy, especially if the couple avoid physical contact with each other during those days.

VENUS IN THE 6TH HOUSE

There are vast differences of opinion among the ancient *acharyas* about this position of Venus. Some say that it causes one or the other small-term illness, domination of the opposite sex in the family and also in outside world, quarrels and enmity owing to strain in relations with opposite sex. It is also attributed to run down vitality in men owing to excess physical relationship, arrival and interference of a third angle in the "husband and wife" relationship.

No doubt that Venus in the 6th house causes wasteful and sometimes beyond means expenditure on items of comfort/ luxury/ fashion etc. On the other hand, some other ancient *acharyas* say that it grants learning and vast and varied experience to the individual especially in medical science or fine arts, generally help the concern for the needy and the suffering or ill. It gives a strong physique, presentable personality, and expertise in solving matrimonial problems of others.

Our experience shows that both the schools of thought are correct, depending on which houses in the horoscope are owned by Venus, and which Rasi is in the 6th house. Also where the lord of the 6th house is placed and what relations exist between Venus and that lord of the 6th house. It also matters considerably what stars are casting full *drishti* on Venus from the 12th house. If Venus happens to own the 3rd, 8th or the 11th house and the 6th house is owned by Moon or Mars or Mars, or that Moon is situated in the 12th house, the unfavourable results stated above will descend on the individual.

On the other hand, if out of Venus-owned Rasis, (a) Taurus is in the 2nd house and Libra in the 7th house, or (b) Taurus in 4th house and Libra in 9th house, or (c) Taurus in 5th and Libra in 10th house or (d) Taurus in 11th house and Libra in 4th house, the favourable results of Venus mentioned above would be there for the individual.

Libra in 2nd house and Taurus in 9th house would give mixed results. However if one of the Venus-owned Rasi is in favourable house and the other is a damaging house, the damaging position would prevail over the favourable one.

One important point with Venus in 6th house is that the 6th house is in 12th position from the 7th house which rules marriage, married life and marriage partner (spouse). It sometimes gives an indifferent attitude to the spouse or to the individual, and the marriage life becomes a subject of artificial compromise between the husband and wife.

If Mars or Saturn or Rahu occupy the 2nd or 7th house they are inclined to break a marriage, Venus in the 6th house would give support to the break-off trend. However if the spouse of such an individual has Venus in the 8th or 12th or even 2nd house, the unfavourable impact of the individual having Venus in 6th house would get mitigated and married life might continue happily. Normally, if nothing else, an individual having Venus in 6th house with no countermanding position of Venus in the horoscope of the spouse would give at least bickerings between the husband and wife.

Another point worth notice is that generally Venus in 6th house brings home greater demands for money from the kids, the girls after the age of 14 and boys after the age of 16. Non-fulfilment of their demands result in arguments, not between the child and a parent, but rather between the parents. It is always better for the parents not to convert the arguments into a serious quarrel.

Venus and Sun, Moon, Mars, Mercury or Jupiter in the 6th House

Reference is invited to the relevant chapters earlier relating to each of these stars in the 6th house.

Venus and Saturn in the 6th House

This combination on one hand reduces the unfavourable results of Venus in the 6th house and on the other, enhances the favourable results attributable to Saturn in the 6th house, irrespective of the Rasi in the 6th house.

It is so because Saturn would overrule Venus, because one of the best positions of Saturn in a Birth-chart or Yearly-chart or Question chart is the 6th house, provided it hasn't shifted position in the Bhava-Chalitam. Saturn would not give chance to the enemies to be effective in causing harm to the individual, whatever the ground of enmity. This position would help an individual in elections too, provided the individual doesn't depend more than 40 per cent on inducements.

Saturn keeps losses under control in any industrial or manufacturing unit, where a majority of employees are females. However, Saturn would not tolerate child labour, specially girls below the age of 14 working in factories and would start giving losses or labour trouble or trouble from a government agency, because the combination indicates these results.

Another factor is that this combination saves damage to the machines, big and small, at least from man-made mischief. Saturn protects the individual from sex-oriented diseases also, and cures the disease quite quickly, provided the individual doesn't take liberty for its repetition, because then Saturn would not come to the relief of the individual.

This combination helps an individual maintain healthy appetite for sex – even into advanced years, for both, men and women. However Saturn's influence on Venus in the 6th house wouldn't stop the individual from meeting persons of the opposite sex, other than the spouse, for satisfaction in bed. Saturn would rather give immoral relationship with an elderly person, senior in age by anything more than 10 years. It could be even marriage or husband-wife-like relationship with an elderly person.

Venus and Rahu in the 6th House

This combination protects an individual from any sex-oriented disease basically. If once the disease afflicts an individual, Rahu isn't of much help in quick recovery.

It is the same case in matters of enemies. It can protect against mild natured enemies, but not so much against enemies of wicked and cruel nature. Similarly Rahu gives romantic ideas, exchange of sweet nothings with the opposite sex, but not the desired chances of physical liberty with each other.

On the other hand this combination creates differences of opinion, sometimes in a severe manner, between wife and husband or between the couple on one side, and other members of the family on the other.

However this combination helps the progeny to work towards riches and life style of comfort, luxury and fashion, provided the parents do not drag them into income-oriented work before the age of 18 years.

Rahu ensures that at election time, the individual's committed supporters would neither betray nor would abstain from voting, whatever the kind of election. Rahu is not of much help in registering help of new supporters, because Rahu is not so powerful as to totally override Venus in the 6th house.

Venus and Ketu in the 6th House

In this combination of Venus and Ketu in 6th house, Ketu would give 40% results of Rahu and 60% results of Mercury, which means that the individual might be caught on the wrong foot for utterances or writings in office or for public consumption.

If a quarrel takes place, Ketu brings it on paper. Sometimes if Sun or Mars or Saturn or Jupiter is also in the 12th house, where naturally Rahu is there, the individual might be charged by anyone for defamation, or with contempt of the court. The individual may suffer in terms of money (penalty or compensation), though it is less likely to lead to any imprisonment sentence.

This combination makes the progeny quite ambitious but without making much effort towards fulfilment of ambitions, unless their own stars are very helpful in the matter.

Ketu neither causes any serious type of sex-oriented disease, nor it is much helpful in curing it. Ketu allows Venus to carry on its functions and stays more or less neutral in the 6th house.

Ketu however doesn't help an individual in securing a third angle or falling a victim to a third angle in married life or love affair. Here too, Ketu stays neutral to Venus influence in the 6th house.

Ketu, during its antardasa in Mars or Saturn main *Dasa* can cause a blunt injury by a fall, but not a serious injury, especially in the case of a male individual.

VENUS IN THE 7TH HOUSE

This is a very important position of Venus. The 7th house rules love affair, marriage proposals, actual marriage, married life, and relationship with spouse in post-marriage period. It rules quarrels between man and woman, or quarrel between persons of the same sex but relating to a third member (of the opposite sex). It also rules the private parts of the body. It rules appearance, personality, complex, built of body, facial formation, neat and clean or unclean habits, nature, to some extent education, and in a sense family background of the spouse.

It is pretty unfortunate that the Ancients have discussed at great length these qualities or lack of these qualities about a bride, but very little has been laid down about the bridegroom. Modern *acharyas* have laid down some outlines about the bridegroom too, but the reality is that it needs a good deal of research, not by quacks but by knowledgeable, learned and experienced astrologers.

Presently astrologers depend to a great extent on their personal limited knowledge and experience to guide an individual, which may lead to maladjustment in marriage and then in rare cases, to ultimate failure of the marriage.

Another problem, at least in India where marriages are arranged, is that sometimes the parents or the mediatory person develop a preference for a particular choice, or the girl and the boy in question start to like one another irrespective of the whether the horoscopes match or not. In such cases, it becomes difficult for the learned and impartial astrologer to advise against the marriage if need be.

There are hundreds of cases within the knowledge of the authors, wherein such marriages conducted against the advice of the learned and impartial astrologer, unfortunately resulted in divorce or death of one of the married couple. (Of course, this observation holds good for the believers who seek astrological guidance.)

In their long experience, the authors have come across several cases where the interested parties 'bought' the opinion of some obliging (unscrupulous) fortune-teller in support of the marriage proposal,(even though the stars of the boy and girl were not agreeable) with disastrous consequences.

Ancient *acharyas* have said that with Venus in 7th house, an individual gets a beautiful and charming wife. If we apply the same rule to bride too, it can be said that a girl with Venus in the 7th house would get a bridegroom, who would be handsome, with a pleasant personality.

Another general rule is that if a male Rasi (Aries, Gemini, Leo, Libra, Sagittarius or Aquarius) is in the 7th house, the spouse would be tall, and if a female Rasi is in the 7th house, the spouse would be of medium height. The question of height would very much depend on the climate of the region where the boy or the girl were born and raised. There are exceptions too, to this rule.

Similarly, the impression is that Gemini, Virgo, Libra, and Pisces in the 7th house get the individual a fair complexioned spouse. This is all a relative term, because in countries nearer to equator, how much fairness would be found in the residents, and in countries above thirty-three degree latitude away from equator, it would be difficult to find dark complexioned original residents. Likewise, original German nationals are very tall, in some countries we find residents very short in height. Therefore while giving a prediction about height or complexion of a matrimonial match, these considerations should be kept in mind.

Similarly some astrologers try to bind the consulting public in direction (East, West, North, South) for finding a matrimonial match, while some others try to restrict the profession or source of income of the matrimonial match. General idea should be given but the choice field for the spouse-seekers should be left open and wide.

There are quite a large number of instances, where an individual received education in a particular discipline and took career or source of livelihood in a totally different field which was poles apart from the discipline of education. With large strides in development of science and technology as also distances in the world becoming easily accessible by means of communications and transportation, the whole concept of these considerations in finding a matrimonial match have changed.

The science of astrology still lacks in scholars keen on doing research without considerations for money or fame. Quacks, and half-baked astrologers do not have the knowledge, learning, and experience to guide or undertake real research. Some learned and really knowledgeable astrologers have too much work on hand; they hardly have the time, energy or platform to undertake research work.

Then the question comes of quarrels, fights, battles, and even wars generated by Venus in the 7th house. Astrologers with learned family tradition in astrology for generations together would examine this question in the rights perspective, otherwise normally astrologers of short standing and little experience would refuse to link quarrels, fights and battles with Venus in the 7th house.

The points to look at are what is the Rasi in the 7th house and where is its lord in the horoscope and what kind of relationship it has with Venus in the 7th house. If Rasis owned by Mars or Saturn is in the 7th house and its lord is in the 2nd, 8th, or the 12th house, a quarrel or fight or even battle is possible. It is so at least during the mahadasa of Venus and antardasa of Mars or Saturn (as the owner of the 7th house), or mahadasa of Mars or Saturn (as the owner of the 7th house) and antardasa of Venus, which might give origin to the quarrel or fight etc. If Saturn or retrograde Mars is in the 2nd, 8th or the 12th house by transit, even then a quarrel, fight or battle might occur. If Rahu be in the 2nd, 8th or 12th house, it might create a temporary shadow of quarrel or fight, but it becomes solvable or compromiseable or end-able (sorry for framing our own terms to give correct exposition to the subject matter).

History is replete with numerous examples, in India and elsewhere, about great battles and wars fought on account of women. The Hindu epic Ramayana has it that the kidnapping of Rama's beautiful wife Sita, by the demon-king Ravana led to the destruction of the demon clan entirely. In the other great epic, Mahabharata, lovely and proud princess Drapadi's insult by Duryodhana and his brother Dushshashana lead to such a war that within a short period of 18 days virtually the majority male population at least of the then North India was wiped out.

Helen of Troy and Cleopatra of Egypt changed the history of Europe and Northern Africa through wars. Rani Laxmibai of Jhansi's revolt against the British, threw out the East India Company and brought the formal rule of the British into India in 1857. No more examples are needed.

It is indeed a very difficult task to predict battles and wars between countries, nations, different races; very high quality of knowledge experience and insight is needed for this. But the 7th house is directly and importantly concerned with wars and battles.

Experience shows that Venus in the 7th house with planetary details stated above (outside the paragraphs in italics) can cause grounds for separation between husband and wife, and ultimately lead to divorce. It may be after a regrettable fight in a court of law or a mutual fight between the two families of husband and wife or between the husband and wife themselves. If there is any other soft planet in the 7th house, like Mercury or Jupiter, the divorce can be by mutual consent too. Otherwise, if the 7th house is owned by a soft planet and the owner is sitting in the 4th or the 1st house, or even in the 5th house, there can be divorce by mutual consent.

One more point may be noted in this regard that the very presence of Mars, or Saturn in the 7th house (irrespective of the Rasi in the 7th house) along with Venus there, would make the marriage a non-workable one, unless the concerned charts of the spouse contain countermanding stars. It is always better to bear the position of stars in mind while matching horoscopes for marriage, irrespective of the fact whether it is the first or second or a third marriage of the individual.

Now where does the difficulty arise? Firstly in the case of love based marriages. One cannot first go and get the horoscope of the opposite sex for marriage and then initiate the love affair. Further, in India as well as many other countries people are losing faith in matching of horoscopes for marriage, because of large failures of marriage after cursory (computer) matching of the horoscopes and secondly, because of families getting uprooted from their original community-base. On this account, matrimonial match finding, for arranged marriages, has become a tedious task. Therefore the discerning look for real learned and knowledgeable astrologers for the purpose.

Matching of horoscopes done by computers is rather misguiding, because the nuances that should be studied by an expert human astrologer have not all (yet) been converted into software!

Another factor of Venus in the 7th house is that one of the couple gets interested, sometimes owing to own volition and sometimes under peer pressure in drinks and a third angle to the married life. This effect is enhanced if Venus happens to be the lord of the 6th or the 12th house. In such an eventuality, if the spouse behaves in an affectionate and firm manner, the fondness for wine or a third angle can be nipped at the initial stage itself, because Venus in the 7th house is always on the side of the spouse (be it wife or husband).

In relevant chapter earlier discussed with harmful effect of Mars in the 7th house (or the 8th house) is also worth re-reading with the above discussion about Venus (alone) in the 7th house.

Venus and Sun, Moon, Mars, Mercury or Jupiter in the 7th House

Please refer to the relevant earlier chapters earlier on each of these stars in the 7th house, which contain sub-headings dealing with combination of Venus with each of these five stars in the 5th house.

Venus and Saturn in the 7th House

This combination has always to be watched in the married life of the individual and in selling and buying activity (particularly for business purposes), as also in matters of quarrel, dispute and fight.

As usual Saturn overrides Venus, and Saturn sometimes becomes intent upon disturbing the married life, specially if Saturn owns the 4th, 8th or 12th house, or it has the support of Mars or Rahu from 2nd, 4th, 8th or 12th house. It has to be noted that being a slow moving planet, Saturn's effect on married life is introduced into the married life slowly and steadily; it normally doesn't strike suddenly.

Relations between wife and husband start getting sour over petty grudges against each other, usually unspoken grudges gaining ground in the mind of one of the two. Biased suspicion also sometimes gains roots about the character of the other partner. Saturn has tendency of whispers in the ear and spying, which also tends to dent the married life. One oft-repeated grudge of the individual is that the spouse does not properly take care of the individual during complaints of health.

If both are in service or one is in service and the other is in business or self-employment, the grudge is about to receiving less attention from the spouse.

One major difference between Mars and Saturn is that Mars starts harming or hurting the married life during the first 8 to 10 years immediately following the marriage, while Saturn starts harming and hurting the married life after at least nine years of marriage.

No doubt if other stars support the evil intents of Saturn on the married life, the damage to married life might start even much earlier. In some cases it has been observed that Saturn with support from other stars hit the married life within the first 19 months or 19 weeks. This is very much true if Saturn was in a damaging transit to the 7th house or Saturn's antardasa was running under Venus mahadasa or mahadasa of a planet which was supporting Saturn in disturbing the married life.

Damage to married life starts much earlier if Venus is in the 7th house and Saturn is casting full *drishti* on Venus from the 1st or the 6th house. Saturn's *drishti* from the 11th or the 10th house is neither so harmful nor harming the married life instantly.

We have several instances where Saturn's *drishti* on the 6th house on the 7th house ended the marriage within 19 days or 19 weeks or 19 months. As a rule, Saturn has full *drishti* on the 2nd house from Saturn's placement.

The next question that arises under this combination is of injury to bone and health complaints of the private parts of the body either to the individual or to the spouse. It is always better to somehow ascertain the physical suitability and compatibility of the boy and the girl before marriage in such cases. If that is not possible, the married couple themselves should adjust to physical suitability and compatibility of each other by openly and freely discussing the matter mutually, and if necessary, seeking professional medical help.

This point has been discussed so precisely here because cases are not rare where the health of one of the two got much damaged owing to physical unsuitability of each other.

If Saturn owns either the 2nd or the 8th house, interference of the family of either of the two would be there and the couple should make it a point not to allow such interference to disturb their married life. Saturn is not given so much to open and free talk, and whenever, one of the two partners in married life notices that some casual touch of disturbance is taking origin in the married life, open and free talk between wife and husband would iron out the disturbing factors.

If the married life is ever dragged to a court of law or family court, it is very likely that cross-examination of the complainant partner would hurt the heart and the prestige. The counsel or advocate of the respondent-partner would be concerned with the fees, not so much with emotional sensibilities of the two parties involved.

The senior author has come across an instance when an advocate advised the petitioner-wife to suggest in her divorce petition an incestuous relationship of her husband with his mother whereas the poor mother had died when the respondent-husband was a boy hardly 14 or 15 years old!

Parents of girls with Venus with Saturn combination in the 7th house should caution their daughter against any kind of male attention that take advantage of her, leading to molestation. This guidance/ caution is best given to the daughter between her 10th to 19th year of age, because this is the period when Saturn might strike an innocent girl with molestation.

Venus and Rahu in the 7th House

Rahu and Venus combine in the 7th house disturbs, not so much the married life, as the confidence of one of the partner in the other in the matter of extra-marital affair. Other grounds of suspicion could be about management of money, social life, about contacts with members of family and friends, about behaviour towards family of the other, about mode of dress and style of talking. Critical remarks may hurt the ego of the partner, and should be avoided, because Rahu is bound to give a sharp sense of ego to the spouse and to a limited extent, to the individual too.

One advantage of Rahu's position with Venus in the 7th house is that Ketu would eventually be in the 1st House, and would always give a sense of correct appreciation of the mind, words, and act of the other partner in marriage. Ketu would thus help married life to run smoothly and amicably.

The individual with this combination in the 7th house should always, at least during the first 9 years of marriage, stay above board in money matters. If the individual is a husband, he should keep disclosing every item of income and expenditure to the wife. If the individual is wife, she shouldn't try to build up secret funds beyond the knowledge of the husband. Contrary behaviour would ultimately hurt the marriage.

If the above precautions are observed, this combination would not give any major chance of marriage running down the hill of life. It would not give rise to any big quarrel, dispute or differences.

If either of the married couple gets involved in confrontation or conflict with another woman on civil grounds, Jupiter's influence should be examined in own horoscope and then steps should be taken towards litigation or to stop it.

Venus and Ketu in the 7th House

Venus rules love, romance, beauty, conflicts and quarrels with anyone and everyone, poetry, music, dance, medicine, herbs, marriage, married life, relations between husband and wife, while Ketu, on pattern of Mercury rules literary thoughts, spoken word, written word, intelligence, wisdom, experience and also patience.

Thus when these two are in conjunction in the 7th house, it can safely be presumed that the wife and husband would have pleasantness in their married life, sweet and musical talks, love and affection not only felt within hearts but expressed in so many words. Some of the individuals prove to be good poets of romantic subjects, devotional songs like those of *Surdas*, *Meerabai* and *Raskhan*, wit in their ideas and expressions like poet *Bihari*.

The individual normally marries a person with talent and understanding as also accommodating, even towards the roughly behaved members of the family of the spouse.

Some of the female involved in the written word who have Venus and Ketu in the 7th house, progress very well in work, but often their credit is stolen by those who have Venus and Mercury in the 7th house, because Mercury is a solid planet, while Ketu is a shadow planet.

However, in case this pair of stars (Venus and Ketu), by chance suffers from direct *drishti* of Mars or Saturn, or if the Rasi in the 7th house is owned by Mars or Saturn, or Sun enjoins Venus in the 7th house even at a distance, the individual might have to suffer a nagging partner like **Isaac Newton** who often suffered the anger of his wife.

VENUS IN THE 8TH HOUSE

This position of Venus needs careful examination, as practising astrologers very often come across cases of maladjustment between husband and wife or between lover and beloved.

The question of extra-marital affair or casual physical relationship might crop up under Venus in 8th house.

(A close friend of the authors, to whom a portion of the draft manuscript of this book was shown, suggested that explicit language regarding relationship between man and woman should be avoided. However, should this advice be followed, it would be unfair to the scientific exposition of the subject)

This point is brought up here because it is important to mention in this context that many a time, differences and dissatisfaction crops up in married life from one partner refusing to adopt certain unconventional methods in the physical relationship. It can happen even between lovers. If a soft star like Mercury or Jupiter is in conjunction with Venus in the 8th house, these misunderstandings do not assume seriousness and the couple understand things and come to mutual adjustment.

However, if Mars, Saturn, or Rahu is with Venus in the 8th house, mutual understanding and adjustment is elusive sometimes beyond amendment, with each partner sticking to his/her stand.

Venus on its own doesn't give any ailment or disease relating to private parts or any other complaints of health related to sex life. But these days we hear a lot about venereal diseases and fatal sex-related diseases like HIV and AIDS in case the individual has conjunction of Mars or Saturn with Venus in the 8th house.

However if it is Rahu with Venus in the 8th, the ailment would not stay for long and be cured with continuity in treatment and preventive care.

One very typical point has to be noted about Venus in the 8th house and that is, that a man with Venus in the 8th house, either has extra capacity to satisfy the female partner in bed, or on the other extreme, is unable to satisfy most the time.

If an individual has Saturn and Venus in conjunction in the 8th house, the individual avoids to bother about the extra-marital affair of the spouse.

However, sometimes, even when both are secretly involved in extra-marital relationships, the more violent of the two (husband and wife) would attempt physical attack on the other which may lead to fatal injuries in some case. Otherwise, bashing one another in fits of rage could be a common; rarely would one be at the receiving end of the other!

Venus in the 8th house attracts an individual in business and trade towards hoarding of medicines, long cloth and allied items, *ghee,* sugar, cotton and cotton seed with intention of profiteering during times of paucity or short supply owing to restrictions on import. The individual has no hesitation on indulging in smuggling, over-invoicing and under-invoicing in import/ export trading.

If it is Saturn or Rahu with Venus in the 8th house within 12 degrees, the individual might directly or indirectly be associated with flesh trade, smuggling of herbs and medicines or their extracts, smuggling of highly technical and surgical instruments.

When the Rasi in the 8th house is owned by Moon, with Venus therein, the individual is likely to suffer food poisoning, illness caused by heavy drinks or any other kind of intoxication. The individual's life may be endangered by floods or by sea-water or by biting by any poisonous insect or rabies. Combination of Moon with Venus in the 8th house is apt to cause mental depression, mental disorder and cynical attitude.

If however Jupiter joins Venus in the 8th house, it can cause cystic fibrosis or any other allied ailment.

The relief in the matter of Venus alone being in the 8th house is that ailment, illness, disease, bad habits, 'viceful' actions, anti-social or illegal activity are not carried on by the individual for long.

Venus and Sun, Moon, Mars, Mercury or Jupiter in the 8th House

Reference is invited to relevant chapters earlier on each of these stars in the 8th house.

Venus and Saturn in the 8th House

Some of the points have been mentioned already in the preceding paragraphs. The important point is that this combination can affect the sex organs of the individual, which might be since birth or might develop in later life owing to some injury or accident or psychological pressure, or even advancement of age.

This combination poses risk to money and person of the individual arising out of jealousy, misappropriation, deceit, cheating, illegal activity, governmental action, mutual quarrels and fights and also non-cooperation of near and dear ones or of friends in litigation and prosecution.

The problem is that Saturn is a slow moving planet, and once the individual gets into the arena of smuggling, kidnapping, trading for immoral purposes, mischief in import and export, it becomes difficult for the individual to come out of the web, notwithstanding the fact that the individual is either a male or female.

The point of relief is that if the individual is sentenced to imprisonment or runs away to a place of hiding to avoid legal action or to escape attack by competitors or opponents, full care is taken of the needs of that individual and family thereof by the gang/association to which the individual belongs or works under.

In case of illness, ailment or disease or injury or wound created by Saturn with Venus in the 8th house, recovery would take longer and would cost substantially.

Venus and Rahu in the 8th House

This combination makes the individual bold in words and action, fearless and courageous in immoral or unlawful activity, rich by marriage or by love affair or any kind of relationship or connection with a member of the opposite sex.

It makes the individual ruthless in personal quarrels and fights, fond of developing romantic (platonic or other kind of) friendship.

If the individual's spouse has charming, attractive, pleasant personality, the individual has to be protective towards the spouse from evil elements and influences, because in these matters education or non-education of the spouse doesn't matter much.

Rahu with Venus can cause ailment allied to venereal disease or AIDS, but the illness gets diagnosed at an early stage, and chances of cure of the complaint are quite good, quick and easy.

Rahu with Venus would not lose its initial tendency of giving extra than normal weight at the midriff, be it a male or a female.

Venus and Ketu in the 8th House

The combination of Venus and Ketu normally brings damage and destruction to an individual's papers and documents of own writings and published works of self.

The combination is also capable of giving trouble from leakage of love letters exchanged with sweetheart.

The senior author personally knows of a case when, in the course of searches of the premises of a business family of six brothers, love letters and photographs of ex-lover of the youngest brother's bride were found by the Revenue Intelligence, Customs and Central Excise officials. But before they could read or seize the love-letters and photos, which were anyway irrelevant to the case, the senior author, who was one of the two senior officers supervising the searches, got them destroyed and advised the young lady to cut off the memories of the past. Had the love letters and photos been seized, it would have destroyed the married life of the young bride.

In so far as any kind of ailment, illness or disease related to sex is concerned, Ketu with Venus causes it in a very mild manner and it is often easily detected and cured.

Ketu doesn't induce (even with Venus) in the 8th house an individual towards dishonesty, criminal, or immoral or illegal activity, because the individual is neither very greedy nor very fond of pomp and show. On the other hand, the individual tries to maintain good moral character and if is at all drawn towards romantic relationship, it stays at platonic level only.

No doubt, Ketu with Venus in 8th house can cause piles with its adverse effect on sex life of the individual causing frustration to the spouse. Another point often noticed regarding influence of this combination is that the individual might suffer from dog bite, snake bite, bite by a camel, kick by a horse or donkey or mule, rabies, injury by jackal or fox or bear, monkey, tiger, boar, lion, wolf or any other animal like crocodile etc.

It is always better for the individual to be careful in this respect, and if any untoward incident takes place, he or she must take resort to medical treatment immediately.

VENUS IN THE 9TH HOUSE

Venus in 9th house gives inclination of romantic ideas towards close relations of self or spouse at the level of brother-in-law or sister-in-law, and whether this romantic approach dies a natural death or is developed depends upon the stars of the person towards whom the romantic approach took origin.

If there is no response but tolerance, the attitude might persist for some time (that is a few months or even years depending upon the proximity between the two). But if the person towards whom romantic approach is made takes serious objection or rebuffs or seeks support of others to stop the nuisance, the matter ends there.

However other influences of Venus in the 9th house are that it makes an individual quite religious minded, be it towards God Almighty, or Goddess or other deities or to lower spirits. On the whole if Venus is in its own Rasi or in exaltation (Pisces), the devotion is generally towards any form of Goddess, more importantly for *Laxmi, Parvati, Durga* or *Saraswati*.

These individuals get associated with religious, charity-oriented or social non-governmental organisations (NGO), and try their best to stay honest in management (if they enjoy any powers in management). But they do not interfere with dishonesty or morality of others in the administration nor do they take any initiative in exposing them.

These individuals always try to prove helpful to brothers, sisters, cousins, uncles and aunts of self or of spouse, and try, to render physical, moral and financial assistance, to the extent financially or physically possible. This attitude outwardly has no romantic link or motives as has been described in the opening para.

In so far as elections and public service are concerned, they are generally helpful to the extent possible for them, but they avoid going out of the way to prove helpful. These individuals get good support from females in their elections or any other kind of pursuits. These helpful females do not normally expect any return for the services rendered.

Unless Mars or Saturn (by presence in the 9th house) puts hurdles, these individuals are able to inherit what is due to them in ancestral or parental property and assets. They are normally very keen to inherit jewellery, precious stones, diamonds, and other costly items of heirloom, and in doing so, they sometimes give up their claim to immovable assets or agree to inherit less share in immovable assets.

These individuals are always keen to run some kind of business as main or subsidiary source of income, and they get good footing and success in trade of cloth, ready-made garments, silver items, cotton, yarn, cottonseeds, refined cotton for textile and silk mills, and medicines too.

They could also be successful in trading cold drinks, beverages, wines, liquors, or any other kind of alcohol items, sugar, bread and butter, *ghee,* medical herbs, cosmetics, costume jewellery, fresh flowers, perfumery, and import or export trading of any of these items. They also prefer to work with foreigners.

If Venus happens to be lord of the 1st or the 7th house, these individuals are more interested in harmless flirting, rather than actual physical indulgence with the opposite sex. This is a very delicate question, and unless consulted, an astrologer shouldn't go deep in this matter, except making some casual observations.

This position of Venus makes an individual fond of pilgrimage to religious places, far and near or even in foreign countries, and if they can do nothing else, they would mix work with pilgrimage, specially to places by the side of ocean, sea, big rivers, gulfs, etc.

The 9th house is directly concerned with fame or defame. Venus, in the 9th house is either in own Rasi or a Rasi owned by Mercury, would help the individuals to earn fame. However, in case Venus is in a Rasi owned by Mars or Saturn, it would bring some kind of notoriety too for any, even minor, act of commission or omission on part of the individual. In case Venus is in Pisces in the 9th house, the fame would get a boost up, but in case Sagittarius is in the 9th house, the results would be either neutral or partly good fame and partly bad name.

Venus and Sun, Moon, Mars, Mercury or Jupiter in the 9th House

Relevant chapters earlier relating to these stars in the 9th house, which contain sub-headings dealing with combination of Venus with each of these five planets in the 9th house may please be referred to.

Venus and Saturn in the 9th House

The problem with this combination of Venus and Saturn in the 9th house is that though intimate friends, Saturn generally tries to dominate Venus, and Venus is more or less helpless to resist.

Saturn would adversely affect relations of the individual with a brother, sister, cousin, uncle or aunt of self or spouse. Whether the individual is at fault or not, pretty often faults are alleged against the individual for her or his talks and actions. Even if the individual proves helpful to these relations, motives are ascribed to it.

Saturn disturbs the settlement of inheritance of ancestral or parental moveable and immovable assets, and it has been observed that the individual gets less than due share. If the individual alone is the sole claimant, outsiders would often try to deprive him or her of at least a part of the inheritance by cheating or buying assets at a throwaway price or create legal or social hurdles in enjoyment of the inheritance.

Sometimes the individual on own accord disposes of the assets or part thereof for negligible price, moreso for facility of migration from the place where the assets are situated.

This combination harms the fame of an individual, more so if the combination is in a Rasi owned by Mars or Saturn, and therefore individuals with Venus and Saturn combine in the 9th house should normally stay alert to protect their name and fame.

In social, religious, charity-oriented organisations too, unwanted, unjustified, unwarranted vague and flimsy blames or allegations are made against the individual, and sometimes these allegations are by such people as have vested interested in making them. The ultimate result often is that the individual withdraws from any kind of active work related to that organisation, and the helpless beneficiaries suffer.

In matters relating to elections, public service, work connected with trade unions and agricultural labour or agriculturists themselves, the individuals adopt very hard line attitude, which proves beneficial to the sections of the society for whom the work is aimed or directed. In this field the individuals do not bother about criticism or blame and allegations.

The individuals gain by import or export of produce of mines and minerals, raw iron, products of iron and steel, petrol, lubricants, machinery parts, items of rubber and allied raw material, jute and its products, machinery and parts thereof, placement services or import/ export of manpower.

Ancient *acharyas* have ascribed hypocrisy to these individuals, from which even father, uncles, aunts and other near relations of self and spouse do not escape. They try to wear their ego on their sleeve a bit sharply, but outwardly only, and give it up according to the need of the hour or need of the situation.

In the same breath, the Ancients have attributed to Venus and Saturn combine in the 9th house of the individual as leaning towards the family and relations of the spouse and getting influenced by them rather than own family.

These individuals prove very useful and successful in organising rallies, demonstrations, public meetings, sit-ins, strikes and hunger strikes or relay hunger strikes; but they expect their price too for the services rendered in this behalf. Likewise they prove very helpful in recovery of loans and dues, again no doubt for their fixed rates of price or commission.

Venus and Rahu in the 9th House

Rahu, when in combination with Venus in the 9th house, is more or less mute observer of acts commissions and omission of Venus in this house, except that Rahu does interfere in the matters of inheritance of ancestral or parental assets, working actually against the interests of the individual.

However, the help or intervention of other members of the family or relations or well-wishers later on solves this trouble created by Rahu.

Rahu keeps the individual in the background in arranging finances, manpower, slogan shouters for organising rallies, demonstrations, public meetings, political pickets, strikes and relay hunger strikes, but unlike Saturn and Venus combine in 9th house, Rahu with Venus take care that no person on hunger strikes is hurt or killed. Rahu is a shadow planet and therefore likes to make a show of things, instead of making it real.

This combination helps an individual to get either a job with or a supply contract from an Embassy, High Commission, their consular offices or foreign firms or multinational companies, with ample opportunities for travel to foreign lands. In the same breath, Rahu and Venus combine deprives the individual of full benefit for lack of integrity or any other kind of lapse in service or work.

If the individual has a roving eye or romantic attitude towards any blood relation or relation by marriage or adoption, Rahu would indirectly help the individual. But in case this attitude of the individual is reprimanded, it would break off of relationship. Rahu provides no protection. On the other hand Rahu would help in enhancing and speeding up the reprimand, rebuke, and break-off of relationship.

Venus and Ketu in the 9th House

When Ketu is in combination with Venus in the 9th house, Ketu protects the individuals from harmful influence coming from outside, but cannot put a stop if the influence is flowing from inside the immediate or wider family itself or from circle of intimate friends.

On the other hand, Ketu motivates others to deal severely with the individual.

If the individual is a medical person, artist, musician, dancer, actor or actress, painter, photographer, designer, writer, poet, journalists, teacher, literary person, private tutor, or runs and/or manages any institution imparting instructions in any of these lines of career, the Ketu and Venus combine would help the individual immensely. Ketu's help is subject to the condition that the individual keeps above board with regard to money and character.

In matters of publication of book, thesis, etc. the writer should stay wary of the women publishers as well as pirates belonging to either gender.

Normally the downtrodden would render help or assistance to the individual in any hour of need, even a brother or sister or cousin of self or spouse might come forward to help, forgiving the past hostile attitude of the individual.

If a female Rasi (Taurus, Cancer, Virgo, Capricorn or Pisces excluding Scorpio) is in the 9th house, the individual's progeny consists of only daughters or more daughters than sons, depending on the stars of the spouse too.

In the case of females, this combination gives pain in the arm or hand or left breast, but helps in recovery of money from relations and friends (not from outsiders). Women associated with religious, charity-oriented or social organisations should try to keep above board, as they would easily fall prey to blackmailers and critics.

Venus in the 10th House

The individual has presentable personality and manner of talking, has expertise in or at least liking for any of the fine arts, painting, music, acting, photography, poetry, and is quick in making friends with unknown persons and foreigners. The individual has taste for imported items even if indigenous products of better quality are available, fond of good company or the company of the opposite sex.

The individual has soft and radiant skin, and makes gestures while talking or extra gestures while dancing. The individual avoids hard games and sports that might cause injury, but in case Mars, Saturn or Rahu is in the 3rd or the 11th house, the individual becomes fond of gambling through chess or card games. He or she might indulge in speculation based on rains and rainy season or on floods and drought, and in rare cases, would indulge in betting at horse races, if facilities exist in the town or city of residence.

These individuals are very fond of trying to know famous actors, actresses, singers and instrumental musicians. Some of them with Mercury in the 5th or the 7th house derive pleasure in talking about romances and bragging about own achievements and failures in no-strings-attached-love and romance.

The individual earns livelihood from any of the subjects mentioned above or the subjects mentioned under Venus in the 1st house. It would sound funny, but sometimes these individuals try to live as parasites on income of wife or other female members of the family of self or spouse. This is particularly true in case Venus has its Rasi (Taurus or Libra) in the 6th or the 12th house, with no hard planet in the 6th or the 11th house.

However if Venus has its Rasi in 1st, 4th, 5th, 9th, 10th or 11th house, the individual would earn livelihood from working for multinational companies or for any foreign firm or Embassy etc. The individual could also earn by trading with foreign countries or by catering to the needs of the foreigners/ artisans/ artists, medical world.

Another main source of income could be functioning as a doctor, *Vaidya* or *Hakim* or curing patients by spiritualism, or running a business in medicine manufacturing or selling or manufacture or sale of musical and medical instruments. It goes without saying that Venus in the 10th house gives better success to all individuals in the medical line or in chemist and druggist business.

Another profession normally given to the individual by Venus in the 10th house is that of working as a career diplomat or politician diplomat or bureaucrat-diplomat, roving ambassador, or getting a job in any outfit of the United Nations or Commonwealth Secretariat. If Jupiter is in conjunction with Venus in the 10th house or Jupiter is situated in the 4th or 7th house, working for the World Bank, International Monetary Fund, Asian Development Bank is also very likely for the individual.

One point has to be noted that Venus in the 10th house gets an individual support from the opposite sex in getting a job or getting promotions in the job so long as the job is in any one of the lines described in the preceding paragraph. It should be noted in the same breath that any harm could also flow to the job or status or prestige from the opposite sex itself, irrespective of the fact whether the individual is a man or woman.

If any soft planet is in the 6th house or a hard planet is in the 8th or the 12th house, the individual should stay faithful to the spouse in physical intimacy or chances of a infection of a sex-oriented disease. This restriction is all the more applicable to those who use their official position as bait for enchanting the opposite sex.

These individuals get easy chances to travel abroad if a watery Sign (Cancer, Pisces, or Aquarius) is in the 10th house, and Venus has favourable relationship with the owner of the 10th house, i.e. *Kendra* or *Trikona* relationship. This is irrespective of the fact whether the lord of the 10th house is a friend or an enemy of Venus.

Venus in the 10th house with malefic influence on it from Mars, Saturn or Rahu in the 3rd or 5th, 9th or 11th house might veer an individual towards smuggling activities, if not actively and directly, then at least indirectly. If nothing else, the individual might help in manufacture, storage, transmission and sale of these contrabands. If one hard planet is in any of these houses mentioned here and another hard planet be in the 12th house, the individual is likely to be booked for offence connected with smuggling, some time of the other.

Another activity connected with the same position of stars is trade in flesh, managing or helping in running a brothel, or trade in call girls (or call boys, which is also assuming the shape of a trade in some white and developed countries). However in this matter, booking of the individual by any law agency would confront him or her, only if Jupiter is in the 6th, 8th or 12th house.

Yet another result of Venus in the 10th house is that the individual would not hesitate in using the influence or personality or connections of the mother, step mother, adopting mother or any woman of the status of a mother for furthering the individual's prospects in profession, job or business. However the scope of such use or misuse is very limited and restricted in self-employment

One special point to be noted with reference to the 10th house is that in respect of every House (other than the 10th house) in the Birth-chart, the elements of mahadasa, antardasa, transit of slow moving planets and the position of stars (with special emphasis on Muntha in the Yearly-chart) count a lot.

In case of 10th house these elements assume much greater importance and relevance for determining progress and prospects, or even run down in source of income, and also for fixing the periodicity of progress or run down taking place.

Venus and Sun, Moon, Mars, Mercury or Jupiter in the 10th House

Please refer to the relevant chapters earlier on each of these stars in the 10th house, which contain sub-heads dealing with combination of Venus with each of these five planets in the 10th house.

Venus and Saturn in the 10th House

Saturn and Venus combine in the 10th house brings into focus all unfairness, dishonesty, cleverness, cunningness, wickedness, illegal touch to the source of earning or livelihood of the individual, with special effort to keep out of the dragnet of law and order machinery.

It is noticed that unless Jupiter is in the 6th or 8th house or Mars is in the 12th house, the individual manages to remain outside the dragnet of law and order despite above type of activity.

These individuals rarely follow the line of profession or main source of livelihood of the father and/or mother or any of the grandparents. The individual finds or makes own path, good or bad, fair or unfair, socially prestigious or non-prestigious. The main aim and ambition is to earn well and live with standards.

In this process of pursuing different line of livelihood or

earning apart from parents or grandparents, sometimes the individual suffers the disapproval of the elders in the family, which might lead to grave differences of opinion or separation between parents and the individual, before marriage or after marriage. Saturn (without bothering about its conjunction with Venus) might lead even to parents disinheriting the individual. Sometimes it makes a difference for the individual, sometimes it makes none at all, and even if it makes a difference, the individual struggles and doesn't bother about being disinherited.

In cases where the mother or step mother or the adopting mother owns substantial moveable or immovable assets (including property), matters and relationship might go worse than just parting of ways. It might lead to be a severe dispute between the mother and the individual. And in case Jupiter is in the 6th or 12th house, the dispute would assume legal angle for solution. This question should be considered with due insight on the 9th house, and if the astrologer is sure about own findings, it is better to caution the mother or the individual before time.

As discussed earlier with relation to the 9th house, if Mars or Rahu be in the 9th house (in this paragraph we are discussing Saturn's conjunction with Venus in the 10th house), chances of a serious dispute between mother and the individual are rather strong. If the mother's chart too has adverse influences in this behalf, matters might go from worse to worst.

However in this regard due attention be paid to the transit of Saturn vis-à-vis the mahadasa and antardasa in the horoscope of the individual. If mother's horoscope too is available, her birth chart and Navamsha, as well as her mahadasa and antardasa be taken into consideration. Then a comparative study of the stars of the individual and mother would give the correct picture for accurate predictions.

In so far as the astrologer is concerned, he or she should be honest to the planetary influences in horoscope of both, individual and mother, but at the same time, the astrologer should not advise in a manner that might aggravate the problem.

Further instances have been noticed when whether dispute

or no dispute, in event of illness or any serious disease or an accident or an injury, sometimes the individual or the parent is unable to tend to the sick parent or child respectively. Reasons could be many, including circumstances beyond control or bitterness or strain in mutual relationship or an atmosphere of distrust too on the two sides.

Another very important influence of this combination in the 10th house is that the individual is deprived of the love, care and guardianship of one of the parents before the individual reaches the age of 23 years. The periodicity of this point depends on mahadasa, antardasa and transit of Saturn, and Saturn's position in the Yearly-chart of the individual concerned.

In case the individual is in politics or trade union or any other kind of public leadership, she or he would achieve success by mixed fair and unfair efforts. These efforts would sometimes get exposed and condemned by the public, moreso if very unfavourable antardasa is running or Saturn or Rahu (or to some extent Jupiter) is unfavourable in transit or in the Yearly-chart.

One special point to be noted is that as compared to all other Houses, the 10th house gets very much affected, for good or for bad, by transit of long-term stars. The placements of important stars in the Yearly-chart also affect it with emphasis on Muntha (rotation of the Janma Lagna in the Yearly-chart).

Venus and Rahu in the 10th House

When Rahu is in combination with Venus in the 10th house, Rahu doesn't have much control over functioning of Venus in the 10th house, except that it creates a shadow of doubt in the mind of the individual about results of own acts of commission and omission.

It also creates a doubt in the minds of others about the work and character of the individual. Sometimes it delays the results of good or bad acts and actions of the individual. It creates a shadow of disloyalty in the mutual relations between the individual and the parents, more with the father than with mother (while if Saturn in 10th house with Venus it does so with the mother or motherly person).

In case the individual is in a public service or in a public sector service (including banks and insurance companies) a shadow of doubt might be created during the mahadasa or antardasa of Rahu itself or antardasa of Saturn or Mars in Rahu mahadasa or vice versa, on the integrity of the individual. It could be on account of the individual's public dealings or morality of character.

It is always better to caution the individual in this behalf, well in advance, because if Jupiter is in transit over the 6th or the 12th house, formal enquiry might be instituted against the individual. Chances are there that the enquiry might lead to legal action or punishment by the department or the appointing authority.

Another typical phenomenon is that Rahu and Venus combine would give extra weight to the spouse, which might ultimately lead to some serious illness, all the more so if the horoscope of the spouse too indicates scope for obesity.

However this combination indirectly helps the progeny in educational and career matters, especially the one who has own favourable stars for education and career.

In matters of gratification and politics, these individuals often face unfulfilled promises by others to them and also by themselves to others. The account is normalised, though this game doesn't happen between the individual and the same "others"; it could be different people, different times, different fields of activity. This rule applies to question of bribes and cheating too.

Rahu and Venus combine generally do not cause loss of one of the parents before the age of 23 years of the individual, as stated above in the case Venus and Saturn combine in the 10th house. But it is very likely that for one reason or the other, someone other than the natural parents might bring up the individual in infancy, childhood and sometimes in years of adolescence. The individual might be put into a boarding school, or owing to circumstances, the individual might have to stay separately from the natural parent(s).

Venus and Ketu in the 10th House

When in combination with Venus in the 10th house, Ketu doesn't interfere at all in the functioning of Venus in that house; rather Ketu supports influence of Venus in every matter and in every field of activity.

In case the individual is capable and competent to produce any literary work or gain efficiency in any fine art or acting or dance or music or painting or photography, in knowledge and application of mantras, in architectural planning, sculpture, practice of medical science, manufacture and sale of medicines and herbs, Ketu simply helps the individual all the way. Ketu also helps Venus bring good publicity and popularity to the individual.

This combination doesn't disturb the individual's relations with either of the two parents of self or spouse, but if any others stars do disturb the relationships, this combination would stay a moot spectator, taking no sides.

If the spouse of the individual is active in bringing normalcy or additional strain in the relations between the individual and one parent or both, these two stars in combination would stay neutral even then. They would allow the spouse and parents to settle disputes, and assume normalcy in attitudes mutually between them.

In the same indifferent manner, Ketu (with Venus in 10th house) would not take any active part in disputes related to family property. However if the property is acquired by the individual or spouse thereof or both, by joint efforts and finances, Ketu would help in favour of the individual or the spouse or both.

These two stars would however be active in social and charitable work for public welfare and service to commoners without reservation on account of colour, caste or community etc. Both are liberal and intellectual stars and open-minded to one and all.

VENUS IN THE 11TH HOUSE

Venus gives good income with continuity, but well-earned income only, rather fairly earned income from any of the sources which have been described in the above paragraphs pertaining to the 1st house and the 10th house. This includes any branch of the fine arts including music, dance, acting, producing films and serials, practice in medical sciences, manufacture and sale of medicines and herbs, dyeing of cotton, silk, woollen yarn, or business in cloth, yarn, ready-to-wear garments and/or wool or woollen items.

It also includes silk and silken items, production by handlooms and/or powerlooms or textile mills of cotton, woollen, silk cloth or that of artificial silk or of woollen waste or of jute or hessian. Sources of income made available to the individual by Venus in the 10th house would include all kinds of paper and paper products, (though not plastic items, as plastic is ruled by Jupiter).

Venus gives good-looking, sharp featured, better than average complexioned spouses to the progeny of the individual. If the stars of the concerned child are helpful, the spouse might be a doctor (in any branch of medicine or medical science or *Vaidya*-system, *Unani* system, *Hakimi* system), or an actor, actress, musician, dancer, painter, photographer, with proper education and qualifications or expertise.

However it may be noted that in case the stars of the concerned child are countermanding the stars of the individual, the above rule might not apply or apply only in a casual manner.

Normally the spouse of the child of the individual would have earning capacity and qualification, actually depending on the stars of the child and spouse thereof.

In some rare cases, Venus in the 11th house brings to the individual an enemy of the individual's enemy for establishing friendly relations with the individual, making true the saying that 'An Enemy's Enemy is a Friend'.

In the modern world of quick break-ups of marriages made on earth itself (Heavens doesn't have scope now for providing life partners for more than two billion human beings), Venus creates adaptability in the mind of the spouse of the individual for step children of the previous marriage of either or of both.

Venus gives politicians and to persons working in the field of films and fine arts a typical greed for the money, assets and property of the spouse, notwithstanding the legal position in the matter.

Venus gives or at least creates the ground for, differences between the mother of the individual and spouse(s) of the child(ren) of the individual, which means differences between grandmother and granddaughters-in-law or grand sons-in-law. It happens rarely but in case Venus is alone in the 11th house and owns the 4th, 5th or the 11th house, this situation is very much possible, though it might last for a short while owing to separate living of grandparents and of grandchildren after their marriages.

In case the individual or any member of the immediate family of the individual is given to drinks or use of drugs (including *Bhang*, *Ganja* etc.), Venus gives the individual a tendency to drink or have drugs at the cost of others.

Venus and Sun, Moon, Mars, Mercury or Jupiter in the 11th House

Reference is invited to relevant chapters earlier in regard to each of these planets in the 11th house, which contain sub-heading dealing with combination of Venus with each of these five planets in the 11th house.

Venus and Saturn in the 11th House

The combination of Venus and Saturn in the 11th house gives a clear-cut touch of unfair and unearned income for the individual, moreso if the individual is a technocrat, scientist, artist, or is a woman.

Saturn may generate side-income by illegal gratification and bribes in cash and kinds, particularly if mahadasa of Saturn falls in the earning years of the individual. When Venus mahadasa runs, the tendency for unearned/ unfair income finds origin during Antardasas from Rahu or Saturn.

As Rahu often gives the results similar to that of Saturn, though less serious in nature, the tendency for bribes and illegal gratification, profiteering, hoarding, under-invoicing and over-invoicing are likely to crop up during Rahu mahadasa too, if it falls during the earning years of the individual.

It is often likely that the individual is qualified or competent or capable for practice in medicine only. But the individual may try to dabble in surgery, orthopaedics and medical termination of pregnancies by physically or surgically operated methods, and may become responsible for death of a patient or at least in creating serious health problems for the patient, on failure of the treatment by the individual in this line.

Another field that these individuals operate is in means of communications by use of latest techniques and scientific methods, and they make very lucrative earnings thereby.

This combination brings the individual in contact with smugglers, particularly those operating between lands separated by sea or ocean. The individuals themselves might not indulge directly in it, but they derive benefits therefrom either by association and providing shelter or by storing and disposing of the contraband. The contraband might consist of opium and other dangerous drugs. It might even be a connection with trade in flesh and smuggling of girls and milch animals.

Another aspect of this combination is that it creates a feeling of distance and jealousy between the grandparents and the grandchildren and/or their spouses, and if it is so, the grandparents are at the losing end, especially the grand mothers.

In such cases, the children of the previous marriage in the case of a second or third marriage, the stepchildren are rather unacceptable to the second or third spouse of the individual. And as stated in the preceding paragraph, there is chance of lack of harmony and affection between the grandparents and grandchildren. Thus if the children from the previous marriage are minors at the time of second or third marriage of the individual, the children of the previous marriage are real sufferers in their childhood and adolescent years of growth, sometimes with and sometimes without after-effects, which can be determined by the horoscopes of the concerned child(ren).

Because Saturn is often protective to the individual when in the 11th house, the individual gets ample protection when involved in acts and actions against the law or the society. However if Mars or Jupiter is in the 12th house or Mars in 12th house and Jupiter in 6th or 8th house, or Mars in the 7th house, Saturn might prove unable to provide protection to the individual. It is at least so when Mars or Jupiter is stronger than Venus or Saturn, and Mars or Jupiter is running own mahadasa or antardasa. This point always needs very in-depth study.

This combination interferes in the educational progress of the progeny unless the stars of a particular child are strong against this combination in the horoscope of one of the parents. If the child is sent to a medical institution, it is always better to examine the stars of the child concerned for successful completion of the medical education and subsequent use and utility of that education. There are several instances where after receiving high-class education in medical science, the individual person (no more a child) drifted away from that specialised education and knowledge.

Yet another point for consideration that comes up in this context is the question of love affair or love-based marriage of a child of the individual. Normally the individual adopts hostile attitude in this matter under pressure from Saturn, which is overriding the presence of Venus in the same 11th house. In such cases it is always better to examine the stars of the child concerned, and also those of the spouse of the individual (parent) who has Saturn (with Venus) in the 11th house.

Unless there are serious reservations about the success of the marriage itself owing to nature, education, culture and family background of one of the two in the love affair, the individual should give up the hostile attitude. If nothing else, a neutral attitude should be adopted by the individual in this matter.

In some cases, especially if a Rasi owned by Venus or Saturn is in the 4th house, the individual becomes critical of the food served, and passes critical remarks on this, which hurt the feelings of the person(s) who prepared or served the food. And once this habit develops, the individual forgets the occasion and the host(s) when the critical remarks are passed, and if mother or any motherly woman is concerned with the preparation or serving of the food, it creates a gulf between the mother and the individual, though often temporarily.

Venus and Rahu in the 11th House

The combination of Venus and Rahu in the 11th house normally gives, to a reduced degree, most of the results described in the above paragraphs relating to Venus and Saturn combine in the 11th house.

The only difference is that the results are not so severe nor so harming nor so hurting. This combine would cast a shadow disturbance in the educational progress of a child, create temporary differences of opinion on the point of love affair or love-based marriage of any of the children.

These two stars together would give a touch of unfair and unearned nature to the income of the individual and a distant connection with people indulging in smuggling or other activity against the given law of the land.

It would give casual and intermittent strain in the relations between grandparents and grandchildren, not with any mentionable after effect.

This combination provides protection against any legal action, but the protection is neither substantial nor stable, and gives way under pressure of investigation and interrogation.

Sometimes ego of the individual stands between the individual and his own progeny or stepchildren and their spouses.

This combination encourages bragging habit of the individual about own personality and physical charms, whether they exist or not! The individual develops a tendency for kind of cheap romantic talks and jokes, and when this becomes a habit, the individual forgets the time, place and the occasion. It often hurts the feelings of the individual's mother (if alive) and other motherly females in the family.

The individual becomes critical about the food served and the unseeming remarks badly hurt the feelings of the person(s) who had cooked or served the food.

Venus and Ketu in the 11th House

Ketu's company with Venus in the 11th house doesn't disturb the functioning of Venus.

However, Ketu does keep a mental account of the acts and actions of the individual under Venus in the 11th house, and when any occasion or opportunity arises, Ketu reminds the individual of past acts and actions, even utterances. Thus any unsavoury habits of the individual is monitored and improvement gets effected.

Further, this combination helps the progeny of the individual in their studies, moreso in attending to home work and written exercises during school education. It also helps improve the handwriting of the progeny if the number of children is limited to two.

If any other star has strained individual's relations with mother, step-mother or any motherly female, this combination helps improvement in the mutual relations. Furthermore, mother or step mother often guides the individual against indulgence in objectionable or such acts and actions as are against the word and spirit of the law of the land or of the civic laws and regulations.

It is very rarely and that too under pressure of other hard stars that this combination gives any undesirable or unfavourable results to the individual. No doubt, it approves intention and plan of the individual and/or spouse for medical termination of pregnancy, and sometimes, Ketu brings about natural loss of pregnancy.

VENUS IN THE 12TH HOUSE

This is a very tricky position for this soft star, and it intentionally imposes unfavourable results on the individual. It leads towards a third angle in married life or a love affair. It gives romantic touch to the very nature of the person. Even slightest pressure or indication from any friend leads the individual to drinks or any other kind of intoxication. It gives a tendency of dissatisfaction over financial position, standard of living, and social status (desiring much more than due or deserving).

It gives greed for gifts in kind instead of cash and expects the gifts to be richer than the capacity or intention of the giver. In case the individual gets involved in any matter leading to investigation or interrogation, the individual surrenders to pressure and torture very easily, rather quickly too. These individuals, by a little persuasion become approvers in criminal cases, and do not hesitate to change sides and change their version in civil cases.

They are generally apt to be won over in matters of election or voting, whether it is for political offices or at general body meetings of industrial and commercial companies, under the slight influence of wine and allied facility.

They may be lured into smuggling and flesh trade, but are not always dependable and trustworthy for the reasons given in the preceding paragraph. Some are good at music, dance, and any branch of the fine arts, architecture, sculpture, but do not hesitate in jumping a contract or agreement or even a bond for work. They (either sex) work well when in the company of the opposite sex, even if they keep romanticism away in that company.

There are often differences between the individual and the progeny over style and standard of living and any romanticism on part of the individual. Differences crop up also over love affair of the progeny during educational stage, but generally these differences are temporary in nature and do not bring about any separatist tendency in the progeny.

It has been discussed above that Venus in the 12th house generally brings extra-marital affair in the life of the individual or at least casual physical involvement or indulgence here and there, certainly outside the knowledge of the spouse. It can be a third angle in a love affair of unmarried boy or girl. Unless there is Aries, Leo or Capricorn or Aquarius is in the 12th house, sooner or later, the third angle becomes known to the person(s) concerned. Then the question arises of either adjustment by the adversely affected partner to the marriage or end of the love affair or of separation, if not legally, at least physically between the married couple or the lovers. Very few people realise that Venus in the 12th house can also bring failure of marriage, even without adverse impact of Mars/ Saturn or Rahu on the married life from 1st, 4th, 7th, 8th or 12th house.

Another on the side and rare influence of Venus in the 12th house is that it gives less sex drive to the male individual for physical indulgence with wife or beloved. The issue of dissatisfaction of the wife, therefore, often looms large on the marriage.

If the basic birthchart has Taurus, Libra or Virgo in the 4th or the 5th house, chances are for regaining the sex drive for mutual satisfaction. However, if a Rasi owned by a hard planet like Mars or Saturn is in the 4th or 5th house, medical treatment brings about some marginal improvement in the male partner.

While matching horoscopes for marriage purposes, the astrologer should invariably examine this point if Venus is in the 8th or the 12th house without company of other stars there. However it is in very rare cases that Venus in the 12th house of the male comes in the way of getting progeny; normally at least one child is sure. There are cases where couples in similar situation could beget four children!

If a Rasi owned by Venus or Mercury is in the 6th or 8th house, and if the individual takes to drinking on a regular basis, it would adversely affect his sex life, more or less positively after the age of 36 years. It has to be noted that Venus in 12th house gives a male immense desire for physical relationship with opposite sex, but it is no proof of a robust sexual life.

Generally Venus in the 12th house doesn't lead an individual towards debts unless drinks or drugs or intoxication of any kind on regular basis overtake the habits of the individual.

Venus and Sun, Moon, Mars, Mercury or Jupiter in the 12th House

Relevant chapters earlier on each of these planets in the 12th house contain sub-headings which deal with combination of Venus with each of these five planets in the 12th house, which may please be referred to.

Venus and Saturn in the 12th House

The combination of Venus and Saturn in the 12th house harms or hurts the interests of the progeny in matters of education, development of personality and quick settlement in life (career etc).

Sometimes there is delay in the individual be-getting children. Loss of pregnancy naturally or by medical method is not ruled out. Sometimes complexion and features of any one of the first two children are far removed from either parent but of course any doubts on this score are baseless.

This combination may lead an individual to bad company and getting dominated by such bad company even in matters concerning the family and management of money. The results include incurring debts, unmindful of repaying the debts, distrust over members of family of self and spouse, and forcing wife to undergo a medical termination of pregnancy. It also includes spending more of spare time outdoors and among friends than with family and at home; disobedience to mother, infidelity by clandestinely having a third angle to the married life.

These individuals also indulge in wasteful expenditure even by incurring debts for the purpose. They have no hitch in indulging in injustice, when holding a position or post of power (be it political or executive or judicial). They tend to earn by unfair means, keep secrecy of money matters from spouse and other members of the immediate family.

Another aspect of this combination is that it can give complaints of health relating to ear, nose and throat in the childhood, sex transmitted complaints in youth, and problems relating to bones at the start of old age, which might include difficulty in walking and free movements of the body. Whenever Saturn is in the 12th house by transit or Saturn has its own mahadasa or antardasa in mahadasa of Sun, Mars or Venus, it is capable of giving fracture of any bone. During Saturn antardasa under mahadasa of Moon (when Moon is in 6th or 8th house), it could be risk from water for the individual, including chances of drowning or financial or material loss by floods, storm, downpour of heavy rains, sinking of boat or ship in deep river, sea or ocean.

Venus and Saturn are capable of exposing the individual to penalty and punishment by law and order system of the land for direct criminal act or abetment to it. If there is a confrontation or conflict at individual's level or at the level of society, community, state or the nation, the individual (if she/ he has the decision-making position of power), would seek path of compromise instead of leading a "fight to the end".

These two stars in the 12th house can make an individual very charitable physically and financially, but in the same breath, entertaining malefic motives too, which ultimately adversely affect the reputation of the individual.

The important point in this context is that Saturn overrules Venus, whatever house they are situated in, and thus Saturn brings loss of reputation to the individual, whatever the reason thereof. Sometimes the kith and kin of the individual or colleagues and friends create the situation for loss of reputation, or at least they spread the loss of reputation.

Venus and Rahu in the 12th House

Rahu is generally not very effective in the 12th house when with Venus. At the most, it disturbs in a mild manner education of the progeny, leads to boastful expenditure coated with miserliness, exhibition of ego amongst friends and wider family, bragging about achievements of self (whether on merit or without merit).

It also gives drinking habit within limits of self-control, ideas and talks of romanticism but often not actual indulgence, and differences with parents of self or spouse after marriage of self.

However Rahu rarely leads to any serious or widespread loss of reputation, and even if there is any mild loss of reputation, people quickly forget it, leaving no mark behind. Rahu with Venus in the 12th house can give sexually transmitted complaints of health, but often of recoverable nature, not serious or long lasted, because Rahu with Venus gives physical contact only with personally intimately known members of the opposite sex.

Venus and Ketu in the 12th House

The results of Venus and Ketu combination in the 12th house are more or less the same as described above in the preceding paragraph under Venus and Rahu combine in 12th house.

The only additional point is that Ketu and Venus in the 12th House cause ill health to the individual now and then, chronically without being life threatening, especially relating to bad stomach, bad throat, congestion in chest owing to cold.

Ketu with Venus can give indebtedness, though of manageable nature, and also intention to repay at the first convenience of the individual.

SATURN IN THE 12 HOUSES

SATURN IN GENERAL

It should be noted that Saturn is a hard planet. It doesn't fail to give results under influence of any planet, not even when it is combust in conjunction with Sun, because Saturn is deemed to be son of the Sun. Every father wishes that the son may prove better in every respect when compared with father. Even in Sanskrit there is a very famous saying:

"Parajayam ichchet Putraadapi Sishyaadapi"

(meaning –'wish for a defeat by your son, or by your student, or disciple'). Only two other planets compare to Saturn in force (strength) and influence, viz., Mars and Rahu. Rahu is a shadow planet, and whenever it is in conjunction with Saturn, Rahu enhances the force (strength) and influence of Saturn, because Rahu is 100% on pattern of Saturn in every matter, whatever it may be.

Saturn is deemed to be a messenger (a rather dignified term used in place of "a labourer"!) among the planets. Because of this classification, Saturn is lord of communications (of every mode and every type, every method), ruler of the labour class, guide and protector of the down-trodden, and of the sufferer-community in social framework. It is also the master of iron and steel, as well as gas (petrol), all kind of edible and mechanical oils, bone-structure in body including bone-frame of the skull. It is common knowledge that a body can survive and work without much flesh or muscle, but it cannot exist without blood and bones.

It is apparent that Mars is the only other solid planet to stand comparison to Saturn, and often both Mars and Saturn work in co-operation. For example, in every communication system, power (electricity), ruled by Mars, is basically needed. And similarly where the body is concerned, Mars rules the blood system and also the 'fabric-cover' of the blood and bones in the shape of skin. In turn, Saturn rules hair on the skin. Mars and Saturn are die-hard enemies but they function in co-operation for helping the animal and human life on the surface of the earth. It might seem odd, but that is the truth, astrologically. Mars is the lord of earth, while Saturn is the lord of mountains, rocks, stones and dust found on Earth. Thus, these two bitter enemies working in coordination with each other for the sake of others.

It is also noteworthy that Saturn is the slowest planet among all those planets that are astrologically recognised for consideration. Though Herschel, Neptune and Pluto move considerably slower than Saturn, but being very far away removed from earth, these three stars do not affect an individual's affairs and life. Although Herschel and Neptune do affect major events in the sky and on the earth, like earthquake, tornado, landslides, large-scale fire (specially in jungles), heavy floods, and the like.

Saturn takes, on an average, two-and-a-half years in transit movement from one Rasi to the next, and completes a round of all the twelve Rasis in roughly 28 to 30 years. Comparatively, Sun normally takes 1 month, Moon 2.25 days, Mars 1.5 months (except when it goes retrograde, then it takes from 6 to 8 months). Similarly, Mercury one month, Jupiter 12 to 12.5 months (13 years to complete a round of the 12 Rasis), Venus 1 month, and even shadow planets Rahu and Ketu take 18 months each, to move from one Rasi to the next Rasi.

While giving predictions about Saturn, one more very important point should be borne in mind. It is about *"Saturn Saadhe-saati"* (more or less 7.5 years' of adverse impact of Saturn's transit over the 12th position from Janma Rasi (Moon's position in Birth-chart), over the Janma Rasi itself and over the 2nd house. In major portion, good or bad results of this 7.5 years phase of Saturn's transit depends on Saturn's position in the Birth-chart (Bhava-Chalitam position) and Saturn's position in the Navamsha-chart too (Trinshansha-chart in case of females).

God Almighty has been kind to the human beings that a Saturn *Saadhe-saati* repeats after a cycle of about 28 to 29 years;

and normally an individual undergoes a maximum three (at the most 4 if anyone had *Saadhe-saati* in childhood) *Saadhe-saatis* in a life time. (The topic of *Saadhe-saatis* has been discussed in detail in our book Star Guide® to Saturn - Transit of Saturn in the 12 Rasis)

IMPORTANT NOTE: since combination of Saturn with Sun, Moon, Mars, Mercury, Jupiter and Venus has been dealt with in each house under the relevant sub-headings in the relative chapter earlier on each of these six planets, the authors' remarks for referring to the concerned chapters earlier on each of the six planets is not being repeated below every house discussions about Saturn.

SATURN IN THE 1ST HOUSE

This is one of the most important positions of Saturn, and since it very much affects the formation of an individual's personality, this position of Saturn assumes importance amongst all other stars occupying the 1st House.

The individual suffers ill health in one manner or the other in childhood, depending upon the family tradition of ill health. Further in childhood, the individual sometimes suffers from constipation or weak digestive system. But the individual very rarely suffers from over-dose of any kind of illness, sufferings, etc.

The individual gets provoked easily and under strong provocation, doesn't hesitate to take serious physical risks. Apart from that the individual is fearless and violent without much preview of the risk involved.

The individual is of firm determination, which in other words can be called obstinacy, rigidity, and stubbornness. The individual doesn't keep many goals in mind during formative years, has only one aim in mind, at least upto the age of 23 years, and pursues that aim with full force, vigour, and undivided attention.

The individual listens to advice and guidance given by one and all, but follows own course of action, after arriving at a decision based on own thinking plus essence of advice and guidance received from others. One important point is that no one can take this individual for granted, and he or she doesn't become a "pocket edition" of anyone, whatever that other person's superior qualities, knowledge, learning, status, achievements, physical strength, and capacity to cause harm/damage.

The individual has the mental and physical capacity and countenance to maintain dignity even in worst possible circumstances.

The individual is rarely impressively dressed, believes more in development of personal qualities securing respect from others on basis of qualities and not based on dress and outer appearance. The individual is polite and respectful to those who deserve it, but not to bogus persons and impostors.

These individuals have a weakness for the opposite sex, because sitting in the 1st House, Saturn has direct and more likely full *drishti* (aspect) on the 7th house. It is likely that they do not have much of physical indulgence, but may often earn a bad name for this weakness.

These individuals are a bit careless about upkeep of their hair, talk a lot, and shift from one topic to another quickly, anxious to exhibit their knowledge and experience to impress the listener with variety of subjects. But in the same breath, they keep notice of the fact whether the listener is interested in listening or not. One of the best qualities of these individuals is their capacity for secrecy, and therefore best suited for functioning as a spy, intelligence agent, person meant for secret investigations, secret messenger between individuals, envoy/ambassador, suitable for commercial intelligence and similar allied jobs. It is not easy to win over these individuals by attractions of money, assets, facilities or even sex; they stay more or less duty bound. However one unfavourable point for these individuals is that very often others pirate the credit for the good work done by these individuals. They mind it but do not bother to take remedial action.

Thus brings us to the question of their friendship. These individuals remain good, sincere and dependable friends so long as the person(s) opposite do not cheat them, though they do not mind exploitation to a certain extent. These individuals are never keen for "give and take" attitude in friendship. But when they find that the other person is trying to be clever or snobbish, they suddenly cut off the friendship, and very rarely allow it to come back in their life. They are often selfless to an extent but do not sacrifice that selflessness at the altar of cheating and cunningness.

Some people might be under the impression that because Saturn is a technical star, these individuals might grow into high-class technocrats. No, it is very rarely so, and it depends on several other factors such as what Rasi is in the 1st house, where the Rasi Capricorn and Aquarius (owned by Saturn) are positioned in the Birth-chart. Also, what matters is the Navamsha of Saturn, and what other stars are in the company of Saturn or otherwise associated with it. No doubt, if these individuals learn science or any technical subject, they gain good command on the subject, because of their undivided study and approach to the subject matter before them gives them efficiency over that subject. They also know from where or whom to get hold of the best and updated knowledge about that subject.

These individuals make successful industrialists. Even as an employee on the management side in any industrial unit, they give a very good account of themselves in management of production and labour force.

Saturn and Sun, Moon, Mars, Mercury, Jupiter or Venus in the 1st House

Respective chapters on Sun, Moon, Mars, Mercury, Jupiter, and Venus under the relevant sub-headings for the 1st house may please be referred to.

Saturn and Rahu in the 1st House

Since Saturn's combination or conjunction with other stars has been discussed in the relevant chapters relating to those stars, now Saturn's combination with Rahu and Ketu only has to be discussed in all the 12 house, starting with the 1st house.

This combination gives a very sharp sense of ego, self-confidence, self-respect, because Saturn alone too gives a strong sense of self-confidence and self-respect to the individual. Therefore Saturn and Rahu together make that sense doubly strong, and in the process the individual suffers severely and several times too.

But the individual would not care about it, and proceed further with fulfilment of aims and ambitions; the individual doesn't sit with bowed head just regretting and repenting over the past. This individual most often looks forward, and looks at the past merely for guidance about the future attitude and actions.

Generally these individuals are "self made" persons, who might have undergone difficulties at the educational stage, and had to find their own path or had to make a path of their own, in matters of settlement in career. This doesn't mean they are 'self-seekers'. No, on the other hand they are more charitable and helpful to one and all, who really deserve it, and these individuals extend help and support more to satisfy their own ego.

Financially too, these individuals rarely seek loans and accommodation, because their ego sits on their nose to make them hesitant to ask for help or loan. They are in most cases accustomed to undergo hardships, and therefore, 'ups' and 'downs' in life do not make much difference to them, because their sense of self respect is neither a borrowed one nor bestowed upon them by others as a favour or alms. At the same time, they are often unable to recover loans or credit-in-business given by them, and it is in their best interests that these individuals conduct their business normally by cash transactions (payments by bank instruments included).

These individuals trust others easily and quickly and thus fall into trap of cheating and piracy by others, whatever their trade, profession or calling or source of income. Because they are more individualistic, even members of their families (including those of the family of the spouse) flatter and exploit them instead of being helpful and serviceful to them. And in an hour of need, these individuals are again ready to help and support those very people who had cheated, pirated or exploited them.

The only relief for them is that they rarely lose their self-confidence and inner power to face the struggle in life.

Saturn and Ketu in the 1ˢᵗ House

The rather important point about this combination is that some of these individuals have literary trends, notwithstanding their educational background or family traditions. If the support of Mercury or Jupiter is available to this combination, these persons turn out to be good authors, journalists, public speakers, ghost writers for politicians and other so-called great people. They can become good '*katha-vaachaks*', priests (whatever religion they follow or preach), office bearers in administrative *panchayats* or *panchayats* of their own community or tribe. And in this *panchayat* position, they are known for their impartiality, honesty of purpose, sense of equity and fairness. However they are not very verbose in their decisions and judgements.

If these individuals have piles in the family history on father's side or the mother's side, they must take preventive steps, whatever country or climate they reside or work.

Their talents as writer, journalist, ghost-writer or *panchayat* office-bearer often develops and gives results in declining years of age, say after the age of 46.

Please refer to the relevant chapters earlier on each of these planets, which contain sub-headings dealing with combination of Saturn with each of these six planets in the 1ˢᵗ house.

SATURN IN THE 2ᴺᴰ HOUSE

While examining this position of Saturn, it has to be borne in mind that it is the 8ᵗʰ place from the 7ᵗʰ House which rules marriage, love affair, married life and relationship with spouse. Further 8ᵗʰ position from any house is considered harmful to that particular house. Thus Saturn often affects the 7ᵗʰ house adversely, especially when Saturn is in transit over the 2ⁿᵈ house (which is normally after about every 28 years), or when Saturn's mahadasa or antardasa is currently running. Whenever it is so, it is always beneficial to predictions to take into co-ordinated consideration the Saturn's position in the Yearly-chart.

In case Saturn is unfavourably placed in the Yearly-chart

too, and adverse relationship is reflected between Saturn and other stars whose mahadasa or antardasa be current during that period, special precaution and preventive measures would be needed for continuance of happy relationship between husband and wife. Steps would also be needed for prevention of any health problem to the spouse.

Further Saturn's 2nd house position sometimes brings in violence in the relationship between husband and wife, all the more so, chances thereof if the 2nd, 7th or 8th house in the horoscope of the spouse has similar star-elements. And violence or no violence between the husband and wife, Saturn's transit over the 2nd house or its antardasa in an adversary's mahadasa can give problems of health to the spouse. These problems would include bone injury, sprain or severe injury to the foot, any other kind of pain to the legs/feet/waist line/lower spine bone as might create difficulty in free and fast movement of the spouse.

However in case Capricorn is in the 1st house, Saturn's position in the 2nd house would be in its own Rasi (Aquarius), and thus it would be less harmful to the spouse. On the other hand, if Capricorn is in the 7th house, it would be Leo in the 2nd house, and then adverse effect to the spouse would be somewhat more serious.

If Aries or Scorpio is in the 2nd house with Saturn in it, the spouse has to be preventive against fire, skin ailment, headache, eyesight, electricity, acids, inflammables and such injury as would cause bleeding. This precaution is more required if Saturn has its antardasa under Mars mahadasa or Mars has its antardasa under Saturn mahadasa.

Saturn in the 2nd house normally gives slow and steady growth of savings, build-up of money and other assets, chances of starting and running any manufacturing or industrial venture. If Saturn happens to own the 11th or 12th house and is in the 2nd house, Saturn becomes all the more beneficial to the individual in matters of savings, money and assets. Sometimes, depending on their own stars, brothers, sisters and cousins expect and receive moral and monetary help/support from the individual, who rarely denies it so long as own condition and affairs afford scope for doing so. In rare cases the individual has to suffer indirect or direct jealousy and envy from these blood relations of self or spouse.

Individuals with Saturn in the 2nd house should take preventive steps against natural loss of pregnancy, and should avoid medical termination of pregnancy as either way it would be injurious to the health of the wife in the long run.

Saturn in the 2nd provides protection against jealousy, blackmail, criticism, or any other harmful action against the individual holding any office in social, charitable or educational establishment.

These individuals do not become diehard enemies on their own, though they do retaliate any physical or moral attack on them. However this theory doesn't apply in the case of their spouse, where the individuals are hard and difficult even if the spouse doesn't deserve it.

These individuals normally get long life, notwithstanding the fact whether they are physically fit for active work or are crippled by old age with this or that complaint of health. Saturn has nothing much to do with the longevity of the spouse, that would depend on the stars of the spouse.

These individuals, when in active politics generally adopt very rigid approach to any personal or social or communal or national matter, and instead of appreciating reason, they try to find out supporters to their viewpoint or their stand.

Normally these individuals are very calculative in spending money or giving money to their own children or giving charity or financial help to needy students. They want full justification for the money demanded or needed.

An individual with Saturn in the 2nd house speaks, when in anger or in a quarrel or in rebuking mood or when threatening, in very measured tone, subdued but firm, creating a sense of fear in the mind of the party opposite

Saturn and Sun, Moon, Mars, Mercury, Jupiter or Venus in the 2nd House

Respective chapters on Sun, Moon, Mars, Mercury, Jupiter, and Venus under the relevant sub-headings for 2nd house may please be referred to.

Saturn and Rahu in the 2nd House

Though Rahu belongs to Saturn's group, and is a shadow star only, in the company of Saturn, it does wield power to interfere with good or bad results of Saturn.

For example, Saturn alone makes the individual criticism-oriented and with a violent attitude towards the spouse, Rahu diminishes the force behind the criticism or violence. In so far as any ailment, disease or injury to any bone or problem in the health of the spouse is concerned, Rahu makes it curable quickly and rather easily.

Some astrologers hold the view that Rahu, being a friend and associate of Saturn, increases the force in criticism or violence or adds to ailment, disease or injury etc., but practical experience shows that it is not so.

No doubt, Rahu adds a few pounds to the body weight of the spouse without degrading the personality or physical appearance of the spouse, unless spouse has stars of own to do so.

Saturn, when alone in the 2nd, sometimes starves the spouse for money but Rahu serves as a remedy to it and keeps routinely needed funds in the hands of the spouse too. At the same time, Rahu helps in scrutinising the demands and actual needs of brothers, sisters and cousins, and sees to it that no unwanted money goes to any of them.

Further Rahu induces the individual to become popular with downtrodden and those living below the poverty line, whatever country of residence, and it encourages Saturn to extend financial help to these sections of the society.

In the same breath, Rahu injects some flexibility into the rigid approach and stubborn stand of the individual in political matters, and thereby saves the face and position of the individual in active politics.

In case the natural mother or step/foster/adopting mother of the individual has independent income of her own, the individual is sure to get a good portion of it during the lifetime and due share in 'leftover' of mother's assets after her death. Rahu helps in creating a bridge in the strained relations between the individual and natural or step or foster or adopting father that might have been created by Saturn.

In brief it can be said that Rahu neutralises the hard effect of Saturn in the 2nd house.

Saturn and Ketu in the 2nd House

Though in combination with Saturn in the 2nd house, Ketu dare not interfere with the effect of Saturn in that house.

However Ketu does extend some other talents to the individual, such as building up, slowly and gradually, a personal library of the individual, and then encourage the individual towards writing, including ghost writing for others. Ketu develops this talent too slowly and gradually, ultimately leading towards writing book(s).

Ketu brings a touch of culture and courtesy in the tone of the individual when talking in measured tone, subdued and firm, and Ketu reduces its impact of fear on the mind of the party opposite. Whether formally educated or not, Ketu makes an individual learned by experience, and that experience of being learned reflects in the talks and threats of the individual.

These individuals make very competent Press Reporters on crime side, defence matters, and at the battlefields. However, normally these individuals do not prefer to function as a photographer too combined with their job of a reporter.

On the minus side, Ketu is capable of giving complaints of health relating to ear, eye, nose, cheek, throat, teeth and tongue, also lips or an injury on the chin, sometimes leaving a scar behind. It is also capable of giving, even without influence of Saturn's company, piles-related trouble to the spouse, specially if the spouse has any history of this trouble on the father's or mother's side.

Because of their impartiality in nature and work, these individuals do not prove a do-good-press-reporter on political front, burdened with the job of supporting a particular candidate at elections, or defending a guilty politician-in-power.

SATURN IN THE 3RD HOUSE

This is one of the best positions for Saturn. It helps the individual to hard work, gives courage and boldness to face difficulties and hard-line opponents. The strategy adopted by the individual often proves correct and successful. The individual can prove an efficient and result-oriented police officer, defence officer, ordnance scientist, surveyor of enemy areas including enemy's defence formations on the border and within the country. In case posted in the armed forces or paratrooper or bombardier, the individual, whether man or woman, proves efficient and successful in discharge of duties and responsibilities.

The individual often extends a helpful hand to brother, sister or cousin, but does not normally exhibit outwardly love and affection for all of them or some of them. In the same manner, the individual suffers, occasionally only, leg pulling by a brother/sister or cousin. However in this context, one thing is sure – either side doesn't hesitate to render physical service/help to one another as and when needed.

However when Saturn is *"Bhatri-karaka"*(ruler of brother and sister element at birth) in the Karaka chart or Capricorn is in the 3rd house, or Mars is occupying the 9th house and casting full *drishti* on Saturn in the 3rd house, there is risk to the life or limb of the younger brother or sister.

The most important part of the 3rd house Saturn is that this is the 6th position from the 10th house, which rules career, profession, business, job, and means of livelihood. Thus this position of Saturn helps in winning over or wiping out enemies, opponents, adversaries etc., without much burden on the purse. It applies all the more for trade union leaders, scientists, technocrats, industry owners, managers in industrial units, defence and police personnel, pilots, locomotive drivers and technicians working on train. It also applies to persons running large-scale agricultural farms, labour-suppliers and persons running placement services, those in the trading of petrol, lubricants, diesel and allied oils etc., also traders in oilseeds.

This individual commands respect in society for hard work, foresightedness and single-aimed progress.

If an individual runs Saturn mahadasa in the prime of youth, or gets Saturn's antardasa in Venus or Mercury or Jupiter mahadasa when the individual is at the threshold of entering into self-earning, it is almost sure, the individual will achieve best success in his work and livelihood.

Saturn in the 3rd sometimes brings jealousy from uncles, aunts, and spouses of brothers, sisters, cousins, or a brother or sister of the spouse. In the normal course these people are unable to cause any harm or damage to the individual except creating heartburn or anxiety or side-worry. It is always advisable for these individuals not to go into partnership business with any uncle or aunt or possess property in joint names with uncle or aunt. If it is a question of inheritance, it is always better to part company when relations are sweet and soft.

Another important point is that these individuals should always maintain respectable distance with spouses of brothers, sisters and cousins, notwithstanding whether the individual is a man or a woman.

In sports and games, at playgrounds, in adolescent or early youth years, these individuals might cause a serious injury or bone injury to a player on own side or other side or to a spectator. A little extra caution is always better on part of these individuals.

These individuals are normally a charge on the personal purse of the natural or foster or adopting mother, but without hurting her feelings. They rarely lose their due share in inheritance from mother's side, and in some cases they get a lion's share openly or secretly.

In student life and competitions, these individuals do not hesitate in use of unfair means, specially because, they do not deem 'unfair means' as unfair; they actually think everything is fair in Examinations!

Saturn and Sun, Moon, Mars, Mercury, Jupiter or Venus in the 3rd House

Respective chapters on Sun, Moon, Mars, Mercury, Jupiter, and Venus under the relevant sub-headings for 3rd house may please be referred to.

Saturn and Rahu in the 3rd House

The first thing Rahu (with Saturn) would do is to cause loss of one or two pregnancies to mother or loss of a brother or sister, before it attains the age of 12 years or at the most 23 years.

In all other matters, Rahu renders tenderness to the approach of Saturn to men and matters!

However Rahu gives a tendency to the individual to scrutinise the needs of help and support, physical and/or financial or moral, asked for by any blood relation of self, and then give the help or support actually and factually necessary. At the same time Rahu reduces the element of jealousy from uncle, aunt, spouses of own brother and sister as well as brother or sister or cousin of the spouse.

In the field of politics, profession, career, job, business and industrial venture, Rahu and Saturn together become very powerful to win over or wipe out cleverly the enemies, opponents, adversaries and competitors too. Saturn alone doesn't touch the competitors.

Rahu reduces the tendency and element of using unfair means in Exams and competitive tests. It is so because Ketu in the 9th house gives the individual capacity for hard work supported with intelligence for grasp of the subject matter of study.

Rahu however in 3rd house with Saturn encourages the individual to bank too much upon getting extra pocket money secretly from the mother, and when grown up, the desire to get a lion's share in inheritance from mother.

Saturn normally gives very good health even in old age, but Rahu in conjunction with Saturn interferes with Saturn effect, adds fat to body and gives all complaints associated to obesity, and gradually leads the individual to less activity and more laziness. In old age, Rahu slightly but adversely affects the facial expression too.

Saturn and Ketu in the 3rd House

The hard natured individual gets a touch of literature and nobleness on account of Ketu's combination with Saturn in the 3rd house.

Sometimes even defence and police personnel turn out to be good writers or poets. And scientists and technocrats quite often turn into authors with good reviews and reputation.

But Ketu too interferes with one or two pregnancies of the mother, though it doesn't concern itself with death of a brother or sister in infancy.

Ketu doesn't encourage the individual towards use of unfair means in Exams and competitions, nor does it create a tendency to win over or wipe out the enemies and opponents. Ketu rather prevails upon Saturn to "mind own business", and not to bother about others, whether friends or foes.

But one weak point of Ketu in 3rd with Saturn is that it induces Saturn too to become less ruthless and more kind-hearted towards defeated enemy at a battlefield, which tendency doesn't meet with approval of War strategists, specially under influence of the last two World Wars.

SATURN IN THE 4TH HOUSE

A difficult position for the individual! It initially interferes with parental protection to the individual in infancy, childhood and adolescence as also in early youth. The reasons may be many, say separation between father and mother, father going away to distant land for livelihood, father or mother's odd hours of work. Other reasons can be the individual has been given away in adoption, or the individual living with grandparents or uncles or aunts due to family circumstances, or death of one of the parents.

There can be other difficulties too, such as lack of means of the parents for proper education or proper upbringing according to standard of neighbourhood or fellow students in the school. It might be second marriage of father or mother leading to living with a step-parent or step-brothers or step-sisters. These events become all the more bitter and unbearable if Saturn mahadasa runs during childhood or early youth.

If nothing else, Saturn in the 4th house gives differences between individual and one of the parents and the individual is charged with disobedience or other faults by an either parent. Sometimes the question of inheritance creates differences between the individual and both parents. In brief, Saturn is not satisfied unless it gives some kind of unpleasantness to the individual with regard to parents.

If the individual is given into adoption, there too one of the above mentioned problems might crop up. Saturn would not spare the individual where strain in relations with natural or adopted parents is concerned.

The question is that the Bhava-Chalitam should confirm Saturn's position in the 4th house, and if Saturn continues its 4th position in the Navamsha-chart, the situation becomes all the more bitter.

In these circumstances, it is always better to get some religious remedy done for Saturn before the child is 12 years old. Experience shows it does reduce the bad effect of Saturn.

Second stroke likely to be given by Saturn in the 4th house is oft-repeated falls and injuries, even accidents, injury to bone, injury or deformity of one of the testicles, hernia trouble in childhood or early youth. Chances are greater if Saturn mahadasa or Saturn antardasa in Venus/Mercury/Jupiter mahadasa occurs before the age of 23 years.

Then it creates problems in competitions for career or

job, entry into profession, entry into active politics (between the age of 23 and 35 years).

Saturn doesn't feel satisfied after creating problems at the initial stage of entry into livelihood. It does try to give problems and harassment in the course of career, profession, job, industrial venture, business etc. Why is it so? Because Saturn causes harm or damage to the house on which it has full *drishti*, and sitting in the 4th house, it would have full *drishti* on the 10th house, which rules father and livelihood (also politics).

Saturn in the 4th house often makes an individual undertake repeated tours and travels, and then it causes inconvenience to the individual as well as to the family. Accidental injury to the individual or his or her vehicle or mode of transport can not be ruled out, when Saturn is in the 4th house.

Saturn doesn't stop here. It causes inconvenience from domestic servants, other employees and labour, sometimes a domestic help gives up suddenly and next help takes time to arrange, and discomfort descends on the individual or the spouse. Pilferage, embezzlement and sabotage at the hands of employees are also not ruled out. But if the mother is alive, she stays in good stead for the individual in such circumstances.

Saturn gives a tendency for accepting (even extracting) bribes and illegal gratifications in kind rather than cash. For example, a lower division clerk in the Central Public Works Department, whose job was just to deliver payment-cheques to the works-contractors, never took even a single rupee as bribe. And he was able to build a four-storied spacious house merely by begging entire construction material, as also borrowing construction technicians and labour force from the contractors! And he had Saturn and Ketu in the 4th house!

Apart from these nasty points, Saturn gives some very favourable results too. It gives the individual a desire and capacity to undertake construction works for social and charitable purposes, with own money or with the financial and active help and support of others. Such projects include school, college, hospital, dispensary, night homes for needy, shelters for widows and destitute women, drinking water stands, ponds and tanks for humans and cattle, sometimes prayer houses, marriage halls, etc. If the individuals do not have own financial capacity, they appeal to others to provide funds for these purposes. These individuals are no doubt closely associated with and active for these purposes of public utility and public service.

Then these individuals are good fighters at any active battle for the nation or the state. They function as expert and dependable spies and envoys.

They make expert engineers, scientists and technocrats in automobile/locomotive/aeroplane industries, but not much in shipping industry. They are not very efficient teachers, but they make efficient demonstrators, practical surgeons, orthopaedic doctors/technicians, works engineers, craftsmen, masons, architects, sculptors, construction workers for high-rise buildings, roads, bridges, and sometimes dams too if Venus too has some kind of link with Saturn in the 4th house.

They often have the tendency and willingness to help persons in difficulty, flood-affected or earthquake affected people, drought-affected people, masses and cattle suffering in famine conditions. They make their best efforts to provide fodder and other eatables for cattle on death-path in drought and famine conditions.

These individual are normally good friends, they make friends slowly (not at the first sight or first meeting) and they try to be sincere and helpful. At the same time they have a forceful tendency for revenge if a friend does any wrong to them, though they are not so revengeful towards a foe.

They own residential property, either inherited or self acquired, but do not enjoy continuous residence in it, because they reside in a different town or state or country, or in a residence provided by the employer or government or local body.

As are chances, if these individuals are in construction line, they build houses and roads of dependable kind, not just fallible pigeon-holes being constructed these days by Development Authorities in every city and town of India.

These individuals have the facility of conveyance, whether belonging to self or by courtesy of others or employers or neighbours or colleagues. Even then they run the risk of being stranded on road or on train route or at the airport, reasons might be any.

And Saturn's last stroke: these individuals, whether men or women, accumulate extra pounds of flesh around waist line, buttocks and upper thighs, which adversely affects their blood system, might give rise to angina trouble and ultimately to a serious ailment of the heart.

These individuals are neither regular nor prompt in medical treatment of self or of others; they are given to a tendency of taking things easy. They are not very choosy and fault finding about food, moreso after they start living away or apart from natural mother.

It is best for these individuals to go for a walk daily, walk for the sake of walking. It will spare them pain in the waistline and trouble with the spine bone, and help in keeping body weight within prescribed medical limits.

Saturn and Sun, Moon, Mars, Mercury, Jupiter or Venus in the 4th House

Respective chapters on Sun, Moon, Mars, Mercury, Jupiter, and Venus under the relevant sub-headings for 4th house may please be referred

Saturn and Rahu in the 4th House

While in some houses, though rather rarely, conjunction of Rahu and Saturn reduces the impact or force of Saturn's influence in that particular house, but in the 4th house, Rahu enhances the influence of Saturn.

If there are differences or misunderstanding with the natural, foster or adopting mother, Rahu worsens the situation. Further, Rahu adds to the sense of ego and self respect in the mother. It also gives obesity to mother, and creates problems for her in the subsequent pregnancies. If mother owns any substantial jewellery, cash or assets in her name and right, and if she has the full freedom to pass it on to any of her children or to anyone other than her own progeny, the factional fight between mother and the individual would further worsen.

However Rahu's conjunction with Saturn reduces the chances of a fracture of the bone(s) in any accident, fall or slipping down, and even if fractures take place, their degree or volume is not so serious on account of Rahu in the 4th house. Further Rahu helps in quick recovery from the injury and it tries its best to leave no invalidity in the individual on account of the injury. When the individual was in the process of receiving the injury or immediately thereafter, and finds the onlookers laugh or jest at him/her instead of assisting or helping, the individual feels hurt and insulted. The impact then and there is great in adversely affecting the consciousness of the injured individual.

In case the individual gives any assurance or makes any promise for any social, charitable, educational medical facilities/construction to be provided for public use and utility, Saturn might induce the individual to back-out of the assurance or delay the matter. But Rahu inspires the ego of the individual to implement the assurance or promise, as far as possible, within the stipulated period.

Saturn in 4th house disturbs the digestive system and gives fatness to the body of the individual; Rahu's combination worsens this situation. If Mars happens to be in the 2nd, 7th, 11th or the 12th house, the individual runs the risk of angina trouble, risky blood pressure and heart ailment or even heart attack. It is always better to examine the mahadasa periods of any of these three stars, and if it occurs during early age or youthful years, it is further advisable to calculate the Antardasas of the other two remaining stars in that mahadasa. Then remedial medical and religious steps for avoidance of any such risk to health should be taken.

Saturn in the 4th house gives friends, but at the same time Saturn tries to expose such friends as are not loyal and helpful in the hour of need. Rahu keeps such nasty and undependable friends unexposed, and thus the individual suffers double pain (mental agony included) in the hour of need.

Individuals with this combination should as far as possible, check up their mode of travel before commencing the journey, make sure about reservation on the train or aeroplane or sailing ship. Chances of being stranded at the railway station, on the road or at the airport are pretty strong for them, especially if during that period, antardasa of Rahu or Saturn is running, or either of these two is in transit over the 4th or the 11th house. In case either of these two stars is in transit in the 12th house, extra money would be able to buy them continuance of their journey.

These individuals are slow in their homework during school days, and have no hesitation in copying from others. But they are often honest in Examinations, unless Mercury is in 6th, 7th, 8th or the 12th house in Birth-chart or Navamsha-chart. Books and exercise books of these individuals are generally stolen or lost or damaged by careless handling and they have no hitch in using books of others or those of the library by fair or unfair means.

These individuals are slow and irregular in medical treatment, and any visible (even partial) recovery makes them stop the treatment, and then recurrence of the same complaint of health is the real warning to them!

They do own residential property but often reside elsewhere either for greed of rent or for other circumstances.

Women should always be very careful about their weight and health of the reproductive organs in postnatal periods generally extending to one year after childbirth.

These individuals are apt to develop pain in the waistline and lower part of the spine bone, but preventive steps can avoid this possibility.

Saturn with Ketu in the 4th House

When in combination with Saturn in the 4th house, Ketu would not normally interfere in the functioning of Saturn there, except that it tries to forewarn the individual whenever any untoward happening is to take place.

Secondly, it gives promptness and talent to the individual

to give full attention to what is being taught in the classroom and also completing the homework regularly during school days. The individual doesn't depend on facilities for studies, they can study even on floor, under a street light.

In case this individual happens to be a writer or contributor to the Print Media, he /she is always keen that the matter/material gets published, payment or no payment.

Ketu makes no contribution either to body weight or to the ego of the individual, it leaves these matters to Saturn's command.

Ketu doesn't approve of Saturn making the individual revengeful towards unfaithful friends, it encourages the tendency to forget the past and look forward to future.

Ketu has no temptation towards ownership of property, by inheritance or self-acquisition or gifted by others. Here too, Saturn has its free will to operate in a manner it likes.

Ketu makes the individual more prompt and regular in medical treatment of others, but keeps rather lethargic and carefree where treatment of self is concerned.

Yes, Ketu is particular about the quality and freshness and purity of the food served. These individuals learn cooking and do not mind trying their hand at it now and then.

Saturn doesn't allow Ketu to interfere in its domain of pain and injuries to the individual.

SATURN IN THE 5TH HOUSE

Saturn makes the individual strong-headed, stubborn, obstinate, generally one-track minded, often non-adoptive to another person's point of view, somewhat slow in grasping studies, less appreciative of literature, though rather open-minded to music and poetry.

If man, his wife and if woman, she herself suffers loss of pregnancy, sometimes more than once, unless the stars of the spouse are helpful otherwise. Unless lord of the 5th house is a male star and occupying a house favourable to the 5th house, she gets a female child first. In other words, the individual has problem in the matter of progeny unless stars of the spouse are powerful and helpful, or otherwise the star controlling the portfolio of progeny at the time of birth (known as *Putra Karaka*) is strong and helpful for the purpose. They have no hitch or hesitation for medical termination of pregnancy, even at a bit advanced stage. Their decision is the main thing.

These individuals, when grown up, may have complaints against the parents and also develop differences of opinion with the parents. There have been cases where the parents overlooked and neglected proper upbringing and education as also settlement in life of the progeny. Thus it could be both ways round.

Some of these individuals get associated with management of industrial venture, manufacturing unit, petrol or diesel or lubricant outlet, placement agency, automobile outfit, establishments manufacturing and/or selling agricultural machinery and equipment. They also may get associated with units manufacturing yarn and cloth (powerloom and handloom cloth included), running agricultural farm, leading trade unions, supply and export of labour, collection of slogan shouters for rallies/ demonstrations/ election meetings.

Some others may be associated with running courier services, or employed as railway train crew or as ground crew at airports. Some of these individuals might be managing loading and unloading of goods and managing transhipment yards at road transport godowns, railway godowns, seaports and airports, managing weighment-centres, or functioning as brokers at foodgrain-*mandi*, vegetable-*mandi* and fruit-*mandi*. They could also be associated with survey of land for map-making or for cultivation or urbanisation.

Now the main point in this connection is that these individuals prove very hard task masters, are able to manage unruly labour, keep the labour organised, as far as possible avoid strike by labour, but in the same breath it is also true that their hard-task-master tendency leads to labour strike. Thus Saturn in the 5th house is a two-edged weapon in so far as labour management is concerned.

These individuals have no high morals, delivery of the job or task undertaken or entrusted is their first and foremost concern.

On their own, they are neither intimate friends nor bitter enemy to anyone without specific cause or purpose. They are friendly with their work only. Similarly they have faith in God, but are not given to any regular prayers etc., unless some difficulty, problem or situation warrants it. Then they are quite regular in prayers, but only till the job/task is accomplished, or the trouble is over.

They rarely have faith in the theory of pure or dirty thoughts or even actions. They think an action necessary in their interest and go ahead with it.

Saturn and Sun, Moon, Mars, Mercury, Jupiter or Venus in the 5th House

Respective chapters on Sun, Moon, Mars, Mercury, Jupiter, and Venus under the relevant sub-headings for 5th house may please be referred to.

Saturn and Rahu in the 5th House

In this house, Rahu helps Saturn in every thought and action, including causing medical termination of pregnancy.

These individuals, often slow in studies, try to make it up by use of unfair means, threats and approaches to teachers, examiners and experts at viva-voce, or experts at clinicals in medical courses of study. But it has been observed that this is the case only upto the age of 19 or at the most 23 years.

If they do not drop out from the school by the 17th year of age, they take their studies seriously and end up with high achievement or high standard of education, especially with relation to scientific, engineering and technical subjects. In a sense it can be said about them that they pick up high level of education and later on its proper use and application in the second phase., which starts from the age of 19 years.

Rahu tries in a very limited sense to reduce the rudeness

and ruthlessness in the administration and management of this individual, moreso in the case of educated employees and skilled labour, not in the case of unskilled labour and manual workers.

Saturn normally leads to silent disobedience whereas Rahu leads to spoken disobedience, which can be classified as insubordination.

Rahu encourages strike from work by labour, supervisory staff, clerical staff, and even staff at junior officer level.

Saturn and Ketu in the 5th House

When in combination with Saturn in the 5th house, Ketu tries its best to add mildness to thoughts, behaviour and action of the individual, which are normally prompted by Saturn.

Ketu also tries to avoid medical termination of pregnancy, though it is unable to help in natural loss of pregnancy.

Saturn and Ketu together in the 5th house influence the individual to issue written instructions in each and every matter of administration and management. Scolding and rebukes are also done in subdued but firm tone. Ketu adds literary softness to the harshness of Saturn in the 5th house.

SATURN IN THE 6TH HOUSE

This is yet another very favourable position for Saturn. It protects the individual against enemies, competitors, jealous friends and relations, normal diseases and illnesses. It helps enhancement of prestige and increases the social circle (which is sometimes disliked by the spouse because it snatches away time and energy meant for the spouse).

Slowly and steadily the family becomes larger and becomes a well-knit unit. It gives capacity for expert management of industrial ventures, manufacturing units, and all other sources of income, some of which have been mentioned in earlier paragraphs.

The individual gets good co-operation from labour and other skilled and unskilled employees as well as domestic help, because they are kept satisfied to a certain extent.

This position of Saturn gives soft relations with labour officers, trade union leaders and inspectors of virtually all departments (excluding Taxation Inspectors, unless Jupiter too is in a favourable position in the Birth-chart as well as in the Navamsha-chart).

The individual is able to establish good rapport with political leaders and bureaucrats, with whom the individual comes in contact or has to deal with them in their official capacity.

If the individual is in defence or police or any allied service, there are less chances of the individual being superseded, unless he/she indulges in some activity or commits an action violating the conduct rules.

If the individual receives any serious injury or fracture(s) of bone(s), this position of Saturn helps in timely medical aid, quick recovery and protects against any permanent invalidity or immobility.

The spouse of this individual easily suspects the individual of infidelity or immoral relations with a third person, whether there is justifiable cause for it or not. Therefore the individual should always act and behave in a guarded manner while meeting or contacting or dealing with opposite sex for sake of harmony and happiness in married life. Then a member of the family of the spouse shouldn't be unwelcome to the individual. And if any of them is a burden in the finances or encroaches upon time and energy of the individual, it is better to discuss the point sweetly and softly with the spouse, instead of showing the door to that member of the family of the spouse.

Further the spouse shouldn't feel that he/she is being starved of money needed for day-to-day living expenses. The individual should take enough interest actively in the upbringing and education as well as settlement in marriage or career, with regard to progeny and other dependants in the family or even outside the immediate family.

If the spouse or progeny dislike any pet animal(s) kept by the individual, it is better to strike a compromise, even by making the pet animal(s) to quit.

This individual is not very fit for upbringing at the house of the maternal grandparents or under their care, because in the long run, the individual is likely to come in direct or indirect conflict with a brother or sister of the mother. It is better to avoid such a situation.

The individual shouldn't feel arrogant because of physical strength of self or physical support of others being available or because of contacts with people in power, and should avoid physical violence, specially towards the spouse and progeny.

Saturn and Sun, Moon, Mars, Mercury, Jupiter or Venus in the 6th House

Respective chapters on Sun, Moon, Mars, Mercury, Jupiter, and Venus under the relevant sub-headings for 6th house may please be referred to.

Saturn and Rahu in the 6th House

There is nothing much to say about this combination in the 6th house, because more or less in every respect Rahu supports Saturn. In addition, Rahu would give extra weight to limbs lower to naval point and in declining years create problem in movement and mobility. Saturn with Rahu in 6th house gives only platonic type attraction to opposite sex other than own spouse, and gives a faint idea of suspicion in the mind of the spouse.

Often the spouse doesn't feel satisfied with money management in the immediate family, and this also adversely affects sweet and soft atmosphere of the house.

Saturn and Ketu in the 6th House

Ketu in a way is unable to interfere with functioning of Saturn, and gives moral support to Saturn in all matters. Saturn is normally a star of few words, whether written or spoken, but Ketu makes the individual react by writing or talking.

Another good thing that Ketu does in the 6th house with Saturn is that the individual doesn't get much physically attracted towards opposite sex other than own spouse and doesn't create circumstances of rift between husband and wife on this account. It also gives tendency of economic approach in money management to the spouse. However it develops difference with mother's paternal family, specially with maternal uncles or aunts. Neither in childhood nor in youthful years these individuals prefer to stay for long periods in the house of the maternal uncles or aunts.

SATURN IN THE 7TH HOUSE

One of the difficult positions of Saturn, because –

(a) it delays marriage.

(b) it sometimes leads to pre-marital affair, specially if it is under any kind of influence of Venus after the age of 14-16 years, and if it is Mercury's influence over Saturn, the affair would be at the stage of school or college life.

(c) adversely affects harmony between husband and wife during the initial years of married life,

(d) it gives quarrels and disputes in deals/transactions involving sale or purchase of any item of high price.

(e) it delays decisions in business transactions with the result that sometimes a good transaction slips out of hand because of the delay.

(f) it encourages the individual towards extra-marital affair.

(g) it also encourages tendency for litigation, without much bothering about results/outcome.

(h) it induces the individual to go out of native town/district/state/ country and settle elsewhere for better scope in life.

(i) Saturn is directly connected with venereal diseases and also with AIDS and allied troubles.

(j) Though normally it is believed that only Mars or Sun give injury with bleeding, but Saturn in the 7th house is fully capable of giving an injury leading to wound, and its delayed recovery.

(k) In *Ayn Rand's* world famous novel, *Fountainhead*, the first husband of the main woman character, Dominique, in a sense strikes a deal to share his wife for $ 2,500,000 with a press tycoon; such a husband must have Saturn in the 7th house to do so. In other words, a husband or wife permits the spouse to share bed with another person for some reason or consideration, which is one of the results of Saturn in the 7th house.

(l) Saturn in the 7th house also causes circumstantial or judicial separation or separate living of husband and wife. This can ultimately lead to divorce, specially if Mars (and sometimes Jupiter too, where more of legal grounds are involved)) extend a helping hand to Saturn in this behalf.

(m) Enemy action on individual level or group level or fighting in a battle or any other kind of fighting leading to an injury or big wound to the individual.

(n) Lack of full or partial sexual vitality in the individual,

(o) Tendency to join or work for criminal or unlawful activity, or to have association with or support to it.

Against all these minus points, the big plus point is that this position of Saturn normally tends to give an upper hand to the individual in all disputes, fights, litigation and transactions, business deals etc.

Saturn and Sun, Moon, Mars, Mercury, Jupiter or Venus in the 7th House

Respective chapters on Sun, Moon, Mars, Mercury, Jupiter, and Venus under the relevant sub-headings for the 7th house may please be referred to.

Saturn and Rahu in the 7th House

The point of importance is that Rahu with Saturn in 7th house gives ego problem first to the spouse and then it travels to the individual too. If both husband and wife are sensible and practical, they try to suppress own ego and make honest effort to satisfy the ego of the opposite party. But if both or either of the two is sentimental and emotional, matters drop down to worse situations. This ego problem if not suppressed and satisfied at the initial stage itself, can sometimes lead to physical separation and the word "divorce" starts surfacing in the process.

In case there is an element of suspicion in the mind of one of the two (husband and wife) about extra-marital affair or casual third angle's appearance in the married life, the accused person prefers to actually develop a third angle in the married life even if it was not there when the suspicion started. In other words it can be said that the element of suspicion plants the idea in the mind of the other partner in marriage.

Further Rahu gives extra fat to the body below the naval, and this adversely affects, though to a small extent only, the mutual capacity for each other in the bed.

Sometimes the ego problem leads to differences between husband and wife over money management, each one wanting to have the first say or the upper hand, depending on the tradition in the family of both. In case no compromise is reached, it would affect other matters in mutual life.

In the case of childbearing women, they should take herbal or medical remedies for restoration of fitness of the body, otherwise Rahu overrules Saturn and leaves the body in a floppy shape, gradually with every childbirth.

Rahu makes the individual easy target for venereal and AIDS problems, and so preventive caution is rather essential.

The ego of the spouse sometimes generates problem of adjustment between spouse and mother of the individual, and father of the individual keeps more or less aloof outwardly and feels hurt inwardly.

Saturn and Ketu in the 7th House

In combination of Ketu and Saturn in the 7th house, firstly, Ketu doesn't follow the footsteps of Rahu and doesn't lead to clash of ego between husband and wife.

Secondly, Ketu doesn't generate suspicion in the mind of one of the married couple relating to a (regular or casual) third angle in the married life.

Thirdly Ketu doesn't concern itself with fatness to the body below the naval point, nor does it adversely affect the figure of the female after every childbirth, provided necessary herbal or medical remedies have been adopted.

Fourthly, Ketu always generates element of wisdom and practical common sense in the mind of the spouse and thus save the married life from onslaught by Saturn in the 7th house.

Fifthly, Ketu encourages the spouse to resumption of studies by husband or wife or by both, especially if element of incompletion has been there. If no regular studies are started by both or either of the two, at least the spouse develops interest in general reading, depending on facility of time and convenience as also availability of material to do so.

Sixthly Ketu develops common sense into the individual with regard to buying, selling, and conducting any business deal or transaction.

Seventhly, Ketu doesn't encourage tendency towards litigation, quarrels, disputes, and false claims merely to harass the opposite party.

SATURN IN THE 8TH HOUSE

This is a mixed position for Saturn, as it is for other hard stars like Mars, Sun, Rahu, Herschel and Neptune to add or reduce the good and bad results of Saturn in the 8th house.

These hard stars distinctly give benefits in terms of source of income, but give minor or major complaints of health, specially when these stars have their mahadasa or antardasa.

Thus Saturn in the 8th house gives higher income, sometimes helps in recovery of old loans and old dues, creates scope for expansion of source of income, all the more so if the source of income is industrial venture or any other element discussed in the beginning paragraphs under Saturn.

However it has to be borne in mind that if Jupiter too is in the 6th, 8th or the 12th house, the individual might be accused of tax evasion, directly smuggling or giving shelter or other accommodation or financial support to smugglers. This position poses scope for searches and seizures, enquiries, surveys, investigations and even legal action against the individual.

In case Saturn owns the 4th, 7th or the 11th house and is in the 8th house, the individual might be accused of petty thefts within the house in childhood and bigger theft/embezzlement or pilferage in adulthood. It is the duty of the parents that if they find such a position of Saturn in the Birth-chart of an infant, they should inculcate into the child, good qualities of honesty and truthfulness. They should let the child know the risks and dangers involved in the bad habit of theft, embezzlement and pilferage.

These individuals prove brave and courageous fighters on battlefield, not given to easy retreat in spite of injuries and wounds. They prove expert and efficient strategists in matters of battle, war, border skirmishes, and are foresighted planners in matters related to ordnance. They prove their skill in managing transport facilities in defence and police services in times of emergency.

They are good at management of labour and problems related to them, created or agitated by labour. These individuals are expert engineers, especially for establishment of new industries, acquiring big and small machines and installation of the machines and commissioning them into production. However their job ends with product getting out of the factory gates. They are not so good at actual marketing.

As regards health, these individuals have always to be careful, especially when Saturn is in transit over the 4th, 8th or 12th house or Saturn has its own mahadasa with antardasa of any star in 6:8 relationship with Saturn or Saturn's antardasa under any such star's mahadasa. Saturn is capable of giving long-term illness including wound(s) going septic or gangrenous. Similarly if it is a case of fracture of bone(s), recovery might take time and some kind of invalidity might still be left behind causing complaints subsequently under climatic conditions. Saturn is also capable of causing tuberculosis, cancer (when getting support in this behalf from Mars or Neptune), venereal disease of any kind (specially if Mars is in 2nd, 7th or the 12th house or Venus is in 6th or 8th or the 12th house).

Saturn is capable of causing invalidity or ineffectiveness of any limb or part of the body. But it has to be carefully noted that Saturn in the 8th house normally grants long life to an individual, notwithstanding any kind of disability, invalidity or ineffectiveness to any limb or part or functionary of the body.

Individuals with Saturn in the 8th house should keep away from freelance attitude with regard to the opposite sex, and also avoid extra-marital affairs or casual contacts with opposite sex for clean and comfortable health. Further, the individual shouldn't be cruel to the spouse, whatever the pressure from the family on either side, because (a) firstly, there is always scope for police or legal action in the matter; and (b) secondly, risk to the life and limb of the spouse. It applies to both husband and wife. Print and visual media often publicise news of wife's torture by the husband or his family, but there are equally substantial cases of wife and her family harassing, blackmailing and torturing the husband and/or his family, though those news hardly find coverage in the media.

Often Saturn gives settlement in a town or district or state or country other than one's native one. But the individual should pay special attention to keep away from any legal problem relating to violence and also from the opposite sex, because the chances are strong for police action including arrest and further legal action in the matter. Thus high income in a town or country other than one's native one would not prove full and fair compensation for the legal problems coming up on account of acts of commission and omission of the individual himself or herself.

There would be good and dependable friends even in foreign places too, and they would come forward in an event of injury to the individual. But rarely a friend would come forward to help or support in case of police or legal action of any kind against the individual.

As has already been suggested above, while examining the position of Saturn in the 8th house in Birth-chart and/or Navamsha-chart, an astrologer shouldn't overlook the contemporary position of Jupiter (and sometimes Mars too) in both, Birth-chart and Navamsha-chart.

Saturn and Sun, Moon, Mars, Mercury, Jupiter or Venus in the 8th House

Respective chapters Sun, Moon, Mars, Mercury, Jupiter, and Venus under the relevant sub-headings for the 8th house may please be referred to.

Saturn and Rahu in the 8th House

Rahu becomes a follower and "yesman" of Saturn in the 8th house when in combination there with Saturn.

Besides adding extra weight to the thighs and knee-region, Rahu gives a touch of ego to the individual, specially whenever the individual is in trouble with police or the law. Chances are that the individual might brag, boast, drop names of important connections, and the more this is done, the greater the trouble for the individual with law or police. In such circumstances, it is better to be polite, unassuming and courteous to the agents/workers of police and/or law set-up, be it in courts or outside.

It has been stated above that Saturn in the 8th house gives higher income, and Rahu helps in building up savings and owning assets (moveable and immoveable), but that too shouldn't make the individual arrogant, careless and misbehaved.

Further Saturn often gives temporary or casual contact with the opposite sex, but Rahu tries to give it a longer and stabilised shape, which ultimately leads to loss of face as well as money. Sometimes Rahu with Saturn might lead an individual to develop connection with a male or female prostitute. These two stars in the 8th stars encourage the individual towards unconventional sex activity.

Rahu in the 8th house delays speedy recovery from any injury, wound, illness, disease, and tries to leave an impact on the mind of the individual. Prevention is better, though very, very difficult to observe.

Rahu inducts interference in the married life from the family of self and the spouse, though not so much on account of differences between husband and wife. If husband and wife are appreciative of this development on parts of the families of both sides, the marriage can be spared troubles and break up.

Saturn and Ketu in the 8th House

Poor creature Ketu! It tries to give good sense and useful common sense to the individual, when in combination with Saturn in the 8th house.

It can be classed as against the influence of Saturn in inducing the individual to wrong deeds. But Saturn is so strong and Ketu is a shadow planet, thus Ketu is rather unable to cut much ice in the matter against onslaught by Saturn in the 8th house.

One rather bad contribution of Ketu is that it leads a wound to go septic or formation of gangrene, and even in comparison to Rahu, makes recovery very much delayed and expenditure oriented.

SATURN IN THE 9TH HOUSE

The important point to be noted about this position of Saturn is that it interferes with the right and claim to inheritance, whether it is property and other assets of natural parents or adopting parents or foster parents or even with regard to gifted property. On account of Saturn the individual gets much less than her/his rights and claims to the inheritance.

Other claimants or non-claimants try to usurp a portion of the due and correct share of the individual by any means possible including false litigation, or encroach upon the share or inherited portion of the property of the individual.

The unfortunate part of the matter is that depending on the owner of the 9th house and its relationship with Saturn sitting in the 9th house, sometimes the uncles or aunts or cousins also openly or secretly act against the interests of the individual in matters relating to property and other assets. Thus the individual has to stay alert regarding matters of inheritance which might include gifts from any source.

And insult to the injury is that burden of repayment of any debts or liabilities descending upon the individual is put on him or her, and sometimes this burden is greater than the individual's share in inheritance. However the spouse of the individual can protect the individual to a certain extent from this evil.

If Saturn is directly aspected by Mars or Jupiter from the 3rd house or Jupiter is in the 6th or the 8th house, generally an allegation is levelled against the individual, by other heirs, co-sharers and claimants, that the individual has been given cash or jewellery in a hidden manner by a parent of the individual or by a grand-parent.

In this particular matter, the individual has also to be blamed to certain extent as he/she gets more intimate and serviceful to the source from which inheritance is to flow down to the individual or to the spouse. It is partly better to keep open relationship and services to the parent or grandparent. And whenever a parent or grandparent breathes his/her last, it is always better to inform all heirs and claimants of the event of death as quickly as possible so as to avoid post-death allegations, charges, and blames.

These individuals are often keen to associate themselves or actively participate in the management of religious bodies, charitable trusts, social establishments etc., and do not try to keep their actions and conduct above board. Then they become an easy scapegoat for allegations of mismanagement of funds, embezzlement, pilferage of assets of that body/trust/establishment. And sometimes the blame is justified as they have a direct or indirect hand in embezzlement or mismanagement.

If Sun or Mars is in the 10th house, these individuals plan to march into the political arena through their association or participation in these religious/ charitable/ social set-ups or organisations.

Coming to other points, these individuals do not normally enjoy very clean image and good reputation with regard to their attitude towards the opposite sex, moreso those within the wider family relations. This is true unless Venus and Jupiter are very favourably placed and are in no manner associated or linked to Saturn in the 9th house.

These individuals, at least in some cases, particularly where Saturn owns the 10th and 11th Houses, do not enjoy good rapport and affectionate relationship with natural, foster or adopting father. The father forms an impression that the individual is too keen to inherit property and assets from the father, even during the father's lifetime.

These individuals brag and boast a lot about their sense of self-respect and honour, but they pocket insult and condemnation mutely or silently where they find that they have vested interests.

These individuals try to use or misuse the influence of social/political/bureaucratic status of their brothers-in-law or sisters-in-law.

Another weak point in these individuals is that they do not repay loans by due date nor in lump-sum. It is difficult even to recover dues from them. They postpone paying their liabilities even when they are in a position to clear them. And they do not mind insults and threats in this regard. If they are manhandled for non-payment or delayed payment of dues, they swallow that too silently.

They are expert at collection of mob for rallies, processions, public meetings, slogan shouting, pickets, political and social drives, religious processions. But they must get their due price in cash, kind or uplift as a reward for these services.

These individuals do not have much faith internally in luck, God Almighty and the Karma-Theory of the previous births. They have greater faith in their own acts and actions, efforts and manipulations or manoeuvres. They have faith in forming groups and gangs, and if Mars is in the 3rd, 6th, 8th or the 11th house, they have no hitch or hesitation in throwing threats and demands at the face of others.

They have less fear for law, order, and system and often feel that they can easily manage law, order and system by money and manpower. This feeling in these individuals becomes stronger in case Saturn in 9th is in Libra (exaltation) or in its own Rasi, or if otherwise Saturn is Lord of the Ascendant (1st house).

If Saturn's Rasi is in the 7th house, these individuals try to bring forward their spouse by fair or unfair means in political, religious or social arena, and sometimes they try to derive benefit under the cover of the spouse. If the individual's spouse is not capable or competent to be placed as 'front cover', they bring in the arena the spouse of a brother/sister or nephew/niece or of a trusted friend or follower for this purpose.

Saturn and Sun, Moon, Mars, Mercury, Jupiter or Venus in the 9th House

Respective chapters on Sun, Moon, Mars, Mercury, Jupiter, and Venus under the relevant sub-headings for 9th house may please be referred to.

Saturn and Rahu in the 9th House

Here in the 9th house too Rahu doesn't have much say against the influence of Saturn, and thus it becomes a 'yes-man' of Saturn. The only new factor Rahu brings into the conduct of the individual is that he/she often tries to help and support persons from own caste or community or religion or faith or camp.

Further the individual doesn't hesitate in telling lies, backbiting, criticising others for own personal interests, mix up with downtrodden too for self-interest and own benefit. The individual doesn't feel ashamed or belittled when exposed for acts/actions of commission and omission.

These individuals do not hesitate from cornering, to own benefit, the credit for works accomplished by others, or partners/colleagues of the individuals. They do not treat piracy in literature, poetry, songs, *geets, ghazals, qawwalis*, in music writing, in tunes in vocal and instrumental music as a crime. They deem it as their due right or rightful property.

Rahu supports and provides a veil or cover to the romantic approach or attitude of these individuals towards opposite sex within the wider circles of the family of self and spouse.

Saturn and Ketu in the 9th House

Like Rahu, Ketu too doesn't interfere with ideas, thoughts, attitudes, acts, actions and utterances of the individual under influence of Saturn in the 9th house.

But Ketu doesn't encourage or approve attitude of piracy in literature, music etc., though it is unable to stop it altogether. Ketu does try intelligently to guide the individual on path of correct and upright attitude and actions.

Ketu further tries to improve upon romantic approach and attitude of the individual towards members of the opposite sex within the wider family circles.

Ketu doesn't encourage the individual to extend a helping hand to any brother/sister/cousin of self or spouse when in need; the maximum it does is to express 'lip sympathy'. On the other hand, the individual doesn't hesitate to secure help and support for own benefit and self-interest from anyone, high or low, big or small, approachable or unapproachable, kind or cruel, even from an enemy by surrender and sacrificing others, friends, colleagues, followers.

Health-wise, Rahu does not create much trouble when with Saturn in the 9th house, but Ketu can give pain, injury, wound or fracture to any portion of the hand from the armpit to the middle finger. Therefore when Ketu mahadasa or Ketu antardasa runs, may be under Saturn mahadasa or any other star's mahadasa, prevention of injury or trouble to hand is rather necessary.

SATURN IN THE 10TH HOUSE

This is rather a delicate position of Saturn, because it can help or hit in the same breath. The individual has to be very careful, alert and cautious in one's acts and actions, keep mind awakened while dealing with employees, subordinates, servants and labour as also followers in politics, religious activities and trade union leadership. In this behalf, some points are very important, viz.,

(a) which houses are owned by Saturn and how those two houses are placed with relation to the 10th house,
(b) which planet is the lord of the 10th house and what is the

relationship, on permanent basis relationship and relationship at the time of birth which is known as *Tatkaalik* relationship, and how are the two stars placed in the Birth-chart and Navamsha-chart with relation to each other. To make the point clear, suppose, the 10th house is owned by Mercury, which is a friend of Saturn in permanent relationship. However if Mercury is positioned in the Birth-chart 5 houses away from the 10th house, it has got enemy-type relationship with Saturn at the time of birth. Because Mercury and Saturn have *Trikona* (5:9) relationship in the Birth-chart, on the whole Saturn would give good results in the 10th house.

(c) Let us take a second example. Suppose Sun is the lord of the 10th house. Saturn and Sun (though believed to be son and father) are enemies to each other in permanent relationship. And if Then Sun is sitting in the 6th place from Saturn (i.e. in the 3rd house), the relationship at the time of birth is also that of an enemy and naturally it would be presumed that Sun would adversely affect good results of Saturn in the 10th house. Normally Sun is favourable in the 3rd house. Sun would give results adverse to the interests of Saturn in the 10th house, mainly because in the Birth-chart Saturn and Sun have 6:8 relationship with each other.

(d) Let us take another example with Sun itself. Suppose Sun is in the 9th or the 11th house, it is friendly with Saturn at the time of birth, and on the whole Sun would not interfere with beneficial functioning of Saturn in the 10th, and Sun would extend some good support to Saturn.

(e) A third supposed position of Sun could be in the 8th or the 12th house. In this position, though Sun is friendly with Saturn in birth-time relationship, Sun would create problems and troubles for the individual because Sun is in the 8th or the 12th house, and the same position of Sun would hinder beneficial functioning of Saturn in the 10th house.

(f) Then suppose Saturn-owned Rasis (Capricorn and Aquarius) are in the 1st and 2nd houses, these positions are very helpful to Saturn's functioning and thus beneficial to the individual. But suppose, these Rasis are in the 12th and the 1st houses, Capricorn in the 12th is detrimental to Saturn's beneficial attitude for the individual, while Aquarius in the 1st house would prove helpful to Saturn in the 10th house. Thus the effect of the Saturn-owned Rasis countermanded each other and Saturn is free to function on its own, with no impact of Rasis owned by it.

Suppose Capricorn and Aquarius are in the 4th and 5th houses or even in 3rd and 4th houses. These positions of Saturn-owned Rasis would prove helpful to Saturn in beneficial functioning for the individual, because ownership of even the 3rd house (in spite of its 6th position from Saturn in 10th house) is beneficial to Saturn's beneficial functioning in an overall manner. But the positions of Capricorn and Aquarius in the 4th and 5th house would not be very beneficial to the individual through Saturn in the 10th house.

Then suppose, Saturn is lord of 5th and 6th houses, the effect is mutually countermanded, because Saturn's ownership of the 6th house is beneficial, while of the 5th house is not.

Let us take another example. Suppose Saturn is lord of the 7th and 8th house. Though 7th house has a *Kendra* relationship with Saturn in the 10th, Saturn's ownership of the 7th house is harmful to the individual, while ownership of the 8th house is beneficial on the whole for the individual, and thus Saturn would give mixed results to the individual.

Yet another example would suffice in this matter. Suppose Saturn is lord of the 11th and 12th houses, its results with regard to the 10th house would be a mixed fare. On one hand Saturn is very favourable being lord of the 11th house, but its favourability is reduced owing to 11th lord occupying 12th house. Otherwise too Saturn's ownership of the 12th house is not beneficial to the individual. Also the unfavourable results of the 12th house having Aquarius in it is because lord of the 12th house (Saturn) is occupying the 11th position from the 12th house.

All this is a very delicate matter and should be studied with full attention keeping in mind all related relationships.

Then the question remains of Saturn being lord of the 10th house itself and the 9th or the 11th house in addition. If it is the lord of the 9th house also, it assumes lordship of both, a *Kendra* and a *Trikona* and thus even being a hard star, it is beneficial to the individual in its own way. It includes gains from charitable, social, religious organisations, gains from side business (if the individual is in employment), gains from leadership in trade-union or any other labour or agricultural organisation. It would also include gains from politics, running or managing an industry, placement service, dealing in old or new auto vehicles, dealing in machinery and their spare parts, and all such other lines as are attributable to Saturn.

However in case Saturn is lord of the 10th and the 11th house, it would ensure success as leader of a trade-union, labour or agricultural organisation or in politics or administrative formation. It helps getting selected or elected to a position of power including membership of parliament, senate, any legislature or *panchayat* or similar public administration formation, higher income than expectation and anticipation by fair and unfair means. At the same time Saturn in 11th house would adversely affect the education and to some extent the general health of progeny, unless the stars of the progeny itself are very strong to countermand the adverse effect of Saturn in the 11th house.

So much emphasis has been given to Saturn's position in the 10th house, because the 10th house mainly relates to source of livelihood and fair or unfair means of income, as also gains or no gains from the father.

Thus it is clear that as compared to other stars or as compared to Saturn's position in other houses, it matters considerably, for prediction purposes, which houses in the Birth-chart are owned by Saturn. Saturn is helpful in the house occupied by it (by both fair and unfair means and methods), it is in a way harmful for the house it aspects directly (it being the 4th house), though indirectly it aspects the 11th, 12th, 6th and 7th houses as well.

It means that while occupying the 10th house, it is in a way unfavourable to the 4th house, which rules mother, conveyance or means of transport, middle parts of the body including heart and digestive system, food, property, friends and domestic happiness or unhappiness.

It has been generally observed that when Saturn is in the 10th house, the individual is deprived of shelter and protection of one of the parents before the individual completes 23rd year of age. Saturn in the 10th could also develop a gulf in communication or in relationship between the individual and one of the parents. The individual could also be brought up or looked after in childhood by some blood relation other than the parents, particularly if Sun or Moon be in the 4th or the 9th house; it can be an adopting father or mother, whether a blood relation or not.

When talking of adoption it is kept in mind that there are growing incidents of newly born babies being abandoned on roads, garbage-bins, at doors of places of worship or orphanages, and therefore it is not necessary that adoption is from relations; it has come to be believed that kids are adopted by any kind of parent (in no way related to the child).

Overlooking this important point would harm the predictive science. In ancient times too, newly born were abandoned by their mothers or others on behalf of the mothers, most glaring examples being those of *Kunti* and *Karna* (in the Hindu epic *'Mahabharat'*), or that of *'Shakuntala'*, whose son's name was *Bharat*, (wherefrom India derived its name *'Bharat-varsh'* are enough. Birth-charts of *Karna* and the beautiful *Shakuntala* are not known now to anyone. Whatever the position of other stars, it can safely be presumed they had Saturn in the 10th house in a strong position. That Saturn in the 10th house adversely affect the 4th house, which ruled, among other things, the natural mother.

Saturn in the 10th house brings support in matters of selection and election of the individual from unexpected quarters too, like labour organisations, caste or communal formations, religious bodies, women's organisations, big farm owners influencing their employees in favour of the individual.

If Saturn is in a watery Sign, there are chances that the individual would go oversees for seeking means of livelihood and big fortune in terms of name, fame and money. If Saturn is in a cardinal Sign (Aries, Cancer, Libra or Capricorn), chances are that the individual would move out of the native village, town, city, district, county or state to other place for seeking better means of livelihood.

It could also for any other reason such as to escape legal action for civil or criminal offence or on account of excommunication by caste, community, religion or the local administration etc.

In other words, it can be said that Saturn in the 10th house, for good or bad, disturbs the individual's constant and permanent relationship with parents and residence at the native village or town. However it has to be noted that in any planetary influence where another person is involved, it should be borne in mind that the stars of the other person would also adversely or favourably or protectively affect the situation. The stars of the other person or persons thus support or countermand the adverse influence of Saturn in the individual's Birth-chart.

However it is abundantly clear that Saturn's position in the 10th house warrants special and concentrated study.

Another interesting point is that Saturn in the 10th house leads an individual to source of livelihood other than that of the parents. Suppose the parents are in the industrial line, the individual might deviate therefrom, while on the other hand if the parental line had no link or concern whatsoever with industrial line, Saturn in the 10th house might induce the individual to adopt industrial line for main or supplementary source of income.

Saturn and Sun, Moon, Mars, Mercury, Jupiter or Venus in the 10th House

Respective chapters on Sun, Moon, Mars, Mercury, Jupiter, and Venus under the relevant sub-headings for the 10th house may please be referred to.

Saturn and Rahu in the 10th House

Whether the individual with Saturn in the 10th house did any wrong or not, Rahu with Saturn is likely to have a finger of suspicion raised against the individual for any act of commission and omission. And despite that, the individual would dare to maintain the sense of ego before colleagues, co-workers, superiors, subordinates, employers, and employees, as also in the public eye.

Rahu doesn't help or support in matters relating to politics, profession, career, business or industry. But it does help in matters related to acts and actions related to mischief, misconduct, dishonesty of any kind, falsehood, forgery, cheating or any other misdeed of the individual, which includes matters relating to inheritance from parents, specially from natural or adopting mother of self or spouse. In case of defeat or loss or setback in any matter, the individual feels deep sense of hurt to the ego and feels depressed and dejected to the extent becoming inactive or withdrawn from active work for a few days. In such a situation, mother or spouse or a friend of the opposite sex of the individual should try to pull the individual out of depression and dejection, because except these three none else can help the individual in a situation like that.

However when the individual is riding the ladder of success, he or she develops quite violent feelings towards others, and sometimes ruthless too where fault or offence or guilt is involved on part of other(s).

Rahu makes an individual quite romantic by spoken word, sometimes indulging in poor or intolerable utterance or remark. It also encourages the individual to usurp money or assets of others to which the individual has no right or claim. Rahu makes a person quite mobile, proceeding on a journey, tour or travel without hesitation, (especially if the journey or tour concerns the individual's job, business, profession or source of income), though Saturn in the 10th house makes a person slow in taking a decision in this regard. Thus, Rahu gains an upper hand over Saturn in the matter of tours and journeys.

Saturn and Ketu in the 10th House

When Ketu is in combination with Saturn in the 10th house, as has been indicated earlier, Ketu adds softness and sweetness to harsh and hard decision, acts or actions of Saturn in that house.

Ketu brings to bear on Saturn humanly fairness, sense of

equity, feelings of sympathy and mercy in the innermost heart and also in outer behaviour and actions of Saturn. However, Ketu joins hands with Saturn in disturbing the care, affection, love, protection and communication between the individual and one or both parents.

Ketu induces the subordinates, friends, employees, domestic help, followers and workers to exploit the individual in money matters, and if scope permits, to indulge in pilferage of assets of the individual. The situation becomes pretty difficult for a single man or woman living alone to manage with plenty household supplies and rich possessions.

If the individual is an author, writer, free-lancer in journalism, risk of inordinate delay in publication hangs over the individual's literary or journalistic works (big or small). If the individual happens to be a teacher, professor or consultant in subjects related to science and technology, the individual, in spite of efficiency in knowledge and teaching, is unable to command discipline over the class or the group, and has to adopt rough and harsh attitude to command discipline.

If the individual functions as a ghost-writer for any important person, the individual gets paid for the speeches, write-ups, articles or even booklets and books produced by the individual. But neither credit nor respect and honour are shown to the individual, by those concerned, for the excellent work done by the individual.

SATURN IN THE 11TH HOUSE

This is one of the best positions for Saturn, whatever Rasi be in the 11th house, and wherever Saturn-owned Rasis are situated in the Birth-chart. The individual is always assured of regular income and earnings. The individual stays active in life for long years, reaching old age. If Mars or Rahu or Herschel is in the 4th house, the individual may have to start earning from an early age, say between the age of 14 and 18 years.

The individual starts with moderate or meagre income but

gradually and steadily reaches high levels of earnings, as well as direct and indirect income too.

The individual doesn't have much distinction between fair and unfair in-flow of money in own hands or in the hands of spouse or other members of the immediate family, as happens often in the case of people in positions of power and authority. The reason is simple. The 10th house rules profession, politics, business, career, vocation, source of income, and the 2nd house from any given house is always of money, savings and moveable as well as immoveable assets.

Further generally it is observed that individuals with Saturn in the 11th house either have more than one source of income or both husband and wife earn actively or the immediate (joint) family has at least two actively earning members. It has to be remembered that Saturn's very nature is "slow and steady". The subjects, that can constitute sources of income for the individual, have already been mentioned in previous paragraphs under the current chapter on Saturn.

However there is no harm in repetition of a few of them. These are industrial ventures, manufacturing units, business or trading in petrol, diesel, lubricating oils, edible oils (specially groundnut, linseed, sesame, and cottonseed oils). It also includes dealing in machinery and spare parts, running labour-supply-agency, placement services, recruitment agency for engineering/ scientific/ technical experts, running courier service, cargo and customs clearance service, trade union leadership, collecting masses for a rally/ procession/ meeting/ demonstration/ picketing etc.

Saturn in the 11th house concerns itself also with blackmailing, smuggling, hoarding, profiteering, kidnapping for ransom or other purposes.

Saturn in the 11th house is a good support in matters of politics and acquiring power by fair or foul means. Because of good level of income, these individuals often make financial contributions or indirect financial support to politicians. If Saturn is very strong in the 11th house and has the support of Sun or Mars, the individual assumes the role of a king-maker at *panchayat* level, district or county level, state level or even at the national level.

In this context it has to be noted that when Saturn is lord of the 12th or the 1st house and is occupying the 11th house. It may be more or less taken for granted that the individual would encash every particle of money spent on politicians or on influencing politics, be it by fair or crooked means and methods.

These individuals are bold, brave, daring and dashing without much fear, whether it is in personal fight and combat, group fighting or fighting for the state or nation. They prove efficient defence strategists and expert in developing useful ordnance weaponry. They make competent police or security officers, but seldom of high integrity.

If these individuals are in the field of industry or manufacturing, they are always keen to exploit the labour force and at the same time to extract higher price for their product or produce. If necessary they will do so by deteriorating the quality, mischief in quantity or adulteration etc., applying all kinds of crude methods.

However there is one obstacle in these underhand activities. In case Jupiter is in the 5th or the 9th house, the individual would hesitate to indulge in mischievous methods to enhance income. This effect is enhanced all the more if own progeny is grown up enough to understand the crude methods, or if a brother or sister of self or spouse is a partner in the activity. But if the brother or sister of self or spouse is nothing more than an employee or salaried manager, that person would not be able to cut much ice in reducing the mischief in the mischievous activity.

Saturn and Sun, Moon, Mars, Mercury, Jupiter or Venus in the 11th House

Respective chapters on Sun, Moon, Mars, Mercury, Jupiter, and Venus under the relevant sub-headings for 11th house may please be referred to for results of these six combinations with Saturn in the 11th house.

Saturn and Rahu in the 11th House

When with Saturn in combination, Rahu becomes a blind supporter of Saturn in the 11th house, whatever the Rasi in the 11th house.

Rahu enhances the income, also helps in mischievous methods of generating big money, proves an additional handle in suppressing labour force, subordinates, scientific and technical employees, domestic help. But Rahu doesn't interfere with the working, work conditions and employment terms and conditions of the office staff and accounts employees.

As the level of income grows higher, Rahu encourages the individual with bragging, boasting and sharp sense of ego. This bragging and boasting sometimes invites the attention of the taxation sleuths and demands for higher gratification from other inspectors of this department or that.

Rahu disturbs one or two pregnancies during the 2nd or the 3rd months, or encourages and induces medical termination of one or more pregnancies.

Rahu encourages dubious investments and unlawful activities for generation of higher income. If the individual is in the political or trade union arena, Rahu with Saturn helps in building up a big bank balance, some of which would be kept in foreign country. Rahu facilitates under-invoicing and over-invoicing, without fear of any routine or serious action as such.

Rahu brings, no doubt with Saturn's support, considerable travel to foreign countries or having a branch seat in a foreign land. Another favourable influence for the individual is that Rahu specially helps the individual to sustain all kinds of pressures, harassment and torture and the individual is able to keep secrets to heart against these odds. In fact, Saturn also helps in the matter, but if Saturn is alone in the 11th house, physical torture might force the individual to speak out the 'secrets of trade'. It is here that Rahu helps the individual.

Saturn and Ketu in the 11th House

Ketu gives more or less the same results as Rahu gives with

Saturn in the 11th house, but Ketu-oriented results are less in quantity and quality.

One precaution essential about Ketu and Saturn combination in the 11th house is that during investigations and interrogations by police or investigating agencies, the individual should avoid at all cost (tolerating the physical and family's torture) giving any written statement in the individual's own handwriting. It has to be so whether the individual volunteers it or is forced to do so.

If the individual gives any written accounts or statement or even any simple explanation at the initial stages of enquiry and investigation, the individual is very likely to land in trouble by his own writing, and subsequently it would be pretty difficult to get out of the self-created situation. Ketu encourages the individual to adopt written word instead of the spoken word. This combination encourages the individual to start writing as a source of additional income, and though the published or telecast or broadcast writings of the individual are well received by the public, the payments for that work are received in parts and that too after long delay or intervals.

Ketu with Saturn induces the individual to high quality wardrobe, going out well dressed and in the case of women, appearing in public adorned with jewellery and ornaments.

SATURN IN THE 12TH HOUSE

This is one of the most difficult positions of Saturn in a Birth-chart for the following reasons.

1. First of all, it often gives a height less than the typical average of that region or that climate or of the family group.
2. Secondly it is likely to give boils on the lower parts of the body in childhood.
3. Thirdly, it adversely affects the digestive system in childhood at least upto the age of 12 or 13 years.
4. Fourthly, it affects adversely the complexion of the individual. In other words, the person loses to some extent the fair

complexion of childhood by the time the person reaches the age of 23 years.

5. Fifthly, the individual reflects a snobbish tendency right from the school days.

6. Sixthly, the individual is capable of telling believable lies with a straight face.

7. Seventhly, the individual considers one's own self as someone different than other members of the family, that she or he is a kind of superior person. The individual adopts this superiority complex (which is not a birth-nature) to evade manual work at home, in the school and at work in initial stages of joining.

8. Eighthly, the individual when out on a buying spree forgets the money content in the pocket or the purse, and at some stage falls short of money for payment and then doesn't hesitate to ask the accompanying person (spouse or relation or friend) to make up the payment. Normally nothing wrong in it, but the individual delays return of that money, or sometimes manages to totally forget the repayment to the friend or relation.

9. Ninthly, the individual does not respond in the same manner. Suppose the same friend or relation on some other subsequent occasion is short of money in the market, the individual instead of "one good turn deserves another" makes excuses that the individual too doesn't have enough money to lend on the spot to the relation or the friend.

10. Tenthly the individual has no hitch or hesitation in telling lies, making false excuses even in routine matters, leave aside the question of being subjected to any enquiry or investigation. However one difficulty is there. These individuals do not always remember what lies they had spoken, and when confronted with their own previous statement, the contradiction in the statements becomes very obvious.

These are just the routine plus and minus points for the individuals with Saturn in the 12th house. They become, at least sometimes, a victim by their own utterances, written statements, and acts and actions of commission and omission, anywhere and everywhere.

They thus drop into the trap of enquiry, investigation and action under rules, regulations and law of the land. Because they are, in many cases, themselves open to illegal gratification or obligation, they try their best to influence the enquiry officer or investigating authority to win over his or her favour leading to their acquittal.

This trick or theory sometimes works and sometimes falls flat with further adverse consequences for the individuals, depending on the position of Jupiter in the Birth-chart and its relationship with Saturn. This point leads us to the conclusion that barring a few, most of these individuals are apt to unfair and unjustified earnings and income, if not in cash, at least in kind or by way of obligations of other kind for self or kith and kin.

It has often been noticed that their money, at least a good part of it, goes the same way, which way it accrued in their hands. They presume, rightly to some extent in modern times, that everyone can be bought, in the same manner in which they themselves can be bought by others through bribes and illegal gifts.

They are often helpful to the members of immediate and distant family but always with an eye for return. And they have no hitch or hesitation in usurping the rightful possessions of others, whether they are friends or members of the immediate or wider family.

These individuals evade taking risk in helping or supporting or cooperating with other members of the immediate or wider family or friends. But they expect that those members of the family or friends must come to their help, support, and relief. Also rescue them without any reservation, restriction or restraint of any kind.

They often keep 'yesmen' quite handy, who would be prepared, no doubt for monetary or any other selfish consideration, to shoulder the responsibility for acts and actions of commission and omission by these individuals. For example, if the owner makes a serious accident by his vehicle killing or very seriously injuring any person, and that owner's chauffeur or driver takes the onus of the crime upon himself.

It is not unknown that mafia bosses never come to light for their nefarious and criminal activities, and it is always their goons who get caught for smuggling, trading in human flesh, unlawful trading in arms and ammunition or in drugs. The mafia bosses maintain the families of these goons when they are in police custody or in jail, and also manage their release or bail. It can go without argument that this type of mafia bosses might be having Saturn or Mars or Rahu or Herschel or any two of these hard stars in the 12th house. No doubt it is also true that these mafia lords do come to suffer the consequences of their acts and actions of commission and omission, sooner or later.

The question then arises is that when do they come under the clutches of law or of bad resultant luck. It is explained below:

(a) First of all, it has to be studied which are the stars in the 12th house with Saturn or whether Saturn is alone there.

(b) Whether Mars or Mercury or Jupiter has direct (*drishti*) aspect on Saturn from the 6th house.

(c) The birth Navamsha-chart should be studied whether it has any hard stars in the 12th house and any soft stars in the 6th house.

(d) Or any combination of hard and soft stars is in the 8th house.

It has also to be determined in this process which stars are most harmful and with how much strength, and when is the likely period of their causing the harm.

(a) Now, whenever the individual comes under mahadasa of Saturn and antardasa of that other planet connected with Saturn, or whenever the other planet has its mahadasa with Saturn's antardasa under it, the individual is likely to suffer consequences of own misdeeds of this birth or of the previous birth.

(b) Whenever **Saturn runs its *Saadhe-saati*** (seven-and-half years bad period by transit), the individual is to suffer consequences of his or her own misdeeds.

(c) Similarly when Saturn is in 4th or the 8th transit from Janma Rasi, that is also distinctively an unfavourable period lasting on an average for two-and-a-half years.

(d) Whenever Saturn is in an unfavourable position in the Yearly-chart.

(e) If Jupiter is lord of the 6th or the 12th house or Mars is lord of the 2nd or the 12th house, trouble can descend upon the individual during Saturn mahadasa and Jupiter sub-period, or Mars sub-period. The sufferings for own misdeeds can descend upon the individual during mahadasa of Jupiter or Mars and sub-period of Saturn thereunder.

It has to be noted that Saturn in the 12th house is capable of giving losses in industrial ventures, manufacturing units, in any other such business or income-generating activity as might be directly or indirectly connected with domain of Saturn.

It can give loss of money by jealousy and misdeed of any member of the family or an intimate friend. It can give loss of money by strike or any other kind of trouble created by labour force or other employees, or by pilferage or by embezzlement or by theft.

Loss of money can be caused due to natural calamity such as earthquake, landslides, drought conditions damaging crops owned by the individual, looting type attack by famine-struck groups of people.

It has however to be noted that unless Moon or Venus has direct connection with Saturn in the 12th house, loss by floods is not attributable to Saturn in the 12th house.

Saturn can lead to arrest or being confined in police or judicial custody. The periodicity is already mentioned above in this regard. If the individual is victim of any attack by a group of people or by a mass of people, it is no doubt attributable to Saturn in the 12th house. Saturn in 12th house, when embittered by direct contact with Mars or Jupiter can lead to sentence of simple or rigorous imprisonment of the individual.

It is often beneficial for the astrologer to judge the receptive tendency of the individual before predicting chances of imprisonment or corporal punishment, as the individual might not take it with an open mind and liberally.

Similarly any prediction regarding major rift within the immediate or wider family should also be given with a pinch of salt to make it digestible to the individual.

One very important point about Saturn in the 12th house is that though it makes bank balance and financial status of the individual fluctuating, Saturn never brings an individual to abject poverty or insolvency or bankruptcy, unless other stars like Sun, Mars or Jupiter are bent upon causing it.

Saturn in the 12th house means it is the 3rd position from the 10th house, which concerns source of income. Thus the individual is often hard working and active where the source of income is concerned. Very often students of astrology overlook this special result of Saturn in the 12th house.

Saturn and Sun, Moon, Mars, Mercury, Jupiter or Venus in the 12th House

Respective chapters on Sun, Moon, Mars, Mercury, Jupiter and Venus under the relevant sub-headings may please be referred to.

Saturn and Rahu in the 12th House

There is nothing much to say about Saturn and Rahu combination in the 12th house, because in this house too Rahu toes the action-line of Saturn.

Rahu adds to the force behind Saturn's results, whether good or bad. Further Rahu creates a kind of remote suspicion in the mind of the spouse about the morality of the individual's character and this ultimately leads to rift between husband and wife, unless it is either a joint family or the family is well knit even if living in separate premises.

Saturn is itself careless about the dress and connected outward appearance of the individual, and Rahu makes the dress more unfitting or unpresentable. It also depends to a certain extent on family background, surroundings, environment, social and professional status, and the kind of work being handled by the individual (physical, manual or intellectual). Then there are in certain jobs dress regulation connected with the work.

Further Rahu draws the attention of the individual towards members of the opposite sex with romantic touch, but at the same time Rahu doesn't induce initial advancement towards the opposite sex, in spite of the fact that the individual is spot-ready to respond.

Rahu carries a touch of ego wherever it is placed. Therefore, in the 12th house too, Rahu gives a kind of ego or vanity about family connections of the individual, capacity for spending money, political and bureaucratic connections (both Saturn and Rahu being in the 3rd position from the 10th house).

Rahu makes the individual over-confident about intellectual and physical capacities and capabilities of self, while Saturn alone gives confidence related to physical capacity only. Thus in this particular field, Rahu assumes a little superiority over Saturn. If Saturn in the 12th house makes an individual ruthless and physically violent, Rahu with Saturn in 12th house mentally encourages ruthlessness and physical violence.

One very special favourable influence of Rahu in the 12th house is that the individual is always able to put up a big and successful show at a low cost, which no other planet in the 12th house is capable of giving. If the individual spends just one hundred, it would appear as if the individual has spent 150 or 200 (choose your currency!) to put up that show with elegance and success. These individuals prove very useful for arranging marriages, parties, receptions, dinners etc. connected with election campaign where even small or cheap gifts offered to ordinary type of voters would make them feel gratified.

Saturn and Ketu in the 12th House

When in combination with Saturn in the 12th house, Ketu tries to improve upon or reduce the impact of bad or harmful or damaging results of the Saturn in the 12th house.

Ketu injects some softness in the hardened attitude of

Saturn towards the individual. Ketu impresses Saturn to think in kind and merciful manner, leading to lessen mutual quarrels and disputes within the family or with friends, or with co-workers and colleagues.

As already mentioned above more than once that Ketu carries the caricature of a soft planet, and therefore it reduces the impact or hurt or injury or loss to be caused by Saturn in the 12th house. Ketu also gives a literary touch to the nature of the individual.

When alone Saturn in the 12th makes the individual unkind, 'feelingless' and sometimes unhelpful or cruel towards others, and Ketu with Saturn in the 12th house brings softness and mercy to the mind of the individual.

In addition, Ketu encourages the individual to associate with charitable, social, public service or religious activities, and the individual feels inclined to donate or contribute financial help too to the public service cause.

There are one or two weak points also attached to this combination. It can cause a minor injury to the eye, specially the left eye, otherwise too, the eyesight of the individual goes weak after the age of 48 years. Sometimes (if Mars or Sun are also linked in some manner with the 1st or 2nd or 12th), there can be loss of eyesight in one or both eyes, if not earlier, at least by the age of 72 years or near about.

Ketu with Saturn in the 12th house disturbs the individual's relations with the maternal uncles and their family, based grossly on some misunderstanding relating to the opposite sex. But since Ketu is a shadow planet, a little careful conduct and behaviour on part of the individual can avoid the misunderstanding and consequent 'run down' of relations. Otherwise sometimes the misunderstanding gets cleared in the long run.

RAHU IN THE 12 HOUSES

Rahu in General

Since Rahu's (and Ketu's) combination with other stars (Sun, Moon, Mars, Mercury, Jupiter, Venus and Saturn) has already been discussed in the earlier relevant chapters, here we are discussing only the influence of Rahu (and Ketu) in the 12 Houses.

It needs no mention that Rahu and Ketu, the shadow planets are always 7:7 apart from each other; therefore the question of their combination with each other never arises.

Being shadow planets, they do not enjoy casting any *drishti* on any stars or any houses, although in modern times, some over-enthusiast astrologers have started attributing and attaching *drishti* to Rahu (and Ketu) too. In Indian astrology, Rahu is the Head of the Demon, and Ketu is Torso (Tail) of the Demon. Therefore logically the body of the Demon cut into two parts can have no *drishti* or Vision as such

Similarly, these two (shadow) stars do not own any house (Rasi) as such, though again some astrologers attribute this or that Rasi as their ownership. But even amongst mid-ancient astrologers there had never been any agreement on which particular Rasi was owned by Rahu (or Ketu) or which Rasi constituted exaltation and debilitation position for Rahu (and Ketu). Evenso, if the readers want to take some Rasi as owned by Rahu (and Ketu), and some other Rasi as house of Exaltation for Rahu, they are free to do so.

They must do so after checking up their viewpoint by critical observation for some years, by study of different horoscopes, of people from different walks of life and if possible from different parts of the world, which is so closely knit now.

Rahu in the 1ST House

The most important point of this position of Rahu is that it gives a sharp sense of ego to the individual, whether male or female, whether rich or poor, whether strong or weak, whether highly educated or less educated or even uneducated, whether well connected or isolated. However the individual doesn't indulge in a lot of bragging and boastful utterances unless Rahu is in conjunction with or aspected by Mercury directly, or occupies a Rasi owned by Mercury.

Normally Rahu alone in the 1st house has the capacity to make an individual very vocal and talkative, but without association of Mercury it doesn't make the individual very boastful and bragging.

Rahu gives reddish touch to the eyes, sometimes an unnoticeable touch of squint, quick tendency to pick up a quarrel, and shouting a lot while in a quarrel.

At the same time, the individual is bold, courageous with tendency to help and assist the people suffering from or under cruelty of wicked and exploitative people, and in so doing the individual is not much mindful of harm or hurt to self.

Rahu generally gives hesitation in starting own business/ industry/ profession or self-employment. But if any of these lines of livelihood were handed over to the individual by a parent, grandparent or anyone else, the individual would certainly settle down in that line. Otherwise if left to self, the individual would seek and adopt safe line of livelihood, like service, partnership in already working unit, living on income from rents and interest from investments.

A good point of Rahu in the 1st house is that these individuals often try to keep away from investment or dabbling in shares and stocks. They rely more on solid business or trading.

Since the question of 'ego' is directly and prominently involved, these individuals often make best attempt to come in contact with, as also try to become intimate with, people in power. And often these individuals make an effort to make such contacts and intimacy a subject of exhibition or common talk, public observation and publicity. Readers might have often seen certain individuals raising their heads and necks in photographs and visual media behind important personalities, just to have their face appear with the important personality, even though they have no concern, no connection to be there in that photograph or visual media!

Students of astrology may take that such individuals are likely to have Rahu in the 1st or the 9th house.

One important influence of Rahu in the 1st house is that in spite of sharp sense of 'ego' but these individuals are not normally disrespectful towards others. On the contrary, they are more respectful towards elders, teachers, parents, and learned or experienced people and also towards the women folk. No doubt these individuals do not tolerate insult of self or parents or teachers or elderly people even by other respectable people, and they do not hesitate to give vent to their feelings.

Rahu and Sun, Moon, Mars, Mercury, Jupiter, Venus or Saturn in the 1st House

Respective chapters on Sun, Moon, Mars, Mercury, Jupiter, Venus, and Saturn under the relevant sub-headings for 1st house may please be referred to.

RAHU IN THE 2ND HOUSE

There are a lot of misconceptions in the minds, not only of the general public but also in the minds of astrologers, that Rahu in the 2nd house is harmful to savings, bank balance and general wealth. No, it is not so. It is well established experience of several generations of astrologers of Madhya Pradesh, Gujarat and Rajasthan that

(a) Mars in the 2nd house at one time or the other in the life of the individual brings huge drop in the wealth and assets of the individual, and might even lead to poverty depending upon the family and social background of the individual, while

(b) Rahu in the 2nd house positively improves and multiplies the money element or wealth (in cash or assets) of the individual slowly, gradually and steadily. Combination of other stars (barring Mars) do not disturb this influence of Rahu, rather the other stars help increase the wealth of the individual in their own manner and method.

(c) If an individual has in the 2nd house both Rahu and Mars, the astrologer must be very careful in giving predictions, because both are strong stars, they have adversary attitude towards each other, and neither of the two would surrender the ground. Then what is the best method to arrive at a conclusion?

First of all, check up the degrees of the two. If they are within 6 degrees to each other, both would assert themselves, especially during their mahadasa and antardasa into each other's mahadasa, viz., Mars antardasa in Rahu mahadasa and Rahu's antardasa in Mars mahadasa. In such a case as this, on one hand, the individual would have good income and savings owing to Rahu's influence, and on the other, would suffer a loss or money gets stuck up owing to influence of Mars.

In case Mars and Rahu combination is within 12 degrees, the results would be more or less the same as when they are within 6 degree combination. However, if the combination is at a distance of more than 12 degrees, sometimes leading to their respective positions being in two different corners of the 2nd house, Rahu would not give much margin to Mars to function. No doubt, Mars would have a say to some extent and adversely affect the current income or level of savings or returns from investments. In doing so it ought to be borne in mind that it is always the position of Rahu and Mars in the Bhava-Chalitam chart which matters.

Then the next important point to judge the respective influence of Rahu and Mars together in the 2nd house is to check up their respective positions in the Navamsha-chart. If it is the horoscope of a female, check up the Trinshansha-chart too in addition to the Navamsha-chart. If in these charts, Mars holds good its influence over the 2nd house, while Rahu didn't hold its influence over the 2nd house, take it that Mars would give once or twice in life of the individual, a big jolt to money content and assets or wealth of the individual, be it a man or a woman. It would also give problems of blood system and eyesight to the spouse of the individual.

However, if Rahu is holding its influence over the 2nd house in the Navamsha-chart (Trinshansha-chart included in case of females) either directly or through its counterpart Ketu, Mars wouldn't find much scope to damage the money content and wealth of the individual. Very likely, both would hurt the health of the spouse or mutual relationship between wife and husband.

Rahu in the 2nd house induces the individual, in a big or a small manner, to share own money and wealth with other members of the family, though not so much with the society or community. This is true unless there are relevant stars to give this kind of result in the 4th and/or 9th house.

Rahu in the 2nd house is liberal towards the spouse to have enough money for spending but normally doesn't hand over full control of the entire purse to the spouse. No doubt, spouse gains weight in social and communal circles on account of growth in money and wealth of the life-partner, so much so that the spouse gains physical weight too, and special efforts are needed to maintain figure.

Rahu in the 2nd doesn't make very faithful lovers, rather slippery or casual ones, where physical contacts and regular meetings are concerned, but so long as the relationship continues, the individual is faithful financially.

These individuals do not have any reservations of caste, colour, creed, status, education etc in the matter of a love affair, but in financial dealings (like partnership or business association or sole representative or selling agent), these individuals keep their own selfish interest on top of everything. While entering into partnership with these individuals, Rahu's position vis-à-vis other stars should be checked, if possible between the Birth-chart of the partners, as is done in the case of matrimonial alliances.

And these individuals normally are not very fussy about upkeep, decoration, neatness, presentability of their premises of residence and work, whether temporary or long term or permanent one.

As stated above, in matters of employment, whether the individual is an employee or employer, caste, colour, creed of the employee or employer doesn't bother the individual, he or she being above these considerations, because the main aim and ambition is money.

Rahu and Sun, Moon, Mars, Mercury, Jupiter, Venus or Saturn the in the 2nd House

Respective chapters on Sun, Moon, Mars, Mercury, Jupiter, Venus, and Saturn under the relevant sub-headings for 2nd house may please be referred to.

RAHU IN THE 3RD HOUSE

This is one of the favourable positions of Rahu in so far as the individual is concerned. Normally success is achieved in whatever is handled by the individual; credit is earned for own work as well as for direct or indirect piracy of work of others. These individuals are often efficient advisers in war strategy, boundary disputes, water sharing disputes between two countries or two states or two counties, disputes between or among heirs or claimants of inheritance and heirloom. These individuals put up a bigger show of their work/ effort/ labour than what it is actually worth.

These individuals are not much sincere and helpful towards their kith, kin and brethren etc., but here too, they do not fail to put up a show as if they actually are sincere and helpful. They do not mind in encroaching upon or usurping due share of brothers, sisters, and cousins, but in doing so they often put up a show of disinterest in the shares of others.

However, they are always very serviceful to own spouse, own children, own employees (at home and at work), and pretty often even to friends. They are not so much serviceful to mother and females equivalent to mother, though they never fail to pronounce from housetops that they are very serviceful to mother.

On the other hand, these individuals often have an eye on getting monetary and other undeserved benefits from the mother or females equivalent to mother.

Though these individuals are not sheer cowards, but at the

same time they are not very brave and courageous. Rahu in 3rd gives the quality of bragging and boasting, and these individuals make best use of this quality.

These individuals are fond of owning one or more vehicles, keeping them in working condition always and replacing them by new and modern models as and when they can afford to do so.

One good quality is that they either these individuals do not borrow money on personal level, leave aside institutional loans etc., and if they have to borrow on personal level, they are careful to repay the loan on the promised date or as soon as possible. Loans given to these individuals do not generally sink as 'bad debt'.

Whether an injury is caused to them on a battlefield, in a dual, or by a fall or accident, immediate anti-septic treatment should be given, besides proper dressing etc. These individuals are apt to suffer from septicaemia or in worst cases from gangrene or allied trouble, all the more so is if Moon or Venus is in conjunction with Rahu within 12 degree-distance.

Rahu and Sun, Moon, Mars, Mercury, Jupiter, Venus or Saturn in the 3rd House

Respective chapters on Sun, Moon, Mars, Mercury, Jupiter, Venus, and Saturn under the relevant sub-headings for 3rd house may please be referred to.

RAHU IN THE 4TH HOUSE

It is generally believed that Rahu (and its counterpart Ketu) give only shadow results, but it has been observed that Rahu in the 4th house gives solid results, both good and bad.

The individual first suffers high expectations of the mother about the individual's performance in studies and in earlier stages of career. Later on, if mother's expectations remain fully or partly unfulfilled, she feels belittled in her own eyes as well as in the eyes of near and dear ones. The individual is often not able to do anything concrete in this regard, except remain a mute spectator.

The individual expects monetary and moralistic boosting from the mother between the age of 14 and 28 years, and if the expectation is unfulfilled, the individual feels frustrated in relations with the mother.

The individual is often very ambitious about own rise in career, bypassing others in competition, owning substantial real estate, making a show of charitable and socialite nature. In case the individual is from low family stock, he or she tries to somehow gain high standing in the social and work circles. The individual is fond of developing contacts with higher-ups merely to show off own status, and doesn't hesitate to pretend contacts with higher-ups even if they are not there. In other words, it is the hidden sense of 'ego' at work again. In this process the individual has no hitch in running down others without their fault, offence or guilt.

These individuals often grow fat around belly, buttocks and breast, while the spouse remains lean and thin, unless the stars of the spouse also indicate otherwise. Further the spouse sometimes suffers from inferiority complex, particularly when in the company of the life-partner. These individuals are fond of good and tasty food, not bothering about their health and body weight gained therefrom. After the age of 36 years, these individuals start complaints of digestive system and by the age of 54, they need regular medication in this behalf.

These individuals are normally careful drivers, but if they make a mistake and commit an accident, they make excuses and try to find a scapegoat to shift the responsibility. They prefer inflated claims on the insurance companies, also for personal injury and damage to the vehicle.

They are very often willing participants in any drive for social, charitable, medical, educational projects of public utility; contribute money too for the purpose, but more than money, they exert themselves for the program or project. By doing so, they seek recognition and respectability in the society.

Rahu's position in the 4th house should be studied properly with regard to progeny (getting children). If the wife is careless during the 3ʳᵈ and 4ᵗʰ months of pregnancy, it can either be termination of pregnancy or may lead to minor defect to the embryo. It is often so if Rahu's antardasa is running in Mars or Saturn mahadasa or Rahu is in transit over the 4ᵗʰ, 5ᵗʰ or 12ᵗʰ house in Birth-chart.

Rahu and Sun, Moon, Mars, Mercury, Jupiter, Venus or Saturn in the 4ᵗʰ House

Respective chapters on Sun, Moon, Mars, Mercury, Jupiter, Venus, and Saturn under the relevant sub-headings for 4ᵗʰ house may please be referred to.

RAHU IN THE 5ᵀᴴ HOUSE

It has to be recalled that the 5ᵗʰ house concerns education, wisdom, intelligence, experience, and also pregnancy; its successful continuance till delivery, health and longevity of the new born, management capacity of the individual. Rahu is a shadow planet, but in the 5ᵗʰ house it is perfectly effective whether in conjunction with a solid star or not. Rahu generates and controls 'ego' in the mind of every individual, even in childhood and school days.

Thus sometimes the child becomes over confident about performance in studies, which ultimately makes the foundation weak and the child suffers setback in education at the final stage of school leaving exams and then in the admission to college for higher studies. Therefore parents of children with Rahu in the 5ᵗʰ house should stay extra careful for laying a strong foundation for studies, check diversion of mind of the child, and supervise effectively the home work. Generally it has been observed that kids with Rahu in the 5ᵗʰ house are given to mild or serious mischief, excuses, interest in games/ playground/ Visual Media/ music/ talking to fellow students and companions, neighbourhood children. If Venus is also in the 5ᵗʰ house, such kids take interest in the gossips among women even in sophisticated families. This element of mischief and diversion prevails upto the age of 16 to 18 years, and warrants greater caution on the parts of parents, guardians and elders.

Another effect of Rahu in the 5th house is that it gives the child a tendency to depend on homework or notes of other students. This attitude converts into unfair means in the examination hall. However if Moon, Mercury, Jupiter or Venus be in the 6th or the 12th house, the mischief of using unfair means during writing an exam gets detected.

In so far as Rahu's effect on pregnancy and progeny is concerned, it may create trouble to the pregnancy in the 2nd, 3rd, 5th 7th and 8th months, and therefore such precautions as are suggested by the medical consultant must be observed strictly. If Saturn is in the 4th, 5th, 7th or 8th house in the Birth-chart or in any of these houses by transit during the pregnancy, the chances of its termination become more prominent. Mars hurts the pregnancy only when it is in the 8th or the 12th house in the Birth-chart, and is also in transit over either of these two houses or an antardasa of Mars is running under any mahadasa.

Rahu in the normal course doesn't create trouble at the time of the delivery of the child. But sometimes a minor mistake is committed by the midwife, nurse, or doctor or anyone attending the delivery process in disconnecting the umbilical cord, which might later on necessitate a minor surgery of the naval button of the mother or the child.

However it may be noted that if Rahu is in conjunction with Jupiter in the 5th house, none of the unfavourable points mentioned herein above would occur. If Venus is within 12 degrees of Rahu in the 5th house, the couple may observe restraint to protect the pregnancy. From the completion of the 5th month, the risk of abortion or termination of the pregnancy by Rahu's influence is starts waning.

However it has been generally observed that the progeny of these individuals may not be kept very tidy in their childhood, at least upto the age of 9 years.

Rahu gives theoretical efficiency in management, but unless Mars, Mercury or Jupiter is in the 5th house or in the 11th house, individuals with Rahu in the 5th house are not so very practical in management, particularly that of an industrial venture or manufacturing unit. If Rahu is alone in the 5th house, the individuals are lenient and liberal in matters concerning wages, allowances, overheads and other expenses, though this attitude reduces the level of profits.

Rahu and Sun, Moon, Mars, Mercury, Jupiter, Venus or Saturn in the 5th House

Respective chapters on Sun, Moon, Mars, Mercury, Jupiter, Venus, and Saturn under the relevant sub-headings for 5th house may please be referred to.

RAHU IN THE 6TH HOUSE

This is a favourable position for Rahu, but Rahu is not very effective in this house if it is alone. It is fully effective if it is in conjunction with a solid star within at the most 15 degrees.

In case it is so, Rahu would give good health, would cure any ailment, illness or disease rather quickly (though not permanently – chances of recurrence hang over).

If the stars in conjunction with Rahu in the 6th house are Mars, Saturn or even Sun or Herschel, Rahu would be helpful and effective in putting down or winning over the enemies, adversaries and opponents or competitors.

If Rahu is in combination with Mars or Saturn or Sun or Herschel it makes the progeny, at least one of them, richer than the parents. In case Rahu is in the company of Mercury, the progeny would be careless about books and exercise books and notebooks. They would be irregular in their homework too upto the age of 14th years.

If Venus is with Rahu in the 6th house, the individual would indulge in extra-marital relationship, which may get detected and hurt the individual's reputation for some time. Sometimes it might lead to loss of face and money both in one go. If it is a case of a female, she might be cheated in matters of money and assets by the paramour.

In case Jupiter is in the 6th house in conjunction with

Rahu, the individual would feel prompted to indulge in litigation, and might win some of the times. In litigation between husband and wife, the responding party would be at an advantage, and if possible such a contingency should be avoided.

There can be loss of money or assets by cheating, theft or speculation or money lending.

If Moon and Rahu are together in the 6th house, though it becomes an Eclipse combination, the individual is at an advantage, as Moon would not be successful in making the individual a brooding person or an introvert.

Individuals with Rahu in the 6th house are generally free from debts and they maintain good prestige in friends' circle and in the market. They often keep a vigilant eye on their budget and try to remain within limits of capacity to spend whatever the occasion. It is not easy to provoke these individuals to spend wastefully.

Rahu and Sun, Moon, Mars, Mercury, Jupiter, Venus or Saturn in the 6th House

Respective chapters on Sun, Moon, Mars, Mercury, Jupiter, Venus, and Saturn under the relevant sub-headings for 6th house may please be referred to.

RAHU IN THE 7TH HOUSE

Often the spouse has a sharp sense of ego, and harmony in married life would depend on the placements of the lords of the 1st and the 7th house and their relationship with Rahu in the 7th house. When soft planets like Moon, Mercury, Jupiter or Venus is in the 7th house, the married life would run smoothly. If Mars or Saturn (to an extent Sun too) be there in the 7th house within 12 degrees of Rahu, the married life would be uneven, often reaching the point of separation or parting company permanently.

In this context, it is advantageous to re-read the influence of Mars or Saturn in the 7th house in their respective chapters earlier.

Since the 7th house concerns business or normal transactions and deals, Rahu in this house assumes importance. The 7th house concerns the seller, and sometimes the seller stands on ego and thereby abruptly misses the finalisation of the deal or transaction, and later regrets it. However, Rahu ensures that both buyer and seller are straightforward in the deal, and no unethical behaviour is involved in the matter. If in a deal, one party is a non-business person and the other party is a regular trader or business person, the non-business person has to stay alert as the regular business person might take undue advantage of the lack of business gambit and tactics of the non-business individual.

As the 7th house concerns quarrels, fights, battles and war too, Rahu in the 7th house, the individual makes empty noises but has less courage and boldness to fight as a fearless person or as a warrior. No doubt these individuals are good strategists, but there too, they give in to a point of dispute rather easily, without much argument or bargain. In case the quarrel or dispute is between husband and wife, the husband would have an upper hand when a male Rasi (Aries, Gemini, Leo, Libra etc) is in the 7th house. When it is a female Rasi (Taurus, Cancer, Virgo, Scorpio etc) in the 7th house, the wife would have the last word.

Rahu in the 7th house can give minor complaints relating to the private parts, provided a hard planet is neither in the 7th house nor has a direct *drishti* on the 7th house (and Rahu therein) from the 1st house. If the hard planet's influence or interference were there, the trouble would be more severe and would take longer time to cure.

And the somewhat ridiculous effect of Rahu in the 7th house is that the individual might make use of the spouse to win favours, to get a certain job done or to earn money or gifts in kind. When Mars is in the 7th house with Rahu, the wife might take it upon herself to do the same with or without knowledge of the individual. However, if Saturn is with Rahu in the 7th house, the individual would show no qualms in pressurising the spouse to use her charms.

An important influence of Rahu in the 7th house is that it affects the sex drive between the husband and the wife.

In case Mars happens to be lord of the 1st or the 7th house and Saturn be in the 1st or the 7th house, or Saturn is lord of the 1st or the 7th house and Mars is in the 1st or the 7th house, the female is likely to get her menopause at an earlier age than normal. Also this type of planetary situation in a female's Birth-chart restricts the number of children she can bear.

The 7th House involves very touchy and delicate questions pertaining to the private life of an individual, whether male or female. The astrologer must proceed with great care and caution in study of the horoscope and expression of views, as often people feel hurt, even if the study and views of the astrologer are correct. It discourages the clients to pay a repeated visit to the astrologer for consultation, and people with hurt feelings tend to bad mouth astrology.

There are very few people who want a frank, honest and correct study of their Birth-chart or that of the spouse.

Rahu and Sun, Moon, Mars, Mercury, Jupiter, Venus or Saturn in the 7th House

Respective chapters on Sun, Moon, Mars, Mercury, Jupiter, Venus, and Saturn under the relevant sub-headings for 7th house may please be referred to.

RAHU IN THE 8TH HOUSE

The first thing Rahu does in the 8th house is to give obesity to the individual, specially during Rahu's own mahadasa or during Saturn's transit over the 8th house. It becomes rather difficult to shed the flab given by Rahu, though by effort, the weight fluctuates, reduces by physical exercise or going for a walk daily; and when the exercise or walking is stopped, the weight returns to its pre-exercise level in most cases.

Rahu gives a fall from higher level, from a raised bed or 'Jhula" in childhood, but unless Saturn is concerned with the 8th house, the injury given by Rahu is not serious and gets cured easily and quickly. In accidents too, when Rahu is alone in the 8th

house, the injury would be less harmful and less severe. But when Saturn too is in 8th or 2nd house it can be a fracture of bone(s).

Rahu in the 8th house, during its mahadasa or antardasa, may give complaints of piles or fistula etc.

Then in some cases, depending on the background of the individual during educational stage and post-education days, Rahu may give a tendency towards smuggling of consumer goods, commodities and in some rare cases, kidnapping and smuggling of kids and grown ups, including trade in flesh. Rahu in this position, may lead to tendency for other crimes too, but much depends on the others planets in conjunction with Rahu in the 8th house or casting *drishti* on Rahu directly from the 2nd house. *Remember that Rahu is a <u>shadow</u> planet, and is capable of giving concrete results only when it is in conjunction with any solid planet like Sun, Moon, Mars, Mercury, Jupiter, Venus, or Saturn.*

Of these, the combination with Moon in the 8th house often leads to mental problems, viz., weak memory, forgetfulness, not remembering faces of persons or their names/ surnames etc., mental disturbance, worry-oriented nature, partial or near-complete mental disorder, sometimes leading to partial or near-complete insanity. In this combination, much depends on the Rasi in the 8th house. If it is Cancer, Capricorn, Scorpio or Pisces, chances of mental disorder are very strong, and preventive measures should be taken in the childhood itself or as soon as even remote possibility of it comes to notice of the parents or guardians.

Another unfavourable effect of Rahu in the 8th house is of an injury to the individual by four-legged animals, snakes and reptiles, crocodiles (if a watery Rasi is in the 8th house or Moon or Venus be in conjunction with Rahu in the 8th house). Rahu can even lead to rabies trouble, in which case, immediate medical treatment is the only remedy.

In the early 1940's, the ruling Maharajah of a princely Indian state (Jhalawar) in lower Rajasthan had Rahu in the 8th house and he was running Rahu mahadasa with Rahu antardasa. During Dusshera festival in October, the elephant the Maharajah was riding suddenly went amuck and there were fears that the Maharajah might be thrown off and crushed under the feet of the *elephant.* One of the horse-riders of the state cavalry, who were also part of the festive procession, swiftly took out his sword and chopped the trunk of the amuck elephant, and thus saved the life of the Ruler of his state.

Rahu in the 8th house, if in watery Rasi, can give risk to the individual from water, (still-water or flowing) pond, tank, well, river, sea, or ocean. The periodicity has to be fixed by checking the mahadasa and antardasa of Rahu and of the lord of the watery Rasi or vice-versa. In such cases, the progressive Yearly-chart gives very correct and specific guidance.

If Rahu is alone in the 8th house, it can give an injury to the individual in any quarrel, fighting, movement, demonstration, procession, mass violence, action by militancy; but Rahu alone in the 8th house would not cause death, not even permanent invalidity, incapacity etc.

No doubt Rahu can cause, even if alone in the 8th house, some long term illness or disease, which doesn't prove fatal so long as another planet's fatal influence does not associate with Rahu in the 8th house.

Rahu in the 8th house can cause differences with spouse or her/ his family over matters related to money and other assets, because Rahu leads to the richness of the spouse, which the individual may or may not cherish, ultimately leading to differences between husband and wife, or between lovers.

Rahu and Sun, Moon, Mars, Mercury, Jupiter, Venus or Saturn in the 8th House

Respective chapters on Sun, Moon, Mars, Mercury, Jupiter, Venus, and Saturn under the relevant sub-headings for 8th house may please be referred to.

RAHU IN THE 9TH HOUSE

Rahu alone in the 9th house is not very effective, unless it is in conjunction with some other planet or it enjoys direct *drishti* from the lord of the 9th house.

Further on account of Rahu in the 9th house, the individual changes colour (of nature and relations with people) according to the planet in conjunction with Rahu in the 9th house. If there be no other planet in the 9th house with Rahu, it would follow in the footsteps of the lord of the 9th house.

In case the planet in conjunction with Rahu in the 9th house is a soft planet, (Mercury, Venus or Jupiter) Rahu would help in advancement of the good luck of the individual. Rahu and its accompanying star would make the individual quite religious by mind and action, and if the accompanying star is lord of the 9th, 10th or 11th or the 5th house, the individual would be associated with some non-governmental organisation (NGO) concerned with charitable, social or religious activity. The same results will be there for the individual if the 9th house is owned by any of these soft planets (excluding Moon) and that lord of the 9th house is occupying the 5th, 10th or 11th house in the birth-chart.

It might have been noticed that while discussing the soft stars in conjunction with Rahu in the 9th house, Moon has not been included. It is not an oversight. It is intentional. Moon in conjunction with Rahu, whatever the Rasi there, constitutes ECLIPSE combination, which means Moon is not free to act in the company of Rahu and it would give merely subdued results of good luck and religious/ social/ charitable activity for the individual. But Moon would give full results if it owns the 9th house and is sitting away from Rahu in the 5th, 10th or 11th house. It has to be noted that if Moon is in bright half of the month, the good results are more or less guaranteed. It is known as waxing process of Moon.

However if the Moon is in waning process (as in the dark half of the month), its' results would be barely half or even less than that, depending on how close it is to the "No-Moon day (*Amaavasya*)".

On the other hand, if Rahu is in conjunction with Mars, Saturn or Herschel (Uranus), the individual would be deceitful in matters related to management of religious/ charitable/ social organisations, and the individual would constantly be making efforts to gain more power and position in the concerned non-governmental organisation(s). In other matters too, the individual would not hesitate to encroach upon rights and possessions of others, including brothers, sisters and cousins.

When the 9th house is owned by Mars, Saturn or Sun and the lord of the house is positioned in the 3rd, 4th, 6th, 8th or the 12th house, the individual will be overpowered by selfish motives and ruthlessness in fulfilment of those motives. The individual would not normally distinguish between whom to hurt and whom to spare. The individual would have no hesitation in piracy of literary, charitable, social, religious works and achievements of others, including fellow workers, colleagues, subordinates and friends too.

The individual would develop the tendency to back-bite others, run down those who do good to the individual (which can be termed ungratefulness), and the individual might have no hitch in harming or hurting the person who has done good to the individual. The individual's selfish motive is on top of everything in life.

It has also to be noted that whether Rahu is alone in the 9th house or is in conjunction with any soft or hard planet, the individual suffers from a hidden sense of fear and timidity. They might fail to prove their worth at a moment and place or at situation warranting chivalry, boldness, bravery and courage.

It is also a quality of these individuals that they are happy with distant relations and try to keep away or remain disinterested in the affairs of real brothers, sisters or cousins. These individuals indulge in flattery and expect flattery, which can hardly be expected from real brothers, sisters or cousins.

If Sun, Mars or Saturn accompanies Rahu in the 9th house, the individual would try to usurp rightful possessions/ assets/ money and wealth of brother, sister, cousin or even an uncle or aunt by unfair/ unjustified means and methods. This is very much true when the individual is running Rahu mahadasa with antardasa of Sun, Mars or Saturn or vice-versa, that is, mahadasa of Sun or Mars or Saturn with antardasa of Rahu therein.

Individuals having Rahu in the 9th house, whether accompanied by any other planet or not, are not very trustworthy and dependable in political matters. They take no time in changing colour and changing party of their affiliation. It's best examples can be found in Indian politics since early 1950's. And in case Moon in waning process is within 12 degrees of Rahu in the 9th house, these individuals would not let their mind known even to their godfathers, patrons, faithful followers and financiers, when they change colour or party of affiliation. In case Saturn is within 15 degrees of Rahu in the 9th house, the individual would take a good portion of his companions, colleagues and followers to the other political party.

Rahu and Sun, Moon, Mars, Mercury, Jupiter, Venus or Saturn in the 9th House

Respective chapters on Sun, Moon, Mars, Mercury, Jupiter, Venus, and Saturn under the relevant sub-headings for 9th house may please be referred to.

RAHU IN THE 10TH HOUSE

It is interesting to note that even when alone, Rahu is quite effective in the 10th house. First of all it gives a sense of ego to the individual, whatever her or his position or power or authority or command or control be in the field of livelihood, earnings or income. Individuals have been noticed having no power or position or direct means of livelihood or self-employment or any touch of career or profession or calling, but wear their ego on their sleeve without hitch or hesitation.

Further, Rahu functions independently in the 10th house without being influenced by other stars in conjunction with it there. Rahu in the 10th house doesn't get influenced by the lord of the 10th house or by Rahu's mutual relationship with the lord of the 10th house.

The individual may have or may not have any position, power or authority or independent source of livelihood, it won't matter much. The individual would indulge in talks and comments on any current or past event or matter or happening of local reference or any event with wider implications and thus try, to the best extent possible, to impress the listeners. At any meeting, gathering or in any crowd, this individual makes best efforts to be noticed by people who matter and would try to come to front-line.

These individuals would try to act or speak or talk in a manner to seek attention of those present and also of those who matter for that moment.

These individuals treat every one else's money, assets and resources as their own, and therefore they do not hesitate in using and utilising those assets or resources for their own benefit. Approval or disapproval of the real owner matters little. But in spite of this tendency of usurping money, assets and resources of others, very rarely these individuals get treated as rich or well possessed, because often it is "easy come" is "easy gone".

Whether they are capable or not, these individuals often try to be romantic by nature, show fondness for music and poetry, if for nothing else, at least to impress others and be noticed in the social and influential circles. Critics might call it an 'inferiority complex' but for them it is not so.

In case these individuals are themselves in active politics, social service, or exponents of vocal or instrumental music or reciting poetry (whether own composition or pirated), they often want to be surrounded or accompanied by members of the opposite sex. Yes, it is so in case of female artists and poetesses too, they desire to be surrounded or accompanied by male followers or friends.

In their desire to be seen with important people in any of the fields mentioned above, and otherwise too for selfish purposes, these individuals often undertake short and long journeys. These individuals prove helpful in gathering crowds for social, political, religious gatherings and meetings or rallies. They do so only when they are sure of their share in the management money or other gains from doing so. If their self-interest or main purpose is not served, they do not hesitate even for a moment from changing sides, whatever the field of activity; and if escape is not possible, they would make excuses and absent themselves from active participation.

Rahu and Sun, Moon, Mars, Mercury, Jupiter, Venus or Saturn in the 10th House

Respective chapters on Sun, Moon, Mars, Mercury, Jupiter, Venus, and Saturn under the relevant sub-headings for 10th house may please be referred to for results of these seven combinations with Rahu in the 10th house.

RAHU IN THE 11TH HOUSE

Whatever the Rasi in the 11th house and whosoever the lord of the 11th house, Rahu is always a benefactor in the 11th house, even if it is alone and not accompanied by any hard planet.

The individual, if given to correct habits and the right company of friends, never suffers from want of money; and unless he or she goes in for big investments, there crops up no cause for incurring debts. In any horoscope the best positions for Rahu to give unconditional financial benefits are the 2nd and the 11th house. There are not many repercussions of Rahu in the 11th house, except that in some cases, it adversely affects the educational progress of the kids, and that too when their own birth stars are unhelpful for their education.

If Aries or Aquarius are not in the Ascendant (Lagna), Rahu in the 11th house gives a pleasing personality, cheerful in personal conversation, impressive in public speaking, with a touch of witticism in talks, not unnecessarily abashed, rather somewhat frank and straightforward.

When the opportunity is there, the individual wouldn't hesitate to be deceitful, clever, cunning and sometimes cheating too in money matters. They tend to give preference to their personal interests over all other matters, on some occasions even to the call of duty.

Where the individual's own interests are not in conflict, he or she is quite helpful, charitable and willing to volunteer service of any nature including physical service to others, whether they are known or unknown, even to animals and birds. In that sense the individual is kind hearted, doesn't brag or boast of the help given or service rendered.

If other planets do not seriously obstruct, Rahu is always helpful to the individual in job, business, self-employment, profession or any other source of livelihood, particularly when Rahu mahadasa or its antardasa or its favourable transit runs. Even losses incurred during any other period get wiped off during Rahu's favourable transit or Mahadasa-antardasa. Rahu stays in a Rasi for 18 months and returns to the same Rasi after its 18-year round.

Rahu and Sun, Moon, Mars, Mercury, Jupiter, Venus or Saturn in the 11th House

Respective chapters on Sun, Moon, Mars, Mercury, Jupiter, Venus, and Saturn under the relevant sub-headings for 11th house may please be referred to.

RAHU IN THE 12TH HOUSE

The principle that applies to this house is that Rahu (or Ketu) alone is not very effective and influential; it would need the company of other solid star to give results.

However it has to be noted that Rahu is rarely helpful in the 12th house to the individual concerned, not even to the individual's progeny; but no doubt helpful to a limited extent to the real father or mother-in-law of the individual.

Rahu in the 12th house encourages an individual to spend money for charity and social work, but the main aim is "name and fame", rather than real sympathy and mercy for the sufferers. And money thus spent for charity and social work is normally not coming out of the individual's earnings by hard work or labour, but from funds derived through unfair means, through participation in or association with illegal activity. This may include hoarding for profiteering, smuggling, and depending on other planet in the 12th house. In few cases, the charity or social service might be to camouflage some anti-social or anti-national activity of the recent past.

Rahu in the 12th house is capable of giving a strong-built body, shoulders, neck, and chest, giving the body an impressive appearance.

Rahu on its own in the 12th house doesn't lead an individual to police custody, prison, imprisonment, or punishment. But if Mars, Saturn, Herschel or even Jupiter, by virtue of its presence in the 12th house is with Rahu, it can lead an individual towards any kind of punishment. Rahu otherwise alone in 12th house leads to punishment in terms of money or confiscation of assets or even a portion of the property, but never imprisonment. Confiscation of immoveable property takes place only when Mars too is in the 12th house.

Imprisonment with hard labour or any punishment severe than that, doesn't normally occur, unless Mars, Saturn or Herschel is also in the 12th house (within 12 degree conjunction with Rahu there) of the individual. At the same time, Mars or Saturn (or to an extent Sun) happens to be the lord of the 3rd, 6th, 8th or of the 12th house itself, and Rahu as well as conjoining planet haven't changed position from the 12th house in the Bhava-Chalitam chart. It is always safe to determine the Navamsha positions of Rahu and its accompanying planet, whether the Navamsha positions are protecting the individual against severe punishment or Navamsha position is increasing the punishment.

As already stated above in this context that Rahu alone in the 12th house, irrespective of its position in Navamsha-chart, doesn't normally go beyond financial penalty, fine, and loss of money or assets.

Rahu and Sun, Moon, Mars, Mercury, Jupiter, Venus or Saturn in the 12th House

Respective chapters Sun, Moon, Mars, Mercury, Jupiter, Venus, and Saturn under the relevant sub-headings for 12th house may please be referred to.

KETU IN THE 12 HOUSES

KETU IN GENERAL

It has to be borne in mind that normally Ketu gives results parallel to that of Mercury, and unlike Rahu, when alone, Ketu rarely gives more than 50 per cent results of its position in any particular house.

Further Ketu is not very operative in the Navamsha-chart, and not at all in the Trinshansha-chart, because in Trinshansha-chart, Ketu occupies the same house as that by Rahu, and therefore it is totally inoperative in Trinshansha-chart. Some learned astrologers do not mention Ketu in the Trinshansha-chart, which chart is very important in the horoscopes of females for study of marriage, married life and relations with husband and his family.

KETU IN THE 1ST HOUSE

The individual is gifted with intelligence and sharp 'grasping power' but without the support of Mercury or Jupiter, the individual is generally not able to make full and apparent use of own intelligence, wisdom and power to grasp a subject taught or learnt. Generally brothers, sisters, cousins and fellow students in school and college and colleagues in career run-down the individual with regard to his or her intelligence and power to grasp, and the individual is to an extent helpless in the matter.

This tendency on part of self and the unhelpful attitude of the near and dear ones develops a sense of fear and timidity in the individual sometimes resulting in withdrawal symptoms. This fear complex prevails to certain degree in the individual even after marriage and even after birth of a child. On the other hand, the individual does not entertain fear from wife and children, though entertains fears pertaining to them.

The individual lacks wickedness and cruelty, and is

sometimes exploited by wicked and cruel persons. Their own brethren also keep aloof in such situations, unless the individual has hard planets in the 3rd, 6th or 11th houses, or soft planets (Mercury, Jupiter and to an extent Venus) in the 5th, 9th or the 10th house.

Another problem with these individuals is that during school and college life, they come to adverse notice for faults and offences of others.

The favourable result of Ketu in the 1st house is that in career, if the individual gets work warranting use of intelligence and experience, he or she gets success and appreciation of those who matter.

Ketu and Sun, Moon, Mars, Mercury, Jupiter, Venus or Saturn in the 1st House

Respective chapters on Sun, Moon, for Mars, Mercury, Jupiter, Venus and Saturn under the relevant sub-headings for the 1st house may please be referred to.

KETU IN THE 2ND HOUSE

The individual is fond of collecting books and magazines - good and inferior, all kinds - some are read, some are glanced at and others are just added to collection. The individual is good in literature, writing and in accounting. But the individual sometimes behaves like a highbrow, given to pretension and vanity. This last attribute leads the individual to differences with the spouse or family thereof, as also presumed misbehaviour with government officials, thereby incurring their annoyance and resultant trouble.

Some of the individuals have to face non cooperation from certain members of the family of self and spouse, have to spend money and effort to prove helpful, to appease such members of the family. Spouse gains weight after marriage, with the result that sometimes the individual is (at least in mind) attracted towards others. In spite of gifted with intelligence and knowledge, the individual is unable to read and understand the mind of own spouse, which leads to partial aloofness in one of the two.

These individuals are careful and tactful in management of whatever money they have got, and therefore they are rarely so short of hard cash as to borrow from others. As far as possible, they avoid borrowing from any member of the family of self or spouse, but they unhesitatingly borrow from close friends. These individuals repay the borrowed money, but rarely by the promised date.

These individuals should always take better care of their ear nose and throat, particularly against any mild injury. And if they are active participants in sports and games, they should take extra care against injury to the skull, lest it might lead to neurological ailment sooner or later in life.

Ketu and Sun, Moon, Mars, Mercury, Jupiter, Venus or Saturn in the 2nd House

Respective chapters on Sun, Moon, Mars, Mercury, Jupiter, Venus, and Saturn under the relevant sub-headings for the 2nd House may please be referred to for results of these seven combinations with Ketu in the 2nd House.

KETU IN THE 3RD HOUSE

The individual with Ketu in the 3rd House makes efforts by own initiative and wisdom, has got beautiful handwriting, can plan and implement a strategy in any confrontation or conflict.

The individual bears impressive appearance and personality, bear the boldness and courage to face difficult persons and difficult situations. They display expertise in management of money of self and employers, are aggressive in any dispute so long as it is limited to spoken or written words, but feel inner timidity where the dispute enters the arena of violence at individual or collective level.

The individual is restrained in coming to the rescue of kith and kin in their difficult moments or difficult situations, but volunteers help, support and relief to friends and colleagues.

The individual might some time or the other suffer pain

or injury in the right arm or armpit or muscles near right ribs or right hand, but the pain or injury is easily and quickly curable. Such injury normally doesn't leave behind any invalidity or non-functioning of the limb, though the story would be different if Saturn influences Ketu (in the 3rd house) by direct *drishti*.

These individuals normally have strained relations with one of the brothers, sisters or cousins of self or of the spouse, on account of either side's doing. It is also likely that if Venus has any association with Ketu in the 3rd house, the individual might develop physical or platonic relationship within the family at own age-level. It happens so because normally the individual is gifted with fast-moving and fast-changing mind with less self-control on romantic side of the mind.

Because of their capacity and expertise in the management of money, these individuals rarely suffer paucity of hard cash, unless they have soft stars in the 6th house or any stars (soft or hard) in the 12th house.

Ketu and Sun, Moon, Mars, Mercury, Jupiter, Venus or Saturn in the 3rd House

Respective chapters on Sun, Moon, Mars, Mercury, Jupiter, Venus, and Saturn under the relevant sub-headings for the 3rd house may please be referred to for results of these seven combinations with Ketu in the 3rd house.

KETU IN THE 4TH HOUSE

Because Ketu is a shadow planet, if alone, it is not very effective in the 4th house, though the individual gets less care and affection from mother in infancy or childhood. It may take the individual away from mother in childhood for schooling or any other purpose, but this is not a hard and fast rule. It might not be so, depending on other stars in the 4th house or position of the lord of the 4th house and that lord's relationship with the 4th house as well as with Ketu.

Same theory would apply to accidental injury, especially injury by any vehicle or a four-legged (pet or wild) animal, particularly dog, fox, jackal, horse, donkey, pony, camel, elephant, cow, buffalo, goat or a fall from an animal while riding it. The injury can be caused on a play-field, whether actually participating in the game/ sport or not. The injury could even be by a wild animal in a circus or in a jungle.

Ketu in the 4th house can cause loss of at least one pregnancy to own mother at a very early stage, which can be called a mere conception. Otherwise too, there might be minor complaints of health to mother within four years of the birth of the individual.

If the mother owned any assets or property in her independent and exclusive capacity, there are strong chances of the individual inheriting full or substantial part of those assets or property, more often, after the death of the mother.

It is also likely that others would throw their claims in the arena of succession, but the individual has better chances of winning the battle, especially with support of documents like gift-deed, will, etc. However, Ketu in the 4th house is rather unconcerned and unconnected with the individual's other inheritance from father or uncle or sources other than the mother. That depends on other houses in the Birth-chart, their lords and planets in the 4th or the 9th house.

Ketu in the 4th house gives greater mobility to the individual, within town, within same province and within the country, and if a watery Rasi is in the 4th house and if its lord is supportive, in foreign countries too. Otherwise too, travel to foreign countries today has become like a travel to a neighbour's garden. No doubt, the individual keeps links with roots in the home country, home town, and if he or she owns any property, he or she maintains the ownership during active life of self, unless other solid stars interfere in the matter.

Individuals with Ketu in the 4th house should always take better care of their digestive system and control their weight.

The individual is charitable and serviceful socially, but in a limited sense because Ketu is after all a shadow star.

Ketu and Sun, Moon, Mars, Mercury, Jupiter, Venus or Saturn in the 4th House

Respective chapters on Sun, Moon, Mars, Mercury, Jupiter, Venus and Saturn under the relevant sub-headings for the 4th House may please be referred to for results of these seven combinations with Ketu in the 4th House.

KETU IN THE 5TH HOUSE

The individual is good at studies, particularly in grasp of the subject taught or read by self, but evasive in homework more or less throughout the schooling. These individuals have very good and impressive handwriting, are very much interested in general reading for the sake of developing vast treasure of general knowledge (if Mercury too is in the 5th house with Ketu, the individual develops knowledge sometimes like a mobile Encyclopaedia). They have got rich vocabulary, and are good at writing essays and compositions, which sometimes develops as a writing talent in later life.

Ketu in the 5th house gives loss of at least one conception, be it naturally or through medical termination. And in the same breath, Ketu gives a full term (healthy child, if the stars of the other partner are not obstructive) as a compensation to that loss of one or two conceptions caused by Ketu in the 5th house.

It is an unfortunate part of Ketu in the 5th house that it gives second thoughts to the individual, and sometimes regret and repentance over one's own mistakes and lapses in planning and in implementation of those plans, and regrets on plans abandoned midway.

Ketu in 5th house can give extra flab around the waistline and lower body especially to females, if not earlier, at least after birth of two children. This extra fat might give, after the age of 54 years, trouble in walking, getting up and sitting down, in terms of gout, arthritis, rheumatism, sclerosis, cicatrix, and allied complaints of health. Otherwise Ketu helps in keeping strong physique and work-oriented health.

Ketu and Sun, Moon, Mars, Mercury, Jupiter, Venus or Saturn in the 5th House

Respective chapters on Sun, Moon, Mars, Mercury, Jupiter, Venus, and Saturn under the relevant sub-headings for the 5th house may please be referred to for results of these seven combinations with Ketu in the 5th House.

KETU IN THE 6TH HOUSE

This is a house where Ketu's results are not parallel to that of Mercury, though in other houses Ketu gives results parallel to those of Mercury. Ketu in the 6th house gives an alert mind, good memory, tendency to follow up past events and actions (but not in revengeful manner). It also gives a healthy body, tendency to work hard constantly and continuously, convenience of means of transport. To those living in rural areas Ketu gives fondness for pets and milch animals, keenness to forgive minor offence or insult by others, but not to forgive or forget serious type of insult and injury.

Along the of Rahu and Saturn, Ketu in the 6th house is capable of giving differences or even dispute with maternal uncles, maternal aunts, in rare cases, based on question of inheritance from maternal grandparents or maternal family. If Jupiter is in conjunction with Ketu within 12 degrees, the differences and disputes might go to the extent of legal action, because Ketu in the 6th house gives narrow-mindedness especially where maternal family is concerned.

Ketu gives quick recovery from illness, provided it is not a bone injury nor fracture or sex-related complaints of health. Individuals with conjunction of Venus with Ketu in the 6th house should try to keep away from extra-marital relationship or free-lance physical relations with any sex.

Ketu and Sun, Moon, Mars, Mercury, Jupiter, Venus or Saturn in the 6th House

Respective chapters on Sun, Moon, Mars, Mercury, Jupiter, Venus, and Saturn under the relevant sub-headings for the 6th house may please be referred to for results of these seven combinations with Ketu in the 6th house.

KETU IN THE 7TH HOUSE

This position of Ketu makes an individual travel a lot, even in childhood (with any member of the family or sometimes alone too). The journeys would not always be comfortable or successful, and minor complaints of health like fever, headache, fluctuation in blood pressure might follow a long or tiresome journey, whatever the mode of travel.

The individual often tends to worry a lot, when away from home for several days, weeks or one or two months. The worry relates to affairs at home and about members of the family including the spouse. When Ketu is connected with Mars or Saturn in the 7th house, it generates a remote sense of suspicion about the spouse, moreso in cases where strain exists in the relationship between husband and wife!

If there is a watery Rasi (Cancer, Aquarius, and Pisces) and Capricorn in the 7th house, the individual should stay cautious about water, be it a tank, pond, swimming pool, river, sea or ocean, or even drinking water storage tanks. The individual should never take risk with water, notwithstanding the individual's capacity and competence in swimming.

Another weak point with these individuals is that they spend heavily under provocation or emotion, and then regret the spending, particularly if the expenditure was meant for spouse or the family. But these individuals do not mind wasteful expenditure on friends of either sex. Their annoyance and anger also remains under control in relationship to outsiders of either sex, though it is not the same at home and with immediate family and wider family.

One school of thought holds the view that Ketu is more favourable when in Scorpio, but experience doesn't confirm it. On the other hand, Ketu in Scorpio gives sometimes pain or a minor sexual ailment and also relating to reproductive system in females.

Ketu and Sun, Moon, Mars, Mercury, Jupiter, Venus or Saturn in the 7th House

Respective chapters on Sun, Moon, Mars, Mercury, Jupiter, Venus, and Saturn under the relevant sub-headings for 7th house may please be referred to for results of these seven combinations with Ketu in the 7th house.

KETU IN THE 8TH HOUSE

Ketu in the 8th house generally gives injury or accident by a vehicle or horse, donkey, mule, camel, elephant, buffalo etc., but if Ketu is not in anyway under the influence of Saturn or Mars, the injury would be minor and easily curable. It can give bite injury by a dog, jackal, fox, monkey, camel etc., which may or may not cause rabies. Sting or bite by a poisonous snake, crocodile, scorpion, or wasp is included in the results of Ketu in the 8th house.

If Ketu is in conjunction with Moon or Venus, particularly in a watery Rasi, risk is involved from water or from food poisoning. Then very often Ketu in the 8th house causes piles (haemorrhoids) trouble especially if there is a history of piles on the father's or mother's side, even two generations away. Fistula or allied ailment would not need any family history.

Another aspect of Ketu in the 8th house is inclination towards unnatural physical contact with either sex. Study of the horoscopes of gays or lesbians would indicate that at least 50 per cent of them would have Rahu or Ketu in the 8th house, very specially Ketu in the 8th house. It has been noticed that some people develop this interest at an advanced age, say beyond 45 or 48 years.

However Ketu, when alone in the 8th house, would not give any serious illness or disease as an outcome of these tendencies. But if Mars, Saturn, or Venus are in conjunction with Ketu in the 8th house, or cast substantial *drishti* on Ketu from the 2nd house, the illness or disease caused would take longer to cure and might leave a scope for recurrence.

Ketu in the 8th house makes the wife demanding in money matters or in physical relationship, which sometimes the husband fails to meet with *in toto*. If a Rasi owned by Mercury or Venus is in the 8th house, Ketu would improve the financial position of the individual as also the social status, provided Mercury or Venus is does not occupy the 1st or the 3rd or the 6th house.

If Moon is in the 2nd house and Mars in the 8th house, Ketu in 8th house can give leukaemia or allied skin ailment. And if Moon is in the 12th house (Ketu in 8th house), it can give neurological trouble, its degree depending upon the distance of Moon from the central point of the 12th house.

Ketu and Sun, Moon, Mars, Mercury, Jupiter, Venus or Saturn in the 8th House

Respective chapters on Sun, Moon, Mars, Mercury, Jupiter, Venus, and Saturn under the relevant sub-headings for the 8th house may please be referred to for results of these seven combinations with Ketu in the 8th house.

KETU IN THE 9TH HOUSE

In this house Ketu assumes the characteristics of Mercury, giving extra intelligence, talent for writing, religious trends and tendencies, association with religious, social or charitable organisations, association with welfare bodies including orphanages, old-age homes, child welfare shelters etc.

Also this position of Ketu creates ghost writers of speeches and sometimes books and other literature too for politicians, big business tycoons and social leaders, and it is unfortunate effect of Ketu in 9th house that these ghost writers are seldom well paid for their wisdom and work.

Sometimes these individuals are victims of romantic advances by opposite sex who can be near relations and friends, which is normally rebuffed by these individuals. In case Saturn or Venus is not associated with the 9th or the 3rd house, the matter ends there itself. However if Venus or Saturn is associated with Ketu in 9th house, declining these advances might result in blackmail or bring bad name to these innocent individuals.

These individuals prove very helpful followers and advisers to political leaders, but they remain victim of short-payments or usurpation of their payments by middlemen in the camp of the political leaders, because in spite of their intelligence, experience and talent for writing, they are neither cunning nor established flatterers.

Generally these people suffer in the matter of inheritance. They do not get their full legitimate share because of usurpation and encroachment on their rights by brother, sister or cousin of self or spouse, and even by distant relations, even by those people who have no relation with the deceased person in whatsoever manner possible.

Where the question of name and fame is concerned, they do not make efforts to claim their due. It has been noticed that mischievous writers and publishers quite often pirate/ plagiarise writings of these individuals, and these individuals rarely seek legal redress or compensation or damages for the mischief done to them and their work.

Normally, lower rank people, the downtrodden in the society and masses come forward to help, support and rescue in difficulties of these individuals with Ketu in the 9th house, as compared to help or support from their own kith and kin, brethren etc.

During Ketu's main period or sub-period or Ketu's transit in the 8th or the 12th house, some of these individuals suffer pain or injury to the lower portion of the hand, i.e. between elbow and fingers of either hand, but not on both hands. It can be averted if any soft planet is in *Kendra / Trikona* or hard planet is in 3rd, 6th or 11th house.

Ketu and Sun, Moon, Mars, Mercury, Jupiter, Venus or Saturn in the 9th House

Respective chapters on Sun, Moon, and Mars, Mercury, Jupiter, Venus, and Saturn under the relevant sub-headings for the 9th house may please be referred to for results of these seven combinations with Ketu in the 9th house.

KETU IN THE 10TH HOUSE

This position of Ketu functions as a curtain of smoke between the individual and father, many times there is less than desired communication between the individual and the father. No doubt, they are helpful to each other physically at the hour of need, but financially, the help is often negligible.

The individual gets inconvenience and discomfort from or about a vehicle or an animal used as means of transport, and thus time schedule or appointment, engagement or catching a train or an aeroplane gets disturbed. Whenever in urgency or important need, these individuals should keep ready a second back-up means of transport. This problem might become all the more acute if Saturn is in transit over the 10th house (which occurs after every 28 years cycle). If Saturn is in 12th house and Ketu in the 10th house, during Saturn's or Ketu's mahadasa or sub-periods mutually under each other's mahadasa, these individuals may avoid long road journeys.

These individuals with Ketu alone in the 10th house have rare chances of reaching the top in active politics, they rather remain back-benchers, supporters of others, and if Mars or Saturn is in the 7th or the 12th house, these individuals sometimes become mere fodder for their patron-politicians. However, these individuals do better and get full credit for their work in social or charitable field, whether they are mere active workers or financiers, or both. They get their due appreciation and name.

In business matters, it is always better for these individuals to have either a godfather, or very dependable and trustworthy manager or second-in-command, who may guide them in major business deals and also serve as a brake when these individuals fear lapse in the decisions and transactions.

When in employment of others, including government or local administration or municipal body or semi-government formations like public sector undertakings, these individuals prove very efficient, competent and honest, as also devoted to assigned or undertaken work or responsibility.

These individuals are good at teaching but not efficient

in controlling a class, and often need a high-handed monitor on their 'beck and call'. Further these individuals are not successful at stocks and shares, neither as a brokers, nor as speculators.

Ketu and Sun, Moon, Mars, Mercury, Jupiter, Venus or Saturn in the 10th House

Respective chapters on Sun, Moon, Mars, Mercury, Jupiter, Venus, and Saturn under the relevant sub-headings for the 10th house may please be referred to for results of these seven combinations with Ketu in the 10th house.

KETU IN THE 11TH HOUSE

The 11th house is also a house where Ketu can give results independently, without the company of any solid planet.

Ketu in the 11th house gives higher income, protects against losses or cheating, gives a presentable personality, pleasing manners, fond of good apparel, and a rich collection in the wardrobe.

Whether high education or not, Ketu makes an individual a talented person, rich in general knowledge, possessing wide experience, gifted with foresight, having capacity for writing. They can be good teachers, but not good at controlling a class of students or a crowd or gathering where they have to speak.

Ketu in the 11th house virtually carries all the good and bad qualities of Mercury in the 11th house. However, these individuals tend to neglect to an extent the educational achievements of their kids, and the children have to become educated by the grace of their own stars and capacity.

If these individuals work for politicians or social or charitable formations, they stay honest and efficient workers, but certainly want full compensation for their work in cash or kind, because they are not very enamoured of fame through this kind of work.

Ketu in the 11th house might delay the first pregnancy, but normally it doesn't disturb the pregnancy till normal delivery of the child. However after the delivery of the child, Ketu indicates better care of the child during its first year of age, at least against cold, cough and problems of respiratory system or fever.

Ketu in the 11th house generally makes an individual less serviceful to mother physically after attaining the age of 22 years, though the individual doesn't hesitate to render financial help or service through servants and nurses etc.

Ketu and Sun, Moon, Mars, Mercury, Jupiter, Venus or Saturn in the 11th House

Respective chapters on Sun, Moon, Mars, Mercury, Jupiter, Venus, and Saturn under the relevant sub-headings for 11th house may please be referred to for results of these seven combinations with Ketu in the 11th house.

KETU IN THE 12TH HOUSE

This position of Ketu gives eye trouble, generally in the young age, till attaining adulthood. Unless Mars or Sun is with Ketu in the 12th house, Ketu alone doesn't give any serious complaint of the eye. Use of spectacles is no doubt becoming very common in modern times of electronic media and computers!

Ketu in the 12th house can give, to many individuals, particularly to childbearing females, pain in the waist region, and it becomes more serious if Saturn is in the 12th house with Ketu or in the 8th house. Mars with Ketu in 12th house would give problems relating to menstrual cycle.

Ketu in the 12th house adversely affects the individual's relations with a brother or sister of the mother, which is more a jealousy-based matter.

Ketu and Sun, Moon, Mars, Mercury, Jupiter, Venus or Saturn in the 12th House

Respective chapters on Sun, Moon, Mars, Mercury, Jupiter, Venus, and Saturn under the relevant sub-headings for 12th house may please be referred to for results of these seven combinations with Ketu in the 12th House.

We conclude with a famous Sanskrit saying:

*"Kavihi karoti kavyani
Rasam aasaadayanti panditaa"*

which means –

'Poet creates poetry
The learned scholar enjoys it.'

GLOSSARY

6: 8 relationship among planets When a planet 'A' is in the 6th position from planet 'B', then 'B' would naturally be in the 8th position from 'A'. For example, assume Moon is in 5th house in Leo, then naturally, if Saturn occupies the 12th house in Pisces, it is in 8th position from Moon. Thus there is a 6:8 relationship between Moon and Saturn. Such a relationship between planets is considered 'extra' harmful to the individual in respect of the subjects controlled by those two planets, and also subjects ruled by the houses occupied by the two planets respectively. As another example, Sun is in the 1st house and Mars is in the 6th house. These two have got 6: 8 relationship with each other because Mars is in the 6th position from Sun, and Sun is in the 8th position from Mars.

Air Signs (*Vayu-Tattwa Rasi*) Gemini, Libra and Aquarius; (Indian names, Mithun, Tula, Kumbha)

Aspect (*Dristi*) Planet or a house within the straight or angular vision of another Planet.

Cardinal Sign (*Char Rasi*) Aries, Cancer, Libra and Capricorn (Indian names, Mesh, Simha, Tula and Makar).

Conjunction Two planets in one and the same Rasi (Sign of Zodiac).

Cusp The line of division between two houses.

Divisional Charts The Birth-chart (the ascendant as well as the planets) are dissected, for purpose of more accurate analysis, on the basis of their degrees and minutes, into several divisions. viz.,

One-half called 'Hora'

One-third called 'Deeshkana'

One-seventh called 'Saptamsha'

One-ninth called 'Navamsha'

One-twelfth called 'Dwadashansha' One-thirtieth called 'Trinshansha' and One-sixtieth called 'Shashtyansha'

Earth Signs (*Prithvi-Tattwa Rasi*) Taurus, Virgo and Capricorn – (Indian names, Vrishabha, Kanya, Makar).

Female Signs Odd Signs of the zodiac. Taurus, Cancer, Virgo, Scorpio, Capricorn, and Pisces

Fire Signs (*Agni-Tattwa* Rasi) Aries, Leo and Sagittarius (Indian names, Mesh, Simha, Dhanu).

Fixed Signs (*Sthir Rasi*) Taurus, Leo, Scorpio and Aquarius (Indian names, Vrishabha, Simha, Vrishchik, Kumbha)

Hard Planet Sun, waning Moon, Mars, Saturn, Rahu, Ketu, Herschel and Neptune.

House (*Bhava*) One of the twelve divisions made in the cycle of the Earth's daily rotation. Each house represents an approximate of two hours period during which one-twelfth of the Zodiac is covered.

Individual and individuals These two terms (in singular and plural numbers have been used exclusively for the single person or group of persons, whose horoscope or the Yearly-chart or any other chart is under study of the astrologer for giving predictions. Or who are under influence of the position of single planet or collective positions of more than one planet is under discussion for guidance and predictions. Unless otherwise mentioned, these two terms stand for both, male(s) as well as female(s) with regard to that rule of prediction.

***Janma Lagna/* Ascendant**   Ascendant, i.e. the Sign of the zodiac rising in the eastern horizon at the time of birth, or at the given time (of the event)

Janma Nakshatra   Constellation occupied by the Moon at the time of birth

Janma Rasi   Sign of the zodiac occupied by Moon at the time of birth

Karaka   Every planet rules some specific aspect of life, which can be called in broad terms as its portfolio. For instance Sun rules the self, Moon rules the mind and Mars rules energy in human body. This distribution of portfolios is of two kinds. One is fixed and the other is according to the degrees and minutes of the seven solid planets at the time of birth. This other distribution is called "Taatkalik Karaka". The Signs of the zodiac occupied by the planet are not taken into account. The planets are arranged in terms of their degrees. The one with the highest degree is the Ruler of the element of "Self", the one with the second highest degree is ruler of "Counsel" and so on till the planet with the lowest degree is taken as the ruler of the Seventh House (spouse). Rahu and Ketu are not included in this rulership of portfolios at birth.

Kendra (Square)   Houses which are in the 1st, 4th, 7th and 10th positions from one another are known as "in *Kendra* to each other, or one another". For example, Aries, Cancer, Libra and Capricorn are in *Kendra* to one another. Similarly, Taurus, Leo, Scorpio and Aquarius are in *Kendra* to one another, and likewise Gemini, Virgo, Sagittarius and Pisces are in *Kendra* to one another. Then any planet(s) occupying one particular Sign of the Zodiac is taken as in *Kendra* with other planets occupying any Sign of the Zodiac of that particular group. For example, suppose Sun is in Gemini, and Mars+Jupiter are in Virgo, all these three planets would be considered in *Kendra* to one another.

Ketu — Descending Node of Moon (also known as Tail of the Dragon)

Lord of a House — Ruler of the Sign of Zodiac (Rasi) of a particular Rasi (Sign of Zodiac) is known as its Lord of that House. See Figure 4 in the beginning of the book for a list of Lords of various Rasis.

Mahadasa and *Antardasa* — Mahadasa is the main period, and antardasa is the sub periods of effects of the planets. The commonly followed system is "Vimshottari Mahadasa" spread over a life span of 120 years. Under this system Sun gets 6 years, Moon 10 years, Mars 7 years, Rahu 18 years, Jupiter 16 years, Saturn 19 years, Mercury 17 years, Ketu 7 years, Venus 20 years (see Figure 11).

These main periods are further divided into sub-periods giving share to all nine planets according to the ratio of total years of each one's Mahadasa with the total period of 120 years of all Mahadasas. This share of each of the nine planets is called the sub-period or Antar-dasa. Each planet's share further varies according to the ratio between its total years with total years of the planet under whose Mahadasa the sub-period is awarded.

Male Signs	Signs of the zodiac with even numbers, i.e. Aries, Gemini, Leo, Libra, Sagittarius and Aquarius.
Muntha	The rotation of the Ascendant at birth in the Yearly-chart (Varsh-Kundali). It has great influence over the results of the Yearly-chart.
Mutable Sign (*Dwi-swabhava*)	Gemini, Virgo, Sagittarius and Pisces (Indian names, Mithun, Kanya, Dhanu, Meena).
Navamsha	'Navamsha' (one-ninth dissection) of any Ascendant (Birth-chart, of the Yearly-chart or Question-chart or Event-chart. It has great importance in Indian Astrology for consideration of any aspect of life, because Ascendant is treated as Body and Navamsha as Soul of the chart. It has important impact on, besides other subjects, on love, marriage and married life for men and on all other events for all, males and females.
Opposite	Any house (or planet) occurring directly opposite, in the seventh position, from the house (or planet) under consideration.
Opposition (between planets)	Permanent relations of friendship, neutrality, and enmity among planets.
Rahu	Ascending Node of Moon, (also known as Head of the Dragon)
Rasi* and *Ansha	Sign of zodiac (Rasi) and its degree are '*Ansha*'
Soft Planet	Waxing Moon, Mercury, Jupiter and Venus
***Swagrahi* Planet**	A planet occupying that very Sign which it rules (See figure 4 in the beginning of the book), and it is considered extra powerful in giving good or bad results.

Trinshansha — 'Trinshansha' (one-thirtieth dissection) of a chart. Considered with Birth-chart, it too has great predictive value on matters of love, marriage and married life of females, (somewhat parallel to Navamsha-chart in case of males).

Water Sign (*Jal-Tattwa Rasi*) — Cancer, Scorpio and Pisces (Indian names, Karkata, Vrishchik, Meena)

Trikona (Trine) — Any Sign of the zodiac in 5:9 relationship to each other is considered to be in *Trikona*. For example, Aries, Leo and Sagittarius are in *Trikona* to one another. Similarly, Taurus, Virgo and Capricorn are in *Trikona* to one another, and Gemini, Libra and Aquarius are in *Trikona* to one another, and Cancer, Scorpio and Pisces are in *Trikona* to one another.

Note: For Planets, the terms 'planets' and 'Stars' have been used interchangeably. Similarly, for Signs, sometimes Signs and sometimes *Rasi* may have been used.

Other books by Astrologer Pandit Parsai

- **Star Guide® to Love and Marriage**
  – by Pandit K. B. Parsai & Ms. Gargi Parsai

  The 7th House in Astrology which is about Love & marriage and all things related to it. In this book the authors expertly steer you from something as basic as the recognition of birth charts to more complex issues like the 'how' and 'when' of a relationship or marriage. Pick this book up to find out all about matching your horoscope with that of a prospective partner, the reasons behind a failed marriage, adjustments in marriage and lots more!

  Available in English and Hindi

- **Star Guide® to Election**
  – by Pandit K. B. Parsai & Pandit D. K. Parsai

  Available in English and Hindi

- **Nirayana Tables of Houses**
  – by Pandit K. B. Parsai & Pandit D. K. Parsai

  (for each Latitude from 1° to 60° for both North & South Latitudes – with Table to cast the 10th House and explanatory notes in English and Hindi to calculate the 12 Houses (Bhavas)

  Available in English and Hind

Forth coming book by Pandit Parsai

- **Star Guide® to Saturn**
  Transit of Saturn in the 12 Rasi's (Signs)
  – by Pandit K. B. Parsai & Pandit D. K. Parsai

  Including chapters on Sani's Saadhe Saati (Saturn's Seven & Half Years Impact) and Mangali Horoscopes.